THOUGHT AND PLAY IN MUSICAL RHYTHM

Thought and Play in Musical Rhythm

ASIAN, AFRICAN, AND EURO-AMERICAN PERSPECTIVES

Edited by Richard K. Wolf, Stephen Blum, and Christopher Hasty

OXFORD
UNIVERSITY PRESS

OXFORD
UNIVERSITY PRESS

Oxford University Press is a department of the University of Oxford. It furthers the University's objective of excellence in research, scholarship, and education by publishing worldwide. Oxford is a registered trade mark of Oxford University Press in the UK and certain other countries.

Published in the United States of America by Oxford University Press
198 Madison Avenue, New York, NY 10016, United States of America.

CIP data is on file at the Library of Congress
ISBN 978-0-19-084149-2 (pbk.)
ISBN 978-0-19-084148-5 (hbk.)

9 8 7 6 5 4 3 2 1

Paperback printed by Marquis, Canada
Hardback printed by Bridgeport National Bindery, Inc., United States of America

Contents

List of Figures and Tables vii
Preface xiii
List of Contributors xv
About the Companion Website xvii

Introduction 1
Richard K. Wolf, Stephen Blum, and Christopher Hasty

1. *Thinking With and About Rhythm* 20
Christopher Hasty

2. *Formative Processes of Durational Projection in "Free Rhythm" World Music* 55
John Roeder

3. *Meter and Rhythm in the Sung Poetry of Iranian Khorasan* 75
Stephen Blum

4. *An Approach to Musical Rhythm in Agbadza* 100
David Locke

5. *Rhythm and the Physical* 146
Eugene Montague

6. *Modern Drum Solos Over Ostinatos* 174
Fernando Benadon

7. *Temporal and Density Flow in Javanese Gamelan* 196
Sumarsam

8. *Layers and Elasticity in the Rhythm of Noh Songs: "Taking Komi" and Its Social Background* 212
Takanori Fujita

Contents

9. *Rhythmic Metamorphoses: Botanical Process Models on the Atlas Mountains of Morocco* 232
Miriam Rovsing Olsen

10. *Mapping a Rhythmic Revolution Through Eighteenth- and Nineteenth-Century Sources on Rhythm and Drumming in North India* 253
James Kippen

11. *Time Changes: Heterometric Music in South Asia* 273
Richard Widdess

12. *"Rhythm," "Beat," and "Freedom" in South Asian Musical Traditions* 314
Richard K. Wolf

13. *New Music—New Rhythm* 337
Christopher Hasty

GLOSSARY 381
BIBLIOGRAPHY 393
INDEX 415

Figures and Tables

FIGURES

1.1. From a) two to b) three claps and the possibility c) of two larger events. 36
1.2. Joseph Haydn, String Quartet Op. 76 no. 4 ("Sunrise"), second movement, bs. 1–16. 39
1.3. Josquin des Prez, *Missa pange lingua*, the opening of *Pleni sunt coeli*, t.1–24. 42
1.4. Josquin des Prez, *Missa pange lingua*, the opening of *Pleni sunt coeli*, repetitions in altus, t.13–23. 46
2.1. Some temporal sensations associated with durational projection and realization. Adapted from Hasty, *Meter as Rhythm* (1997, 87–89). 57
2.2. Projective analysis of the introduction (*darāmad*) to the classical Persian chant (*āvāz*) of an extract from *Bīdād* from *dastgāh homāyun*, sung by Afsāne Ziā'i with Hoseyn Omumi, *ney*. 58
2.3. Projective analysis of the first seven cycles of "Flute," performed by Zinzir, *tatarore*. 63
2.4. Two possible kinds of realized durational projections in "Flute" (under the assumption of parallelism). 64
2.5: Projective analysis of the opening (0:07–0:55) of the *ālāp* on *rāga* Pūriyā-Kalyān performed by Budhaditya Mukherjee, *sitar*. Transcribed by Richard Widdess, adapted and annotated by John Roeder. 68
3.1. One quantitative poetic meter as represented in (a) the system of Arabic and Persian prosody, and (b) a simplified notation of attacks and durations in rhythmic cycles, which can also be used for poetic meters. 79
3.2. Moḥammad Ḥoseyn Yegāneh (d. 1992) singing a Persian quatrain to *Šāh Xaṭā'i*. 81
3.3. Initial quatrain of a *monājāt* (an intimate communication with God). 82
3.4. The guše of *Šāh Xaṭā'i* in the dastgāh of *Navā*, as sung by Maḥmud Karimi. 83
3.5. Quatrain from the story of *Šāh Esmā'il*, sung by Moxtār Zambilbāf, 1972 (AWM RL 16245). 85

3.6. Quatrain from the story of *Šāh Esmāʿil*, sung by Moxtār Zambilbāf, 1972 (AWM RL 16245). 85
3.7. Two lines from Ferdowsi's *Šāh-nāma*, sung to a 12-beat cycle by Ḥāj Ḥoseyn Xān Yāvari (age ca. 60) of Xarv Olyā (AWM RL 16234). 88
3.8 One verse of a fable from the *Būstān* of Saʿdi as sung by two *naqqāls*: (a) Ṣādeq ʿAli Šāh (AWM RL 16211, and *Naqqāli in Northern Khorāsān*, track 6, 4:23–4:35); (b) Moḥammad Ḥasan Naqqāl (AWM RL 16225). 89
3.9. Two verses from the *Šāh Nāma*, sung by Sayyed Ḥasan Naqib Zāde (age 43), the *moršed* of a *zur-xāna* (men's athletic club) in Sabzevār, 1995. 90
3.10. The same verses as in Figure 3.9, sung by Ḥasan Salaḥšur (age 18), a *naqqāl* active in tea houses of Bojnurd, 1969 (AWM RL 16208). 91
4.1. Rhythm of Agbadza dance movement. 103
4.2. Resultant rhythm of bell phrase with four-feel and six-feel beats. 109
4.3. Support drum function: articulation of offbeats. 110
4.4. Support drum phrase: accentuation in the metric matrix. 111
4.5. Music setting of drum language of the time parts. 112
4.6. Response drum themes for items 1–25. 114
4.7. Response theme, item 24: motion and accentuation "in four" and "in six." 119
4.8. Lead drum: key to notation of strokes. 120
4.9. Lead drum themes for items 1–25. 121
4.10. Lead drum form: excerpt from complete score of item 1. 126
4.11. Modes of anhemitonic pentatonic scale. 131
4.12. Modes of hemitonic pentatonic scales. 132
4.13. Song-drum affinity in item 19: time-point 1.2. 137
4.14. Song: drum interaction in item 15. 139
4.15. Song and drums in item 16: cascading entrances, reinforcement of lexical meaning. 140
5.1. Eight ways to notate the *son clavé* rhythm, after Toussaint (2005). 149
5.2. A score of the first page of "Pianistes" from Saint-Saëns, *Le carnaval des animaux*. 153
5.3. A rhythmic analysis of the Piano I part at the opening of "Pianistes." 154
5.4. A gestural-rhythmic analysis of the opening of Chopin, Étude in C major, Op. 10 no. 1. 158
5.5. Spans of the right hand in Chopin's etude. 159
5.6. Calculating the stretch of each handspan in the basic instrumental gesture of Chopin, Op. 10 no. 1. 160
5.7. Stretching the hand: relative stretches of each of the three handspans A, B, and C in the first three phrases of Chopin, Op. 10 no. 1, measures 1–8, 9–16, and 17–24. 161
5.8. Three-voice counterpoint (bass line plus span C, the topmost two in Chopin, Op. 10 no. 1, measures 1–8). 162
5.9. A diagrammatic representation of the drummer's gestures in a typical measure of "Straight Edge" by Minor Threat. 164

5.10. An interpretation of the metrical structure of the first four lines of "Straight Edge." 166
5.11. An interpretation of the metrical structure of Mackaye's performance of "Straight Edge." 166
5.12. An interpretation of the durational structures of Mackaye's performance of "Straight Edge." 167
5.13. A rough alignment of the drum and vocal rhythms in the opening lines of "Straight Edge." 167
5.14. A general analysis of the rhythmic relationships between voice and drums in the first section of "Straight Edge." 168
6.1. Configurations in "synchronization space" for three- and two-element groups. Elements inside a circle are in synchrony with each other; d = drums, m = meter, o = ostinato. 175
6.2. Steve Gadd, "Quartet No. 2, Part II" (9:14). 177
6.3. Trilok Gurtu, "Belo Horizonte" (3:49). 181
6.4. Gurtu's accent placements in the measure cycle. 182
6.5. Dave Weckl, "Master Plan" (3:12). 183
6.6. Vinnie Colaiuta, "Live at Catalina's" (2:51). 184
6.7a–b. Vinnie Colaiuta, "Live at Catalina's" (2:11). 185
6.8a–d. Jojo Mayer, "Jabon" (5:09, 5:19, 5:56, 6:11). 187
6.9. Gadd, clave solo (2:21). 189
6.10. Ostinato (top) vs. polymeter (staggered 2+3 pairs) vs. meter (vertical lines) in the first five measures of Figure 6.9. 191
6.11. Gadd's 15-subdivision group and two "rational" approximations. 193
6.12. Drum notation key. 194
7.1a. A song for accompanying a deer dance: the original song. 199
7.1b. A song for accompanying a deer dance: Sindusawarno's version of the melodic skeleton of the song. 200
7.2a. Example of the melodies of elaborating instruments (*rebab, gender, bonang*) and *kendhang* (drum) in *irama dadi*. 205
7.2b. Example of the melodies of elaborating instruments (*rebab, gender, bonang*) and *kendhang* (drum) in *irama wilet*: gendèr rangkep, bonang imbal, kendhang ciblon. 205
8.1. Original configuration of poetic syllables in *hira-nori* rhythm (a song from Noh *Ataka*). 213
8.2. *Su-utai* performed by amateur singers, at the amateur recital held on August 9, 2009, at the Noh theater in Otsu city. 215
8.3a. The libretto notation of a song in *Ataka* by Kita school published in 1924. 216
8.3b. Singer's rhythm image of a song in *Ataka*. At the syllables with accent signs (ʎ), choral singers have to extend the syllables to go with drumming pattern. 217
8.4a. *Mitsuji* pattern of *o-tsuzumi* and *ko-tsuzumi*. 218
8.4b. *Tsuzuke* pattern by *o-tsuzumi* and *ko-tsuzumi*. 218

8.5a. "Waving" modification of a drumming pattern in the dance music *kakeri*. 219
8.5b. "Contraction" of beats 2 and 4 in the entrance music *shidai*. 220
8.5c. *Mitsuji* pattern in "blur" modification, *norazu*. 221
8.6. Analysis of a *hira-nori* song in *Ataka*. 223
8.7. Alternation model of synchronization and detachment in a passage. 226
8.8. An amateur woman dancing with professional musicians at the back and choral singers at the side of the stage July 31, 2011, at the Noh theater in Otsu city. 228
9.1. The beginning of *amarg* sung by a soloist. 249
9.2. *Amḫllf*. The beginning of the two female choirs. 249
9.3. *Amḫllf*. Introduction of the first verse in the female choirs. 249
9.4. *Amḫllf*. Beginning of the drum ming and the dancing. 250
9.5. *Tamssust*. The same tune as before is sung alternately by the two choirs. 250
9.6. *Tamssust*. Rhythmic transition in the percussion instruments. 250
9.7. *Tamssust*. Introduction of a new melody. 251
11.1. *Dāphā* song *He Śiva Bhairava* as sung by the Dattātreya and Bhairavnāth temple *dāphā* groups, Bhaktapur, Nepal. 282
11.2. Singers of the Bhairavnāth temple *dāphā* group singing *He Śiva Bhairava* at the start of the Biskāḥ festival. The chariot of Bhairav can be seen in the background. Bhaktapur, Nepal, 2003. 283
11.3. Changes of metrical cycle in *dāphā* song *He Śiva Bhairava*. 285
11.4. *Dāphā* song *Girīhe nandinī* as sung by the Dattātreya temple *dāphā* group, Bhaktapur, Nepal. 287
11.5. The Dattātreya temple *dāphā* group, Bhaktapur, Nepal, 2012. 289
11.6. Proportional structure in *dāphā* song *Girīhe nandinī*. 290
11.7. *Maṇḍala* of Cakrasaṃvara. Painting on cloth, Nepal, c. 1100. 293
11.8. Singers making time-keeping gestures while performing *Mahārudra Gvārā*. Ikhālakhu Nekujātrā and Matayājātrā group, Patan, Nepal, 2011. 295
11.9. Proportional structure in *Mahārudra Gvārā*. 296
11.10. Structure of *pāṇikā* song. 299
11.11. The Ikhālakhu Nekujātrā and Matayājātrā group, Patan, Nepal, 2011. 306
11.12. Page from a modern notation-book showing heterometric structure of a *gvārā* song (Śākya 1995). 309
12.1. *Ādi tāla* with 2 *kaḷā*. 319
12.2. 12.2a: Tiruganāṭ basic version on tabaṭk, "one-beat" (*or aṛy*). 12.2b: Tiruganāṭ variation on tabaṭk, "two-beat" (*eyṛ aṛy*). 12.2c: Tiruganāṭ variation on tabaṭk, "three-beat" (*mūṇḍ aṛy*). 322
12.3. 12.3a: Do mār. 12.3b: Tīn mār. 324
12.4. The *kalmah*, a beat pattern corresponding to the Muslim statement of faith in one god. 329
12.5. Approximate oscillation rhythm on *svara ma* in *nīlāmbari*. 334
12.6. Approximate oscillation rhythm on *svara ma* in *śankarābharaṇam*. 334

13.1a–b. Scheme for simple durational projection. 340
13.2a–e. Schemes for compound projections. 342
13.3. Scheme for triple unequal projection (deferral). 344
13.4. Pierre Boulez, *Le Marteau sans maître*, no. 9, "bel edifice et les pressentiments" double bs. 1–4. 349
13.5. Anton von Webern, *Six Bagatelles for String Quartet*, Op. 9 no. 6, bars 1–6. 350
13.6a–b. Lewin's representation of a) Bamberger's stimulus and b) her subjects' interpretation (modified). 351
13.7a–b. Toru Takemitsu, *Rain Tree*, a) second section bs.1–8 (bottom of page 6); b) interpretation of figure X. 352
13.8. Salvatore Sciarrino, *Muro d'orizzonte* bs. 13–22. 355
13.9. Salvatore Sciarrino, *Muro d'orizzonte* bs. 1–12. 357
13.10. Toru Takemitsu, *Rain Tree*, first section bs. 30–45 (page 5 of score). 360
13.11. Toru Takemitsu, *Rain Tree*, opening bs. 1–29. 363
13.12. Morton Feldman, *Spring of Chosroes* bs. 1–7. 367
13.13. Morton Feldman, *Crippled Symmetry* first system (bs. 1–9). 369
13.14. Morton Feldman, *De Kooning* first system. 370
13.15. Morton Feldman, *De Kooning* final system. 372

TABLES

2.1. Distribution of ratios of successive durations marked by grace-note-group onsets. 71
2.2. Distribution of ratios of successive durations marked by long-note onsets. 72
4.1. Agbadza dance cadence "in four." 104
4.2. Agbadza dance cadence "in six." 104
4.3. Supporting instruments: implicit Ewe texts. 107
4.4. Agbadza kidi phrases: patterns of bounce and press strokes. 117
4.5. Lead drum: palette of strokes. 120
4.6. Agbadza songs: musical form, call-and-response, and duration in bell cycles. 133
4.7. Agbadza songs: nuanced form of melody with call-and-response. 134
5.1. The lyrics of Minor Threat's "Straight Edge." 166
9.1. Temporal development of a "womens' *aḥwaš*": the order of contributions to the performance. 246
9.2. The sung poetry reconstructed in its literary form from the performance of the *aḥwaš*. 247
9.3. The sung poetry transcribed as expressed in performance. 248
10.1. The three categories of *tāl* in the *Sharḥ-i risāla-yi qawā'id-i ṭabla*. 263
11.1. Levels of pulsation in Tīntāl (cardinality 16). 275
11.2. Levels of pulsation in Jhaptāl (cardinality 10). 276
11.3. Text and translation of *dāphā* song *He Śiva Bhairava*. 284

11.4. Text and translation of *dāphā* song *Girīhe nandinī*. 288
11.5. Proportional structure in *Girīhe nandinī*. 291
11.6. Proportional structure in *Mahārudra Gvārā*. 297
12.1. Beat structure of *cāl*s performed by *ḍhol* group in Hyderabad, Sindh, Pakistan. 325

Preface

EARLIER VERSIONS OF the essays collected here were presented at a Conference on Rhythm held at Harvard University, March 3 and 4, 2012. The conference was planned in conjunction with a seminar on cross-cultural rhythm taught by Richard Wolf and Christopher Hasty during the spring semester of 2012; Stephen Blum was also involved in organizing the conference. We are grateful for financial support for the conference provided by the Harvard University Department of Music, the Provostial Fund for Arts and Humanities at Harvard, the Reischauer Institute of Japanese Studies at Harvard University, and the South Asia Initiative (now South Asia Institute) at Harvard.

We first conceived of the introduction as a conversation among the three of us, which we began to draft the day after the conference. When that plan proved unworkable, Richard Wolf made an outline of six topics that seemed to draw together themes from all the chapters, and these served as the basis of the introduction as it appears here. The opening section and the treatment of "Representations" and "Qualities" are Wolf's work; Blum wrote the sections on "Units" and "Interactions"; and Hasty those on "Periodicity and Cycle" and "Meter." Some topics are necessarily discussed in more than one section, just as the three of us are continually returning to them in our conversations.

We would like to thank the Harvard University Music Department for support during all stages of this project, and particularly Lesley Bannatyne, who assisted preparing the final manuscript.

—RKW, SB, CFH

Contributors

Fernando Benadon is Professor of Music at American University.

Stephen Blum is Professor of Music Emeritus at the City University of New York Graduate Center.

Takanori Fujita is Professor of Ethnomusicology at the Research Centre for Japanese Traditional Music at Kyoto City University of Arts.

Christopher Hasty is Walter W. Naumburg Professor of Music at Harvard University.

James Kippen is Professor of Ethnomusicology at the University of Toronto.

David Locke is Professor at the Music Department of Tufts University.

Eugene Montague is Associate Professor of Music at the George Washington University.

Miriam Rovsing Olsen is Associate Professor Emeritus of Ethnomusicology and Member of the Center for Research in Ethnomusicology (CREM-LESC) at the University of Paris Nanterre.

John Roeder is Professor at the University of British Columbia School of Music.

Sumarsam is Winslow-Kaplan Professor of Music at Wesleyan University.

Richard Widdess is Professor of Musicology at SOAS University of London.

Richard K. Wolf is Professor of Music and South Asian Studies at Harvard University.

About the Companion Website

OXFORD UNIVERSITY PRESS has created a password-protected website to accompany *Thought and Play in Musical Rhythm: Asian, African, and Euro-American Perspectives*. Readers may stream or link to recordings and videos referenced in the book via this site. The reader is encouraged to take advantage of these additional resources. Examples available online are indicated in the text with Oxford's symbol: ⊙

We welcome feedback and suggestions for additional content based on readers' experiences with arts programs. Readers can contact us through the following email address: www.oup.com/us/thoughtandplay.

THOUGHT AND PLAY IN MUSICAL RHYTHM

Introduction

Richard K. Wolf, Stephen Blum, and Christopher Hasty

THOUGHT AND PLAY in Musical Rhythm seeks to explore representations, ideal types, and implicit theorizing of rhythm in relation to aspects of performance that "play"—that pull against these ideal types, resist objectification, and/or are elastic. Our aim has been to incorporate a diversity of musical traditions and scholarly approaches, embracing those of performers, music theorists, and music ethnographers. The performance dynamic implicit in "thought and play" can, with some imagination, be recast in terms of a larger dynamic in scholarly discourse on rhythm and music more generally—that between "universalizing" and "local" approaches. The former include efforts to create overarching models that accommodate the diversity of music and to gain insight into human cognition generally, as well as craft terminologies (meter, beat, etc.) that apply cross-culturally. Local, by contrast, signals attention to musical systems and practices as they are constituted in one region, however narrowly or broadly defined; attention focuses on the specifics of musical interaction, uses of language, and regional histories. Most music scholars attempt to bring out the historical and regional specificity of what they study while also contributing to general knowledge about musical process.

One of the first challenges in writing about and teaching "rhythm" is constituting rhythm as an object of study in the first place. Some concepts of rhythm rely on the presence of regular, perceivable recurrences, making possible such statements as "X is more rhythmic than Y." When rhythm is understood as the patterning of events in time, all music has rhythm and the problem is to describe or represent rhythm when the patterning is less than obvious. The commonplace elision of two senses of the word—"rhythm" as a structural abstraction and "rhythms" as specific instance—creates another form of confusion in definition, particularly when what is meant by "rhythms" is "drumming patterns." The challenge of commonplace terminologies remains for the authors of this volume, who do not always agree to use terms in the same ways. For this reason, we provide a glossary highlighting not only local-language terms, but also some differences in usage for English words across the volume.

Etymologies (in various languages) have stimulated imaginative thinking about rhythm. For example, the derivation of "rhythm" from the word "to flow" in Greek supports, via the image of "waves," intuitive ideas of rhythm as regular, yet elastic and full of movement (see also Stephen Blum's chapter in this volume). Émile Benveniste has revealed the flaws in this etymology, pointing out that the term in question for "flow" was used at the time in Greek for the movement of a river or a stream and not for the recurrence of waves in the sea (Benveniste 1971, 281–82). Benveniste suggests that a modern sense of rhythm can be traced back in Greek at least to the time of Plato's Socratic dialogue *Philebus* (4th c. B.C.E.), which draws an analogy between "intervals" in music and the timing of bodily movements, the numerical regulation of which was called "rhythm" and "measure" (Benveniste 1971, 286).

Despite its dubious historical veracity, the "wave" etymology resonates with various intuitions about rhythm shared by many writers on music and time. It may call forth the tensions between "pure duration" versus "measurable time" in Henri Bergson's formulation (Bergson 1965 [1922], 50), "inner time" versus "outer time" in that of Alfred Schütz (1951), and time without parts versus time with parts in the *Maitri Upaniṣad* (6.15–15, cited in Rowell 1992b, 180). The unbroken motion of water in a wave is analogous to the continuity and absence of articulation in inner time, while the sound of each wave lapping onto a piece, boat, or segment of shoreline, creating semiperiodic attacks, may suggest a form of time measurement and division. In understanding rhythm as both a musical and cultural phenomenon, then, it is helpful to keep both operational definitions and local ideologies closely in mind.

This idea of moving among different views on rhythm could fruitfully spill over into more holistic accounts of music generally. Unfortunately, in music textbooks one commonly encounters rhythm, alongside harmony and melody, represented as an "element" of music. This fundamental act of separating rhythm from musical process is, in our opinion, detrimental to understanding the fullness of musical experience. In a similar vein, in *Rhythm and Tempo* Curt Sachs alludes to "pure melody"—a melody that can recur with different rhythmic settings (Sachs 1953, 18; compare with a similar move by Sindusawarno as discussed by Sumarsam in this volume). But does pure melody exist? In each and every instance melody must have a rhythmic form. Without accounting for the passage of time, "pure melody" could be no more than an ordered set of pitches—though it is hardly possible to think about "order" without invoking time or space. The point is that no actual passage in music is possible without rhythm.[1]

It would be equally problematic to suggest that rhythm could exist without sounding vehicles that produce sameness and difference in timbre, tone, and vertical relations (harmony, etc.). An account of rhythm that embraces musical experience requires attention to much more than the relations among abstracted points in time. It may call for analysis of attack and decay, envelope, interactions among musicians, physical gestures overlapping parts, microtiming, silent reckoning of beats and pulses, and so forth. Africanist scholars of rhythm, accustomed to the subtleties of interaction among instrumentalists, dancers, and singers, have long recognized rhythm's many facets—what David Locke has called "simultaneous multidimensionality." But the musical traditions of Africa merely provide salient examples of what is more generally the case. We wish to highlight the many ways musical rhythm persists multidimensionally. A responsible account of rhythm in any one case will allude to this, while recognizing that certain kinds of reduction in complexity are inevitable in putting pen to page.

The authors of the present volume explore what rhythm is and can be across a spectrum of musical traditions. In rejecting the kind of abstraction that removes "rhythm" from musical process and experience, we nevertheless recognize that the very consideration of rhythm as a topic involves a set of terminologies, methodologies, assumptions, efforts at generalizing, and yes, abstracting that point toward a music-field-wide effort to understand rhythm better per se. In this sense, the "universalizing" writings of Justin London, Michael Tenzer, Jeff Pressing, and others who seek overarching ways of representing rhythm as part of human music-making and cognition provide useful reference points for inspiration as well as resistance. Counterposing these efforts are those of some ethnomusicologists and theorists who have elaborated theories of rhythm or time specific to one civilization, region, or culture—such scholars as Alan Merriam, Ruth Stone, Simha Arom, and Meki Nzewi for Africa; Lewis Rowell for India; Judith Becker for Indonesia; José Maceda for Southeast Asia more generally; and a host of anthropologists with regard to time in a broader range of cultural behaviors and institutions. Clifford Geertz (e.g., 1973) and Nancy Munn (e.g., 1986) provide salient examples of culturally constructed time (and space), while Alfred Gell argues against notions of different kinds of time (Gell 1992). In thematizing the universalist-versus-local tension we ask the reader to question what is to be gained in emphasizing one end of the spectrum or another at any given analytical moment.

Rather than introduce the chapters one by one, we will discuss aspects of these contributions in terms of six broad topics pertinent to the universalist-local dynamic:

Representations, Units, Periodicity and Cycle, Meter, Qualities, and Interactions.

REPRESENTATIONS

Representations of rhythm and its parts highlight this dynamic, for the choice of an analytic vocabulary shared by a scholarly community accomplishes something quite different from highlighting the terms, metaphors, or myths drawn from a particular repertoire.

Many of the discussions negotiate broad and focused views on rhythm via forms of "translation." "Rhythm," already multifaceted in English, may have similarly multifaceted analogues in other languages or no analogues at all. Rhythm may also play a relatively major or minor part in the way a particular repertoire is identified and valued—whether by practitioners themselves or by broader reputation. African music has long been identified with rhythm in the popular imagination—especially in the Western world. Despite the enticing potentials of the tabla and other drums, rhythm is subordinated to melody in the world of South Asian classical music because of a longstanding ideology there favoring the voice. At a more local level, Sumarsam explains, the melodic identity of particular pieces in Javanese gamelan resides in particular levels of rhythmic texture and density (*irama*).

Terms such as rhythm in English, *laya* in Indic languages, *īqāʿ* in Arabic, and *irama* in Javanese operate synecdochically, referring to one part or aspect of a musical structure as well as to a more abstract, general idea of rhythm. The fact that performers in many traditions use some version of the English word "rhythm" does not make it a transparent term for cross-cultural analysis, but it does alert us to the kinds of translations taking place all the time when performers put musical process into words.

In understanding the regulative role of cycles, whether in Javanese gamelan (Sumarsam), folk drumming (Richard Wolf), African time-lines (Locke), or ostinatos (Fernando Benadon), as well as their hierarchical implications, we engage theories of meter, but it remains an open question as to how we translate local representations of such structures. In Indian musical studies, opinions vary on the extent to which the regulative cyclic framework of *tāla* ought itself to be considered as musical meter. Richard Widdess and James Kippen do allow for this equation. Taking a narrower frame of analysis: *mātra* in South Asian music refers to a subdivision of the *tāla*, a unit of a cycle. Sumarsam cites a Javanese usage of *mātra* (and also *gatra*) as meter, the ordering of alternating movements with contrasting weight. These usages pinpoint segments of contrasting length. The possibility of a *mātra* being akin to meter would depend on how short it is.[2] If two levels of grouping exist below that of the *mātra* (e.g., beat and pulse), one might view it as metric in the sense developed by London (2012, 46–47).

Commonplace understandings of meter in Western classical music rely on the listener's inference of repeating units differentiated by strong and weak beats. In Indian classical music, strong and weak beats in the music are not necessarily meant to be guided by claps in the *tāla*. Justin London's "many meters hypothesis" (meter as skilled behavior involving many context-specific, expressively nuanced tempo-metrical types) takes in expressive microtiming at lower levels of the metric hierarchy and questions the dichotomy of structure-versus-expression. Hence, at different tempi and in different styles, a meter with X number of beats can vary considerably. In the case of *tāla*, were one to grant metric status to the structure in an ordinary sense, how might one account for different feel patterns of a single *tāla*? In North India, the *ṭhekā* allows for such variation and yields differently named *tāls*. In South India, one particularly common groove within the 8-count *ādi tāla* has its own name, *deśādi*, which would seem to support London's more inclusive concept of meter, but in South India generally, groove patterns are not considered part of the definition of *tāla*.

Beat remains a difficult concept to translate across various musical styles. Determining the placement of "beats" is essential in attempts to employ Western staff notation, and is usually important in representing meter as well. In Locke's analysis dance movements determine the beat, and he uses beat numbers to indicate the location of every pulse in the musical flow. This makes it possible to allude to time-signature-like representations of meter: "this piece is 'in four.'" Widdess regards the beat as an isochronous division of the metric cycle while Miriam Rovsing Olsen allows for a drum pattern of 5 beats of equal or unequal length. Some nonisochronous notions of beat derive from the more fundamental idea of a "strike," with some implication of accent within a larger structure, but not necessarily implying a regularly recurring pattern (Kippen, Wolf). The term becomes even more problematic in Japanese, when we learn that terms for beat need not refer to attacks, but also to time points to which performers attend as well as to the interval between one time point and the next (Takanori Fujita).

Representations of rhythm often involve metaphorical projections that extend beyond notation. Here we mention three: body, space, and object. For Eugene Montague, Rovsing Olsen, Widdess, and others, rhythm is the product of bodily agency. Reminiscent of Hornbostel's early insights into African rhythm as composed of physical movements as well as sounds, Montague argues that rhythm and its notation carry traces of the physical gestures with which they were learned, and on down the line so that any pattern implicates a history of gestures. In Rovsing Olsen's analysis, the complexity of Berber rhythmic texture arises from principles of bodily movement, "shifting/intertwining" and "trembling/restlessness." This latter principle militates against "shifting" and is marked by a stop or jolt.

Considering the relation between attacks and pauses (or sustained durations) turns out to be fundamental to rhythmic thinking in many societies including those of South Asia (*laya:* Wolf, Kippen) and Java (*irama:* Sumarsam), and West Asia (e.g., in the rhythmic practices discussed by the Central Asian polymath Al-Fārābī in the tenth century C.E.; Sawa 2009, and Blum this volume). On a small scale, these representations of rhythm are linear. But rhythmic representations often project into space. For example, according to Locke, African teachers emphasize circular conceptions of time that tend to destabilize a single notion of beat 1 in a cycle. Yet the time-line also extends forward in virtual horizontal space—it is linear, while sustaining "vertical" relations with other parts in 3:2 proportions. One can hardly mention "projection" without taking into account Christopher Hasty's theory of rhythm, which involves the listener or player predicting durations based on ones heard before. In thinking through the potentials of this theory, as John Roeder does in this volume, it is almost inevitable to spatialize time in the form of diagrams.

A third type of metaphorical projection relates rhythm to concrete objects, organs, or figures. Fujita, for instance, points to a rushing stream and the relation of lord to servant as prominent rhythmic metaphors in Noh. Rovsing Olsen describes models of barley and date-palm growth as fundamental to Berber rhythmic ideas. And Sumarsam notes Javanese instances of widespread tendencies to describe rhythm in relation to breath and heartbeat. This selection of metaphorical projections provides a sliding scale of relations between the universal and the particular.

Another category of representation might be labeled the organological: rhythm embodied in things. Here we encounter the distinction between something *having* rhythm—however defined—and *being* rhythm—as is often the case in representing drum patterns. Versions of this distinction can be found in the tendency of European/American trained music scholars to represent rhythm as "in" such and such a time signature, as opposed to representations of musical process in relation to concrete patterns (*usuls*, *ṭhekās*) and gesture sequences. Benadon's discussion of drum-solo-ostinato relations brings out these issues of rhythmic embodiment and counterpoint.

Another aspect of the organological concerns mechanisms of counting or timekeeping, whether they be such abstract constructs as written measures or *tālas*, or such concrete structures as those marked by gongs, metallophones, and other gamelan instruments, West African bells, drums and hand claps, and responsorial hand claps (Benadon). These abstract versus concrete aspects of timekeeping foreground the difference between unsounded and sounded aspects of rhythmic structure, important to Hindustani concepts of "empty" beat (Kippen) and Japanese "taking komi" (Fujita). Roeder (this volume) and Wolf (2010) also allude to the possibility that *cikārī* and *tāla*-string plucks, normally thought of as forms of punctuation in *ālāp/ālāpana*, provide projective potentials for hearing future attacks as if they are "on time" (Roeder).

"Oral notations"—mnemonics for tones, drum timbres, and other instrumental sounds in African, Indian, Indonesian, and many other traditions—are tools for rhythmic representation, teaching, practice, and memorization. They have the advantage of helping one to think musically without musical instruments at hand.[3] In the Ewe tradition Locke describes, oral notation is not merely an iconic representation of instrumental sounds but constitutes its own language with semantics that comment on aspects of performance. Whereas oral notations may aid one in performance (i.e., are "prescriptive") and provide culturally specific ways of reducing the complexity of musical process, complex "descriptive" notations, such as those of microtimings in Benadon's chapter, help us bring into focus musical details whose systematicity may be difficult to grasp in the heat of performance.

In the study of rhythm, elastic rhythm has been a particularly challenging topic when it comes to notation. Indeed, one author's interest in the "problem" of so-called free rhythm arose from attempts to notate it (Widdess 1995, 79). It's a catch-22: to analyze the sound object one wants to put it on paper, but to put it on paper one must make decisions about temporal relations/groupings that should, properly, be part of the analysis and not prior to it; this is arguably true for all transcription and merely more obvious here. Wolf (this volume and 2010) attempted to circumvent the enforced precision of the written note—especially problematic in South Indian classical music—by providing a recording with his finger snaps as a tactus, allowing listeners to compare their own subjective responses to his in real time. South Indian classical *ālāpana* provides a great density of melodic movement, which would call for detail at the level of pulse and subdivision thereof in a notation. Slow *ālāp* in North India can often be represented in terms of long pitch durations that are equal to or exceed that of a possible pulse (Widdess 1994 and Roeder this volume). Widdess used time measurements along with Ritwik Sanyal's own sense of pulse in his performance to create a notation. Roeder in this volume uses Widdess's data to recast the analysis in terms of Hasty's projection theory.

In this volume, Christopher Hasty explicates rhythm in terms of what he calls R1—realtime experience of rhythmic process—and R2—objectifications or representations of rhythm encountered outside the musical event. In this discussion of representation, we have encountered processes that engage both R1 and R2—oral notation (which could be written down), embodiments of metrical form through instruments or hand gestures, encounters with metric moments that are signified by absence, and in some ways a return to the Socratic idea of rhythm as time interval in the movement of bodies.

UNITS

Units pertinent to the experience of rhythm, as perceived and performed, are recognized as they recur (or acquire that potential)—in a continuous succession on one occasion, or serving similar or different functions on new occasions. A *projected duration*, as that term is used in the chapters of Hasty, Roeder, Blum, and Montague, is a unit whose recurrence is felt as possible, perhaps even highly likely, but not yet actual. Units with well-established identities and histories include the *gesture patterns* of claps and waves that have long been codified in Sanskrit treatises (Widdess) and the *practiced gestures* of instrumentalists whose acquired habits enable them to reproduce the right gesture at the appropriate time (Montague). Thinking and playing with their voices, musicians often isolate *phonemes, syllables, words, formulas*, and *figures* as units that can be articulated at will, distorted or otherwise varied, juxtaposed with other units, or imitated on an instrument. Musicians may experience the intervals of rest or preparation between two articulations as units requiring as much attention as the articulations (see Fujita on Noh and Hasty on "New Music").

The extent to which terminologies identify the units that musicians learn to recognize in performance varies greatly from one musical practice to another. Terms for units may designate musicians' actions (or moments of rest), results of those actions, or both at once (e.g., a conductor's *beat* or one *part* in a four-voice chorus). Many terms identify a *series* of actions, a *path* for musicians to follow in the course of performance. Common metaphors that pedagogues and theorists have appropriated as terms for musical units (and defined in various ways) include *point, line, cycle, slot, grid, frame, groove, stream, wave, way, mode*, or *matrix*. Many units are compounds, composed for example of a set number of pulses, moras, syllables, strokes, counts, beats, or groupings of these, and a fair number of languages have terms for compound units at two or more hierarchical levels and for certain of their constituents. How those terminologies have been or might be compared across languages is a topic that continually turns up in these chapters (see Kippen on Indo-Persian treatises; Wolf on derivatives of Tamil, Sanskrit, Persian, and Arabic terms in several South Asian languages; Sumarsam on

Indian musical concepts as a stimulus to gamelan theory; and Blum on Arabic analogues of ancient Greek terms).

We encourage readers of these chapters to reflect on differences between universalizing and locally relevant terminologies, and on limitations as well as strengths of music theoretical terminology in English. One universalizing term used in several of these chapters, *cycle*, can be defined as an ordering of constituent moments that recurs as a recognizable unit and functions to orient the actions of performers. Units at higher hierarchical levels tend to bring that function more strongly into play, for example a *gongan* in Javanese gamelan (composed of a given number of *gatras* or *matras*), or a 32-bar *chorus* of a popular song (composed of four 8-bar *phrases*) on which jazz musicians play solos. As a general term, *cycle* may designate either a compound unit like a *gongan* or *chorus*, or what Gerhard Kubik (2010, 41) terms a *short cycle*, such as a drummer's short ostinato (see Benadon), one unit in Agbadza with 4 beats and 12 fast pulses (see Locke), or a single measure of a song in 4/4.

Each realization of a cycle defines or confirms a predictable duration or a relatively fixed sequence of events in at least one stratum of the texture. As one such duration is succeeded by the next, performers may attempt to reproduce the same sequence of movements and sounds, perhaps for as many times as a ritual protocol or a composition requires. More often, some performers maintain a constant pattern through each recurrence of the cycle and some make changes from one cycle to the next; many performance roles carry responsibilities of both types. Each term that has been glossed as *cycle* carries its own implications in the relevant musical practices; consecutive cycles may or may not follow one another without interruption, for example. In current usage, a cycle is commonly a sequence of isochronous beats and/or fast pulses, registered in various ways by performers who make certain beats or pulses audible or visible but may perceive others as not requiring or permitting action. Three exceptions to isochrony discussed in these chapters are the "fixed series of 5 long pitches" that is cycled in a bamboo flute solo from Papua New Guinea (Roeder), the common "8-beat meter (cycle or unit)" of Japanese Noh where the timing of beats is extremely flexible (Fujita), and a rhythmic cycle to which verses are sung in Iranian Khorasan, in which the timing of stressed syllables is only sometimes predictable (Blum). Performers of many European dance genres know both the prescribed number of beats in each measure, and the subtleties of timing that dancers in a given locality expect, as in the Polish *mazurka* where more time must elapse between the onsets of beats 2 and 3 than between those of beats 1 and 2. If attacks at certain levels of a cycle are isochronous, those at lower or higher levels may not be (see Polak 2010; Polak and London 2014; Kippen and Wolf in this volume). When the fastest pulse is isochronous, musicians may identify it with a sequence of syllables rather than an abstract term such as *beat*, *stroke*, or the *protos chronos* ("primary duration") of ancient Greek rhythmics.

Terms that denote or index actions of performers, results of those actions, units like cycles or measures that orient the sequencing of action and rest, and phases of a composition or performance must be understood in relation to one another and to concepts that control the relationships among units, such as *irama* and *laya* (discussed by

Sumarsam and Wolf). In many languages, a single term refers to units of two or more types (e.g., *beat* in American English; Arabic *dharb* and its Persian equivalent, *zarb*, discussed by Kippen and Wolf; Kota *dāk* and Tamil *aṭi*, discussed by Wolf). A term or name may designate a class of units, one member of a class, or one portion of a larger unit: each Hindustani *tāla* has its own proper name (e.g., *tīntāl*), and each is structured as a cycle (*āvart*) with a given number of beats (*mātrā*) grouped into sections (*vibhāg*) whose initial beat is marked with either a clap or a wave. *Tīntāl* gets its name from the "three" (*tīn*) claps that mark the first, second, and fourth of its four *vibhāgs*.

Ways that names and numbers can represent rhythmic units are a central concern of Kippen's and Wolf's chapters. Kippen glosses the term *sam* as "a beat in a *tāl* considered to be a point of confluence or resolution," noting that in its earliest documented uses it did not always designate the first beat of a *tāl* as it does today. Widdess analyzes a heterometric song composed of "timespans of proportionally related lengths," achieved by repeating cycles of 4, 14, 4, and 10 beats enough times to produce a sequence of 32, 28, 24, and 20 beats, in the proportion 8:7:6:5. The assumption that rhythm emerges from simple proportions among units that allow for enumeration has a long history in European and South Asian music theory; indeed, the Latin equivalent of Greek *rhythmós* was *numerus* (see Seidel 1980 for the history of both terms).

While counting is a common way to name the constituents of a larger unit, pedagogies vary in the extent to which attaching numbers to beats, strokes, or larger units is deemed helpful in early stages of learning (or at all). Teachers may insist that movement patterns relevant to the constituent moments of a cycle, matrix, or schema are best learned without counting (cf. Locke on Agbadza and Fujita on "ignoring the basic 8-beat meter," as the songs of Japanese Noh are taught). Teachers and theorists also differ in the extent to which they find it useful to attach names to musical units. Whatever the pedagogy, performers must internalize the sequences of action and inaction (including cues or preparations for action, as in Noh drumming) that could prepare them to assume a specific role in performance. This inevitably entails learning how one may, must, or must not perform specific actions at certain moments in a sequence, in order to differentiate those moments from others.

Musicians often create so many varieties of accent and salience that performers and other listeners may choose to focus on certain of these as especially relevant to their experience of rhythm during one phase or at one moment of a performance. Locke describes "beat one" in Agbadza as "a moment of both rhythmic closure and initiation," as well as "a moment of temporal orientation." Fujita explains that Noh musicians understand "beat one" in the 8-beat cycle as the time interval that separates it from beat 8 and prepares its articulation. The numbers assigned to beats in a cycle or measure often register differences between odd-numbered and even-numbered beats—for example, odd or even as *active-enlarged* or *subdued-shortened* in Noh; *light* or *heavy, soft* or *loud* in gamelan according to Sindusawarno as quoted by Sumarsam; nonweight-bearing or weight-bearing in Agbadza.

Rhythmic units defined by a recurring configuration of accents include gestures coordinated with a regular series of beats, such as the drummer's gestures in a typical measure of Minor Threat's *Straight Edge* analyzed by Montague and the "quick contraction-expansion torso movement" of dancers that generates several types of accent on the twelve fast pulses of a four-beat measure in Agbadza. Locke's gloss of *accent* as a "qualitatively different feeling tone" is pertinent to these and many other examples. Even when listeners are not actively performing, they may respond to the "qualitatively different feeling tones" in a short configuration of accents, imagining how it might feel to produce them, or making what E. M. von Hornbostel, writing on melody as "an act of motility" and "one of the elements that determine rhythm," termed an involuntary "motor reaction" to an "acoustic impulse" (Blum 1991, 11–12). Several contributors to this book see rhythm as dependent on what Locke terms "aural and kinesthetic perception."

PERIODICITY AND CYCLE

To the extent rhythm involves the repetition of durations, rhythm will involve questions of periodicity and cycle. "Periodicity" implies continuous repetition or recurrence at regular or same intervals of time, again and again. Music and poetry can provide intricate and exquisitely varied ways of experimenting with fairly large and complicated periodic repetitions of various scales and levels of complexity. Indeed, music can far exceed unsung poetry in scale and complexity. By slowing speech, singing can bring language into larger scales of duration. Music as theorized can suggest ways of experimenting with conceptual issues repetition might raise. One way of measuring the same temporal interval is by count—a growing length of time measured by units. Temporality here enters as the growth of the interval, unit by unit. (When we speak of the growth or expansion of space we are also speaking of temporality.) The completion of the cycle or count is a returning to the same place as a mark of beginning, or rather as a mark of beginning-again, the beginning of a *new* "cycle" that by definition is repeated, or at least repeatable. This beginning has many names: "*sam*," "*thesis*," "metrically accented," "one," "downbeat," and so forth. The counts of a cycle, though they can be named by number, must be qualitatively differentiated if they are to be sensed—they occupy special places. For instance, in Hindustani music the cycle (*tāl*) is characterized or qualified in detail by its repeated and identifying *ṭhekā*, a very specific and intricate patterning of the cycle through each of its counts. The counts of the cycle are composed of complex and thus highly characteristic patterns made of stroke patterns, timbral differences, and physical-instrumental gestures—movements of the two hands striking the two drums. Moreover, even the semblance of numerical count is questioned by the introduction of an empty beat (not zero) and the resultant numerical disarray—as in tintal: X 2 0 3. ("Tintal" = beats: X 2 3.) Further compounding multidimensionality are the *bols*, the spoken patterns.

How temporal or in what ways terms are temporal is also various (among less temporal options, think of the periodic table). It might be said that all the many musical names for something like periodicity are specific choices for thinking about temporality understood as humanly experienced. And different musics explore the endless variety of possibilities for experiencing repetition. Indeed, any of these musical and music theoretical constructions of repetition might help to deepen the notion of periodicity. In this volume Fujita in his discussion of "*haku*" or "*hyoshi*" points to a notion of beginning that can, from outside, seem puzzling or counterintuitive—that beat 1 as the initiation of a succeeding 8-beat cycle might be thought as "measured from" the preceding beat 8 or perhaps be felt as the issue of beat 8 itself the culmination of the preceding cycle. Moreoever, as Fujita's examples show, the 8-count cycle need not be composed of equal durations. It suffices that the 8 counts are distinguished by their numerically and qualitatively unique positions in the series. If questions of repetition or periodicity are endless, then endless (in principle) too are musical and music-theoretical cultures that can provide ways of experiencing and thinking about temporal process.

Notice that if we want to refer to individual repetitions we use the word "cycle," not "period." A period need not imply repetition, as for example when we speak of "a period of time" or "the classical period." We can speak of "a cycle" as either one round or as an entire series (e.g., the everlasting cycle of birth and death) or as a complete set (e.g., an epic cycle or song cycle).

The symbolisms of the ouroboros, samsara, "eternal return" (Eliade 2000) and others speak to perennial questions of permanence and change by proposing a mediation, an act of returning (change) to the same (permanent, eternal) place or the same originative moment (the mouth eternally swallowing the tail). If we think about music in terms of such symbolisms music can seem to reenact the drama of rebirth in its cyclic returns. Music can in this way be given mythic importance and be aligned with general human and supra-human repetitions ("the music of the spheres").

It is a common trope to oppose "cycle" and "line" as symbols for an Eastern mentality of stasis (or "eternity") and a Western mentality of movement (or "progress"). But even if there were some such (and certainly less crude) difference of mentality and geography, the symbols "cycle" and "line" taken in temporal terms are not so clearly opposed. If "line" is taken as the "time-line" conceived as number line, then it is a symbol for the annihilation of tense or movement (as it has been for classical Western physics) and for the denial of the reality of time. On the other hand, "cycle" is the affirmation of a real stretch of time (duration) even if it is necessarily closed off in order to be *a* duration. Moreover, it is closed off in the periodic and continuous or unbroken return to a new beginning. Thus periodicity opens this cycle to a becoming beyond itself, in the proliferation of cycles. Thinking about things in this way could make "line" a symbol of timelessness (Western mechanism) and "circle" a symbol of temporal opening as circulation and continuation.

METER

Conceived most abstractly as number, cycles are closed, autonomous units. As units, cycles are countable—for example, cycles per second. Here it is only the repetition of quantity that matters. Such units of quantity are simple and uniform or unpatterned. To give rise to patterns, cycles must be differentiated in some way, for example as accented/unaccented or strong/weak. Meter can be understood as a way of opening cycle to the great variety and complexity of patterning found in music. Thus meter is often understood as a complexity of cycles or of cycles-within-cycles, and so introduces the notion of hierarchy as faster-moving cycles grouped or organized or unified by higher-level, slower-moving cycles. For example, in Western notation "3/4 (or quarter-note)" meter is the grouping of quarter-note pulses in threes, resulting in a larger/slower cycle and thus a higher level. In this case, the hierarchy can extend down into various cyclic divisions of the quarter-note pulse. The hierarchy might also extend upward to cycles larger than the central or "prototypical" (Rosch 1973) measure, to "hypermeasures" or measures of measures. In any case, at whatever level we wish to focus on, the others are always in some sense available. To keep the measure is to be open to the possibilities of more than one level (see Fujita). In this sense, keeping the measure is not a matter of following equal measure with equal measure. It is rather a readiness to enter into well-learned metrical behaviors. In high art forms such behaviors can become highly complex in their possibilities and thereby require great skill achieved through special practice.

A theme of this volume is metrical possibility as such. Thus, even if meter is regarded as in some sense mechanistic, it is a mechanism that is implicit rather than explicit and subject to deformations and reversals. Benadon calls meter "implicit-unchanging." To be unchanging in that music in which it can be obscured and momentarily quite forgotten, meter must be implicit rather than explicit. Benadon indicates this intermittence of meter by showing how, in the context of improvised drum solos, meter's effects can be relativized in the ever changing configurations of a global "synchronization space" that meter shares on equal footing with ostinato (explicit-unchanging) and drums (explicit-changing). Hasty points to a similar relativization in the influence *tempus* has in Renaissance music where this central "ruling" metric can nonetheless suffer all sorts and degrees of complication and even occasionally quite disappear. In the music Benadon and Locke consider, units are very precisely isochronous, as they must be to accommodate their particular energetic and fine-grained complexity in which the hierarchy of beats focuses on very small divisions. Complex isochronies can then be distinguished from one another by being out of phase, and thus distinguished can constitute a veritable (polymetric) polyphony.

Other kinds of music allow a less strict and perhaps less obvious isochrony (e.g., Fujita's "elasticity of beats" in which the same beat might pass more quickly or slowly). And it is in such cases that a strictly numerical understanding of meter may be criticized as over simple. To call such music nonmetrical is to miss an opportunity to understand meter as a *universal* category and not the possession of one music or another, one style or another. Several chapters in this volume claim for meter situations that are much more complex than strict isochrony would allow. Hasty, citing Paul Fraisse, argues that meter is very robust and quite difficult to suppress, as in New Music. Central to this debate is the connection of music and poetry where complexity/variability of speech rhythms, tamed but not always strictly ruled by the strictures of a more dance-like prosody, can draw slower music into complicated temporal relationships that are not reducible to numerical, unit-based isochrony but metrical nonetheless—or perhaps especially metrical to measure such intricate differences.

QUALITIES

Relations between universalist and local approaches to rhythm can also be apprehended in terms of qualitative aspects of rhythm—that is to say, through an emphasis on experiences as opposed to representations of rhythm. A single "piece" of music can be experienced in terms of either R1 or R2 in Hasty's theory, and often in terms of both—when one is reading a score, for instance. Montague's chapter in particular reminds us of the degree to which studies of rhythm, which sometimes pay lip service to experience, tend toward formalism and abstraction rather than subject-centered considerations of the body feeling rhythm. A moment in Sumarsam's chapter highlights this pivotal distinction in pointing out that the effect of the gong is not merely to mark coincidence (or a point in the colotomy), but also to communicate "moods" having to do with the play of melody and time preceding and following that point. Wolf's discussion of anchor points in Kota music (Wolf 2005) concerns a similar affective relation to salient moments in time and space.

Elasticity in rhythm may lead the listener to feel a tension between aspects of grid versus flow, particularly in efforts to describe it. On the part of the performer, it may be an expression of "freedom"—in the case of South Indian classical musicians, freedom from the world of rhythm as defined by *tāla* theory and metric constraints of a performance. Most metric theories growing out of Western European scholarship subsume ideas of regularly occurring beats and in that sense leave little room for subjective differences in experiencing the beat. The authors of the present volume provide more leeway in this regard, providing multiple definitions of what a beat can be (in different languages and contexts) and suggesting, perhaps, that counting, anticipating, and looking back on "beats" are activities with feeling tones that depend on genre. Qualities of rhythm take on a particular prominence when one experiences moments of textural change, such as change in *irama* (Sumarsam), meter in a heterometric piece (Widdess), and through the various stages of performance described by Rovsing Olsen.

In some theories of Noh drama, alternating moments in the temporal structure are imbued with qualities of yin and yang such that even-numbered beats are dark and subdued while odd-numbered ones are light, active, and "large" (having wide intervals preceding them); similarly at the level of drum patterns, the second-halves are small or compressed compared to the larger or temporally extended first-halves. In her case study of music in the Anti-Atlas, Miriam Rovsing Olsen points out the problems of relating the agricultural terms performers use "as metaphors" to components of performances "stemming from [Western] music theory." Instead, she contends that these terms focus on aspects of performance not emphasized in Western music theory, but rather on situated moments of temporal passage that villagers can "complete" mentally—that is, project.[4]

A commonly recognized failing of most notation systems concerns timbre, but it is precisely through timbre that performers are able to create critical distinctions in rhythmic texture, and in a larger sense rhythm generally. Benadon notes that different timbres of a drumset create separate audio streams that are best understood by listening to the recording while reading his transcriptions; the overall effect is one of "fission," persistent separation of drum solo, ostinato, and meter within "synchronization space." Locke, who deals with a more limited set of discrete timbral components, isolates the "bounce" and "press" strokes of the response drum to show the timbral morphology of 25 kidi phrases. Rovsing Olsen describes a process referred to as "inserting" or "adjusting" or "budding," giving a sense of advancement or growth. On the drums, this comes about from the contrasting timbres and attacks of two drums, one that strikes three times alternating with the other that strikes twice.

Other qualities of rhythm pertinent to this book's chapters include perceptual ambiguity in discussions of Benadon and Locke, and what Locke terms "rhythmic personality." While issues of perceptual ambiguity are raised in comparative, universalist approaches to musical rhythm, one might ask whether subject-centered studies of performers in context would yield similar expressions of ambiguity. This is not a question that can be answered once and for all, but should rather urge us to continue to seek accounts of experience in the many contexts where analysts might perceive ambiguity. Moreover, one might distinguish between the idea of choosing different ways of hearing or emphasizing rhythmic activity at different moments, and the idea of inexactitude or lack of clarity. The former might be a participant's strategy and the latter an aspect of ambiguity felt by a less acculturated listener.

INTERACTIONS

The music-making of individuals and groups depends on interactions that are guided by and generate rhythm. In many languages, the pertinent terminologies identify the responsibilities (and relative status) of participants in a performance genre and potential results of their interactions. Rhythmic theory is likewise a product of interactions, commonly involving musicians and theorists with diverse backgrounds. Reflecting on the gamelan theory generated through interactions between Dutch and Javanese scholars, and between musicians with traditional training and those trained in conservatories, Sumarsam speaks appropriately of "inside and outside looking in and out" (see also Sumarsam 1995).

Performers often discuss challenges they face in coordinating movements of different parts of the body and in responding to feedback received from their instruments, fellow performers, and auditors. In many practices they must also respond to instructions conveyed by notations or voiced in rehearsals, possibly treating a notation as "an invitation for creative experimentation," as Hasty notes in the book's final chapter. By describing music notation as "an ingenious device for capturing an improvisation, in order to allow for its rebirth" (1974 [1916], 26, trans. Blum), the composer-pianist Ferruccio Busoni encouraged performers not to endow notations with an authority that might prevent, instead of assisting in, a rebirth.

Responsibility, coordination, response, renewal, and *authority* are thus key terms for thinking about rhythmic interaction. Montague analyzes the constituents of a compound gesture involving right hand and forearm, which pianists subsume within a larger gesture as they respond to Chopin's notation of an etude. Rovsing Olsen's notations of *aḥwaš* show how Moroccan women in the central Anti-Atlas coordinate their articulation of sung syllables and their dance steps in performance genres they conceptualize in terms of plant growth, naming actions and responses performed in *aḥwaš* with terms used for phases in the cultivation of barley and date palms. At the right moments, for example, a performer or a plant may become "one who intersects, adjusts, replaces."

Sumarsam, quoting Supanggah, emphasizes "the importance of dialogue" in the musical process of gamelan (as when the *kendang* player cues changes of *irama*); Locke describes "the hand off of melodic fragments between leader and group" in Agbadza; and Wolf gives numerous examples of "rhythm as a trade in utterances," in several of which leaders of drum ensembles cue a change of pattern. Without using the term *hand off*, Rovsing Olsen notes that in performances of *aḥwaš*, male and female poets convey their verses to women's choirs in quite different ways: female poets by whispering, male poet-singers by singing. In a women's *aḥwaš*, a male poet-singer may return to the audience before the choir responds to his verses, but in a men's *aḥwaš* he must continue the improvised exchange if he is to uphold his reputation.

Wolf's chapter opens with another key term for analysis of evolving rhythmic interaction: *background* or *reference system*. More than one such system or configuration is potentially relevant to rhythmic interaction: the physical habits of performers, norms of social behavior, and assemblages of musical resources for use in teaching and performance, to name three that are considered in these chapters. Wolf's interest in South Asian reference systems for rhythm is not limited to the *tāla*s of Karnatak and Hindustani music, though he draws on *tāla* theories (old and new) in developing a framework for comparative discussion of "nonclassical" genres. Performers in drum ensembles may be expected to maintain a background that supports the leader's improvisations, and to adjust quickly when the leader cues a change of pattern. In some instances, "the ebb and flow of group reactivity" transpires over a background of social relations rather than with reference to a system that regulates the timing of moves in the manner of *tāla*.

Changes in social relations may well have consequences for systems that regulate the timing of moves. Fujita suggests that as the relationship of Noh drummers to singers changed from one of subordination to relative equality, drummers developed the practice of taking *komi* to assert their rhythmic independence from singers; furthermore, singers with professional ambitions are no longer prevented from taking lessons in drumming. In the final chapter, Hasty examines efforts of twentieth-century

Western composers "to limit or break inherent doubling of durational measure," with the result that listeners faced "a rapid and demanding flux in presentation." Among the many general questions raised by such discussions are the following: How are potential participants in a performance motivated or encouraged to join in what Widdess terms "a concerted religious effort"? Do some or all participants in a performance entrain to a background with one or more pulse streams? Does the timing of performers' actions make it difficult or impossible for listeners to entrain to a background? Do the performers encourage clapping, dancing, or other regular movements from listeners and onlookers? Do some or all of the latter regard such responses as inappropriate on their part?

In chapter 1, Hasty discusses "the complexity of event formation," noting that "there are always multiple 'hierarchical levels' of relevance at work in any situated event." As we attend to shifting relationships among levels, performers and analysts often rely on referents that we may describe as a "meter," a "cognitive schema or template" (Widdess); a "gridlike substratum" or "abstract metrical frame" (Wolf); a "groove" (Montague, Wolf, Widdess); an "unchanging and often syncopated foil for the drummer's rhythmic invention" (Benadon); a "cyclical space" in Hindustani music that the drummer's *ṭhekā*s endow with "a recognizable musical character" (Kippen); a "cyclic structure conceived as background" (Sumarsam); or "a latent, implicit and tacit dimension that is available to consciousness as a factor in a listener's perception" (Locke). All these metaphors relate to what Hasty describes as "internal measurement": "the take on the past, the background, potentality, virtuality (however we might choose to name and characterize the situation something new is born into) that offers the new event all that it has to go on." Hasty's language acknowledges that those of us engaged with music will continue to make disparate choices, one issue being how we understand a background in relation to potentiality. An engagement with the potential, the virtual is fundamental to musical experience, in the course of a single performance or when seeking to identify major changes in a music's history. Locke's conception of a *metric matrix*—"a multidimensional dynamic condition in which several beat streams (metric fields) coexist simultaneously"—directs attention to "the potential [of each phrase] to recast a listener's perception of the overall polyrhythm." Kippen describes a "sea change" in the practice and theory of Hindustani music through which *tāl* gained an "ability to reflect the animated rhythmic flow of a metric cycle."

Moments when actions of two or more performers coincide are often highly salient, all the more so when they are relatively infrequent as in Noh or when "instrumental layers need not take their measure from one another" (as in the passage from Boulez's *Le marteau sans maître* discussed in Hasty's chapter "New Music—New Rhythm"). In a survey of music terminology in two Mande dialects of Guinea, Mali, and Senegambia, Eric Charry (2000, 313–17) registers multiple uses of the verb *ben* "to meet, agree," which he contrasts with the common (though questionable) derivation of Greek *rhythmos* from the verb *rhein* "to flow" (xxvii). In many musical practices, performers learn when and how two or more sequences of sounds might or ought to meet, as well as when and how they are best kept apart. Fujita describes situations in which a Noh drummer must remain detached, rather than synchronizing specific strokes with sung syllables. Expectations of coincidence may allow for a degree of flexibility, as when gamelan musicians who entrain silently to a stream of beats or fast pulses time their attacks to come slightly "early" or "late" (Sumarsam). Benadon analyzes the thought and play of three drummers within what he calls a *synchronization space*, a concept he illustrates by diagramming five possible states in which the three elements of drum, ostinato, and meter are either apart, together, or in "variable (a)synchrony" with two elements together and one apart.

The compositional thinking responsible for so many rituals and ceremonies in the course of human history plays continually with relationships of *apart, together*, and *variable (a)synchrony*. In a classic study of Stravinsky's *Les Noces*, Margarita Mazo drew attention to Stravinsky's remarkable insight into phases of Russian peasant wedding rituals when two "layers are improvised independently, each within its own framework and with no fixed idea as to note-to-note correspondences and harmonic coordinations between them," pointing to such passages as nos. 24–27 and 68–70 in *Les Noces* as evidence of Stravinsky's interest in that aspect of peasant ritual practice (Mazo 1990, 133). Geneviève Dournon recorded a wedding dance of the Muria Gonds of Bastar, India, in which boys and girls move to independent pulse streams which they maintain on double-headed drums and small iron cymbals, respectively (Dournon 1980, side A, track 3). In a study subtitled *Time, space, and music in the lives of the Kotas of South India*, Wolf (2005) treats moments when musicians synchronize attacks (in contrast with those when they do not) as one variety of *anchor*, a term that denotes "a value-laden point of reference that affects events or places surrounding it" (237). And in the New Music of the second half of the twentieth century, Hasty identifies compositional concerns that have much in common with those explored for so long by ritual specialists. In Morton Feldman's *De Kooning* (1963), for example, performers are responsible for the durations of events, and in his *Crippled Symmetry* (1983) the notation "fosters" interactions among the performers without "controlling" them. Modes of musical interaction extend from those requiring tight synchronization of all actions to those allowing for considerable independence in different domains of activity, extending beyond the production of sounds (see Ellis 1985 on *interlock* in Australian Aboriginal performance). The long series of collaborations between Merce Cunningham and John Cage was informed by what Cunningham termed "the underlying principle . . . that music and dance could be separate entities independent and interdependent, sharing a common time" (Meade and Rothfuss 2017, 34). Each chapter of this book explores some of the ways humans interact as we share a common time.

ORGANIZATION

In organizing the conference from which this book developed, we aimed simply to invite scholars whose work we find especially interesting, without trying for comprehensive coverage of world regions or of approaches to analysis of rhythm. We will be pleased if readers find the variety of approaches represented here a stimulus for thinking about how local theories and practices relate to universalizing methods, and vice versa. The six sections of our introduction offer general statements that readers may wish to assess in relation to the local theories/practices or universalizing methods that are central to their musical experience.

We have arranged the thirteen chapters to bring out issues addressed by more than one author. Questions about temporal experience raised in the opening chapter by Christopher Hasty turn up in several of the remaining chapters: explicitly in chapters 2 through 7, 9 and 12 (by Roeder, Blum, Locke, Montague, Benadon, Sumarsam, Rovsing Olsen, and Wolf), and implicitly elsewhere. Roeder finds Hasty's concept of projection useful in hearing a vocal *darāmad* that initiates a performance of Persian classical music, a flute solo from Papua New Guinea, and a Hindustani *ālāp*. Blum's chapter opens with a discussion of Arabic rhythmic theory in relation to Hasty's concern with how duration comes to be determined.

Locke offers the most sustained discussion of one of the book's primary concerns, the multidimensionality of rhythmic experience. Montague pursues that theme with a focus on the bodily experience of performers with instruments, and Benadon with an analysis of five drummers' actions within what he terms a *synchronization space*. Benadon, and later Widdess, are the two authors in our collection who draw significantly on current work in music cognition. Sumarsam and Fujita draw attention to the flexibility of timing in relation to very different types of cycle in Javanese gamelan and Japanese Noh theater. Rovsing Olsen returns to the topic of bodily experience, in this case that of singers and dancers in the agricultural labor that provides the concepts with which they theorize about musical performance.

Musicians trained in other practices have long admired the rhythmic inventiveness of South Asian musicians. Examples in our group of three chapters extend from Nepal in the north to the Nilgiri Hills in the south. Kippen's study of the treatment of a "rhythmic revolution" in theoretical sources provides new insight into the historical development of several terms that are now central to the theory of Hindustani music. Widdess pursues several interesting questions about practices that allow for more than one time-cycle in a single composition or performance; his chapter brings out the relevance of sociological analysis and work on music cognition for the writing of South Asian music history. Wolf describes multiple manifestations of what he terms "a family of common rhythmic conceptions," with attention to connections between these representations (Hasty's R2) and subjective experience (R1).

Like Kippen's and, more briefly, Fujita's chapters, Hasty's final chapter considers implications of a break in musical practice, one that in this case was marked with the term "New Music." None of the chapters is consistent with the stereotyped view of rhythm as but one "element" or "dimension" of music.

NOTES

1. Powers describes essentially the same phenomenon as rhythm, here referring to the drum mnemonics *ta din giṇ ṇa tom*, which can appear in different durational configurations in cadential passages: "Musical rhythms whose fundamental property is the number of attacks in the pattern need not be connected with either speech or accentual rhythm" (Powers 1986, 705).

2. P. Sambamoorthy locates *mātra* at an intermediate level, equivalent to the 4-count *laghu* of Karnatak music. Depending on the structure of a given *tāla, mātra* could in that case be understood as having three levels of hierarchy: the *mātra*, the *akṣara*, and the *naḍai*. However, the length of the mātra in Indian music varies according to theorist and performer (Sambamoorthy 1958, 110).

3. Wegner considers the related practice of "shadow singing" in reconsidering the phenomenon of inherent rhythms: "one might ask whether shadow singing will have given preference to percepts which mirror musical material actually sung in different musical contexts" (1993, 222). This reminds us that vocalization of instrumental music serves different purposes, and can foreground varying features, in different contexts.

4. Chernoff makes a similar point in writing that certain kinds of metaphors he encountered in West Africa "do not easily lend themselves to Western descriptive terminology" (1997, 22).

1

Thinking With and About Rhythm

Christopher Hasty

IT IS CUSTOMARY to begin an essay on rhythm with the problem of definition. As Paul Fraisse (1982, 189) writes: "The task of those who study rhythm is a difficult one, because a precise, generally accepted definition of rhythm does not exist."[1] The same might be said of practically any term, but rhythm seems especially problematic in that its uses point in two directions that are difficult to reconcile. On the one hand, rhythm can be understood as objective pattern that can be represented, named, and described; for example, in music and poetry, abstract patterns of duration and relative accent. This is the dominant sense of the word favored in dictionaries and in technical studies. On the other hand, rhythm can name something experienced or felt apart from such representation, something we might call the engaging course or flow of things. This sense of rhythm might be called qualitative, or aesthetic, or subjective. Because it is connected to value and meaning and speaks of quality as well as (or perhaps, as yet, unseparated from) quantity, rhythm in this second sense resists quantitative analysis and is rarely encountered in technical discussions.

The first sense objectifies rhythm as an extractable component, as when, for example, we speak of *the* rhythm *of* say, a passage of music or poetry; that is, when "rhythm" is a substantive or a definite noun or noun phrase. The second, "subjective" sense can be perhaps most clearly heard when we use rhythm as an adjective—as when we speak of a rhythmic gesture or movement, or a rhythmic performance. This difference can be seen as, among other things, a difference of part and whole. In the first case, rhythm is understood as a self-standing entity or pattern, *a* rhythm, separable as one among many other components of the music or poetry (e.g., melody, sonority, timbre, form, theme, semantic meaning). In the second case, there is no separation, no rhythm apart from the object or ongoing activity that is called rhythmic and that involves all dimensions of sense and feeling that can come into play. Thus a rhythmic performance may be valued as such for its spontaneity, its quality of movement, its expressiveness—all of which involve all the components or factors we might name (and perhaps many more).

Thinking in terms of actual performance is thinking in terms of process in which there is both the articulation and the integration of anything that can come into play in a here and now situation. By contrast, thinking in terms of product, *a* rhythm as an entity can be imagined separable from its carrier and repeatable just as itself. Thus different things can have the same rhythm (e.g., iambic). Such a rhythm is timeless in its power of "appearing" at any time and being conceived (named, described) apart from any actual appearance. The ongoing activity or process that is rhythm*ic*, however, has no rhythm apart from its actual appearance. Indeed, calling a gesture rhythmic implies particularity, a quality that inheres in just this gesture (*this* gesture qualified as rhythmic). A rhythmic drawing, for example, has its rhythm (a rhythm we see by looking) as does a rhythmic performance of a poem, a dance, a "piece" of music.

Although the difference between an artifact such as a finished drawing, a composed or notated poem, or piece of music and a performance may seem striking, it must be remembered that artifacts must first be made and made to be worked with, again and again. To *be* an artifact is to be repeatable, and each repetition is a new performance. The object or activity here is not separable from the rhythmic in the way an abstract pattern such as, for example, short-long is separable from its host, an actual here and now utterance of ultimately unfathomable complexity. A drawing or a composition may be said to be many more things than just rhythmic in the sense that all sorts of categories can be applied (costly, damaged, Impressionistic, orchestral), but it can't be understood apart from rhythm if it is to be seen, heard, felt. Rhythm in this sense brings us always to time and the course of experience—to the "adverbial" question of *how* (how it goes) rather than a "substantive" or nominal *what* (what it is).

If adverbial rhythm points to the temporal, we will have to make room for the complexities of becoming as well as the analytic naming of parts. One of the virtues of rhythm is its problematic mixture of "objective" and "subjective," or of representation and actual, ongoing, present experience—a dominant, objectivist reduction to formal determinacy haunted by an opening to the spontaneity of performance. In this chapter I will argue for a reversal of value to promote performance and to question the powers of form. I begin by suggesting that what I have called the "subjective" sense of rhythm is broader than the "objective" and can thus help motivate a critique of the narrowness of objectification and its exclusionary claims.

RHYTHM AND PASSAGE

Rhythm as something experienced or lived involves movement, change, ongoing activity. As such, rhythm is unthinkable apart from temporal passage. There is no immobilized rhythm, no rhythm without change, no timeless rhythm or rhythm at an instant. In the case of rhythmic experience, actual passage is unavoidable. Life goes on, and the word "rhythm" can point to the dynamics or the characterful shaping of that going on. By temporal passage I mean the fact that time doesn't stop, that the world keeps pouring in, in unceasing novelty in a now or present that is always on the move, always new. The tense of "present" here should be understood specifically as present progressive. Indeed, the new or now is always being shaped by what is or has been, but it exceeds that *what* by moving forward, becoming something different as it goes. To be involved in the present, what is past must in a sense be repeated, but to be repeated it cannot return as the same. Without difference or differing there could be no passage, no movement from one to another. Let's say that rhythm is the particular course, the characterful, eventful "how" of differing or becoming—becoming precisely different.

What rhythm adds to words like "movement," "change," "process," and "activity" is a focus on moments of repetition and difference in the creation of events that are palpable, felt in their very becoming. Rhythm points to the sensible course of events which to be events must be differentiated but which, nonetheless, create a flow or course. There is no word that speaks more urgently of eventful becoming and that more sharply engages the problems such becoming poses for thought. In his entry for "rhythm" in the *Harvard Dictionary of Music* (1969), Grosvenor Cooper offers the following definition of rhythm giving primacy to what I have thus far characterized as a secondary meaning: "In its primary sense, the whole feeling of movement in music, with the strong implication of both regularity and differentiation."[2] "The whole feeling of movement" might be called a fluid articulation in which rhythm is both a separating and a binding. In this articulation successive events come into being and attain their duration as they give way or give birth to new events, but there is no break in the movement one to another. In its unbroken movement rhythm mixes traditional categorical distinctions of succession and continuity, articulation and flow, holding and moving, separating and binding, repetition and novelty (or difference). Taken in Cooper's "primary sense" or in a sense that takes temporal passage seriously, rhythm exposes such paradoxes of time and passage. Such paradoxes can be averted if time is simplified so as to allow time to be conceived as pure order or arrangement (*taxis*). But if time is reduced to a linear order of essentially separate parts (units or instants) rhythm will be deprived of its problematic power to stimulate thought of temporal complexity.

THE GENERALITY OF PROCESS

In the paradoxical or problematic pairings just listed, the second terms—*continuity, flow, moving, binding, novelty*—are dynamic, processive terms consonant with the rhythmic-experiential terms I first suggested as a way of focusing on temporal passage (change, passage, ongoing activity). The first terms in this list—*succession, articulation, holding, separating, repetition*—point to objects, things carved out of process. Such thing-terms are also at home in a "subjective" (experienced, felt) sense of the rhythmic that requires change and therefore some sort of differentiation or heterogeneity (a rhythmic performance can't do without articulation and succession). If rhythm is flow it is a characterful, patterned, shaped flow. But these first-named carving terms are exclusive for an objective rhythm that requires objective (external) measure and discrete units for measuring.

If subjective rhythm gladly accepts both sets of terms, objective rhythm doesn't return the favor. Serving the needs of analysis or the naming of parts, objective rhythm is fully invested in the particulate and so must resist a dynamic-kinetic that exceeds division and separation. This disparity reveals a sense in which subjective rhythm is a broader category than objective rhythm, justifying Cooper's "primary sense" and his privileging of movement over regularity and differentiation. The disparity will come as no surprise if it is seen that the realm of form inhabited by objective measure and pattern is one built of an essentially static, dead image of an abstract time in which passage is eliminated and consequently nothing can actually happen or become. Indeed, nothing can actually happen apart from an emerging present situation, a now (*actuel*) that is always new. If this is granted we can now say that rhythm, most broadly and generously conceived, speaks to the liveliness of this situation.

The subjective-experiential sense of the rhythmic is broad and generous because it accepts time and becoming. Indeed, if thought is nothing outside or apart from passage then thinking with and about forms itself is not immune from a becoming that static form itself would deny. Our invention of forms, fixed patterns, schemata, representations—all those things that would defy passage by staying the same—is, as invention, always on the move, always actually said and heard "in time," always different, always changing sayer and hearer, changing practice, making new values that both endure and perish "at the same time." Theorizing and analyzing are rhythmic acts, and the theories and analyses that they deposit are nothing apart from their various entertainments or enablings, much as musical or poetic artifacts—written or not—are nothing apart from the possibilities for experience they afford. Confusion, however, arises if the out-of-time abstraction of theory is taken to be the timeless basis for performance, an underlying structure to which our reading, playing, hearing, saying, feeling, sensing, doing, and making of music or poetry ought conform. This confusion is the work of reification or what Whitehead (1967) calls "the fallacy of misplaced concreteness," the error of mistaking the abstract for the concrete, thereby denying the irreducible complexity and the temporality of the concrete.[3] Why should (and how could) a temporal-concrete conform to an atemporal representation from which the temporal has been abstracted? And why should we grant a one-way relation that gives power only to the representation? Why not ask instead that representations or theories of the actual, temporal-concrete conform to actuality which always involves process, temporality, becoming?[4] Why should the objective be asked to rule the subjective?

These are meant as rhetorical questions that ask for a reversal of values in which abstractions of theory would subserve the deliverances of experience marked by particularity and novelty and not held apart from passage. Posed nonrhetorically, as questions of the status quo in which novelty and passage are customarily dismissed, they ask for reasons, for cultural-historical answers that would turn our attention to overriding values of control, especially the scientific-technological control that has proved so successful precisely by eliminating the reality of time, or time's arrow and so predicting and controlling a future (and thus simplifying, as in "controlling for").[5] So pervasive are habits of spatializing and quantizing or "unitizing" time, of thinking in terms of substance rather than process, of objects rather than events, it is difficult to imagine other ways of thinking.[6] The simplifications of theoretical and analytic reduction are certainly useful—perhaps nothing if not useful—and can perhaps be most efficiently used when accepted without question and by the rule: follow this procedure, expect this result. But if we can see abstractions precisely as useful devices with their particular limitations, we may be free, if we wish, to look beyond these abstractions to explore other ways of seeing things—indeed, other forms of limitation or abstractions (theories, concepts) but ones that might be more useful for imagining and working with rhythm as something that actually happens.

To think with rhythm as happening necessarily involves criticism of doctrines that deny it, specifically, the commonly accepted notions of 1) a linear time and 2) separate, substance-like things that pass through or are contained in this "time." These notions are so pervasive they can seem unquestionable, transparent, intuitive—simply the way things are. To call them into question will involve stepping outside them to see how limiting and, indeed, counterintuitive they are if we take time and actual experience seriously.

There is a long tradition of pointing to the limitations/fictions of "a block universe" (James), "the cinematographic method," "the spatialization of time," "the logic of solids" (Bergson), the fallacies of "simple location" and "misplaced concreteness" (Whitehead), the "muddle of assuming fixed classes of objects, each defined by its common features" (Gibson), "common and good sense" (Deleuze), and the old "classical Western unit model" (Gendlin). These and many other critical voices belonging to what is generally called "process thought" suggest alternatives—ways of thinking about the ongoingness of the world that would replace mechanistic and deterministic doctrine in which actual passage into novelty is made an impossibility.

If nothing escapes passage into novelty and if passage always involves things/events that succeed one another in their coming into being and passing away, then nothing escapes rhythm. Thus rhythm, very broadly, could be more or less synonymous with time, passage, becoming, change, movement, and process—but adding to these relatively "smooth" dynamic terms, much as Cooper adds "differentiation" and "regularity" to "whole feeling of movement," an explicit reminder of the pulsed and often violent complications of eventfulness: continuity and articulation (discontinuity), joining and separating, returning and departing, remembering and forgetting, moving and holding, becoming and being.[7]

If left "merely" subjective and ineffable, such an eventful rhythm would seem to be an affront to reason. By opening to the indeterminacies of actual passage in which nothing can be held as the same and where any attempt at representation is already a new creation, rhythm is a great threat to reason if reason's aim is the discovery of a clear and distinct path for thought and for the thought of how things must proceed, a given path or course that can be the same for one and for all, once and for all, present, past, or future. This would be a way that all right-thinking performers/sensers—that is, "competent" listeners/speakers/readers/viewers—should pass. The univocity of a stabile underlying structure (won by the denial of passage) can claim to be the foundation for any actual experience and, as fundamental or founding, can claim to be "prior" to any actual experience. Such a foundation can be imagined to function as a general or universal "it" with the power to rationalize or give order to the countless particularities of individual performances that in their uncontrollable multiplicity can seem precisely irrational. If the objects of analysis are seen as ultimate rather than as fictive, "made-up" abstractions, the complications of particularity must be seen as needless distractions. If the goal of analysis is to identify the way people hear, understand, or process the same thing, we must present different individuals the same thing—again an objective, self-same thing that objectified can be the same, time to time and person to person, an external, universal thing whose substance and properties we already know *about*. In this top-down sort of way the local is denied importance. In this way we must control for, or rather against, difference.

COMING OUT

To allow rhythm the breadth that I suggest is its due, let's say that rhythm, most broadly conceived, is a here and now process of event formation that can be felt, sensed, heard, seen. Event is a "coming out" (from the Latin *e-venire*); it is something we can follow or stay with as it continues to come out, for us. Events are the things that emerge in the course of ongoing experience—in music things such as phrases, sounds, beats, motives, things that begin and end and so have duration. Beginning and ending may or may not be clearly articulated; events may overlap and are always nested, smaller events happening within or in the course of larger events (e.g., in the course of the piece of music, or in the course of the ceremony of the larger performance event). Events are held for a while and then pass into others. If event formation is rhythm, why introduce the term "rhythm"? What does the word "rhythm" contribute? I suggest that "rhythm," generously construed, might sanction a way of interpreting repetition and measurement as categories of event formation that cannot be detached from questions of value and feeling (or sensing). Valuing implies selection—selecting this over that, focusing on one or another formation according to our attractions and the intensity of our involvement. Here events are seen not as external givens but as products of desire. If "rhythm" refers to a process of event formation and if all experience emerges in events then all experience is rhythmic, or we might say rhythmic to some degree if there can be variation in "eventfulness," that is, variation in intensity of or attentiveness to what is going on.

As an abbreviation, let R1 stand for rhythmic experience—actual here-and-now feeling, sensing, moving (the online activity of making rhythm), and let R2 stand for an apparently out-of-time (offline) description, analysis, or explication *of* rhythm as something that can be held apart as a there-and-then object already made. This R1/R2 distinction is not a dichotomy. We might think of R2 as a species of R1, a second order (meta-) experience defined by its "aboutness." But R2 description is not less a here-and-now activity than is R1. It is only in being regarded as separate, cut off, that R2 can appear timeless by a sort of trick of intellect or imagination. Moreover, descriptive, explanatory concepts can in various ways and to various degrees inform practice, most especially in their pedagogical applications. Concepts entertained—as they must be to be actual holdings on or holdings onto (*con-cepere*)—are events. Indeed, the human was never before language, and "practice" is never before/outside "theory." As Blum (1975, 218) puts it, "any musical practice . . . presupposes an underlying theory."[8] We might say that R1 and R2 are mutually implicit and interactive. In this case, it is important that R1 and R2 not be separated, even conceptually. Yet such separation has been the overwhelming temptation of R2, taking as it would, "*meta-*" to mean "above" rather than "after" or "between." Thinking in terms of process, "after" and "between" might evoke time and rhythm, images of following on from or of moving back and forth between.

REFORMING R2: REPETITION AND MEASURE

All music involves some form of repetition and measure (generously conceived). Here let's say that repetition delivers difference and that difference or differing is measured or felt. In much music the repetition of more or less equal beats is a significant feature. Conventionally, this later characteristic has been taken as rhythm proper. Such propriety is expressed in the distinction of "*free* rhythm." "Rhythm" is the dominant or unmarked form carrying the implication of equal or strict measure. "Free rhythm" is the marked and thus marginalized form distinguished by its relative deficiency in repetition and regularity. In attempting a broader understanding of rhythm I do not wish to invert this asymmetry in favor of free rhythm but rather to question the terms of the opposition and to seek a temporal or processive redefinition that might obviate the opposition.[9] Here repetition will not refer to the return of the same, and measuring will not refer to a counting of objectified time spans, but rather to a sensing or "taking the measure" of events. Again, we're allowing that repetition produces difference, and difference is precisely measured or felt. Both repetition and measuring will be referred to the ongoing and continuous creation of events which, to be events (comings-out), are always newly created.

EXPERIMENTING WITH REPETITION AS PROCESS

If repetition is "the *same again*" and if rhythm involves the ongoing course of events, could we think of rhythmic repetition as recurrence of the same event? From a temporal or processive perspective, the "again" or "*re*-" as a return or going back is clearly problematic. From such a perspective, "the same" is certainly no less problematic. Clearly, the two events—the first and its follower (*secondus*), the one and the other—must be different "in time." Without this difference the necessary novelty of temporal passage would be denied. To forestall this denial let's hold off on the question of "the same" and its implication of identity and univocality. As an experiment, let's think of "again/*re*-" as the emergence of something new, other, different, though not separate or independent from its predecessors, near and distant. If there were such a separation time would stop, nothing could follow. As for "again," we might think "against" as a reminder of actual succession as the coming-out of the new rather than as a "going-back." "Against" might serve as a reminder of the act, effort, decision, adventure of making or embarking upon a second, following, new event. In this preliminary sense, repetition could come out against a background as something new and focal, or it could be the coming (again/against) of a new, succeeding event as a sort of birth or regeneration—one creature coming out of another. Whatever its defects, this latter metaphor suggests a way of conceiving similarity as a kind of inheritance. It remains to be explored how similarity or likeness might emerge and be felt.

In this experiment I am suggesting that repetition (a nominalized verb) be conceived as a process by which events are actually formed rather than as a similarity relation of already-formed objects. Such already-formed objects (thus conceived as "substances") are separate individuals that stand out, each against one another. As individual, separate things, such objects have or contain properties (from Latin *proper*, each its own), properties that can be compared across objects as relations, measured one against another in terms of similarity/difference. I would like to call this sort of measuring "external measure"—"external" in two senses: 1) the outside-one-another of objects, and 2) the implication of an external observer who makes a comparison, takes a measure from outside. Thus, external measure concerns (separate) objects and their objectification by an observer. By contrast, "internal measure" or "self-measure" would concern events and experiencing "subjects" inseparable from events.[10] Subjects shape and are shaped by events.[11] Here measure (or measuring) is a process in which events are formed by taking measure of one another. If repetition is the production and emergence of events, what we might call similarity or dissimilarity is an accomplishment, not a comparison. Indeed, the sense of repetition as regeneration I suggest need not privilege similarity or likeness—contrast or difference can emerge from repetition. To fully appreciate this affirmation of difference (a denial of identity as separation) it must be understood that "the same" is sustained by difference.

MEASURING DIFFERENCE

Something new has begun, coming out of and against the old. Will it be similar, how similar, in what respects? Such questions cannot be answered in advance without denying the spontaneity of actual experience. Whatever respects we might name in which the second event is similar/dissimilar to the first will come out in the emergence of the second. We could then in retrospect reflect on the two and say in what respects they were same or different. Such a saying would be an account of objects and their relations, a decision about what properties and, indeed, what objects we wish to identify. But can we reflect on the emergence of events? Emergence is a present activity—when it is past (no longer an activity) reflection is powerless to bring it back as it was when it was present. Here reflection must be speculative (not ineffable), a general inquiry into the possibility of emergence or how emergence might be possible. How might we think of an internal measuring that is constitutive of events? What might an event take into account (what is measured) and how might it be taken into account?

These are difficult questions that can provoke any number of responses. As a first step I would suggest a reflection on the complexity of events as a way of thinking about the what. This new event, this new move, is deeply embedded in a history of moves, a past that it cannot but take into account.[12] The past it takes into account may be relatively deep or shallow. It is, in any case, selective. Its taking into account involves a selection of relevancies, exclusions as well as inclusions. Think of the next musical move. The way it is precisely (actually) made comes out of the situation it finds itself in and carries on, or changes. "The situation" is inherently complex and changeable. We don't need to and usually can't afford to reflect on what's involved, precisely because so much is involved.[13] To single out one thing can cut the whole process short. And yet singling out, abstracting, cutting short is not necessarily a bad thing. Such analysis or cutting short can be useful if it is held onto in creative repetition—held and, at the same time, allowed to move. Think, for example, of refining or relearning a skill where you have to take apart and so lose the continuity of your habitual, already-learned facility in order to gain a new facility, which when gained returns a new continuity and a new complexity. In such a relearning you might, for example, focus on just one aspect of your playing—say, hand position. The new position you're asked to master will be awkward at first, a painful violation of hard-won habit. If your retraining works properly, over time you will no longer have the awkward, painful experience of isolating your hand; over time the new facility can gradually become integrated with all the other elements of your technique (thereby changing all those other elements). Such cases are productive—an alienation is progressively healed through repetition as a practice. But in the short term, abstracting or isolating can be merely destructive. Think, for example, of stage fright when your performance becomes detached from you and becomes captive to an externalizing and immobilizing fear of judgment. Or think of noticing something that leads to a train of thought (even thought *about* music) that takes you out of a more integrated and intense musical experience. These are, I would suggest, examples of withdrawing from the rhythmic understood as a sort of fluency and full-bodied engagement. The relativity of engagement could thus be a measure of the more or less rhythmic—with more engagement, more rhythm, energy, involvement, intensity, or "eventfulness."

Rhythm, to be intense, must involve gradations in intensity of relevance and distinctions of "focal" and "subsidiary" awareness.[14] Value and relevance imply difference—a difference of attention, differences of how we attend and, indeed, intend. And yet focusing on one aspect "over" another need not imply exclusion of the others. Rather, we might substitute for "over," "through" or "by means of"—focusing on one aspect through or with the aid of another (functionally subsidiary) aspect. If all aspects or dimensions work together, close attention to one (say, timbre) can lead to a keener sense of the others as they pertain to the one. But before turning to a closer inquiry into aspect or dimension, I would like to return briefly to the broader question of "situation"—the environment in which an event finds itself.

ENVIRONMENT

Thus far I have focused (abstractly, schematically) on "immediate succession"—a "first" followed by a "second." But what "follows" (*sequi*) follows on infinitely more than the immediate predecessor, not only because that predecessor has inherited from all its predecessors but also because "immediately" is already multiple—there are always multiple hierarchical levels of relevance at work in any situated event—events "within" events. Moreover, events are not just private. They are products of a world—an environment, culture—in which they take place (and change); as products of the world, they take place always in contexts created through interaction with other people.[15] Musical events have most often involved a group of people intensely working and feeling together—playing together and dancing together, hearing with the players and seeing with the dancers. All the factors that come into play come together, each affecting and being affected by all the others. Complexity in this sense is a mutual involvement of influences folded or woven (*plicare*) together, not separated. If rhythm is the course of events in their emergence as events then rhythm involves all the factors that can enter into (everything that can be felt in) the formation of an event, all working together in the creation of the event. The new event is, let's say, its own take on its own situation, the world it finds itself in and for a moment owns. The situation is "part" of the event and a partition, the event's perspective on the world that it takes place in and changes. Thus the new event itself *is* in a sense "separate," not as a timeless object but as a new creature born into a world that it inherits and moves on from as it sees (we see) fit. Indeed, there is no other option, for "this world" is changing, precisely through a new birth, a new event that will forever change the world, however imperceptibly. Internal measurement would then be the take on the past, the background, potentiality, and virtuality (however we might chose to name and characterize the situation something new is born into) that offers the new event all that it has to go on.[16] Internal measurement to be "internal" will not submit to analysis any more than subjective rhythm can be reduced to objective rhythm, but this fact of life need not invalidate the analytic enterprise, which trades in objects.

CATEGORIES/DIMENSIONS

In music what is measured might be the qualities of, say, tone, timbre, volume, contour, intonation, scale-degree, interval, duration . . . whatever categories of difference we might choose to name (perhaps an unlimited number). Such categories refer to real distinctions grounded in feeling, but they need not be taken as universal (or even as stable). We define categories in a variety of ways, refine them as clusters of subcategories, apply them differently in different situations. Take, for example, interval. Is interval the "distance" between two pitches (how measured—"steps," semitones, unit numbers of cycles per second), or a vector or movement from one pitch to another, or an operation or transformation mapping one pitch into the other, or a relative distinction of size (large/small), or a distinction of place, or one of color, or of mood or "character"? Interval may comprise a variety of types that include or exclude certain other qualities: for example, absolute (or registral) interval, interval class, interval modulo 12, directed interval. Moreover, since interval depends on pitch, definitions of pitch will come into play as in distinguishing in-tune from out-of-tune, possibly leading to a different category in-between named pitches (for example, a quarter-tone interval). Moreover, situation matters. The ostensibly same (named) interval, say perfect 4th, might sound quite different in different contexts by, for example, involving different scale degrees (e.g., scale degrees 1 and 4 vs. 5 and 8 (1), or even scale degrees 1 and 4 in the different scales of major and minor). In different cultures interval might be defined quite differently: for example, highly regulated in classical Western music and less (or differently) regulated in cultures for which intervals of the same tune might vary from instrument to instrument, or singer to singer, or time to time. These questions concerning the category "interval" point to the unstable, problematic nature of music-theoretical categories—a nature far from natural kind. Other categories, such as texture or timbre or rhythm, present different problems.

There seems no end to the ways music can be carved up into categories, though each appropriate way can be grounded in feeling and thus "carved at the joint," as Plato puts it, and so serve practice as a device for learning ("now I can hear the difference"). Indeed, learning opens the idea (category) of category to the complexity of actual experience, which far exceeds naming. The feeling of what we might call interval as a quality that can enter into the here-and-now event is something learned in countless past experiences. This complexity together with the complexity of the immediate situation is what determines the measuring of interval. The now relevant past may have included practice with categories as a regime of training. For example, for someone trained in the Western classical tradition learning to sing from notation may have begun with learning an interval type from a familiar tune—for the ascending perfect 4th, Wagner's "Bridal Chorus" from *Lohengrin* ("Here comes the bride"), and for the descending perfect 4th, Schubert's "Unfinished Symphony" have been favorite examples. These are good examples not only because of their familiarity to students but also because each begins and ends with the interval (Wagner, emphatically with a flourish or turn). Although such practice has become common in Western music education, it should be noted that many cultures do not isolate something like interval as a category for naming and learning. Moreover, interval is not a very stable category. Interval is highly style specific. Even within Western music moving from one learned style to another ("tonal," "modal," "atonal") can require a significant shift in hearing.

Once again, I am not denying the usefulness of music-theoretical (R2) categories but rather suggesting the importance of taking into account their limitations and thus suggesting the reversal of an accustomed order in which such categories can seem to logically, ontologically, or temporally precede experience (present and past). In fact, the logical, global, theoretical is always posterior, dependent on and deriving from the empirical, experiential world, which can found innumerable categorical schemes. Complexity is the ground upon which the simplifications of conceptual abstraction are constructed and reconstructed in their own infinitely complex ways. R1 and R2 are intricately interactive, something the "objectivity" of R2 generally overlooks when it seeks hegemony as "objective."

If R1 and R2 can be interactive and can thus take measure of one another, they are nonetheless incommensurate in their measuring. The difference of analytic/descriptive categories and the kinds of feeling that can be taken into account in event formation is not due to a difference in the number of possible distinctions, which is in both cases limitless. Rather, the difference is due to a difference in kind. Descriptive categories are separate and fixed. They are distinctions (as in my earlier lists) that must be held the same in order to apply to different situations. In the actual emergence of event things are quite different. In internal measuring the whole situation is felt for what it can offer or afford. R1 categories are mobile, kinds of feeling that change in their very becoming of categories. For example, in actual sight singing we read ahead, searching for the new pitch or pitches that are forming into moments of this emerging figure, or phrase, or period. Perhaps we draw on our familiarity (i.e., past experience) with a certain harmonic progression or figure. Such familiarity is born of previous encounters all intermeshed and held in our changed and changing bodies (nerve and muscle tissues). If we were to draw on "Here comes the bride," which "Here comes the bride?"—in the past, they are not separate. On the nearer end, perhaps we draw especially on a previous pitch to sing, say, a step higher because that's the best thing we have to go on right now; or perhaps we search for the coming "scale degree," a quality that emerges from a variable constellation or field of pitches working together and from our acquired sensitivity to such qualities. Moreover, the pitches are not detached from duration and metrical placement or any other qualities that come into play—timbre, tempo, breath, intonation. And precisely how we sing now will have consequences for the next bit and "indirectly" for a subsequent attempt at sight-singing ("have I gotten better at this?"). In all this there is no fixity and no ultimate separation. Although our choices in forming the event are specific selections (this sound, this long) they are nothing apart from the unsegmented world they emerge from and are not separate from their contributions to future events.

All the ways an event can draw on, use, and measure its world might be called *dimensions*—ways of measuring-out (*di-metiri*)—measuring out of and in to. Music, like any other activity, is always multidimensional. The hypothetical singing example named several possible dimensions. Since namable, these would appear to be separate. But none need be taken to work alone, outside the here-and-now situation which necessarily involves many dimensions (duration, breath, etc.), or to be taken as a single, separate event apart from the nested complexity of many hierarchic (or heterarchic) event-levels, all folded into one another. Moreover, our hypothetical "strategies" for singing might work together in various ways and also involve other strategies unnamed. We might call these ways essentially separate "kinds" (*what* kinds); but "way" is also useful in linking the notion of path and manner: *how* (in what way) rather than *what* (kind). The challenge here is to conceive of multiplicity (always many dimensions) together with a complexity in which all factors are interwoven and not separate, and thus to conceive of an unseparated multiplicity where "many" does not mean countable as discrete "units."[17] What we might call "factors" are not separate because each "one" changes what the others truly are, and this change is continuous. If music is multidimensional in the sense I suggest then its dimensions are innumerable, though again for specific purposes of description and pedagogy, dimensions can be named and held separate.

Although dimensions are unseparated both in their potential for being brought into play in new events and in their actual working together in the new event, they are not unordered either *in actualis* (the way they come out in the activity of event formation where measuring takes place) or *in potentia* (the past, background, implicit, or virtual that applies a definite constrain on an actual). The world the new event continues and changes (if ever so slightly) is formed of habits or channels of behavior that are deeply sedimented in the past. Since the term comes up in several chapters of this volume, "matrix" might be a useful word for thinking about paths of inheritance. In its etymology matrix can return us to the generative and regenerative implications of repetition. The Latin *matrix* meant womb, the environment in which new life is formed prior to birth and separation. Inheritance from the past is not simply (oversimply) due to a fund of dimensions as kinds of measurables (much less, a fixed fund of dimensions); inheritance is also a route, a channel or way for present becoming opened by innumerable prior becomings. Thus the notion of matrix can lead to a way of thinking about multiplicity not oversimply as a mere aggregate or amalgam of qualities, kinds, intensities; nor abstractly as a timeless and mathematical order; but rather generatively as a process in which innumerable possibilities inherited from countless generations actualize in innumerable real beings. The word "matrix" can also evoke ideas of a mold or fixed set of constraints or a fixed (two-dimensional) order of relationships and thus lead to the idea of pattern as something timelessly given. But thinking of pattern as habit can help to keep the temporal dimension alive. Think of the becoming of event as an active searching that involves a narrowed or focused selection of potentials that have come to be ordered or structured in specific, characteristic ways as behaviors or habits that persist in repetition. Thus, matrices might be understood as persistent patterns or behaviors that bring their own (multidimensional) complexities to bear in shaping new events. But not to abandon the temporal picture, we should grant also that the pattern-habit-behavior is itself mobile—a sort of pattern or patterning that is ongoing and that sustains itself and also changes as it goes, changing (evolving) as it goes from birth to birth.

Musical matrices ("forms") are learned and worked with again and again. As Stephen Blum writes in this volume (chapter 3), a musical matrix can be used for "mastering sets of constraints" and thus to "increase performers' sensitivities." We can name/describe matrices, but like the dimensions they pattern and bring into play there is no end for the possibilities for naming. For example, David Locke's metrical matrix for Ewe drumming is in any actual performance situation inseparable from countless other dimensions (emotional, spiritual, interactive-personal, etc.) that are informing every gesture. Of course, to describe (write down) a matrix we will have to limit such multiplicity; and indeed, as patterns, or likenesses in certain respects, matrices are limited or selective in the dimensions they bring into focus. More problematic is to describe such matrices in terms of time and process.[18] How can matrices be in some sense fixed (as forms) and yet change and give rise to changeable performances? How can matrices be both closed and open? This problem haunts all accounts of form (for example, the music theorist's sonata from, or the poetic prosodist's iambic pentameter).[19] Here I would like to suggest a way of beginning to work with the problem.

Let's say a matrix is a constellation of rules as habits (inherently flexible, context-sensitive rules, i.e., rules of thumb) rather than as a set of rules as algorithms. In R2 we might identify some such rules and some of the ways they work together. In their working together we will find new questions to ask. But we needn't stop with here with the rules as givens. We could go on to ask about their histories, how they might have emerged in their working together, and why they might have persisted or survived as patterns. This set of questions suggests movement, from a Linnaean classificatory to a Darwinian evolutionary perspective, but one that celebrates a Lamarckian cultural inheritance of acquired characteristics. Presumably, artistic forms persist because of the efficient advantages they offer as opportunities for intense, valued feeling, and they persist for however long such feelings are valued with sufficient intensity to keep them alive. For example, in the domain of poetic line, the "iambic pentameter" matrix has survived for hundreds of years. This form would not have been so often repeated (to become a form) if it did not offer something of value. In its long history, the form has been chosen again and again, and the choice has been made on the basis of complex and changing cultural values. Many writers have pointed to the values of complexity and spontaneity as opportunities afforded by the iambic pentameter line and its openness to more fluid discursive speech. Derek Attridge (1995, 159) has specifically linked these qualities to its escape from the four-squareness and closure of tetrameter (2x2 beats).[20] One conspicuous value that emerges from iambic pentameter is a flexibility and variability with regard to "grouping" and timing that is designed to allow or promote significant departures from strict isochrony. In a sense this line was a path to "free verse." But the species, or creature, iambic pentameter exceeds what we might call the structural. Iambic pentameter has worked as a complex potential made of countless lines "internalized" (learned, memorized) and recited by poets and readers. I would suggest that such a form does not work as an out-of-time abstraction (except in pedagogical contexts) but instead as a repertory of many past experiences constrained by a canalizing rule or habit that is always made anew.

FOCUSING ON DURATION

Since, for better or worse, rhythm is usually identified with duration and timing, I would like to try out some of the categories I have proposed for taking durational quantity as a dimension.[21] This attempt is firmly situated in R2 naming, but R1 can remind us that naming is itself rhythmic, an actual adventure in thinking or trying to think about rhythm, or even about naming. In an attempt to bring duration into line with event as dynamic process I would like to conceive of duration in a broad sense that includes but is not limited to quantity. To think of duration as process, rather than as an attribute or property of event (and to continue thinking of event as a process rather than a substance or object), we might try hearing durat*ion* as a noun denoting activity (like "act*ion*"), as if coming from a verb to "durate." To imagine the activity of "durating" we can recall the Latin *durare*, to harden or solidify. Thus duration could be thought of as a process of hardening or solidifying as an event, becoming event. The character of "harden*ing*" might also point to the fluidity of the event as it is becoming and to a sort of congealing as it gradually comes to be determined or ended. The event endures throughout (during) its becoming, and we might say that when the event is finally become—congealed, no longer fluent—it can endure in the past for active, new events to take into account.

In this sense duration can include any dimensions (or dimensions coordinated as matrices) that might come into play. And so if we identify one dimension as quantitative/durational then we need not (and in principle, cannot) exclude all relevant other dimensions, quantitative and qualitative. Dimensions ought not be separate from one another. Again, identifying/naming a dimension is never a clear cut—whatever distinction we might draw can be variously redrawn as we attempt to take more complexity into account. The rhythm of naming never really stops. Even when we use the same name again, the context, situation, meaning changes. But to make a beginning, let's focus on durational quantity where quantity names a measuring of how *much* or how *long*. These categories (much, long) can be measured externally by units, which bring the quantitative dimension of how *many*. But let's not confuse these categories at the start. Confusion stops the rhythm of a naming that would attempt to accommodate complexity.

AN EXPERIMENT WITH QUANTITATIVE DURATION

Think of an acoustic event of brief duration, say a hand clap. Or better, try clapping. The sound lasts as long as we can hear it. If we attend carefully we notice that we can continue hearing this clap, however faintly and tenuously, as a sort of echo, through a process Ulrich Neisser (1967) named "echoic memory." As it becomes more difficult to hold onto the sound we may find ourselves repeating ("rehearsing") it in order not to lose it. But eventually it is gone as is our attempt to keep it going. Now let's clap again, following a first clap with another clap a second or two later. With attention we might notice some difference—the second sound might be louder or softer, more or less resonant, different in timbre, longer or shorter. We might think of the difference in terms of comparison, but we don't need to go back and forth between the two sounds—the difference could be just the particular quality of the second sound, something it has inherited from the first by taking measure of the first, and indeed by opening dimensions as ways of taking measure. Moreover, a new *quantitative* dimension will have been opened.

With the second clap a first event, lasting from the first up to the second clap, will now have been formed. With the second clap a first event is now fully determined and in itself past, become and no longer becoming. What is the duration of the new event initiated with the second clap? If we pay attention we can notice a new difference. Unlike the silence after the first clap (without a second), the silence after the second clap is a measured duration; it is palpable in a new way, thickened or filled in a way that the silence after the first was not. The echoic continuation was a different sort of "filling of time." Echoic continuation is serial, a sequence of fading snapshots, a focus on images or a single image repeated *al niente*. In contrast, the silence following the second clap is unsegmented (though endlessly segmentable). I would describe it, perhaps fancifully, as a force, like the flow of water through your fingers or the like the power of moving through a viscous medium. This thickening/filling is, I suggest, the feeling of duration being made. By "duration" I mean duration-being-made, that is to say the process of solidifying, thickening, filling that is the new, now event. With our second clap we can experiment with this streaming and solidifying.

The new, second event in its growth has a more or less definite duration even as it goes on. In the absence of a third clap, definiteness of feeling or feeling of definiteness will attenuate continuously and will, like the serial continuation of echo in the absence of a second clap, fade to nothing. We might try to hold on to this feeling of solidity or becoming solid, but it will eventually dissipate. Though it will be hard to say precisely when it ends, the duration of the second event will be on the order of the duration of the first event, now past. This present durat*ion* (again, as a process) is the active measuring of the second event, taking into account all it has to go on, which in this simple situation is the determined duration of its immediate predecessor. Such measuring is a feeling of how much time is left until the new duration runs out, or how much time remains before a new third event if for any reason we are interested in a possible successor. Since a successor will make the duration of the second event determinate, we might feel the measuring of the second event very precisely in feeling that the third clap came, say, slightly early or late, or just right.

In this experiment if we focus our attention in this way on these larger events, then the differences of the two sounds (timbre, volume, etc.) we began with may seem irrelevant to or separate from these larger durations. Could we not produce the same durations apart from the particular sounds of the two claps? No, not if duration is the actual becoming of events. Whatever specific difference or particularity of sound we pick up on cannot be separated from the complex feeling and precision of our timing. Relevance is nothing if not connection and nothing if not variable—it depends entirely on the situation. But it is not negligible, unless we choose for descriptive purposes to neglect it. The "attentiveness" I have suggested, as a way of picking up more sonic detail, can lead to an intensified feeling of duration or, more generally, a heightened rhythmic engagement. But there cannot be an event/ situation in which we pick up on nothing—if no new perspective on the world, no event.

To carry our simple and easily doable experiment a bit farther (and to introduce the topic of metrical hierarchy), let's add a third clap when the time seems right, that is, when it seems the duration of the second event is about to expire. The event initiated by a third clap could inherit or take its measure from its immediate predecessor, the second event. But let's say that the third clap as the initiation of a new event takes for its measure not the second (determined/past) event but a larger event comprising the first two events together. (Experimenting with "tempo" may be useful.) In this case, the third clap would sound the emergence of a second (*secundus* following) event, which as a second could only take its measure from its predecessor—the event of the first two clap-initiated events together. This new event is, at the same time, a new togetherness of the first two—now one. The second clap is now an earlier phase in a larger event comprising the two clapped events. I offer Figure 1.1 as an (R2) attempt to represent this process diagrammatically:[22]

The symbol "┌" represents claps and the continued horizontal lines represent silences filled with more or less definite durational quantity. The vertical line (|) here marks or symbolizes the initiat*ion* of an event, an initiating that belongs to the whole event and that is inseparable from the event as a whole. Although the | is placed at the beginning

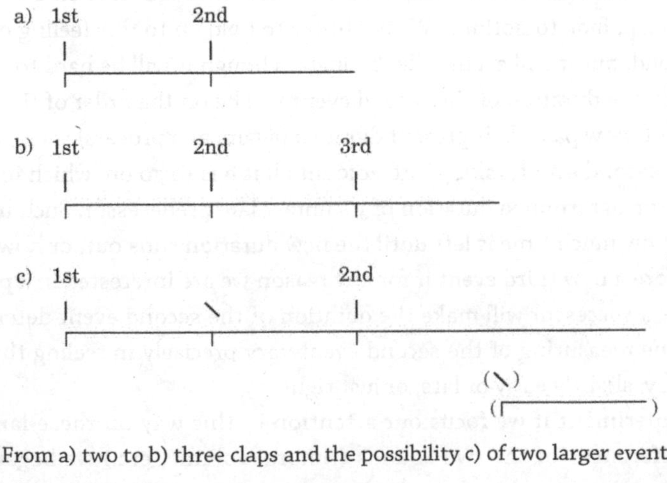

FIGURE 1.1 From a) two to b) three claps and the possibility c) of two larger events.

of the graphically represented event, the | does not refer to the initiating clap itself, much less to an instant of beginning. Rather, | continues—it lasts as long as the event continues. The backward-directed diagonal line \ symbolizes the second clap as an event that functions as a continua*tion* of the larger first event. Continuation is a creative process (that of duration) and, again, inseparable from "beginning." There is continuation all along, but with the second clap continuation is articulated— \ is a *mark* of continuation, as | is a *mark* of initiation or beginning of the event. We may justly say that there are now two parts, two "beats." But it is important here to note that the symbol | does not refer to a first beat. It labels the entire two-part event. The internal articulation does not end the becoming of the larger event initiated with |.[23] The next initiation (|) does end the larger composite event and can take its own measure from its predecessor. Since the first larger event was articulated, its successor can inherit an articulated continuation. (Remember, dura*tion* is always complex, more than a "time span.") Thus, we might in certain circumstances feel some trace of a "silent" continuation in the second (shown in parentheses). That is to say, we might take advantage of this complex measuring potential to try to hold on to the second duration. Notice the difference of this perspective from one that would posit the operation of an autonomous (unitary) beat or beat-train that, infinitely repeatable, runs on inertia. I suggest that habit is more complex and situation/context sensitive. Habit is not mechanical; as habitus it is fully worldly.

COMPLEXITIES OF DURATIONAL QUANTITY/QUALITY

Thus far I have not spoken explicitly of equality or isochrony. Doing so now will return us to questions of strict and free rhythm and provide an opportunity to question the separation of quantity and quality. Taking measure need not result in equal durations measured by the clock (in any case approximate—how accurate, by the clock, do we care to/can we be?). A second duration felt to be just right might be quite different from a clock-measured, and thus externally measured-compared, first.[24] Moreover, a feeling of shorter/longer (or simply, short/long) is not a freedom from the constraints of a predecessor; it is rather a precise feeling of the predecessor's influence or "inflow." In the case of acceleration, events could be described as progressively shorter; but it might also make sense to say that they come faster—the "same" durations but faster. This later formulation will seem contradictory only if same means a same (externally measured and unit-based) amount of clock time.[25]

Quantitative measuring in the complexity of more properly musical situations (more complex than our clapping exercises) can lead to a great variety of (types of) feeling. A new event may come *too* soon as an interruption or *too* late resulting in the failure of the preceding event to offer a measure for the new event (hiatus). Moreover, since durations are ongoing and in the process of "solidifying" or becoming determined, and since there are always many events going on (at different hierarchic/heterarchic levels), feelings are fluid and mutable. What began as a continuation can break off to become a new beginning, or vice versa. For example, what may at first seem a new phrase or section can turn out to be an extension of the phrase or section we're in when the "real" phrase or section emerges. Events are not instantaneous; it takes time for them to emerge. This fluidity cannot be seen from the score, though we can attempt to describe it. By way of illustration, I will relate an anecdote I found instructive. Some years ago (October 2012), the Ying Quartet came to a graduate seminar to discuss a piece they were to perform later that week. The piece was the second movement Adagio of Haydn's "Sunrise" quartet Op. 76 no. 4, the beginning of which is shown as Figure 1.2.[26]

After they had played the opening phrase I asked the quartet if they felt it in triple or duple. They immediately answered something like "triple—the piece is notated in three-four, and of course that's how we play it." I asked them to play it again, and the violist noticed that he was actually feeling duple meter. (Interesting that it was the violist; did he feel a *shift* from triple to duple?) With more playing, all the members of the quartet came to acknowledge that they had always heard in duple. The clue to their actual and *tacit* measuring (which, again, took some time to make explicit) came from listening to the duration of the fermata in bar 2. When the players paid close attention to how long they were holding the fermata they immediately recognized the duple feeling. The quartet had consistently held the fermata approximately "four quarters" long. This meant that the fermata was taking its measure from an immediately preceding event. But to say the fermata lasted "four quarters" is misleading. Such a manner of speaking is a creature of R2 notational discourse (as, of course, is the conviction that the opening is in three-four). The players certainly were not explicitly counting to four. They were just feeling how long to hold, when it felt just right to move on.[27]

Since the phrase very clearly ends in triple, it seems fair to ask if we've started with duple, when does duple become triple? I suggest that unless we intervene by trying to enact the notational record (as we might try to do in bars 1–4, conducting or counting in threes and feeling the fermati as hiatus, or too long), it will not be clear precisely when the change is effected. Somewhere in the neighborhood of bar 6 things can change—one kind of measuring (duple) can be heard gradually to have slipped into a new (triple) kind of measuring.[28] Evidence that the new measuring is shorter/faster/more condensed can be felt in the complex speeding up or contracting/condensing/intensifying that leads to a moment of cadence or ending, a process that involves many dimensions working together. This stylistically favored gesture for phrase formation (acceleration to cadence) is intimately connected to a precise, syntactic sense of harmonic progression: beginning with a long 2-measure (not bar) tonic, followed by a similarly long measure of supertonic (functionally, "dominant preparation," i.e., strongly implying dominant to come), followed by a new "second" and larger event, prolonging supertonic and thus delaying its resolution, resolving in bar 7 to the characteristic "cadential dominant" (a resolution delayed in the cadential "six-four" suspension, first in violin 2 and viola, and then farther delayed in violin 1, which, syncopated, pushes its leading tone, d1, forward to the very last eighth), and finally resolving into, ending

FIGURE 1.2 Joseph Haydn, String Quartet Op. 76 no. 4 ("Sunrise"), second movement, bs. 1–16.

with tonic.[29] Bar 8 can be taken as continuation of a measure begun with bar 7. This continuation (\) can relax in the perfunctorily arpeggiated tonic that will, as the ending of a large phrase-event, be followed by a move into a second phrase, a beginning-again (second violin) now high and clearly triple. Again, acceleration leading to cadence is a characteristic feature of this style. I would suggest that this feature proved so robust because it can work so well to hold together relatively large phrase events toward the end when they are threatened with dissolution or a failure to solidify (with this possibility in mind "duration" might be variable not just in length but also in coherence—or rather in duration *as* coherence).

Having spent so much time with the first phrase, it would be a pity to ignore its second. As a second, the new phrase necessarily inherits the immediate world just left to it by its first, the phrase now past. One way of speaking of inheritance would be in terms of contrast or difference. With no fermati, the opening of phrase 2 is moving at the pace of the end of phrase 1 and not at the slower pace of the beginning. Gone now are the two long, stately events that opened the first phrase (bars 1–4). Now (bars 9–12) there are no fermatas; what was duple is now freely running triple. Notice also in the second phrase the new rate and character of harmonic change and the connection of the two smaller (4-bar) phrases in the focal connection of bars 12 and 13, and also the intricately covered rhyme of bars 13 and 15. (The rhyme of 12 and 13 taken together with that of 13 and 15 or 12–13 and 15–16 presents a fascinating complication, we might say, of "levels.") If they work at all, these factors must work together and with countless others.

For the transition between the two phrases bar 8 is crucial. In the emphatic closure with the very beginning of bar 8 there is no trace of anacrustic impetus for successor. With bar 8 this sounding event is closing—the focus is on closing. The imagination, however, since it is not tethered to sound, can entertain a new event as a *what if*. And here the pause or relaxation in bar 8 provides an opportunity perhaps to think ahead and to imagine if ever so vaguely the advent of a new phrase, or at least to momentarily open oneself to a new phrase event. If this inclination is there it will not take much to give it shape and habitation; imagination is eager to be led by something concrete. In bar 8 the first violin begins leaving the cadence to become the focus of transition to the new phrase leading into a very different sonic world (high and mobile, wide-ranging) and "at the same time" to a beginning again. The first violin's arpeggio in bar 8 can but need not be perfunctory. In the Kuijken recording the first violin articulates the last three notes (*d2-e♭2-g2*) as syncopated anacrustic group (/) to the new phrase intensifying the move to the new, high register (with *b♭2*). This move, among other things, picks up on the beginning of bar 8 with anacrusis (*d1-e♭1-g1-b♭1*) and on the syncopation (hemiola) in bar 7 (*d1-a1-d1*) itself a large anacrusis to bar 8. Moreover, this emerging anacrustic figure can prepare or motivate the first violin's anacrustic and syncopated *b-c-b♭* in bar 10. The Kuijken Quartet's intricate and lively (I would say, highly "rhythmical") interpretation continues the acceleration into the new phrase and so doing contributes to the character of the new phrase.

EXPERIMENTING WITH RHYTHMIC PLAY IN A PASSAGE FROM JOSQUIN DES PREZ'S *MISSA PANGE LINGUA*

To leave the Haydn and simultaneously to continue exploring durational quantity and some of the methodological issues it raises, I would like to experiment with a composition that can offer more resistance to a received theory based in eighteenth- and nineteenth-century European practices. "*Pleni sunt coeli*" (the second of three sections of the larger *Sanctus*) from the *Pange lingua* Mass (c. 1515, Figure 1.3) comes from a distant world as an artifact of musical notation mediated to a limited extent by the writing of contemporary theorists. How to engage with this record is an open and creative question. Living informants are the performers (singers and conductors) and the historical musicologists who continue to sing and to sing of the old compositions. "Continue" is, however, not quite accurate because there is no continuous performance tradition passed down from singer to singer, and because historical musicology is a relatively recent field of scholarship. Josquin's music was found/rediscovered/invented with the advent of modern historical musicology in the late nineteenth century and remains an ongoing artistic project for performers and scholars. The following rhythmic interpretations to be experimental are intended be tried out, performed by the reader with the understanding that not only singing but also listening to a recording is a performance.

The full text is "*Pleni sunt coeli et terra gloria tua*" ("full are heaven and earth of thy glory"). Text placement here is taken from the *New Josquin Edition* (1987, ed. Willem Elders). Text placement was not prescribed by the composer but was a decision made by performers according to their understanding of the rhythmic possibilities allowed to/provided for them. Indeed, a different text placement might lead to rhythmic events different from those I shall suggest. For the reader's convenience I have used modern clefs (altus sounds an octave lower than written). I have, however, retained the mensural notation to avoid misleading ties for longa (misleading because of the implication that the held duration is composed of actual shorter durations) and to resist the notion that "minim," for example, is the same as a "half note."[30] For convenience, but problematically, I have used two highly anachronistic notational devices: 1) the aligned presentation of both voice parts together in score form ("score" as cut/mark/bar/, a symbol of division), and 2) *Mensurstriche*, vertical lines drawn between the two staves marking what we might think of as "bars."[31] Indeed, this is one device. Putting two or more voice parts together diagrammatically involves a diagrammatic coordination that can nevertheless work to obscure felt rhythmic complexity. In the mensural world of Renaissance polyphony the absence of bar lines and score can (even today) promote complexity in timing in which "bar-units" marked by *Mensurstriche* need not always be clearly or simply felt and in which the opening of a variety of measures can call for challenging, creative play from the singers. Rather than using the word "bars" to refer to places in the score, I will refer to "tempora"—abbreviated as "*t*." Tempus (sing.) is here a breve ⊟ understood as a focal measure on the order of the later graphic marking or scoring of the bar.

FIGURE 1.3 Josquin des Prez, *Missa pange lingua*, the opening of *Pleni sunt coeli*, t.1–24.

The *Mensurstriche* I have drawn have consistency as breve markers of the proportional notation ¢ corresponding more or less to our $\frac{2}{1}$ signature.[32] In ¢ the tactus implied by the notation is the breve 𝅜, beat with two equal hand motions. However, singers might in appropriate circumstances choose to focus on smaller beats—a semibreve 𝅝 tactus or focal "beat" composed of two minim 𝅗𝅥 beats; but what is felt as focal might be variable and variable in degree. For example, in the opening of Figure 1.3 tactus might be felt as breve and later (around *t*.13–14) change to semibreve. How and to what extent tactus was felt is of course an open question. But it seems clear that measuring was (and is) highly nuanced and flexible and allowed for actual, felt measures that might in one way or another depart from the globally prescribed mensuration of tempus and notationally prescribed tactus (i.e., notated in the mensuration signature).[33] Since the tactus did regulate or conform to the "placement" of dissonant passing tones and suspensions and cadences (but not the placement of the dissonant *cambiata*), its presence could often be clearly felt.[34] But in a passage without dissonant minims, tactus might be able to change. The widespread practice of voices imitating at the interval of a semibreve (*imitatio per arsin et thesin*—for example, in the second large phrase of *Pleni sunt coeli, t*.32) argues for the possibility of a departure from the prescribed tempus in a semibreve "performance" tactus. My event-metrical interpretation in Figure 1.3 shows in *t*.12–22 many departures from tempus and a lack of coordination between voices before the reset with the cadence (*t*.22–23) at the end of the large phrase. But before turning to these developments I would like to consider the possibility of an earlier and less clear-cut departure from tempus in options open to altus and speculate on the play or slight looseness that might be involved in measuring.

In *t*.4 altus begins "*-li*" as continuation (\) suspended into a long holding. Here some sort of counting might come in handy, 4 or 2x2 semibreves. In the course of counting, could not a feeling of tactus shift so that "*sunt*" (*t*.6) might be felt now as beginning (|)?[35] If so, the reset with t.8 will have created a triple measure (| -\).[36] Meanwhile, playing off this altus "*-li*," the focal superius sustains the climactic, opening, anacrustic tone, *c*2. This long, variously sustained *c*2 begins at the end of *t*. 4 as suspended (unresolved or syncopated) anacrusis. With this highly energized, continuative and sustained *c*2 at the very end of *t*.4, a new behavior and possibly a new event is beginning to take shape. In superius there now emerges a new, compressed and "stuck" behavior repeatedly focusing on *c*2, in which none of the beginnings (|) of the three following prescribed tempi (*t*.5-7) is articulated. But how energizing then to come back to a suspended continuative anacrustic *c*2 in *t*.6. Does altus pick up on this to sing a continuative "sunt" or does he wander into triple (| -\)? Rather than ask for a correct choice, let's ask for the difference a choice might make. Forgetting the continuative-anacrustic beginning with "*-li*" will result in a sort of hiatus for the altus and an acceleration to the new small phrase beginning with "*coe-*" (*t*.8). On the other hand, remembering suspended continuation with "*-li*" will result in a long-deferred resolution to the new beginning with *t*.8. But need this be such a clear-cut R2 distinction? For R1 the situation could be complicated and changeable.

However this juncture is negotiated, it is a juncture. The "suddenness" (in either of our two R2 scenarios) of the new event beginning with *t*.8 is a powerful way of intensifying this crucial moment in which the two voices overlap in beginning and ending: altus in *t*.8 (felt as a breve tactus) begins a new, "*coeli*" phrase: *f-e-d/f-e* and also (at "the same time") echoes the superius figure beginning at the end of *t*.4: *c-b-a/c-b*.[37] Superius quasi-cadentially closes its phrase below altus on *d1* introducing a new sonority. This moment is a big change for the course of the piece, a movement into a second phrase or phase which, I would suggest, comes to function as a sort of transition, an approximately 4-5 tempus door (*t*.8–12) into a very new (perhaps obsessive or ecstatic) behavior, a properly second phase/phrase event significantly labeled "*et terra*," *t*.13–23, in which homogeneous measuring is strained. This intense, highly engaging event-mensural complexity resolves very smoothly but quite suddenly in the final, cadential "*terra*" measure, the triple (| —\ in altus) measure that ends in a turn (but not necessarily return) to tempus with the ending with the first true cadence (on *A*), *t*.22-23. This *clausula vera* figure has only one metrical interpretation marked especially by a suspended dissonance resolving to consonance.

In Figure 1.3, I've labeled the cadential intervallic succession as follows: 6-6-6-7-♯6-8. In this succession of intervals, following a run of parallel 6ths, 7 is the suspended (syncopated, held up) cadential dissonance, resolving to ♯6 which then itself resolves in the closing 8, the perfect octave on *A*. This last move to *A* breaks the parallel 6ths by introducing contrary motion: the lower voice forces the upper voice to move down then "back" up again to the same pitch (*a2*) that was just now dissonant and was forced to resolve to the leading tone; this same pitch (*a2*) is now redeemed and sustained as consonant in the perfect octave, a perfection (*per-facere*, thoroughly or completely made or done) in which nothing more needs be done for the becoming of this large phrase. I dramatize here because this is a dramatic moment—the ending of something, and the promise of something new. Stylistic conventions especially dramatize the moment of ending, each style in its own way saying something about ending and beginning. In "this style," parallel 6ths (four here) signal preparation for the cadential suspension. As a characteristic marker, parallel 6ths can give some advance notice of ending and, at the same time, expand a present *moment* of ending. Indeed, ending an event takes time; ending is not the same as being ended, cut short, stopped; ending belongs to the event. But much music shows us that we don't need much time to prepare for ending. A moment of ending can be very expansive (see, for example, the extended ending of the immediately preceding movement, the first part of the *Sanctus*) or fairly sudden. Hearing the acceleration and intensification of this first large phrase and the suddenness or concentration of this close (and the turn to triple meter in altus at the very end), I suggest that this ending has some unspent energy that can help to motivate the launching of the new phrase, a second large and contrasting phrase more or less commensurate with the first (here a second *pleni sunt coeli*).

All these more or less sensible interpretations (sensible to the extent of being actually, sensibly tested) are speculative because we have so little to go on in trying to hear a music that when it was new had much more to go on, more to go on than we shall ever know. But our record shows a rhythmic complexity that must itself have been of high value to singers and hearers. In the entire phrase there are no dissonant minims and only one suspension, the cadential 6-7-♯6-8 at the end. This absence of orienting dissonance means that the music can freely depart from the ¢-prescribed tempus and tactus. It does so in ways that can make it difficult and interesting for the two singers who would closely attend to one another. At *t*.13 we enter into a new behavior. The two voices imitate at the "distance" of a minim, and they alternate in "5-minim" and "4-minim" measures. At this tempo (say, semibreve = 60-72) the "5" will be composed, more or less distinctly, of two smaller measures, duple and triple—but in what order, 2+3 or 3+2? Moreover, the ordering of duple and triple in altus and superius might be different. Since the two voices are out of synch such a difference need not be especially confusing for the singers. What matters immediately is how to sing your own part, using all the resources at your disposal. These resources may involve close attention to your partner for coordination, or not. I imagine that, singing from parts, the severe dissociation of altus and superius in *t*.13–21 could be challenging, virtuosic, and perhaps exhilarating. I imagine that for a master singer everything that could be sensed would matter or ask to be valued. The "decision" or choice in the moment of performance to articulate the 5-minmim figures 3+2 or 2+3 would then be motivated by sensations in the immediate past and the contemporary present (i.e., the other, "contemporary" singer).

To envision one scenario (perhaps the less likely of the two), let's say that by *t*.13–14 new relevancies are emerging in altus that might shift things to favor triple followed by duple. Precisely when such a shift might take place, we can't say. Perhaps there could emerge a subtle play of 2+3 and 3+2 quite unlike the either/or and discontinuous situation of Necker cube experiments, but perhaps not entirely unlike the graphic experiments of Escher which explore an intensely rhythmic vision and can manifest a subtle and engaging neither/nor or both/and oscillation and thus perhaps question neither-nor/both-and. In any case, the way each of these 5-beat events is performed is motivated by a context in which the immediately past event is especially powerful. As an experiment, I would like to suggest a way in which the novelty of this new configuration might be prepared or made less abrupt. In altus let's experiment hearing the semibreve *e*1 ("*-li*") at the end of *t*.12 as initiation (|) rather than continuation (\), say as a shift from rising seconds to falling thirds. In this case, the preceding three minims *e-f-d* can have become a triple measure (| \—\) and indeed the beginning of a 5-mimim measure *e-f-d-e* concluding with "*-li*" if the following "*et*" begins a new measure.

I haven't attempted to specify projective functions in detail in this fluid "*et terra*" event. To do so would lead to more complexity and would require much more analytic detail. Asking more questions would lead to problematic openings and to some of the opportunities for play this artifact affords. Such opportunities are dramatically enhanced by playing with another. I would suggest (in part, based on my singing altus in this passage with students) that if you are secure in your own part, you can confidently afford to focus on your partner's part. This can be a risky but very exciting experience and quite profound if we imagine, in Polanyi's terms, making our singing selves subsidiary to a focal partner as a sort of "indwelling," dwelling in another's singing. Let's imagine that our conscientious altus would, given the opportunity, spend time with this part (and his partner) discovering opportunities for hearing/singing in rewarding ways. "Rewarding" might mean attending to one another without losing one's way and engaging in a complex play of sensations and feelings that asks for, demonstrates, and advances one's mastery.

Certainly, the rhythm of this large phrase, even in the domain of durational quantity, involves much more than the sort of measurings I have proposed. The reappearance of figures can be an important factor in event formation and is a striking feature in this highly patterned phrase. Beginning *again* quickly articulates a new event as a focus of attention. In Figure 1.4 I have identified a sort of network of beginnings-again in the altus in the second ("*et terra*") part of the phrase. It will, of course, take some time for this fairly large event to emerge as a second, that is to break off from (forget) what had first emerged as a second phrase/phase, the second "*coeli*" event in the neighborhood of *t*.8, heard in the overlapping of closing in superious and (re-) opening in altus.

In the new second (or third) phase emerging around *t*.13 I have labeled four large altus events A, B, C, and D. Here the altus begins with the first of what will become two complex figures, A and B, each made of two strongly contrasting parts or phases ("*et*" and "*terra*"). The beginning-again with event B ends or concretizes A which is taken as measure for the present B in a clear feeling of repetition. A more or less new pattern emerges in the following "*et terra*" (C). The superius (see Figure 1.3, *t*.17) now goes off in a new direction breaking from the preceding iteration, but oddly remembering (with the complicity of altus, *t*.19–20) a bit from what I conceive as the transition to what emerges as a second half of the phrase. (Compare superius *t*.12–13 and *t*.19–20

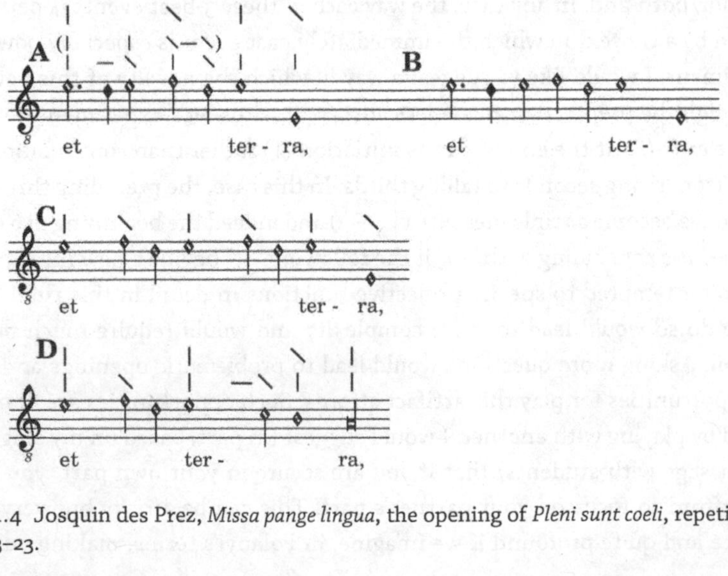

FIGURE 1.4 Josquin des Prez, *Missa pange lingua*, the opening of *Pleni sunt coeli*, repetitions in altus, t.13–23.

in conjunction with altus *t.* 12–13 and *t.*18–20.) The altus doesn't take this departure (though he can hear it). Instead, altus begins again with a compression of its predecessors, repeating in smooth equal measures a simplified version of the earlier (unequal, 3+2 or 2+3) 5-minim figures. Compression can be felt in C's feeling/measuring of *its* own(-ed) or relevant(-ed) progenitors. Thus, the first event of what will become C gets to its second, semibreve "tactus" beat (beginning with *f*1) a minim sooner than A and B. But this initial compression/acceleration turns out to become (complexly) wedded to an expansion with the event of a concluding octave "*ter-ra*." The next "*et ter-ra*" event D begins with the promise of reproducing its predecessor, a promise enhanced by the repetition A-B. And yet, this promise is denied by a sudden turn to cadence. This denial is part of the relevance of many preceding events in the construction of a feeling of the suddenly focusing and truncating turn to closure of this huge, demanding, and possibly exhilarating phrase—exhilarating if only in the accomplishment of having stayed together in the face of so many challenges, and perhaps augmented with gratitude to God for the gift of having made some beautiful moves along the way.

It might be argued that such feelings will be lost with familiarity as the singer-listener comes to "know" what will happen and no longer "expect" the larger continuation, no longer be "surprised" by the turn of events (or that seeing the notation, the singer will never have expected anything different). But I would argue that such feelings as I have attempted to describe are opportunities for rhythmic engagement and intensity that can be enhanced and not dulled with practice. To "know" in advance, to expect a determinate outcome, to lose surprise with the knowledge of what will be—these are all expressions of a deterministic perspective that runs counter to a temporal perspective in which real novelty is inescapable, though certainly dulled by inattention and insensitivity. In the actual practice of music-making, familiarity, borne of habit, is stillborn if it does not lead to new, creative, adventurous practice.

CONCLUSION

If artifacts of music (written or not) are endless in their possibilities for actual occasions of rhythmic experience (R1), they are also endless in the observations they can elicit and the questions they open or problems they pose (R2). Imagine that observations leading to questions/problems are affordances of artifacts, and that these are no less affordances than are the multitude of aesthetic experiences that things have to offer. If things/artifacts afford both modes of experience, then why should not the two have commerce? In the R2 analyses I have selected a few details that I trust can be sensed in singing or hearing others sing. If sensed they will actually have been entangled with countless other sensible distinctions that might in turn be pointed out (and, indeed, all sorts of sensible distinctions for which we have no names, as yet).

Analysis as a separation and naming of parts is immediately destructive of meaning understood as the performative, creative working together and working out of differences in the "moment"—a moment or movement that is a working together of what we call "present, past, and future." With its imaginative out-of-time ("diagrammatic") separation of "factors," analysis must destroy the actual intricacy of our ongoing involvement with a changing world. And yet, since we can't really get out of involvement while we're alive, an imaginative separation or taking apart will have consequences for us (and consequences that can come to seem to have their "own" life as ideas). In this case, analysis or thinking-about can be productive as a loosening that can lead to new thinking/hearing/feeling. This process might be called learning, in which a focus on one or another detail, temporarily separated or alienated from its involvement in countless other details, might lead to a special sensitivity, or focus, or skill that once achieved might be "creatively forgotten," that is to say, incorporated into a change of skill and so loose its separation to rejoin a whole that it now changes and hopefully enriches (though no guarantees). Again, this is a process familiar to practicing musicians and to artists in general. It is possible, however, to get stuck in this process by dwelling on separation. Thinking *about* can then seem something *separate* from the thinking—an object of thought that can be viewed as something that (while I might be changing) remains self-same, something that is just itself, a self insulated from intrinsic interdependence and change. Such separation is a fiction and, indeed, a very useful fiction. In fact, laws, rules, and structures are in practice, as things entertained and used, changeable from time to time (or culture to culture) and from person to person. (What did the rule of a fixed "theoretical tactus" and the consistency of system of proportional notation depositing an invariant tempus mean for Josquin and for contemporary singers? When, where, to whom?)

Both R1 and R2, or "with" and "about," are fully temporal (if time is real) and always mixed. Indeed, their mixing might be conceived as a sort of rhythmic exchange in which new meanings are made. The general difference of "with and about" understood temporally could, I think, be useful as one way of thinking about a variety of differences (perhaps even the highly problematic differences of sound and sense or music and language). But such a project would require far more thinking with and about than I have attempted here. In any case, such a project has not been the focus of this chapter. My aim has been more generally to urge that the word/concept "rhythm" be taken as a way of thinking and speaking about music (and things in general) that would validate the activity, the on-goingness, the actuality in which music is made.

NOTES

1. Fraisse continues: "This difficulty derives from the fact that rhythm refers to a complex reality in which several variables are fused . . . Most generally, we say that there is rhythm when we can predict on the basis of what is perceived, or, in other words, when we can anticipate what will follow." Fraisse here touches on two issues that will be focal for the present essay: 1) "fused" or continuous *complexity*, and 2) experiential temporality as an ongoing responsiveness to opportunities for the actualization of emergent potentials, a process I will call "passage," a process that involves anticipation but in its temporal complexity exceeds anticipation pure and simple. As we shall see, the problem of definition reveals the profound gap

between actual experience and out-of-time representations that make no room for complexity and temporal passage. This is, of course, a general problem of description and analysis. But "rhythm," because of its unavoidable temporal implications, can bring problems of description and analysis into especially sharp focus.

2. I imagine that by "regularity" Cooper here means repetition of "the same lengths of time" and by differentiation the markings of accent that give rise to pattern and coordinated hierarchical "strata."

3. "This fallacy consists in neglecting the degree of abstraction involved when an actual entity is considered merely so far as it exemplifies certain categories of thought" (1985, 7–8). See also Whitehead (1967, 64 and 72).

4. By "actual" I mean present and ongoing. This sense has been largely lost in English, but it persists in the French *actuel*. The OED gives the following etymology: "Latin *actualis* active, practical, exhibited in deeds (5th cent.), real, existing (from 13th c in British sources), current, effective at the time . . . classical Latin *actus* physical movement, motion, mode of action, movement, action, activity, doing, duty, work, transaction, performance, administration, conduct, method, employment, performance (of a play), representation, delivery (of a speech), part or division of a play, session of a discussion, moral conduct, behaviour."

5. "Control" comes to us from the fourteenth-century Anglo-Norman *contreroller*—to count; but more specifically, to check accounts with a *duplicate register*. Randle Cotgrave (1611) defines *contrerolle*: "To controll; observe, oversee, spie faults in; also, to take, and keep a copie of a roll of accounts; to play the controller any way." I bring up this history to suggest a deep and abiding connection of writing technologies or notations that give us a way of "predicting and controlling a future" with *duplication* (identifying the same in representation) and getting back the same via a *register*.

6. In many publications Milič Čapek has traced the elimination of time throughout the history of western science and philosophy. See especially Čapek (1961).

7. John Dewey (1887, 197) writes: "In its broadest sense, rhythm is identical with the apperceptive activity of the mind." Notice the difference in saying "the rhythm of thought" compared to saying "the movement or process of thought." Rhythm seems to speak to a qualitative dimension that involves a manifold of moments involving repetition and difference (and perhaps a sort of oscillation, a "sinusoidal" version of the hermeneutic circle).

8. Blum (2009a) develops this idea with the notion of the "implicit theories" that need not be assumed to be identical for individuals working within a shared practice. This is a perspective that takes actual, here-and-now, variable practice into account (and that resists an R1/R2 dichotomy).

9. Strict and free might then be relative, comparative terms or perhaps ideal limits. In this case, it would be useful to try to understand the terms of difference as defining a scale of intensity. One possibility might be to think of free as more of an imaginative stretch (and perhaps sometimes a leap) than strict, or to continue the metaphor, to think of strict as more vivid, closer up, or more in focus than free as something receding or stretching into the distance. Need we think of these two terms or end points (*termini*), strict (not free) and free (not strict), on a value scale of positive and negative? Which would be positive and which negative?

10. I take the general distinction of internal and external measurement from Koichiro Matsuno (1989, 32): "Internal measurement is inherent in realization of a particular pattern of interaction between an arbitrary pair of interacting bodies in the absence of an external observer . . . In contrast, external measurement . . . assumes an intervention of an external observer." For a specifically tense-temporal interpretation see Matsuno (2000, 332–49). Although

I adapt these terms to situations quite different from those Matsuno considers, the understanding I present here is, I trust, more or less compatible with Matsuno's. In asking for a turn to internal measurement Matsuno replaces one-to-one mapping with one-to-many mapping.

11. In a sense subjects *are* events. For a development of "subject" along the lines of Whitehead's process theory, see Hasty (2013).

12. "It" is an abbreviation for it/we. Again, "event" here is not something outside the experiencers.

13. In his lecture-performance "Thinking Twice," Stefan Wolpe (1967, 297) writes of the complexity of situation in terms of composing: "It is good to know how not to know how much one is knowing."

14. The terms "focal" and "subsidiary" refer to Michael Polanyi's theory of tacit knowing. See Polanyi (1969) for a concise explanation. As an example: I point with my index finger to a diagram on the blackboard. You see the diagram focally, but you have also seen my act of pointing subsidarily. You are no less aware of my finger and gesture of pointing, but this is not the focus of your awareness.

15. By "world" I will mean something specifically human and cultural. This sense can be heard for example in the Old Saxon *werold: wer* meaning "man" (akin to the Latin *vir*) plus *old* (age), what we might call history or tradition. In the sense I intend, "world" should not be understood as separate from environment, which includes nonhuman and nonliving agents and opportunities (e.g., the air we breathe, the sun that warms us, the food we seek, etc.).

16. "Situation" here may be compared with Searle's "background," Whitehead's "potentiality," and Bergson's and Deleuze's "virtuality."

17. In his theory of implicit meaning, Eugene Gendlin (1962, 148–72) writes of a "nonnumerical" or "unseparated" multiplicity carvable in many as yet unspecified ways.

18. Time here can be problematic in the positive sense of stimulating new thinking (Greek *problema* as a throwing forth, similar to the Latin *projectio*). In his descriptions of Ewe drumming (2010, paragraph 2) Locke vividly speaks of process. For example, in describing the metric matrix he invokes time and the dynamic metaphor of resonance: "Beat *streams* in the matrix act like sympathetic strings: just as a tuned string will *resonate in response* to a melodic pitch, *a specific feeling* of musical groove *will activate* when sounded accents coincide *with a flow* of tacit beats in the metric matrix" (emphasis added).

19. Take the (classic) example of chess. In chess the allowable, separate moves permitted the pieces constitute a closed set of rules. If we were to depart from this set we would no longer be playing chess. But what if we were to alter this set slightly, say by making the opening move obligatory and determined by a coin toss—would this no longer be (a form of) chess? At what point of an alteration of rules would the game no longer be called (a form of) chess? Certainly, in this continuum of the practice of chess there is no single, measurable point. But the broader problem is that of locating these ideal moves in the human. Such moves/rules of the game do not determine the actual course of a game which is infinitely complex and which involves innumerably more rules than the set of allowable moves of the chess pieces. Beyond the rules of play are the larger rules (if we wish to call them that) of pattern, strategy, and behavior carried out by people in actual, full bodily motion. If we can't connect allowable moves (say, broadened to include all the classic plays) with people *playing* chess, we've done little more than read the instruction booklet, however infinitely detailed it might be.

20. For speculation on the historical valuation of iambic pentameter in cultural-social terms see Antony Easthope's *Poetry as Discourse* (1983).

21. For worse to the extent that "rhythm" is deprived of its service in properly naming many courses of event formation (e.g., visual arts, thinking, interacting) where durational quantity is not foregrounded. If quantity of "time" and especially the sequential reproduction of such quantity as "the same" defines rhythm proper, then a host of other eventful activities will be marginalized as merely "metaphorically" and not properly rhythmic. Again, the decision to define rhythm narrowly has its virtues, but I am arguing that this word presents opportunities for thinking about time or process that cannot arise from narrower definitions.

22. This very primitive diagram is not intended to address the many problems raised by a processive or temporal perspective. For a set of more explicit diagrams, see pp. 338–42 of this volume (my second essay, chapter 13).

23. Thus, the symbols | and \ (and later /) do not label beats conventionally understood as separate entities, much less "strong" and "weak" beats. The notion that dynamic or stress "accents" are the foundation of meter, at least in European musical traditions is, I believe, false and also misleading in its cultural implications. Contrasting a western and non-Western feeling of rhythm-meter, Gerhardt Kubik (2010), for example, writes: "In jazz the term [beat] is understood in a sense that does not imply stress accents on 1 and 3, as in Western 4/4 meter. Sometimes it may appear that 2 and 4 are accented. Using the word 'beat' in the jazz sense, we can apply it to the (inner) reference beat" (36). "A difference between African metrical schemes and European measures is that the former do not include the notion of stress" (38). I would argue that the situation Kubik accurately describes for African and Afro-American musics might serve as an antidote for theories of Western music that make stress (and separation) fundamental. I do, however, whole-heartedly agree with Kubik's conclusion: that "The habit of associating metrical schemes with notions of stress is so deeply rooted in European cultures that *observers* trained in classical music often find it difficult to separate the two" (38, emphasis added). I do not intend to single out Kubik for criticism, but rather to draw on his articulation of a perspective that I think is representative of much ethnomusicological thought. This thought, in running counter to received Western theory, might be more productively used as a critique of that theory than used as another opportunity to essentialize actual musical practices.

The marks | and \ as marks are irredeemably separate, but the functions they would symbolize are not oppositions of properties such as accented/unaccented, strong/weak, good/bad. My terms "initiation" and "continuation" as nouns of action from verbs (to initiate, to continue) are meant to point to process. And yet, calling | "initiation" or "beginning" can be misleading by implying a separable beginning part or phase. To be more precise we might speak of "an articulated continuation of a beginning," or "the beginning's continuation" where each belongs to each. It is interesting that it is so difficult to find easy verbal expressions for involvement and lack of separation.

24. "Comparison," as I intend the term here, means an out-of-time, external measure, that is to say, out of the (R1) event-time it would represent. But again, because there is nothing really outside time, even an apparently out-of-time comparison in the sense I suggest here is temporal, in its own (R2) way—indeed, hopelessly temporal.

25. In several informal experiments in seminars and lectures asking a group of (5–40) people to clap a fourth after I have clapped three times where each clap comes sooner than the last, the group's fourth claps are always highly synchronized (apart, sometimes, from a few outliers who I think were not quite prepared for this exercise). In these experiments I have always proceeded from clapping once (and asking how long the clap has lasted, with some more tries leading to a feeling of "echo" and farther to a kind of "echoic repetition") to clapping twice (ca.

mm = 60) and asking for a third clap from the audience. Finally, I clapped an accelerated or somewhat shorter third and ask for a fourth clap. What I find especially telling is that from two of my claps on, I observe people preparing for their action in highly complicated ways—first putting a pencil down, moving a hand from under the table, putting a notepad aside. All this intricately timed motor activity is carried out within the "span" of about 1–2 seconds (less for acceleration).

26. I would recommend two widely available recordings: Kuijken Quartet (Dennon CO-18045-46) and Kodaly Quartet (Naxos 8.550129).

27. This is not to say that some form of "counting" was not active. What sort of "counting" would be an interesting question to pursue. A part of my motivation for pointing to a difference between what the players actually felt (R1) and what they said they were doing from an R2 perspective is to suggest a Western parallel in some respects with Richard Wolf's (2010) experiments with South Indian musicians' feeling and understanding of alepana.

28. Along similar lines, it is likely that the duple vs. triple question in the first four bars is more complicated. It is possible that the players (and especially the viola player) did initially feel the beginning of bar two as a downbeat (|), the initiation of a new event, but that at some point during the fermata the situation changed as the offbeat (continuative) tonic harmony came to be felt as a second event. Precisely how all this was felt by the four players and how this larger 2-bar event colored the feeling of the next event (and how these feelings changed from one rehearsal, one performance to the next) is R1 and so beyond analysis, but not beyond thinking about or at least acknowledging.

29. Here I introduce a new symbol "/" to mark anacrusis (or more specifically "anacrustic continuation") as a sort of pointing forward. The distinction of \ and / (arsic and anacrustic continuation) is one of orientation, a feeling of how much time is left until the new duration runs out, or how much time remains before a new third event if for any reason the move to a new event is or becomes relevant.

30. The connections of note names and graphic notations are as follows: longa [𝆷], breve [𝆸], semibreve [𝆹], and minim [𝆹𝅥].

31. Again, bars are notational devices that may or may not correspond to (felt) measures. Likewise, *Mensurstriche* (a modern device dating from the 1920s) need not mark felt or keenly felt measures, but in any case are used here for notational reference, that is, to locate places in the score. Another way my notation misrepresents (or rather can't represent) part notation concerns spacing—in part notation relative duration length is not represented spatially; for example, adjacent semibreves are spaced no farther apart than are adjacent semiminims (four times shorter in duration).

32. The mensuration symbol ¢ that marked *tempus imperfectum diminutum* specified the following: *imperfect* (binary) rather than *perfect* (ternary) in the choice of the number of semibreves for *tempus*, and by implication an *imperfect* (two minim) "prolation" for the semibreves. The "cut" (*diminutum*) signified a quicker tempo than c. Although prolation is generally defined as *division* of semibreve, *prolatio* had quite different connotations—bringing forth and enlarging (and also delaying or postponing).

33. The rhythmic fluidity of Renaissance vocal polyphony has been widely acknowledged. Curt Sachs (1953, 250), for example, imagines that without accent a great variety of measures might arise in performance: "In vocal polyphony 'norms' and 'regularly recurring accents of the first beats' were almost nonexistent, and hence any 'abnormal syncopation' as well. The truth is that Renaissance polyphony, very far from our normal recurrent accents, relies on an unrestrained polyrhythmic writing, on a continual almost erratic change from duple to triple

groupings, with or against the other parts, with or against the time signature." Giving more weight to the norm and regularity presumably guaranteed by the ruling proportional signature in the sixteenth century ("and perhaps even earlier"), Knud Jeppesen (1946, 18, 26–28) introduced the terms "macro rhythm" and "micro rhythm" (the former "total," the latter "partial"). (Other scholars have invoked the influence of chant with its "free rhythm.") Gustave Fredric Soderland (1947, 7), without referring to Jeppesen, explains the difference thus: "There was a system of accentuation known as the greater, or Macro, rhythm which defined, in $\frac{4}{2}$ time, the first and third beats as strong, the second and fourth beats as weak. The greater rhythm acted as coordinator, or regulator assigning the location of different devices such as suspensions, cadences, and passing tones to certain beats. On the other hand, secondary, or Micro, rhythm was the irregular rhythmical grouping of each individual voice part." The terms "macrorhythm" and "microrhythm" have now become standard, though scholars differ in their understanding of these terms. Often the implication is of the macro as a system of global constraint, always at work throughout the piece, rather like the current notion of modern time signatures and their bars providing an autonomous and invariant grid against which secondary irregularities can be counterpointed (say, as "metrical dissonances"). This is the sort of understanding that led the Quartet to assume they were playing in ¾ throughout. I contend that measuring/timing in many styles (ancient and modern) is variable and context-sensitive. This understanding does not deny the power of the reigning tempus; indeed, it honors that power in recognizing its ability to endure (as a conceptual order) sometimes quite extreme disruptions. Ruth DeFord (2015), a singularly enlightening guide, identifies three measurings for music of this period in terms of tactus or "beat." These are, in brief: "theoretical tactus" (for example, the two semibreves per tempus ordained in the signature ¢ and shown by the homogeneous and numbered *Mensurstriche* in Example 2), the "compositional tactus" (a more flexible metrical situation the composer allowed for in the intricacies of notation and counterpoint), and a "performative tactus" (the tactus in its particularity, or in its performative particularizing of "compositional tactus"). My suggestions, because they aim for a particularity tested/made by the reader, aim problematically for a "performative tactus," a tactus actually made. DeFord provides a much more nuanced discussion of the possibilities of mensuration than I can here. See especially her analysis of the Benedictus from the *Missa Pange lingua* (108–113).

34. In this way suspensions and dissonant minim passing tones can keep or save the tempus. Without these markers the tactus is free to shift from the prescribed mensuration. The practically obligatory suspension at cadence guaranteed a reset. In view of the abstract, shadowy nature of a ubiquitous tempus, however, we might ask what "keeping" means—when, where, for whom?

35. The altus here might be in a situation similar to Haydn's violist in bars 1–3 of the Adagio: violist moves out of beginning into continuation (|→/), altus moves out of continuation into beginning (\→|).

36. To indicate triple measure I show a second continuation (—\) prolonging the duration. Since triple differs from duple measure arises in *not* creating a new initiation with a third beat, I call such situations "deferral" to speak of process rather than count or proportion.

37. The sense of repetition here would be significantly enhanced in memory of the importance of a pedagogical practice for these singers, beginning in childhood—the mastering of solmization, a system of pitch naming that assigned to both figures, superius, *c-b-a/c-b* the later altus, *f-e-d/f-e* the same names *fa-mi-re/fa-mi*. Although I will say very little about them here, dimensions of pitch, register, and contour are crucial in shaping durational quantity-quality. As one example, consider the opening gesture of altus, repeated an octave higher in

superius. The ascent "*Ple-ni sunt coe-*" from *e* up to *c* is intensified in various ways: the repetition of the interval of the fourth *e–a* in *t.*2 twice as fast, immediately followed by a higher fourth *g–c* exposing a higher register in hexachordal "registral space." The initial *e–a* is in the "normal" hexachord (*c–a*). With the appearance of the high *c* (followed by half-step *b*) a movement is made to the "hard" hexachord (*g–e*). This change or mutation here might be initiated with the *a* in *t.*2, especially if this *a* gets the new text syllable "*coe-*" (and right away the sense of heaven). The lengthening and suspension of the continuative *c* into the next measure (*t.*3) is the momentary apogee of this line which in *t.*4 returns to *c* and moves up to *e* (*la* in the hard hexachord), an octave above its beginning. Here the *e* (completing "*coe-li*") lends intensity to superius *c* and energy to the long holding pattern around *c* that begins with this initial, suspended *c*. (Incidentally, when altus repeats *e* in *t.*6 "*sunt*," this *e* returns to the normal hexachord as *mi*.) In the context of the preceding *Sanctus* section, which ends on C with *e*1 in superius (and a languid extension of the cadence), the quick, accelerating ascent in *Pleni* to *g–c* can seem an energizing return or arrival.

2

Formative Processes of Durational Projection in "Free Rhythm" World Music

John Roeder

IN A 1996 survey of the ethnomusicological literature, Martin Clayton identified around seventy musical genres across the world in which rhythm seems to be "free," ranging from those "apparently without pulse of any kind to those with a clear pulse but no higher level periodicity" (Clayton 1996, 324). Many scholars had observed this phenomenon, particularly in a "continuous, loosely related cultural zone" extending from North Africa to East Asia where "free rhythm is an essential, genre-related characteristic" (Frigyesi 1993). Clayton's special concern, however, was why the music had attracted so little analysis. He attributed its neglect to a lack of appropriate theory:

> The absence of adaptable concepts and methods in conventional (Western) musicology, where rhythmic analysis generally presumes the existence of metre, appears to have inhibited the development of ethnomusicological methods. . . . Most non-Western cultures, too, appear to lack theories of free rhythm, and the fact that ethnomusicologists have in general found no such indigenous theories to report has also stood as a barrier to this study. (Clayton 1996, 325–6)

Although theories of meter have been enriched lately by consideration of the timelines and nonisochronous beats that are common in world music (Agawu 2006; Polak and London 2014), such concepts still do not apply to situations in which pulse and pulse hierarchy are too irregular, sporadic, or slow to be entrained, or even absent. For analyzing free sung poetry, theories of prosody suggest grouping durations into poetic feet. For instance, Tsuge (1970) observes in Persian music how singers tend to alternate long and short syllables in a loosely iambic pattern (see also Azadehfar 2004 and, for a related repertoire, Qureshi 1969). This kind of description helps explain some of the generative strategies of performers but does not define large-scale form or engage with the specific durations of syllables, phrases, or sections.

Just a year after Clayton's article appeared, however, a promising possibility presented itself. In the book *Meter as Rhythm*, Christopher Hasty posited an elemental process of temporal perception that he called "projection." The top row of Figure 2.1 represents it symbolically as it might manifest in a succession of sounds, represented by thick line segments. The onset of the second sound makes definite a duration, denoted by a solid arc, that began at the onset of the first sound. At this same moment, indicated by the head of the arrow on the arc, Hasty says, listeners mentally "project" this duration into the future. The projection, symbolized by the dashed arc, acts as a measure by which listeners may assess the timing of upcoming events. For instance, if an event appears that same duration after the second onset, the projection is felt to be "realized." The sensation of meter, then, as defined in this theory, does not involve pulse hierarchies or entrainment, but simply an assessment of durational reproduction.

Grounded in process philosophy, the concept of projection is intuitively appealing, because it captures a familiar and compelling aspect of temporal cognition: our ability to direct our attention toward a future moment contingent upon an immediately past duration, and so to discriminate differences between successive durations. Hasty developed it into a rich, hierarchical theory of metrical "particularity" that can express, for example, the complex temporal sensations afforded by modernist Western art music. Considering Clayton's conundrum, however, it is worth investigating how the concept *tout simple* can support analysis of free rhythm.

At first glance it appears promising: listeners may perceive and project durations even in the briefest, most irregular succession of events, and the theory provides a way to characterize the time-sensations that they afford. Some of the nature and variety of these sensations are demonstrated by the rhythms analyzed in Figure 2.1, which are adapted from Hasty's exposition. The realization of a projection, shown in the top row, offers a sense of temporal continuity, specifically, that the realizing event-onset is extending an ongoing process, perhaps a nascent stream of pulse. This continuity may be nuanced if the event-onset is heard to realize the projection slightly early or late, as represented at the top of the second row: acceleration deemphasizes the present moment and directs attention toward the future, while slowing makes the present seem more weighty and terminal. A sense of termination arises more strongly when an event fails to materialize within the scope of a projection, creating metrical "hiatus" and discontinuity. Some event successions foster a change of scope, in which the listener decides to subordinate a second event in order to focus on a longer duration. Other rhythms, shown at the bottom of the second row, may encourage the listener to reorient attention toward the second event-onset, and the shorter or longer duration it begins, as more salient than the first. Lastly, as shown at the bottom of the figure, an event may be heard as subordinate, functioning more to continue an already becoming duration than to initiate a new one; the later it occurs in the duration, the more it heightens, as an anacrusis, the anticipation of the completion of the duration.

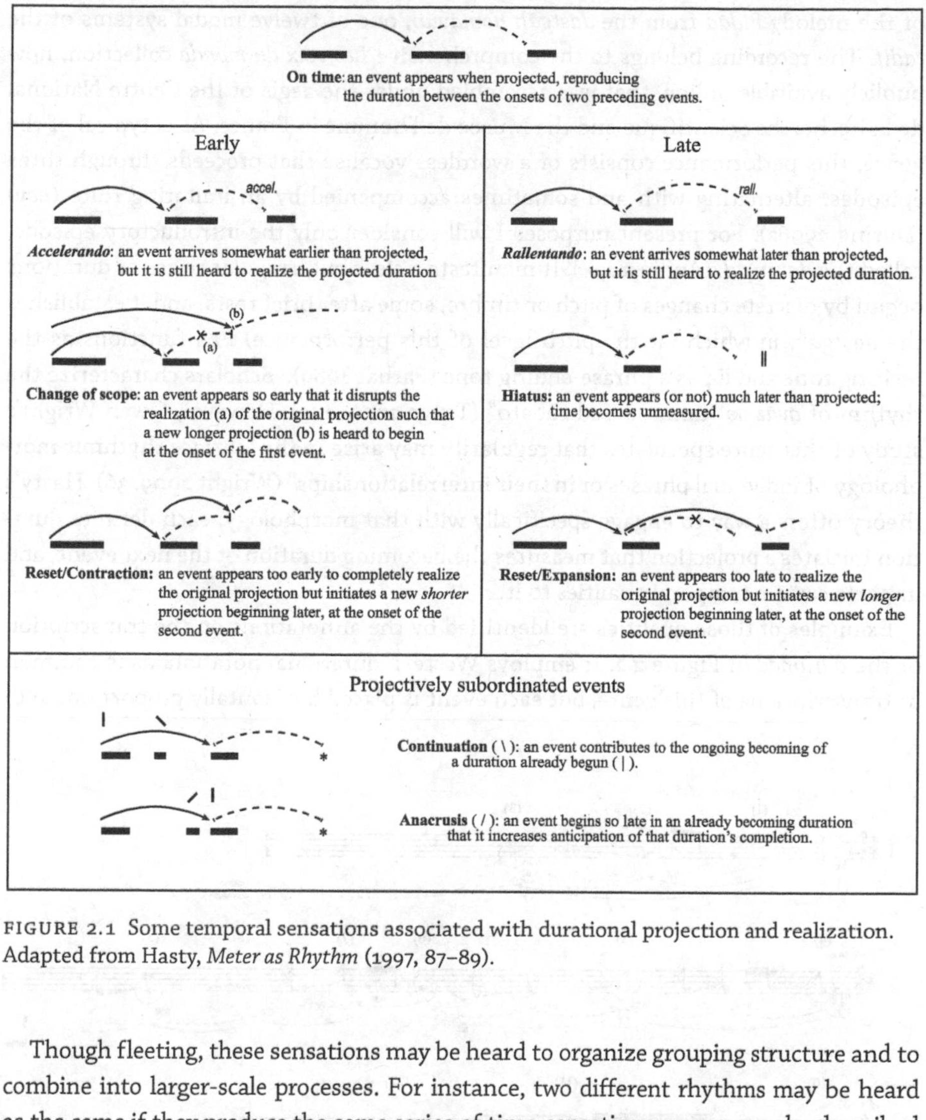
On time: an event appears when projected, reproducing the duration between the onsets of two preceding events.
Early
Late
accel.
Accelerando: an event arrives somewhat earlier than projected, but it is still heard to realize the projected duration
rall.
Rallentando: an event arrives somewhat later than projected, but it is still heard to realize the projected duration.
(b)
(a)
Change of scope: an event appears so early that it disrupts the realization (a) of the original projection such that a new longer projection (b) is heard to begin at the onset of the first event.
Hiatus: an event appears (or not) much later than projected; time becomes unmeasured.
Reset/Contraction: an event appears too early to completely realize the original projection but initiates a new shorter projection beginning later, at the onset of the second event.
Reset/Expansion: an event appears too late to realize the original projection but initiates a new longer projection beginning later, at the onset of the second event.
Projectively subordinated events
Continuation (\ ): an event contributes to the ongoing becoming of a duration already begun (|).
Anacrusis (/): an event begins so late in an already becoming duration that it increases anticipation of that duration's completion.

FIGURE 2.1 Some temporal sensations associated with durational projection and realization. Adapted from Hasty, *Meter as Rhythm* (1997, 87–89).

Though fleeting, these sensations may be heard to organize grouping structure and to combine into larger-scale processes. For instance, two different rhythms may be heard as the same if they produce the same series of time-sensations, or one may be described specifically as a variant according to the way that its projections vary those of the other. Realization, acceleration, slowing, and hiatus may be heard to create and articulate a directed temporal flow to which some events contribute but others may come as surprise, forcing retrospective reinterpretations of the importance of beginnings and durations.

Perhaps the reason that the potential of this theory for analyzing free rhythm has not been appreciated is that not enough work has been done to show how such music can direct and organize these elemental sensations that it describes. To foster that appreciation, this chapter examines how the durational successions in three examples of "free rhythm" world music may afford perception of process, pitch structure, and form.

To give concrete examples of the time-sensations represented in Figure 2.1, and of their formal functions, and also to consider some methodological questions, I will refer first to an item of Persian classical music: Afsāne Ziā'i's vocal performance (*āvāz*) of the melody *Bīdād* from the *dastgāh homāyun*, one of twelve modal systems of the *radif*. The recording belongs to the comprehensive *Les voix du monde* collection, now publicly available online, that was assembled under the aegis of the Centre National de la Recherche Scientifique and the Musée de l'homme in France. As is typical of the genre, this performance consists of a wordless vocalise that proceeds through three episodes, alternating with and sometimes accompanied by an imitating flute (*ney*) (During 1996a). For present purposes I will consider only the introductory episode, called the *darāmad*. (Audio.2.1 ▶). It manifests a clear but irregular series of durations begun by discrete changes of pitch or timbre, some after brief rests, and it establishes the *dastgāh*, in which (at the pitch level of this performance) F#4 functions as the reciting tone and E4 as a phrase-ending tone (Farhat 1989).[1] Scholars characterize the rhythm of *āvāz* as "unmeasured rubato" (Tsuge 1970, 205). However, Owen Wright's study of this genre speculates that regularity may arise in the "surface rhythmic morphology of individual phrases or in their interrelationships" (Wright 2009, 36). Hasty's theory offers a way to engage specifically with that morphology: each definite duration initiates a projection that measures the becoming duration of the next event, and imparts certain temporal qualities to it.

Examples of those qualities are identified by the annotations on the transcription of the *darāmad* in Figure 2.2. It employs Western durational notation, as is common in transcriptions of this genre, but each event is placed horizontally proportionate to

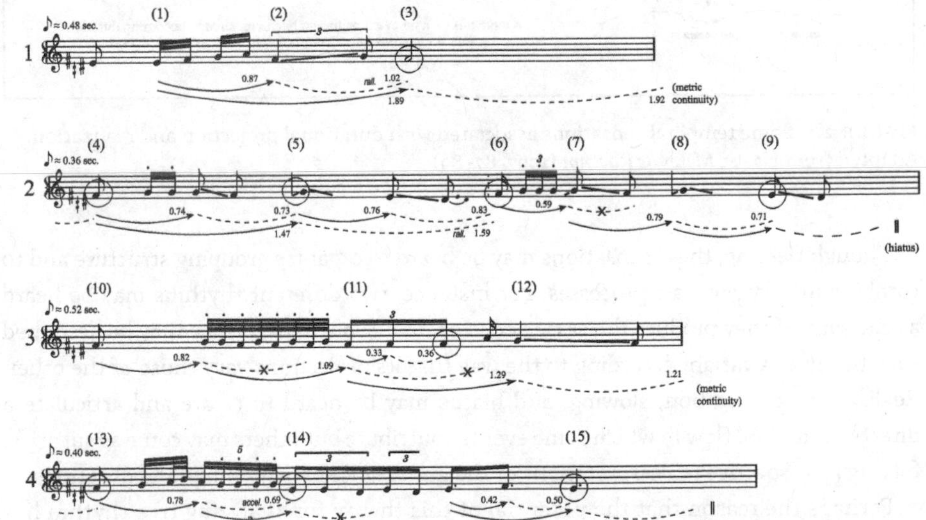

FIGURE 2.2 Projective analysis of the introduction (*darāmad*) to the classical Persian chant (*āvāz*) of an extract from *Bīdād* from *dastgāh homāyun*, sung by Afsāne Ziā'i with Hoseyn Omumi, *ney*. Transcribed by John Roeder.

its onset time, with a notehead that approximates its duration with reference to the tempo mark at the beginning of its respective staff, so that the durations of identically notated events may differ. The arrows and arcs indicate durations that may be heard to participate in projections. To clarify certain comparisons, numbers on the arcs label these durations quantitatively to the nearest hundredth of a second but, as I shall discuss, it is only the comparisons, not the chronometric timings, that are relevant to the analysis. The grouping of the events into four systems reflects my hearing that the projective processes form the *darāmad* hierarchically into two pairs of phrases.

Before proceeding, however, let us take the opportunity this music provides to consider the appropriateness of the analytical method. Within many of the durations asserted by the transcription, timbre, loudness, and pitch vary continuously. How valid is it, then, to quantify and compare them? Judit Frigyesi trenchantly demurs:

> The idea that one can scientifically measure the duration of a note is pure illusion: in reality, most sounds present a complex schema of internal life with subtle variations in loudness, timbre, vibrato, and pitch. Ornamentation and the coordinated action of multiple instruments make the image more confused, just like the presence of breath, vibrato, and text pronunciation in vocal music. At a very subtle level, the act of deciding when a note begins and ends is already influenced by our preconceived perception of the internal periodicity of a particular style. (Frigyesi 1999, 61; par. 23 in online version)[2]

If she is right that "scientific" measurement is unjustifiable, then one must find other ways of describing free rhythm, for example as contours of stress, as Frigyesi herself has done with her characterization of "flowing rhythm" in Jewish *nusah*, or as patterns of "intonations" (Asafiev 1947; Chashchina 2013).

However, the fact that sounds are complexly varying ensembles of qualities does not preclude hearing and comparing the durations begun at their onsets. Indeed, Frigyesi's description affirms the essentially processive nature of durational perception that Hasty's theory advocates. For instance, the moment (2) is clearly articulated by the sudden change in pitch, and although the pitch and vocal timbre vary continuously immediately afterward, the moment (3) is also clearly articulated by a discontinuity in those same features. Thus the duration from (2) to (3) can be perceived as a whole, complete process, whose "subtle variations" are what make its becoming so compelling. Moreover, a listener need not quantitatively measure it to perceive whether it replicates the equally perceptible duration from (1) to (2). What I take from Frigyesi, then, is not a renunciation of duration per se but an exhortation to consider the "internal life" of projections and how they color the durations' functions. Some examples will be considered in the analyses that follow.

Furthermore, projective analysis can address some of the well-known problems of transcribing free rhythm that are implicit in Frigyesi's critique (see also Clayton 1996, 326 and Frigyesi 1993, 60–62). For instance, the indication of gliding pitches and ornaments of *āvāz* using Western-style note heads, which imply the beginnings of discrete events of fixed pitch, suggests durations that are not really present. Figure 2.2

compensates for this weakness by using projective arcs to group together symbols that appear to represent two or more distinct events—such as the G4-to-F#4 just before (5), the E4-to-embellished-D#4 just before (6), the G4-to-F#4 at (12), and the accelerating pitch ascent at (13)—into a single longer duration of varying pitch. The arcs show that it is the longer durations that have metrical function in the analysis, not the briefer processes that combine into them.

It is harder to counter Frigyesi's objection that beginnings and ending of sounds are not objectively measurable but are perceived with reference to a stylistic context. But she seems to be referring to styles in which there is some explicit or implicit conception of periodicity. There are many genres that insiders claim to be aperiodic, and so her assertion may simply be taken as a mandate to focus on them.

Having addressed these methodological questions, let us listen in the *darāmad* for the various projective time-sensations of Figure 2.1, and consider their formative functions. On several occasions, the song affords hearing the most elemental process in Hasty's theory, a realized projection. Consider the moment labeled (15) on the last staff of Figure 2.2. The E beginning then sounds on time if we hear the duration that it completes from the onset of the preceding F#, shown by the dashed arc, to reproduce the duration from the earlier E to that F#, shown by the solid arrow.

When successive durations differ somewhat, we may still hear a realized projection but understand the realizing event to be slightly rushed or delayed. For example, consider moment (2) on the first staff. At the attack of F# then, the duration beginning at (1) is made definite and is projected forward. The singer holds the F# slightly (150 ms) longer than the duration she projected (870 ms), bending it upward in pitch to G4 before stabilizing again on a sustained F#4 starting at (3). Her return to F# realizes the projection, but slightly late, giving a temporal sensation of *rallentando* that is indicated on the dashed arc. This process gives the F# at (3) a metrical priority, enhanced by the delay, beyond the stress it accrues through its duration alone. It also makes the duration (1.89s) from (1) to (3) available, as indicated by the long dashed arc, to measure the duration of the long F#. Attending to projections, then, we may discern a rhythmic strategy in this opening. Although singer employs a variety of durations, the effect is not arbitrary. She concisely realizes projections of increasing length, culminating in a long F# that is thereby affirmed both as a modally significant pitch and as a promise of continuation and connection to the following music.

She fulfills that promise by beginning her next event, at (4), on time (within 3 ms) as measured by the projection she set up at (3). However, her succeeding utterances come more quickly than at first, making it impossible to perceive a constant pulse carrying on from the first system. The new projective processes mark the moment (4) as an important beginning, and (5) and (6) as moments of realized projection, forming a durational hierarchy that recalls the time sensations she introduced from (1) to (4). Yet she also develops them: right away she introduces a distinctive glottal tremolo (*tahrir*) on G, indicated by the staccato articulation marks, as part of the becoming of the first projective duration; and she begins to associate sounds with similar "internal life" with particular projective functions by placing descending semitone glissandi (G4 to F#4 and E4 to D#4) as the realizations of the short projections at (4) and (5).

At (6) she starts to repeat the events of (4),[3] but she changes her timing in a way that introduces new projective sensations. At (7), the projection of the duration from (6) is nearly 200 ms shorter than the preceding projections, breaking the metrical continuity. As the *tahrir* tremolo now recurs more intensely, it seems to cause this disruption. The next event (8) comes too late to realize it, even as a *rallentando*. The following chain of events affords the "reset/expansion" sensation cataloged in Figure 2.1: we reorient our reference to a later beginning, and the duration we project is longer than the previous one. Specifically, if we change our reference to consider (7) as a beginning, we can hear a realized projection when the 790 ms duration from it to (8) is closely reproduced by the 710 ms duration from (8) to (9). In this way the singer gives the onset of the realizing E, circled at (9), an emphasis that it did not have the first time around, before (6). Since the E functions in this *dastgāh* as a phrase-ending pitch, this emphasis is appropriate, but then she glides away from it, denying it stability. With the projections that she has set up at (9), she has the option to make the next onset sound on time, and thus to create the kind of durational continuity that she did at (4). But her next entrance, at (10), is far too late to reproduce the duration from (8) to (9). This dissolution of projection offers the sensation of "hiatus" described in Figure 2.1, and it allows her next phrase to begin relatively uncontingent upon past durations.

Capitalizing upon that distinctive quality, she sings a contrasting series of events that thwart any attempt to hear durational reproduction but still appeal to listeners' memories and experience of what she has just sung. Her *tahrirs*, whose disruptive powers were foreshadowed at (6), now recur and continue beyond what we could project, thus initiating a succession of reset/expansions at (11) and (12) that might be heard as development of the earlier one at (7).[4] At (13), which realizes the projection at (12), she offers us a sense of longer durational predictability, but then accelerates into another ambiguous passage with *tahrir*. In this context, her last and clearest reproduction of duration at (15) restores temporal order, makes the phrase-ending pitch E4 sound "on time," and sets up another hiatus into which the flute can enter uncontingent upon her timing.

My narrative of this *darāmad* shows how the theory of projection distinguishes and precisely characterizes several types of "freedom" in its rhythm, each affording a distinctive temporal sensation.[5] In one type, definite durations are not immediately reproduced, such as following (6). In another, there are successive realized projections, but the reproduced duration is different, such as is shown by the lower arrow-arc pairs between (1) and (6). Also, there are moments of hiatus when no projections are active, such as just before (10). Projections may have qualities of *rallentando* or *accelerando* such that events sound late or early, such as at (3) and (14) respectively. Or events may simply seem too long or too short, and so disrupt projection or encourage the listener to reorient to other moments and durations, as at (8) and (11).

The varying qualities and presence of realized projections form the *darāmad* into two pairs of phrases, the second of each pair beginning with the succession F# to G after a long duration. Consistency of projective processes, such as from (1) to (4) and (4) to (6), binds events together into groups, and those groups are separate by change of projective duration, such as at (4) and (13), and contrast of process, such as at (10).

The single hiatus during the vocalise creates the strongest discontinuity, and the hiatus after it sets up the entrance of the flute solo. Lastly, pitches that are highlighted at moments of durational reproduction in this otherwise unpredictably timed music form a meaningful process. Realized projections introduce and reinforce F#4 as reciting tone, establish G4 as an important upper neighbor (and as an agent of metrical disruption, because it is the site of the glottal tremolos) and, except for a brief preview at (9), hold off emphasizing the modally referential tone E4 until the end.

This account shows how it is possible to coordinate the observations about durational projection in an analysis that attributes purpose to every event in its time. The theory's orientation toward process is especially apt for evoking the vivid presence of this *darāmad*, in which each moment is charged with possibilities of realization and denial that the performer creates by her timing.

To see whether durational projection is analytically productive for other sorts of free rhythm, let us consider an item with no known connection to the highly developed world of classical Persian music. On a recording made in 1976, Zinzir, a member of the Gizra people in Waidoro, southwestern Papua New Guinea, performs a solo on bamboo flute (*tatarore*) (Audio.2.2 ▶). While it is said that this item was traditionally "played only during the rainy season to announce the coming of the southeast winds" (Laade 1979), I have not found any account of emic conceptions of periodicity, if there are any in this tiny isolated community. *Pace* Frigyesi, then, the "scientific measurement" of duration is the only access we have into its rhythmic processes.

Fortunately the durations in this solo are simpler in organization and kind than those of the constantly varying sounds in the *darāmad*. They simply cycle repeatedly through a fixed series of five long pitches in a variable nonisochronous rhythm. Each pitch is sustained between 1.8 and 2.4 seconds, and is preceded by what I will call a "grace-note group" of two or more fleeting pitches. Figure 2.3 shows the first seven iterations of the cycle, transcribing the long pitches with open note heads and the grace-note groups with smaller solid note heads beamed to suggest their relative durations, and it labels each grace-note-to-long-note gesture alphabetically. The cycle is articulated by breaths, notated as rests, that performer usually takes after long notes W, X, and Z, and by the distinctive, consistent content and timing of the first grace-note group. The transcription is time-proportional, such that the positions of the long pitches and of the incipits of the grace-note groups correspond to their onset time relative to their respective cycle-incipits, which are aligned vertically at the left. Dashed vertical lines connect corresponding pitches in successive cycles. The way that they diverge and converge shows how the durations between the onsets of the grace-note groups and the long notes vary as grace notes are added, omitted, or modified in duration, and makes evident why it is hard to hear a persistent beat.

Nevertheless, a listener may sense some regularity. The total duration of each cycle remains remarkably consistent for its first five iterations, varying no more than 1.4% (200 ms) from 14.45 seconds. Perhaps the performer maintains a silent internal pulse or perhaps, after much practice, he has settled into a physical routine, but neither seems likely since he varies the contents of the cycle.[6] Moreover, these variations

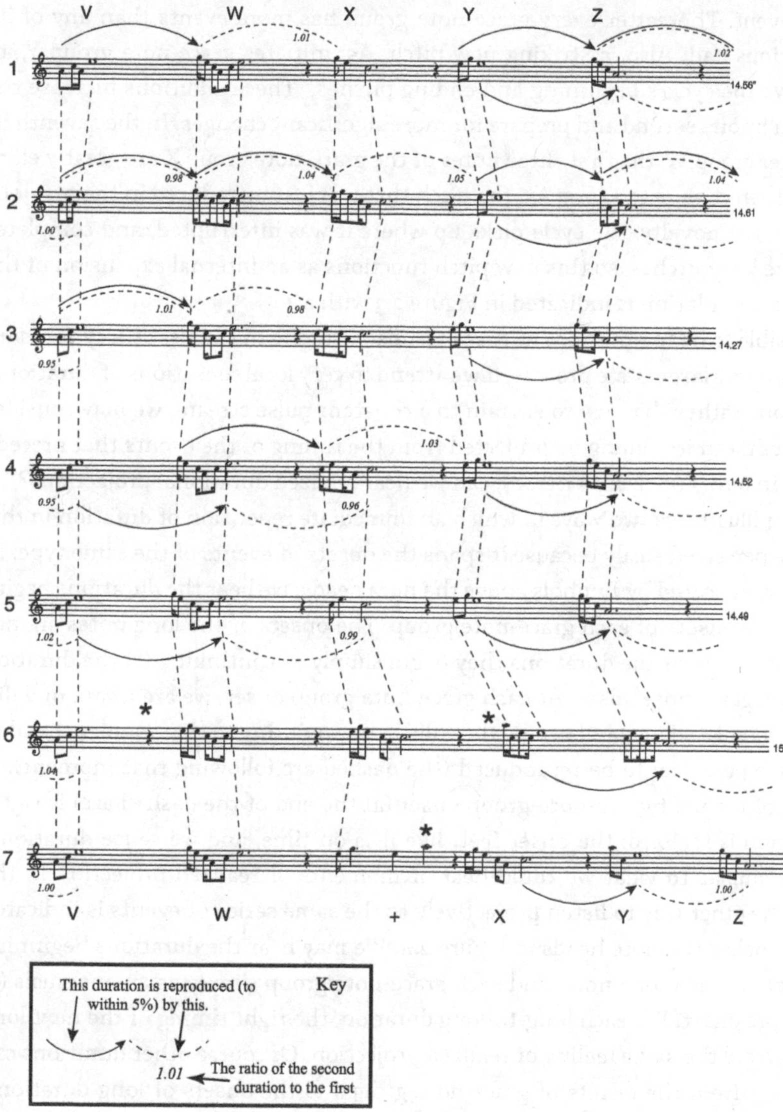

FIGURE 2.3 Projective analysis of the first seven cycles of "Flute," performed by Zinzir, *tatarore*. Transcribed by John Roeder.

produce trends of timing, inconsistent with a pulse stream, that are apparent in the specific way that the lines diverge and converge. For example, across the first five iterations the duration of long note V diminishes and the onset of grace-note group W appears successively earlier; across iterations 3–6 the onset of grace-note group X appears successively later.

Starting in the sixth iteration, as the listener may begin to feel lulled by the languid repetition, the variants become more overt; the most noticeable changes are indicated by asterisks on the transcription. For the first time, the performer breathes after the first long event. Thereafter every grace-note group has more events than any of its earlier versions had. Also, a striking new pitch, A5, initiates grace-note group Y, an octave above the cycle's beginning and ending pitches.[7] These additions increase the cycle length by one second and prepare for more significant changes. In the seventh iteration, after group W, the first three notes of the grace-note group X are greatly elongated, and then change to a long A5, the pitch that was just introduced in the previous cycle. After that novelty, the cycle picks up where it was interrupted, and completes its last three long pitches, so this new pitch functions as an internal expansion of the cycle.[8] The interpolation is indicated in Figure 2.3 with a +.

It is possible to hear a purpose in these trends of timing in the first six cycles, supporting the item's large-scale process, if we attend to very local sensations of durational reproduction. Rather than try to entrain to a constant pulse stream, we may consider for each event: can its timing be projected from the timing of the events that precede it? That is, in terms of Hasty's theory, can we hear realized durational projections?

Figure 2.4 illustrates two ways in which an immediate repetition of duration in this item can be perceived easily because it spans the onsets of events of the same type. In the first way, indicated by symbols above the note heads, we hear the durations beginning (|) at the onsets of each grace-note group. The onsets of the long notes are not as important; we hear the durations they begin simply as continuing (\) the duration begun at the grace-note onset. At each grace-note-group onset, we are aware of a duration just completed (symbolized by the solid arrow pointing to that moment) and of its projective potential to be reproduced (the dashed arc following that moment). If the timing of the next grace-note-group onset (at the end of the dashed arc) is right, the projection is realized: the onset feels like it is on time, and we sense durational continuity, similar to what we could hear at moments of realized projection in the *darāmad*. The other way to listen projectively to the same series of events is indicated by symbols below the note heads in Figure 2.4. We may hear the durations beginning at the onsets of each long note, and each grace-note group simply as an anacrusis (/) to a long-note onset. For each long-to-long duration, the right timing of the next long onset will afford the same feeling of realized projection. Of course other durations can be heard, say, from the onsets of grace-note-groups to the onsets of long durations, and vice versa, but it is obvious from the spacing of the vertical lines on Figure 2.3 that

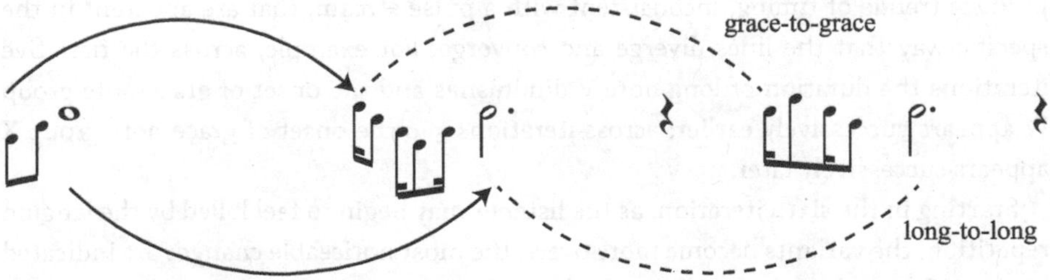

FIGURE 2.4 Two possible kinds of realized durational projections in "Flute" (under the assumption of parallelism).

successive durations of this type are not equal; others are harder to hear because they are so long and involve different types of events.

Although both these ways of listening are concerned simply with the immediate reproduction of duration, they attribute quite different sensations to any given event. In the flute performance, because of the varying timing, one of these readings is usually preferable to the other, because the durational reproduction is more exact. Accordingly, depending on how the timing changes from cycle to cycle, an event that sounds like an important beginning in one cycle may sound in another cycle like a continuation or anacrusis, and an event that sounds on time in one cycle may sound early or late in another. I hear these variations in metrical function and specificity to enliven the cyclic process that might otherwise be depreciated as mere rote repetition.

The annotations on Figure 2.3 document the basis for such a hearing. Each pair of solid and dashed arcs indicates a durational projection that is realized by three successive events of the same type. Arc-pairs *above* the staff indicate projections realized by the onsets of *grace-note* groups, and arc-pairs *below* the staff indicate projections realized by the onsets of *long* notes. Different solid arcs generally correspond to different durations—they range from 2.4 to over 4 seconds—so a succession of them does not indicate a steady pulse stream. The figure shows only those projections in which the second duration is within 5% of the first duration. This is a fairly stringent standard, but also selective: with only a few exceptions, no other pairs of successive durations are nearly that equal. For readers interested in a fuller justification, the appendix to this chapter describes the results of statistical tests that give some confidence that the distributions of durations are not a matter of chance, and cites psychoacoustic research about subjects' ability to discriminate differences in successive durations.

The arcs on the figure help us to identify which durations are immediately reproduced, and to correlate the varying presence of projection with the overall form. Several correlations seem especially salient:

- Below the end of *every* cycle is a dashed arc that continues into the next cycle. This means that in *every* cycle, the attack of the first long E5 realizes the projection created by the attacks of the last two long notes of the previous cycle. That is, if we measure time after the onset of long note Z with reference to the duration to it from the onset of the previous long note Y, the next long note V at the beginning of the next cycle sounds exactly on time. Realized projection forges continuity across every cycle's grouping boundary, thus binding the separate iterations into a larger-scale process.
- In *no* cycle does a solid arc ever span the rest after long note X. This means that durations from the events of group X to the corresponding events of group Y are *never* reproduced, so that the timings of the onsets of the grace-note group and long note of Z always feel unpredictable. However, as observed earlier, every long note Y initiates a span of time that can be felt as measured, lasting until at least the beginning of the next cycle. The consistent lack of measurement just before long notes Y may help the listener feel the ensuing realizations more keenly. In any event, the time sense coming into Y differs

from every other moment, making the temporality during each cycle more variegated than a simple succession of five short groups.

- During the first three iterations, starting from the first long note Y, *every* duration that is reproduced is between the onsets of the *grace-note* groups (above the staff), aside from the special boundary-spanning projections mentioned earlier. At the beginning of the solo, then, it is rewarding to focus on these onsets, because we can hear the projections (the dotted arcs) of the durations they initiate (the solid arcs) to be realized. In this way of listening, the long notes during this passage function to continue those projective durations, not to initiate new ones.
- In contrast, during iterations 4 and 5, as the performer adjusts the timings and contents of the events, it is the durations between the *long* notes that are reproduced (as shown by arcs *below* the staff). Their onsets become the more important beginnings, and the grace-note groups now sound like anacruses to them. Thus the relative metrical importance of grace-note-group onsets and long-note onsets reverses as the cycle repeats. In particular, the first and third long E5s take on a more metrically definite character, and all the grace-note groups sound anacrustic.
- As the changes continue into the sixth and seventh iterations of the cycle, *no* duration (except the boundary-spanning one) is reproduced as exactly as the earlier durations were.[9] We enter a time of metrical uncertainty that may function to help the listener accept, after group W in iteration 7, the interpolation (+) of the greatly slowed grace-note group and the unprecedented high long note. Thereafter, duration begins to repeat again.

Just by attending to the realization of projections in "Flute," then, without even contemplating the more complex time sensations of Figure 2.1, we may observe consistencies and systematic variation in this performance that help us to hear formative processes over a time scale that transcends that of the individual cycle iterations. Just as in the second phrase of the *darāmad*, event-series are repeated but with different timings that affect the larger continuity of the item. The *darāmad* also demonstrated how grouping structure can be created in the absence of repetition through local projective effects, especially hiatus. It is also possible, however, for grouping structure to be perceived if the music reiterates or varies a distinctive pattern of projective time-sensations.

A fine example of such sophisticated control of temporality is the beginning of an *ālāp* on *rāga* Pūriyā-Kalyān performed by Budhaditya Mukherjee (Audio.2.3 ▶). Richard Widdess's intensive analysis (2011) of this studio recording focuses on the strategies by which the sitarist, playing with listeners' conscious and unconscious expectations of pitch, exposes contrasting aspects of the *rāga* and structures the musical discourse both locally and across longer passages. Although Widdess finds no "regular pulse" and therefore says little about rhythm, he makes the intriguing suggestion that "most listeners will compare each duration only with preceding durations, not with any perceived constant unit of duration." Hasty's theory is concerned precisely with such comparisons. By considering how each event seems to come on time, or earlier, or later than could be expected from the durations immediately preceding it, I will identify some consistent rhythmic strategies by which the artist seems to play with listeners' projections of durational repetition to structure the musical discourse.

My hearing is presented on Figure 2.5. It adapts Widdess's meticulous transcription of the passage (his Figure 5.3, 197), retaining its symbols and time-proportional layout but adding analytical symbols associated with Hasty's theory as well as alphabetical labels of certain points in the passage to which I will refer. (I have added symbols for two events—both chords near moment (m)—that he seems to have inadvertently omitted.) As in the "Flute" transcription just discussed, each solid arc represents a definite duration, completed at the head of the arrow, that has a projective potential to be reproduced, represented by a dashed arc following that moment. With a few exceptions that I shall explain, the figure shows only those projections that are realized to within 5%, in other words, where the first duration is immediately reproduced by another perceptibly identical duration, as was the case in the analysis of "Flute." Again, the number under each dotted arc specifies the ratio of that duration to the duration indicated by the preceding solid arc, calculated from onset timings determined from the recording.

At the beginning of the performance, durational projections can be heard to be created and realized by *cikārī* (drone-string) chords. Starting at moment (a), the attack of each new chord completes, to within 5%, a duration that replicates the duration spanning the preceding two chords. Although the durations are long and varied, precluding a strict pulse, this consistent realization of projections nevertheless gives each chord a sense of appearing on time. As soon as this process is evident, Mukherjee complicates the rhythm by arpeggiating the *tarab* (resonating) strings *downward*. His attacks are quite regular, creating a clear repetition of the medium-length duration shown by the arrows below the staff. Complementarily, at (b), after the onset of the following chord, he arpeggiates the *cikārī* strings *upward*, creating a shorter but also definite and projective duration. Again we may sense a potential for the replication of shorter durations within the becoming of a longer measured duration. However, as shown by the two vertical strokes, nothing occurs to realize the projection. Instead there is a sense of hiatus at the shorter time scale, even as the longer duration is about to be reproduced.

The regular pattern of durational reproduction breaks at (c) when the sixth chord comes much earlier than the projection of the previous long duration. Directly thereafter the melody enters, as shown in solid notes on the score. The faltering metrical continuity of the chords heightens its salience. A seventh drone-string chord follows much sooner than could be expected, as the cutoff dotted arc indicates, but the shorter duration set up by the reset/contraction is not reproduced either. Through this demeasured time the soloist leads his melody to a long-held tonic, attacked simultaneously with another chord at (d). This strong coincidence is also too soon compared to the most recently completed duration from (c) and, although it suggests that the duration from (c) to it might be heard as projective, no event occurs at that duration after

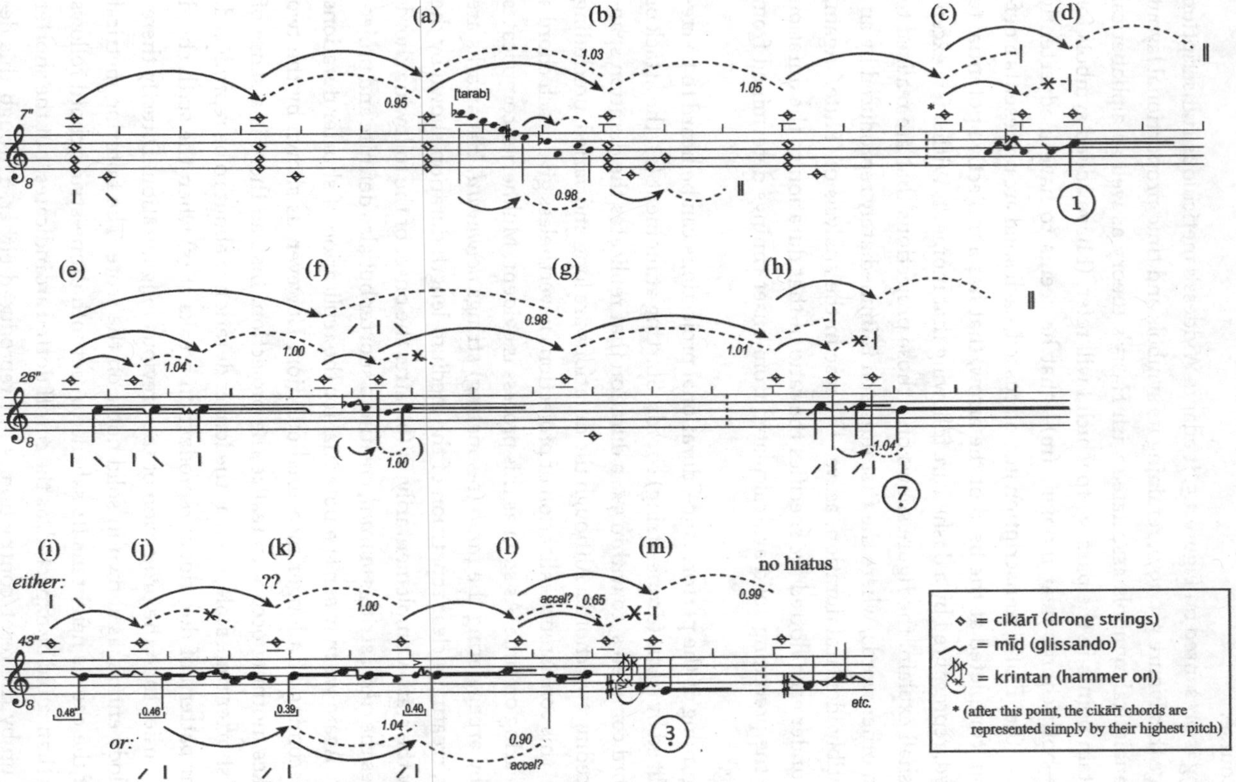

FIGURE 2.5 Projective analysis of the opening (0:07–0:55) of the *ālāp* on *rāga* Pūriyā-Kalyān performed by Budhaditya Mukherjee, *sitar*. Transcribed by Richard Widdess, adapted and annotated by John Roeder.

it. So any sense of durational reproduction falls into hiatus, and so the next attack at (e) stands out as a fresh beginning.

The following passage, shown on the second system, enacts the same general temporal process—establishing a pattern of durational reproduction, disrupting it as a new sustained pitch appears, then sinking into hiatus—with some intriguing variations. First the artist recalls the idea of a quickly reiterated chord. However, rather than using it to *disrupt* meter as he did at (d), he now reestablishes a large-scale *continuity* by playing the chord-pairs regularly enough for us to perceive durational replication, as at first. The duration from (e) to (f) repeats immediately from (f) to (g), and the duration from (g) to (h) replicates the immediately preceding chord-to-chord duration.

Mukherjee also enriches this medium-scale process with his placement of the melodic pitches. Whereas on the first system they seemed out-of-time, now they *interact* with the chords to produce and replicate shorter durations. Notably, from (e) to (f) appear two nested levels of shorter realized projections between the attacks of chord and melody pitches, making a quadruple meter. At (f) the timings of chords and melody also afford two sensations of durational replication, although not in such a hierarchy. These processes parallel the smaller-scale projections after (a) and (b), but involve the melody instead of the drone and *tarab* strings.

The subsequent projective processes strengthen the parallelism with the opening music, as is evident in the similar arrangements of solid and dotted arcs at the ends of the first and second systems. After (h), as after (c), the pattern of durational reproduction breaks down as events come much sooner than could be expected. Through the de-measured time, the artist again leads the melody to a long-sustained pitch—now, the important seventh scale-degree of the *rāga*—and holds it long enough to dissolve any expectations of durational reproduction, just as he did when he introduced the tonic.

Starting at the next *cikārī* chord (i), the same medium-scale metrical process is reprised and condensed: a passage of durational reproduction gives way to a series of unpredictably shorter durations that create a passage without pulse, into which a new sustained pitch is injected (now the third scale degree). The broad similarity of the series of projective symbols to those on the first and second systems indicates the reprise.

However, the specifics of this process are varied again, in a way that suggests a larger-scale strategy in the artist's development of durational successions. Rather than creating projective durations solely between chords, as at first, or between the chords and the melodic notes, as on the second system, Mukherjee now alternates chords and melody in a way that affords a figure-ground-like shift in metrical perspective akin to the one that I attributed to the flute solo. At first it is possible to hear the *cikārī* attacks as initiating and realizing durational projections that the melodic notes continue, just as they did at first. The symbols *above* the system at (j) express that hearing. Then, however, the onsets of the scale degree 7s become more important, initiating projective durations within which the *chord* attacks may be heard to function as *anacruses*.

This reading is expressed by the symbols *below* the system. Several factors incline me toward it. The duration projected by the chord at (j) is not realized, as indicated by the X through the dashed arc. Rather, the lengthening and decoration of 7 after (j) draws attention to its onset, and to the duration from it to the onset of the next post-chord 7 at (k). That attention is rewarded when the latter duration is immediately reproduced. Meanwhile the duration from each chord to the subsequent attack of 7 shortens, becoming more anacrustic to the lengthening 7s. Thus, just as the long scale degree 7 marks the first departure of the melody from the tonic, the timing of its onsets in this particular rhythmic context seems to invest the melody with energy to wrest the metric initiative away from the *cikārī* strums.

The artist has carefully prepared this shift of metrical initiative. At the beginning of the improvisation, he followed each *cikārī* chord quickly by an attack of the lowest, tonic, drone string, whose duration simply continued (\) the longer one initiated by the chord; so the chordal strums seemed to be the most important beginning. During the second system he clearly developed this idea by substituting a melodic tonic for the low drone event after each chord. He also suggested twice that the melodic tonic, as the realization of a projection, could itself be an important beginning. The possibility is renewed at the first appearance of 7 at the end of the system, which, unlike the tonic at the end of the first system, follows a chord and realizes a local projection. It is fully accomplished on the third system, when the chords become anacrustic to the melodic 7s.

That an inflection point has been reached is evident from the projective processes after (l). As we might now expect, they strongly resemble those around the introduction of tonic: three chords appear too quickly to hear as realized projections, the last two too rapidly to comprehend as an acceleration. It is therefore difficult again to attribute metrical function to the new scale degree that is sustained. However, this time around Mukherjee does not dally: the duration completed from (l) to (m) is reproduced from (m) to the next *cikārī* chord, and so the music is now able to maintain its continuity past the held melodic pitches, without hiatus. Now the *ālāp* is convincingly underway.

This sort of analysis has the potential to account for many aspects of this music in addition to the important processes of unveiling the *rāga*. For example, it gives an active role to the attacks of the *cikārī*, which otherwise might seem to be a featureless background. More generally, the three systems of Figure 2.5 show how the artist structures rhythm in three similar but progressively developing stages. Interestingly, these correspond well with Widdess's segmentation of the passage into three phrases, indicated by the dashed bar lines, which he derived "heuristically" by considering "distinctly perceptible changes" of pitch (Widdess 2011, 193). The correlation suggests that durational and pitch discourses are closely linked at the outset of this improvisation, perhaps showing how "the performed rhythm is felt to optimize the reception of melodic information and cognition of melodic structure" (Clayton 1996, 330–31).

My detailed analysis of these three items begins to answer Clayton's call to provide models for understanding "free rhythm" in world music. However, I do not claim that the patterns I observe in these examples are characteristic of their respective genres.[10] That would be generalizing Hastily. I have simply demonstrated that the concept of projection, and its attendant sensations, can be used to construct a coherent narrative of extended passages of music that distinguishes and attributes purpose to the specific free rhythms it features. In the R1 sense advocated by Hasty in chapter 1, and true to the vivid improvisatory presence of the items, the analyses I presented focus on "the online activity of making rhythm." To the extent that they seem cogent, we may say that in these various examples we hear the performers regulating their free rhythm to create musical form.

APPENDIX

A premise of the analysis of "Flute" is that the immediate reproduction of duration to within 5% has a special significance in the ongoing process of this item. This appendix provides a rationale for that assertion with reference both to statistical properties of the timings and to psychoacoustic research into the perception of difference in successive durations.

First let us consider the durations from the onset of each grace-note group to the onset of the following grace-note group. These are the durations shown above each staff in Figure 2.3. Table 2.1 shows how the ratios of successive durations of this type are distributed.

Table 2.2 is concerned with the durations from the onset of each long note to the onset of the following note. These are the durations shown below each staff in Figure 2.3. The table shows how the ratios of successive durations of this type are distributed.

Both tables show that many ratios fall within a narrow band around exact equality (1.0). The half-widths of the central bands, 3.5% and 4.5% respectively, are consistent with the results of a finding (Fraisse 1952, 44) that listeners judge durations of two successive events to be equal that differ by up to 125 ms, which corresponds to a 4.3% difference in the average 2.9 second flute duration.

On either side of those bands, there is a gap of about the same width (7%) where very few ratios fall, but past that gap, there are again many ratios. In other words, it

TABLE 2.1

Distribution of ratios of successive durations marked by grace-note-group onsets

Ratio	(76%)	91%	98%	105%	112%	(154%)
# of pairs with ratios in that range	11	2	11	0	1	

TABLE 2.2

Distribution of ratios of successive durations marked by long-note onsets

Ratio of second to first duration	(52%)	88%	95%	104%	113%	(150%)
# of pairs with ratios in that range	10	2	11	2	12	

appears from these histograms of the ratio distribution that successive durations of the same type either are very nearly equal, or else are clearly not equal, with very few ambiguous cases.

To gain confidence that this distribution is not the result of a natural random variation, we need to establish that the dataset is different than could be expected if the player were replicating each duration with a degree of accuracy that follows a normal (random) distribution, with most attempts close to success. This can be achieved with a standard statistical method. Under the null hypothesis that short-to-short duration-ratios constitute a sample from a normal distribution, the value of the Shapiro-Wilk test statistic W is 0.9410 with corresponding p-value 0.04105. At a 95% confidence level, then, we reject the null hypothesis, in other words, the short-to-short duration-ratios are highly unlikely to be a sample from a normal distribution.

There is no such clear evidence that the long-to-long duration-ratios are not: under the null hypothesis that long-to-long duration-ratios constitute a sample from a normal distribution, the Shapiro-Wilk test statistic W is 0.98104 with p-value 0.7412. However, a time-series analysis shows that every fifth durational ratio is significantly correlated, in other words, that the durational ratio at a given position in one cycle is correlated with the duration in the same position in the previous cycle.[11] One aspect of this periodicity is evident in the consistent reproduction of duration that Figure 2.3 shows from the end of one cycle to the next.

Much of the research into listeners' ability to discriminate difference between successive durations has focused on longer series of empty durations articulated by short beeps. Summarizing the studies to date, Madison and Merker (2002) cite a range from 3.5% to 8%, which is consistent with Fraisse's results cited earlier. Under certain conditions studied mainly for short intervals associated with speech (200 ms), listeners underestimate or overestimate the second of two durations, and the error is not simply due to perceiving durations categorically (Nakajima et al. 2014). Prior expectations and knowledge of its possible range can influence how a duration is perceived then reproduced (Jazayeri and Shadlen 2010). I would hedge, however, that the stimuli used in this psychological research are much simpler than the kinds of musical situations analyzed in this chapter.

NOTES

1. The scale is sung a minor third lower in the recording than Farhat writes it, so the transcription in Figure 2.2 renders it accordingly.

2. My translation of the French original: "L'idée que l'on puisse mesurer scientifiquement la durée d'une note est une pure illusion; en réalité, la plupart des sons montrent un schéma complexe de vie interne avec des variations subtiles de leur dynamique, de leur timbre, de leur vibrato et de leur hauteur. L'ornementation et l'action coordonnée de plusieurs instruments rendent l'image encore plus confuse, exactement comme la présence de la respiration, du vibrato et de la prononciation du texte dans la musique vocale. À un niveau très subtil, le fait de décider quand commence et quand finit la note est déjà influencé par notre perception préconçue de la périodicité à l'intérieur d'un style particulier."

3. The sense that she is repeating a distinctive and fairly fixed succession of events is strengthened by the flute's flexible doubling from (6) until (10).

4. In texted *āvāz*, in contrast to the situation here, *tahrir* usually ends the phrases, but it seems also to have an effect on temporal continuity for, according to Tsuge (1970, 222), "the whole energy which has sustained the melody is actually discharged in the *tahrir*."

5. Bruno Nettl (1987, 33) offers some more general distinctions of free rhythm in Persian music.

6. The question of whether Indian performers maintain a pulse in *ālāp* is a complex one. Both Widdess 1994 and Wolf 2010 have demonstrated that a regular pulse can in some cases be heard, but performers themselves do not acknowledge it. In a personal communication, Richard Wolf wrote me, "I would venture to say that any competent performance of raga alapana in Karnatak music maintains a steady pulse, and that many of the obvious deviations of attacks from the 'on beats' as it were can be accounted for by the same concepts as are used in music regulated by tala. That is, emphasizing a beat by hitting an offbeat (before or after) is a recognized and theorized part of tala based music" (p.c., October 26, 2016).

7. Since the A5 is produced by overblowing, we may hear its appearance at this moment as the culmination of a process in which the performer has blown progressively harder, resulting in a series of ghosted notes that progressively approach a full-bodied A5.

8. The recording contains three further cycle iterations not transcribed in Figure 2.3. They act as a reinforcing reprise: the eighth cycle is like the first six; the ninth contains the additional long pitch, like the seventh; and the tenth cycle returns again to the original series. The overall process of the complete performance—establishing a cycle, gradually introducing variants that led to significant alterations, returning to the original form, then briefly reprising the departure and return—exemplifies one effective way to shape cyclically organized time.

9. The performer sets up the surprise of the added group in another way: after the incipit of W has been growing successively closer and closer to the long note of V in each preceding cycle, in this seventh cycle its timing reverts to exactly what it was in the first cycle. We might expect, on that basis, that the grace-to-grace duration from V to W would be reproduced, as it was in the first cycle, but it is not—the incipit E5 of the inserted new group appears too late.

10. Nevertheless, my accounts of *āvāz* and *ālāp* do support, for these two specific examples, Frigyesi's assertion (1993, 64) that "the[ir] rhythmic styles . . . would strike even the uninitiated listener as fundamentally different."

11. Thanks to Geoffrey Roeder for running and interpreting the Shapiro-Wilks test and the autocorrelation function on the datasets.

DISCOGRAPHY

Mukherjee, Budhaditya. 1991. *Ālāp* in *Rāg* Pūriyā-Kalyān. From *Inner Voice*. Audiorec ACCD 1014 compact disc.

Ziā'i, Afsāne, vocals, with Hoseyn Omumi, *ney*. n.d. *Āvāz* (classical Persian chant): *Bīdād* from *dastgāh homāyun*. *Les voix du monde: une anthologie des expressions vocales*, CD 2, track 18. Le Chant Du Monde CMX 3741011. http://archives.crem-cnrs.fr/archives/items/CNRSMH_E_1996_013_001_002_018/.

Zinzir. 1979. "Flute." From *Australia: Songs of the Aborigines and Music of Papua, New Guinea*. Lyrichord LYRCD 7331 compact disc. The PNG music on this CD is a reissue of part of an earlier LP recording made by Frederic Duvelle, titled *Traditional Music of the Gizra and Bine People: Papua New Guinea, Western Province*. Paddington, NSW: Larrikin, 1978.

3

Meter and Rhythm in the Sung Poetry of Iranian Khorasan

Stephen Blum

IN THINKING ABOUT the sung poetry that is so highly valued throughout the world of Iranian civilization, one would be foolish to ignore the ways that theorists writing in Arabic developed conceptions of rhythmics and metrics assimilated from their Greek predecessors. Prominent among these theorists are the philosophers Abu Naṣr al-Fārābī (d. 950) and Avicenna (980–1037), both born in the eastern Iranian world, and both superbly well-equipped to approach the study of rhythm and meter with the tools of Aristotelian logic. Fārābī's four essays on rhythm constitute a body of work that far surpasses, in scope and depth, the ancient Greek rhythmic theory that was one of his points of departure.[1] I fully concur with George Sawa's judgment that Fārābī's writing on music "offers proper tools for the analysis of contemporary Middle Eastern music" (Sawa 2015, 131), not least with respect to analysis of rhythm.

In addition, as a reader of Fārābī and Avicenna, and as a listener engaged with the sung poetry of Iran, I am deeply indebted to Christopher Hasty's reconsideration of *Meter as Rhythm* (1997) and to his recommendation that we attend to rhythm as both subjective experience (R1 in his "Thinking With and About Rhythm," chapter 1 in this volume) and objective pattern (R2), treating R2 as a species of R1 and moving between them with no reservations or inhibitions.[2] Fārābī and Avicenna might well have agreed with Hasty's observation (1997, 69) that "How duration comes to be determined is the question that emerges when we inquire of process."

Fārābī's writing on music and poetics treats verse and melody as complementary parts of a whole. In a short text on poetry (Fārābī 1959, 91; see also Heinrichs 1969, 142), he maintained that verses become more complete when they are "melodized" (*mulaḥḥana*), in other words endowed with the communicative force that poetry acquires when sung. Fārābī placed the "melodizers" (*mulaḥḥinūn*) of verse in the second class of specialists, that of "expositors" (*ḍawū'l-alsina*), which also includes orators, poets, secretaries, and upholders of religion (Fārābī 1971, 65 and 2001, 37). Although they employ types of reasoning that are inferior to the demonstrative syllogisms of philosophers, Fārābī argued that the "imaginative representations" of expositors provide the next-best means of access to the truths of philosophy.

In the section on theoretical music in his *Iḥṣā' al-'ulūm* "Classification of the Sciences," Fārābī likewise distinguished between "perfect melodies" (*al-alḥān al-kāmila*) that join tones (*nağam*) to poetical utterances (*al-ši'riyya al-aqāwīl*) and melodies composed merely of tones (Randel 1976, 175–76).[3] The two parts of the final major section of Fārābī's *Kitāb al-mūsīqā al-kabīr* [*Great Book on Music*] treat first the composition of melody apart from verse, then the more complex demands of composing melodies for voices, which can exploit the full range of qualitative differences among sounds, not merely their differences in acuity (*hidda*, Greek *oksytēs*) and gravity (*thiql*, Gk. *barytēs*) (Fārābī 1967, 1063–65; French translation in d'Erlanger 1935, 53–55; English translation in Madian 1992, 261–63). As a theorist of rhythm, Fārābī realized that he could not describe the qualitative differences relevant to sung poetry without modifying and extending the Arabic terminology that had been developed for analysis of verse meters (*awzān*, sing. *wazn*), in part by incorporating Aristotle's definition of *syllable* (as discussed in the section on "Concepts of Duration and Cycle").[4]

The verbal noun *īqā'* is the closest Arabic equivalent to Greek *rhythmos*, though it differs from the Greek word in that besides serving as a general term for rhythm, it denotes a compound cycle with which the periodicities of verse meters are to be coordinated in singing.[5] In Fārābī's rhythmics, an *īqā'* comprises two cycles (*adwār*, sing. *dawr*) of like duration (*zamān*) and structure, comparable to the two hemistiches (sing. *miṣrā'*) that constitute a line (*bayt*) of verse, although both hemistiches of a line need not be given equal duration in performance. With respect to Fārābī's chapters on rhythm in the *Great Book*, Sawa glosses *īqā'* as "rhythmic mode," by analogy with Latin *modus* in Medieval European theory; in Fārābī's later treatises, where the fundamental *īqā'* is a compound cycle of "attacks . . . separated by equal durations," Sawa (2009, 236) equates *īqā'* with "meter." The term can also be glossed as "metric cycle" (emulating Clayton's gloss of *tāl* in Hindustani music: 2000, 215) or as "rhythmic cycle."[6] In this chapter I have opted for the latter as the more inclusive.

CONCEPTS OF DURATION AND CYCLE

Fārābī approached the question of how duration (*zamān*) comes to be determined from two angles: first, as a "movement" or "progression" (*nuqla*, Gk. *metábasis, phorá*) initiated by one attack and concluded by a second attack, a "passage" (*intiqāl*, in other contexts "modulation") from one "now" (*ān*, Gk. *to nūn* "the now") to the next.[7] The two attacks function as "a prior and posterior limit" by which, as Aristotle put it (*Physics*,

Book Delta, 219a), we become "aware of the measuring of motion" and hence "may say that time has passed" (trans. Wicksteed and Cornford 1963 [1929], 387). This definition makes Fārābī's *zamān* a close equivalent to *interonset interval*, which is likewise delimited by "the attack-points of successive events" (London 2012, 4).

In addition, a duration progresses from the motion (*ḥaraka*, Greek *kínēsis*) of "striking" (*qār'*, comparable to Gk. *plēgē*) through the subsequent pause (*waqfa, wuqūf, sukūn*; Gk. *ēremía*) as the sound produced by the strike continues or decays.[8] This conception was possibly modeled on Greek *ársis* "upward motion" and *thésis* "downward motion" or perhaps "letting the hand rest" in Fārābī's interpretation (Neubauer 1994, 112 and 1998a, 415).[9] The "shortest perceivable time" between two attacks will be the duration of "the fastest perceivable motion existing between two attacks" (Sawa 2009, 326; Arabic text in Neubauer 1998a, 306). In adopting the basic premise of Aristoxenian theory, that rhythm is created by and guides actions of the feet, hands, and vocal apparatus, Fārābī modifed the Aristoxenian list of analogies between constituents of speech (letter, syllable, word), music (tone, interval, system), and bodily movement (signal, position) (Aristoxenus, trans. Pearson, 1990, 6–7, 22–23): in Fārābī's rhythmics the analogue of letter (Gk. *grámma*) and signal (Gk. *sēmeion*) is attack or stroke, rather than tone (Gk. *phthongos*, Ar. *nağam*). Aristoxenus was interested in bodily movements of dancers, Fārābī in those of instrumentalists and singers.[10] Since stroke is logically prior to tone, we might broaden Fārābī's conception of *laḥn* "melody" as a sequence of durations determined by attacks to encompass the two categories that Richard Wolf, later in this volume, distinguishes as *stroke melodies* and *tone melodies*.

Reading Fārābī, I am reminded of Hasty's discussion of projective potential in *Meter as Rhythm*. When an attack is made prominent in some way and the next attack stands out in a manner we relate to the first, we can choose to recognize what Hasty calls projective potential in the duration determined by the two attacks: anticipating a third attack that would determine a second duration equivalent to the first, we can prepare to make a move that would coincide with that attack, which may or may not occur as anticipated. A "past and determined duration" that is not too long may remain present "as a definite potential" on one level of passage while other levels remain mensurally indeterminate.[11] Fārābī spoke in general terms (1967, 1182) of the expectations that listeners form with respect to the course of a melody, to which the progression will be either "faithful" (*wafiy*) or "deceptive" (*khātil*).

Like Hasty's discussion of projection, Fārābī's conception of listening is consistent with a fundamental premise of the theory of melodic construction that Aristoxenus developed in his *Harmonic Elements*: "Comprehension [*synesis*] of music comes from two things: perception and memory: for we have to perceive what is coming to be and remember what has come to be. There is no other way of following the contents of music" (Book II, 38–39, trans. Barker 1989, 155; Greek text ed. Rios, 1954, 48).[12]

Treating durations as determined by attacks is consistent with a fundamental premise of Arabic prosody, as formulated in the eighth century C.E. by al-Khalīl ibn Aḥmad: the smallest constituent of verse was a consonant (*ḥarf*), qualified as "movent" (*mutaḥarrik*), that is, vowelled; or "motionless" (*sākin*), that is, vowelless, depending on whether or not it is followed by a short vowel.[13] Their combinations, all of which begin with a movent letter, were labeled various types of *sabab* and *watad*, terms with a long history in rhythmic theory after al-Khalīl used them to identify the sequences of feet in sixteen poetic meters.[14] In all sixteen, each line (*bayt*) is composed of two hemistiches that share the same sequence of four feet.

Discussing the composition of melodies for voices in his *Great Book on Music*, Fārābī confronted these constituents of Arabic verse with Aristotle's definition of *syllable* as "a meaningless sound composed of an unvoiced and a voiced element" (*Poetics* 1456b), in order to make several distinctions he deemed pertinent, such as which of the voiced (*muṣawwit*) and unvoiced (i.e., vowelless) elements can be "prolonged" (*tamtad*) in singing.[15] He also recognized that since the constituents of an *īqā'* differ from those of a poetic meter, al-Khalīl's system of prosody (*'arūḍ*) did not provide an adequate basis for a theory of rhythmic cycles (*īqā'āt*) in music (Neubauer 1998b, 81–82; Sawa 1989, 38). Although he retained the Greek distinction of short and long syllables (respectively *al-maqṭa' al-kasīr* and *al-maqṭa' al-tawīl*),[16] in music theory Fārābī often preferred oppositions with a third, intermediate option. Hence, a sung syllable might be "prolonged," "shortened," or "in between" (1967, 1071; trans. Madian 1992, 270), and an attack might be "strong" (*qawiyya*), "moderate" (*mutawassiṭa*), or "soft" (*layyina*) (Sawa 2009, 166–67, 261; Arabic text in Fārābī 1967, 986). The latter typology is presumably based on differences in timbre, loudness, and envelope that are perceived early in the passage (*intiqāl*) from one attack to the next. Fārābī also classified attacks as fast, medium, or slow according to the durations they define, proportionally related as 1:2:4 respectively (Sawa 2009, 237, 261–62).

Noting our inclination to think of the beginning of a sound as "a durationless instant from which we can measure duration," Hasty (1997, 70) aptly describes that instant as "a potential beginning" which "only by *becoming* past . . . *becomes* a beginning." The attacks that Fārābī qualified as strong, moderate, or soft are not durationless; his representation of attack as "point" (*nuqṭa*, Gk. *stigmē*) refers to "the contact of the striking and struck objects" that produces a sound (Sawa 2009, 565 and 136–37) as well as to "the now" that creates both a present and a past.[17] Geometry was one of several source domains for imagery (*takhayyūl*) relating to sounds and the actions that produce them, a second example being the vocal timbres represented as "circular" (*mustadīrah*) or "rectilinear" (*mustaqīmah*) (Fārābī 1967, 1071; trans. Madian 1992, 270–73 and d'Erlanger 1935, 58–59). Some vocal timbres may have become "circular" as singers took advantage of the nine Arabic diphthongs (see note 15). Other source domains of terms for potential qualities of a passage from one attack to the next relate to "senses other than hearing" (Sawa 1989, 99), such as clarity, muddiness, coarseness, smoothness, softness, harshness, and firmness; a tone might be shaken, broken, stable, free, or "slightly accelerated in the manner of a trotting horse" (100). Still others describe "specific ways air passes through the organs": humidity, dryness, complete nasality, half-nasality, and so on (101).[18] Certain of these qualities could only emerge as listeners perceive changes during the passage from an attack that initiates a sound to the next attack.

As a sequence of clearly defined durations, expressible as ratios of rational numbers, the compound cycle *īqā'* is also a passage from the first attack in a series to that which initiates either the next cycle or an interval (*fāṣila*, Gk. *diastolē*) separating two cycles.[19] The term *zamān* may refer to the total duration of a cycle, to each duration within the cycle, or to the duration of the interval separating two cycles. Since the greater duration of an *īqā'* afforded musicians ample opportunity to engage the interest of listeners with a compelling traversal of the passage initiated by the first attack, Fārābī devoted far more attention to ways of embellishing each species of *īqā'* than to singers' options in vocalizing on individual syllables.[20]

Despite the differences between an *īqā'* and a poetic meter, both have long been represented in treatises as circles. Al-Khalīl ibn Aḥmad classified the 16 meters of Arabic verse into five circles (*dawā'ir*, sing. *dā'ira*) in order to display relationships among meters, including what we would call rotations (two or more meters beginning at different moments in the same sequence of long and short syllables). The set of syllables used since his time to represent poetic meters differs from the set devised for rhythmic cycles, which in its simplest form posits an isochronous pulse at the level of the mora (either a consonant with a short vowel or the consonant *n* alone).[21] No such isochronous pulse is necessarily implied by the syllables for poetic meters, formed from the verbal root *F'L*; isochrony is merely an option. In this system, a consonant with a short vowel represents a short syllable, and a long vowel is represented by a consonant with a long vowel or by consonant, short vowel, final consonant. Both sets indicate groupings of syllables into feet, marked in Figure 3.1 with slashes. At present, Iranian musicians often use the *atānin* syllables for Persian poetic meters as well as for musical rhythms (Azadehfar 2006, 71); see Figure 3.1 for representations of one poetic meter in both systems.

In treatises, syllables from both sets are often inserted within a single circle, which does imply isochrony (see, for example, Abdurashidov's 2009 study of *robā'ī* (quatrain) meters in Persian). Important though that option has been, Iranian musicians have not always wished to limit the matrix of possibilities associated with a poetic meter by insisting that durations relate to one another through easily perceptible proportions.

a. AFĀ'IL 11 syllables: ¯ ˘ ¯ ¯ / ¯ ˘ ¯ ¯ / ¯ ˘ ¯
fā – 'e – lā – ton / fā – 'e – lā – ton / fā – 'e - lon

b. ATĀNIN 19 morae: . . . . / . . . . / . . . . .
ta-n ta -na-n ta-n / ta- n ta - na-n ta-n / ta-n ta - na-n

FIGURE 3.1 One quantitative poetic meter as represented in (a) the system of Arabic and Persian prosody, and (b) a simplified notation of attacks and durations in rhythmic cycles, which can also be used for poetic meters.

CYCLING POEMS TO TUNES

As I reflect on how the sophisticated theoretical work of Fārābī and certain of his successors might relate to the theorizing and practice of Iranian performers in the twentieth and twenty-first centuries, I remind myself that performers may voice long-standing concerns in unconventional ways. Studying the fate of inherited theories, we are likely to find that bits and pieces have been restated, reworked, forgotten, deliberately abandoned, or reinvented (to name but five of the possibilities). We know little as yet about ways that singers of verse in each of Iran's regions have drawn on inherited terminologies and concepts in talking about their performance practices. This contrasts with an abundance of recent work on the theoretical foundations of the music that is labeled "traditional" or "classical." In what follows, I discuss certain practices of one region, Khorasan, at various times in the past half century, and I comment on a few respects in which the singing of verse in this one "regional music" (*musiqi-ye navāhi*) relates to that in the nation's better-known "traditional music" (*musiqi-ye sonnati*).

Moxtār Zambilbāf, a bard (*baxši*) active in Iranian Khorasan with whom I conversed at some length in 1969 and 1972, told me that when a *baxši* performs quatrains within a narrative, "every five poems are cycled to one tune (*har panj-tā še'r be yek āhangi čarxide miše*)"; "it's like this, that we cycle every five poems to one tune (*in tur ist ke, har panj-tā eš'ār rā be yek āhangi bečarxānim*)" (conversation of August 25, 1972, AWM RL 16243, side 1, 46:46–47:16).[22] The verb posits a relation, that of cycling, between verse and *melody*, not between verse and *music*, on the assumption that a *baxši*'s presentation of a melody involves both his voice and his *dotār*, a long-necked lute with two strings. Of the three key terms in Moxtār's statements, *še'r* "poem" is borrowed from Arabic, and both Persian words have Arabic equivalents or analogues with long histories in music theoretical writing: the verb in both statements is derived from the Persian noun *čarx* "circular motion, cycle," equivalent to Arabic *daur*, and some uses of Arabic *laḥn* are equivalent to Persian *āhang* "tune," though other meanings of *laḥn* embrace tune and verse as an integral whole. Fārābī had the latter sense in mind when he defined *mūsīqī* as *alḥān* (one plural of *laḥn*) in the first sentence of his *Great Book on Music* (Fārābī 1967, 47).

I have not seen or heard any other uses of the noun *čarx* or its verb in theorizing about performance of sung verse. Moxtār's choice of this verb made explicit an understanding that was implicit in *āhang* and in such related terms as *ṭarīqa* ("way," borrowed from Arabic), *rāh* (Persian equivalent of *ṭarīqa*), *raqam* ("manner, kind," borrowed from Arabic), *now'* ("kind, type," also borrowed from Arabic), and *jur* (a Persian equivalent of *raqam* and *now'*). In the usage of Moxtār and his contemporaries, any of these terms might designate a procedure that was used cyclically in singing poems, with rhythmic and melodic features that distinguished it from other such procedures. In the late 1960s and early 1970s, a *ṭarīqe* or an *āhang* might also bear a proper name like *Šāh Xaṭā'i*.[23]

As a musical term in Arabic and Persian, *ṭarīqe* has often referred to a rhythmic cycle that supported one or more tunes.[24] The *ṭarīqe* that Moxtār knew as *Šāh Xaṭā'i* (pen-name of Šāh Esmā'il, founder of the Ṣafavid dynasty, r. 1501–1524) was a small group of tunes performed to a rhythmic cycle well suited to Persian or Khorasani Turkish verses in one poetic meter: the 15-syllable *ramal* is shown in Figures 3.2 and 3.3 with its four feet separated by slashes. In any rendition of this *ṭarīqa*, sung syllables are distinguished both as long or short and as stressed or unstressed (though no short syllable is stressed). One option is to stress each odd-numbered syllable, maintaining a cycle of eight beats (numbered in Figure 3.2) that allows for extra beats between the lines. Before and after each quatrain, the performer of Figure 3.2, Moḥammad Ḥoseyn Yegāneh (d. 1992), played figures on his *dotār* that were clearly derived from the basic four-syllable unit of the poetic meter.

Most tunes to which Moxtār and Yegāneh cycled quatrains are composed of initial, medial, and final phrases, which share a limited number of melodic formulas. My figures use a cipher notation that shows the scale-degree(s) to which each syllable is sung, while avoiding any implication of isochronous beats or subdivisions. Syllables sung to the same degree are marked with dots, so that the rhythm created by changes of scale degree will be easily visible. A *baxši* tunes one string of his *dotār* to scale-degree 1 and the other either a fourth or a fifth lower; Yegāneh (Figures 3.2 and 3.3, Audio 3.1 ▶ and 3.2 ▶) always tuned to a fourth; Moxtār (Figures 3.5 and 3.6, Audio 3.4 ▶ and 3.5 ▶) to a fifth. All phrases may descend to scale degree 1 (as in Figure 3.2), though more often the descents in initial and medial phrases pause on degrees 3 or 2 (as in Figures 3.3, 3.5 and 3.6) and the final phrase (to which only the fourth, or both third and fourth lines of the quatrain may be sung) completes the descent. The *Šāh Xaṭā'i* tunes mark the caesura at the mid-point of each line with a change of pitch (often an ascent, as in Figure 3.2).

While the rhythmic cycle denoted by the name *Šāh Xaṭā'i* determines whether each syllable is to be heard as long or as short and also places constraints on stress, in

beats: 1 2 / 3 4 / 5 6 / 7 8
– ⏑ – – – ⏑ – – – ⏑ – – – ⏑ –

degrees: 7 5 . . . . . 4 5 6 7 5 54 5 43
yak na-zar bar ab-ri kar-dam, ab-re bā- rī - dan ge-reft

5 4 . . . 3 . . 4 5 43 4 3 2 1
yak na-zar bar yā-ri kar-dam, yā-re nā- lī- dan ge-reft

3 . 4 . . . . 3 4 5 4 . 3 2 1
tek- ke bar dī- vā-re kar-dam, xā-ke bar far-qam ne-šast

5 7 5 . . 4 3 2 4 . . 3 3 2 1
xā- ke bar far-qaš ne- šī- nad, har ki yār az man ge-reft

I glanced at a cloud, a cloud engaged in raining,

I glanced at a lover, a lover engaged in weeping,

I cut into the wall, dust lay on the crown of my head

May whoever takes from me my lover have dust on the crown of his head!

FIGURE 3.2 Moḥammad Ḥoseyn Yegāneh (d. 1992) singing a Persian quatrain to *Šāh Xaṭā'i*. From *Music from North of Khorassan: Maestro Mohammad Hossein Yeganeh, dotar and vocals*. Tehran: Anjoman-e Musiqi-ye Irān, ANJ-008, tr. 4, 0:41–1:24 (Audio 3.1).

timing the attacks of successive stressed syllables performers are not obliged to create isochronous durations. Yegāne took advantage of that freedom in performing Figure 3.3, where the stresses fall only on syllables 3, 7, 11, and 15. The sequence of stresses supports the parallelism of the quatrain's verses, each of which groups the syllables as 3 + 4 / caesura / 5 + 3. If the first stressed syllable is heard as initiating a relevant duration, the second stressed syllable determines a projective potential that is denied by the "late" arrival of the third stress but is realized as the fourth stress determines the new duration that was initiated by the third. The entire progression then provides a relevant measure for the following three lines.

In both excerpts, rhythmic figures associated with *Šāh Xaṭā'i* provide an instrumental referent with which to measure Yegāneh's articulation of the verses. Baxšis of lesser skills are dependent on a regular series of beats, whereas those who are respected as masters treat the presence of a predictable beat as a variable, as Yegāne does, appropriate at certain moments and necessary in the *dotār* interludes played between quatrains, but not indispensable.[25]

Šāh Xaṭā'i is also the proper name of one unit (*guše*, "corner") in the *dastgāh* repertory that is now regarded as Iran's "traditional" or "classical" music (as distinguished from "regional" musics such as that of Khorasan).[26] Here as well, the name designates a procedure for performing verses in a single poetic meter: the eleven-syllable *ramal* of the great *Masnavi* of Jalāl al-Din Rumi (1207–1273 C.E.) rather than the fifteen-syllable

[vocables: a ha hay janımı]

stresses: 1 2 3 4

– ˘ – – / – ˘ – – / – ˘ – – / – ˘ –

degrees:

7 . 2 . . . . . 4 . 3 4 3 2 . 32
ey mə-nim kög-lüm a- lan, qəm-ən go-da- zı, har-da-sın?

6 5 6 5 . . . 4 . 3 4 3 . 2 . 4 3 2
mər-hə-me ya- ğı di-lom, ruh o rə-van-ım, har-da-sın? [har-da-sın?]

2 3 4 . . 3 4321 3 2 3 4 3 2 . 1
ha - li- mə rəhm ey- lə- gin, ey şəh-sə-var-ım, har-da-sın?

2 3 4 . . 3 4 3 2 . 4 3 2 . 31
mub-tə-la ol- dum bu-gün, bu- gün a- ğar-ım, har-da- sın?

[Oh my beloved!] O, my heart, captured, melted from sorrow; where are you?

A cure for my rebellious heart, my soul, my spirit; where are you?

Have pity on my condition, oh my sovereign; where are you?

Now I'm afflicted with distress, today I'm so weighted down; where are you?

FIGURE 3.3 Initial quatrain of a *monājāt* (an intimate communication with God), adapted into Khorasani Turkish from a Turkmen text of the story of *Adham-e divāne* "Crazy Adham"; performed to *Šāh Xaṭā'i* by Yegāne and recorded by Ameneh Youssefzadeh, who also transcribed and translated the text (Audio 3.2).

FIGURE 3.4 The guše of *Šāh Xaṭā'i* in the dastgāh of *Navā*, as sung by Maḥmud Karimi. Notation from Massoudieh 1978, 180 (Audio 3.3).

ramal of the *baxši*'s *Šāh Xaṭā'i*. Rumi's poem begins with a line that epitomizes a fundamental Iranian understanding of musical experience:[27]

beš-no ***az*** *ney* / *čun ḥe-* ***kā****-yat* / *mi-ko-nad* **Hear this flute / as a tale / it relates,**

az jo- ***dā*** *- i - hā* / *še-* ***kā****- yat* / *mi-ko-nad* of separations / a complaint / it utters.

In Audio 3.3 ⊙, the distinguished performer and teacher Maḥmud Karimi (1927–1984) sings this line to the *guše* of *Šāh Xaṭā'i*, and Figure 3.4 reproduces a transcription of that recorded performance (Massoudieh 1978, 180). The rhythm and profile of the initial melodic figure give a longer duration and a higher pitch to the third syllable in each of the first two feet. Once again, I suggest that the second of these stressed syllables creates a projective potential that is denied when the hemistich ends with a continuation rather than a new beginning. The hemistich's three feet form a sequence joining an imperative verb and its object (*bešno az ney*) to a second clitic group (*čun ḥekāyat*) and a verb (*mikonad*). When word groups coincide with feet, singers may choose to mark the beginning of a new word group and a new foot by renewing or transforming the melodic figure adopted for the initial foot,[28] an option that the *Šāh Xaṭā'i* melody encourages. A singer who knows *Šāh Xaṭā'i* will sing the first hemistich twice, to essentially the same tune with differences in timing and grouping like those shown in Massoudieh's transcription. As he repeats the hemistich, Karimi reduces its total duration from approximately twelve seconds to approximately eleven, and he attaches the fifth syllable to the first foot. The second hemistich and the tune to which it is sung retain the articulations of the first with one change: the initial clitic group and corresponding melodic figure extend into the second foot, and the syllable *-hā* is sung on the same pitch as the earlier *ney* and *-yat*.

MOUNTING NEW RHYTHM UPON THE OLD

In his commentary on Aristotle's *Poetics*, Avicenna was careful to distinguish the "*īqā'* that measures" (*īqā' awzāna*) from the "additional *īqā'*" (*īqā' zā'id*) that enhances sung verse in performance (1966, 44; Eng. trans., 90). Another eleventh-century theorist, al-Ḥasan al-Kātib, urged musicians to use rhythmic cycles that would differ from, rather than "agreeing with," the meters of the verses they were setting or performing (al-Ḥasan 1975, 69; French trans., 108). The structural correspondence between an *īqā'* composed of two cycles and a line of verse with two hemistiches may well have encouraged musicians to play with what we might call "rhythmic counterpoint."

When he spoke of the "superinducing or *mounting* of a new rhythm upon the old" as "something answerable to counterpoint in music," the poet Gerard Manley Hopkins (1967 [1918], 46) described the composition of poetry in terms we might extend to the singing of poetry, in which both the old rhythm and the new are multidimensional. Each poetic meter serves poets as a template for composing verses by "mounting new rhythm" on rhythms of morphemes, words, and phrases; and singers learn additional ways to mount new rhythm in the course of performance.

Singers of Iran's "traditional" and "regional" musics must develop an intuitive sense of how to coordinate what I will call the "order numbers" of syllables (first, second, third, etc.) with the contours of specific melody types. Yegāneh's conception of the *Šāh Xaṭā'i* tune outlined in Figure 3.2, for example, may have called for a melodic ascent on the ninth syllable. Such skills of coordination are normally acquired without explicitly assigning numbers to syllables or stating the principle involved, though the two sets of syllables illustrated in Figure 3.1 have presumably been helpful to countless singers of traditional music. The order numbers of syllables are as pertinent in verse composed to quantitative meters like the eleven-syllable and fifteen-syllable *ramal* as they are in verse where any syllable may be long or short so long as each line has the same number of syllables (apart from the occasional exception). Most verses that *baxšis* sing in Khorasani Turkish are of the latter type, generally with lines of eight syllables grouped as 4 + 4, 3 + 5, or 5 + 3, or lines of eleven syllables grouped as 6 + 5 or 4 + 4 + 3. Such groupings are readily associated with changes in melodic direction.

Figures 3.5 and 3.6 are two quatrains in Khorasani Turkish, drawn from the story of *Šāh Esmā'il*. Articulating the eight syllables in each line of the quatrain in Figure 3.4, or the eleven syllables in each line of the quatrain in Figure 3.5, creates one level of periodicity having no necessary connection to an isochronous pulse. If listeners are to accept the performance as an enactment of the emotional state of one character in the story, the *baxši* must insert vocables (bracketed in Figures 3.2, 3.5 and 3.6) at pertinent moments, and these can be all the more effective when they do not coincide with the beats of a rhythmic cycle. A *baxši* has the option of coordinating the articulation of the syllables with a regular sequence of beats *and* with predictable moments of coincidence between beats and syllables, as in Figure 3.5, where after the first four syllables, syllables 5, 8, 1 and 4 always coincide with beats 3, 4, 1, and 2, respectively. He has many options when it comes to coordinating syllables with scale degrees, and he also has the option of a flexible beat, as in Figure 3.6, or none at all.[29] He may choose to repeat lines or segments of lines so long as he does so to an appropriate unit of the tune. And he has the option of tapping on the belly of the *dotār*, either at moments that coincide with beats, syllables, or both (as in Figures 3.5 and 3.6), or at unpredictable moments that rarely or even never coincide with other actions. In Figures 3.5 and 3.6, the tapping functions, above all, to mark final syllables of certain lines; in other performances it is not limited to that function and becomes a distinct stream of activity.

beats:
(no pulse here) 3 4 1 2 3 4
7 7 7 7 76545342 3 3 3 4 32 3 3 3 432 3 4 32 32
[ey] dağ-lar ba-şey du-tub du-man [ey] nə yul- dey Gul- zar il- le - re
taps: **x x x**

1 2 3 4 2 3 4
7654 4 3 3 432 3 3 3 432 3 3 3 432 3 3 32 32
[ey] dağ-lar ba-şey du-tub du-man nə yul-dey Gul - zar il- le- re
taps: **x x**

1 2 3 4 1 2 3
65453 4 3 3 432 3 3 3 432 4 3 3 4 4 3 2 1
[ey] rə- qi-bə ver - mi-rəm ə-man nə yul-dey Gul-zar il- le-re

1 2 3 4 1 2 3
1 1 1 432 4 3 3 432 4 3 3 4 4 3 21
rə-qi-bə ver- mi-rəm ə- man nə yul-dey Gu l- zar il - ler
taps: **x x**

Fog covered the mountain tops. What path has Golzar taken? (2)
I'll show my rival no mercy. What path has Golzar taken? (2)

FIGURE 3.5 Quatrain from the story of *Šāh Esmā'il*, sung by Moxtār Zambilbāf, 1972 (AWM RL 16245) (Audio 3.4).

x 1 3 3 3 3 4 4 4 3 4 3 4 64 3 4 32
[hey] qo-va qo-va [ey] bir mə-ra-li gə-tır-dım [gə-tır-dım ə]
taps: **x x**

7654 3 3 4 4 4 3 4 4 4 3 4 64 3 4 32
[ey] qo-va qo-va bir mə-ra-li gə-tır-dım [gə-tır-dım ə]
taps: **x x x x**

1 3 3 4 4 4 43 4 4 4 3 4 64 3 4 32
i-tir-dim cey-ran-ım [ey] bu-ra-yə gəl-dım [can gəl-dım ə]

1 3 3 3 3 4 4 3 4 64 3 3 3
sə-ni gör-di-mi aq-le hu-şim bay-dır-dım [ey]

6 5 5 4 4 4 3 3 3 4 3 21
bay-dır-dım hu-şi-mi bu-ra-he gəl-dim [ə]
taps: **x x**

3 4 4 4 4 4 3 3 4 4 3 3 4 4 3 3 4 3 21
bay-dır-dım hu-şi-mi bu-ra-yə gəl-dim [ha-lı Ley-li can gəl-dim oy]
taps: **x x x x x x x x**

[As he hunts, Shāh Ismā'il enters a garden looking for a gazelle that has eluded him, and he is overwhelmed by the beauty of Golzār, daughter of an Armenian khoja.]

FIGURE 3.6 Quatrain from the story of *Šāh Esmā'il*, sung by Moxtār Zambilbāf, 1972 (AWM RL 16245) (Audio 3.5).

Singers who have learned the *dastgāh* repertory of Iran's traditional music will know one or more units (*gušes*) with which they can sing verses in any of the quantitative meters of classical Persian poetry, though a small number of units (*Šāh Xaṭā'i* among them) are suitable only for verses in a single meter. The prominent singer Mohammad Rezā Shajariān maintains that with those few exceptions, "any poem may be sung to any gushe" (Simms and Koushkani 2012, 191). Other singers and theorists have posited compelling affinities between melody and poetic meter, as expressed in the title of Naṣir Forṣat al-Dawla Shirāzi's treatise, *Boḥur al-alḥān dar 'elm-e musiqi va nesbat-e ān bā 'aruz*, "Meters of melodies in the science of music and their relation to the system of poetic meter" (Shirāzi 1966 [1914]).[30] The heart of any performance of Persian traditional music is the singing (*āvāz*) of a *ğazal*, during which one instrumentalist at a time provides "responses to the vocalizing" (*javāb-e āvāz*), an art that requires instrumentalists to recognize the poetic meter and project the duration of each group of syllables to which they must respond.[31]

Performers who specialize in one of Iran's regional musics are less likely to sing verses in a large number of quantitative meters. The singers whom I recorded in Northern Khorasan generally knew one or more tunes for verses in each meter represented in their repertory, such as the *ramal* meters illustrated earlier and the eleven-syllable *motaqāreb*, the meter of Ferdowsi's *Šāh-nāma* (Iran's national epic) and many other works. Singers had conflicting opinions on whether the attributes of a tune (*āhang*) or a "way" (*jur, rāh*) of singing made it an appropriate choice for a given poetic genre or for verses on a particular theme.

In my limited experience, a decade before the Revolution of 1979, the Khorasani singers most interested in comparing "ways" of singing were those, called *naqqāl* (literally "transmitter"), who inserted sung verse within prose narration as they performed episodes from the *Šāh-nāma* in tea houses.[32] They evaluated ways of singing according to conceptions of the ethics of vocal performance. Among the pertinent ethical considerations were constraints on how singers could best engage the attention of listeners in a given set of circumstances, and how best to use one's voice in genres of praise and lament.[33] Singers of those genres are appropriately considered "expositors" (*ḍawū'l-alsina*) in Fārābī's sense of that term (mentioned at the outset of this chapter), alongside "orators, poets, secretaries, and upholders of religion": the "imaginative representations" of all expositors must be evaluated by ethical criteria, whether or not one follows Fārābī in deriving those criteria from the demonstrative syllogisms of philosophers. In his commentary on Aristotle's *Poetics*, Avicenna described "melodious intonation" (*talḥīn*) as "a sort of action" (*fi'l*) which "imitates significant actions" by "imitating the mode which the agent must have—the agent who possesses a certain moral character and thought which give rise to such action" (Avicenna 1966, 45; trans. Dahiyat 1974, 90). One *naqqāl* active in Mashhad described the *Šāh-nāma* (completed around the year 1010 when Avicenna was thirty years old) as "a book full of advice" (*ketābi pandamiz*), adding that his narration of its episodes "acts on the comportment of the intellect" (*ru-ye raftār-e 'aql 'amal mikonad*) (conversation of April 28, 1969 with Moḥammad Ilxāniān; the recording on AWM RL 16251 does not include these remarks). A naqqāl of higher social status, who belonged to the Šāh Ne'matollāhi brotherhood, believed that public performance of the epic was essential if Iranians "were to know the high rank of national affairs" (*bedunand maqām-e olyā-ye omur-e mamlekat*). In 26 years of public performance, initiated with a public blessing from the master he claimed to have served for twelve years (a conventional number), he had avoided "inappropriate words" (*kelām-e nāšāyeste*), speaking only those that were "true" (*saḥih*) and "correct" (*dorost*).

A third singer, Moḥammad Ḥasan Naqqāl, maintained that verses from the *Šāh-nāma* must be sung to a "warlike" (*razmi*) tune and wished to distinguish "the way (*jur*) that I wish to sing/recite" from that of the another *naqqāl*, whose *Šāh-nāma* performances were broadcast once a week on the radio station of Mashhad. The latter, Ṣādeq 'Ali Šāh, was also known as a specialist in performance of *moṣibat*, a genre of lament for the martyred imams of Shi'ah Islam, and his critics saw that as a reason for what they deemed his failure to master the "honorific" (*tajlili*) way of singing or the "warlike" tunes appropriate to Ferdowsi's verses. He himself took pride in his ability to attract and hold the interest of listeners (see further Blum 2003, 180).

In our conversations, a *naqqāl* would identify a "way of singing" with a proper name like *Šāh Xaṭā'i*; a generic term like *ṭarīqe*, *jur*, or *rāh*; an epithet like *razmi* or *tajlili*; any combination of these, or none of them. Each singer might have his own conception of the features that distinguished one "way" from others (see Blum 2009b, 92 for a list of five common features), though for *naqqāls* differences in the timing of vocal attacks, and passage from one attack to the next, were clearly pertinent distinctions. *Naqqāls* with more or less extensive training in performance of *Šāh-nāma* verses, and amateur singers as well, tended to stress the final syllable of each foot (i.e., the third, sixth, ninth, and eleventh syllables of each eleven-syllable hemistich in the *motaqāreb* meter). This habit was so widely shared among Khorasani singers that I consider it an attribute of the "old rhythm" on which each singer could mount "new rhythm."

Ḥāj Ḥoseyn Xān Yāvari, an amateur singer who struggled to remember the fourteen verses he kindly sang at my request on the morning of June 25, 1969, sang each three-syllable foot to the same rhythmic figure: the attacks of the first and third syllables established a duration that remained relevant through the cycle of twelve beats on which he sang each hemistich (Figure 3.7, Audio 3.6 ▶). Yāvari sustained the third syllable of the first two feet through two beats of the cycle before articulating the initial short syllable of the following foot on the next beat, and he moved more quickly to the initial syllable of the fourth foot after the final syllable of the third foot. The moments when the periodicity of the eleven attacks intersects with that of the twelve beats are consistent throughout the performance, and the "interval of disjunction" (*fāṣila* in Fārābi's terminology) that precedes some renewals of the cycle can be heard as a thirteenth beat. Rather than playing with the rhythmic options offered by a matrix of possibilities, Yāvari adopted a *template* or *scheme* that remained constant from one line to the next.[34] (Yāvari and the other singers of *Šāh-nāma* verses discussed here occasionally replaced the long vowel *ā* with *ū*, a substitution that is common in vernacular Persian.)

beats (ca. 88):

1	2	3	4	5	6	7	8	9	10	11	12 [13 or *fāsila*]

˘   –   –   /   ˘   –   –   /   ˘   –   –   / ˘   –   [hiatus]

scale degrees:

<u>5</u> . 1   1 <u>6</u> 1   2 1 2 . 1

če Ros-tam   ga- z an-dar   ka-mān rān - de zūd

<u>6</u> . 1   2 1 <u>6</u>   2 1 2 . 1

be-dūn-sūn   ke Sī – mor -   ğe far- mū - de būd

1 2 3   3 2 1   2 1 2 . 1

be-zad tī-   re bar češ -   me Es - fan- di-yār

<u>6</u> . 1   2 1 <u>6</u>   2 1 <u>6</u> . 1

ja-hūn šod   si- yā pī-   še ūn nā- m-e-dār

Then, as the Simorgh had ordered him, Rostam drew back his bow.

Aiming at Esfandyar's eyes. he released the arrow,

and for the Persian prince the world was turned to darkness.

(trans. Dick Davis, Viking Penguin, 2006, p. 414)

FIGURE 3.7 Two lines from Ferdowsi's *Šāh-nāma*, sung to a 12-beat cycle by Ḥāj Ḥoseyn Xān Yāvari (age ca. 60) of Xarv Olyā (AWM RL 16234, reproduced on the CD *Naqqāli in Northern Khorāsān*, track 4, 1:54–2:31) (Audio 3.6).

Figure 3.8 compares two ways of singing one verse from a moral fable composed in the *motaqāreb* meter by the thirteenth-century poet Sa'di: those of Ṣādeq 'Ali Šāh and one of his critics, Moḥammad Ḥasan Naqqāl (Audio 3.7a ◉, 3.7b ◉). Both men coordinated the eleven syllables of a hemistich with six (at times seven) rather flexible beats, though Moḥammad Ḥasan chose a much slower tempo. In Ṣādeq 'Ali Šāh's performance, the attack of the third syllable, *d*, initiated the duration that would be defined by the attack of the sixth syllable, *b*, and would remain a relevant measure throughout the cycle. Although Moḥammad Ḥasan did the same, the slower tempo allowed him to solicit his listeners' attention by lengthening or shortening the projected duration. In his judgment, Ṣādeq 'Ali Šāh's way of singing did not bestow the appropriate weight on the moral message of Sa'di's verses.

A second role associated with performance of verses from the *Šāh-nāma* is that of the *moršed* (literally "guide"), whose singing and drumming guide a sequence of exercises in the men's athletic clubs called *zur-xāne* (literally "house of strength").[35] The verses are called for at a specific moment, as the athletes stretch out horizontally

```
(a) beats, ca. MM 76:
         1          2    3      4     5   6    7       8 9  10     11 12   13
degrees:
5  .  4  3 5  .       3   32 1  32     1 .   .  3   2 3 2 1  7   1  321
˘  ¯  ¯  ˘ ¯  ¯   ˘   ¯   ¯  ˘  ¯      ˘ ¯   ¯  ˘   ¯ ¯ ˘ ¯  ¯   ˘  ¯
ze-nax-dūn fo-rū bor- dᵉ čan-dūn be jeyb / ke Bax-šan-de  rū-zi ra-sā-nad  ze ğeyb

(b) beats, ca. MM 46:
         1        2    3       4    5  6      7       8      9   10     11  12
degrees:
2  3  432 .  .  3      32 3 .  2      1 2  3  1   . 3 1 23  2  1  ,
˘  ¯   ¯  ˘  ¯  ¯  ˘    ¯ ¯ ˘  ¯      ˘ ¯  ¯  ˘   ¯ ¯ ˘  ¯  ¯  ˘  ¯
ze-nax-dūn  fo-rū -b as-tᵉ   čan-dīn be jeyb / ke Bax-šan-de rū-zi  ra-sā-nad ze ğeyb
```

He lowered his chin to his chest / [asking] that the Bestower send his daily sustenance

FIGURE 3.8 One verse of a fable from the *Būstān* of Sa'di as sung by two *naqqāls*: (a) Ṣādeq 'Ali Šāh (AWM RL 16211, and *Naqqāli in Northern Khorāsān*, track 6, 4:23–4:35); (b) Moḥammad Ḥasan Naqqāl (AWM RL 16225) (Audio 3.7).

to do push-ups (*šenā*, "swimming"), with their hands on a small board and their toes touching the floor. The *moršed* alternates between singing eleven syllables for about eight seconds as the men remain stationary, and drumming for another eight seconds as they do a push-up; hence each cycle of approximately sixteen seconds begins with the first syllable of a hemistich. Performing the two lines transcribed in Figure 3.9, a *moršed* in the city of Sabzevār treated the first two syllables as upbeats to a rhythmic figure which he then reproduced with the remaining two three-syllable constituents (Audio 3.8 ▶). His figure scrupulously respected the distinction of long and short syllables, though he was willing to split apart words. The beginnings marked on the third and sixth syllables of each hemistich in Figure 3.9 determine a projective duration which is not realized with precision by the attack of the ninth syllable, yet serves as a measure that allows small differences to register and the final long syllable of each melodic constituent to be heard as a continuation. All three melodic constituents are variants of the same figure, and each *begins* with the onset of the *final* syllable of a poetic foot.

Ḥasan Salaḥšur, a young Kurdish *naqqāl* who sang these same two lines as he would perform them in a tea house, was not obliged to consider the timing of push-ups and needed only about four and a half seconds for each line (Figure 3.10, Audio 3.9 ▶). In the first line, the attack of the sixth syllable determines a duration whose projective potential is not realized; instead, the attack of the eighth syllable (*gar-*) determines a shorter duration whose projective potential is then realized with the articulation of the ninth and again with that of the eleventh syllable. Salaḥšur then sings the second hemistich to the same rhythmic cycle. For the second line, he adopts a new cycle, in which beginnings that determine durations occur on the sixth and ninth syllables, but not on the eighth. Whereas in the first cycle the attack of the ninth syllable determines a duration whose projective potential is realized with the attack of the eleventh, that b = beginning; c = continuation

			b		c	b^{1}		c	b^{2}		c
degrees:	3	.	32	1	3	32	1	2	21	7̲	123
	˘	–	–	˘	–	–	˘	–	–	˘	–
	a-	zūn	nā -	m^{e} -	dā- /	rā-	n^{e}	gar-/	dan -	ke-	šān
	3	.	.	1	3	32	1	2	21	7̲	1
	ka-	sī	ham	ba -	rad /	sū-	ye	Roś-/	tam	ne-	šān
	3	.		2	3	.	1	2	21	7̲	1
	ke	Soh-	rā -	b^{e}	košt-/	ast	u	af - /	kan-	de	x^{w}ār
	3	1	32	1	3	.	1	2	21	7̲	1
	ke	Soh-	rā -	b^{e}	košt-/	ast	u	af - /	kan-	de	x^{w}ār
	3	.	32	1	3	32	1	2	21	7̲	1
	ha-	mī	x^{w}ās-	t^{e}	kar- /	dan	to	rā /	x^{w}ā -	s^{e}-	tār

[Sohrab, before realizing that the man who has fatally wounded him is his father,

Rostam, imagines how his death will be reported to Rostam:]

"A hero from among this noble band will take this seal

and show it to Rostam:

'Sohrab's been slain and humbled to the earth,'

he'll say, 'This happened while he searched for you.'"

(translation from Clinton 1987, 153, with punctuation altered)

FIGURE 3.9 Two verses from the *Šāh Nāma*, sung by Sayyed Ḥasan Naqib Zāde (age 43), the *moršed* of a *zur-xāna* (men's athletic club) in Sabzevār, 1995 (Audio 3.8).

does not happen in the second cycle, where the eleventh syllable is "early" and can be heard as a continuation of the previous beginning (as in all four lines of Figure 3.9).

Ḥasan, unlike his eight illiterate brothers, had attended a madrasa for six or seven years after their father was killed by a bandit, after which he spent three years learning from a poet-singer how to perform episodes of the *Šāh-nāma* as well as *ğazavot* (narratives of religious wars) composed in the same poetic meter. He used the same melodic models for both genres and did not seem concerned with the objections to "inappropriate" modes of performance voiced by *naqqāls* who claimed or aspired to a higher social status on the basis of their family background, education, affiliation with a Sufi brotherhood, or all of these.[36]

CONCLUSION: ILLUSIONS OF ABSENCE, NEGLECT OF PRESENCE

A short chapter on rhythm in an introduction to the traditional music of Iran by the late musician-scholar Dariush Safvat (1922–2013) and Nelly Caron opens by distinguishing

slow cycle:		1		2						
faster cycle:				1	2	3	4	5	6	7
degrees:	2 3 4 3 2			4 3 .		.	.	. 2		

a- z īn nā - mᵉ- dā- / rū - nᵉ gar-/ dan - ke- šūn

		1		2	3	4	5	6	7	8	9
	2 3 4 3 2			3 .		.	.	. 2			

ka- sī ham ba- rad / sū- ye Ros-/ tam ne- šān

cycle 2:		1		2		3		4
	1 2 3		2 3 .		2 1 . 2		

ke Suh- rā - bᵉ koš-/ t-as- t u af -/ kan- de xʷār

		1		2		3		4
	1 2 3		2 3 .		2 1 7 1		

ha- mī xʷās- tᵉ kar- / dan to rā / xʷā- sᵉ- tār

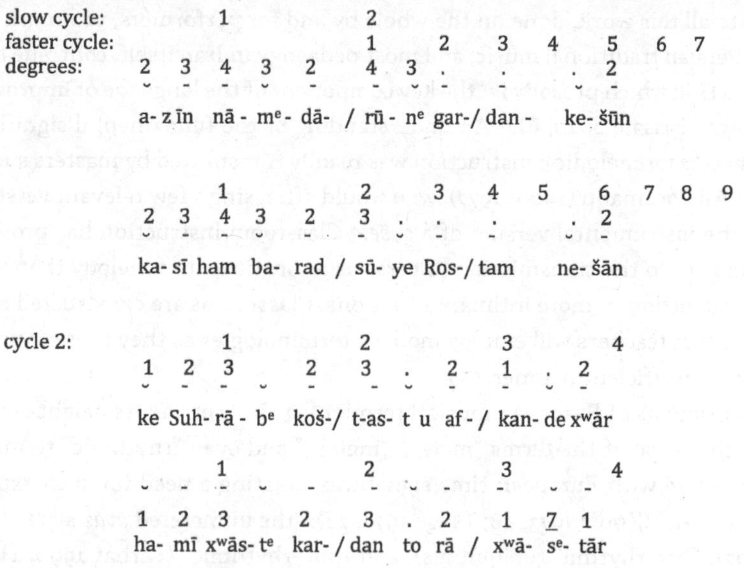

FIGURE 3.10 The same verses as in Figure 3.9, sung by Ḥasan Salaḥšur (age 18), a *naqqāl* active in tea houses of Bojnurd, 1969 (AWM RL 16208; also available on the CD *Naqqāli in Northern Khorāsān*, track 2, 0:06–0:28) (Audio 3.9).

rhythms "independent of poetry" from those "dependent on or inspired by" poetic meters, noting that the latter are "at times salient, at times concealed" (*tantôt accusé, tantôt caché*) (Caron and Safvate 1966, 133–34).[37] Passage between salience and conceal-ment often occurs more than once within a single *guše*. Dariush Talā'i (b. 1952), now an established master of Iran's traditional music, devoted his master's thesis at the Sorbonne to analysis of traditional music through prosody (Talā'i 1983) and went on to produce outstanding pedagogical and analytic publications in which prosody is not neglected. The late Moḥammad Rezā Loṭfi (1947–2014) told students of tār and setār that they could not learn melodies or improvise on them without remembering verses that complement the melodies (Amoozegar-Fassaie 2010, 8). Indeed, throughout the Persian-speaking world, instruction manuals for music students (e.g., Dehlavi 2000; Tahmāsebi 2001; Abdurashidov 2002) outline the system of poetic meter (*'aruz*) as indispensable preparation for composition or performance of melody, reaffirming the conception of verse and melody as a unity that has long been a major premise of music theory in Arabic and Persian. The initial chapter of the published version of Moḥammad Rezā Āzādehfar's doctoral dissertation on "Rhythmic Structure in Iranian Music" is devoted to "rhythmic aspects of Persian poetry" (2006, 9–66), building on and correcting the pioneering dissertation of Gen'ichi Tsuge (1974). Nearly three decades after Talā'i's Sorbonne thesis, a young performer-scholar once again made the intimate connection between prosody and Persian classical music the topic of his mas-ter's thesis (Amoozegar-Fassaie 2010). In his words, only the musician who develops "an ear for poetic meter (*guš-e 'aruzi*)" will understand the ways in which meter "proj-ects the music forward" (personal communication, May 21, 2017).

Despite all this work, done on the whole by and for performers, too much scholarship on Persian traditional music, and most pedagogy in Iran itself, continue to ignore the respects in which prosody is "the key component of the language of improvisation" (Amoozegar-Fassaie 2010, 8).[38] An understanding of the fundamental significance of poetic meters for melodic construction was readily transmitted by masters such as the late Nur 'Ali Borumand (1906–1977), who would often sing a few relevant verses before playing the instrumental version of a *guše*.[39] Classroom instruction has proven to be less conducive to the transmission of verse as a constituent of melody than was face-to-face instruction in more intimate situations. Classrooms are constructed in the expectation that teachers will employ modern terminologies as they present up-to-date theories in an efficient manner.

Appropriations of European musical terminology in Iran and its neighbors have restricted the scope of the terms "meter," "metric," and even "rhythmic" to music that can be notated with European time signatures, creating a need for such expressions as "non-metric" (Zonis 1973, 48; Tsuge 1974, 24), "the unmetered *āvāz* style" (Nooshin 2015, 102), "free rhythm" (ubiquitous), and "non-rhythmic" (Farhat 1990, 111). Talā'i opened his thesis with an attempt to dispel these illusions of absence (1983, 2): "In our days, Iranian musicians call pieces built on a succession of equal measures (hence susceptible to percussion accompaniment) 'rhythmic music' . . . Most Persian music, not following that rule, is thus considered 'non-rhythmic,' despite carrying within itself a rhythm."[40] Amoozegar-Fassaie (2009, 152) likewise notes the tendency of contemporary Iranian musicians to think within the "framework and method of Western musicians." In neighboring Azerbaijan, a distinction between music *with* or *without* "measure" (*vəzn* or *bahr*) was formulated and disseminated in the period of Soviet hegemony (notably in Hajibeyov 1988 [1945], 126–27; English trans. 1985, 129–31); Iranian versions of that distinction resulted from various types of contact with Western European musicians (reviewed in Darvishi 1995).[41] As borrowings from European languages, *rhythm, rhythmic, meter*, and *metric* are now current in both Azerbaijani and Persian alongside derivatives of the Arabic terms *baḥr* (pl. *buḥūr*) and *wazn* (*vəzn* in Azerbaijani, *vazn* in Persian), both of which have long histories of usage in prosody and in the music theory that treats verse as a component of melody. The fact that the traditional meanings of both terms remain relevant to a great many cultural practices in Iran and its neighbors is a good reason not to make either of them nothing more than a synonym for *meter* in conventional Western musical terminology.

The revised version of Talā'i's analytic notation of the Persian *radif* (a repertory of models, briefly described in endnote 24), published in 2016, reserves the term *vazn* for poetic meters that are "salient" (rather than "concealed") in certain units (*gušes*) of the radif.[42] Earlier, in his *New approach to the theory of Persian art music*, Talā'i spoke of "flexible [*en'etāf-pazir*] melody . . . especially with the widespread and very common unmeasured melodies [*meludihā-ye bedun-e mizān-bandi-ye ritmik*], in which the rhythm depends on the meter of the poetry [*ritm az vazn-e še'r peyravi mikonad*]" (Talā'i 1993, 11 [English], 16 [Persian]; 2002, 867). Whether *peyravi mikonad* is translated as "depends on" or as "follows," multiple options are available to singers and instrumentalists as they realize this "following" or "dependence," including the options of "concealment" that were noted by Safvat and Caron. Talā'i's term *flexible melody* can be interpreted as encouraging attention to changes within a *guše* or melody type, including those that reproduce a projective duration once or twice before abandoning it, and the passages between salience and concealment mentioned earlier.[43] His use of Persian *bedun-e mizān-bandi-ye ritmik* (literally "without rhythmic articulation of measures") for "unmeasured" is a better choice than the Azerbaijani terms *vəznsiz* or *bahrsız* (both meaning "without meter") or the more recent Persian *metr-e āzād*, "a translation of free-metred" (Azadehfar 2006, 188).

Experiencing meter as rhythm (to cite once more the title of Hasty's pathbreaking book), and meter concealed within or emerging from rhythm, can direct our attention to the many ways in which sequences of sounds become rhythmic. It is for that reason that Evan Rapport, in an excellent study of performance styles of Persian-speaking Jews (2016), finds *prosodic rhythm* a more appropriate term than *free rhythm*: rather than positing an absence of constraint, we can attempt to recognize pertinent constraints that are audible or implicit. The best analytical work on Persian traditional music, that of Talā'i in particular, provides an excellent foundation for analytic studies of Iran's regional musics, which will be best carried out by Iranian scholars who find opportunities to learn regional languages well enough to recognize some of the ways in which verses are "melodized."[44] Conversely, encounters with masters of regional musics may provide Iranian scholars of traditional music with opportunities to observe methods of transmission that have not been designed for classrooms.

ACKNOWLEDGMENT

I wish to thank Ameneh Youssefzadeh for our two decades of collaborative research on sung poetry of Khorasan; Christopher Hasty for the continuing inspiration of his writings and conversation; Richard Wolf for indispensable criticism of errors in an earlier draft of this chapter; and Farzad Amoozegar-Fassaie for conversations that are clarifying issues I've been reflecting on for many years. In revising the paper distributed at the 2012 colloquium, I have drawn on a study of Fārābi's poetics and politics of music that I drafted for a conference on "Fārābi from the music point of view," planned for 2010 by the Iranian Academy of Arts only to be indefinitely deferred, and on a paper presented to the Ethnomusicology Colloquium at Brown University in September, 2016.

NOTE ON TRANSLITERATION

For transliteration of Persian words, I have used the 2012 version of the Iranian national system, with two modifications: dots beneath *ḥ*, *ṣ*, and *ṭ* to distinguish them from the letters transliterated as *h*, *s*, and *t*; and macrons over *ī* and *ū* in figures where this might help readers readers recognize the distribution of long and short syllables in a poetic meter. Elsewhere, long *i* or *u* in Persian does not require a macron, since the short values of those vowels are written as *e* and *o*, respectively. In transliteration of Arabic, however, *i* and *u* are short unless marked with a macron; transliteration of a few Arabic consonants must also differ from that of Persian (e.g., Arabic *'aruḍ*, Persian *'aruz*; Arabic *wazn*, Persian *vazn*). In transcribing Khorasani Turkish from recordings, I use the modern Latin alphabet for Azerbaijani. In the section on "Cycling Poems to Tunes," the Arabic and Persian consonant transliterated in the preceding sections as *kh* is transliterated as *x* (as in "*baxši*") for consistency with Khorasani Turkish. I have retained common spellings of geographic names, rather than altering them in conformity to these transliteration conventions. Proper names in the text and references are spelled in ways that I hope will assist readers in locating them.

NOTES

1. Two chapters on rhythm in Fārābī's *Kitāb al-mūsīqā al-kabīr* [*Great Book on Music*] (1967, 435–81, 983–1055) were followed by the *Kitāb al-īqā'āt* [*Book of Rhythms*] and the *Kitāb iḥṣā' al-īqā'āt* [*Book for the Enumeration, Classification and Basic Comprehension of Rhythms*]. Sawa 2009 includes English translations of all four texts with commentary, and the three-part translation of *iḥṣā'* as "enumeration, classification and basic comprehension" is his. Eckhard Neubauer's German translations of the *Kitāb al-īqā'āt* (1968–1969) and the *Kitāb iḥṣā' al-īqā'āt* (1994) likewise include illuminating commentary; both are reprinted in Neubauer 1998a with facsimiles of the Arabic texts.

2. In a comment appended to Regina Bendix's essay "The Pleasures of the Ear: Toward an Ethnography of Listening" (2000), Don Brenneis speaks of "the self-imposed split, which scholars often make between their powerful personal responses to the acoustic and the impersonal terms within which they conceptualize and write about cultural expression as professionals."

3. *Al-alḥān al-kāmila* is the Arabic equivalent of Greek *teleion melos*, as used for example by Aristides Quintilianus (*De musica*, Book I, ch. 12; ed. Winnington-Ingram 1963, 28; trans. Barker 1989, 430). The premise that music cannot realize its full potential in the absence of words was for centuries as fundamental to Arabic and Persian music theory as to that of Europe, and was supported from time to time with references to Plato and Aristotle, as in Zarlino's *Istitutioni harmoniche*, Part Two, chapter 7 (1573 [1558], 83–87).

4. In an illuminating study of "Rhythm and Meter in Ancient Greek Music," Mathiesen (1985, 167) lists three functions of meter, two of which depend on the concept of syllable: "measuring certain grammatical elements"; "measuring syllables in words, which are quite variable"; and, quoting Aristides Quintilianus, measuring "feet compounded of dissimilar syllables, symmetrical in length." In the *Rhythmic Elements* of Aristoxenus (ed. and trans. Pearson, 1990, 6–7, 22–23), a syllable is analogous to a musical tone and a performer's signal or cue.

5. *Īqā'* is the verbal noun of form IV, the causative ("to let fall") of the verb *waqa'a* "to fall, occur." A basic image is that of a person using a stick to mark beats in one of the compound cycles called *īqā'āt*, the plural of *īqā'*.

6. Clayton (2000, 36) cites the limits of immediate memory as a reason to avoid equating *tāl* with European *meter*, since "*tāl* cycles are rarely as short as 3 seconds"; presumably *metric cycle* draws attention to the variability in length.

7. Neubauer (1994, 114–15) diagrams three conceptions of "the course of a single tone" in Fārābī's rhythmics. He notes (1998a, 401) that for Fārābī *nuqla* is equivalent to *phorá*, a term for "local movement" in Aristotle's *Physics* 243a (trans. Wicksteed and Cornford 1963 [1929], 217), and to *metábasis* in the rhythmics of Aristoxenus (trans. Pearson 1990, 22, citing Michael Psellus on movement [*kinesis*] as a "shift" [*metábasis*] from one position [*schema*] to another, one tone [*phthongos*] to another, one syllable to another).

8. Avicenna argued that the attack terminating the interval of time (*mudda*) initiated by an earlier attack should occur before we lose the memory of the first attack (El Hefny 1931, 66 for Arabic text, 92 for German translation) since the pleasure we feel on the inception of an attack dissipates as the sound continues or decays, to be renewed as we perceive the next attack.

9. Sawa (2009, 88n1) suggests that theorists writing in Arabic adapted the Greek distinction of *thésis* and *ársis* to signify, respectively, "putting down" a full cycle and pausing before putting down the next cycle.

10. The emphasis on attacks is consistent with the view that Fārābī adopted from Aristotle (*Physics* 194a; *Posterior Analytics* 78b, 36–79a, 2), that harmonics and by extension the rest of music theory are applied rather than pure mathematics, having more to do with the physical than with the mathematical sciences even as terms and concepts from mathematics remain indispensable (Haas 2006, 645, 686–95).

11. In Hasty's estimation (1997, 283), durations that remain present in a musician's or listener's immediate memory do not normally exceed "an upper limit of three to five seconds."

12. See Levin 1972 for an illuminating discussion of the Greek term translated here as *synesis*, one of the central concepts of Aristoxenian theory, which Levin glosses (1972, 211) as "'musical intuition' or 'competence,' i.e. an inherent mental capacity comprising one's implicit musical knowledge."

13. Applying a distinction first made by the Russian linguist Prince N. S. Trubetzkoy (1969 [1939] 173–81), Dmitry Frolov (2000, 73–78) sees Arabic as a language whose minimal unit of prosodic length is the *mora* rather than the syllable, though in discussing the "Equivalence of Ḥarf and Mora" he notes that "The notion of *ḥarf* is not fully analogous to the notion of *mora*" (77). I have adopted Sawa's translations of *sākin* and *mutaḥarrik*; Madian (1992) and others translate *sākin* as "quiescent."

14. Of particular importance in this history is chapter 13 of the *Kitāb al-adwār* of Ṣafī al-Dīn al-Urmawī (d. 1294); see James Kippen's discussion of eighteenth-century Indo-Persian treatises in chapter 10 of this book. In Urmawī's codification of earlier theory, the primary constituents of rhythmic cycles are the heavy *sabab* (two attacks, represented as *ta<u>n</u>a*), light *sabab* (an attack on only the first of two morae, *tan*), *watad* (attacks on the first two of three morae, *tatan*), and small *fāṣila* (attacks on the first three of four morae, *ta<u>n</u>atan*) (Urmawī 2001, 173–74; see also Wright 1978, 216–18).

15. In our terminology (cf. Wright 1983, 445), these are the liquid and nasal consonants L, M, and Z; the three long vowels; and nine diphthongs formed of their combinations (*ay, ai, aw, yi, yā* or *ya, yū* or *yu, wi, wā* or *wa, wū* or *wu*) (Madian 1992, 274–75 n44).

16. *Maqṭa'* is Fārābī's term for syllable in the *Great Book on Music*, though in his *Commentary and Short Treatise on Aristotle's* De Interpretatione (1981, 41 n1) and in his short book on poetry (Fārābī 1959), he transliterated Greek *sullabē* directly into Arabic (Madian 1992, 50, 276).

17. Fārābī's use of the *point* metaphor in rhythmic theory is based on the discussion of time in the fourth book of Aristotle's *Physics*. See the excellent summary by Daniel Heller-Roazen (2007, 52–53 and 307 n24): "All sensation occurs in time and, more precisely, at one time in particular—namely, 'now.' . . . Aristotle defines 'the now' (*to nun*) as the ultimate element of

time (*khronos*) and he characterizes it, in terms that recur throughout the history of philosophy as both a 'point' (*stigmē*) and a 'limit' (*horos*), conceivable in relation to both the line (*grammē*) of temporal succession and the circle (*sphaira*) of eternity." In Aristotle's *De anima*, a point "can be one or two by virtue of its position as a 'boundary' or 'limit' (*peras*)."

18. Fārābī's roster of distinctive attributes of tones was recapitulated and extended, presumably in the eleventh century, in the *Kitāb kamāl adab al-ghinā'* of al-Ḥasan al-Kātib (1975, 78–84, 124–125; French trans. by Amnon Shiloah, 1972, 121–131, 174–175). Sawa (1989, 98–102) reproduces the Arabic terms added by al-Kātib.

19. Karlheinz Stockhausen's distinction of *Zeitdauer* "duration" and *Einsatzabstand* "interval of entry" (1963 [1955]) may serve as a reminder that entries on many rhythmic levels (not merely on the three that Fārābī identified as varieties of *zamān*) may determine durations that become relevant as we experience subsequent events in a musical process.

20. See Sawa 2009, 263–302 and 339–409 for the relevant sections of the *Kitāb al-īqā'āt* and the *Kitāb iḥṣā' al-īqā'āt*, and Sawa 1989, 40–71 for a summary.

21. Fārābī's procedures for notating rhythmic cycles allow for representing a heavy attack with a long syllable (*maqṭā'*) such as *tan, tā, nan*, or *nā* (Sawa 2009, 260–61, 336–38). Explicit analogies between the constituents of rhythmic cycles and syllables are rare in rhythmic theory after Fārābī, and even where that analogy is made *tā* and *nā* are redundant. Azadehfar (2006, 49–113) provides good explanations of both systems as currently used by Persian musicians, many of whom do use *tan* and *nan* to represent the long syllables in poetic meters.

22. Recordings identified with AWM RL numbers are housed in the Harvard University Archive of World Music and can be accessed through website maintained by the Loeb Music Library for "The Stephen Blum Collection of Music from Iranian Khorasan" (http://nrs.harvard.edu/urn-3:hul.pos:MUS).

23. After the Revolution of 1979, *maqām* became the most frequently used alternative to *āhang* in most regions of Iran, and the number of proper names used by Khorasani *baxšis* seems to have increased. Ameneh Youssefzadeh, whose fieldwork in Khorasan began in 1987, found *baxšis* using those two terms, rather than *ṭarīqa, rāh, raqam*, or *jur*. Standardization of terminology is one consequence of official interest in the nation's regional musics (see Massoudieh 1992).

24. Eckhard Neubauer has discussed the early history of *ṭarīqa* as a technical term in Arabic writings on music theory (Neubauer 1994, 404–05; 1995–1996, 276–77 and 283–84; 1998b, 74–76). Shiloah (1972, 17–18) had earlier drawn attention to the term's focus on rhythm, which was not adequately recognized at the time he was writing. A few melodies called *ṭarīqa* are notated with durations in the final chapter of the *Kitāb al-adwār* by Ṣafī al-Dīn al-Urmawī (2001, 86–89, 186–90). Different manuscripts of the treatise have two, three, or four such melodies, with variants in notation that Wright (1978, 217–31) has transcribed. For examples of the term's uses in Persian music theory and poetry, see Setāyeshgar 1374-75, 2: 161–62.

25. For further discussion of rhythm in the practice of Khorasani baxšis, see Youssefzadeh 2002, 250–58; Blum 2006; Youssefzadeh 2010, 232–37; Rahāti 2012a, 49–55; and Youssefzadeh and Blum 2016. For further analysis of *Šāh Xaṭā'i* as performed by Khorasani baxšis, see Rahāti 2012b, 50–55 and Youssefzadeh 2002, 203–05, 224–26, 236–37.

26. Iran's "traditional music" is based on a repertory of units (*gušes*) organized into seven sequences called *dastgāh* "system," two of which have secondary sequences called *āvāz*. The full repertory of units, many of which are models allowing for considerable recomposition in performnce, has been known since sometime in the nineteenth century as the *radif* "row," versions of which differ according to instrument (or voice) and line of transmission (*revāyat*).

27. An alternative to this familiar reading of the *Masnavi*'s initial line is that of the Konya manuscript of 677 AH (facsimile in Rumi 1992 [1371]), adopted in Este'lāmi's edition (Rumi 1990) and Mojadeddi's English translation (2004): *Bešno* ***in*** *ney čun* ***šekāyat*** *mikonad / az jedā'i-hā* ***hekāyat*** *mikonad* "Hear *this* flute as a *complaint* it utters / of *separations* a tale it relates" (differences are indicated in bold) It dramatizes a rather different act of listening: on hearing a complaint, we infer a tale, rather than hearing a tale and interpreting it as a complaint. I prefer the former scenario as an entry into Rumi's world.

28. Wheeler Thackston's advice "to think of the [Persian] meters, without reference to the foot-divisions, as a set sequence" (1994, xx) is more relevant to meters with a variety of feet than to those like the eleven- or fifteen-syllable *ramal* in which one species of foot is continually renewed as the line proceeds.

29. Male pronouns are used here as women have not been active as *baxšis* of northeastern Iran (in contrast to neighboring Turkmenistan), with the partial exception of Golnabāt Moqimi (recorded on *Iran: Bardes du Khorassan*, OCORA C560136 [1998], track 4).

30. For more information on this important work and the question of its authorship, see Binesh and During 1989 and Khazrā'i 2012.

31. Tahmāsebi 1995 is an instruction manual on *javāb-e āvāz* for players of *tār* and *setār*, based on Massoudieh 1978. A recording of *Āvāz-e Abu'Aṭā* in which 'Ali Akbar Šahnāzi plays responses to the *āvāz* of the great singer Eqbāl Āḏar (c. 1869–1973?) is readily available online (*iranicaonline.org*, "music sample" under the entry "Eqbāl Āḏar"). Any recording of Persian traditional music that features a vocalist will include *javāb-e āvāz*. For exceptionally beautiful exchanges between two long-time friends, listen to the performance in the dastgāh of *Rāst-Panjgāh* on the *Anthology of Persian Music, 1930–1990* (details under "Recorded Sources").

32. *Naqqāl* comes from the same root as two terms mentioned earlier in discussing Fārābi's rhythmics; *nuqla* "progression" and *intiqāl* "passage." For further information about *naqqāls*, see the notes to two CDs listed under "Recorded Sources": *Naqqāli in Northern Khorasan* and *Shāhnāmeh-khāni in Iranian folk music*.

33. Differences between genres of praise and of lament remain just as central to Iranian conceptions of the ethics of vocal action at present as before the 1979 Revolution. I regard the configuration of those differences as a variant of the longstanding polarity between "strong" and "soft" genres in Arabic and Persian theory (see Blum 2013, 107–10 and 113–14).

34. Elsewhere in this volume, Widdess speaks of *schemes* of greater dimensions than the "*template* or *scheme*" that Yāvari adopted for each hemistich in his performance of *Šāh Nāma* verses (which might also be termed a *schema*). In studies of sung verse, I tend to reserve *template* for schemes of relatively short duration (as in Blum 2006, 41); I would not apply that restriction to *scheme*.

35. Only one of the five singers included on the CD *Naqqāli in Northern Khorāsān* was a *morshed* in the sense described here, and the track list (prepared and published without my approval) anachronistically applies that term to the others. Three of the singers followed the profession of *naqqāli*, and the fourth was an elderly villager, ailing and unemployed at the time of the recording.

36. For excellent recordings of *Šāh-nāma* verses as sung in other regions of Iran, listen to *Shāhnāmeh-khāni in Iranian Folk Music* (details under "Recorded Sources").

37. Lloyd Miller, who worked closely with Safvat, lists the meters of all the verses sung by Maḥmud Karimi in his recording of the vocal *radif* (Miller 1999, 239–51). Students new to the subject should find Miller's list helpful in recognizing ways that vocalists "conceal" poetic

meters as they work with Massoudieh's transcriptions of the Karimi recording (Massoudieh 1978 and 1997).

38. For example, Laudan Nooshin's monograph on *Iranian Classical Music: The Discourses and Practice on Creativity* (2015) has very little to say about prosody or rhythm more generally.

39. An extended sample of Borumand's teaching is available on a set of four CDs, *Descriptive Analysis of the dastgāh of Māhur by Ostād Nurali Borumand* (see list of "Recorded Sources"). In demonstrating the guše *Azarbāyjāni*, for example, Borumand sang a verse from one of the religious dramas called *ta'ziye* to a tune included in that guše (disc 2, track 2, 1:49-2:34).

40. "De nos jours, les musicians iraniens appellent musique rythmique des pièces construites sur la succession en mesures égales et donc susceptibles d'être accompagnées par une percussion. . . . La majeure partie de la musique persane, ne suivant pas cette règle, est donc considérée comme non rythmée, bien qu'elle porte en elle un rythme."

41. In an excellent recent monograph, Owen Wright (2009, 36) posed the question "is unmetred music really unmetred?" noting "the pervasive complicating factor (not least because of the terminological overlap) of poetic metre." He acknowledged, as many have, that "the metrical structure of the verse will have an effect on the rhythmical structure of the melody," a general point that should inspire specific studies of those effects.

42. Talā'i's analytic notation of the *radif* was published in an English edition (Talā'i 2000) that prints the analytic remarks separately from the musical notation. In the 2016 Persian publication, the analytic remarks are significantly expanded and are printed alongside the notations to which they refer. In both publications, related segments of each *guše* are aligned so as to display their relationships to one another, as well as to a poetic meter, where relevant.

43. Azadehfar (2006, 177–87) uses the term "stretchable or elastic metre" in a somewhat more restricted sense than Talā'i, placing it between "fixed metre" and "free metre" in order to assign each *guše* to one of the three categories. Talā'i's "flexible rhythm" invites attention to changes within a *guše*, which are extremely significant in performances of Persian traditional music.

44. Their work should serve to correct errors in the publications of non-Iranians like myself, who lacked sufficient opportunities to attain the necessary competencies.

RECORDED SOURCES

Adham-e divāne ("Crazy Adham"), narrative (*dāstān*) performed in Persian prose and Khorasani Turkish by Moḥammad Ḥoseyn Yegāne (d. 1992), voice and *dotār*, recorded by Ameneh Youssefzadeh (Audio 3.2 ▶).

Anthology of Persian Music, 1930–1990. CD included with book *The Art of Persian Music*. Washington, DC: Mage Publishers, 1991, track 11, *Rāst-Panjgāh*, performed by Hātam 'Askari (b. 1933), voice and Dariush Safvat (1922–2013), *setār*.

Descriptive Analysis of the Dastgāh of Māhur by Ostād Nurali Borumand. Recordings and interview by Hormoz Farhat. Tehran: Māhur, 2005 (M.CD-176). Four CDs with notes (Persian and English) by Hooman Asadi.

Ğazal, "Bar xiz bedeh jām če jā-ye soxan ast," performed in the āvāz of *Abu'Aṭā* by Eqbāl Ādar (c. 1869–1973?), voice, and 'Ali Akbar Šahnāzi (1897–1984), *tār*. Music sample attached to entry "Eqbāl Ādar," iranicaonline.org.

Iran: Bardes du Khorassan. Recordings and notes (French and English) by Ameneh Youssefzadeh. Paris: OCORA, 1998 (C560136), track 4, "Sakine," performed by Golnabāt 'Aṭā'i, voice and *dotār*.

Music from North of Khorassan: Maestro Mohammad Hossein Yeganeh, Dotar and Vocals. Tehran: Anjoman-e Musiqi-ye Irān, 1999 [1378] (ANJ-008), track 4, *Šāh Khaṭā'i, laḥn-e digar* ["*Šāh Khaṭā'i*, another melody"] (Audio 3.1 ▶).

Naqqāli in Northern Khorāsān. Recordings and notes (Persian and English) by Stephen Blum. Tehran: Māhur, 2007 (M.CD-227, Regional Music of Iran, 19): Track 2, Verses from the story of Rostam and Sohrāb, sung by Ḥasan Salaḥšur (Audio 3.9 ▶). Track 4, Verses from the story of Rostam and Esfandiyār, sung by Ḥāj Ḥoseyn Xān Yāvari, (Audio 3.6 ▶). Track 6, Fable from the *Bustān* of Sa'di, sung by Ṣādeq 'Ali Šāh (Audio 3.7a ▶).

Shāhnāmeh-khāni in Iranian folk music. Recordings (made in 1997) and notes (Persian and English) by Moḥammad Rezā Darviši. Tehran: Māhur, 2014 (M.CD-391, Regional Music of Iran, 46).

The Stephen Blum Collection of Music from Iranian Khorasan. Recordings made in 1968–1969, 1972, 1995. Available on a website maintained by the Loeb Music Library of Harvard University, https://library.harvard.edu/collections/stephen-blum-collection-music-iranian-Khorasan. RL 16211, Fable from the *Bustān* of Sa'di, sung by Ṣādeq 'Ali Šāh (Audio 3.7a ▶). RL 16223 (s. B), *moṣibat* on the death of Imām Rezā, sung by Moḥammad Ḥasan Naqqāl. RL 16225, Fable from the *Bustān* of Sa'di, sung by Moḥammad Ḥasan Naqqāl (Audio 3.7b ▶). RL 16243, Conversation with Moxtār Zambilbāf. RL 16245, *Šāh Esmā'il*, performed by Moxtār Zambilbāf, voice and *dotār* (Audio 3.4, 3.5 ▶). RL 16251, Conversation with Moḥammad Ilxāniān.

Vocal Radif of Persian Classical Music, 5, Navā & Rāst Panjgāh. Maḥmud Karimi, *voice*. Tehran: Māhur, 2003 (M.CD-129), track 28, *Šāh Khaṭā'i* (Audio 3.3 ▶).

4

An Approach to Musical Rhythm in Agbadza

David Locke

THIS CHAPTER ADDRESSES the subject of musical rhythm in Agbadza, a type of performance art of the Ewe-speaking people of West Africa (Ghana/Togo), which is profoundly shaped by an ostinato bell part that has become an icon of West African culture (see Figure 4.1). My main argument is that Agbadza's rhythm, emerging from the interaction of many different musical factors, is resistant to one-dimensional interpretation, and compliant to dynamic ways of listening.[1]

Traditionally performed at life-cycle rituals associated with death, Agbadza's expressive means are dance, vocal music, and drum-ensemble music. The instrumental music of Agbadza features musical interactions based on precomposed implicit Ewe-language texts between lead drum (*sogo*) and response drum (*kidi*). Vocal music consists of many different Agbadza songs, each with a poetic lyric that is set to a tune and arranged for call-and-response between lead singer and choral group. The specific music under discussion here is a recorded performance of Agbadza by Gideon Foli Alorwoyie and the Afrikania Cultural Troupe of Anlo-Afiadenyigba, Ghana. This recording of twenty-five "items" of Agbadza music emphasizes Alorwoyie's creative juxtaposition of song and drum materials that he chose from the inherited tradition. In each item of vocal/instrumental music, described in the next paragraph, Alorwoyie paired singing with drumming on the basis of the meaning of a song's lyrics and the meaning of the drum language.[2]

There is no handy term in English that denotes the fusion of vocal and instrumental music in Agbadza. In the online monograph *Agbadza: The Critical Edition*,[3] I use the word "item" to subsume both components and gave each item a proper name based on the associated song lyrics.[4] Each item of Agbadza music is extensively documented with an audio file, complete note-for-note transcription in staff notation, interview with Alorwoyie about the meaning of the drum language and song lyric, and other more detailed information. In this chapter an "item" of Agbadza refers to the music itself as well as the documentation in the online monograph. The full list of items with links to constituent documents and recordings can be accessed at http://sites.tufts.edu/davidlocke/agbadza-items. This chapter draws on select items and their associated recordings and figures. Here, each audio recording is numbered according to the item number, so for instance item 4 corresponds to Audio 4.4 ▶, Item 5 to Audio 4.5 ▶ and so forth. The recordings can be accessed according to this numbering system via this book's companion website. In addition I refer to lead sheets for songs 12, 13 and 20. These should be accessed via the correspondingly numbered items in the online *Critical Edition*.

I begin with a review of the fundamental temporal framework, giving emphasis to (a) the impact of dance; (b) the importance of implicit, unsounded metric structure; and (c) the effect on accentuation and grouping of what we will call the "time parts" in the drum ensemble: bell, handclap, rattle, and support drum. The chapter then examines the response drum and lead drum parts with particular attention to issues of accentuation and motion. Next, I consider the rhythm of vocal music. Finally, I discuss the relationship of songs to the themes of lead and response drums. By integrating the performance modalities of dance, song, and drumming, the chapter hopes to make a contribution toward a holistic analysis of Agbadza's musical rhythm.

TEMPORAL FRAMEWORK

The Musical Impact of the Agbadza Dance

Writers on African music rightly have sought in dance clues to vexing analytic challenges in topics such as meter, grouping, accent, and form (see Agawu 2006).[5] The discussion to follow shows that key features of Agbadza's musical rhythm are indeed given tangible shape in dance figures and choreographic pattern. But in my view, the scholarly literature tends to dwell on rather elementary patterns of footwork, overlooking the multifaceted nature of dance and the capacity of dancers, like musicians, to play creatively with basic temporal structures (see Ladzekpo and Pantaleoni 1970).[6] To illustrate the capacity of dance to inform the analysis of musical rhythm, I begin with a detailed discussion of *dzimeɣe*, the basic Agbadza dance (lit. "dance of the middle-of-the-back").[7]

The Agbadza dance movement, centered in a quick contraction-expansion torso movement, marks elapsing musical time with brief units (beats). The temporal proportions are 2:1; that is, the expansion is twice as long as the contraction (see Figure 4.1). In other words, the dance shapes the flow of time into a series of ternary beats that most scholars have notated with dotted quarter-notes (three pulses per beat). The dance maps four beats into the time span of the bell phrase, enabling us to say that Agbadza is "in four" with time flowing ONE-two-three, TWO-two three,

THREE-two-three, FOUR-two-three. The equation 4 x 3 = 12 describes Agbadza's basic musical period: four beats each containing three faster pulses. In the written analysis that follows, the set of three pulses within each of the four ternary beats will be given as 1.1, 1.2, 1.2, 2.1, 2.2, 2.3, and so on. In other words, the marking 4.2 indicates the second twelve-pulse (time-point) within the fourth beat. Similar marking will designate the two fast pulses within the six-feel beats (quarters) and the four fast pulses within three-beats (half-notes). Two-step footwork repeats on each side of the body's midline: (1) touch with the right, (2) step on the right, (3) touch with the left, (4) step on the left.[8] An upward foot gesture and bodily contraction invariably precedes the foot going down and the body expanding out from its center core.

The dance confers qualitatively different feelings (accents) to the three pulses within each unit of movement, as well as provides a pervasive sense of beat-to-beat motion.[9] Normally expansion expends energy while contraction is a moment of recovery, although this kinesthetic accentual pattern can be inverted for artistic effect. Within each contraction-expansion dance unit, the torso's powerful "pop" achieves musical prominence by its longer duration (agogic accent) and its coincidence with the onset of the count (commetric accent) (see Kolinksi 1973). In contrast, the snapping torso "tuck" has the twin feeling of (a) coming just before an onbeat (contra-metric accent) but also (b) leading toward the subsequent "pop" (pickup). The second fast pulse within each count (beat zone) is inherently less prominent (unaccented). Shaped by this pickup-to-onbeat pattern in the dance, time in Agbadza flows in a lop-sided, short-long manner: "a-**1**-y, a-**2**-y, a-**3**-y, a-**4**-y" (the bold font notates metric accent).

For listeners attuned to the dance, each of the four counts within a cycle of the bell phrase feels unique. Count one is distinguished from the others as the first unit in the set (downbeat), count three is the midpoint (upbeat), and count four leads toward the beginning of the next cycle ("turnaround"). The second unit in the set of four units, which fills time between the downbeat and upbeat, is metrically weak like the unaccented second pulse (afterbeat) within each ternary beat.[10]

Patterns of foot movement and weight transference have musical significance not only for rhythmic grouping but also for patterns of accentuation and motion that follow on from it. Because the dance reflects the bilateral symmetry of the human body (right-right/left-left), the four counts separate into two pairs, (one-two) + (three-four), with emphasis on counts one and three (grouping accent). These two-beat sets establish a slow-paced half-note motion between the two halves of the bell cycle; the first half calls for response from the second half that follows (call-and-response). Antecedent-consequent progression occurs within each half-measure, as well, but at twice the speed: one toward two, and three toward four. Furthermore, since counts two and four (backbeats) bear the body's weight, they literally feel heavy in contrast to the lighter quality of the nonweight-bearing touches on counts one and three. From this perspective (dynamic accent), the pattern of accentuation is one-TWO-three-FOUR. We observe that backbeat accentuation, a well-known hallmark of black music, dualistically counters the grouping accents on beats one and three.

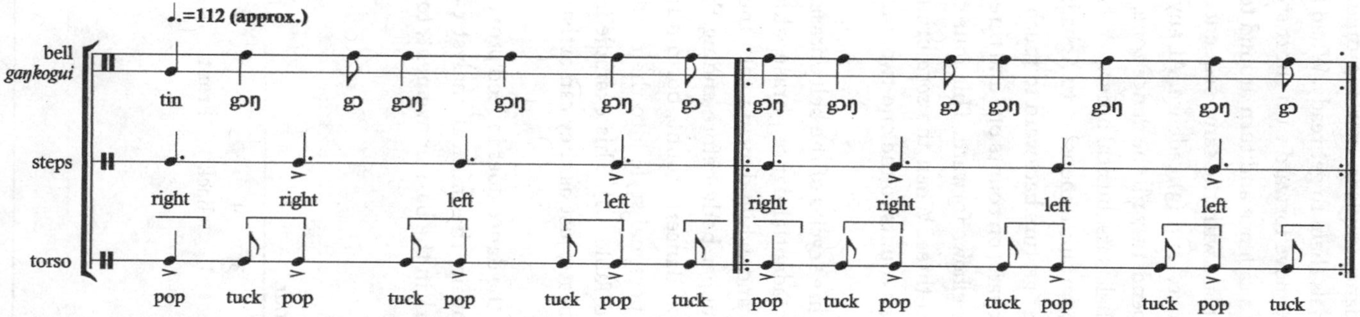

FIGURE 4.1 Rhythm of Agbadza dance movement.

The choreography of the dance adds to Agbadza's rhythmic foundation and musical form.[11] Sitting on the perimeter of the dance area, people rise to dance usually in small groups. At first they dance in place, marking time until the lead *sogo* drum plays a rolling passage that signals them to get ready. When the *sogo* sounds the drum language, the dancers gradually move forward with short steps. At the far side of the performance area they execute a cadence and turn around to face where they started. Then they dance back to their place with the same sequence, that is, (1) waiting step, (2) forward with the basic "move," and (3) cadence. At any point of time during an event many small groups independently fill the dance zone, giving the performance a decentralized appearance that belies its musical order.

The waiting step adds an important dimension to Agbadza's temporal framework. On counts two and four dancers gesture backward to touch the ground with one foot as they swing their elbows backward; on counts one and three they step in place on the active foot as they swing their elbows forward. This four-count waiting step shapes the flow of time four-one, two-three. When the *sogo* brings in the drum language, the dancers regroup the elapsing counts to the one-two, three-four pattern discussed earlier.

The cadence moves within three cycles of the bell phrase. Dancers tend to develop a personal trademark for the cadential dance phrase, although everyone does the basics—stop moving forward and, while dancing with the feet in place, gesture to both right and left with the upper body before ending the dance with back-front leaning (see Table 4.1; top row: dancers' count; bottom row: upper body gesture). Among the ways dancers put personal style into their cadence is to move at a rate of 6:4 to the basic counts (see Table 4.2). This example indicates that dancers can fluently change their flow of beats, just as they can artistically pattern their accentuation and grouping.

My point here is that while the dance does indeed provide important insight into core patterns in Agbadza's music, the musical analyst cannot rely upon one feature of dance, such as footwork in the basic movement, to resolve complex analytic

TABLE 4.1

Agbadza dance cadence "in four."

1	2	3	4	1	2	3	4	1	2	3	4	1
R	R	L	L	R	R	L	Back	Front	-	-	Back	Front

TABLE 4.2

Agbadza dance cadence "in six."

1	2	3	4	5	6	1	2	3	4	5	6	1	2	3	4	5	6	1
R		R	L		L	R		R	L		B	F					B	F

questions about temporal framework. The Agbadza dance shows that the "four-feel" is deeply engrained within Ewe music culture; a person enculturated to Ewe traditional culture will very likely know intuitively, or perhaps the better word is "feel," the musically correct placement of four onbeat moments within the music's temporal flow. But the dance also indicates that other recurring patterns of accentual marking also are explicitly present in performance (slower tempi in ratios of 1:2, 4:1, or 3:2 (cut time, in-one, and polymeter, respectively). I argue for the value of thinking of meter as a matrix of beats, but hierarchy is also present: if musicians need to identify one time-feel as most fundamental, it is without doubt the four-feel.[12] We may hypothesize that Agbadza's rhythmic sophistication depends upon a music culture in which competent performers and listeners easily locate and maintain the "four-feel groove."[13]

Hand Clapping and the Six-Feel

Far from being insignificant or incidental, handclapping is the main way that singers, dancers, and members of the audience actively participate in and contribute to the instrumental music of Agbadza. A defining feature of the Agbadza recorded by Alorwoyie is handclapping "in six" (see Figure 4.5). Given the importance of the four-feel groove (dotted quarter-notes), the claps (quarter-notes) have the wonderful musical effect of always bringing into sonic prominence the feeling of 6:4 (two sets of 3:2) within the time span of one bell cycle. In-six clapping suffuses the music with the temporal duality of three-in-the-time-of-two. The constant presence of 3:2 challenges music scholars who assert a monometric order to this kind of Ewe music (see Agawu 2006; Anku 2000; Burns 2010; 2012; Nzewi 1997).

Meter as a Matrix of 3:2 Beats

If the steadily recurring bell phrase suggests the idea of measure, and the unit of dance seems equivalent to the idea of metric beat, where should bar lines be drawn? The question can be reframed, "What does the idea of ONE mean in the cyclic context of Agbadza music?"[14] For now, we can answer, "ONE is a moment of both rhythmic closure and initiation." And, "ONE registers in musical consciousness as a moment of temporal orientation." But as I already have suggested in discussion of the dance and the handclap, the ternary-quadruple metric frame is only a single dimension among many that comprise the music's syntax.

Although the concepts of measure and beat find equivalents in Agbadza, meter needs to be understood within this context. Meter, as a theoretical concept and analytic tool, need not be universalized as a unitary concept. For most world musics, meter will refer to spans of musical time, patterns of accentuation, and qualities of temporal musical motion, but I argue here that each music culture, or even idiom of music, may have its own particular metric features. Certainly, meter as a heuristic concept for types of Western art music cannot be simply imposed upon other types of music without adjustments.[15]

This chapter regards meter as a matrix, that is, a multidimensional dynamic condition in which several beat streams (metric fields) coexist simultaneously (see Locke 2009). The metric matrix in Agbadza arises from the simultaneous interpretation of a span of time as having two equal parts and three equal parts. Action on the musical phenomenal "surface," so to speak, always can be felt "in two" and "in three" (see Jones 1954). Two sides of the same coin, the time-feels are inextricably intertwined and define each other.[16] We regard Agbadza's meter as an unsounded facet of structure; its reality is cognitive and kinesthetic—a matter of mind and body.

The 3:2 ratio occurs at different speeds—twice per bell phrase (quarters with dotted quarters, the 6/4 standard), four times per bell phrase (eights with dotted eighths; double time), and once per bell phrase (half-notes with dotted half-notes). In Agbadza, the ratio of 3:4, a derivative of 3:2, is less prominent but important nevertheless. The metric matrix is the interplay of streams of beats at four levels—four-feel beats, six-feel beats, three-feel beats, and eight-feel beats. I will term the twelve quick units within a cycle as "pulses," or "fast pulses," not beats.[17] Each four-feel beat contains three fast pulses (ternary morphology, dotted quarter-note); each six-feel beat contains two fast pulses (binary morphology, quarter-note); each three-feel beat contains four fast pulses (quaternary morphology, half-note); each eight-feel beat contains three super-fast pulses (ternary morphology, dotted eighth-notes).[18] I suggest that all time-feel layers in the metric matrix exist in a latent, implicit, and tacit dimension that is available to consciousness as a factor in a listener's perception.[19] The play between what we may call the music's surface and its "underneath" is crucial to Agbadza's music.[20]

In addition to their normal "onbeat" positions, the four different streams of beats in the matrix also have "displaced" or "offbeat" locations within the time span of the bell phrase (see Locke 1982). The durations of what I will refer to as "shifted beats" are identical to their unshifted counterparts but their onsets happen on different time-points within the twelve-pulse span of the bell cycle. Since 3:2 or 3:4 can occur between streams of beats in both normal and displaced positions, the metric matrix is deeply multidimensional. An important aspect of the expressive power of the musical surface, I argue, derives from the way its patterns of accentuation occur in relation to the implicit metric fields. It is as if the sonic designs in sounded events make reference to the various beat streams within the metric matrix. I argue that performers and listeners ("perceiving subjects," if you prefer) are aware in mind and body of the power of metric fields to confer musical meaning to what is heard and seen. The affect of the music derives much of its power from this dynamic relationship.

This chapter sidesteps the question, "How do they hear it?"[21] First, I emphasize the observable domain of musical action—what people do in performance rather than what they say in language about what they do. It is the work of intercultural scholarship to translate between cultures and between modalities of representation.[22] Second, my aim is to render musical sound into the graphic form of staff notation. Accordingly, the concept of metric matrix has heuristic value for finding order in Agbadza music; that is, it is a precondition for relevant notation and analysis. I argue the following proposition: In their onbeat and offbeat positions, beat streams interwoven in proportions of threes and twos provide a basis for organizing the aural and kinesthetic perception of Agbadza's music. The metric matrix, I posit, is a tool that directs attention to significant features in the music while also providing a theoretical basis to explain its syntax.

SUPPORTING INSTRUMENTS: TIME PARTS

The music of the drum ensemble is made from the simultaneous play of five instruments that exist in a texture we will term "polyrhythmic." Enculturated listeners expect Agbadza music to be a multipart texture; thus it seems reasonable to refer to "Agbadza's polyrhythm" as an ethnographically real musical phenomenon.[23]

Drum Language

The phrases of bell, handclap, rattle, and support drum create musical time in Agbadza. Vernacular texts for these phrases given by Alorwoyie establish Agbadza's context of origin—urgent action in military struggle: bell and rattle say that the group will meet the challenge, while support drum extols courage (see Table 4.3).

While language shapes the music of songs and lead-response drumming, texts do not precisely determine the musical phrases of the time parts. As evidence that its musical rhythm is not controlled by drum language, Alorwoyie gives the same language

TABLE 4.3

Supporting instruments: implicit Ewe texts.

	Implicit Ewe Text	*English Translation*
gaŋkogui bell		
• first time	Do mayi makpo teƒe mava mayi!	Get out and see for yourself.
• all other times	Mayi makpo teƒe mava mayi.	I will go to witness the thing and return.
axatsɛ rattle		
• first time	Tsia mayi makpo teƒe mava mayi!	Get up quickly and see for yourself.
• all other times	Mayi makpo teƒe mava mayi.	I will go to witness the thing and return.
kagaŋu support drum	Míayi ava yia afia	We shall go and show (our bravery).

for the high-pitched support drum in both Agbadza and Atsiagbekor even though the details of the part are different (see Locke 1978). The drum language of the time parts *does* shed light on issues of phrase shape and meter, however.

Bell

The bell phrase is both an audible part of the music and an abstract musical idea that is a source of creativity for composers and performers. Even if it is not actually being played, the bell theme serves as the players' basis for musical orientation and as a stimulus for musical ideas.[24] The musical force of the bell phrase derives both from its sequence of time values and from its relationships to beats in the metric matrix. To employ a spatial analogy, the bell phrase exists in horizontal space as a musical line and vertical space as the intersection of that line with the layers of beats in their 3:2 proportions. Motion in the bell part is eternally circular but also a linear experience in elapsing time. For any other part in Agbadza music, musical interactions with notes in the bell phrase are a significant feature of accentuation. A note may be offbeat in relation to a layer of beats in the metric matrix but in unison with bell strokes (offbeat but onbell, so to speak). This interplay of accents is among the multidimensional aspects of the syntax of Agbadza music.

The bell's seven strokes mark proportions of time in a distinctive sequence—long-long-short-long-long-long-short—that may be understood additively as 12 = 2+2+1+2+2+2+1. One of these strokes, which we shall number as stroke one, may be played on the larger of the instrument's two bells, its lower pitch marking the special time-point in the circling rhythm: ONE. The bell phrase begins either on stroke one or on stroke two. If the bell phrase is conceived to begin on stroke one, notes within the phrase move toward a goal moment on stroke six, with stroke seven functioning as a pickup to the ONE of the next cycle (see Lehmann 2002). If the bell phrase is conceived to begin on stroke two, notes within the phrase move toward stroke one like an arrow toward its target. Since this is the ONE of the next measure, we may call this "phrasing forward over the bar line." Like the bell, many musical phrases in Agbadza often begin in a musically unresolved condition and move toward tonal and rhythmic resolution at their conclusion.

The bell phrase functions as an interface to the metric matrix, a go-between that connects explicit and implicit dimensions of the music.[25] Just as in geometry where two points define a line, two bell strokes accentuate a flow of beats. In this way, the bell phrase alludes to the tacit matrix of beats in their onbeat and offbeat positions. For example, bell-strokes six and one mark four-feel beats four and one, while bell strokes one to three and four to seven mark onbeat and upbeat positions of the six feel. As suggested by the design of the dance and the handclap part, the resultant rhythm of the bell with the four-feel beats and the six-feel beats is second nature to an adept Ewe musician (see Figure 4.2). As in any figure-ground perception, a listener's experience of the rhythmic motion of the bell phrase differs depending on the time-feel (or absence of time-feel in favor of an unmarked flow of elapsing time).

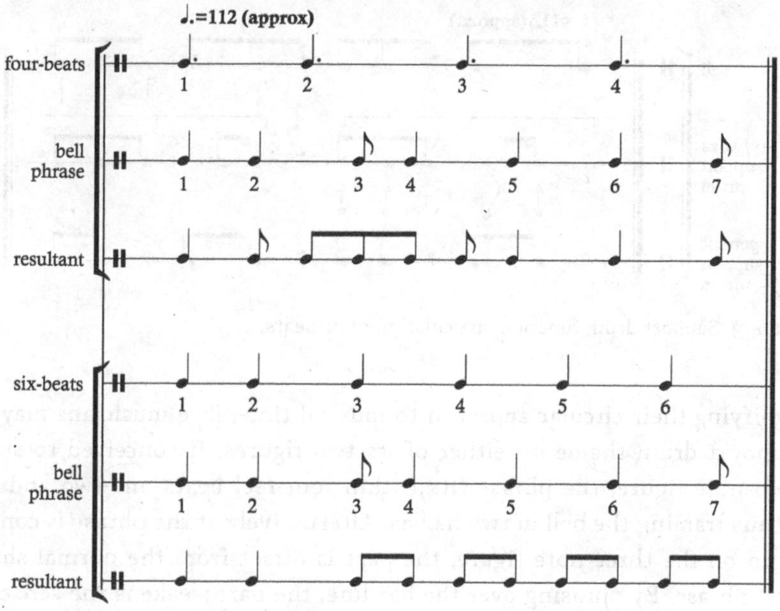

FIGURE 4.2 Resultant rhythm of bell phrase with four-feel and six-feel beats.

Rattle

The spare texture of the bell phrase enables its rhythmic design to morph in relationship with the beat frameworks of the metric matrix and in polyrhythm with other parts. The dense texture of rattle part, on the other hand, makes it less amenable to what might be called "rhythmic shape-shifting." Coming at the end of the phrase, the rattle's only long tone reinforces the impression that the bell phrase starts on stroke two and moves to conclusion on stroke one. Hands move in a distinctive kinesthetic pattern: downstrokes are in unison with the bell, while upstrokes occur between bell strokes in line with the onbeat six-feel.

Support Drum

Two long thin sticks hit flat on the drumskin, giving the high-pitched support drum crisp articulation and a dry timbre that cuts through the ensemble's overall sound. Rhythmically, the theme contrasts intensely with the other drum parts and the singing. In Ewe dance-drumming as a whole, ensemble textures usually include an instrument whose main musical function is to mark offbeats within each four-feel beat. The phrase in Agbadza accomplishes this essential offbeating function in a rather complex way (see Figure 4.3).

The support drum part exerts manifold impact on the overall music of Agbadza. We offer the following observations to exemplify the way one short motive shapes the music's sounded texture and alludes to its silent but lively "underneath."

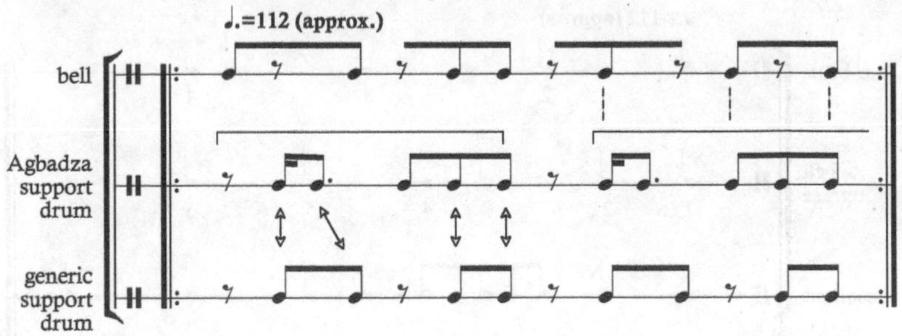

FIGURE 4.3 Support drum function: articulation of offbeats.

Exemplifying their circular approach to musical time, Ewe musicians may begin the support drum theme on either of its two figures. If conceived to start on the two-note figure, the phrase fits within four-feel beats one-two and three-four, thus framing the bell in two halves. Alternatively, if the phrase is conceived to begin on the three-note figure, the part is offset from the normal shape of the bell phrase. By phrasing over the bar line, the part weakens the sense of arrival inherent to ONE and keeps the music moving forward on its circular path. First strokes in the three-note figures match four-feel beats two and four, creating backbeat accentuation. Over the first half of the bell, drum's strokes tend to be offset from the bell strokes; over the second half of the bell the two parts share moments in unison. Because each of the two iterations of the support-drum phrase has a distinct polyrhythm with bell, the two parts continuously refresh each other.

Strokes in the support-drum phrase sound out many of the beats in the implicit metric matrix (see Figure 4.4). The three-note figure flows with the twelve pulses, thus bringing that implicit timing referent into explicit sonic reality. The kinesthetic pattern of the strong hand steadily accentuates the upbeat six-feel. From an "in four" perspective, the part articulates the second time-point within every four-feel beat; that is, it accentuates four-feel beats displaced by one eighth-note. Within four-feel beats one and three, the timing of the second onset in the two-note figures brings the eight-feel perspective into sonic reality.

Musical Impact of Drum Language of the Time Parts

Both bell and rattle phrases share the same text, confirming their close musical affinity. The drum language for the bell confirms its two phrasing shapes: starting either on stroke one or stroke two. When Alorwoyie starts the bell and rattle parts, he usually begins with a stroke on time-point 1.1, a style explained by the implicit text (see Figure 4.5). The drum language of the first notes—the bell's "do" and the rattle's "tsia"—change the sentence to a command: "Get up!" and "Go quickly!" The text of subsequent passes through the temporal cycle is phrased to end on time-point 1.1, which accords

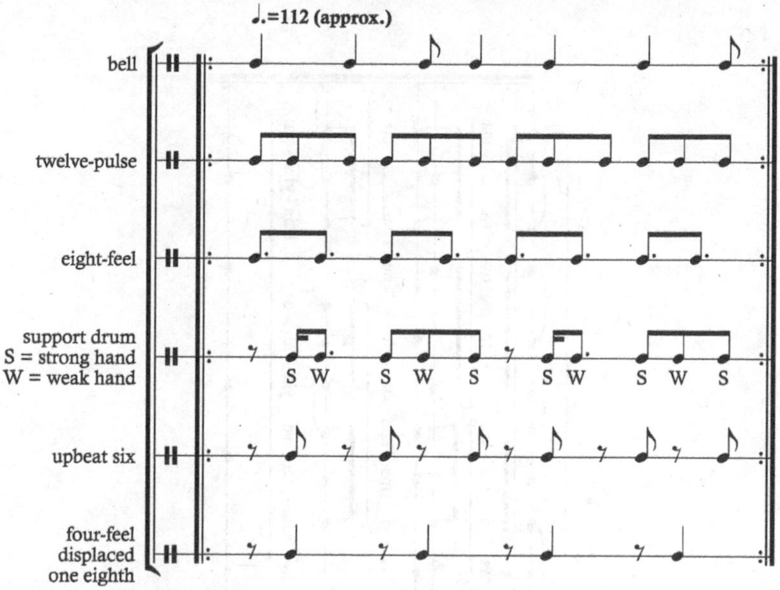

FIGURE 4.4 Support drum phrase: accentuation in the metric matrix.

with our musical analysis of these parts. Because the text includes syllables that coincide with the unsounded four-feel beats two and three but fails to mark time-point 4.2, which coincides with the sixth six-feel beat, the drum language corroborates the primacy of the four-feel groove.

LEAD AND RESPONSE DRUMS

Although musical logic might dictate that we discuss the lead part before the response part, analysis of response themes helps clarify the musical parameters within which the lead drum's part functions. Thus, I will begin with the response and follow with the lead.

Response Drum

The themes played on *kidi*, the medium-pitched response drum, serve two main functions in performance: (1) answering the lead drum's calls, and (2) contributing a musical component to the polyrhythmic texture of Agbadza's drum ensemble music. Response drum phrases are built with the homogeneous time value of the twelve fast pulses; its steady articulation makes response themes especially susceptible to shape shifting between the four-feel and the six-feel. Response drum phrases use only two timbres, resonant bounce strokes and dampened press strokes; bounce strokes highlight moments within the flow of musical

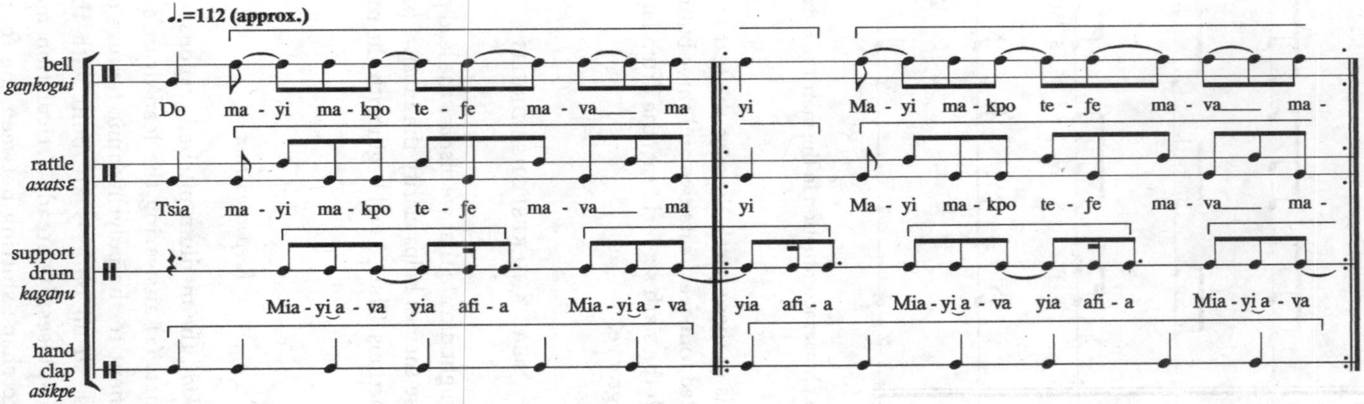

FIGURE 4.5 Music setting of drum language of the time parts.

time, creating points of accent that energize the other components of Agbadza's overall music rhythm.

Response Drum Themes

Variety is the striking characteristic of the twenty-one different response-drum themes in Alorwoyie's Agbadza project (see Figure 4.6). Each phrase has a distinctive musical character that has the potential to recast a listener's perception of other parts as well as the overall polyrhythmic composite. I will address the following features: the duration and placement of a response phrase on the bell phrase (alignment), design of bounce strokes and press strokes (morphology), stroke-for-stroke interaction with the bell (polyrhythm), and pattern of onbeat-offbeat accentuation (displacement, polymeter).

Alignment within Bell Cycle

Alignment with bell is a crucial feature of a response drum theme. Phrase duration has impact upon the reciprocal influence that bell and response drum cast upon each other. In response phrases shorter than the bell (three- or six-pulse spans), bounces and presses fit with different bell notes in each repetition within the cycle. In long twenty-four-pulse phrases, on the other hand, the bell phrase stays steady over two cycles as the drum strokes change their relationship to the bell's notes. Six-pulse response phrases can make it seem like the bell is playing two different six-pulse patterns, while a phrase that stretches over two bell phrases can reshape the bell into one twenty-four-pulse phrase. The unique twenty-four-pulse theme of item 25 (Audio 4.25 ▶) can reshape a listener's perception of the twelve-pulse bell pattern into three eight-pulse motives.

A response theme's entry into the polyrhythmic texture is relevantly described by the relationship of its first bounce stroke to three factors: bell strokes, twelve-pulses, and four-feel beats. We observe response-drum themes in Alorwoyie's Agbadza project that begin on every bell stroke and on every twelve-pulse except pulse four (beat 2.1). Phrases are launched from all beat zones with slight preference for beat four.[26] Seven *kidi* phrases begin in phase with the bell part on stroke two, but the others are out of phase with that very important "shape" of the bell phrase. Strikingly, two phrases begin with a highly syncopated solitary bounce on pulse twelve that highlights bell stroke seven, but only one phrase starts on ONE.

Internal Design and Polyrhythm with Bell

The pattern of its bounce and press strokes (timbral morphology) shapes the rhythmic line of a response drum theme.[27] Table 4.4 displays timbral patterns as an equation of bounces + presses whose total equals the duration of the phrase. As was true of their duration and alignment, variety once again is the outstanding feature of the response drum phrases in Agbadza. The only patterns that occur more than once are 6=3+3 and 12=(2+3)+(2+5).

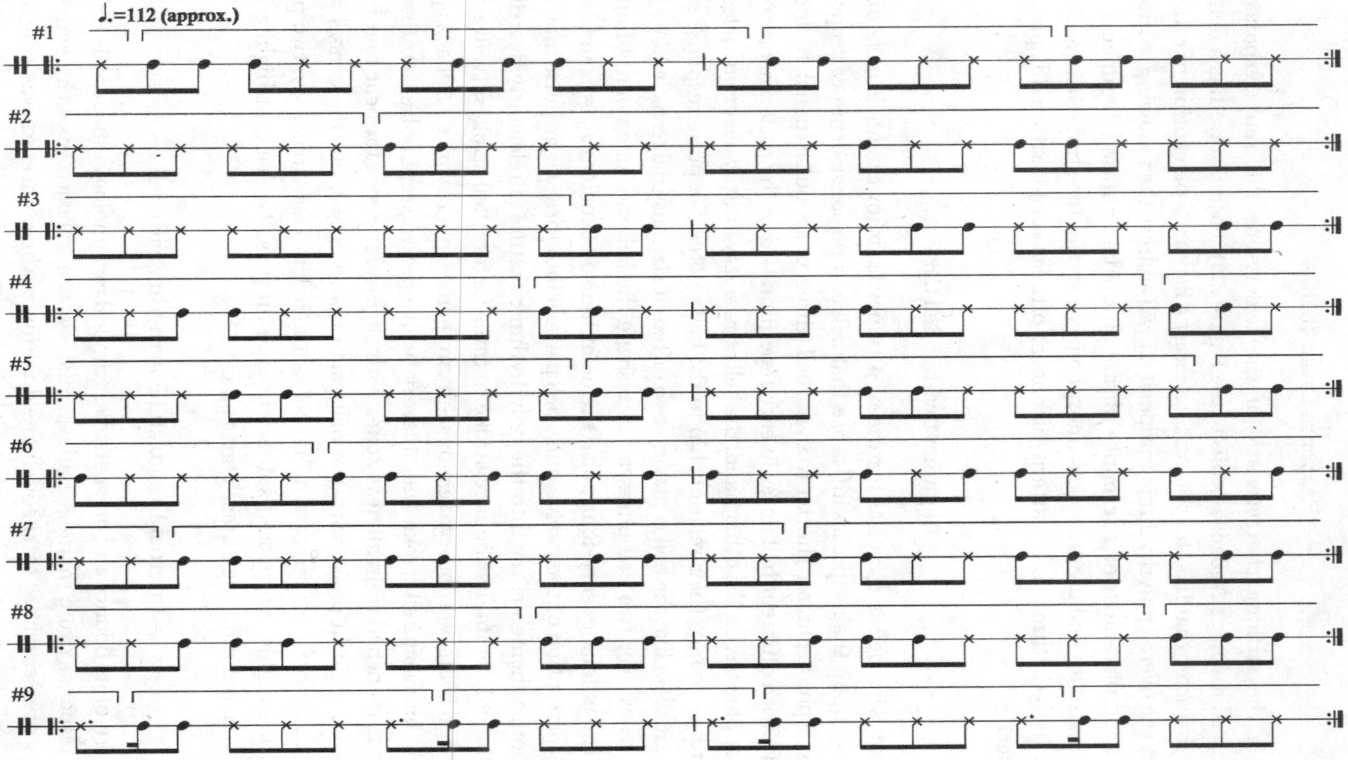

FIGURE 4.6 Response drum themes for items 1–25.

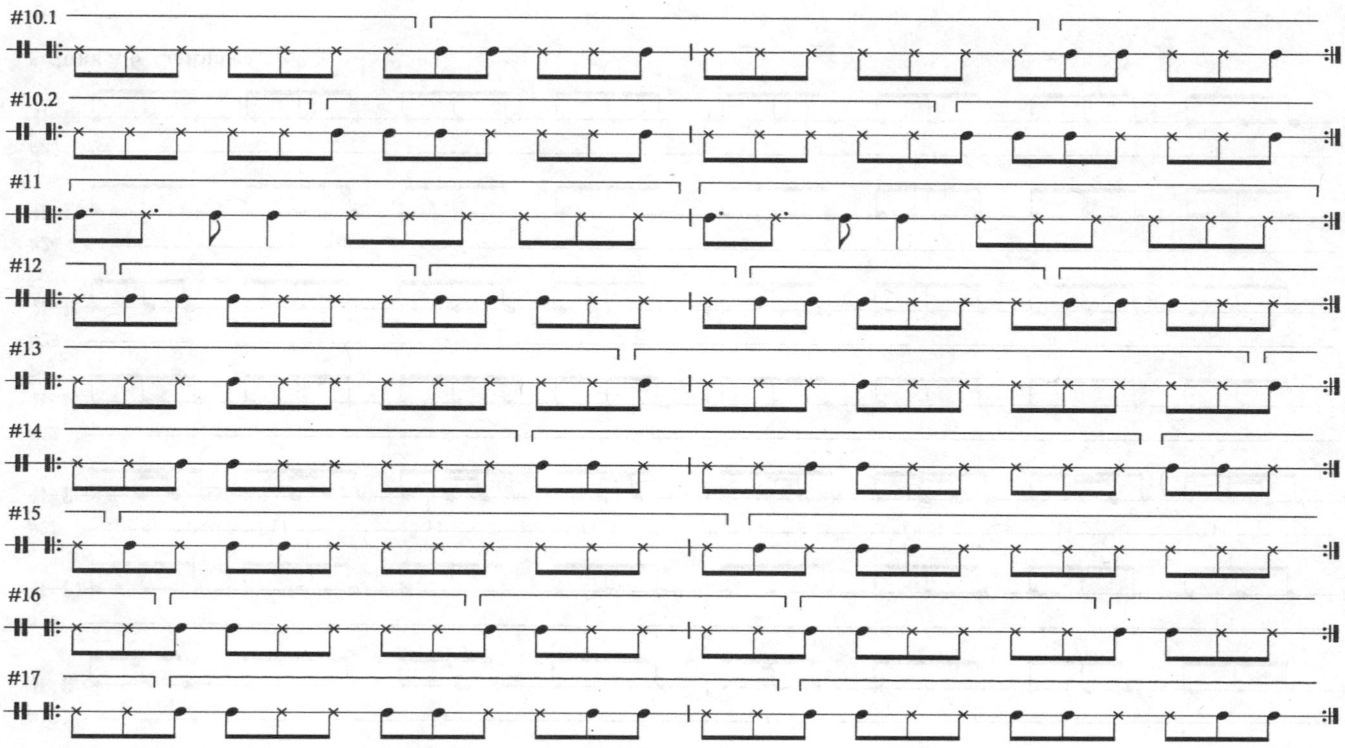

FIGURE 4.6 Continued

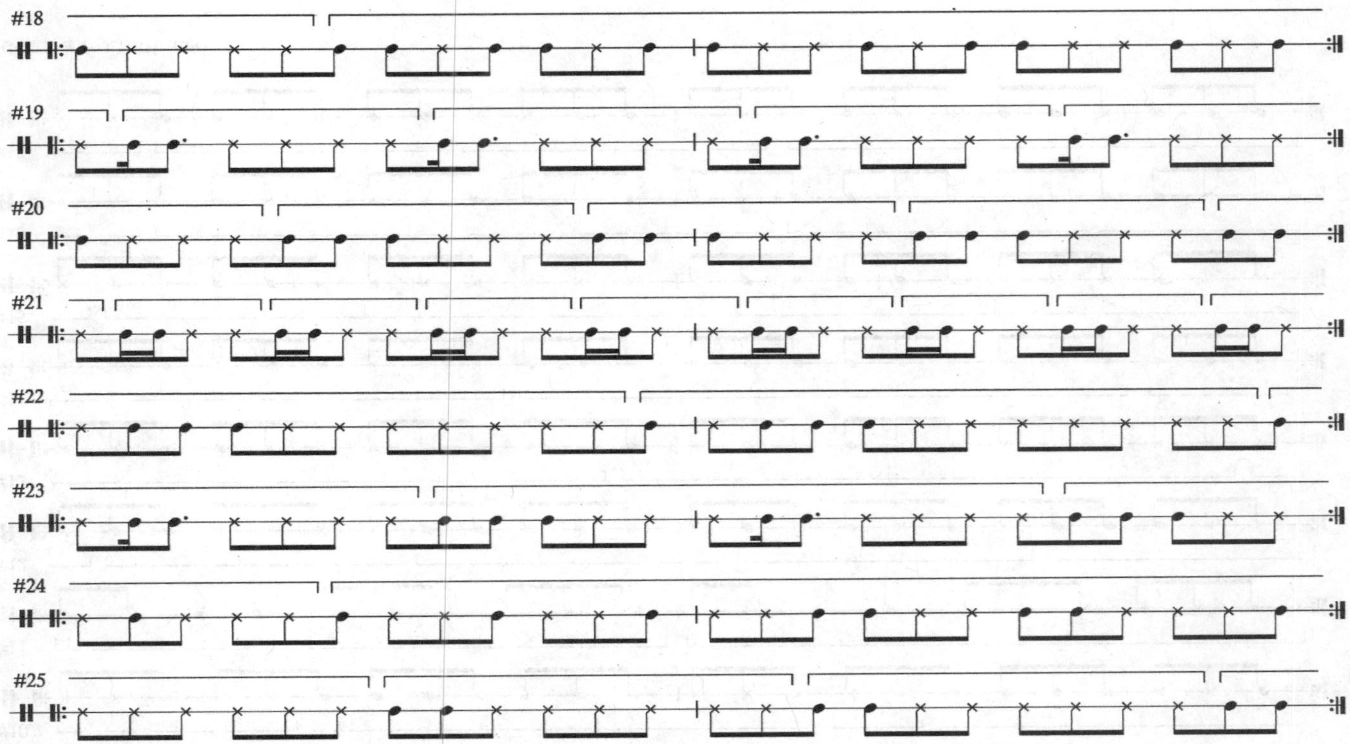

FIGURE 4.6 Continued

TABLE 4.4

Agbadza kidi phrases for items 1–25: patterns of bounce and press strokes.

#	duration	bounce+press
1	6=	3+3
2	24=	(2+7)+(1+2)+(2+10)
3	24=	(2+4)+(2+4)+(2+10)
4	12=	(2+3)+(2+5)
5	12=	(2+3)+(2+5)
6	24=	(2+1)+(2+1)+(2+4)+(1+1)+(2+2)+(1+1)+(2+4)
7	12=	(2+2)+ (2+2)+(2+2)
8	12=	(3+2)+(3+4)
9	6=	1+5
10.1	12=	(2+2)+(1+7)
10.2	12=	(3+3)+(1+5)
11	12=	(1+2)+(2+6)
13	12=	(1+3)+(1+7)
14	12=	(2+3)+(2+5)
15	12=	(1+1)+(2+8)
16	6=	2+4
20	6=	3+3
21	3=	1+2
22	12=	(1+1)+(3+7)
23	12=	(3+3)+(2+4)
24	24=	(1+2)+(1+2)+(1+2)+(2+2)+(2+3)+(1+1)+(1+3)
25	8=	2+6

Bounce strokes of the response drum weave in and around strokes on the bell, creating timing relationships of coming before, coming after, or matching exactly. These temporal interactions are essential to Agbadza's polyrhythmic experience. Unison between tones of response drum and bell creates a moment of weight or accentuation in the music's overall texture but an offset relationship also can produce a powerful effect. Since each bell stroke has its own special quality, the musical flavor of a response drum-bell duet will be affected by the particular bell strokes involved, as well. In theme #22, for example, a solitary bounce lands on pulse twelve (see Figure 4.6). While the bell part treats this moment as a pickup to ONE, it functions as an offbeat accent on the third time-point of four-feel beat four for the response drum. Polyrhythmic relationships affect each of the next three bounce strokes: the first fills the gap between bell strokes one-two, the second matches bell stroke two, and the third is the onbeat goal moment in the figure (time-point 2.1). Every response drum rhythm participates in this sort of dynamic interaction with the other components of the performance.

Rhythmic Motion and Accentuation

Variety in types of rhythmic motion within response drum themes and the widespread distribution of cadential moments in response drum themes over the span of the bell phrase maintains the music's forward drive.[28] Given my suggestion for the multideterminant nature of meter in Agbadza, I posit that no phrase will have just one pattern of accentuation. At minimum, each response drum phrase can be analyzed in terms of how it works with bell phrase and the four-feel and six-feel beats in their onbeat and displaced positions; as I will discuss, offbeat features in one time feel may be onbeat in other time feel. For example, theme #24 has nine bounce strokes distributed over twenty-four pulses, that is, the span of two bell phrases (see Figure 4.7). In measure 1, bounces one, two, and three accentuate third fast pulses within four-feel beats two, three, and four. In measure 2, bounce four also comes on a third fast pulse but instead of functioning as another offbeat accent, it serves as a pickup to bounce five that is right on the second four-feel beat. Bounces six-seven repeat the two-note figure idea sounded by bounces four-five, but shift its metric position. In the phrase's final rhythmic gesture, bounce eight returns to the idea of third fast-pulse timing that characterized measure 1; stroke nine, however, confounds expectations with a delayed landing on an afterbeat (1.2). Strokes eight and nine dramatically surround ONE, imparting a highly offbeat, syncopated, and unresolved feeling to the phrase. Not only does the theme's pattern of onbeats and offbeats make a well-designed rhythmic line, the artful arrangement of unisons and offsets between bell strokes and response-drum bounces give the theme depth. My analysis argues that relationships to the four-feel beats and the bell phrase are a vital aspect of the musical personality of every response drum phrase.

From the six-feel perspective, three types of accentuation occur with equal frequency: (1) consistent accentuation of onbeats, (2) consistent accentuation of upbeats, and (3) movement between onbeat and upbeat accentuation. Consistent accentuation makes a response drum phrase feel rhythmically homogeneous and unified. Conversely, phrases like the *kidi* part in item 24 (Audio 4.24 ▶) that have both onbeat and upbeat accentuation have an elusive, slippery rhythmic quality (see Figure 4.7). Finally, response drum phrases may strongly accentuate 3:4 (half-notes: dotted quarters) through bounce-press patterns based on some variety of the formula 12 = 4 + 8 (see items 7, 10.1, 12, and 13; Audio 4.7, 10.1, 12, 13 ▶).

Lead Drum

Musical Role

The low-pitched *sogo* drum is the leader of the drum ensemble. Its main musical functions are (1) to state drum language compositions, (2) to improvise melodic-rhythmic lines that connect with the medium-pitched *kidi* response drum and make exciting interaction with the other instrumental parts in the ensemble, and (3) to provide a musical line that moves in tandem with the song melody. In full performance with

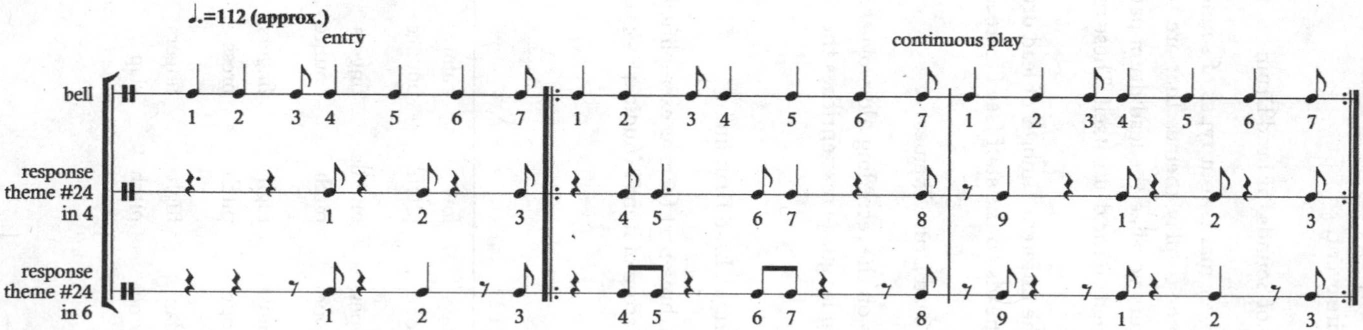

FIGURE 4.7 Response theme, item 24: motion and accentuation "in four" and "in six."

dance, the lead drummer keeps close eye on the dance space, using rolling figures to cue dancers to begin the Agbadza step and controlling his musical energy to maintain the overall momentum of the entire event.

Palette of Sounds for Lead Drum

With two bare hands, the *sogo* player makes four types of sound (see Table 4.5). This tonal palette enables the drummer to play themes that are tonally, timbrally, and rhythmically varied. Ewe drummers vocalize the lead drum part using vocables that represent the types of strokes played on the drum itself. These recitations are a system of oral notation.

Staff notation can represent the different timbres of lead drum strokes by type of notehead and by location of noteheads on the staff (see Figure 4.8).

Lead Drum Themes

For each of the twenty-five songs on the recording Alorwoyie has selected a composition for *sogo* and *kidi* whose drum language text enriches the message carried by the song lyrics (see Figure 4.9).

Form in Lead Drumming

The music of the lead drum has a three-part form as exemplified in the following brief excerpt taken from the complete score of item 1 (Audio 4.1 ▶; see Figure 4.10).[29]

TABLE 4.5

Lead drum: palette of strokes.

ga (strong hand) da (weak hand)	bass tone	low pitch	palm bounce	full volume
de (strong hand) gi (weak hand)	open tone	middle pitch	fingers bounce	full volume
dzi (strong or weak hand)	mute tone	high pitch	fingers press	full volume
tsa (strong or weak hand)	slap tone	high pitch	fingers slap	variable volume

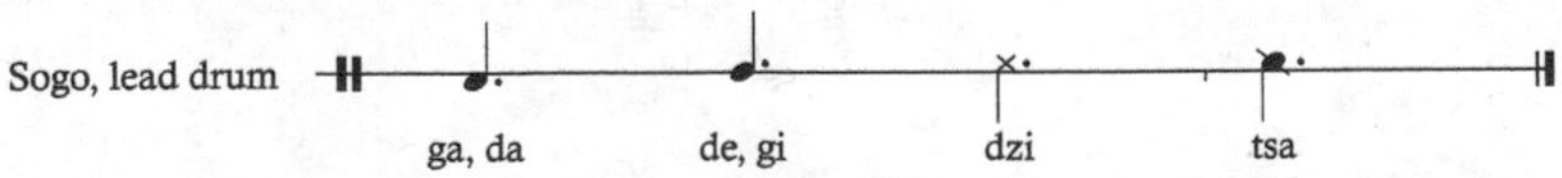

FIGURE 4.8 Lead drum: key to notation of strokes.

FIGURE 4.9 Lead drum themes for items 1–25.

FIGURE 4.9 Continued

FIGURE 4.9 Continued

FIGURE 4.9 Continued

FIGURE 4.9 Continued

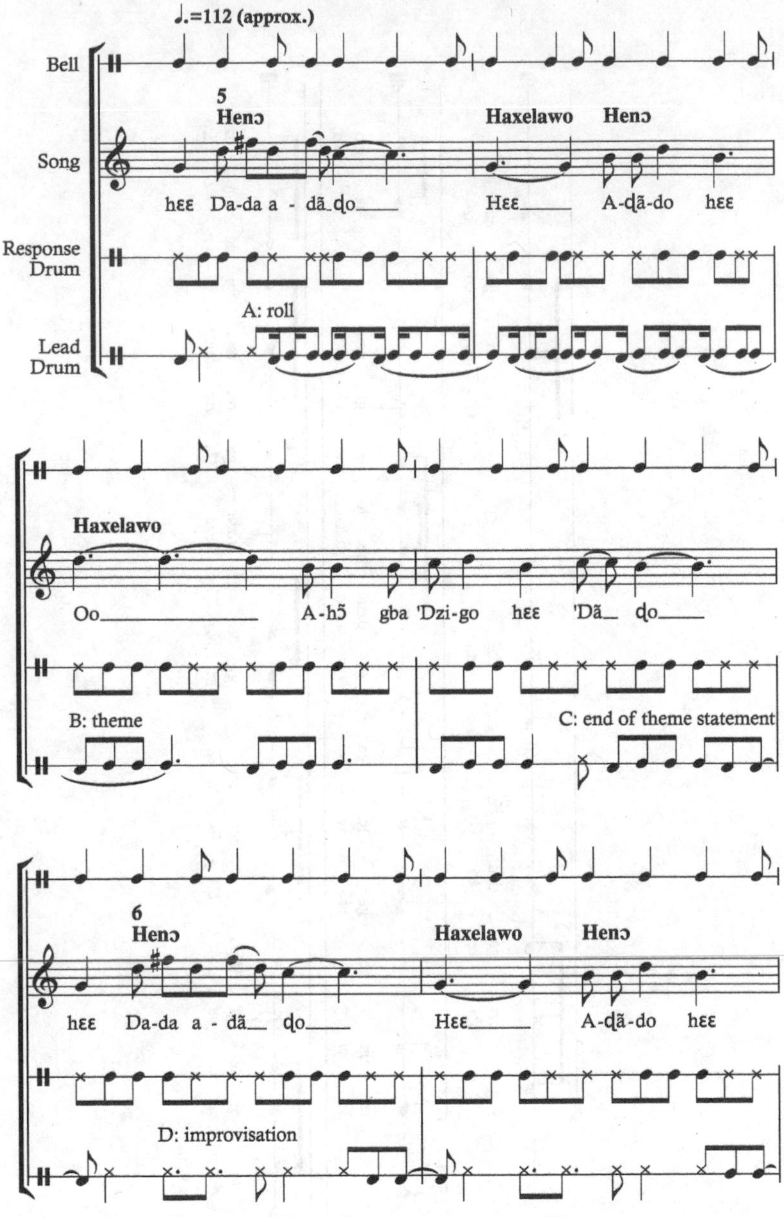

FIGURE 4.10 Lead drum form: excerpt from complete score of item 1.

Rolling passages of quick notes, notated in sixteenths and eighths, signal that the drummer is about to play the drum language theme (see A, mm. 1–2). When the roll ends and the theme is announced, dancers begin the tuck-pop torso movement (see B, mm. 3–4). After playing the theme a few times, the lead drummer cuts off the statement of the drum language (see C, m. 4) and begins a section of improvisation (see

FIGURE 4.10 Continued

D, mm. 5–9). In the recorded performance, Alorwoyie carefully aligns his rolls to the musical form of the song, usually timing the theme to coincide with the beginning of the poem/tune.

Musical Relationship of Lead and Response Drums: Overlap and Interlock

Themes stated by lead and response drums may be said to "overlap" and "interlock." Interlock refers to cases in which the loud tones are offset, making for exciting quick interchange between the two drums (see items 2, 4a, 4b, 5, 8, 9, 10.1, 10.2, 16, 19, 25; Audio 4.2, 4.4, 4.5, 4.8, 4.9, 4.10.1, 4.10, 4.16, 4.19, 4.25 ▶). Overlap indicates themes in which *sogo* and *kidi* play in rhythmic and melodic/timbral unison, which creates less of what could be termed musical "pressure," "tension," or "excitement" between lead and response parts (see items 1, 3, 6, 7, 11, 13, 15, 20, 21, 22, 23, 24; Audio 4.1, 4.3, 4.6, 4.7, 4.11, 4.13, 4.15, 4.20, 4.21, 4.22, 4.23, 4.24 ▶).[30] When improvisation is factored into the analysis, it becomes evident that interlock characterizes the relationship between lead and response drums; after stating a drum theme, the *sogo* player's improvisation usually weaves the loud sounds of bass-toned "ga" strokes and open-toned "de" strokes before and after the *kidi*'s bounce strokes, which usually match the sogo's quieter mute "dzi" strokes.

Disciplining Frameworks: Bell Phrase and Metric Matrix

Lead drum themes are inspired and constrained by the musical framework established by the bell phrase and the metric matrix. For example, the time span of a *sogo* theme, like its response drum partner, must be proportional to the duration of the bell phrase. In this collection, the most common duration of a lead-drum theme is one bell phrase (thirteen themes). Themes that are either twice or half the duration of the bell phrase occur with equal frequency (five themes of twenty-four-pulse duration, four themes of six-pulse duration). One unique theme is a very short three pulses in duration (see item 21; Audio 4.21 ▶).

How do lead drum themes move within the ternary-quadruple metric framework inherent to the ever-present ostinato phrase of the bell? Only three themes begin and end within a single bell phrase; most themes begin within one bell phrase and end somewhere within the next bell cycle. This staggered fit of *sogo* theme on bell phrase serves to enhance the forward-feeling drive of the music.[31]

Lead drum themes tend to be offset from the phrasing of the other instruments in the ensemble. By far the most common moment for a *sogo* theme to start is at the midpoint of the bell phrase, that is, four-feel beat three or its pickup (eleven themes). A lead drum theme that starts on ONE is rare, indeed. Not surprising given the propensity for lead drum themes to be out of phase with bell, four-feel beat two often serves as the cadential moment (seven themes). Although *sogo* phrases tend to add a fresh sense of motion to the ensemble's music that differs from qualities of motion that are structurally embedded in Agbadza's temporal framework, some themes reinforce these familiar patterns. Motion from four-feel beat one toward beat four occurs in two themes (see items 1 and 7; Audio 4.1, 4.7 ▶); motion from four-feel beat three to beat one is found in two themes (see items 6 and 24; Audio 4.6, 4.24 ▶).

In addition to accentuating the motion of four-feel beats, *sogo* themes frequently accentuate beats of other duration, as well. The eight-feel framework enables the *sogo* drummer to move through the ternary four-feel beats in binary fashion; six themes use this type of rhythmic motion (see items 2, 4b, 8, 9, 11, 2; Audio 4.2, 4.4, 4.8, 4.9, 4.11, 4.20 ▶), predominantly within four-feel beats one and three. Nine themes regularly and consistently place accented strokes on the six-feel timing (see items 3, 4a, 5, 7, 10a, 15, 16, 23, 24; Audio 4.3, 4.4, 4.5, 4.7, 4.10, 4.15, 4.16, 4.23, 4.24 ▶). Significantly, it is more common to articulate six-feel beats over the second half of the bell phrase, which creates an interlocking relationship between strokes of *sogo* drum and bell. Six themes highlight the upbeat six-feel flow (see items 4b, 8, 10b, 13, 20, 25; Audio 4.4, 4.8, 4.10, 4.13, 4.20, 4.25 ▶). Four lead drum themes have strong three-feel beat flavor (see items 7, 10a, 13, and 25; Audio 4.7, 4.10, 4.13, 4.25 ▶).

Many themes accentuate the offbeat positions of the four-feel and six-feel beats, sometimes consistently over the entire theme but often in heterodox fashion by first accenting one time-feel and then switching to another. A few themes so persistently accentuate offbeat moments that a listener may feel that the position of the onbeat has shifted or been displaced. Items 3 and 19 (Audio 4.3, 4.19 ▶), for example, strongly accentuate second time-points of four-feel beats, while item 6 (Audio 4.6 ▶) confers accentuation to third time-points. Either quietly marking time or loudly energizing the ensemble, Alorwoyie regularly places improvised slap "tsa" tones on the flow of eight-feel or six-feel beats in both onbeat and upbeat positions, as if to intentionally keep in play all strata of the metric matrix.

Variety in Accentuation

The drum language themes sounded by the lead drum and its response drum partner generate focused moments of musical excitement—"accents," if you will—on all locations within the music's temporal framework. Patterns of accentuation in lead and response drum parts derive from features of compositional design, including setting on bell, overall duration, morphology of shorter figures, tonal/timbral contour, and patterned use of different time values. Each theme works with the bell phrase in a distinctive manner—placing notes before, after, or on bell strokes, echoing rhythmic figures made by several successive bell strokes, or highlighting several nonsuccessive bell strokes.

In the music of Agbadza, the interplay of symmetry and asymmetry looms large, the prime instance being the asymmetrical bell phrase set within the symmetry of the implicit metric matrix. Lead drum themes in this collection exhibit both properties with equal frequency (11 symmetrical themes, 12 asymmetrical themes). Asymmetrical themes occur in two additive patterns: 12=7+5 (see items 4a, 5, 13; Audio 4.4, 4.5, 4.13 ▶) and 12=4+5+3 (see items 4b, 8, 15, 16, 22; Audio 4.4, 4,8, 4.15, 4.16, 4.22 ▶). Two themes treat a 6-pulse period as 6=4+2, which I feel as symmetry (ditto the 2+1 pulse structure of item 21; Audio 4.21 ▶).[32] Symmetrical themes usually are based on ternary pulse structure: 6=3+3, 12=6+6, or 24=9+6+9 (seven themes). Two themes segment their musical period into three quaternary units, thus producing strong 3:2 and 3:4 effects: 12=4+4+4, 24=8+8+8 (see items 7 and 25 respectively; Audio 4.7, 4.25 ▶).

SONGS

Agbadza songs may be regarded as poems set to tunes, with poetic qualities being both sonic and semantic (rhyme and metaphor, respectively). Songs associated with Agbadza tend to be historically old—people will say, "I was born to meet it"; that is, the composer is an unknown forbearer—and the lyrics tend to refer to the occasion of battle and the affect of death. The songs are widely known and may be performed on many occasions even though people steeped in tradition will know them to be "Agbadza songs." Men and women usually double each other at the octave, singing loudly with a somewhat nasal and noisy timbre that cuts through the strong sound of drumming. In order to maintain energy and passionate intensity, female singers periodically interject nonmelodic exhortations. The song leader decides the order in which songs are performed, sings the loosely timed introductions, and bears the main responsibility to raise the song leader's portion of the call-and-response. After the instruments have started, one or two other singers act as assistant lead singers, helping to carry the tune or intertwining a contrapuntal line. The songsmiths who originally created the lyrics expressed themselves poetically with language rich in sonic play, figures of speech, allusion, and proverbs (see Anyidoho 1983; Frishkopf 2007).[33] The musical setting of the words may augment their semantic effectiveness.

Every song has a distinctive musical identity but no song is sung in an identical way twice. Stable factors include lyrics, form, rhythm, and tonality; variable factors include melodic contour, intonation, and harmony/counterpoint. In performance, the tune should be recognizable but rendered with tasteful variation. The tunes of Agbadza songs are similar in musical style to songs from other named items of repertory with roughly equivalent tempo and form.[34] Discussion in this chapter emphasizes the contribution of songs to Agbadza's temporal dimension: call-and-response, form, meter, design of phrases, melodic rhythm, melodic shape, and tonal motion.

Pitch

The "writing free" music culture of Agbadza operates without explicitly theorized systems of tuning (temperament), standardized sets of pitch classes (scales), or pitch-class sets inflected with melodic and tonal function (modes). In this oral tradition, singers remember how a melody should go and how the overall music should sound. At the moment of performance, the song leader's introduction establishes a specific tonality (key) that is then picked up by the whole group. In other words, from one rendition to the next a song's exact pitches may change, but the shape of the tune always is kept in mind. Melodic intervals, time values, and a sense of tonal motion give a tune its identity.

Alorwoyie and the Afrikania Troupe sing pitches that are frequently "sharper" or "flatter" than any standardized tuning system. Furthermore, the tendency is for those pitches to drift upward during repetitions of a song in performance. Despite these tendencies, staff notation is a reasonably accurate tool for transcription and analysis. In transcription, notes written on the five-line staff approximate the Agbadza tunes heard on the sound recording. In order to facilitate comparison, the songs consistently are set on G above middle C, except for several songs that are transposed down to D to minimize ledger lines.

Scale and Mode

Songs in this collection conform to two basic types of scales: (1) five pitches without a minor second interval (semitone), that is, anhemitonic pentatonic scale (see Figure 4.11); and (2) five pitches with a minor second interval, that is, hemitonic pentatonic scale (see Figure 4.12). Two different hemitonic scales may be found in this collection of Agbadza songs. In any given song, certain scale degrees serve as pitches of tonal

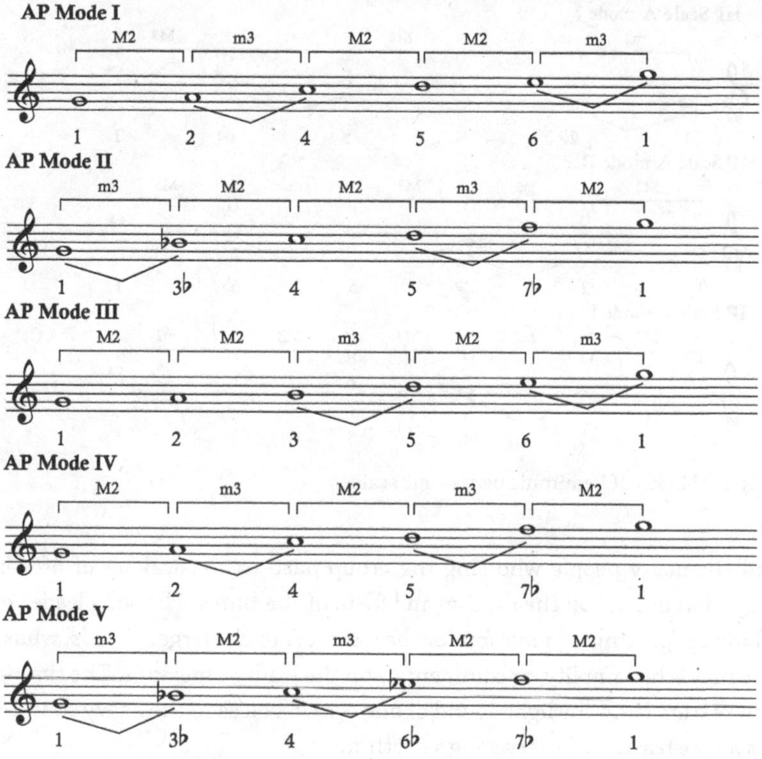

FIGURE 4.11 Modes of anhemitonic pentatonic scale.

stability and melodic repose, while others serve as pitches of tonal instability and melodic action. When scale degrees are weighted with this information about their melodic and tonal functions, we find different modes in both types of scale. Shifts among modes of a scale are a component of Agbadza's musical rhythm.

The melodies of Agbadza songs are pentatonic in nature. In other words, a tune makes only three consecutive "steps" (seconds) in ascent or descent before it "leaps" an interval of a third or greater. Other characteristic pentatonic melodic actions include steps or leaps away from and back to a pitch (pendular motion), descending or ascending motion via interlocking leap-steps figures, successive leaps, or step-leap sequences (see Nketia 1963). Although composers may use additional pitch classes as a means to create melodic sequence or to enable cadential motion toward a new tonal center, melodic motion remains pentatonic even if a song has more than five pitch classes.[35]

Call and Response

Musical sociability between song leader (*hen*ɔ) and singing group (*haxelawo*) is central to the experience of Agbadza.[36] Exchange between the few people who sing the lead

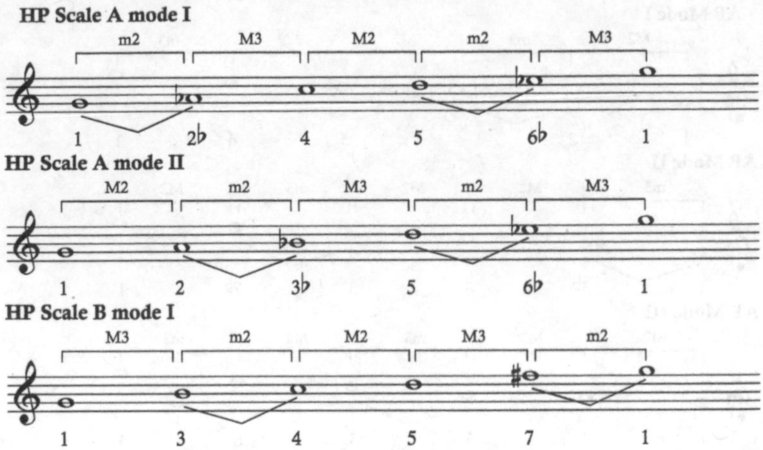

FIGURE 4.12 Modes of hemitonic pentatonic scales.

part and the many people who sing the group part—a musical act of offering-and-receiving—has impact on the rhythm and form of the tunes. The song leader part lifts the melody up, putting it in motion for the hand-off to the larger chorus, whose words and tune may echo, amplify, or comment upon the leader's message. The timing of this switch in texture from the light sound of one or two voices to the heavy sound of many voices is a core feature of every song's rhythm.[37]

Composers find a great many different ways to use this antiphonal exchange as a resource for the setting of melody and lyrics, giving each song a distinct aesthetic personality (see Table 4.6 and Table 4.7). In some songs, a musically complete phrase by the leader is answered by a similarly whole phrase by the group (see item 9; Audio 4.9 ▶). In others, a complete melodic idea requires the hand off of melodic fragments between leader and group (see item 13; Audio 4.13 ▶). The nature of the song lyrics exerts impact. Short poems provide an opportunity for rapid trading of phrases, while longer poems enable development of contrastive musical sections. In a "classic" ABA form that is used widely in Ewe dance-drumming music, a song opens with a section of longer phrases in smoothly flowing rhythm; next comes by a passage whose call-and-response moves in shorter phrases with more percussive rhythmic quality; lastly, leader and group join together to close the song with material drawn from its first section (see items 4, 5, 10, 11, 18, 19, 20, 22; Audio 4.4, 4.5, 4.10, 4.11, 4.18, 4.19, 4.20, 4.22 ▶).

Form: Linear and Rounded

Two types of musical form describe these twenty-five tunes: (1) linear progressive form, and (2) ternary rounded form (see Table 4.6). In progressive forms, the overall tune is created from phrases exchanged by leader and group without repeats or reprises (see items 1, 3, 6, 7, 8, 9, 13, 14, 15, 21, 23, 24; Audio 4.1, 4.3, 4.6, 4.7, 4.8, 4.9, 4.13, 4.14,

TABLE 4.6

Agbadza songs: musical form, call-and-response, and duration in bell cycles.

In column B, a cohesive melodic unit receives its own capital letter, with its constituent shorter phrases identified with a number. Linear form is thus marked with one letter only, but a sequence of numbers. Rounded form is marked ABA, but typically expanded to show phrases within each lettered section. Hyphens are correlated to the marking of call-and-response in column C. In column C, the letters L, G, and A mark material sung respectively by leader, group, and all (leader and group together). Hyphens are correlated to the marking of melodic form in column B. In column D, the duration of a song is measured in number of time spans of the bell phrase. Item 25 is marked "not appropriate" because its duration is dependent upon the impromptu decisions of the lead singer about how many times to repeat its two separate parts 25.1 and 25.2.

item	melodic form	call-and-response	bell cycles
1	Linear: A1-A2-B1	LG-LG-A	4
2	Rounded: A1-B1-A2	LG-L-G	4
3	Linear: A1-A2	LG-LG	4
4	Rounded: A1-A2-B1-A3	LG-LG-A-A	16
5	Rounded: A1-A1-B1-B2-A1	LG-LG-LG-LG-A	23
6	Linear: A1-A2	L-G	4
7	Linear: A1-A2	L-G	4
8	Linear: A1-A2-A3	LG-LG-A	4
9	Linear: A1-A2	L-G	8
10	Rounded: A1-A2-A3-B1-A4	LG-LG-A-A-A	10
11	Rounded: A1A2-A1A2-B1-A2	LG-LG-A-A	14
12	Rounded: A1A2-A1A2-B1B2-C1-A2	LG-LG-LG-LG-A-A	9
13	Linear: A1-A2	LG-LG	2
14	Linear: A1-A2-A3	LG-LG-A	6
15	Linear: A1-A2-A3-A4	L-G-L-G	4
16	Linear: A1-A2-A1	LG-LG-A	6
17	Rounded: A1A2-A1A2-B1B2-A2	LG-LG-LG-LG-A	14
18	Rounded: A1A2-A1A2-B1B2-A1A2	LG-LG-LG-LG-AA	19
19	Rounded: A1-A2-B1-C1-A1	LG-LG-A-A-A	13
20	Rounded: A1-A2-B1-B2-A3	LG-LG-A-A-A	12
21	Linear: A1-A2	LG-LG	4
22	Rounded: A1A2-A1A2-B1B2-A1A2	LG-LG-LG-LG-A	16
23	Linear: A1-A2	L-G	4
24	Linear: A1-A2-A3-A4	LG-LG-A-A	8
25.1	Special	LLL-G	na
25.2	A1A2A3-A4	L-G	
	B1-B2		

4.15, 4.21, 4.23, 4.24 ▶). Rounded forms have some type of reprise. A few songs begin with two contrasting sections of call-and-response and then close with a reprise of material from the opening section that may be sung together by all the singers (items 2, 11, 16; Audio 4.2, 4.11, 4.16 ▶). More frequent is a form that extends the middle portion of the song with additional melodic material before returning to phrases from the opening section (items 4, 5, 10, 12, 17, 18, 19, 20, 22; Audio 4.4, 4.5, 4.10, 4.12, 4.17, 4.18, 4.19, 4.20, 4.22 ▶).

The social nature of Agbadza singing creates opportunities for composers to distribute a tune's phrases between song leader and singing group in many different ways. A sense of the formal and melodic variety in these songs emerges when call-and-response and melodic form are combined. Nine types of "nuanced" form emerge from this more complex analysis (see Table 4.7).

TABLE 4.7

Agbadza songs: nuanced form of melody with call-and-response.

1. Leader sings a melodically complete phrase; group sings another melodically complete phrase (4 songs, items 6, 7, 9, 23).
2. Leader and group alternate twice to make one complete melodic unit (1 song, item 15).
3. Leader and group alternate phrases to make a first complete melodic unit and alternate again to make a second complete melodic unit (3 songs, items 3, 13, 21).
4. Leader sings three phrases in melodic sequence; group responds with one phrase that completes the progression (1 song, item 25; compare to item 10, which also repeats its opening phrase three times).
5. Leader and group alternate to complete a melodic idea; leader sings a new idea; group sings a new phrase that reprises the first section (1 song, item 2).
6. Leader and group alternate to complete a melodic idea; this happens again to make a second complementary melodic phrase; then group (or all) sings a third phrase that completes the tune (3 songs, items 1, 8, 14).
7. Leader and group alternate phrases to complete a first section; they alternate again to complete a second section; then group (or all) sings two or three additional sections (7 songs, items 16, 24, 4, 11, 10, 20, 19).
8. Leader and group alternate phrases to complete a first section; they alternate again to complete a second section; then group (or all) reprise from opening section (4 songs, items 5, 17, 22, 18).
9. Leader and group combine to sing two sections twice each; then group (or all) adds a new section before singing reprise from opening section (1 songs, item 12).

Duration and Alignment of Phrases

The length of songs varies greatly. As shown in Table 4.6, nine songs are four bell-cycles long, but no other duration is shared by more than two songs. Short songs have a drone-like tonal quality and insistent drum-like rhythm (see items 13 and 21; Audio 4.13, 4.21 ▶). In medium-length songs of four-to-eight bell cycles in duration, leader and group usually exchange complementary phrases. Typically, the leader's phrase lies within a higher register and ends without achieving rhythmic or tonal closure; the group's phrase lowers the tune toward the final pitch, which usually comes within four-feel beats one or two. Longer songs feature repetition and extended sectional form. No matter what their duration, songs tend to have downward melodic motion both in terms of the progression of tessituras and phrase finals, as well as direction of melodic intervals.

Location within the temporal framework—that is, when phrases start and end—is highly variable. As is true of lead-drum phrases, the most frequent position for a phrase to start is four-feel beat three, followed in order by beats two, one and four. On the other hand, most phrases end within four-feel beat one, followed in frequency by beats two, four, and three. Interestingly, more phrases end on the second of the twelve fast pulses (time-point 1.2) than on pulse one (time-point 1.1 or ONE).

Melodic Rhythm

Rhythm in song is as cleverly designed as rhythm in the instrumental ensemble. Temporal features of songs include call-and-response, form, meter, duration of phrases, patterns of metric and tonal accentuation, and the motion of time values in rhythmic figures. The basic rhythm of the words to a song is preset and shared by all singers (isorhythm). Although the songs are sung in rhythmic unison, precise treatment of certain rhythmic figures is open to an individual's nuanced inflection, especially in the lead singer's part; for example, within ternary beats (notated as dotted quarters) singers often stretch a short-long triplet figure toward a duplet interpretation, that is, an eighth-quarter figure "swings" toward two dotted eighths.[38] As ever in Ewe music, the duet with the bell phrase is a core feature of a song's rhythm.

Each song has a strong rhythmic personality. Through their use of time values and the nature of their melodic movement, some songs consistently accentuate only one time-feel; for example, song 13 strongly articulates onbeat six-feel time by its use eighths and quarters and the timing of its pitch changes. More commonly, composers artfully shift between consistently accentuated time-feels. For example, song 12 is entirely "in six" until it surprisingly shifts to an "in four" feel in order to musically dramatize the poem's comparison of male and female death.[39] The song returns to the six-feel at the reprise of the opening section.

Rather than this type of consistent articulation of one time-feel, most songs either move among layers of the metric matrix or else have timing that readily can be felt in several meters simultaneously. Rhythmic figures drawn from the bell phrase are a ready source of rhythmic ideas in songs, as is 3:2 between quarters and dotted quarters in its many phrasing shapes. Song rhythm may articulate displacements of four-feel or six-feel beats; for example, in song 20 the song leader's opening phrase flows with the upbeat six-feel in unison with bell strokes four-to-one.

Melodic Shape

Register is an important resource in the construction of melody. Long melodic lines, sometimes lasting over several bell cycles, are built from shorter phrases whose notes are limited to a modest portion of the overall range of pitches. Typically, a tune begins toward the upper end of the song's gamut of pitches and works downward to a low pitch that usually feels like the overall tonal center of the pitch set (tonic). In the majority of songs, the tune never descends below the low tonic but six songs do explore tonal territory in this lower end of the range (see items 2, 6, 9, 10, 19, 23; Audio 4.2, 4.6, 4.9, 4.10, 4.19, 4.23 ▶).

Just as the final note of the whole tune usually establishes the song's central tonal gravity, each phrase has its own tonal goal. Songs with longer ABA forms often modulate upward during the shorter second section before reestablishing the tonal feeling of the song's first section in the closing reprise. However, since the songs are rather short and always are repeated, the tonal stasis of the final phrase is short-lived and quickly followed by another trip through the tune's progression of phrases. Tunes that do not end on a tonicized pitch feel propelled forward into the song's next iteration (see items 2, 4, 12; Audio 4.2, 4.4, 4.12 ▶). Motion between tonal goals is an important component to the melodic identity of any particular song.

RELATIONSHIP OF DRUM THEMES TO SONGS

Serendipity

The Ewe ancestors who composed the drum themes are anonymous; Alorwoyie is responsible for pairing them with specific songs in this collection. Although he put them together on the basis of language, not musical aesthetics, he reports being well aware of musical relationships between drumming and singing (see Interviews, online Agbadza Project). The "melo-rhythmic" interaction of song and drumming is of core importance in the music of Agbadza (see Nzewi 1997).

As a closer listener, I find many wonderful facets to Alorwoyie's arrangement of Agbadza compositions for singing and drumming. In item 19 (Audio 4.19 ▶), for example, drummers and singers both work with time-point 1.2, which is structurally the weakest pulse within the implicit temporal framework (see Figure 4.13). For one of the only times in this collection, the lead singer's call begins on that supremely offbeat moment and, as if to lend support to this unusual timing, the phrases of lead and response drums both accentuate the same pulse. Even if this brilliant rhythmic fit was not Alorwoyie's primary intention, we can be thankful for this sort of musical serendipity.

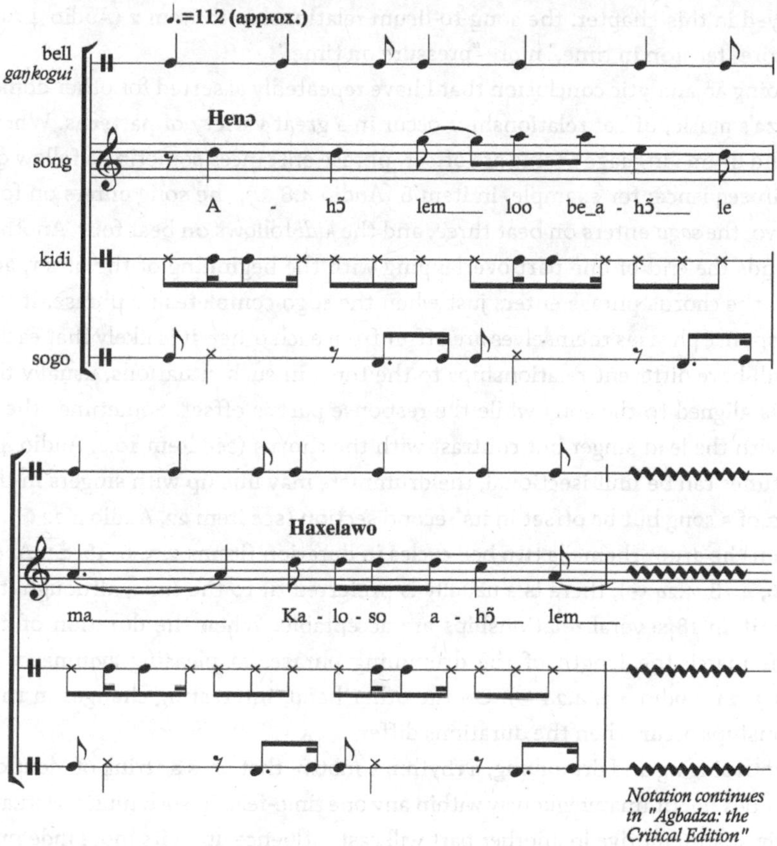

FIGURE 4.13 Song-drum affinity in item 19: time-point 1.2.

Aligned or Offset

The same two types of musical relationship that characterize the rhythmic relationship of lead and response drum are in play between the drum-language themes and the tunes: phrases of singers and drummers are either aligned together or offset in an interlaced fashion.[40] Tunes and drum themes in alignment enter the bell phrase together, use phrases of identical duration, have many moments of unison, and flow to the same time-feel. For example, in item 24 (Audio 4.24 ▶) both song and drum have phrases that are twenty-four pulses in duration, enter on bell stroke four, employ pickup-to-onbeat rhythmic motion, accentuate third partials, and are "in four." On the other hand, tunes and drum themes in offset relationship begin on different moments within the bell cycle, use phrases of contrasting duration, place accents and cadences in contrapuntal fashion, and accentuate alternative time-feels. For example, in item 2 (Audio 4.2 ▶) the song begins on four-feel beat three exactly when the drumming theme ends, the *kidi*'s first bounce figure enters just after the chorus's first reply, and the *sogo* uses duplet figures when the song has triplet rhythms. In the parlance employed in this chapter, the song-to-drum relationship in item 2 (Audio 4.2 ▶) creates more "tension in time," more "pressure on time."

Echoing an analytic conclusion that I have repeatedly asserted for other domains of Agbadza's music, offset relationships occur in a great variety of patterns. When song tune and drum language theme are offset, phrase entrances sometimes follow one another in sequence; for example, in item 8 (Audio 4.8 ▶), the song enters on four-feel beat two, the *sogo* enters on beat three, and the *kidi* follows on beat four. Another pattern finds the end of one part overlapping with the beginning of the other; again in item 8, the chorus phrase enters just when the sogo completes its phrase. If the lead and response phrases themselves are offset from each other, it is likely that each drum part will have different relationships to the tune; in such situations, usually the lead drum is aligned to the song while the response part is offset. Sometimes the drums align with the lead singer but contrast with the chorus (see item 10.1, Audio 4.10 ▶). Since tunes can be multisectional, the drummers may line up with singers in the first section of a song but be offset in its second section (see item 22, Audio 4.22 ▶).

When the drum theme is two bell cycles in duration (items 2, 3, 6, 18, 24, Audio 4.2, 4.3, 4.6, 4.18, 4.24 ▶), there is a usually is preferred fit to the tune, although it seems that in item 18 several relationships are acceptable. When the duration of a tune's phrases match the length of the drumming phrases, a pleasing symmetry results (items 3, 24, Audio 4.3, 4.24 ▶). On the other hand, interesting changes in rhythmic relationships occur when the durations differ.

In both singing and drumming, a rhythmic motive that uses a string of identical time values does not fit unambiguously within any one time-feel. In such musical situations, a strongly shaped motive in another part will cast influence upon its more indeterminate companion. In item 16 (Audio 4.16 ▶) for example, the *kidi* clearly accentuates the six-feel (2 bounces + 4 presses) and confers a similar shape of time to the steady flow of eighth-notes in the tune. Songs with strong rhythmic personality can create vivid counterpoint with the drums. For example, in measure one of item 15 (Audio 4.15 ▶), the tune's melodic rhythm is three-then-two (quarters: dotted quarters) while the *sogo* theme pushes the four-feel, yielding 3:2 over four-feel beats one and two (see Figure 4.14). Making matters even more intense, the *kidi*'s first open tone on time-point 1.2 is tightly interlaced with the leader's entrance on time-point 1.3, which also is bell stroke 2 and the second six-feel beat.

The moments when singing and drumming come together may help drive the music forward; in song 13, for example, the first note of the drum theme comes precisely when the chorus's first response ends and the second leader call enters. This highly offbeat moment within the temporal framework—fast-pulse twelve, bell-stroke seven, time-point 4.3 or 6.2—becomes the focal point of the entire composition for singers and drummers.

Mutual Enhancement of Lyric Meaning and Musical Excitement

The ensemble's time parts and the metric matrix provide a predictable rhythmic setting for all the songs, while the different drum themes create distinctive moments of

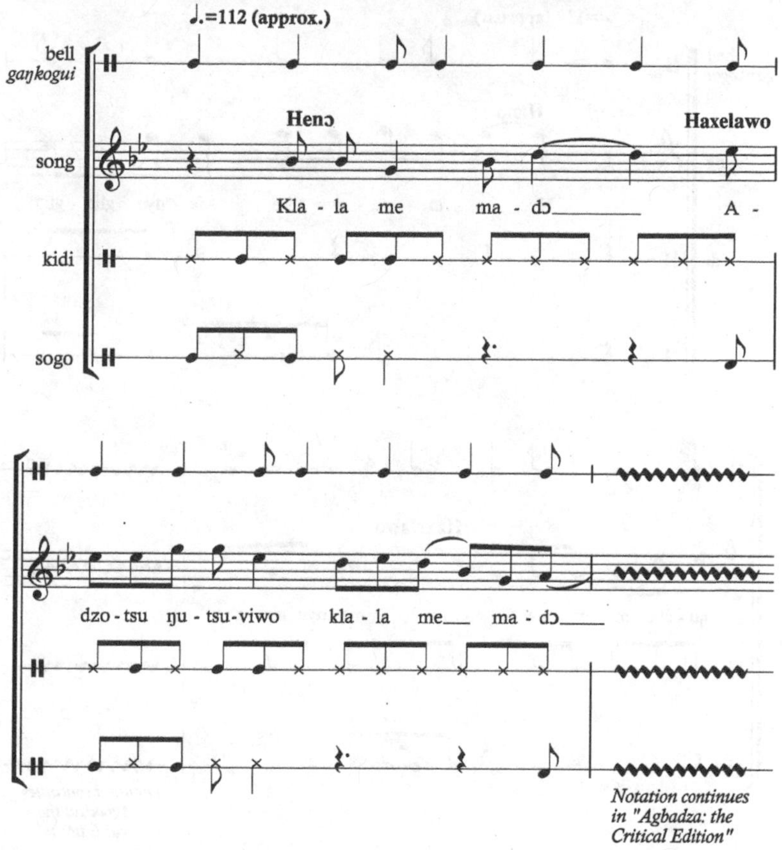

FIGURE 4.14 Song: drum interaction in item 15.

intensity and patterns of accentuation. I get an aesthetic charge when words in a poem occur in unison with rhythmic figures in the drumming theme. For example, in item 16 (Audio 4.16 ▶), tune, *sogo*, and *kidi* enter in cascading sequence (see Figure 4.15).

A pair of bounce strokes on kidi that mean "gbidim" (finish him off) match the lyric "menye" (is not), while the sogo open tones that mean "koko" (by all means) match the singers' "gbɔgbɔ" (journey). The drums thus give special attention to words in the song lyrics that are crucial to the poem's message: soldiers must accept that going to war may be a journey of no return. Thus, even when tune and drum theme are rhythmically independent, their fleeting unisons may significantly enhance the semantic meaning of Agbadza's music.

CONCLUSION

I assert that my analysis is of general heuristic value for finding culturally relevant patterns of temporal order in Agbadza music. Although I believe the theory and the analysis are empathetic to a "culturally inside" perspective of persons enculturated within

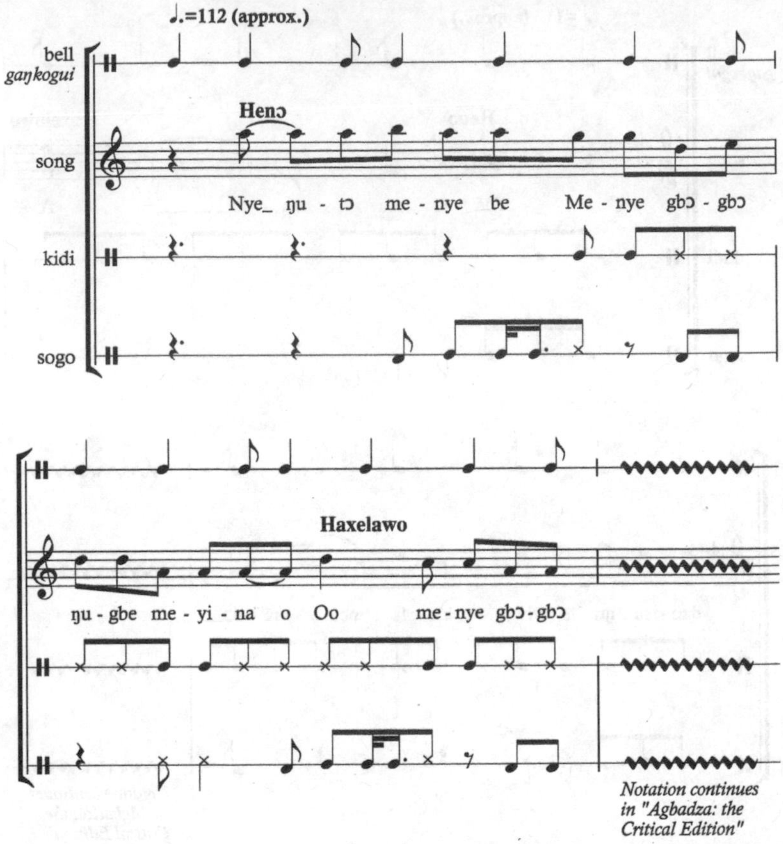

FIGURE 4.15 Song and drums in item 16: cascading entrances, reinforcement of lexical meaning.

Ewe music culture, articulating an answer to the question, "How do they hear it?" is not my goal. Perhaps the elements of a syntax of musical rhythm suggested earlier may be taken as hypotheses for "an Ewe way of hearing" that could be the basis of further investigation into an insider perspective. I do suggest that this chapter indicates the range of performance modalities that should be considered if an analysis if to be considered "comprehensive": dance (special figures and foundational movement vocabulary), drumming (time parts, lead-response themes, improvised elapsing lines), song (tonality, tonal motion, melodic shape, call-response arrangement, polyrhythmic relationships), and language (drum language, song lyrics). These tangible components of performance, I have shown, acquire depth and coherence in relationship to intangible forces in body and mind of meter, time-feel groove, grouping, phrasing, and motion. I have argued that a temporal condition of multidimensionality is established by the simultaneous presence of many perceptually multistable musical components within in an interactive network that is set within a matrix of metric fields. For listeners who may perceive it, the dynamic interplay creates an iridescent musical image.[41]

Implicit in this chapter is my belief that the outlines of a theory of Ewe music now are relatively well understood. The chapter intends to model a textual and graphic language that can represent Agbadza music in ways that are relevant to local and cosmopolitan culture-bearers alike. The chapter intends to illustrate the sorts of interesting questions that might be addressed by scholars going forward:

- contribution of musical factors to expressiveness of song lyrics, viz. metric shift linked to meaning of lyrics, or musical setting of words in lyrics.
- design of lead drumming.
- relationship of lead drumming to song in matters of form, phrase design, and accentuation.
- impact of language on rhythmic design of lead and response drum parts.

I would like to close with a word to readers less interested in an explication of one culturally specific item of repertory and more interested in global comparison of musical temporalities in the academic context of scholarly discourse on musical rhythm. As must be obvious, my heart lies with close attention to performance materials; I elect to concentrate on ethnographic study of music in context, transcription of recorded music, analysis of scores, and formulation of general principles. I listen to teachers who lament threats to the sustainability of cherished items of repertory like Agbadza and assert that ours is an ethical response to our historical condition of rapid change, often resulting in the weakening of traditional performance idioms. That said, I hope that this chapter will be useful to those who would undertake comparative projects leading to conclusions about the musical rhythm of humankind.

NOTES

1. Ideas expressed here emerged from the author's decades-long struggle to achieve ethnographic understanding of Agbadza and effective ways to communicate this understanding to an audience of cosmopolitan musicians. Working within the cosmopolitan sphere, other scholars have developed similar arguments; see especially the work of Justin London (2004) and Jeff Pressing (2002).

2. A succinct version of the Alorwoyie-Locke Agbadza Project has been published in format of book/CD (Alorwoyie with Locke 2013).

3. This chapter is adapted from *Agbadza: The Critical Edition*, a longer work available online (http://sites.tufts.edu/davidlocke/agbadza/). The site also contains comprehensive audio files of the music discussed here and ample information about song texts and drum language.

4. The names of the songs, by item number, are: #1) Dada Ada Do; #2) Miwua Agbo Mayi; #3) Kua Ve Mi Dada Kue; #4) Mekua Menye Nukpe O; #5) Nutsuvi Nya Miegblor Na; #6) Laga Dutor Du Bese Be Akia Wudzo; #7) Kaleworda Wowui De Dzogbe; #8) Eku Menye Nu Wokpor Nuti O; #9) Ahorbo Di Lo Gadzedzo; #10) Akpabli Horsu Wodo Da Hee; #11) Xeke Le Dzifo Masi Worda Worda Tula Sa Bo Gbe; #12) Dzogbe Milador Be Dzogbe Milador; #13) Kaleawo Dzogbe Dzie Nya Le; #14) Adidi Magbe Torkor Nugbe Mayi O; #15) Klala Me Mador; #16) Nye

Nutor Menye Be Menye Gborgbor Nugbe Meyi Na O; #17) Ahor De Lia Gba Adzigo; #18) Morxe Nue Bla Gbadza; #19) Ahor Lem Lo Ahor Le Ma; #20) Kundoviwo Tsor Ameta De Tu Me Di O; #21) Dzogbe Nye Nusu Tor; #22) Kawo Nue Torvi Norvi Kawo Nue Mado Dzi Do; #23) Ana Wowui Lo He Foawo Fia Ada; #24) Amekor Mekorwo Va Anyigba; #25) Tenge Mado Amede Wenya Gbor.

5. Agawu (2006) observes that the weight-bearing steps of dancers may be regarded as marking significant moments within the flow of time that may be taken as "onbeats" (specifically, four-feel beats that may be notated as dotted quarter-notes in 12/8 time signature). This chapter intentionally complicates Agawu's thesis by showing that other aspects of dance align to contra-metric or polymetric temporal patterns.

6. Hewitt Pantaleoni's (1970) pioneering scholarship on Ewe music deserves continued inclusion in scholarly discourse. He sounded warning about the dangers of using staff notation, and the concepts that it implies, as the basis of analysis. His notation system adopts the staff concept from Labanotation to ingeniously display the all-important duet between the bell and each other instrumental part in the Ewe drum ensemble.

7. A good video of the Agbadza dance is at https://www.youtube.com/watch?v=wht_IWFIryM (see 4:50–5:30 for a particularly clear view).

8. In terminology drawn from Labanotation "touch" denotes nonweight-bearing contact of the foot to the ground while "step" denotes a weight-bearing foot action.

9. My thinking about musical motion is influenced by Christopher Hasty's idea of projection (1997). Each marked temporal moment, in this case each onbeat, projects its force toward the next moment in the series of those units. But because this music is premised upon the recurrence of the time parts in the drum ensemble, projection is both "forward in time" but also "backward in time." This kind of projection occurs between all music acts in Agbadza that entail "looping" repetition. Although I do not bring their arguments into this chapter, my thinking about musical accentuation has benefited from readings in the discipline of music theory, especially works by Kramer (1988), Krebs (1999), Lester (1986), London (2004), Rothstein (1989), Schachter (1976), and Yeston (1976).

10. Implicit here is a critique of the contrastive binary "quantitative versus qualitative." In my view, quantitative description *enables* analysis of music's affective impact, i.e., its qualitative aspect to be found in human response to music. Ethnographically informed transcription and analysis can integrate the so-called qualitative and quantitative dimensions of music. This chapter aspires to that condition.

11. Although not about Agbadza, a sense of its choreography and performance scene may be seen on the video "A Performance of Kpegisu by the Wodome-Akatsi Kpegisu Habobo" (White Cliffs Media, 1992).

12. The author has yet to meet an Ewe performer who is much interested in abstract discussion of theoretical musical concepts in the English language. Especially in classroom settings with unenculturated students, I have observed many times the opposite: resistance to analytic questions and discourse. Countless observations confirm the primacy for competent local musicians of the four-feel groove that is presented in this chapter. The concept of meter as a matrix is contextualized by this important factor.

13. This chapter may be taken as providing ethnographically rich corroboration of Pressing's ideas about "groove" and "feel" in the huge domain of Black Atlantic rhythm (see Pressing 2002).

14. In my experience, Africans who teach traditional music in school settings tend to discourage the counting of beats, saying that such an approach is antithetical to the local cultural

practice. Instead they encourage feeling the musical groove. Although the distinction is subtle, counting exaggerates the role of meter, interrupts musical flow, and requires inward personal focus; feeling, on the other hand, limits the hierarchical implications of meter, enhances the projections that are exchanged among beats, and asks the player to listen outwardly to the interactions among parts.

15. My thinking about meter is based on practical and contemplative experience with several idioms of traditional African music (primarily Ewe, Dagomba, and Shona). The impact of secondary source scholarship on musical rhythm is relatively limited, as is comparison to non-African music. For better or worse, we try to explain the musical rhythm of Agbadza by means of musical ethnography, not comparison.

16. In terms of how the mind's musical ear organizes musical rhythm into coherent patterns, there is an important distinction between 3:2—three-in-the-space-of-two—and 2:3—two-in-the-space-of three. Consider the handclap. When oriented to the underlying four-feel beats, the clap is 6:4 (six quarters in-the-span-of four dotted quarters) but when oriented to the clap the four-feel beats are 4:6 (four dotted quarters in-the-span-of six quarters). When the lead drum plays two even strokes within one four-feel beat (dotted quarter), I consider it as 2:3 (two dotted eighths: three eighths) since the most typical internal morphology of a four-feel beat is ternary.

17. Because I do not want to term the twelve-feel durations as "beats," I resist simply adopting without reservation the standard so-called "compound" time signatures such as 6/8 or 12/8; hence I say the four-feel beats are "approximate to 12/8." Furthermore, the conventions of Western music "in 12/8" often are irrelevant and possibly misleading to Agbadza music.

18. Eight-feel beat onsets 2, 4, 6, and 8 cut between the twelve-pulse flow, implying a faster structuring of the bell phrase into twenty-four super-fast pulses (sixteenth-notes). Significantly, the eight-feel beat, which sets up quick motion with the other metric levels, is accentuated much more frequently in drumming than in singing.

19. I cannot confidently explicate the journalistic questions—if, when, how, and why—as they pertain to musicians utilizing beat streams in the metric matrix, although I have phenomenal experience of their existence. I do suggest, however, that this chapter demonstrates the heuristic value to analysis of this theoretic concept. Simply put, patterns of accentuation in dancing, drumming, and singing may align in unison with beats in the unsounded metric matrix, thus adding materiality to their otherwise immanent presence. Listeners may derive affect from these relationships.

20. The term "underneath" is not actively used by Ewes; I use it here in a poetic manner to contrast the unsounded and implicit features of Agbadza's metric structure with the sounded phenomena of musical events. This contrast of surface: underneath is inspired by Steven Feld's ethnography among the Kaluli people of New Guinea (see Feld 1982).

21. This question, so natural and commonplace to most readers, is among the most vexing responses to our attempts at explaining musical experience across the boundaries of culture. Who, one may ask, is "they"?—as if all Ewe people may be reduced to a singularity! And, why should we expect the verbalized responses of Ewe culture-bearers to be formulated in terms that will be germane to the sort of technical discourse attempted here? A reader's resistance to analysis makes sense, however, once we acknowledge the history of suffering and continued oppression of peoples in Africa and the African diaspora at the hands of non-Africans.

22. Axiomatic to this methodology is the necessity of acquiring "ethnographic understanding" or empathy with the scholar's Other. This chapter makes the claim that its author has developed this empathy for Agbadza's music, as well as with the music culture of those

who would read and makes sense of it. I do not seek confirmation in what Ewe culture-bearers say but rather in the accuracy and validity of the notation and the cogency of the analytic argument.

23. Meki Nzewi (1997) suggests terming the multipart texture of African ensemble drumming its "ensemble thematic cycle," or ETC, in order to counteract the emphasis on rhythm conveyed by the term "polyrhythm." He rightly notes that music made on African drums has melodic and harmonic dimensions. I resist coining neologisms, so tend to stick with "polyrhythmic texture."

24. Following its coining by J. H. Kwabena Nketia, the term "time-line" has become widespread in the scholarly literature. We do not find the connotations of this English language term to be particularly germane to music, so eschew its use. I also prefer "bell phrase" or "bell theme" (or simply "the bell") to "bell pattern" in order to reserve "pattern" for other uses.

25. Here and throughout the analysis, I present the multiplicity of ways Agbadza music can be "heard." Each perceiving subject may hear the music differently; the music's design seems to encourage this quality of multidimensionality. I assert that a goal for analysis is to reveal important facets of the music's potentiality. But through the process of enculturation, listeners with ethnographic understanding always are able to orient themselves within the music's temporal condition. As discussed in the chapter, the four-feel beat meter (ternary-quadruple or approximate to 12/8 time signature) is the foundational metric orientation known to all well-enculturated musicians.

26. The term "beat zone" denotes the time span between successive onbeats, as well as the pickup that leads toward the subsequent onbeat. According to the equidurational system employed in this chapter, time within a given "beat zone" may be shaped into one, two, three, four, and six units; a nonequidurational approach to temporal analysis also is possible and is likely to yield fascinating insights not addressed here.

27. From the performer's perspective, "handedness" has an impact on the musical quality of a *kidi* phrase. As a rule, the *kidi* player alternates hands. As a consequence, six-feel time—two fast pulses per beat—is carried in successive strokes of strong and weak hands, while four-feel time—three pulses per beat—emerges from the crossover between strong and weak hands.

28. The aesthetic quality of "forward motion" manifests at many temporal levels, short and long (from figure, to phrase, to episode, to entire performance). Faith Conant reports from Lomé, Togo that this sense of steadily building energy was among the qualities denoted by the local term "sona hua" (Conant 1988).

29. See Burns 2012 for an excellent discussion of the impact on form of the cultural context of a live performance.

30. My thinking about aesthetic forces in Ewe music is influenced by John Chernoff's *African Rhythm and African Sensibility* (Chernoff 1979); as I understand Chernoff's argument, "pressure" is the embodied feeling generated by one part "cutting" another.

31. Although many, if not all, kinds of music may be said to "move through time" toward an endpoint, Ewe musical phrases tend to have a strong sense of motion toward a goal moment; likewise, an entire performance event tends to develop a momentum that builds from mellowness toward intensity.

32. Simha Arom has proposed a formula to account for asymmetry in African music: $N=(1/2N + 1) + (1/2N - 1)$. The math works for the equation $6=4+2$, but I still hear it as symmetrical (see Arom 1991).

33. Michael Frishkopf (2007) provides extensive information about the process of song composition in the liner notes to this CD; contact Michael@KinkaDrum.org.

34. The Agbadza Project materials not only have complete scores that show how Alorwoyie and the Afrikania troupe actually performed these songs on the occasion of the recording session, but also lead sheets that posit a hypothetical "standard" version of each tune.

35. This sort of melodic information suggests that these songs are not "hexatonic," even if their set of pitch classes has six different pitch classes are involved (see Dor 2000).

36. See Locke 2013 for an extended discussion of the call-and-response style of "deploying choral forces" in Agbadza singing. The system of musical analysis known as "Cantometrics" provides unusually detailed ways to discuss kinds of social and musical relationships in ensemble singing (see Lomax 1976).

37. My thinking about "handing off" is influenced by Nzewi's idea of "relay race" (see Nzewi 1997).

38. The word "swing" references the musical practice in jazz of interpreting in performance the time values written on a lead sheet or score. Time values, as performed, follow stylistic norms within a tradition.

39. Although scholars of Ewe music seldom, if ever, connect musical and semantic aspects in this way, close analysis of Agbadza songs suggests the practice may be widespread. For example in item 19, the lyrics about the hopping of a frog are set to a short, recurring melodic figure that sonically mimics the animal's action. The dearth of this sort of observation, we suggest, is due to paucity of relevant theoretical concepts that could serve as tools for analysis.

40. Items I hear as being in alignment are 1, 6, 12, 18, 20, 21, 24 and 25. Items that I hear as being offset are 2, 7, 8, 9, 13, 15, 17, 19, and 23.

41. Ewe culture seems to thrive on uncertainty, ambiguity, disputation, rivalry, unreconcilable antimony, paradox, enigma. In many aspects of life in Eweland, one can never be too sure of anything (see Friedson 2009). As my musical analysis has emphasized, the sonic surface of a song or drum phrase can be heard in different ways.

5

Rhythm and the Physical

Eugene Montague

NOTATING (AND ABSTRACTING) RHYTHM

Of all aspects of music, rhythm is the one most closely associated with physical experience. Rhythm is linked to dance, as a bodily response to music, and to manual work, as a way to synchronize group efforts. Rhythms are felt in the body, as pulsating, energizing, lazy, or propulsive: adjectives thick with physical experience. The scholarly literature on musical rhythm draws heavily on such experiences in both metaphorical and literal ways. Thus David Burrows, writing on music's relationship with time, describes rhythm as "where the bodily warmth of music comes to a focus" (Burrows 2007, vi). And Justin London, in the "Rhythm" entry of *Grove Online*, characterizes rhythm as "the way that we have a sensible, toe-tapping grasp of the periodicities" (London 2001). Such evidence suggests that the concept of rhythm is founded, at least in part, on bodily experiences; and these experiences also play a fundamental part in empirical research on the subject. Psychological studies have long drawn on physical movement as a prior form of evidence of rhythmic response. For example, the classic investigations of Paul Fraisse were founded largely on the physical activity of tapping along with music (Beauvillain and Fraisse 1984; Fraisse 1987). Nor is this a methodology of the past: a recent study that argues for a novel psychological condition in some people's perceptions of rhythm, described as "beat-deafness," infers the presence of this affliction by observing a subject's inability to synchronize physical movements with music (Phillips-Silver et al. 2011). Clearly, the links between physicality and rhythm are deep and vital, from both conceptual and practical perspectives.

Despite these widely acknowledged connections between the rhythmic and the corporeal, systematic accounts of musical rhythm often demonstrate a marked tendency toward abstraction, with little or no attention paid to any physical aspects. Much of the credit or blame for this tendency lies in the practical necessity of notating rhythm, especially when it is considered as separate from pitch, timbre, and other sonic qualities. Notating rhythm necessitates a transfer of temporal qualities to spatial frameworks on paper or other means of visual representation. In this process, rhythmic effects become associated with sequences of neutral symbols, such as dots or dashes, or more sophisticated systems such as the noteheads, dots, and rests of Western notation. Such symbols are taken to stand in for the production of sound, so that any one given symbol can mean the start, and perhaps also the duration, of a particular rhythmic event.

These rhythmic symbols, in general, do not specify the method of production of the rhythm.[1] Such a quality can be beneficial within a performance context (pedagogical or other) in which rhythms are produced in different ways, such as speaking, singing, clapping, or playing different instruments. In such a context, the neutral symbols become real and apparent rhythms, obvious physical phenomena to everyone present. Indeed, the notated rhythm then becomes a recipe for bodily action. In following this recipe, some performers will learn to sound the rhythm easily and some may struggle, feeling the rhythm at odds with their bodies. Some may speak it with facility, while stumbling when clapping it. Some may play with the notation, using the sound it inspires as a ground for further music-making in improvisatory or related contexts. Through all this activity, the notation of the rhythm becomes the foundation for a temporal and physical experience—whether that experience is pleasant or not. The production of rhythm notated as X is just how it is to *do* what X directs.[2] And the notation functions as a stimulus to action and production, rather than as a representation of the rhythm qua object. To use this stimulus, students and performers engage in a physical and temporal series of actions, for only through such actions is the rhythm learned and internalized. Thus, the physical conditions of producing a rhythm become practically associated with its qualities. The neutral notation becomes a stand-in for the physical act of producing the rhythm which itself, as a learned skill, bears all the traces of its previous instantiations.

By contrast, in a nonperformative context, the effect of using neutral marks as a representation is to translate a rhythm into something whose form of materiality and method of realization seems not to matter. In such case, rhythmic experience can easily collapse into abstraction, and the notation, instead of functioning as a cue for experience, becomes taken for the structure of the actual experience itself. Once this occurs, rhythmic notation becomes seen as fundamentally representational. This slippage from a pragmatic system of communication to an ontology is completed in the many systematic theories that represent what rhythm is by employing a variety of neutral symbols as representations of musical events. In such texts the pedagogic foundations of rhythmic notation are obscured, and, with a representational status accorded to notation, the physicality of sounding rhythms is lost.[3]

The existence of this aporia in the theorization of rhythm is perhaps not surprising: it is a gap that is often created by the transition from temporal to written. What is less obvious is how we might recoup the essential physicality of rhythm in a manner that is theoretically cogent.[4] For if the precision of durational symbols gives way to the fuzziness of rhythmic production, with all its complexities of body and brain, do we have anything left to hold on to? Is it not more profitable to insist on the primacy of the rhythm as object, as something that can be precisely notated, because this characterization of rhythm is as much as we can study and analyse? Is the physical aspect of rhythm integral to its nature, but also something that we can only approach indirectly through metaphor and allusion, something that is closed to any more systematic theory?

In this chapter I will suggest a more positive role for systematic approaches through a focus on an approach to rhythmic productions as essentially physical. I will argue that we can and should speak of rhythm as a conceptually separable part of musical experience, and that we can also identify and discuss specific rhythms as particular objects, objects that exist to provide particular temporal experiences. In discussing such objects, however, we should treat them as inherently active, with a necessary physical character. This physicality can be recouped through close attention to the processes that condition the learning and performance of a rhythm.

I have suggested that the practice of learning and performing specific rhythms is physical, and ingrains particular patterns in body and brain. Thus each rhythm and its associated notation carries a particular history of gesture, which history includes the conditions of production for that rhythm. Certainly, such conditions will to some extent vary for each musician who plays this rhythm, but there will be certain core necessities without which the rhythm will not be played. Musical rhythms, conceived in this manner, are not a product of an instant, but emerge through long periods of practice and repetition. Studies in the rhythm of motor movements show that any practiced gesture defines its own rhythm through the process of becoming habituated (Hikosaka et al. 2002; Sakai et al. 2004). This must also be true when the gesture produces a rhythm, so that the performance of a rhythm creates its own physical traces. These traces or "shadow" rhythms of gesture will repeat every time the rhythm is resounded, given the same instrumental conditions. These traces, these "conditions of production" for rhythm, are what I seek to illuminate in this chapter.

LEARNING THE SON CLAVÉ

As a brief example of the outline for such an approach, which also serves to supplement my argument, I turn to a consideration of what might be considered a prototypical example of a particular rhythm: that of the *son clavé*. I will draw on the work of computer scientist Godfried Toussaint and two pedagogical videos that focus on the *son clavé* rhythm in order to contrast a spatial representation of this rhythm with the conditions in which this rhythm is practiced and produced.

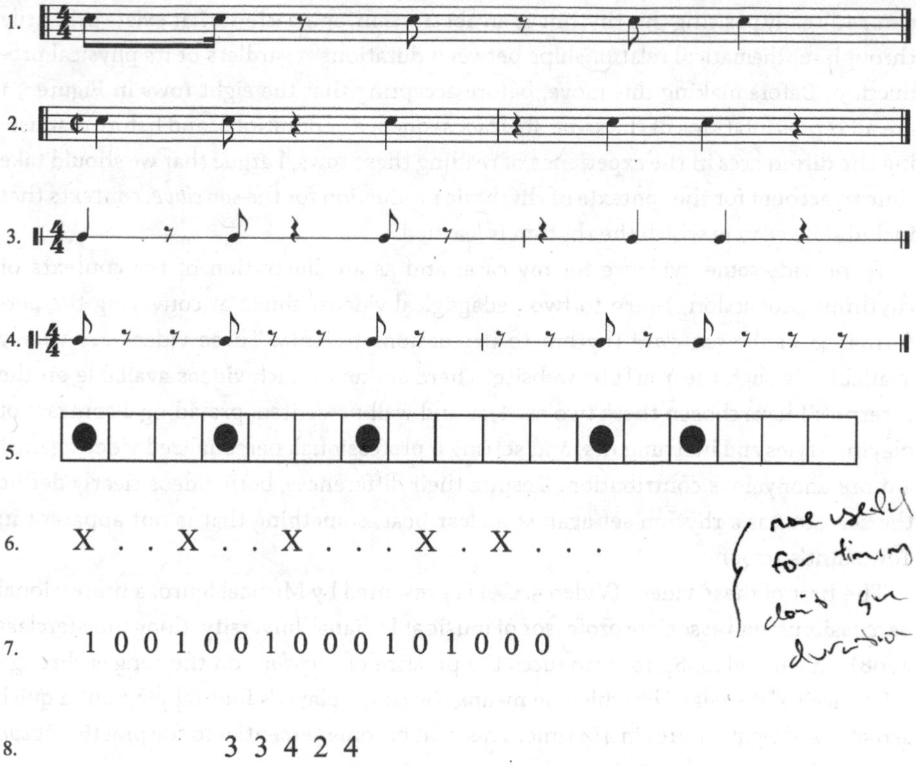

FIGURE 5.1 Eight ways to notate the *son clavé* rhythm, after Toussaint (2005).

Figure 5.1, after a chart created by Toussaint, illustrates eight different methods to notate the *son clavé* (Toussaint 2005, 199). While Toussaint notes that each notation method is used in distinct contexts, in both his paper and his later volume of the same name, methods 1 through 4 are almost never used, while 6 and 7 are likewise absent (Toussaint 2013; 2005). Despite this marked preference for one notational method, what is clear in both this illustration and the accompanying discussion is that each Toussaint considers each notation as a (more or less useful) representation of the same rhythm. This assumption, which follows from the consideration of a rhythmic sequence as an object, is problematic because it ignores the temporal process of producing the *son clavé*: by which I mean both the ways in which the sequence might be learned and the ways in which it might be read. As an example, if we engage with these eight different notations as performers, rather than as readers, and use each notation to produce an instance of the rhythmic cycle, then I argue that we will find the experience of "playing" is quite different from row to row. And in particular, the difference between reading rows 1 through 4 and rows 5 through 8 is sharply defined. What to make of such differences? Toussaint might perhaps argue that they are inessential to the rhythm and that they may even be imperceptible to a listener. Of course, he would be correct to point out that the durational qualities, considered as spatial patterns, may well be the same between different readings. Yet in acknowledging this similarity, we are already positing this rhythm as an abstraction, as a pattern that exists primarily through mathematical relationships between durations regardless of its physical production. Before making this move, before accepting that the eight rows in Figure 5.1 are all representations of the same abstract sequence of durations, and before dismissing the differences in the experience of reading these rows, I argue that we should take time to account for the contexts of rhythmic production for the *son clavé*: contexts that include the ways in which the rhythm is learned.

To provide some evidence for my case, and as an illustration of the contexts of rhythmic production, I turn to two pedagogical videos, aimed at conveying the performance of the *son clavé* rhythm to percussion students. These videos are widely available through the YouTube website. There are many such videos available on the Internet; I have chosen these two as clear and well-presented, providing a contrast of playing styles and instruments, and setting a professional, personalized video against a more anonymous contribution. Despite their differences, both videos clearly define the *son clavé* as a rhythm set against a clear beat, something that is not apparent in Toussaint's account.

The first of these videos (Video 5.1 ▶) is presented by Michael Spiro, a professional percussionist and associate professor of music at Indiana University (Congamasterclass 2008). In this video, Spiro introduces the practice of *son clavé* on the congas through reference to "the beat," by which he means the conga player's foot tapping out a quick sequence of eighth-notes in 4/4 time. This beat becomes essential to the practice of *son clavé*, as Spiro attests:

"Particularly for beginners . . . we have to take time learning how to play *clavé* really strong . . . so that it becomes part of our body, practically . . . The first place that we always start is to learn to play [*clavé*] against the beat, quite literally" (Audio5.1, Congamasterclass 2008, 0.19"—1:05). Spiro then assigns his foot to play the part of "the beat," tapping to the count of "1, 2, 3, 4," while then demonstrating how to practice the *clavé* rhythm through clapping hands while tapping his foot. "What you are trying to do really is make a combined melody . . . of the *clavé* with the downbeats," Spiro attests (Congamasterclass 2008, 2:30–2:45). He goes on to demonstrate this combined melody through vocalization before applying it to the congas, using his hands, with one hand playing the 4/4 beat, while the other sounds out the *son clavé*. Throughout this video, therefore, the practice of *son clavé* is treated as a rhythm that is thoroughly imbued with the 4/4 beat, and hardly exists independently of it.

The second YouTube-hosted video I want to discuss here (Video 5.2 ▶) is posted by an author who posts using a pseudonym (Rqshquesada 2010). Rqshquesada takes a slightly different approach to the teaching of clave rhythm, both instrumentally and conceptually. He uses *clavé* sticks rather than hands, and splits the rhythmic sequence into two measures, each to be learned individually. Yet the practical function of what he calls a "cut-time" framework is indispensable, as it was for Spiro. Rqshquesada begins by explaining the relationship between the *clavé* strokes and the "1 & 2 &" framework. He then carefully and slowly—much more slowly than Spiro—marks out the first half of one of the *son clavé* patterns against this framework, aligning the sticks with the "&"

or the number as appropriate. He then does the same with the second measure of the rhythm, and it is not until three minutes of the short video have elapsed that he puts "both halves" together and adopts a slightly faster speed. Even with these changes, however, the background of counting is never lost.

Both videos, therefore, present the *son clavé* as a rhythmic sequence that is produced, in practice and performance, within the context of a regular 4/4 framework. It seems integral to the experience of the rhythm that the sounding events occur on beats 1 and & and 4 of the opening measure, whether that "&" is counted out and sounded or merely tapped by foot or another hand. The rhythm never appears or is sounded as a "3 + 3 + 4" grouping.

To be sure, one *can* play, practice, and experience the sequence "3 + 3 + 4" as a rhythm. But is not this latter rhythm something rather different from the *son clavé*? Perhaps it is *not* "3+3+4" that drives so much of Latin musical repertoires.[5] If so, this is because to understand the *son clavé* as "3 + 3 + 4," as Toussaint does, is to lose the physical and temporal aspects of the rhythm.[6] It is arguable that this loss is worthwhile, to be compensated by the insights made possible through a spatialization of durational pattern. Yet it is also worth noting that something vital has been lost in the translation.

The gap between notation and experience is not merely a conceptual one, as the videos indicate. In both cases, the background of a 4/4 meter or beat is not an abstract device employed by the percussionists, but a vital and live physical presence that synchronizes with the *son clavé* and becomes, I argue, inseparable from it. This meter may be brought about through a spoken "1, 2, 3, 4," or through a tapping foot, or through another percussion instrument, or by an independent dancing body, or by all of these. However it is sounded, it becomes a central physical element in the performance of the *son clavé* rhythm, and thus integral to its make-up as a rhythm.

It is no accident that the framework that becomes a central element of the *son clavé* is essentially metrical. For meter, understood in an active, productive sense, is integral to the control and regulation of physical activity and the development of motor skills. The achievement of motor skills is pedagogically associated with the implementation of periodic movement, and its definition includes reference to alternating periods. Such movement has little to do with metronomic precision, but a great deal to do with meter as a guide for making movement. It is through the relationship of meter to training, therefore, that the metrical framework of the *son clavé* lessons shed light on the physical aspects of the rhythm, as it is felt and heard by both performer and listener.[7]

This approach to rhythmic quality separates itself from an approach such as that taken by Toussaint. There is, of course, a fixed rhythmic concept—a "thing" if you will—that is the *son clavé*. This thing can be played on different instruments, and it will involve the same sequence of durations. When we want to think of the *clavé* as a thing we are going to produce, we might think of it as this sequence of durations. However, when we want to describe the full quality of the rhythm, to reflect on its performance, or to describe its "feel," we cannot take refuge in the abstraction of its written durational representation. For the context of the sound, both the way that it is played and the way that it is learned, has a direct and vital influence on what this rhythm is. Through cultural context, and through the inevitable physical realization and manipulation of sound, the *clavé* emerges as something quite different than a sequence of abstract durations.

In what follows, I use three case studies to explore similar instances of the complex relationships between rhythms and the gestures through which they are produced. Through close attention to the contexts and conditions of rhythmic production, I aim to show that it is possible, at least in these cases, to recoup the physical qualities of rhythm from a musical performance. Further, I argue that by understanding these rhythms in this way, we gain considerable insights into musical meaning.

RHYTHMS OF PRACTICE: *LE CARNAVAL DES ANIMAUX*

The first study takes as its subject a movement from *Le Carnaval des Animaux* (*The Carnival of the Animals*) by the French nineteenth-century composer Camille Saint-Saëns. *Le Carnaval* presents a number of brief vignettes of animals, including kangaroos, hens, and roosters, and tortoises among others. It is often cited as a highlight among his compositions, and Daniel Fallon in *Grove Music Online* comments that it "remains his most brilliant comic work, parodying Offenbach, Berlioz, Mendelssohn, Rossini, his own *Danse macabre* and several popular tunes" (Fallon 2001). The eleventh vignette continues the comedy with an induction of "Pianistes" to the carnival. Saint-Saëns justifies this inclusion of humans in this work through a direct reference to the typical practice habits of pianists. The score for the opening measures is shown in Figure 5.2.

From a glance at the score, the rhythm of the first few measures might seem both monotonous and repetitive, and indeed such qualities would be largely characteristic of the tradition of exercises. However, despite the regularity of the sixteenth-note motion in both piano parts, there is a sense of development over the course of the opening four bars, as shown in the analysis in Figure 5.3.[8]

In measure 1 the repeated use of a two-note motive creates a physical sense of metric projection based on the gesture of alternating fingers, shown as [a]. This projection changes to a four-note projection [b] in measure 2, the dashed line here showing the initial projective event, followed by the realized projection. In turn, [b] yields to an eight-note duration [c] with the return to the lowest note C, followed by the repetition of the five-finger figure. In measure 3 the length of the meter again increases as the scale first continues [c], but the repetition of the eighth-note C and the continuing ascent to a 2-octave span suggests a potential whole-note duration for the felt pulse [d]. This potential is confirmed in measure 4 when the second piano rejoins the first in contrary motion.

Thus, despite the visual simplicity of the durational values, these four measures present a continuous rhythmic growth in which the opening brief eighth-note cell

FIGURE 5.2 A score of the first page of "Pianistes" from Saint-Saëns, *Le carnaval des animaux*.

quickly becomes a whole-note metrical expanse. This growth can be heard as an iconic feature of the music: as the rhythms expand, so too do the technical and musical abilities of the pianists. The apparent toil of these pianists leads to quick improvement. They begin by laboring a small detail: two fingers alone engage

FIGURE 5.3 A rhythmic analysis of the Piano I part at the opening of "Pianistes."

the keyboard. Not just any fingers, but the first two on the right hand playing in octaves with the last two on the left. The physical requirements of this gesture are telling, not for their particular difficulty but for their implicit demand that the two hands must be equal partners, regardless of the physical differences between the thumb and second finger of the right hand compared to the fifth and fourth finger of the left.[9] There is comedy in training the fingers to perform what they are physiologically quite ill-equipped to do, and this is brought out in the slow rhythm of alternation between the two notes. The regularity of this rhythm, however, transcends the comedic impulse to suggest that the pianist has indeed succeeded in this training. Equality having been achieved, the felt rhythm broadens out, more fingers come into play, and the pianist begins to conquer more and more of the piano's territory in the ascent of measure 3. The rhythm, therefore, does not merely suggest but actually demonstrates the pianist's discipline, training, and skill. As the four measures provide a broad overview of pianistic development, the experience of playing these rhythms likewise defines much of the quality of successful practice.

The relationship between rhythm and gesture in this music is also one that is characteristic of much instrumental practice. If learning the complex duration of the *son clavé* demands the use of a regular meter, Saint-Saëns's pianists present a more direct instance of meter in practice, for the physical movements that produce these notes also mark out a regular meter. This meter is created by the alternating fingers in movement that synchronizes with the meter formed by the sounds. Thus, though musical rhythm and gestural rhythm exist in conceptually distinct forms, in this experience they become united. This unity is of particular importance in learning and developing instrumental skills. In playing an instrument, whether internal or external, a musician develops abilities that are not markedly dissimilar to those practiced by athletes and other skilled workers who innervate motor skills into routines. Practice, insofar as it makes perfect, does so through the discovery of regular relationships between physical gestures and sounds. This regularity, based on periodic movement, emerges through producing and listening to meter and metrical unfolding.[10]

PRACTICE AND METER

This interpretation of the rhythms of the opening of "Pianistes" depends upon the physical demands of playing these measures: demands that create a particular relationship between gesture and sound. In these characteristic forms of instrumental exercises—scales, arpeggios, and the like—the need for regularity in the relationships between body and instrument takes on a potential that is at once rhythmic and metrical. The rhythms of these musical practices are clearly apparent within the many technical exercises that exist for each instrument, over a variety of genres, exercises that often consist of repetitions of a single motive or pattern, transposed over a number of octaves or positions. In the context of such exercises, the coherence between physical movement and musical sond creates a regular connection between sound and movement, and a one-to-one isography between the two. Just as important, both sound and body generate musical meter: the metrical processes evident in the sound are also produced by the movements of the body.

The contexts for the production of the rhythms of Saint-Saëns's piece thus exemplify the habituation that occurs through the activity of practice. These rhythms train pianistic bodies in a process that naturalizes the activity of playing. Maria Talero describes the chronology of this general process: the "earliest stages of our efforts to learn" involve the task of sticking to "the meaningless form imposed on our struggling and reluctant bodies until something happens, and it becomes suddenly easier and more natural" (Talero 2006, 196). It is only through this process of "sticking to" a particular activity by persistent repetition, that a body will innervate the necessary gestures to the point where a skill can be said to be achieved.

Once this achievement occurs, and "something happens," the nature of the relationship between subject and skill undergoes changes. Following tradition, Talero characterizes this change in terms of a shedding of conscious control, no longer necessary given the success of practice. For Talero underlines, "our body takes over and learns for us . . . [in] that distinctive automatism of habit that one day allows us to step out of our struggles as if they were molted skins, and emerge anew, our bodies endowed with fresh powers" (Talero 2006, 196). There is no longer any sticking to but rather a type of letting go, in which attention to the details of the desired movement is relegated to the background of consciousness. Indeed, as Alva Noë reminds us, this relegation is something of a necessity: "Novices and experts have qualitatively different manners of involvement with what they are doing . . . The expert's performance flows from an engagement with the larger activity that is necessarily unavailable to the novice. Paying too much attention to what he is doing, to the mechanics of the task—in other words, behaving like a novice—will interrupt the flow and likely cause the expert to choke" (Noë 2009, 100).

Such insistence on the nonconscious status of such habitual skill has been recently questioned in work by Carrie Noland, Tim Ingold, and Sally Ann Ness, among others (Ingold 2011; Ness 2008; Noland 2009). Yet whether or not the establishment of habits takes bodily skills out of conscious control, it is clear that the process of establishing such skills is closely tied to the production and maintenance of meter. Such metrical practice becomes the default way in which instrumentalists relate to their instrument, the way in which they create, reinforce, and renew their relationship with this tool. Beginning each practice by warming up through repetitive exercises becomes almost standard. The regularity of meter is a home, a comfort that is both physical and sonic. The inherent self-referentiality of this activity is part of its attraction, and also part of its humor for Saint-Saëns. These rhythms of practice are symptoms of the well-functioning instrumental player.[11]

LOCATING SAINT-SAËNS'S ANIMALS

Hearing "Pianistes" in this way has implications for the performance of the movement. If the score includes no verbatim quotations of actual exercises, this music, as I have argued, stands in for the activity of playing exercises by pianists. This "standing in" could be thought of as an icon of an absent presence, as in most of the other movements in the work. For example, the ponderous waltz of the fifth number, "The Elephant," evokes the heavy tread and swaying gait of its eponymous animal through its sonic qualities, without, of course, the actual presence of the animal in the hall. Yet in the case of "Pianistes," the situation is different because the sounds have immediate references in the presence of the performing pianists. Unlike the others, these "animals" are present and performing, doing what they do.

Hearing these pianists as physically "here," connects closely to hearing these exercises as movement, for to hear the pianists at work is to acknowledge their bodies as the meaning of the sound: the music means the activity of producing it. Within this, the transposition of the pattern four times in ascending half steps emerges as another, more refined, joke. The repetition of the same rhythm in C, D ♭, D, and E ♭ majors underlines the ways in which the embodied meters typical of practice tend to equalize the notes of the chromatic scale, regardless of the physical differences in playing them. The injunction "play in every key" is a familiar one in learning such exercises, an order, like that of equality between the fingers, that goes against the material realities of hand and keyboard. For playing in D ♭ is quite different from playing in C major, but the demands of equal temperament, apparently merely theoretical, result in quite real obstacles in the vital interaction between player and keyboard. As Saint-Saens makes clear, no sooner has facility in C major been gained than all must stop and begin again in another key, in this case the key of the next half-step up.

Many performances of "Pianistes" include a practice whereby one or both of the pianists make some mistakes in their parts, perhaps mimicking the inefficiencies of a young beginner. Indeed, this tradition seems at least partially rooted in a suggestion included in the first published edition that the pianists "should imitate the hesitant style and awkwardness of a beginner."[12] If we consider the link to real-life pianists as to absent others, then these slips may be intended to increase the humor of the mood. However, if the performers are here and present, as I have suggested, then such errors seem to have little point. To introduce mistakes to "reveal" the (imperfect) body behind the sound is, certainly, to play to the gallery for some cheap laughs. However, in the light of the discussion of control, these errors can be seen as an attempt to recoup the consciousness of the performer, to dismiss the animalistic pianists as if unworthy of the stage, while returning the real flesh-and-blood pianists to the stage, albeit in a flawed form. In this case, perhaps the creation of mistakes arises from a nervousness about the devolution of control to the body, an unwillingness to allow the body its due? Whatever of this, these mistakes break the regular meter of the exercises, deforming the physical reality of the rhythms and distracting from the metrical growth apparent in each pattern, removing something of the point of Saint Saëns's humor.

This reading of the opening rhythms of "Pianistes" does not seek to defend their simplicity by suggesting that they have layered formal complexities. On the contrary, it is clear that in terms of the structures of reproduction, these rhythms are uncomplicated and straightforward. Yet to hear these sounds as products of bodily movements is to reframe the activity of exercising in "Pianistes" in a way that has relevance for instrumental practice in general. Therefore, in this first case study, the inclusion of bodily rhythms as a constituent part of musical rhythms deepens our understanding of the sounds. No rhythmic "problems" are solved, perhaps—what would such problems be? But the hearing of bodies controlling sounds in habitual fashion poses relevant and musical questions about what kinds of things it is that these "animals" called pianists do and, of course, to what extent these are animals at all. This brings different nuances to the experiences of playing and listening to this music. Without losing the humor of this movement, one may yet take seriously the experience of these rhythms, the ways in which they reflect on the foundation of musical rhythm in performance, and the ways in which meter may supports and define the formation of a performing and rhythmic body.

STRETCHES AND SPANS IN A CHOPIN ÉTUDE

The link between regularity and exercises develops in quite different directions through the rhythms of my second case study: the opening of Chopin's Étude in C major, Op. 10 no. 1. In this music, the relationship between the étude's surface repetition, the work of the hand in stretching laterally, and the contrapuntal voices in the music creates a complex layering of rhythms, rooted in the movement of the hand on the keyboard. Here, it is the very stretching of the pianist's hand across the keyboard that founds a dynamic process that informs and changes the experience of the piece's continuous sixteenth-notes.

The physical rhythm at the foundation of this étude is defined by the two gestures marked as projective in Figure 5.4.

In contrast to the developing variety of gestures in Saint-Saëns's composition, though in common with many other examples of piano études, there is a central basic gesture that becomes the habit for the pianist.[13] This gesture is an arpeggio spread over

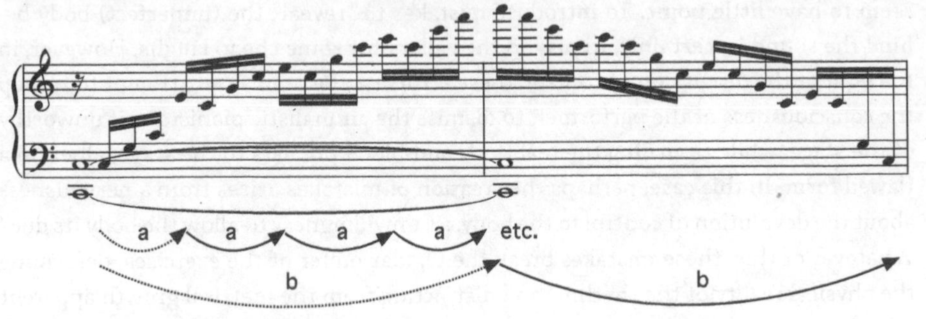

FIGURE 5.4 A gestural-rhythmic analysis of the opening of Chopin, Étude in C major, Op. 10 no. 1.

a large interval (a tenth in the first measure), which demands an outward expansion of the hand; the repetition of this gesture through the first two measures establishes the projective duration [a]. This expansion is achieved through spreading the fingers outward to widen the gaps between them, by an abduction from the metacarpophalangeal joints, stretching the transverse metacarpal ligament. Such abduction, however, will not be enough by itself to allow a smooth connection between the notes, unless the pianist's hand is very wide. Therefore, the central gesture of this étude must also include a lateral movement of the forearm, a gesture that includes radial deviation of the wrist and ultimately involves the whole arm moving in the direction of the notes on the keyboard. In basic terms, the first gesture requires the fingers to spread outward, while remaining flexible, while the hand moves rightward in order to encompass a larger span of a major tenth from the thumb, on C3, to the fifth finger, on E4.[14] These separate gestures of hand and forearm become fused together as the central instrumental gesture of the étude, a gesture that is required in nearly every measure of the piece

Over the course of the first measure, this central gesture is repeated four times, each time ascending the keyboard. This repetition creates a second, large gesture that is defined at its start by an overall rightward movement from C3 to E7. This large gesture is physiologically quite distinct from that of the arpeggio, involving the whole arm moving from the shoulder, as well as a sideways movement of the torso. The descending version of this large gesture, in measure 2, realizes the projective rhythm [b] as shown in Figure 5.4. This descending version, of course, demands a reversal of the gesture in terms of direction, likewise the elements of hand expansion and forearm movement in [a] are also reversed. However, the physical details of these gestures include some flexibility in terms of the exact shape of the arpeggio, the position of the hand on the keyboard, and the question of whether the third or fourth finger is used to play the third note of the arpeggio. Thus, the act of repeating these gestures in a metrical series includes some variety, and it is this variety that allows the meter to play a complex and multivalent part in the musical performance.

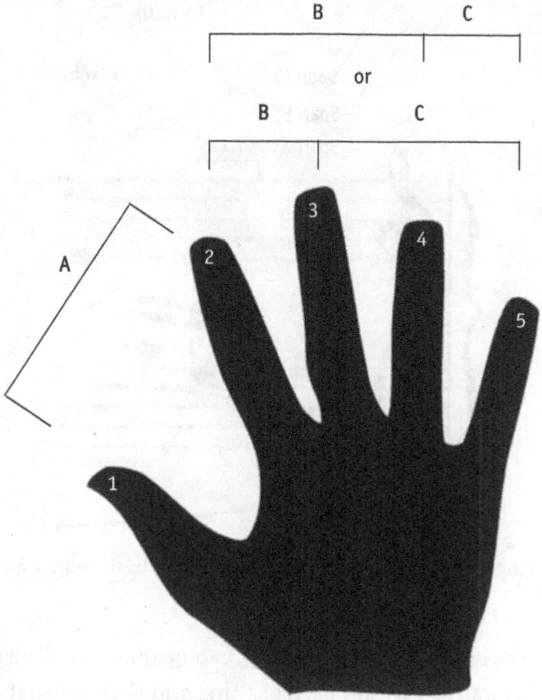

FIGURE 5.5 Spans of the right hand in Chopin's etude.

To analyze the physical context of this musical meter, I begin with the basic gesture of Chopin's étude, which divides the hand into three active spans, labeled A, B, and C in Figure 5.5.

In each instance of playing gesture [a], only four fingers of the five can be active, as the arpeggio consists of only four notes. Given the physical shape of a human hand, and the relatively large spans demanded in each arpeggio, fingers 1, 2, and 5 are always active, with either 3 or 4 completing the quartet. From this, my tripartite division follows, with A as the lowest or leftmost section of the hand, marked by the thumb and second finger. B is the middle span, marked by the use of the second, plus either the third or fourth finger. C is the top-most span, marked by the use of the fifth finger, plus either the fourth or the third.[15]

While my scheme implies the equality of the three spans of the hand, it should be noted that hand physiology determines that these spans are not equal. Not only is the span between 1 and 2 much larger than the spans between the other pairs of fingers, but in addition, the breadth of spans B and C will alter relative to each other depending on the choice of second finger: the span from 2 to 4 is clearly greater than that from 2 to 3. Despite these physical differences, the even sixteenth-notes of the piece establishes each span as an element of equal duration in the overall arpeggio, thus it is inherent in the work of the player to compare and equalize them in terms of their

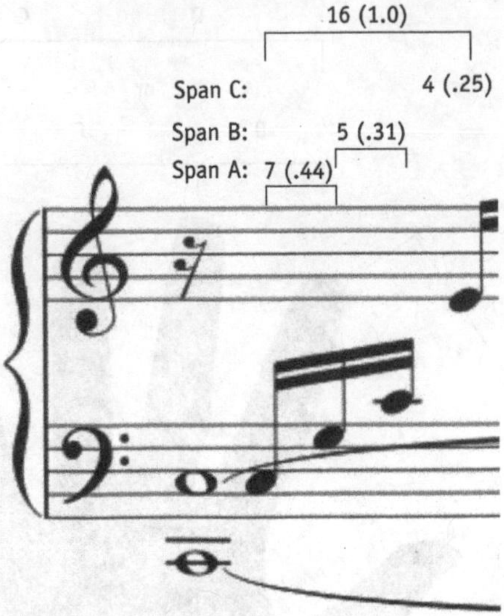

FIGURE 5.6 Calculating the stretch of each handspan in the basic instrumental gesture of Chopin, Op. 10 no. 1.

contribution to the overall sound.[16] This work can be quantified through determining the amount of the overall stretch for each gesture, and then calculating the percentage contribution of each of the finger-spans within that compass. This process is set out visually in Figure 5.6.

In Figure 5.6 the complete four-note arpeggio covers 16 piano keys, a major tenth. This overall span is comprised of 7 notes or 44% in span A between fingers 1 and 2, 5 notes or 31% in span B between fingers 2 and 4, and 4 notes or 25% in span C between fingers 4 and 5.[17] Proceeding with this analysis through the first three phrases of the étude, from measure 1 to measure 24, generates an account of the physical demands of this étude that suggests interesting conclusions about their systematic nature. This account, shown in graphic form in Figure 5.7, suggests that from the start of the piece each 8-measure section in turn takes one of the spans A, B, and C and treats that span as the focus for stretching within the overall extension of the hand. Thus, the steady rhythm of [b], with its exercise-like alternation of ascent and descent creates a longer-term rhythm of eight-measure stretches. Within these stretches, one of the three spans of the hand becomes the focus of the most intense activity, as it is called on to undertake the widest spans on the keyboard.

Figure 5.7 shows these three sections of eight measures each, with the horizontal line showing the degree to which each of the three parts of the hand contributes to the overall span. These sections are not merely arbitrary divisions, as they also form three musical phrases, defined by harmonic and registral return. Thus, a stretching routine for a portion of the hand is defined through musical phrase as well as physical exertion. As the graph shows, measures 1–8 include a dramatic increase in the percentage of area covered by span C, culminating in measure 8, where it becomes the widest span of the three. Span B then becomes the widest stretch in the next section, with its

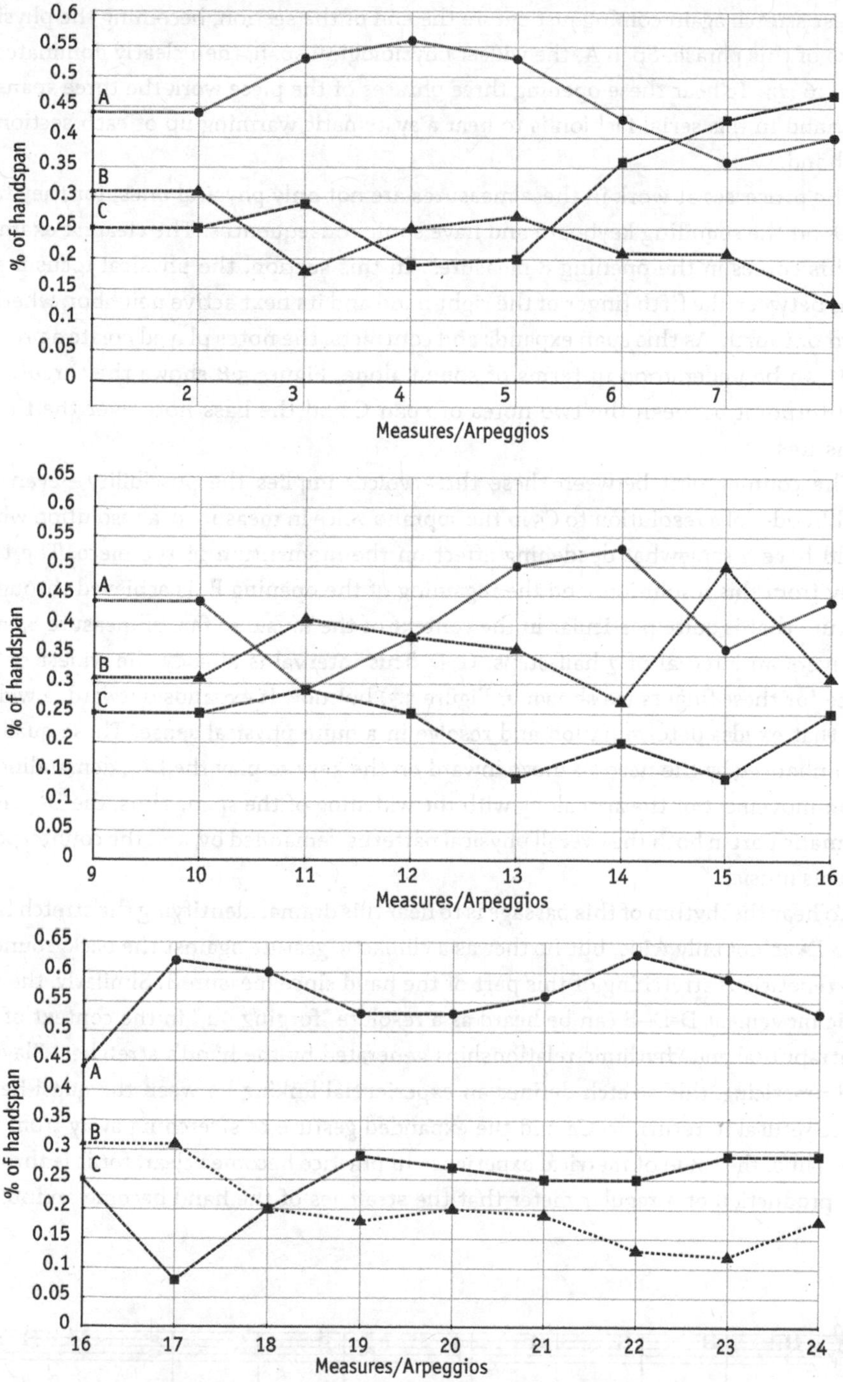

FIGURE 5.7 Stretching the hand: relative stretches of each of the three handspans A, B, and C in the first three phrases of Chopin, Op. 10 no. 1, measures 1–8, 9–16, and 17–24.

widest stretch again coming just before the end of the section, becoming the physical focus of this phrase. Span A, the widest physiological span, then clearly dominates in mm. 16–24. To hear these opening three phrases of the piece work the three spans of the hand in this serial fashion is to hear a systematic warming-up of each section of the hand.

The processes at work in these measures are not only physical ones, for they take place on the sounding keyboard and have sonic consequences. The clearest example of this comes in the opening 8 measures. In this section, the physical focus is the span between the fifth finger of the right hand and its next active neighbor, whether third or fourth. As this span expands and contracts, the notes played create a process that can be understood in terms of sound alone. Figure 5.8 shows the three-voice counterpoint between the two notes of span C and the bass note over the first 8 measures.

The counterpoint between these three voices implies the possibility—even the likelihood—of a resolution to C5 in the soprano voice in measure 9, a resolution which could have a somewhat deadening effect on the momentum of the piece. The turn away from this resolution, and the regaining of the opening E, is achieved through a gesture that is quite particular in the context of the music so far. In measure 8, span C covers an interval of 7 half-steps, G–D. This interval is already the widest of the piece for these fingers (as shown in Figure 5.7) but now it expands outward, a widening that exudes determination and resolve in a quite physical sense. These qualities are enhanced by the need to move inward on the keys to play the D♯4, demanding an extra movement of the arm along with the widening of the span. Thus, the D♯ plays a dramatic part in both the overall physical patterns demanded by, and the counterpoint of, this music.

To hear the rhythm of this passage is to hear this drama, identifying the stretch from G to D♯ as not only wide, but further as a climactic gesture against the background of the repetitious stretching of this part of the hand since measure 1. Similarly, the melodic movement D-D♯-E can be heard as a resolute "forging on," in the context of the contrapuntal and rhythmic relationships generated by the hand's stretches. Playing, and practicing, this stretch defines an experiential linking between the quasi-heroic sonic refusal to return to C4 and the expanded gesture of stretching away from this key. Thus, the value of metrical experience in practice becomes clear, for it is through the production of a regular meter that the stretches of the hand become an integral

FIGURE 5.8 Three-voice counterpoint (bass line plus span C, the topmost two in Chopin, Op. 10 no. 1, measures 1–8).

element in the musical processes of these opening measures. This meter brings an immediacy that animates the musical experience, giving a material basis to the structure of the three-voice counterpoint. In this way, the detailed analysis of meter and its physical qualities allows for a deep understanding of the rhythmic qualities of this passage, qualities that emerge from the interaction of meter, physical movement, and rhythm.

VOICE AND BODY IN MINOR THREAT'S "STRAIGHT EDGE"

In the previous two case studies I have focused on the relationship of meter to rhythm in examples from the repertoire of Western art music, arguing that close attention to the metrical qualities inherent in the playing of these examples provides a way to recapture the physical aspects of their rhythms. Much of this argument has revolved around the development of skills through practice, practice that demands a metrical, physical regularity. In this repertoire, the acquisition of skill is a fundamental necessity for performance, a necessity that plays a large part in defining many of the values of the Western canon such as long hours of (regular and regulated) practice, the hallowed rituals of performance, and the sharp distinctions between these two activities. What, then, of other genres, including those that may not demand a similar commitment to a daily regimen of physical disciplines? Can a similar investigation into the physical demands of meter illuminate rhythm in such musics?

My third and final case study examines this question by turning to a song from the hardcore punk tradition of the early 1980s. "Straight Edge" is perhaps the most iconic song of the short-lived but influential Washington, DC foursome Minor Threat. Like many of their songs, it is extremely short, and is characterized by frenetic speed and a sense of chaos, qualities that came to define the then-emerging subgenre.

Perhaps the most obvious musical feature of "Straight Edge" is one that also serves as an important generic marker of hardcore: the speed and intensity of the drumbeat. The drumbeat of this song, with its relentless drive, could be notated as a series of equal durations: perhaps a sequence of eighth-notes within a 4/4 meter. Three instruments in the drum set are central to this beat: snare, high-hat, and pedal drums, with occasional additional crash cymbals. The parts of all of the main three instruments are characterized by a high degree of regularity, with the high-hat being played as each eighth-note while the bass and snare alternate in synchrony with the high hat. Each instrument will correspond to one particular physical gesture by the drummer—often the snare hit by the left hand, high-hat right, and the pedal with the right foot. Thus, in many ways the metrical demands of the drummer's part in "Straight Edge" demands a similar type of regulation to that of the exercises in Saint-Saëns's "Pianistes." In both examples, repeated gestures are performed in synchrony with a meter, and as a result this meter and the gestures that go with it become thoroughly integrated into the musical rhythm.

FIGURE 5.9 A diagrammatic representation of the drummer's gestures in a typical measure of "Straight Edge" by Minor Threat.

Figure 5.9 provides a representation of the drummer's movements in playing a measure of this groove. It is somewhat idealized, as all such representations must be, but it is important to note that this is not intended to be a neutral representation of the rhythm of the drum part. Rather, through delineating the different hand and foot gestures in terms of shapes as well as rows, the image provides a way to conceptualize the physical work of a drummer playing "Straight Edge." Figure 5.9, read left to right, may be seen as a picture of the drummer's progress through the measure: in this case, the page should be held vertically, and the viewer should imagine that she is placed directly behind the drummer.[18]

In common with many other hardcore songs, the sheer speed of this drumbeat is something that cannot be ignored, and speed is of course an assertion of physical achievement: "Look, and hear, what I can do." To play at this speed demands both considerable stick control and the ability to relax the appropriate muscles in arms and foot. However, this drumbeat, unlike the solo repertoire of a virtuoso, is played within a group and therefore becomes part of a musical situation that must also include the rest of the band. In Chopin's étude it is the physical space of the keyboard and its demands upon the body that pose a challenge to the pianist, but in "Straight Edge" it is the frenetic pace of the drums that constitutes the challenge to the other band members. In effect, this rhythm becomes a metrical challenge to which the other band members must synchronize or perish in the attempt. In the following analysis, I will track the ways in which the vocalist responds to this challenge. In presenting this analysis, I will treat the song as a text—that is, as a potential for performance—rather than analyzing a performance as a completed entity. In this, my analytic approach is not far removed from that of my other two case studies, where I looked at scores of the pieces in order to discuss the rhythmic effects of their performances. However, as no score of the song exists in the same way as for the other two pieces, the "textual ground" of my analysis is constituted by previous recordings of the song, inasmuch as they provide clues to how the song has been and will be performed.[19] The recording I have listened to most in this regard is the version released on Minor Threat's eponymous first EP, released in 1981. This is reproduced, with to my ears minimal remastering, on the band's recording *Complete Discography* issued by Dischord in 1988, several years after the band had broken up. The vocalist in this recording is Ian MacKaye, the drummer is Jeff Nelson.

If, as suggested earlier, the meter of the drumbeat becomes a type of metronome for the physical movements of the other members of the band, the vocalist, as the focus of the audience and the carrier of the song's lyrical message, is perhaps the most challenged. Responding to the drum's rhythm, the vocalist exercises his body to produce sound in much the same way as the pianist of Chopin's étude. Yet as a vocalist, he leaves no physical, visual trace such as the movement of hand or finger. The only material left to us to study the vocal rhythm is, in this case, the structure and characteristics of the lyrics. For this analysis, then, it is the articulation of the lyrics, and the implicit demands they make on the body, that supply the physical material through which the vocal rhythms are produced.

Rather than synchronize to Nelson's drumming phoneme by phoneme, which task might be difficult enough, the central way in which Minor Threat's Ian MacKaye creates rhythm in both sound and body is through the rhyme of the lyrics. In general, the pronunciation of rhymes forms perhaps the clearest example of the repetition of bodily states for a singer. In the same way that the repetition of particular hand shapes on the keyboard requires that the pianist create repeated physical gestures, the rhyming of syllables at the end of each line of verse ensures that the vocalist must form the same physical shape with his voice box each time a line ends. Thus, much as the *son clavé* illustrated a regular rhythm set both against and with the regular 4/4 meter, the repetition of vowel sounds across the lyrics generates a quite clear rhythm that is set against the frenetic repetition of the drumbeat. The performance of the lyrics, shown in Table 5.1, therefore becomes an important part of the rhythmic life of the song, in addition to their semantic value.[20]

In terms of what might be called the inherent rhythmic structure of the lyrics, the first eight lines imply a rather balanced tetrameter, alternating as they do between 7 and 8 syllables in a line: "I'm a person just like you/But I've got better things to do." If spoken, the words would most naturally fall into an iambic metrical foot, with the opening weak syllable dropped, as shown in the interpretation of Figure 5.10.

The metrical interpretation shown in this figure actually corresponds closely to vocal performances in some of the slower cover versions of "Straight Edge," such as those by NOFX and the Whiskey Daredevils. In these recordings, the final accent of each verse tends to fall on or around the downbeat of the second measure of the drumbeat, providing a rather extended pause after each line, and contributing to the relaxed mood of the song in these covers. Within the context of Minor Threat's performance, however, vocalist Ian MacKaye has no opportunity to draw upon this "natural" sense of word rhythm. Given the fast pace of Nelson's drums, there is literally no time to squeeze in an entire line within a measure. Rather, under the pressure of the drumbeat, McKaye's declamation establishes what is closest to a dactylic meter in terms of stress. This interpretation is shown in Figure 5.11.

As this figure implies, this dactylic meter requires some syllables to be omitted altogether, omissions that emerge almost naturally out of the helter-skelter race with the drumbeat. Thus, this organization emphasizes the rushed condition of this rhythm as it is combined with a durational pattern that suggests an anapaest, which contradicts the dactyl and ensuring that the most stressed syllable, the first, is also among the shortest. This pattern is shown in Figure 5.12.

TABLE 5.1

The lyrics of Minor Threat's "Straight Edge" (reproduced by permission of Ian Mackaye and Dischord Records).

I'm a person just like you
But I've got better things to do
Than sit around and fuck my head
Hang out with the living dead
Snort white shit up my nose
Pass out at the shows
I don't even think 'bout speed
Thats something I just don't need

I've got (the) straight edge

I'm a person just like you
But I've got better things to do
Than sit around and smoke dope
Cause I know I can cope
Laugh at the thought of eating ludes
Laugh at the thought of sniffing glue
Always gonna keep in touch
Never want to use a crutch

I've got the straight edge

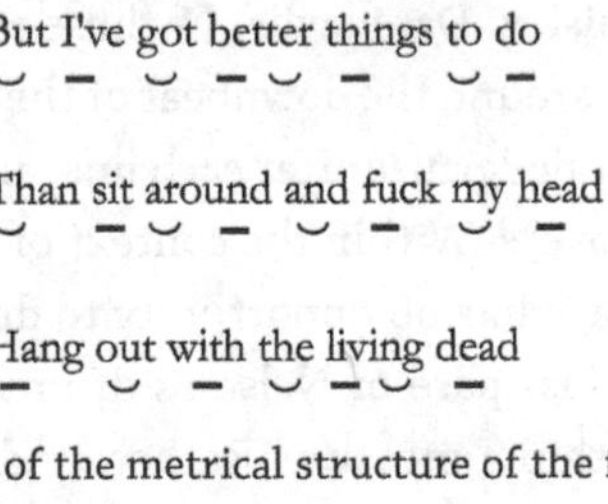

I'm a person just like you
But I've got better things to do
Than sit around and fuck my head
Hang out with the living dead

FIGURE 5.10 An interpretation of the metrical structure of the first four lines of "Straight Edge."

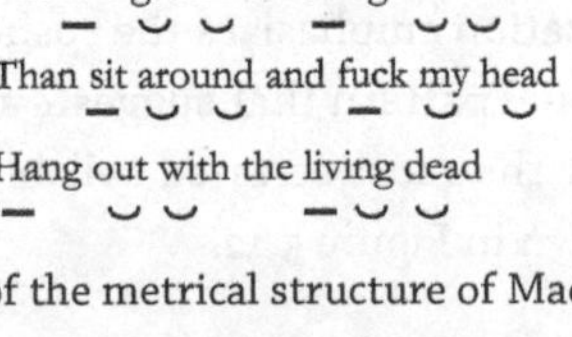

I'm a person just like you
But I've got better things to do
Than sit around and fuck my head
Hang out with the living dead

FIGURE 5.11 An interpretation of the metrical structure of Mackaye's performance of "Straight Edge."

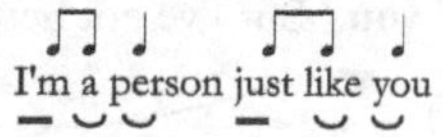
I'm a person just like you

FIGURE 5.12 An interpretation of the durational structures of Mackaye's performance of "Straight Edge."

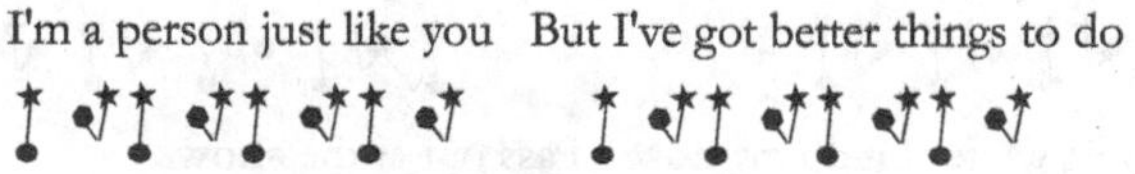
I'm a person just like you But I've got better things to do

FIGURE 5.13 A rough alignment of the drum and vocal rhythms in the opening lines of "Straight Edge."

The patterns of the vocals suggested in Figure 5.12 attest to the conditions in which the lyrics are half-shouted, half-sung. The rhythms of stress and duration do not only contradict themselves, they also contradict the inherent meter of the verse, as suggested in Figure 5.10. These are words that are squeezed out forcefully because the body producing this voice is under pressure, forced to keep up with the mad pace of the drums. It is only in the context of the drum pattern that this lyric declamation makes any sense. Thus, Mackaye as the vocalist takes his measure from the drum as a background, just as the 4/4 beat became the measure for the *clavé* player in my opening example. The relationship between drumbeat and lyric is shown in Figure 5.13.

The neat dots of Figure 5.13 should not be taken as indicative of a tightly structured reciprocal relationship between drum and voice. For Mackaye, as noted earlier, does not easily slip into the groove of the drum. His voice alters the common rhythms of speech, and abandons clear pronunciation in its race to adjust to the drumbeat's speed. Many of the syllables in the printed text are dropped or clipped mercilessly short in the performed version, so that coherence is often at risk. Given this, the importance of the rhyming organization of the words becomes emphasized: these create moments that form a sonic and a physical point of arrival and repetition. Clearly, the strong end-rhymes of each line of the lyrics provides a sense of arrival and balance. This sense, as argued earlier, is a physical activity: the enunciation of each line of the lyric involves a physical rhythm. As the drumbeat materializes through the sticks and skins of the various drums, so the skin and muscles of the mouth forming rhyming syllables constitute the heard rhythms of the voice.

These fleshly facts of vocal performance are determined by the rhymes in the verbal organization, considered not primarily as sounds per se, but as symptoms of similar bodily acts. For example, the rhyme between "you" and "do" at the ends of the first and second lines, respectively, must be produced by a similar activity of the vocal cords and oral muscles. Therefore, this rhyme calls for two similar physical acts on the part of the vocalist. For the vocalist, these repeated physical actions are measured against and produced with the onrushing meter of the drumbeat. These physical bases for rhythm are shown in Figure 5.14 using the same projective arrows as in previous figures.

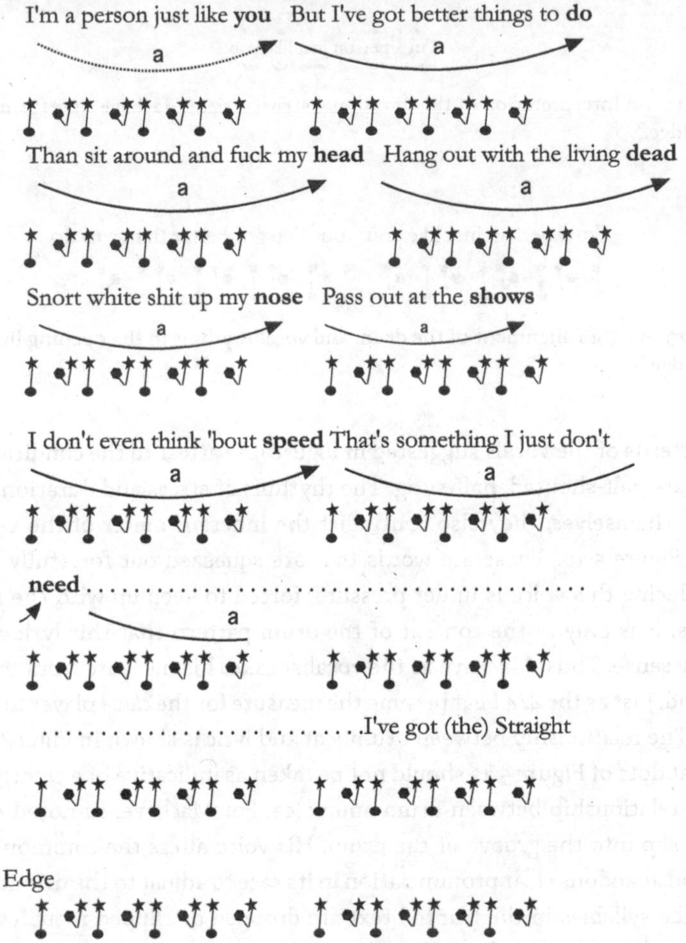

FIGURE 5.14 A general analysis of the rhythmic relationships between voice and drums in the first section of "Straight Edge."

The effort to keep up with the drums' pace stretches the rhythm of declamation in a fashion similar to the way in which the effort to accommodate the keyboard stretched the hand of the pianist in Chopin's étude. To account meaningfully for this quality of this musical rhythm, it is necessary to take into account the physical conditions of rhythmic production. For the interest of the song does not reside in reproducible matters and a purely structural account of meter cannot capture the materiality of the performed rhythm. Partly, perhaps, this is because the song itself does exists within a genre where the note-for-note accurate reproduction of a text is not necessarily as a desirable attribute. More important, I think, the energetic value of the song resides in the performative relationship between drums and voice, a relationship that is necessarily physical, and that is not easily captured in imagistic terms. Thus, the rhythmic energy of "Straight Edge" emerges as a product of the relationships between drumbeat and voice, ending with the moment in which the voice declaims "I've got straight edge" and in doing so wins out over the drums. Figure 5.14 gives an overview of the temporal relationships between drum and voice: its value for this analysis is in the broad picture in conveys of the overall rhythmic relationships between these two physical activities, not in the details or niceties of temporal placement, which are not the focus of this discussion.

At the start, the strong rhymes "you," "do," "head," and "dead," shown in bold in the figure, consistently keep the voice within the cycle of 2 drum measures, chaining the rhythmic declamation of the line to the count of the drum and generating the projective meter [a], shown by the arrows on Figure 5.14. As the first verse continues, the characteristic rush of the vocalist's declamation changes, becoming even more frenetic. In the third line, the pitch of intonation moves sharply upward, a rough octave leap, intensifying the sense of urgency, this is supported by an ascent of a fourth in the supporting guitar harmonies. The speed of enunciation also increases, with "nose," "shows," and then "speed" sounding earlier in the drum count than the rhyming syllables before.

The seventh line has seven syllables, ending with the long vowel "ee" of "speed," and this lengthening proves important, for the six syllables of the next line abandon the previous rough metric organization to stretch out over the drum beat. This causes the next rhyming event to be placed, for the first time, *on* the beginning of the drum count rather than before it. This placement of the word "need" opens up a very different relationship to the drums, for it arrives on a downbeat of a new group of 2 measures. With it, Mackaye breaks out of the confines of the 2-measure units in which all the lines were previously contained. The projective duration [a], tied to the drum beat and to the activity of rhyming, is now abandoned and, as if in celebration, the word "need" is now extended and stretched out, the body reveling at being close to the finish line. Rather than the drums pressurizing the body, it is now the voice which can measure itself against the drums, listening and enjoying the opportunity to place the one-line chorus, the words "I've got the straight edge," exactly where necessary so that the "edge" comes just before the drums arrive at a new cycle. At this point, each of the four accented syllables of the chorus's words ("the" being implied but either weakly enunciated or ignored altogether) become long durations, forming an engaging counterpoint with the repetitive meter of the drums. The final "edge" in the chorus, announces the physical independence of the vocalist from the drum beat, a fine consequence of this music.

The second verse of the song recapitulates the physical relationships between drummer and vocalist, returning to a sense of vocal hurry and precipitate speed at the start, with a gradual assumption of control by the vocalist at the same point in the verse structure. As if to solidify the victory by the vocalist, the final line is repeated four times. This repetition allows the rhythm of the voice to emerge as dominant, defined again in rhyme through the recurrent statements of "edge." This moment of vocal triumph serves appropriately as the last of the song, as "edge" sounds alone, the drums being finally silenced.

This analysis of "Straight Edge" as a duet of conflict between drummer and vocalist grounds the vocal rhythms of this music in physical activity and competition. In this hearing, "Straight Edge" becomes a type of game, a game in which the vocalist wins—at least in the recorded version. This interpretation should not be seen as detracting from the serious intent of the song: the advocacy of a lifestyle that emphasizes personal responsibility and the freedoms that come with it, that eschews dependence on drugs such as alcohol and tobacco, and that promotes abstention from casual sexual activity.[21] For to experience a musical performance as a competition or game, whether as a listener or as a performer, is not in any way to lessen the value of the music or the words that may accompany it. Rather, to hear "Straight Edge" as a physical engagement between drummer and vocalist is to provide one way to understand the infectious energy of the song. Indeed, to hear Mackaye engage in battle with Nelson in a sense enhances the value of the words he sings, they become, as it were, tested and true.[22] Moreover, situating the rhythmic conditions for a performance of "Straight Edge" as a central aspect of its appeal also explains the attractions of the song beyond its doctrinal qualities. In this connection, it is relevant to mention that Minor Threat as a band, and lead vocalist Ian MacKaye in particular, seem to have quickly tired of the intensity and rigidity of those who saw the straight-edge movement as a strict ideology with this song as its anthem (Andersen and Jenkins 2003, 113, 201). To allow a physical perspective to the song, then, is to trace out one way in which a performance of this music creates meaning in addition to the semantic values of its lyrics.

IN CONCLUSION: RHYTHM AND PHYSICALITY

I began this chapter by remarking how the physical qualities of musical rhythm are often celebrated in general accounts, but are often lost in the details of analysis. The three analyses I have presented attempt to overcome this problem through close attention to the conditions under which rhythm is produced in three quite contrasting musical situations. In describing these conditions I have given a prominent part to the movements by which performers learn and produce rhythms and, through these means, bring physical qualities to the fore in analyzing rhythmic structure and meaning.

One common thread within these case studies has been the role of meter, conceived in processive terms as a regular projection of temporal durations.[23] In all three, meter has played an important part in the pedagogy of movement that produce rhythm. Whether as a counted "1-2-3-4," as a tapping of toes, or as a metronome, meter has served a very pragmatic role. Through the physical qualities that it regulates, meter comes to be part of the meaning of each of these examples of musical rhythm. I do not think it coincidental that meter has such a strong relationship with the physical side of rhythmic events, though this chapter's conclusion is not the place to begin a theory of this relationship. As the scholarly truism has it, more work needs to be done, but the three examples in this chapter suggest an interesting physical ground for our understanding of meter as used by performing and practicing musicians.

A further suggestion to emerge from these studies connects our notion of rhythm in performance with the construction of bodily habits. As is clear in all the analyses, to learn a rhythm is to acquire a habit, a disposition of the body. This in turn suggests that the activity of playing music can be understood as a habit, and as such it has physical meaning for the performer and listener. Understood in this way, music and musical rhythm may offer the potential to develop, alter, and re-experience the body. Thus, stretching the outer fingers through an étude will alter the body, creating both new habits and new music. Stretching the voice to entangle, snare, and finally conquer the fleeing and fleeting beat forms a new bodily habit, and defines the energy of a song. Such new habits, which might be glossed as feelings of physical achievement through the body, are motivated by rhythmic processes in sound. Rhythm in general, and rhythms in particular, could then be heard as ways to change a body through music, as the three studies in this chapter have argued. If rhythms may be heard in this way, at least some of the time, then the project to rediscover the physical within musical rhythm has met with some success.

NOTES

1. Once interpreted (i.e., played) by a musician, of course, this agnosticism is lost.

2. Such a context gives immediate relevance to the connection between rhythm as a specific musical property and rhythm as a quality of life or feeling. See Hasty (1997, 10–13).

3. A wide variety of theoretical approaches to rhythm, including insightful and classic works on rhythmic structures employ such notational practices, such as (Cohn 1992; Cooper and Meyer 1960; Krebs 1999; Lerdahl and Jackendoff 1983; Rothstein 1989; Yeston 1976). It should be noted that the systematic representations used by these writers are not equally agnostic as to material. In addition, if the neutral symbols are sounded out, then some measure of physicality is of course restored, though the particular qualities of instrumental gesture are still lost.

4. In this use of the term physical, I refer to the type of bodily action which is necessary to produce sound, and which is usually, I think, implied in the kinds of connections between rhythm and physical movement drawn by the writers mentioned in the opening. I do not mean to imply that modes of response such as imagining sound or still and silent audiation are not physical at base—I am not attempting to sneak in a strong form of dualism. However, activities that do not involve visible or otherwise apparent bodily actions are not usually taken as characteristic ways to engage with musical rhythm. To imagine dancing to music is not the same as bodily, physical dancing: however many neurons are moving and muscles are priming for movement, there is a real distinction to be made.

5. John Chernoff has in various places pointed out the centrality of a repeated pulse to rhythms rooted in African traditions, such as the *son clavé* (Chernoff 1979, 1991; Johnson and Chernoff 1991). While Chernoff's characterization does not make the cut-time framework of the YouTube videos essential to the rhythm, it does suggest that the *son clavé* cannot be understood merely as a single rhythmic line of durational ratios.

6. It should be noted that Toussaint might perhaps agree with this argument, to the extent that he is not interested in physical and temporal aspects of rhythm in his work. Indeed,

he specifically sets out to analyze musical rhythms as "purely mathematical, culturally independent, binary symbolic sequences" (2005, 7).

7. The use of a 4/4 reference in these videos should not, I think, lead to the conclusion that such a meter is in some way natural, or that it pre-exists the *son clavé* in any but a practical sense. The network of "cut time" invoked by both percussionists exists to allow for physical practice of sound. It does two things, the first physical—it allows for close control of the physical actions of playing the sticks—and the second temporal—it creates a sense of the *clavé* rhythm as a counterpoint to another rhythm. This is useful, as the large majority of practical contexts for playing this rhythm will be in musical situations where the sticks establish an independent rhythm that syncopates with an existing 4/4 meter. So, this cut-time meter exists as I practice the *clavé*, and it may exist when I perform the *clavé*, should I hone my technique to the point where I might join in an ensemble. In this sense, the metrical counterpoint is a practical, de facto element in the experience of the *son clavé*.

8. In this example I use a symbolic system of curved arrows to represent metrical projection following the method developed by Hasty (1997). This system has the advantage of focusing attention on the material aspects of the score without the use of extra symbols for rhythmic events. My approach differs somewhat from that of Hasty's analyses in his book (1997) due to my concern with the movements of the body and the rhythms they produce. The basic notion that meter is created through the projection of precise temporal measure remains the same. The analysis is shown as applied to the first piano part, but similar projections can be heard in the second piano part, where it follows the first.

9. A requirement for equality between the fingers was, and still is, a tenet of many technical approaches to piano technique.

10. David Sudnow, in his book recounting his experiences of learning to play jazz piano, has aptly referred to this as the forming of a "music-making body," emphasizing that the agency of the music-maker is located at least as much in the body as in the brain. After long hours of practice, he finds success in the following way: "I specifically recall playing one day and finding . . . that I'd expressly aimed for the sounds of these next particular notes, that the sounds seemed to creep up into my fingers . . . [realizing] a specific sound I'd gone there to make" (Sudnow 2001, 40). Through regular practice, Sudnow's fingers learned, of their own accord, the required gestures, and thus the instrument—at least on this reported occasion—becomes now an extension of his body.

11. It is noteworthy that Charles-Louis Hanon, who wrote the quintessential book of nineteenth-century exercises in *The Virtuoso Pianist* (1873), described his exercises in language that is close to the medicinal. The preface to this book maintains that "pianists . . . need only to play these exercises for a few hours in order to regain all the dexterity of their fingers . . . [If the volume] be repeated daily for a time, difficulties will disappear as if by enchantment" (Hanon 1928).

12. This suggestion appears in the first edition of the work, published after the composer's death in 1922 by Durand & Cie in Paris. The fair copy of the manuscript used for engraving, dating from 1886 and held by the Bibliothéque Nationale de France, does not include this sentence. It is not clear what authorial intent to ascribe to this addition, particularly as it appears that Saint-Saëns did not want the work published.

13. For more on gesture in such études, see (Montague 2012; Wason 2002).

14. The basic physiological aspects of the étude are well illustrated by Paul Barton's YouTube tutorial on playing the piece. One does not need to subscribe to the worth of his detailed

exercises in order to benefit from his illustration of hand movement in the étude, especially in regards to the aims of this paper (Chopin 2013).

15. In the reversal of [a] in the descending portions of the arpeggio, these spans remain the same, but will be played as C—B—A instead of A—B—C.

16. This equalization of what is physically quite different through meter compares to the equal treatment of right and left hand in Saint-Saëns's movement, as noted earlier.

17. Using 4 rather than 3 here is supported by all editions of the études of which I am aware, including such widely used and authoritative editions as those of Karl Klindworth, Carl Mikuli, and Hans von Bülow. However, since fingering can be a matter of personal choice, it is possible that a pianist with a large hard could use 3 instead of 4 on the third note of this arpeggio. This alteration is accommodated within my analysis as spans B and C may use either 3 or 4 without changing the data. Using fingers other than 1, 2, or 5 on the first, second, and fourth notes respectively will invalidate my analysis, however, such fingering would be so dramatically odd as to constitute an aberration in the physical response to the demands of the score.

18. This diagram supposes a conventional layout of the drumset, with the high hat played by the left hand, the snare by the right, crossed under the left, and the bass drum played by a foot pedal. Video evidence from Minor Threat concerts suggests that this was a layout often adopted by Nelson.

19. There are, it must be said, many cover versions of "Straight Edge" in existence, extending from a slow, ironic ballad by punk's professional jokesters NOFX to a fast blast of derisory sarcasm by Australian death metal group Blood Duster. Without delving further into the complex ontology of the pop song and the problems of analyzing it, I will claim that my analysis speaks to "Straight Edge" in the performative tradition established by Minor Threat, without direct reference to performances of the song that seek to undermine, comment on, or mock that performative tradition and the overall ethos of the song.

20. Lyrics copyright Dischord Records, reproduced here by kind permission of Ian MacKaye.

21. This is not to deny that a direct semantic reading is one important historical meaning for the song, which played a large part in the rise of the term "Straight Edge" to describe a subculture of mostly young people who chose to follow some or all of these principles. For more on this see (Blush 2001) and (O'Hara 1993).

22. As a generic marker, this rushed and often unintelligible delivery of lyrics is characteristic of hardcore—indeed, MacKaye's diction is rather clearer than most hardcore singers, enhancing comprehensibility for his message. However, the rhythmic interchange between drummer and vocalist and the sense of a victory for the vocalist at the end are, I think, quite particular to "Straight Edge." There are certainly other songs with similar physical battles in and out of the hardcore genre, just as classical piano études have many examples of rhythmic stretching.

23. This concept of meter follows the theory outlined in Hasty (1997).

6

Modern Drum Solos Over Ostinatos

Fernando Benadon

INTRODUCTION

This chapter explores phrasing strategies and idioms used by modern drummers in their improvised solos. The focus will be exclusively on solos over accompanimental ostinatos: cyclical patterns that provide an unchanging and often syncopated foil for the drummer's rhythmic invention. Since the ostinato is accentually distinct from the underlying meter despite being carved from it, the drummer interacts with two unchanging layers, giving rise to a variety of possible configurations that can be schematized in "synchronization space." The top of Figure 6.1 presents five idealized states involving drums (d), meter (m), and ostinato (o). Inclusion in the circle denotes rhythmic togetherness; for example, in the top leftmost state, there is total asynchrony between the three elements, whereas in the next one to the right, meter and ostinato are together but in rhythmic counterpoint to the drums. This assortment of three-way interactions affords exponentially greater interplay than in a simpler rhythmic binary, where the constituent pair is either apart or together.

Phrases and sections can thus be heard as ongoing rearrangements of the d-m-o grouping. In one common scenario, the drummer weaves between meter and ostinato, alternatively joining with one but not the other—or with neither—before arriving at a triply shared point such as a downbeat. Clearly, the discrete states of Figure 6.1 are but representative cases along a vast continuum of possible interactions. Such reductionism enables us to conceptualize how different solos exhaust those interactions through various juxtapositions and pacing approaches.

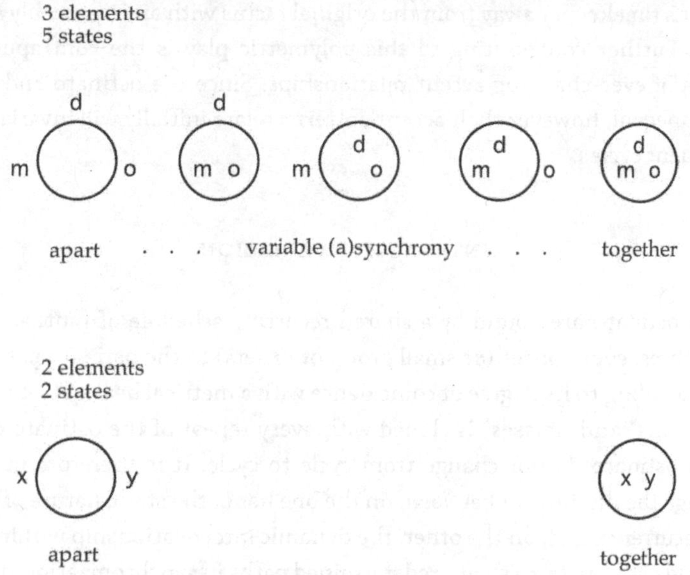

FIGURE 6.1 Configurations in "synchronization space" for three- and two-element groups. Elements inside a circle are in synchrony with each other; d = drums, m = meter, o = ostinato.

The following analyses focus on solos by Vinnie Colaiuta (b. 1956), Steve Gadd (b. 1945), Trilok Gurtu (b. 1951), Jojo Mayer (b. 1963), and Dave Weckl (b. 1960). Consummate musicians with distinguished discographies and large fan bases, these drummers have been featured at least once on the cover of *Modern Drummer*, the leading trade magazine.[1] (Gadd in particular is revered as a quasi-deity: the cover caption of his 2004 feature reads: "GADD ALMIGHTY!") Beyond the shared credit of having played a lot of fusion (itself a broad term) throughout their careers, and apart from the common attribute that none of them identifies with a single primary genre, their résumés differ significantly.[2] To be a "modern drummer," then, is to have firm grounding in jazz and rock, to be fluent in several musical styles, to be musically literate, to possess superlative technique, and to have mastered the ability to alternate effortlessly between supportive and soloistic roles.

Since polymeter is a common tool of this trade, much of what follows is devoted to polymetric passages that highlight specific sets of rhythmic states in the d-m-o network. Polymeter's capacity to confound listener expectations through metric ambiguity has been noted in a wide range of musical contexts and experimental paradigms (e.g., Butler 2006; Cohn 2001; Folio 1995; Krebs 1999; Locke 1982; Magill and Pressing 1997; Mirka 2009; Poudrier and Repp 2013; Pressing 2002). In the examples considered here, polymetric drumming betrays a sense of virtuosic playfulness. While the meter and ostinato cycles are looping mechanistically in sympathetic phase, the drummer's polymeter also loops mechanistically but mischievously out of sync, tempting the listener's timekeeper away from the original tactus with an irrevocably short-lived thrill ride. Further contributing to this polymetric play is the contrapuntal phantasmagoria of ever-changing accent relationships. Since the ostinato and polymeter cycles are unequal, however their accent patterns relate initially will invariably change on subsequent cycles.

INTERACTIVE VARIATION

Meter and ostinato are bound by a shared recurring schedule of mutual encounters and departures: every onset (or small group of onsets) in the ostinato pattern can be assessed according to its degree of coincidence with a metrical beat.[3] The resulting succession of "hits" and "misses" is cloned with every repeat of the ostinato cycle, since meter and ostinato do not change from cycle to cycle. It is therefore important to acknowledge the distinction between, on the one hand, the static nature of the meter-ostinato recurrence and, on the other, the dynamic interrelationship within each cycle as meter and ostinato trace their predetermined paths in synchronization space. These paths define the terrain that the drummer must roam during the solo.

Steve Gadd's solo on "Three Quartets" provides introductory examples (Figure 6.2; a key to drum notation appears in Figure 6.12, in the appendix). The solo comprises nine four-measure "stanzas" (labeled with encircled numbers) of a piano-and-bass ostinato. Beginning in earnest in stanza 2, the ostinato's characteristic figure goes: (1) sixteenth-note pickup, (2) on-the-downbeat attack, (3) anticipation of beat two. The first two onsets of each three-onset unit fuse into a meter-concordant subunit, whereas the third onset stands out as a clear cross-accent. These two "on-off" states alternate throughout the four-bar cycle, doubling in frequency on bar three of every cycle, where the figure appears twice. Like any other meter-ostinato pairing, this one presents to the improvising drummer a set of specific and recurring possibilities for rhythmic interaction.

Stanzas 1 and 2 are mostly an introductory warm-up, with Gadd first testing the waters and then gradually establishing a groove. We skip, then, to the solo's ninth measure. Throughout the third stanza, Gadd remains closely aligned with the ostinato through a series of calls-and-responses, but generally refrains from matching the ostinato's anticipations into beat two, an action that would alienate the meter. The overall status of stanza 3 is therefore one of general conciliation between all three parties—a neutral outgrowth of the prior two stanzas.

By contrast, the fourth stanza brings about disunity via polymeter as the drums settle into a 6/16 pattern. Notwithstanding the occasional alignments with respect to the ostinato (marked with arrows), the drums are for the most part off on their own. Moreover, detachment from the meter is maximized by the phase beginnings of the polymetric drum cycle, whose starting note always falls on the beat's weakest sixteenth-note subdivisions: either (. x . .) or (. . . x).[4] Since, as has been observed, this

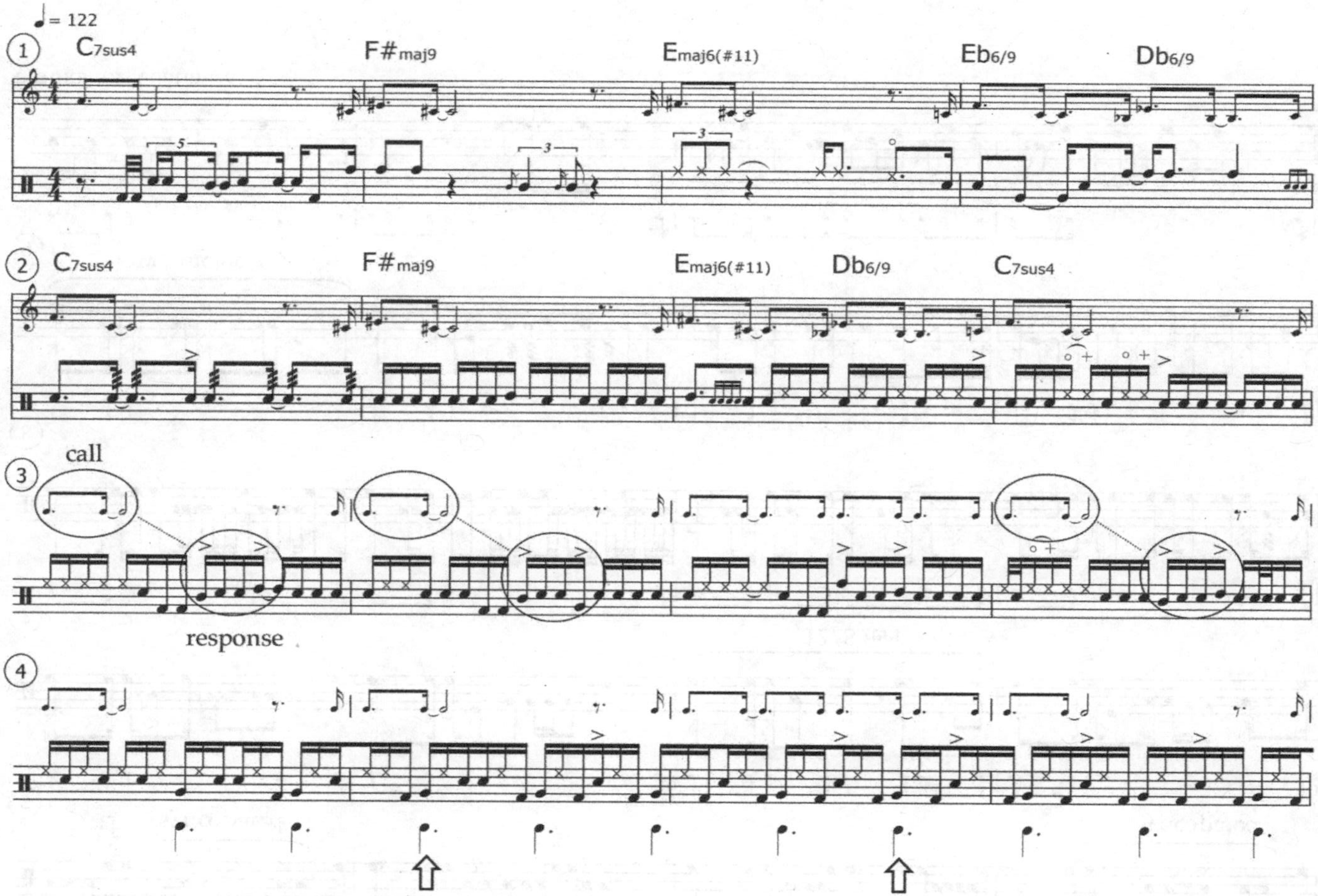

FIGURE 6.2 Steve Gadd, "Quartet No. 2, Part II" (9:14).

FIGURE 6.2 Continued

meter-ostinato pairing alternates between junction and disjunction, stanza 4 features the two leftmost three-way configurations from Figure 6.1.

The balance shifts again in stanza 5, where Gadd is more in line with the ostinato than with the meter, as represented by the center configuration in Figure 6.1. The first instance of the drums-ostinato pairing (the arrowed anticipation into beat two) occurs at the ending boundary of the polymeter we just examined, suggesting that arrival points need be neither a downbeat nor a three-way convergence.[5] In addition to cementing the bond between drums and ostinato at every beat-two anticipation within this stanza, Gadd averts synchronization with the meter by way of prevalent syncopation (marked with horizontal brackets). An exception occurs when the accented fourth beat of bar two creates a strong pickup into the following downbeat, promoting a transitory kinship between drums and meter—Figure 6.1's fourth configuration. For additional instances of drums-meter pairings at the ostinato's expense elsewhere in the solo, we can point to the forceful articulation of each beat at the start of stanza 8 and to the solo's final pickup accent. We have now sampled all five configurations presented in Figure 6.1.

A critical issue brings us back to the fifth stanza. Note how the synchronization between drums and ostinato in the third measure differs from the corresponding location in the next stanza. In the third measure of stanza 5, every attack in the ostinato is matched by a drum accent, whereas in stanza 6, the alignment is approximate as a result of Gadd switching momentarily to a 12/8 feel. Substituting the reigning quaternary pulse for a ternary one embellishes the ostinato's attacks with microtemporally early drum onsets (marked with asterisks).[6] Depending on how we interpret things, drums and ostinato are either tightly knit or hopelessly asunder. Cold measurement between their mostly aligned onsets supports the former view, but it indirectly contradicts the notion that sixteenths and triplets are essentially different percepts. Therefore, to say that two elements are or are not aligned can amount not only to an oversimplification of the gradations of (dis)unity that can exist between them, but also—and more crucially—to a potential disavowal of the conceptual apparatus by which we assess closeness. For that reason, the remainder of this chapter will become progressively less concerned with determining whether rhythmic layers are synchronized (in itself a difficult problem), and more invested in the listening experiences that emerge from what are, in most circumstances, continuously fluctuating interactions. Our interest lies in the musical ramifications of those relationships rather than in the relationships themselves.

TRILOK GURTU: "BELO HORIZONTE"

One way to achieve varying configurations between drums, meter, and ostinato entails embedding the same rhythmic motive at different metric locations within the ostinato cycle. Insofar as it consists of a fixed pattern reappearing in varying metric positions, this method resembles the polymetric cases we will study later. However, here the drummer has the freedom to adjust and readjust the motive's position with respect to its two counterparts (meter and ostinato) without having to follow a strict polymetric regimen.

Figure 6.3 shows how Trilok Gurtu variously positions three variants of a basic gesture in order to achieve contrasting interactive configurations. The bass-and-guitar ostinato contains two rhythmically identical halves, each spanning one 3/1 measure, that differ only in their ending harmonic/melodic cadences (the first in A major, the second in E major). Each of the boxed regions in the transcription contains a unique combination of meter, ostinato, and one of Gurtu's three variants (shown above the transcription). There is complete three-way fusion at B but not at the corresponding location at D, where the same drum pattern now occurs three eighth-notes later. At E, drums and ostinato are perfectly aligned while off the beat. Highly concentrated variation occurs at A, C, F, and G, where Gurtu achieves various alignment configurations within very narrow windows of time. Between these zones of continuously shifting states lies a static expanse: starting on the third stanza and into the beginning of the fourth, Gurtu's eighth-note rock beat allies itself with the meter while paying no heed to the ostinato.

The horizontal brackets show that Gurtu probes different regions of the measure whenever the ostinato rests, such that the drums never repeat themselves at the same location. This is also generally the case when the ostinato is not resting. The near-saturation of the metric grid can be seen in Figure 6.4 which marks the cumulative occurrences of the snare-plus-cymbal (or cymbal only) accent from Gurtu's main motive within the 24-eighth-note measure.

For instance, the first two >'s correspond to the accented second and third eighth-notes in stanza 1's second measure; the next two >'s correspond to the accented fourth and sixth eighth-notes in stanza 4's second measure; and so on. The area is 75% blanketed, a remarkably high percentage in light of the limited number of redundancies—only three—and given the fact that the vacant first slot is usually reserved for prominent phrase boundaries, such as the accented start of stanza 3. All of this results in a fully explored set of contrapuntal options, a situation aided by the rich combinatorial possibilities inherent in three-way interactions.

DAVE WECKL: "MASTER PLAN"

Absent prefabricated rhythmic patterns (either embedded polymetrically or sprinkled arbitrarily), the drums can interact freely and unsystematically. The transcription in Figure 6.5 shows a solo by Dave Weckl that contains no recurring drum patterns. This example is especially intriguing because the four-measure ostinato, despite being in 4/4 and composed primarily of eighth-notes, is itself metrically ambiguous. A suggested hearing is shown above the transcription. The ostinato's most prominent notes fall on hardly prominent spots within the metric hierarchy: the low B on the "and" of beat three, the A-flat on the "and" of two, and the low C on the "and" of four. If Weckl

FIGURE 6.3 Trilok Gurtu, "Belo Horizonte" (3:49).

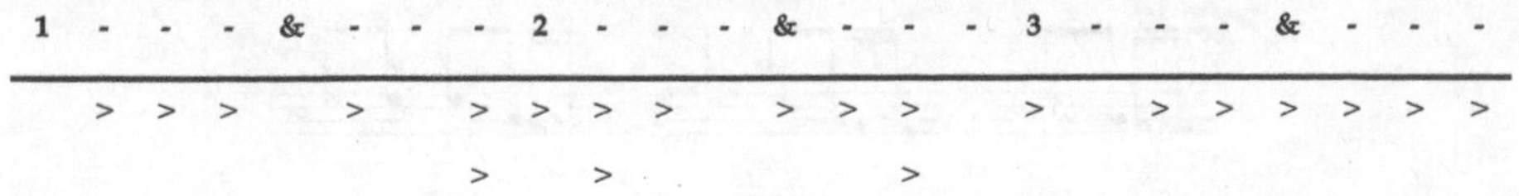

FIGURE 6.4 Gurtu's accent placements in the measure cycle.

accents these notes, he is associating with the ostinato and keeping away from the meter. Conversely, supporting the meter would automatically single out the ostinato.

For the most part, Weckl does neither. It is clear that the underlying 4/4 gains no support from the drums. In addition, the crossed-out arrows reveal a series of missed possible encounters with the ostinato's accents, although occasionally Weckl leans tepidly on the ostinato's eighth-notes (as indicated by the dotted brackets). In terms of the synchronization states introduced in 6.1, this example demonstrates how an extended passage may present a limited surveying of synchronization space, for most of the action here is constrained to only two configurations (those that exclude meter from the circle). The passage zooms by like a ferocious whirlwind, reserving the only point of salient alignment for the ostinato's last note.

Weckl's extended divergence owes much to the drumset's collection of contrasting timbres—the roughly ten instruments in the set plus the multiple hues that each one can produce. These readily split into separate auditory streams as Weckl alternates instrumental timbres at the very rapid rate of about ten onsets per second (Bregman 1990). Given the fast tempos that govern all the solos in this study, we can say that the odds are generally stacked against synchronization even if the drummer plays fairly straightforward subdivisions. As long as the drumsticks are traveling freely around the kit, fission is likely to ensue.

From here on, we will examine polymetric patterns only. Polymeter's famously disorienting effect is particularly effective in three-way scenarios because its shifting phase ensures automatic and continuous change vis-à-vis the meter-ostinato complex. The type of interaction status conferred on the three-way network depends on the nature of the polymeter: where it begins, how often it cycles, and what syncopations it contains. Indeed, the polymetric types populating a solo can be most diverse.

VINNIE COLAIUTA: "LIVE AT CATALINA'S"

The solo by Vinnie Colaiuta that we examine next features numerous polymetric passages. We will focus on two excerpts, both involving a piano-and-bass ostinato that spans a single 4/4 measure. Two of the ostinato's three chords land on a beat; the third chord anticipates beat three. The resulting pattern (on-on-off, on-on-off, etc.) constitutes a fixed set of relationships. Unleashing the polymetric drums creates an expanded set of relationships that varies continuously as the performance unfolds.

Our first example concerns the capacity of the three-way network to expand its number of elements. In Figure 6.6, Colaiuta breaks into a fast punk-rock pattern

FIGURE 6.5 Dave Weckl, “Master Plan” (3:12).

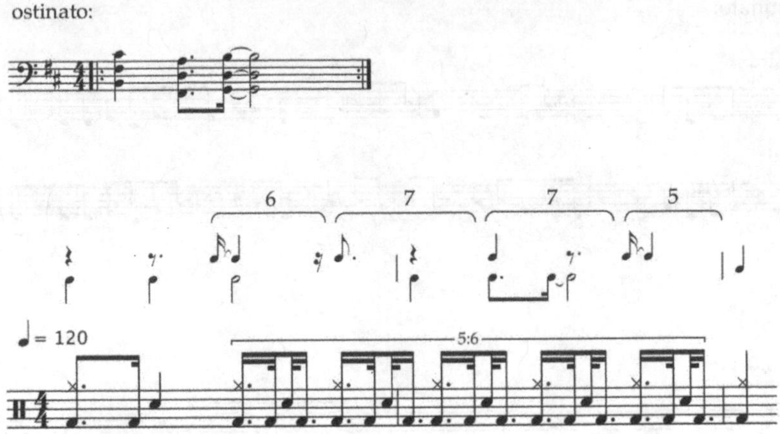

FIGURE 6.6 Vinnie Colaiuta, "Live at Catalina's" (2:51).

that compresses ten beats—rocket-propelled versions of his first two beats—into the space of six before disemboguing into a downbeat resolution. Meanwhile, the piano ostinato splits into two roles. This temporary bifurcation expands the number of total participating elements from three to four, thereby adding a layer of richness to the auditory scene. In addition to the ostinato chord sequence in the low register (shown with downward stems above the transcription), there is now an independent series of accented high-register chords (upward stems). The upper register chords' durations are 6, 7, 7, and 5 sixteenth-notes, a ticking that is sounded in near isochrony before the downbeat resolution. The addition of these four onsets in the space of (just over) six beats increases the overall complexity of the polymetric fabric already present in the 5-to-6 ratio of the drums-meter pairing. In short, even though an ostinato's primary function is to provide a reliably unchanging referent, it can at any time emerge from its accompanimental hypnosis to play a more active part in the rhythmic dialogue.[7]

Figure 6.7a shows how Colaiuta abruptly locks into a slow, slightly swung rock beat that is staggeringly unrelated to the governing tempo: 5½ eighth-notes to the bar.[8] (One way to grasp this ratio is to think of the drummer's sixteenth-note as a slightly slowed down eighth-note triplet, yielding 11 instead of 12 subdivisions.) Colaiuta (1987) refers to this process as "superimposed metric modulation," which involves

> a sort of temporary change in time signature, or the *illusion* of the tempo shifting when in fact it is not. . . . I say "superimposed" because one pulse, or time feel, is layered onto another already existing pulse, and because the layered pulse creates an effect of the time changing, I say "metric modulation." . . . The original time base remains intact (the tempo doesn't shift), and the second or layered pulse *does not take the place of the already existing pulse.* (emphasis in original)

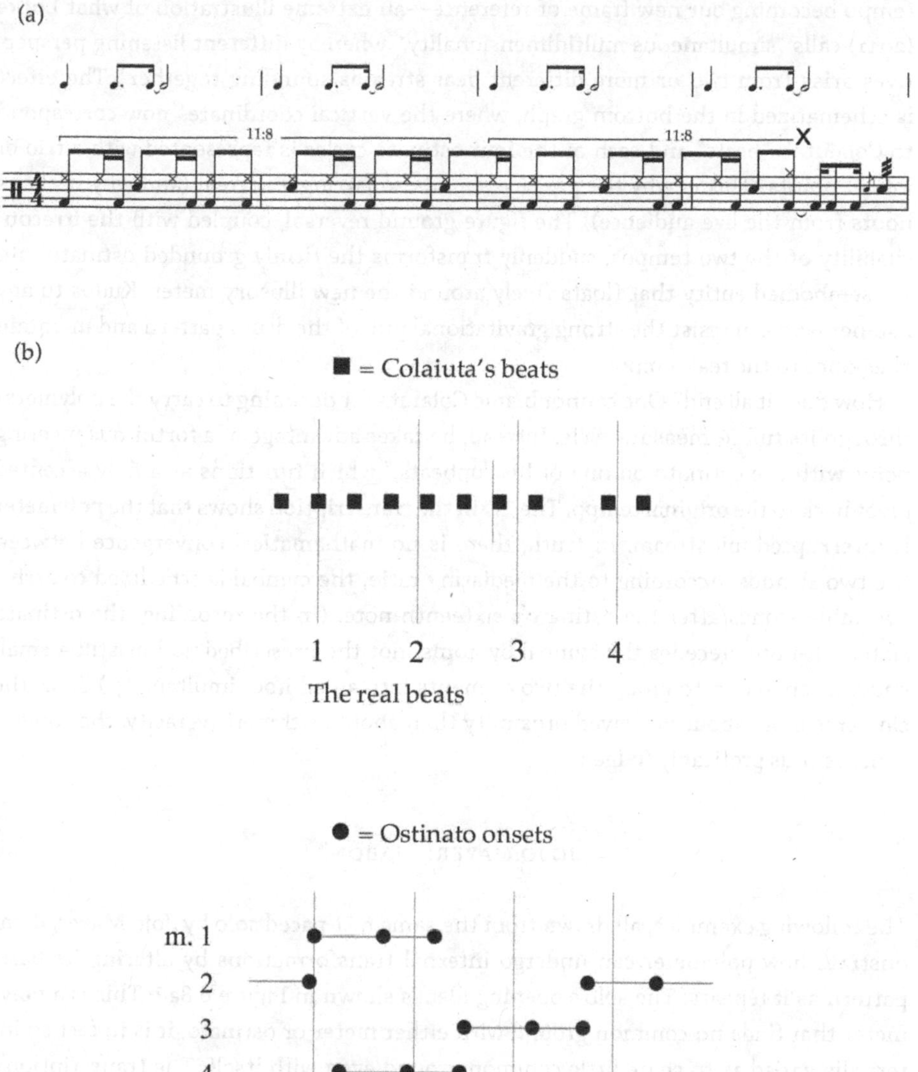

FIGURE 6.7a–b Vinnie Colaiuta, "Live at Catalina's" (2:11).

The cross-rhythms are outlined in Figure 6.7b. The top graph collapses the four measures in order to show the drum pattern's dislocation from the ostinato. With the exception of the opening downbeat, Colaiuta's "quarter-note beats" (the squares) hover around but never coincide with the measure's beats (the vertical coordinates) or with the ostinato's syncopated note (the short vertical line). More importantly, the perceptual reality of this passage is in fact reversed as a result of the drummer's tempo becoming our new frame of reference—an extreme illustration of what Locke (2011) calls "simultaneous multidimensionality," whereby different listening perspectives arise from two or more different beat streams sounding together.[9] The effect is schematized in the bottom graph, where the vertical coordinates now correspond to Colaiuta's "beats" and each of the four ostinato cycles is represented with a trio of joined points. This is why the passage sounds so jarringly surreal (and why it elicits hoots from the live audience). The figure-ground reversal, coupled with the irreconcilability of the two tempos, suddenly transforms the firmly grounded ostinato into a disembodied entity that floats freely around the new illusory meter. Kudos to any listener who can resist the strong gravitational pull of the drum pattern and maintain allegiance to the real tempo!

How does it all end? One cannot blame Colaiuta for declining to carry the polymeter through its full 16-measure cycle. Instead, he takes advantage of a fortuitous meeting point with the ostinato on one of his "upbeats," which functions as a duly accented pivot back to the original tempo. The "x" in the transcription shows that the polymeter is interrupted midstream. In truth, there is no mathematical convergence between the two strands. According to the mediating ratio, the cymbal is scheduled to arrive ~20 milliseconds after the ostinato's sixteenth-note. (In the recording, the ostinato sixteenth-note precedes the cymbal by 40ms, not the prescribed 20 but still a small enough separation to group the two elements into an ad-hoc simultaneity.) Since the ear cares more about perceived proximity than about arithmetic veracity, the convergence is thus profitably fudged.

JOJO MAYER: "JABON"

The following examples, all drawn from the same fast paced solo by Jojo Mayer, demonstrate how polymeter can undergo internal transformations by altering its basic pattern as it repeats. The solo's opening idea is shown in Figure 6.8a.[10] This is a polymeter that finds no common ground with either meter or ostinato; it is in fact so internally varied as to share little common ground even with itself. The transcription's triplets reveal the ternary logic driving Mayer's mental clock; this is the sense in which the passage can be thought of as polymetric. (The rhythm sounds strikingly alien despite the triplets' innocent visual appearance.) The first half of the opening phrase features two destabilizing properties: the pulse displacement caused—and subsequently undone—by the insertion of an eighth-note, and the accented flams whose locations in the sequence follow no apparent design other than to disrupt regularity. Two ostinato cycles later, the process is repeated more or less in retrograde and fanned out to the tom-toms (Figure 6.8b). There is a fundamental difference in how the drums reach the downbeat in the two examples. Internal regularity follows irregularity in one case (Figure 6.8a), while the reverse occurs in the other (Figure 6.8b).

Later in the solo, Mayer halves a polymetric pattern to emphasize the ostinato's upsurge in syncopated activity as it approaches the end of the hypermeasure

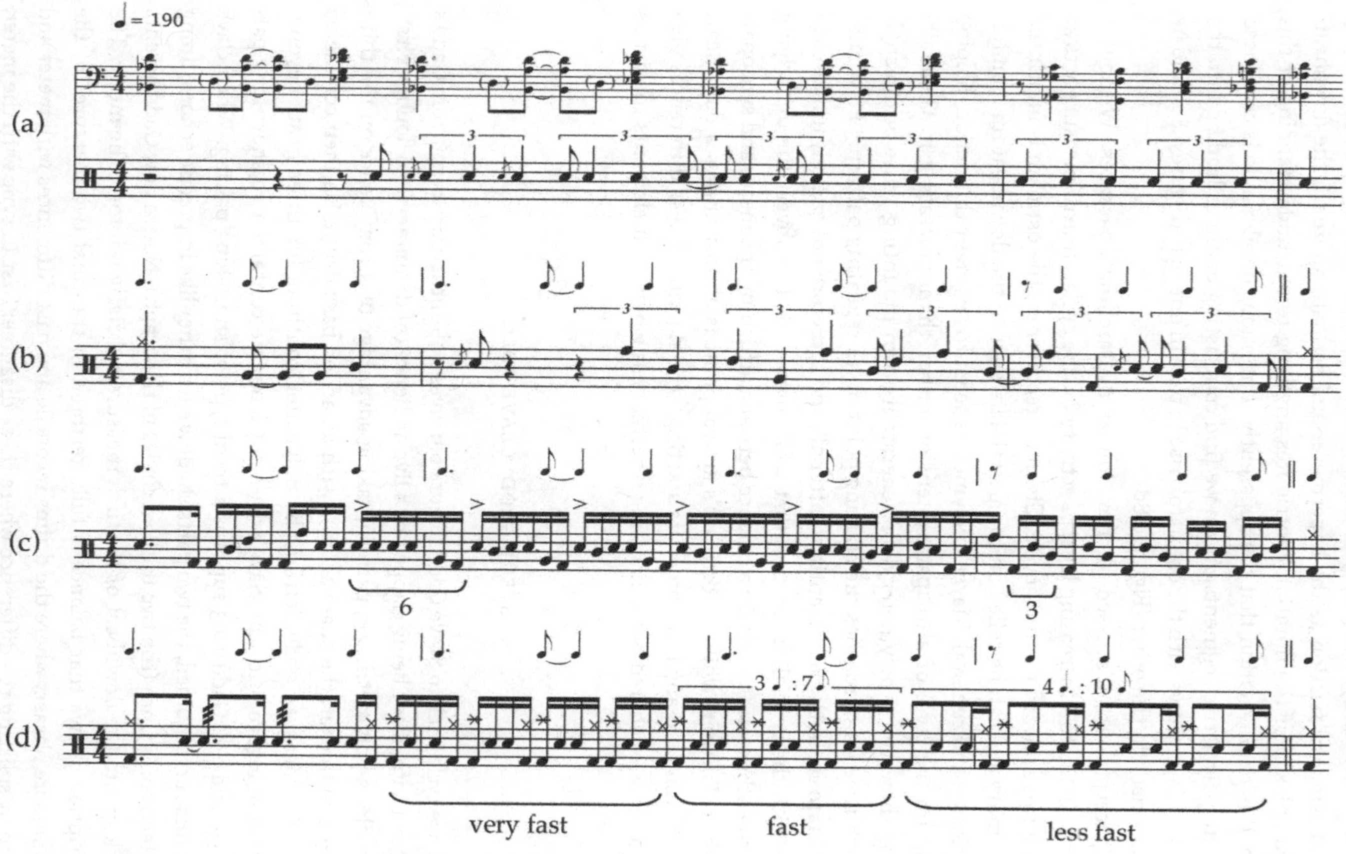

FIGURE 6.8a–d Jojo Mayer, "Jabon" (5:09, 5:19, 5:56, 6:11).

(Figure 6.8c). While the two layers are almost entirely out of sync throughout, there is a sense of sympathetic parallelism as the drums track and react to the ostinato's goal-driven motion. Finally, the polymeter in Figure 6.8d downshifts gradually, creating a kind of temporal friction as the hypermeter and ostinato approach the downbeat. If the complexity of the notation contributes anything to our understanding of this passage, it is the revelation that the apparently continuous decelerando is composed of discrete polymetric segments. Again we find contrasting energies leading into the downbeat: Mayer flows with the ostinato's rise in pace in one case (Figure 6.8c), and he grinds against it in the other (Figure 6.8d).

The excerpts just discussed all function as overarching anacruses. Without a doubt, the ostinato's increasing level of activity on the cycle's fourth measure acts as a driving force toward the next cycle. Given its recurrence, the ostinato is imprinted onto memory and can be relied on to carry the listener to the downbeat for simultaneous closure and renewal. Mayer's polymeters seem to augment this action, helping to ramp up the level of anticipatory tension rather than generating it. Generally speaking, however, a polymeter does generate its own mounting sense of directedness each time it approaches the starting point of its repeating pattern.[11] Polymeter and ostinato are both cyclical entities, after all, and therefore not entirely unlike each other—with the crucial distinction that while one tends to subvert the underlying meter, the other tends to strike a balance between affirming the meter and syncopating with it. Further, while an ostinato's arrival point is almost always a downbeat, polymeter can take any location as its starting/arrival point. These differences give rise to a sense of shared but conflicting directedness when both elements coexist as anacruses.

STEVE GADD: CLAVE SOLO

To end, we cycle back to Steve Gadd. Figure 6.9 gives a 28-measure excerpt from Gadd's solo over a Latin clave being clapped by a live audience (of drummers, no doubt). First, Gadd cycles a polymetric 2–3 pattern, taking advantage of a confluence on the third downbeat to thicken the snare accents with an added bass drum. He then completes the full five-measure cycle, letting the polymeter continue for three beats beyond. As shown in Figure 6.10, the clave's 3-3-4-2-4 template contains two short-long patterns: 3-4 and 2-4. Gadd's 2-3 supplies a third type of short-long pairing. When clave and drums are combined, the two parts shadow each other like imprecise echoes, lining up perfectly only once (the two unfilled circles in the graph). Notice how Gadd accents the pickup into the downbeat of the fifth measure to briefly reinforce the meter. The transcription shows that balance is fully restored in the final two measures of the eight-measure phrase, where the drums reconcile any past differences with meter and ostinato by splitting the difference where these disagree: first in sync with the meter, then with the ostinato.

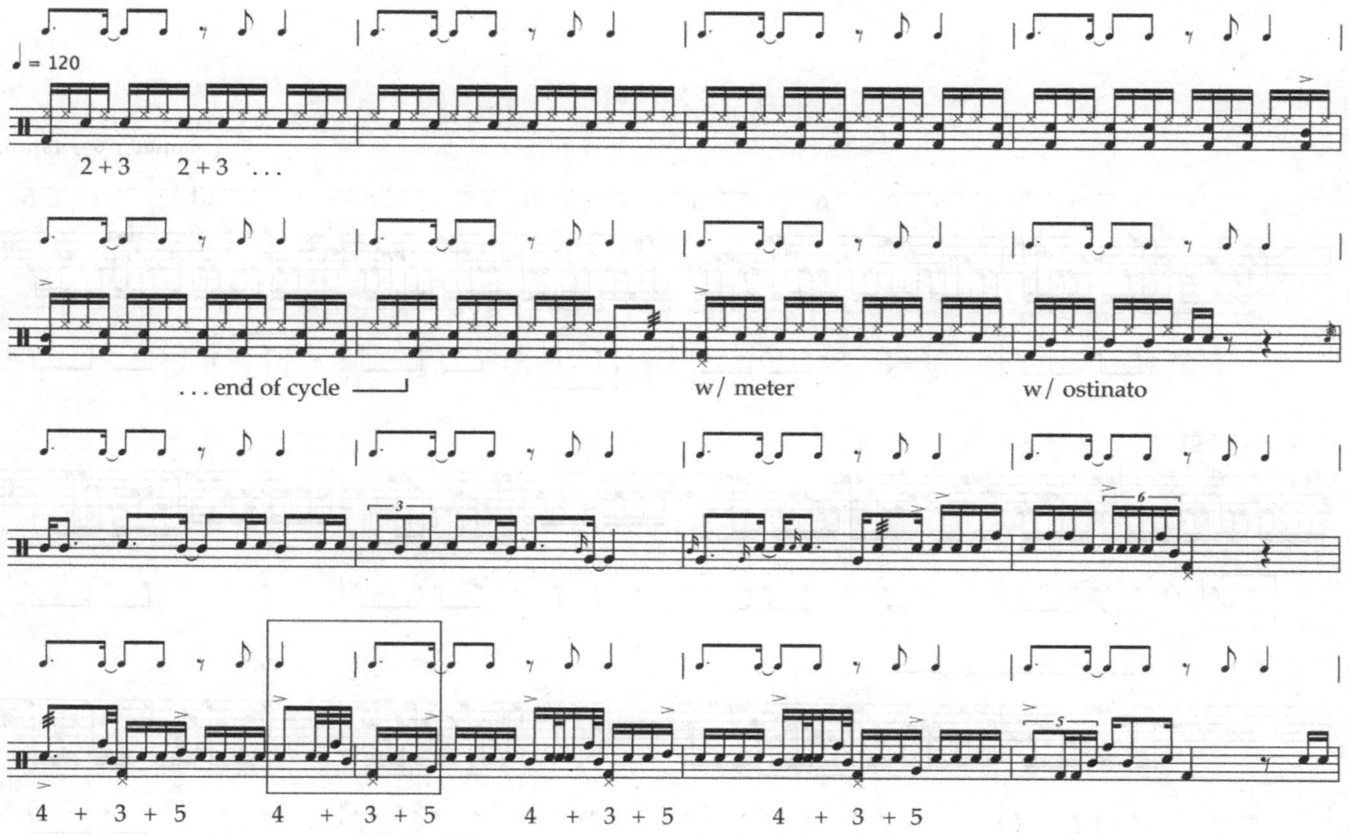

FIGURE 6.9 Gadd, clave solo (2:21).

FIGURE 6.9 Continued

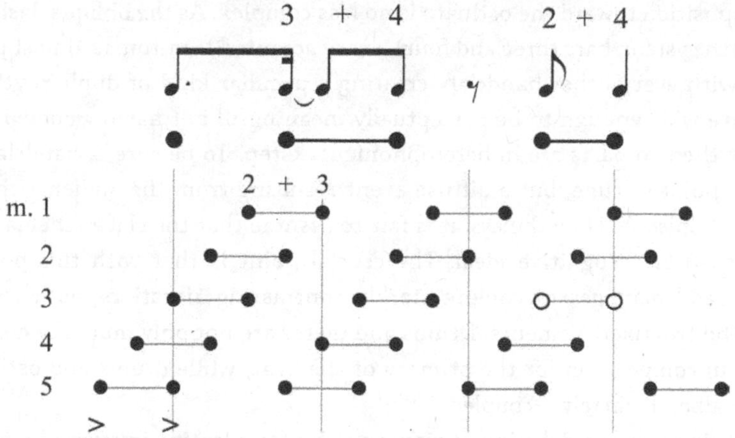

FIGURE 6.10 Ostinato (top) vs. polymeter (staggered 2+3 pairs) vs. meter (vertical lines) in the first five measures of Figure 6.9.

A different polymetric passage ensues at the transcription's fourth system. The cycled pattern (4-3-5) is again a misshapen portion of the ostinato (3-3-4), causing an eerie reflection between the two parts. The boxed-in area in Figure 6.9 points to the only prolonged congruence in an otherwise hocketed exchange where drum and clave onsets rarely coincide. But even this brief convergence is imperfect, for the first item in the drum pattern is yoked to the last item in the clave, and the other two pairings in the box are similarly mismatched in terms of their ordering.

The final three systems in the transcription offer our last exhibit of polymetric play. Following two brief polymetric gestures in the first two measures, Gadd settles on a sequence of sextuplets (marked with solid horizontal brackets) that will dominate the next ten measures. On paper, this rhythm looks fast but straightforward. The pattern begins with sixteenth-note triplets and repeats every three eighth-notes, landing alternatively on beats and upbeats—by no means a radical metric disposition given the 4/4 framework. Though this is likely how the pattern was initially learned and subsequently applied in performance, the ear favors the accented tom-tom (shown with stems down) as the initiator of each cycle. From this perspective, every other cycle begins on the last sextuplet of the beat. This is far more complex than a classic case of displacement or syncopation. At this tempo, the extremely rapid (80-ms) sextuplets mesh into a blur and are in no way suited to accommodate subdivision slots, let alone heavily accented ones. The other tom-tom starting point is only marginally better anchored: it falls on the second triplet of the beat, but in an environment completely devoid of triplets. This polymeter seems tethered to imaginary metric locations.

Its disposition toward the ostinato is no less complex. As the oblique dashed lines show (fifth system, bars three and four), every accented tom-tom is almost perfectly aligned with every other handclap, creating a peculiar kind of duple rhythm. The offsets are wide enough to be perceptually meaningful but narrow enough to suggest that the two parts are in heterophonic lockstep. To be sure, a handclap is not a precise point in time, but a diffuse event resulting from the audience members' attempted unisons. Nonetheless, it is fair to assume that the clave schema remains unperturbed as a cognitive ideal. The crucial point is that with this polymetric phrase, Gadd manages to conjure starkly contrasting situations with respect to each of the two fixed elements. Drums and meter are not only mutually disengaged but also in competition for the primacy of the beat, while drums and ostinato are tightly—albeit bizarrely—coupled.

Were this a fleeting delusion, it would suffice for a lasting impression. But Gadd is merely setting the stage for the unveiling of a truly mesmerizing rhythmic contraption. The dotted brackets beginning in the penultimate system show that what was previously a nine-unit pattern is now fifteen. (Though this has an intimidating ring to it, nothing more than a beat has been added.) Groups of fifteen begin to alternate with groups of nine, summing to the requisite twenty-four sextuplets of a full measure. The six added notes are there to accent the ostinato pattern's last two notes (boxed in), resulting in an abrupt reawakening to the tangibility of the fourth beat and its preceding anacrusis: "AND FOUR!" The experience is relived twice more in the first two measures of the last system. In the midst of highly antimetrical surroundings, this sudden spotlight on the ostinato's most meter-friendly portion is cause for bewilderment. From the ostinato's perspective (that is, for the listener who is latching on to the clave), the polymeter's faithful but uncommitted company culminates with an unexpectedly emphatic "I do!" From the polymeter's perspective (for the listener who has been lured by the periodicity of the tom-tom's nonuple cycle), the beat seems suddenly stretched and, as explained in the following paragraph, strangely subdivided. Which of the two realities do we choose? Since they cannot reasonably coexist on the same plane, we are left to flicker back and forth between them.[12]

Within the illusory 15-subdivision beat demarcated by the tom-tom, we are hard pressed to find a clear-cut arrangement for the polymeter's "and four" accents. Two feasible templates are presented in Figure 6.11, neither of which provides a very good fit. There is little hope of hearing a metrically "rational" subdivision of Gadd's beat. Of course, there is no reason why one *should* settle on a clear-cut arrangement of internal proportions; it is well known that musicians can subdivide beats in all manner of ways. However, this rhythm is neither a flexed version of a simple pattern (such as a "laid back triplet") nor an isolated, freely timed sequence. Gadd's improbable subdivision pattern is unique in that it emerges from a precise physical routine—itself derived from a precise numeric formula—that guarantees exact replication.

FIGURE 6.11 Gadd's 15-subdivision group and two "rational" approximations.

CONCLUSION

We have identified a variety of approaches by which modern drummers play with and against ostinato accompaniments. The five drummers studied here fall under no unified genre. Yet they speak a pervasive and immediately recognizable language whose grammar is shaped by the fluidity of jazz, the forceful drive of rock, the energized syncopations of funk, the metric intricacies of Afro-Cuban percussion, and a great many other individual stylistic influences. In the context of this eclectic performing tradition, the present chapter makes two primary contributions to our broader discourse on rhythm.

The first contribution is technical. Though this is not a study of polymeter per se, the analyses amount to a serviceable field guide of polymetric types and their capabilities. These (often overlapping) capabilities include undergoing internal transformation, redrawing different interaction routines in synchronization space, forming ephemeral rhythms, and holding up a refracting mirror to the ostinato's features. A running theme has been that it is not enough to point out that a polymeter results from the drums being in this or that unrelated meter, as this paints a woefully incomplete picture of the actual realization of rhythmic events. The precise arrangement of onsets matters.

The chapter's second contribution is conceptual: the idea that drummers negotiate the synchronization parameters set by meter and ostinato in a particular kind of three-element theater. What is particular is the fundamental dissimilarity between the attending elements—between that which is implicit-unchanging (meter), explicit-unchanging (ostinato), and explicit-changing (drums). When polymeter is used, the progression of shifting relationships is at once structured (given the polymeter's stable internal makeup and the fixed meter-ostinato pairings) and complexly unpredictable. Viewed this way, the interactive processes of ostinato drum solos provide a useful conceptual backdrop for the characterization of improvised music-making in other ensemble settings.

APPENDIX

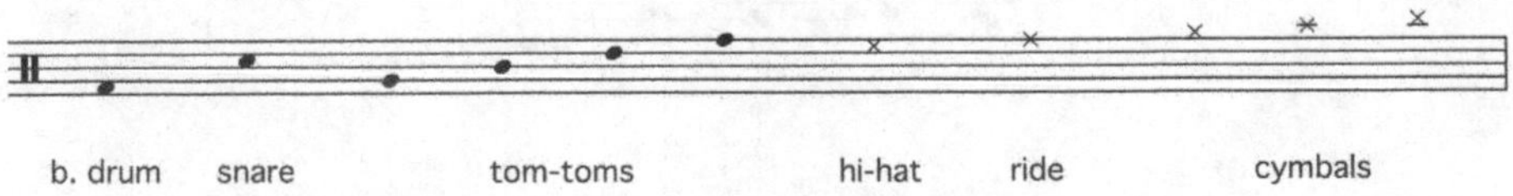

FIGURE 6.12 Drum notation key.

NOTES

1. The years of the issues in question are as follows. Colaiuta: 1982, 1987, 1993, 2007, 2013; Gadd: 1978, 1983, 1996, 2004; Gurtu: 1992; Mayer: 2015; Weckl: 1986, 1990, 2001, 2004, 2015.

2. Colaiuta has worked out of Los Angeles since the late 1970s; beyond session work with numerous jazz, rock, and fusion musicians, he has worked closely with Sting and Frank Zappa. Based in New York, Gadd has done extensive touring and session work in jazz, rock, pop, and funk since the early 1970s. Gurtu was born and raised in Mumbai, where he learned the tabla before taking up the drumset and subsequently touring and recording as a jazz, fusion, and "world music" drummer/percussionist. Mayer relocated to New York from Zurich in his late twenties, shifting his focus from jazz to experimental funk and electronica. Originally from St. Louis, Weckl played jazz and fusion in New York clubs in the early 1980s; he has toured with Simon and Garfunkel and recorded nine albums with Chick Corea's Elektric and Akoustic Bands.

3. We will do this assessment intuitively. To quantify degrees of consonance between patterns, one could measure distances between rhythm vectors using a variety of similarity metrics (e.g., Colannino et al. 2009; Demaine et al. 2009). See also Huron and Ommen (2006) for a method to quantify syncopation scores.

4. This is an instance of simultaneously occurring grouping dissonance and displacement dissonance (Krebs 1999).

5. Another example of a polymeter that cadences on a nondownbeat metric location occurs in this solo's final two measures, where the resolution is on beat four (the pickup to the next section).

6. Only the first and third ~40ms anticipations materialize in the performance; the math dictates a similar anticipation where the middle asterisk lies, but the performance gives a rhythmic unison instead. A similar effect occurs in stanza 8, where the third measure's second half is a tripletized retelling of the first half.

7. This occurs numerous times throughout Colaiuta's solo. Among others, Berliner (1994, 348–86) and Brinner (1995, 173–80) have addressed the flexible nature of predetermined roles in ensemble performance. Brinner's notion of an "interactive system" is especially relevant to the present work.

8. The idea that alternate tempos are a form of polymeter is explored in Benadon (2009).

9. Unlike the current example, in Locke's analyses the streams conform to cycles of equal length, such as four beats versus six in a bar of 12/8. Moreover, whereas these streams "exist in a latent, implicit and tacit dimension that is available to consciousness as a factor in a listener's perception" (p. 106, this volume), Colaiuta's tempo—which he revisits at 2:34 and 4:09—surfaces out of the blue and promptly vanishes. Locke's discussion (chapter 4, this volume) of

the fluid interactions between lead drum, response drum, bell time-line, and implicit meter in Agbadza music can be seen as a four-element d_1-d_2-m-o framework.

10. The transcriptions in Figure 6.8 omit Mayer's hi-hat pedal on every beat.

11. Kramer's "multiply-directed time" (1988, 46) and Hasty's "anacrustic continuation" (1997, 122) are relevant here.

12. A literary analogue is Julio Cortázar's "La Noche Boca Arriba" (a modern version of Chuang Tzu's well-known butterfly dream), in which the protagonist alternates between two dream-like states.

DISCOGRAPHY

Figure 6.2: Chick Corea, "Three Quartets." Stretch Records (1981). Chick Corea, piano; Eddie Gomez, bass; Steve Gadd, drums.

Figure 6.3: John McLaughlin Trio, "Qué Alegría." Verve (1991). John McLaughlin, guitar; Dominic DiPiazza, bass; Trilok Gurtu, drums.

Figure 6.5: Dave Weckl, "Master Plan." GRP Records (1990). Chick Corea, keyboards; John Patitucci, bass; Steve Gadd & Dave Weckl, drums.

Figures 6.6–6.7: Pasqua/Patitucci/Colaiuta, "Live at Catalina's, track7." Unissued (nd). Alan Pasqua, piano; John Patitucci, bass; Vinnie Colaiuta, drums. The bootleg recording was uploaded to the forum www.houseofdrumming.com by a member drummer (Steve Holmes, personal communication, 8/5/13).

Figure 6.8: Jojo Mayer & Nerve, "Modern Drummer Festival 2005." Hudson Music DVD (2005).

Figure 6.9: "Steve Gadd." Hudson Music DVD (2008).

7

Temporal and Density Flow in Javanese Gamelan

Sumarsam

COMPARED WITH THEORY of other musics such as Chinese and Indian music, gamelan theory has a short history. It began to emerge only in the late nineteenth century with the writing of Dutch scholars, such as the work of Groneman and Land (1890). The writing expanded in the early to mid-twentieth century with the work of both Dutch and Javanese scholars, such as Djakoeb and Wignyaroemeksa (1913), Radèn Bagoes Soelardi (1918), Jaap Kunst (1973[1949]), Ki Hadjar Dewantara (1930), and Ki Sindusawarno (1955).

It is worth noting that some of the concepts developed by gamelan theorists are not used by musicians, or are used differently. In some cases theorists who were not gamelan practitioners, such as Sindusawarno, had close relationships with musicians. There are also important differences in perspective between conservatory-trained musicians and those with traditional training, although nowadays traditional musicians intermingle closely with conservatory-trained musicians.

As a consequence of the burgeoning of ethnomusicology, in the mid-twentieth century gamelan theory was gaining momentum. Concurrently, more and more cross-cultural and interdisciplinary approaches to gamelan theory developed. For example, Judith Becker's work on the melodic structure of *gendhing* (gamelan composition) was inspired by the study of Albert Lord (1960) on Serbo-Croatian epics singing. Becker's research, in collaboration with Alton Becker (1979), draws on linguistics. For another example, Sutton (1993) asserts a parallel in musical processes between gamelan melody and Gregorian chant.

Also in the mid-twentieth century, there was a tendency for Western scholars to search for indigenous gamelan theory. The prevalence of a Western perspective in the production of gamelan theory ("outside looking in") might have been the reason for this trend. The most crucial aspect in indigenizing gamelan theory has been the search for the musicians' perspectives. Their perspectives were seen to represent "insider" or "emic" understanding of the music—"inside looking in."

In light of this development, I suggest that the study of gamelan theory should not be only about "outside looking in," but also "inside looking in and out," or, better yet, "inside and outside looking in and out." In any event, this challenging emic-etic consideration should be part of the investigation of gamelan theory.

To a certain extent, Indian musical concepts have given impetus to the development of gamelan theory. We learn from history that Indonesian culture has long been heavily imbued with Buddhism and Hinduism, starting in the early centuries before the Islamization of Javanese people in the fifteenth century. Many aspects of Hinduism were synthesized into Indonesian culture. For example, stories from the Indian *Mahābhārata* and *Rāmāyaṇa* epics have been told in the Javanese shadow puppet show (*wayang*) until today. The hand gestures of Indian dancers, *mudras*, can still be found in Javanese dance, although they have lost their meaning. A few Javanese musical terms that can be traced back to Indian terms are still used in gamelan theory, for example *kekawin*, from *kawya* (poetry); *laya*, from *lay* (tempo); and *irama*, from *wirama* (pauses).

In spite of the significance of Indian cultural influence on Indonesia, Indian music has only marginally impacted gamelan and gamelan theory.[1] One of the Indian terms stands out, however, namely *irama*. The term became an important concept in gamelan rhythm, although its original meaning has been localized.

IRAMA AND RHYTHM

As Indonesia has long been exposed to Western music, Western musical terminology is not alien to many Indonesian gamelan theorists, although traditional gamelan musicians have only a limited or no understanding of them. Use of the term rhythm (Indonesian, *ritme*) is very limited. As Supanggah states in his recent book (2011, 104), the concept of rhythm is not too well-known in *karawitan* (the art of Javanese gamelan and vocal music). I must say, however, that his understanding of "rhythm" is rather ambiguous.[2] In any event, he feels that *irama* encompasses everything about time and space in gamelan; hence the term *irama* represents the term rhythm as well.

Writing in the late 1950s, a theorist at the gamelan conservatory, Ki Sindusawarno,[3] begins his discussion of *irama* by stating that

> Nowadays, the word irama is commonly used to translate "rhythm." However, originally, the term used in karawitan is wirama, the meaning of which has never changed. The term wirama has its specific meaning. Irama in European music, in the sense of rhythm, has a different meaning. Irama also has another meaning in every day conversation. (Sindusawarno 1955, 31–32)

Sindusawarno then uses the term *matra* (Indonesian) to indicate meter in music and literature. The Javanese term *gatra* is preferred when referring to a unit of four notes in gamelan composition; *matra* is used when discussing music generally. According to Sindusawarno, *matra* or *gatra* is the ordering of alternating moments perceived as light-heavy-light et cetera, or soft-loud-soft, et cetera. He then explains the meaning of *wirama*. Implying the same meaning as the Indian term, he defines *wirama* as pauses between the pulses, the absence of activity, or the moments of silence. This means that *wirama* refers to the length of pauses between the pulses during the movement of a *gatra*. In playing a *gendhing* (gamelan composition), the moment of silence between the pulses is filled with the forms of playing intended to fill in the pauses. Thus, *wirama* is a musical process in which certain instruments fill in the pauses in between the basic pulses.

Sindusawarno goes on to say that the determining factor to fill in the pauses is a change of the *laya* (tempo) of the piece. I should mention that although Indonesian gamelan theorists use the term *laya*, musicians don't use this term. *Laya* (from *lay*) is also an Indian term, usually referring to temporal flow. Clayton (2000, 75–92) points out, however, that *lay* actually encompasses both temporal and density flow, similar to the concept of *irama* in gamelan. In any event, the tempo itself is one of three different speeds (fast, medium, and slow), but the density of the pulses that fill in the pauses stays constant. Only when the density level of some instruments changes, can one say that a *wirama* has changed. In other words, two processes are working hand-in-hand in *wirama*: temporal flow (the duration of the successive pulses) in coordination with the changes in density level of certain instruments. Benamou (2010, 225) argues convincingly that *irama* is one of the most confusing concepts in Javanese gamelan, with no equivalent in Western music,

> The closest analogy in Western music to a section of a *gendhing* played in multiple *irâmâs* might be a set of variations in different time signatures but with all variations having the same number of measures and a fairly constant eighth-note value, so that the variations would take varying amounts of time to perform. The *irâmâ*, in this case, would then correspond to the ratio between the density of the melodic figuration and the length of the measure (or, say, the harmonic rhythm). Imagine, for instance, a 2/2 variation with eighth-note figuration going to a 4/4 variation with sixteenth-note figuration: the "theme" would be twice as long in 4/4 as in 2/2, but the figuration would be going by at about the same speed in both.

In gamelan conversation and in subsequent writings on gamelan theory, the word *wirama* used by Sindusawarno is not common; instead, the term *irama* becomes the encompassing term for both temporal flow and density changes. In other words, within the context of a conversation, musicians will know whether one is talking about the change of temporal flow or the change of density level.

The change of temporal and density flow—the changes of pulses in relation to the basic beats—explains *irama* only on a technical or mechanical level of analysis; change in melodic aspects of the piece is actually more essential to the concept of *irama*.

IRAMA AND MELODY

As I mentioned earlier, Sindusawarno asserts in passing that *irama* in gamelan differs from rhythm in Western music. However, in the same work he also says that *irama* could have a sense of a Western rhythm, though he admits that it is difficult to explain. He illustrates this point by first showing a lively song for accompanying a deer dance in a scene of the *Rāmāyaṇa* dance drama staged in front of the Prambanan temple (although he does not mention this source). This lively song is full of syncopated beats (see Example 7.1a). He explains:

> Some of the tones in this melody are low; others are high. Some are loud and some are soft. . . .The tones are alternating in an orderly manner (*bergilir-ganti*), going up and down, coming and going. The tones move in the matra. Against the matra, some tones fall precisely on the beat, slip about the beat, going slightly ahead of, or behind the beat. There are moments when the tones crowd together in an orderly manner like stringbeans (*urut kacang*); there are times when they are dispersed. They move, they flow, they are alive, because of irama. (Sindusawarno 1955, 39, as translated by Hatch in Becker 1987, 356 with a few modifications)

So to him rhythm is a lively, irregular phrasing, and unsteady pulses of the movement of tones against *matra* (meter). To prove his point, he eliminates the syncopated rhythms in the piece, resulting in only the skeletal melody of the song on steady pulses (compare the original song, Figure 7.1a, with Sindusawarno's version, Figure 7.1b). Then he asks his readers to compare them. He suggests that the second melody has lost its rhythm; hence, rhythm is a patterned configuration of beats conceived and perceived against meter.

It seems that this definition resonates with the definition of rhythm in a general sense of Western rhythm: rhythm is the pattern of movement in time, inextricably linked with meter and tempo. Furthermore, rhythm "is necessarily a part of the pitch and textural aspects of music, and one can speak of durational rhythm, accentual rhythm, textural rhythm, harmonic rhythm, melodic rhythm, or timbral rhythm,

```
| 6   6 | . 5 5   6 1̇ 6 | .   0   1̇ 2̇ 1̇ | .65 2   .   0 |
| 2   2   2 3 2 | . 6̣   . 51 2 6̣ | .   0   2 3 1 | . . 0 5   6 |
| . 1̇ 5   3   2 | . 6   . 51 2 6 | .   . 5 6̣ 1 2 |
| . 3 5 2 3 2 2 1| 6̣ 1 2   1   6̣ | . 5̣ 1   6̣   5̣ | .   0 ||
```

FIGURE 7.1a A song for accompanying a deer dance: the original song.

|6 6 | 5 5 6 1̇ | 6 1̇ 2̇ 1̇ | 6 5 2 2 | 2 2 3 2 |

|6̣ 5̣ 1 2 | 6̣ 2 3 2 | 5 6 1̇ 5 | 3 2 6̣ 5̣ | 1 2 6̣ 5̣ |

|6̣ 1 2 3 | 6 2 3 2 | 2 1 6̣ 1 | 2 1 6̣ 5̣ | 1 6̣ 5̣ ||

FIGURE 7.1b A song for accompanying a deer dance: Sindusawarno's version of the melodic skeleton of the song.

depending on which aspect is to the fore in any particular context" (Powers 1986, 701). I would say that one can discuss gamelan rhythm in terms of all of these, except harmonic rhythm.

Returning to gamelan, *irama* in the sense of the coordination of temporal flow and density adjustment brings about a processual dynamic of rhythmic and melodic interplay among the multiple layers of a gamelan ensemble. What follows is an elucidation of how *irama* works and in what ways it has an impact on the melodies and the ensemble's interplay.

There are four levels of *irama: tanggung, dadi, wilet*, and *rangkep* (see Figure 7.2 for the density level of the elaborating instruments in relation to the pulses of the melodic skeleton).[4] A transition from one *irama* to another is led by the drum. First, the drum leads the ensemble to gradually speed up or slow down the tempo. In the case of changing to a more expansive *irama*, when the elaborating instruments reach a point where playing their instruments is uncomfortably too slow, then they have to make an upward adjustment of their tempo, accompanied by expanding the number of pulses within the *gongan* structure of the piece. In essence, when an *irama* changes, the tempo returns back to the same tempo before the change, but the piece becomes more expansive since the *gongan* structure is expanded.

The change of *irama* has wider musical implications than the change of temporal and density flow alone. As Becker (1981) rightly pointed out, it allows a single piece to assume different lengths, different degrees of instrumental or vocal embellishment, different playing styles of some instruments, and therefore, a different mood. Here is where the identity of the melody of a *gendhing* becomes a moot question. Focusing on only one of the multiple-lines of gamelan composition, namely *balungan* (melodic skeleton), previous gamelan scholars paid less attention to this identity of melody of *gendhing* and the interactions between the instruments in the ensemble. Recent works have explored the interconnection and interplay of the instruments in this multilayered ensemble (Sumarsam 1995; Sutton and Vetter 2006; Perlman 2004) and the melodic sources from which a *gendhing* is composed (Sumarsam 1995). Regarding the latter, my research leads me to conclude that the original identity of the melody of most *gendhing* resides in *irama dadi* or *wilet*.

It is beyond the scope of this chapter to say more about this topic, but it is important to mention it, as we cannot ignore the aspects of melody in discussing *irama*.

What is clear is that the interaction, interconnection, or interplay among the instruments is the heart of gamelan playing; hence, the execution of melody in coordination with *irama*. That is, a shift in one musical domain can both trigger idiomatic changes in instrumental performance style and produce a change in the entire ensemble's interplay. A shift in *irama* means a process of change in temporal and density flow, a transformative renewal, bringing about the change of the elaboration, the moods, and the identity of the melody.

In his article on "Temporal Transformation in Cross-Cultural Perspective," Tenzer (2011c, 170) refers to this temporal transformation as musical augmentation. He asserts that "the moment of augmentation is often a goal of the individual composition, while the clarity it confers is a goal of musical perception itself." According to him, in Bali, this musical augmentation attains a strong association with the sacred.

The moment of augmentation in Javanese gamelan, especially in a composition with an expansive structure, brings about a different kind of aural disposition. As Keeler (1987, 225) observes, "As one passes from *wirama* one to two to three to four, which is like shifting gears, the strokes on the *saron* and *slenthem*, which play the skeletal line, become rarer. This permits the other 'inner' or embellishing instruments—the *gendèr, gambang, clempung,* and *rebab*, each of which has a highly distinctive tonal quality—plus the female singer (*pesindhèn*), to superimpose increasingly long and complex variations."

It is true that the augmentation in the more expansive *irama* brings about a greater aural richness, but less aural clarity (Keeler 1987, 225). However, to the musicians, this does not mean that the melody becomes less clear. Unlike in Balinese music as explained by Tenzer, the expansive augmentation does not necessarily signify deeper spiritual experience. On the contrary, it could bring about lively, animated musical moods, such as in the augmentation that happens when a composition is performed in *irama wilet* and *rangkep*.

Now I would like to explain *irama* in the context of the interaction between instruments, especially the impact of drumming style in the ensemble's play. Different styles of drumming affect the rhythmic and melodic configuration of other instruments. There are four drumming styles, each corresponding generically to the mood of a *gendhing* (or a section of it), the character of a dance, or the mood of a theatrical performance. These drumming styles consist of rhythmic patterns ranging from the repetition of a simple pattern with an underlying regular beat (*kendhang satunggal* and *kendhang kalih*) to elaborate patterns with an underlying regular but elusive beat (*kendhang ciblon* and *kendhang wayangan*). In playing a *gendhing* or in a medley presentation, two or more *kendhang* styles may be employed. For example, in playing the first section of *ladrang* Pangkur, *kendhang* plays a less elaborate configurative rhythmic pattern of the *kendhang kalih* style; *gendèr* plays in the *lomba* technique (see Figure 7.2a and b; Audio.7.1 ▶) and *bonang* plays *pipilan*—the player plays each pair of the notes in moderate tempo, anticipating and guiding the melodic skeleton (*balungan*). When the drum cues the ensemble to change to *irama wilet* (by guiding the ensemble to slow down, using the more lively *kendhang ciblon* style), the *gendèr* will change its playing from *lomba* to *rangkep* style; and the *bonang* playing changes from *pipilan* to *imbal* (interlocking) technique (Audio 7.2 ▶), an excerpt of ladrang Pangkur, from the introductory movement to *irama tanggung, dadi*, and *wilet*.

Listening guide I to Audio 7.2
Recording of *ladrang* PANGKUR *Sléndro Sanga*, focusing on the *gendèr*—see the earlier discussion and musical examples of this piece.

0:00—0:07 *Senggrèngan*, a brief melodic cue from the *rebab*, announcing the tuning system of the piece.

0:07—0:16 *Buka*, an introductory movement of the piece played on *rebab*. *Gendèr* and *kendhang* join in. At the end of the *buka*, on the stroke of the large *gong*, the other instruments join in.

0:17—0:25 The piece begins in *irama tanggung*. Immediately, the drum cues the ensemble to slow down gradually, moving toward *irama dadi* after the stroke of the first *kenong*. During the *irama* transition and in *irama dadi*, *gendèr* plays less elaborate rhythmic configurations in moderate tempo—*lomba* style; *kendhang* plays simple rhythmic patterns in a moderate tempo, using two drums—*kendhang kalih* style.

0:25—0:54 The piece stays in *irama dadi*. On the stroke of the third *kenong* the drum switches to an animated *ciblon* style.

0:54—1:13 The *ciblon* drumming signals the ensemble to slow down gradually, moving toward *irama dadi* on the *gong*. After the stroke of the *gong*, the piece enters *irama wilet*.

1:13—3:11 During the playing of *irama wilet*, *gendèr* plays lively and elaborate rhythmic configurations in fast tempo—*rangkep* style; *kendhang* plays animated rhythmic patterns in faster tempo—*kendhang ciblon*—based on the patterns that accompany lively movements of *gambyong* dance.

3:11— If you continue listening to the piece past 3:11, you will hear another transition from *irama wilet* to *irama rangkep*, with a number of *andhegan* (a stop in the middle of the piece, which resumes again after a *pesindhèn* singer sings an interlude), back to *irama wilet* until the end of the piece.

Listening guide II to Audio 7.1
The same recording but focusing on the *bonang*.

0:00—0:07 *Senggrèngan*, a brief melodic cue from *rebab*, announcing the tuning system of the piece.

0:07—0:16 *Buka*, an introductory movement of the piece played by *rebab*. *Gendèr* and *kendhang* join in. At the end of the *buka*, on the stroke of the large *gong*, the other instruments join in—you can hear clearly both *bonang barung* (middle-range *bonang*) and *bonang panerus* (high-range *bonang*).

0:17—0:25 The piece begins in *irama tanggung*. Immediately, the drum cues the ensemble to slow down gradually, moving toward *irama dadi* after the stroke of the first *kenong*. During the *irama* transition and in *irama dadi*, *bonang* plays less elaborate rhythmic configurations in moderate tempo—*lomba* style (the player plays a pair of notes, anticipating and guiding the skeleton of the melody, *balungan*.

0:25—0:54 The piece stays in *irama dadi*. On the stroke of the third *kenong* the drum switches to an animated *ciblon* style.

0:54—1:13 The *ciblon* drumming signals the ensemble to slow down gradually, moving toward *irama dadi* on the *gong*. After the stroke of the *gong*, the piece enters *irama wilet*.

1:13—3:11 During the playing of *irama wilet*, two *bonang* play animated interlocking patterns (*imbal*), with lively rhythmic configurations performed at cadences.

3:11— If you continue listening past 3:11, you will hear the piece making another transition from *irama wilet* to *irama rangkep*, with a number of *andhegan* (a stop in the middle of the piece, and resuming again after a *pesindhèn* singer sings an interlude), back to *irama wilet* until the end of the piece.

The fact that a single piece can be played in different *irama* implies the fluidity of its melodic identity. As I suggested earlier, the original melodic identity of most pieces resides in *irama dadi* and *irama wilet*. This means that the other *irama* have particular performative functions. In most cases, *irama tanggung* is a temporary *irama* used for particular purposes: (1) to make a transition from one section to another or from one piece to another; (2) to accompany a section of dance which requires lively drumming in a repeated short cyclic structure; and (3) to be applied to a section of a piece, such as the *sesegan* section in an instrumental piece *gendhing bonang*, a section that should be performed in loud-style playing as the conclusion of the piece.

For *gendhing* composed in longer *gongan* or colotomic structure, two major sections (*Mérong* and *Inggah*) constitute a composition. The *Mérong* is performed in *irama dadi*. The *Inggah* can be played in *irama dadi* or *irama wilet* (the latter with the animated *ciblon* drumming). In many cases, the original melodies of the *Inggah* reside in *irama dadi*. In fact, many *Inggah* melodies derive from the corresponding *Mérong* melodies. The need to accompany animated dance movements, whose drumming requires the lively style called *ciblon*, has originally been the reason for playing *Inggah* in *irama wilet*. The rhythmic patterns of this drumming are directly related to the rhythmic movements of the dancer. Playing *Inggah* in *irama wilet* with *ciblon* drumming became common practice in *klenèngan* (gamelan performances for listening), albeit without the presence of the dance. It is a way to create a lively mood as musicians creatively augment and embellish their melodies. In doing so, musicians of the elaborating instruments focus more on the treatment of individual patterns: a single *gatra* pattern becomes two patterns. To create a lively mood, musicians will change their technique and melodic ornamentation accordingly. For example, in a piece played in *irama wilet* with animated *ciblon* drumming, *gendèr* will play in lively *rangkep* style and two *bonang* will play *imbal* (interlocking).

(a) balungan	2 1 6 5
rebab	2 2 1 2 1 2 1 6 5
gendèr right hand	5 .3 5 6 . 5 6 5 3 2 3 6 . 5 6 5
gendèr left hand	. 1 2 . 16 1 1 1 .6 5 3 2 . 3 . 5
bonang barung	2 1 2 . . 1 2 . 6 5 6 . . 5 6 .
bonang panerus	212.212.212.212.656.656.656.656.
kendhang	ρ ∘ b ρ b k ∘ k ∘ k ∘ k

(b) balungan	.	2	.	1	.	6	.	5
gendèr right hand	.5..35.6	.3.5.6.5	.6.656.i	..6.6.65	.3.5.3.2	.3.5.3.2	..3.23.5	..6.6.65
gendèr left hand	..12.161	2.165.5.	.6.6.5.6	.1.2.16.	1.16561.	1.16561.	.3.3.2.3	.5.6.1.5
bonang barung	.6.2.6.2	.6.2.6.2	.6.2.6.2	.6.2.6.2	.6.2.6.2	.6.2.6.2	.5.6.1.2	.216.1.5
bonang panerus	1.3.1.3.	1.3.1.3.	1.3.1.3.	1.3.1.3.	1.3.1.3.	1.3.1.3.	5i56i6i2	22i656i5
kendhang	.ρℓ∘ρktρ	tρℓ∘ρktρ	.kρtρℓdρ	ℓbdbdbdb	.∘.bdbd.	b.ρρℓbd.	bktɓ.bLk	b.ρtρρ.ρ

FIGURE 7.2 (a) Example of the melodies of elaborating instruments (*rebab, gender, bonang*) and *kendhang* (drum) in *irama dadi*. (b) Example of the melodies of elaborating instruments (*rebab, gender, bonang*) and *kendhang* (drum) in *irama wilet*: gendèr rangkep, bonang imbal, kendhang ciblon.

Key to Figure 7.2a and b: the strokes of the kendhang drum

b = dhe	t = tak	ρ = thung	ℓ = lung	d = dang
L = lang	ɓ = dhet	° = tong	k = ket	. = rest

Believed to be the most recent invention, *irama rangkep* gives rise to the most lively melodies and moods. Irama *rangkep* does not transform a single pattern to become two patterns, however, but doubles the density level of the existing melodic patterns by repeating sections of a pattern and adding more whimsical melodic ornamentation. Since this *irama* does not change the melodic content of the piece—that is, the players of an elaborating instrument only whimsically repeat different sections of each pattern—*irama rangkep* might not be considered as an *irama*, but a "treatment" (Supanggah 2011, 295). In fact, any piece in whatever *irama* can be performed in *rangkep*. In any event, in *irama rangkep* the drum plays animated rhythmic patterns associated with dance movements, repeating and extending each pattern, and playing them in a faster tempo than that of *irama wilet*.

Other common practices which contribute to the lively moods of the performance of *irama rangkep* include the following: (1) *andhegan* (a stop in the middle of the piece, which resumes again after a *pesindhèn* singer sings an interlude); (2) highlighting certain evocative melodies or rhythms of elaborating instruments and singers, an occasional jocular pattern created by elaborating instruments and *kendhang*; and (3) male singers performing playful *senggakan* (stylized cries) while doing interlocking rhythmic claps.

To recapitulate: the rendering and shaping of melody and rhythm in gamelan music are determined by the changes in temporal and density flow. This makes gamelan rhythm distinctive from that of other music. On the face of it, according to Powers (1986, 724), the "Javanese concept of *irama* (temporal density) seems more complex than Hindustani *laya* (tempo) or European rhythm (patterned succession of attacks), not only because tempo is always coordinated with *irama*, but also because two layers of attack pattern are explicit, a primary sequence moving faster perceived against a secondary sequence moving slower. But in fact, both tempo (*laya*) and rhythm (in the sense of 'a rhythm') also imply at least two layers of motion even where only one is explicit."

Powers also emphasizes the necessity of understanding rhythm as a part of the pitch and textural aspects of music; hence one can speak of durational rhythm, accentual rhythm, textural rhythm, harmonic rhythm, melodic rhythm, and timbral rhythm. I would say that durational and accentual rhythms are directly connected to the rendering of melody. That is, musicians can vary the duration and pulsation of the succession of notes to express a certain rhythmic play. In this regard, a gamelan theorist and composer, Supanggah, offers us a concept called *rampak-rempeg*.

> Unity and synchrony (rampak-rempeg) is a concept which involves working together and togetherness but not sameness. In karawitan, when the musicians play together, they follow a horizontal line. All of them are moving or oriented toward a particular goal: the sèlèh or gong note, not paying much attention to the vertical line. . . . Examples which shows a preference for "non-togetherness" can be seen in the clasing sound of a sekatèn performance, in a suwuk or ending, and in aesthetical terms or expression such as nggandul (playing late: for the gong, kempul, kenong, sindhèn, gendèr, rebab, and so on), nungkak (playing early or anticipating): for the bedhug and rebab), mbanyu mili (like flowing water, foe the gambang), nyelå irama (offbeat, for the handclapping or keplok), and so on. (Supanggah 2011, 103)

Supanggah's elucidation parallels Feld's idea of "*simultaneously in-synchrony while out-of-phase*" (emphasis in original). By "in-synchrony," Feld means "that the overall feeling is of togetherness, of consistently cohesive part coordination in sonic motion and participatory experience. Yet the parts are also 'out-of-phase', that is, at distinctly different and shifting points of the same cycle or phase structure at any moment, with each of the parts continuously changing in degree of displacement from hypothetical unison" (Feld 1988, 82). Feld's descriptions suit well the overall processual dynamics of the multilayered gamelan ensemble, a musical style which is in line with his characterization of the dynamic in Kaluli music that creates "nuances of *textural densification*—of attacks and final sounds; decays and fades; changes in intensity, depth, and presence; voice coloration and grain; interaction of patterned and random sounds; playful acceleration, lengthenings, shortenings" (82, emphasis in original).

As can be seen from the foregoing discussion, *irama* (in the sense of both temporal and density flow) guides the player in the overall rendering of melodies to impart the specific character of a *gendhing* or its different sections. Musicians know that a particular *irama* determines in what way a *gendhing* or section of a *gendhing* should be rhythmically and melodically treated. Supanggah (2011, 134) sees the importance of *irama*; so much so that he thinks of it as the "breath" of gamelan. Furthermore, aside from confirming the function of *kendhang* as the leader of *irama* (*pamurba irama*), he sees the steady and constant pulses of a composition, which are constantly present in the mind of a *kendhang* player (overtly or implied), to analogically represent the beats of human heart, the *keteg*.

IRAMA, A MACRO FORM

Earlier I mentioned Sindusawarno's point on perceiving *irama* as alternating patterns of tones and pulses. He also sees this alternating pattern in the natural world (for example, the occurrence of day and night, the rising and setting of the sun, the appearance and disappearance of the moon) and in human behavior (sleeping and walking [wakening], eating and excreting, etc.). This is all connected to a notion that all things have opposites and occur in alternation—that is, dualism. He says that this is the rhythm of our life. Therefore, "the creations of man are also rhythmically ordered, for example, darkness and light in painting, movement and stillness in dance, loudness and softness in melody, fastness and slowness in pace," and so on.

It seems that Sindusawarno's proposition of a macro-rhythm resonates with the meaning of rhythm in general. Hasty observes that rhythm is not limited to phenomena that exhibit periodicity. "We speak of the rhythm of a tickling clock, the rhythm of the seasons, and the rhythm of birth and death," but in addition, "we can use the word rhythm to characterize phenomena in which periodicity is not apparent: a fluid gesture of the hand, a still life, the course of a narrative, the 'shape' of a musical phrase" (1997, 4). Hasty relates this second usage to aesthetic judgment. Sindusawarno explains the same phenomenon as follows: each time an alternation of elements happens, "there is certain to be a difference—perhaps in time, perhaps in form, perhaps in the environment, the atmosphere, or the condition" (357). It is in these "differences" that one of the keys to understanding rhythm lies.

In gamelan, musicians have known the melodic identity and character of the piece, its *gongan* structure, its *pathet* (modal classification), and the idiomatic vocabularies of each instrument and of singing that musicians apply to the piece. All of these are to be made audible and to be manifest in accordance to the kind of interrelationship and interaction between the instruments—the networking that evokes the ensemble's play, which I mentioned earlier.

Two of the differences constituting the musical processes in gamelan are textural (thick and thin) and timbral (soft and loud) change. Now I would like to illustrate the rhythmic flow as a manifestation of this textural and timbral change by examining a process during which a *gendhing* is performed from the beginning to the end, from the introduction proceeding to different sections, or from one set of *gendhing* to another. With regard to the timbral change, the general practice is as follows: when the piece is performed in a fast temporal flow (say, in *irama tanggung*), the musicians play their instruments (especially the loud-sounding instruments) louder. When the piece is performed in a slower temporal flow, a softer sound of the loud-sounding instruments is required as the softer-sounding instruments play a central role in the aesthetic. What follows is a description of a performance of the piece called *Jaladara*, from beginning to end. This performance is by musicians of the Institute of the Arts in Surakarta, directed by Rahayu Supanggah, recorded in a CD titled *Mengenang Empu Karawitan Pasca Merdeka* (Commemorating Post-independence Masters of Karawitan). The piece was composed by the late R. L. Martopangrawit, one of the most prominent musicians, gamelan theorists and composers of Java (Audio.7.3).

Listening guide III to Audio 7.3 ⊙

I. The piece begins with the *rebab* playing a *senggrèngan* (0:00–0:06), a brief melodic cue, announcing to the musicians what will be the tuning system (in this case *pélog*) of the piece to be performed. Then the *rebab* plays *buka*, the introductory movement of the piece (0:06–0:34). Traditionally, this introduction is the only hint for the musicians to figure out what piece they are about to perform.

II. In the middle of the introduction, the drum joins in with the strokes of low sound, *dhah* (0:27) and *thung* (0:30); and thereafter the drum initiates a steady pulse. At this moment, the *gendèr* joins in (0:29). As the introduction is about to conclude, the rhythmic play of the whole ensemble begins: the large *gong* is struck with a slight delay from its beat, and the other instruments play the *gong*-tone slightly after the stroke of the *gong* (0:35). This kind of rhythmic play is a standard practice for any piece composed in a longer structure (with 64, 128, or 256 pulses per *gongan*). In the intro, we also notice a textural change: the melody of the solo *rebab* is then joined by the *kendhang* and *gendèr*. The thick textural disposition happens on the stroke of the gong when all instruments play simultaneously with their *gong*-tone. The *senggrèngan* and the first half of the introduction is in free rhythm. Then the drum sets the steady pulses of the introduction, a precursor to the pulsation of the piece; this happens in *irama tanggung*, a transitional *irama*.

III. After the *gong*-intro, the drum cues the ensemble to gradually slow down. At a certain point, after about ¾ of the first *kenongan* (one *kenong* phrase = 32 beats), the *irama* changes to *irama dadi* (*dadi* means "settled in"). This is the *irama* of the rest of the first section (*Mérong*) of the piece, before the drum cues the ensemble for a transition to the second section (*Inggah*). During the *Mérong*, every time the *kenong* stroke is about to arrive, the ensemble slows down slightly and the *kenong* plays with a slight delay (2:18; 3:28; 5:52; 7:04). When the piece approaches the *gong*, on and after the *gong* stroke (4:34–4:41), the same kind of rhythmic play happens as when the ensemble approaches the *gong*-intro, which I mentioned earlier.

IV. The entire *Mérong* section is repeated. In about one *gatra* after the second *kenong* (7:14) the drummer cues the ensemble to accelerate gradually, a signal for the ensemble to make a transition to the *Inggah*. When the piece reaches a little after the first half of the third *kenong* (7:41), *irama dadi* changes to *irama tanggung*. The piece moves to *Ompak*, a transitional section (7:48). As the piece approaches the *gong* (beginning at 8:08), it slows down and changes to *irama dadi* on the *gong* (8:21).

V. In the *Inggah*, each stroke of the *kenong* is always slightly delayed, but the ensemble does not slow down as much as in the *Mérong*. When the piece approaches the second *kenong* (11:18), the drum cues the ensemble to slightly speed up, keeping the piece in a moderate tempo. As the piece reaches the middle of the third *kenongan* (15:04), the drum once more cues the ensemble to slightly speed up. The drum cues them to speed up again before the *kenong* (15:18). The piece continues in this moderate tempo, but gradually speeds up. Three *gatra* before the *gong* (15:50), the piece changes to *irama tanggung*. After the *gong* (16:01), all soft-sounding instruments (*rebeb*, *gendèr*, *gambang*, and *suling*) drop out. After the gradual speed up occurs, the ensemble gradually changes to louder sonic presentation. After the *gong*, the piece is in the fast and loud style of playing—the *sesegan*. Here the interlocking of *demung*, which started earlier, becomes prominent. In the meantime, the *slenthem* changes from playing a regular *balungan* to a form of abstraction of the *balungan*—it plays on every other beat.

VI. The *sesegan* is the climax of the piece. It is a treatment of the *Inggah*, in which the musicians are playing from moderately bright (16:01–17:00) to extremely loud (17:18–18:58) as this section goes through different tempos. The intense, percussive sound of the bronze becomes the focus of the enjoyment.

VII. At a certain point in the *Inggah*, when the piece approaches the third *kenong* (i.e., in the middle of that *kenongan*), the drummer cues the ensemble to slow down (19:56)—a signal for *suwuk*, ending the piece. The ensemble responds by playing the loud-sounding instruments softer—the timbral change. As the tempo slows down more, on the stroke of the *kenong* all soft-sounding instruments resume. Toward the end of the piece, the tempo continues to slow down gradually. The final *gong* (19:51) is struck on an extremely delayed beat, followed by the stroke of the *gong*-tone by all of the instruments in the ensemble (19:52).

VIII. As a postlude, a free rhythmic and nonmetric *pathetan* is played by a small ensemble of *rebab*, *gendèr*, *gambang*, and *suling* (19:56–22:28)—a textural and timbral change from large ensemble to small ensemble.

The changes of *irama* can be seen as a rhythmic flow of the composition from the beginning to the end; metaphorically it is like the rhythm of life. All sorts of rhythmic configurations come to the fore as the drummer changes the *irama* of the piece.

CONCLUSION

> Musical time exhibits two complementary aspects. One is periodicity, regularity, and recurrence, corresponds to the domain of metre, and gives rise to the concept of cyclicity. The other is gestural, figural, and (in principle) unpredictable and relates to the domain of rhythm. (Clayton 2000, 23)

Ethnomusicologists have noted the importance of the cyclic recurrence of the melodic/temporal unit, the colotomic structure in gamelan composition (*gongan*). The assumption is that the gamelan system always consists of multiple cycles operating simultaneously. When the cycle and subcycles are coinciding, meaning and power are created (Becker 1979).[5] Another side of the system is a process of interaction or networking of different instruments in the ensemble, resulting in the gestural, figural, and unpredictable transformation that Clayton refers to. *Irama* is a concept that concerns regulating the working process of this binary system, hence the life of the music in continuing transformation of its rhythmic and melodic configurations. In other words, the *gongan* structural system and the networking of various instruments are working in tandem; one provides a subjective or formal reality, the other is the domain of immanence, existential, or practical.

The change of *irama* is the change of density and temporal flow. But most significantly, as I mentioned earlier (quoting Becker 1981), the change of *irama* allows a single piece to assume different lengths and different degrees of instrumental or vocal embellishment. As it usually requires different playing styles for some instruments, it affects melodic and rhythmic content, and thus effects changes in mood. Thus, a shift in one musical domain can both trigger idiomatic changes in instrumental performance style and produce a change in the entire ensemble's interplay. This is a musical process that relies on, in the words of Supanggah, "the importance of dialogue."

The notion of musical dialogue is so deeply engrained in the gamelan system that even the large *gong*—the instrument whose function is limited to marking the end of *gongan* structure—also participates in this dialogue as the *gong* is struck with a slight delay from the beat of the piece. The point of coincidence in gamelan is not only to mark the flow of time toward the point of stasis and stability, but also to tell the listeners the moods of that coincidence as shaped by the playfulness of temporal and melodic treatment surrounding the *gong*. In essence, the cyclic motion in gamelan is not really an absolute "steady state" without any sense of linearity.

This is not to deny that cyclic structure pervades gamelan music, but the music often consists of a series of recurrent cycles. As one cycle move to another, with the alteration of *irama* as well as timbral and textural change, the listeners perceive a sense of linear motion, as our listening to *gendhing Jaladara* indicates. The sense of linearity in experiencing time is revealed as the instruments are interacting with each other, following the alteration of *irama*, textural and timbral changes, and fashioning the instruments' rhythmic configuration.

Perhaps any musical system allows for both linear and recursive or cyclical experience. It is in the degree of linearity or recursiveness that one system differs from another. In gamelan, the cyclic structure maintains its function as a subjective or formal reality of the music. But as the music passes through a series of recurrent cycles and changing *irama*, bringing about variegated transformation of melodic and rhythmic configurations, the cyclic structure is only conceived as background.

NOTES

1. For a possible historical link between Indian music and gamelan during the *Nāṭyaśāstra*'s time, see Richard Widdess's "*Sléndro* and *Pélog* in India" (1993).

2. It seems that to him a rhythm consists of repetitions and regular rhythmic patterns: "The concept of rhythm is not too well-known in karawitan, although when playing together or individually, each instrument uses fairly complex, even irregular, rhythms. Rhythm is a part of melody; this means that a melody is created because there is pitch and rhythm. Perhaps only the bonang barung, bonang panerus, and siter play repetitions of regular rhythmic patterns" (Supanggah 2011, 104).

3. Sindusawarno was a student at the Bandung Institute of Technology. He was also affiliated to the indigenous Javanese educational system (Taman Siswa). Moving to Solo, he became the head of the Central Department of Culture. He was one of the founders of the gamelan conservatory in Solo, which was founded in the 1950s. I don't know what literature he read about Indian musical culture, but occasionally his writing refers to Indian music and uses a few Indian musical terms. He read and spoke Dutch and English. Most likely he read Jaap Kunt's *Music in Java*. He befriended Mantle Hood, who did his research in the late 1950s and early1960s. As a student at the conservatory taught by Sindusawarno for three years, I know that he was not a gamelan practitioner. It is important to mention, however, that his knowledge about gamelan came from his close relationship with musicians and gamelan teachers at the conservatory, mostly Javanese but also Balinese and Sundanese musicians.

4. Sindusawarno identifies one more *irama: irama lancar*, the ratio of which is one beat of elaborating instruments per one beat of the *balungan*. But this *irama* is only used in passing, for example the piece has to go through this *irama* briefly after the *gong* of the *buka* (introduction) and *suwuk gropak*, ending the piece in a fast speed. The only sustainable *irama lancar* is the playing a piece in the *lancaran* structure (eight pulses per *gongan*) in which the elaborating instruments play two beats per one beat of the *balungan*.

5. Contextualizing gamelan in this teleological domain is a thought-provoking and very persuasive argument: human actions are inherent in the rest of nature; the coincidence in the gamelan musical processes parallels the coincidence of two or more different days of Javanese calendrical systems. As I will explain, complementing this notion is a notion that human actions bring about interaction or social networking. In music, this is manifested in the interaction of different parts in the ensemble.

8

Layers and Elasticity in the Rhythm of Noh Songs

"TAKING KOMI" AND ITS SOCIAL BACKGROUND

Takanori Fujita

INTRODUCTION

Noh drama, one of Japan's traditional performing arts, is well known for its rhythmic complexity. The rhythm of Noh singing is especially hard to grasp. For the most part, chorus members sing the songs and two drums, *o-tsuzumi* ("large" drum) and *ko-tsuzumi* ("small" drum) accompany them. If we are interested in Noh rhythmic theory and ask a master, we would immediately be given a simple explanation: the drummers articulate an eight-beat meter that dominates the music of a Noh performance. In songs, both singers and drummers share this eight-beat meter (cycle or unit) as a metrical frame. Delving deeper into the scholarship, we encounter a theory that explains how performers adjust a poetic line to fit an eight-beat meter, notated as in Figure 8.1.[1] However, actual performances of the songs sound very different from what one might imagine and expect from the notation. Singers seem to produce a rhythm that deviates from the basic eight-beat meter, while drummers produce a variation of the eight-beat meter that treats intervals between beats with extreme flexibility. In all, the rhythm of Noh songs consists of sung and drummed layers and involves an elasticity of beats.

Over the course of twenty-plus years as a participant observer of Noh, I gradually began to pay close attention to the drummers' playing technique, called *komi* (lit. "to charge" or "get into"). In order to explain its function, I will focus on *hira-nori* (lit. "standard-riding-on"), thought to be the most complicated of all Noh-song rhythm types.[2] To untangle this complexity, I will first offer a theoretical explanation of *hira-nori* and describe how singers study *hira-nori* songs. Second, I will focus on the drummer's playing technique. Drummers add various modifications to the regular

```
     1     2     3     4     5     6     7     8    (1)
     x     x     x     x     x     x     x     x          8beats
  x  x  x  x  x  x  x  x  x  x  x  x  x  x  x  x  (x)    16slots
  --------------------------------------  ------------------------ (--)
  area for first hemistich (beat 1 to 4)  area for second hemistich (beat 5 to 8)

     1     2     3     4     5     6     7     8
  a  ya   shi me ra   ru na me    n  me  n     to           Line 1
  ---------- 7 syllables ----------  ------5 syllables--------

     1     2     3     4     5     6     7     8
          be  n  ke    i  ni i    sa me ra     re (te)      Line 2
          ---5 syllables--------  ------6 syllables---------

                      (omit)                                Line 3

     1     2     3     4     5     6     7     8
             sa ra    ri to ma    to  i shi    te           Line 4
             ---4 syllables-----  ------- 5 syllables--------
```

FIGURE 8.1 Original configuration of poetic syllables in *hira-nori* rhythm (a song from Noh *Ataka*).

drumming patterns. I will identify the basic modification types that are tacitly understood by drummers. Third, I will analyze the interaction between singers and drummers in *hira-nori* singing. Finally, I will ask what social aspects are relevant as a basis for developing this interaction.

THE THEORY OF *HIRA-NORI*

Theoretical discussions typically describe the *hira-nori* rhythm in terms of lines composed of two hemistichs each, the first of seven syllables and the second of five (Line 1 of Figure 8.1). This is a typical metrical structure in Japanese song texts. Before looking into the configuration patterns of syllables in *hira-nori* we note two general points. First, a hemistich always consists of a meaningful phrase or a compound of phrases. This means that even though seven and five syllables are the standard, the number of syllables actually composing a set of two hemistichs may differ from line to line. In Japanese, a syllable is usually composed of a consonant and a vowel. However, single vowels such as /a/, /i/, and /u/, and nasal consonants such as /n/ and /m/, may also constitute syllables.[3] All syllables are regarded as having equal time values.

Second, Noh drama's eight-beat meter is represented with sixteen slots in the notation in order to serve as the basis for the syllable layout. Noh musicians and scholars commonly refer to events in the intervening slots as "half" beats or "upbeats" to the time points they precede; so, for example, "eight-and-a-half" means "upbeat to the time point of beat one." The syllables of song texts, *kake-goe* (drum calls), and strokes are all placed in these slots at regular intervals. In Figure 8.1, the syllables of lines 1, 2, and 4 of the song "Ataka" are laid out regularly in a cycle of eight beats that are in theory isochronous (Audio 8.1 ▶).[4] The group of two beats accommodates three syllables in a dactylic sequence: long-short-short. In line 1, the first syllable, "a," is in an upbeat position preceding beat 1 and is followed by three dactylic groups of syllables "ya---shi-me," "ra---ru-na," and "me---n-me."[5] In line 1 the positions of syllables look like component parts of a cycle of eight beats and seem to help us recognize the eight-beat meter. However, our perception of the meter is hampered in the following lines because the starting position of each sung phrase changes according to the number of syllables in the first hemistich and the degree of embellishment on some syllables. If the number of syllables in the first hemistich of a line is less than 7, say 5 or 4 (lines 2 and 4, Figure 8.1), the meter of the line starts not with the sung text but with a space filled with the sustained note of the last syllable in the previous sung phrase. Consequently, it is difficult to perceive the cycles of eight beats from the configuration patterns of syllables alone.

THE SINGER'S MODIFICATION OF THE EIGHT-BEAT METER AS A RESULT OF TRAINING

The actual performance of a song never sounds as it is represented in Figure 8.1 because singers deliver the actual rhythm differently in relation to the eight-beat meter. I will first explain the performance context out of which this difference in rhythmic delivery emerged. Then I will describe the conventions for training singers.

In the performance of a full play of Noh drama, metrical songs are always accompanied by drumming patterns on the *o-tsuzumi* and *ko-tsuzumi*.[6] However, on some occasions Noh songs are performed without instrumental accompaniment. This "bare or simple singing" format, *su-utai*, has been popular for over 400 years in performing ritual songs for the new year, marriage, housewarming, and funerals. The *su-utai* format has also been employed in banquet settings as a convenient means for creating casual entertainment, mainly among amateur singers. Because of its simplicity, *su-utai* practice has been popular among commoners since the eighteenth century. In such performance contexts, the basic eight-beat meter was pushed aside and then ignored in song lessons as well as in recitals. Figure 8.2 is a picture of a performance scene on stage by amateurs.

Four systematic constraints in the teaching process ensure that students avoid following the basic eight-beat meter. First, singers are not allowed to count beats by moving their bodies—neither their toes, their fingers, nor their hands may move—even when their teacher claps his hands and indicates the basic eight-beat meter in front of them. Second, the students do not see the meter written out. The libretto notation for singers (Figure 8.3a) contains only the song texts and accompanying signs representing the relative pitch and duration of each note, which mostly correspond to syllables. The notation does not help students understand the underlying meter. Third, the lesson-style emphasizes the textual lines as units rather than the metrical

FIGURE 8.2 *Su-utai* performed by amateur singers, at the amateur recital held on August 9, 2009, at the Noh theater in Otsu city (Photo by the author).

cycles. In the initial stage, students are asked to imitate their teacher's singing phrase by phrase. For example, after the teacher has sung the first line, "A-ya-shi-me-ra-ru-na-me-n-me-n-to-----," the student repeats the phrase, while looking at her or his libretto notation. As soon as the student finishes the phrase, the teacher proceeds to the next line, "Be-n-ke-i-ni-i-sa-me-ra-re-te----," without indicating where the metrical cycle begins. Finally, tradition too plays a role, for according to one saying, "If you study the underlying rhythm in the first stage of your training, you will not make further progress" (Hoshino 1978, 201). Thus, students are initially discouraged from obtaining a clear picture of the underlying meter.

Modern singers would think that the best way to learn the underlying eight-beat meter is to learn drumming. However, singing students are always prevented from taking drumming lessons, regardless of their eagerness to do so. Irmgard Johnson reports that a diligent student in professional track "begged for *taiko* lessons for two years before being permitted to begin at the age of seven—permission granted on the condition that it would be 'for life'" (Johnson 1977, 193). Students, whether they are amateurs or in professional track, are forcibly trained to ignore the underlying meter for a considerable period in the first stage of their lesson. It means that they can never be fully responsible for the underlying meter. In this sense, Thomas Hare is right in terming this process "a kind of infantilization" (Hare 1996, 339). Interestingly enough, he relates the infantilization to the "natural" beauty that can be found in the aesthetic

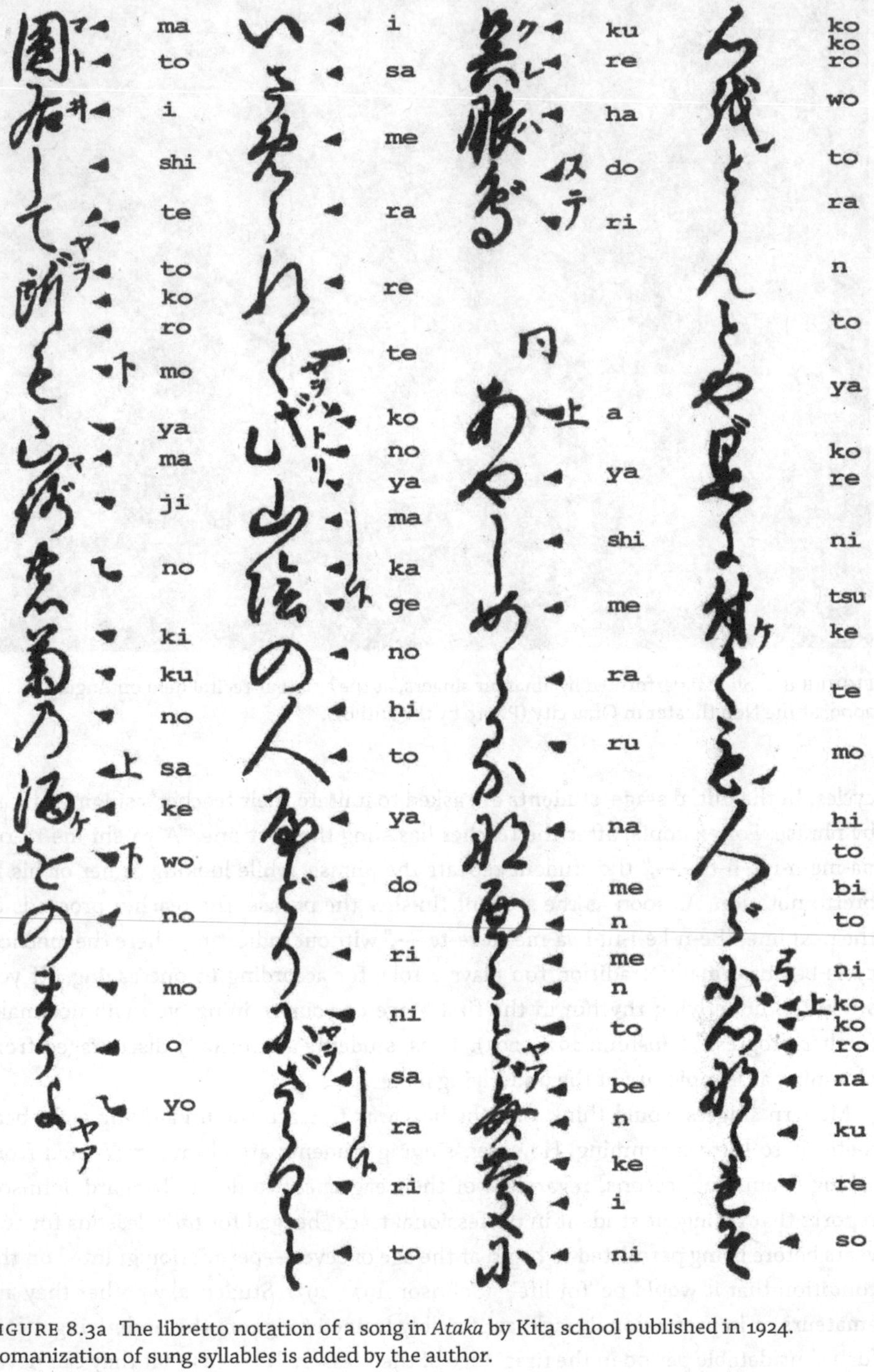

FIGURE 8.3a The libretto notation of a song in *Ataka* by Kita school published in 1924. Romanization of sung syllables is added by the author.

```
A---- ya shi me ra ru na / me n me n to ----------(breath) (7+5)

^      ^          ^
Be n ke i ni / i sa me ra re te -----------(breath) (5+6)

                         ^        ^              ^
Ko------no----- (breath) ya ma ka ge no / hi to ya do ri ni---------(breath) (2+5+5)

      ^          ^
Sa ra ri to / ma to i shi te-----------(breath) (4+5)

      ^            ^
To ko ro mo / ya----   ma ji no-------(breath) (4+4)

   ^        ^
Ki ku no sa ke wo /no mo o yo----------------(breath) (6+4)
```

FIGURE 8.3b Singer's rhythm image of a song in *Ataka*. At the syllables with accent signs (ʌ), choral singers have to extend the syllables to go with drumming pattern.

theory of Noh.[7] In the same way I want to relate this to an aesthetic value in performance that singers have to detach themselves from drummers and vive versa, which I will describe later in the analysis of a piece.

In Figure 8.3b, I offer my own graphical image of the rhythm that singers would obtain from the libretto notation Figure 8.3a, the corresponding section in Figure 8.1 (Also listen to Audio 8.2 ⊙, which corresponds with Figure 8.3). We should note three points. First, from the singer's point of view, each phrase starts from the first syllable in a line, although from the drummers' and theoretical viewpoints shown in Figure 8.1, the starting point is the first beat of the eight-beat meter. Second, since most phrases end with a prolonged syllable, singers recognize the *hira-nori* rhythm as an alternation of rushing syllables and a prolonged space. This might be compared to an image of "alternating stream and backwater." Third, the durations of syllables that compose a "stream" are equal in theory. However, in actual performance a phrase tends to accelerate from the beginning to the end.

The accent-shaped signs added to certain syllables in Figure 8.3b are particularly notable. So long as singers sing in the *su-utai* format without drummed accompaniment, they do not have to synchronize with the drums. However, when they sing with the drum they have to treat some syllables in a special manner: those syllables sung with the drums need to be prolonged (Audio 8.2 ⊙). This treatment is called *mochi* in the noun form or *motsu* in the verb form, meaning "to hold on." Singers learn this treatment not through systematic explanations or notations such as that in Figure 8.1, but simply through repeated participation in Noh as chorus members. After all, singers incorporate the eight-beat meter into their singing just through the repetition without any clear marks of beats to which they can fit their song rhythm.

THE JAPANESE CONCEPT OF BEAT

Before entering into an explanation of drumming patterns and playing techniques, it is important to know that the concept of beat in Japanese musicological terminology, termed *haku* or *hyoshi*, embraces the temporal interval from the end of the previous beat to the point of articulation of the beat in question. For clarity, I will distinguish beat as "time point" from beat as a temporal interval between time points. However, the native conception—which obscures this distinction—is important to grasp: Japanese Noh musicians refer to beat 1 as the space or time interval separating beat 8 from beat 1. This interval is sometimes filled with a *kake-goe* (drum call) by the drummer as well as a stroke of the drum. As we shall see, the Noh musician's concept of beat takes on a qualitative significance depending on its time interval and how it is filled.

THE BASIC MODIFICATION TYPES OF AN EIGHT-BEAT CYCLE

In most scenes in a Noh piece, a cycle of eight beats is produced by both the *o-tsuzumi* and the *ko-tsuzumi*. Among hundreds of drumming patterns that produce a cycle of eight beats, the *mitsuji* and *tsuzuke* patterns are the ones most frequently used (Audio 8.3 ▶ and Audio 8.4 ▶ which correspond with Figures 8.4a and 8.4b). In the *mitsuji* pattern, beats 2, 4, and 6 are silent, lacking drum sounds. Beat 1 also lacks a drum stroke but is filled with a sustained *kake-goe* (drum call). The first line of a song in *hira-nori* always begins with the accompaniment of the *mitsuji* pattern, although some *kake-goes* are commonly omitted and the pattern may be named differently, as seen in the first line of Figure 8.6.

Tsuzuke (lit. "continuing"), another representative pattern, produces or marks all eight beats with strokes. *Kake-goes* do not occur in the intervals preceding the time points of beats 2 and 4, but they do precede strokes on all the other beats. In a song, *tsuzuke* is used after the second line repeatedly, marking the beats of the song actively with drum strokes (also see Figure 8.6).

```
        1     2     3     4     5     6     7     8
   yo-----     ho X                               x        o-tsuzumi
                             yo X     ho x ho X            ko-tsuzumi
```

FIGURE 8.4a *Mitsuji* pattern of *o-tsuzumi* and *ko-tsuzumi*: large X: strong stroke, small x: weak stroke, yo and ho: *kake-goe* (drum calls).

```
        1     2     3     4     5     6     7     8
     yo X      ho X     x yo X ho X                       o-tsuzumi
              X         x yo x      X ho X ho X           ko-tsuzumi
```

FIGURE 8.4b *Tsuzuke* pattern by *o-tsuzumi* and *ko-tsuzumi*.

Also of note are the varying *kake-goes*. The *kake-goe* "yo" falls on the "upbeat" position of beat 1 (i.e., eight-and-a-half) and beat 5 (four-and-a-half), which suggests that one of the original roles of the drummer's call was to signal to the singers or flutist what position they had reached within the eight-beat meter. Looking over the different drumming patterns, we may also notice that the *kake-goe* "ho" announces the coming of beats 3 and 7 as well as 8. Beats of an even number often come without a *kake-goe* and often without a stroke. However, when they carry a *kake-goe*, it is mostly "ho." We should not forget another *kake-goe*, "iya" (see lines 3 and 4, Figure 8.6). Different from "yo" and "ho," the *kake-goe* "iya" always starts on a "downbeat," normally on even-numbered beats.[8]

From the descriptions here, we may note that all the drumming patterns can be simply illustrated as particular combinations of strokes and *kake-goes* over the eight-beat meter frame within the 16 slots. In performance, however, the drumming patterns are modified in different ways, according to the musical context in the drama. It is sometimes impossible to excavate the eight-beat meter.

Taking the basic drumming patterns as examples, I will describe three types of drumming modifications which I shall call "wave," "contraction," and "blur." Musicians identify all these types of modification but do not necessarily name them. Only the modification type I have termed "blur" carries the name *norazu*, which means literally "not-to-ride-on." *Norazu* is contrasted with its positive form, *noru*, which in modern usage is associated with music having regular meter, such as in *hira-nori*.

A WAVE-IMAGE CAST OVER A METRICAL FRAME

In some scenes, or in some phrases in a scene, the flow of the eight beats seems uneven, fluctuating in the manner of a wave—like a car going down a slope and ascending again. Figure 8.5a shows a drumming pattern that typically appears in pieces of music that accompany the main actor's dance such as *kakeri*. The flutist plays an unmetered melody that does not share the same flow of beats, and the actor walks over a bridge to the stage or dances on the stage to a rhythm that differs from that marked by the drums.

In actual performance, this pattern often takes a wave shape. The interval between beats 8 and 1 is prolonged. As musicians would put it, "Beat 1 becomes 'bigger or larger'

(8)	1	2	3	4	5	6	7	8	
yo	X ho	ho	X	X yo	ho	X			*o-tsuzumi*
		X ho	X		x X	X ho	X		*ko-tsuzumi*
|	|	|	|	|	|	|	|	|	

(8)–1	1–2	2–3	3–4	4–5	5–6	6–7	7–8	
	1.16	1.15	1.00	0.95	1.05	1.22	1.35	
1.50	1.18	1.11	0.95	0.85	1.00	1.36	0.99	
1.33	1.17	1.06	0.89	0.81	1.00	1.21	0.86	
1.37	1.12	1.05	0.86	0.95	0.93	1.17		(sec)

FIGURE 8.5a "Waving" modification of a drumming pattern in the dance music *kakeri*.

than the previous beat." The succeeding beats are then accelerated and slowed down again before the next interval spanning beats 8 and 1 is reached. In Audio 8.5 ▶ (corresponding to Figure 8.5a),[9] the interval from beat 8 to beat 1 is the largest one (1.50, 1.33, and 1.37 seconds), and interval between beats 4 to 5 is the smallest (0.95, 0.85, 0.81, and 0.95 seconds).

"TAKING *KOMI*"

In our example of "wave" modification in drumming, there is no stroke on beat 8 (Figure 8.5a). While performing, the *o-tsuzumi* player counts the beat (here beat 8) in his mind by silently uttering "n," "m," or "tsu." This silent utterance, called *komi*,[10] is the basis for timing the subsequent *kake-goes* and strokes. I estimated the interval between beat 7 and beat 8 as 1.35, 0.99, and 0.86 seconds, based on the drummer's slight expiration sounds involving small vocal sound "n" producing beat 8.

When a drummer "takes" *komi* it cannot be recognized from her or his bodily movements unless the player is a beginner undergoing training before a teacher. Generally, only the *o-tsuzumi* player strikes the first beat in the basic patterns that appear in this chapter's notated examples. We may say that the intervals between time points of the beats fluctuate when one drummer, either the *o-tsuzumi* player or the *ko-tsuzumi* player, fills the beat with a stroke (and possibly a *kake-goe*) and the other does not. The slowdown from beats 7 to 1 is created exclusively by the *o-tsuzumi* player while the acceleration from the interval preceding beat 2 and the slowdown beginning on the intervals preceding 7 are created by the *ko-tsuzumi* player. Although not all variations result from the interlocking of the two drum parts, the interlocking framework helps to facilitate fluctuations between adjacent beats.

CONTRACTION OF EVEN-NUMBERED BEATS

The intervals preceding the time points of even-numbered beats are sometimes reduced to half or less than half their lengths. This is typical in *shidai* entrance music, in which the *tsuzuke* pattern (Figure 8.4b) is modified as shown in Figure 8.5b (Audio 8.6 ▶). *Shidai* entrance music is used to accompany the actor's steps over the bridge to the stage with less metrical regularity than the other entrance music types.[11] Comparing Figure 8.5b with Figure 8.4b, we see that the *o-tsuzumi* player does not strike on beat

(8)		1		2		3		4		5		6		7		8	
	yo	X			ho	X			yo	X	ho	X					*o-tsuzumi*
				X				x	yo	x		X	ho	X	ho	X	*ko-tsuzumi*
		|		|		|		|		|		|		|		|	
			1.57		2.40		0.89		2.35		2.37		2.15		2.13		
	2.32		0.82		2.58		0.87		2.47		2.49		1.95		2.07		
	2.48		0.75		2.57		0.65		2.45		2.33		2.04		1.81		
	2.44		0.75		2.35		0.62		2.32		2.30		2.00		1.89		(sec)

FIGURE 8.5b "Contraction" of beats 2 and 4 in the entrance music *shidai*.

4 in *shidai*. Moreover, we also observe in Figure 8.5b that the *ko-tsuzumi* player alone articulates the time points for beats 2 and 4, and that the intervals preceding these time points do not contain *kake-goes*. In the absence of these filler calls, the intervals are contracted to half-length and disrupt the stream of even beats.

An underlying, usually hidden philosophical idea has been used to justify this contraction. A private treatise written in the eighteenth century explains the rhythm of Noh in terms of *yang* and *yin* components, odd numbers being "yang" and even numbers, "yin."[12] Odd-numbers such as 1, 3, 5, and 7 are "as bright as the sun" in this framework, while even numbers are "as dark as the moon." In musical terms, odd-numbered beats are perceived as active and their preceding intervals (for example, the interval between beats 8 and 1), which are mostly filled with *kake-goes*, are enlarged. In contrast, even-numbered beats are subdued, their shortened intervals often lacking *kake-goes* and strokes. I personally envision this as crouching onto the even beats, and jumping up for the odd beats.

BLUR

When accompanying a song without fixed meter, drummers repeatedly play the *mitsuji* pattern (Figure 8.4a). However, they play as if the pattern does not follow an even series of beats.[13] A typical performance modification may be seen in Figure 8.5c (Audio 8.7 ▶). The pattern starts with the *o-tsuzumi*'s small stroke that marks the time point of beat 8. This stroke is followed by the *kake-goe* "yo," which takes 3.51 seconds on the first round of the audio example. Beat one is not marked at all. It is obscured by the prolonged *kake-goe*. Before the next *kake-goe* "ho" starts, there is a brief silence in which *o-tsuzumi* "takes *komi*," saying "n" in her or his mind. This silence marks beat 2, which the *o-tsuzumi* player articulates by her or himself without synchronizing with any other parts. In moving toward the stroke that marks the time point of beat 3, the *o-tsuzumi* player fills a space of 4.78 seconds with a long *kake-goe*.

This is followed by another 4.54 second interval that is, in theory, two beats long. The beginning of the interval is marked on the time point of beat three by the *o-tsuzumi* player and the end of the interval is marked by the *ko-tsuzumi* player on the time point of beat 5. In between, just after the *o-tsuzumi* stroke, the *ko-tsuzumi* player takes *komi* in preparation for the *kake-goe* "yo" and stroke "x." This point of *komi* marks beat 4, which involves no sound. This "double" interval between beats 3 and 5 is actually

```
(x) yo--o-----    ho--o------X                          x     o-tsuzumi
                                yo-----X  ho-----x  ho----X    ko-tsuzumi

 |              |           |          |         |        |
 8              2           3          5         7        8    (beat number)
      3.51          4.78        4.54       3.64      3.08
      3.84          5.58        3.85       3.34      3.07
      4.08          5.67        3.57       3.54      2.75
      4.03          6.04        3.60       3.39      3.12   (sec)
```

FIGURE 8.5c *Mitsuji* pattern in "blur" modification, *norazu*.

smaller than the "single" interval between the preceding beats 2 and 3. The interval that follows beat 5 (i.e., between time points for beats 5 and 7) is also two beats long and lasts only 3.64 seconds, even smaller than the preceding one.

The *mitsuji* pattern too is often explained in terms of *yang* and *yin* components, here referring not to the contrast of odd and even numbers, but to that between the first and second halves of the drum pattern. The first half of the pattern, where the *o-tsuzumi* takes the main role, is conceptualized as "large." In fact, beats 2 to 3, especially, are extremely extended. On the other hand, the second half, which involves the *ko-tsuzumi*, is conceptualized as "small." Parallel to this contrast in interval size, and also conforming to the *yang-yin* relation, the *o-tsuzumi* drum is sometimes seen as male and the *ko-tsuzumi* female.

The interval between beats 7 and 8 is produced by the *ko-tsuzumi*. With this series of two strokes in quicker succession, we might sense even beats emerging. However, this is not sustained because the pattern comes back again to the *o-tsuzumi*'s prolonged *kakegoe* "yo" after the time point of beat 8, which once again obscures the perception of beats.

THE INTERACTION BETWEEN SINGERS AND DRUMMERS: ANALYSIS OF A SONG IN *ATAKA*

Having explained how singers and drummers modify the eight-beat meter, we will analyze the interaction between them (Figure 8.6), using a recorded example that corresponds to Figures 8.1 and 8.3. In the Noh drama *Ataka*, the main character starts a monologue describing the ambivalent emotions he experienced after having been celebrated and supported by the person who was meant to be his interrogator.[14] The recording is found on track 22 of the CD accompanying *Music in Japan* (Wade 2005). This track begins with the main actor's monologue in speech mode, composed of 7+5-syllable lines that are not yet fixed to an eight-beat meter:

Ge-ni-ge-ni-ko-re-mo/ko-ko-ro-e-ta-ri.
Hi-to-no-na-sa-ke-no/sa-ka-zu-ki-ni.
U-ke-te-ko-ko-ro-wo/to-ra-n-to-ya.
Ko-re-ni-tsu-ke-te-mo/hi-to-bi-to-ni.
Ko-ko-ro-na-ku-re-so/ku-re-ha-do-ri.

When the main actor's monologue in speech mode ends, giving way to choral singing in the *hira-nori* rhythm, the main actor concentrates on dancing.

Line 1, Figure 8.6

The chorus begins singing in a way that might make it difficult to perceive the eight-beat meter. To give the first stroke, the *o-tsuzumi* player takes *komi* (says "n" in his mind) on the third syllable, "shi." Since this is an internal process that makes no sound and involves no bodily movements, the singers (if they have no experience of drumming) have no idea that the *o-tsuzumi* player is synchronizing with the syllable they sing. The coming stroke

```
line 1 starting on beat 8
A-----  ya  shi  me  ra  ru  na  me  n   me  n  to-----
            n        X                          n        (uchidashi)
                             n       x   n   ho  x  ho X (uchidashi)
            |  1.2  |0.5|  1.0  |0.4|  1.2  |  1.1  |
8       1   2        3   4       5   6       7      8

line 2 starting on beat 2
--------    Be----   n  ke  i----   ni  i  sa----  me  ra  re  te
yo  X  ho   n   ho   x      X  yo   X  ho  X              n       (tsuzuke)
    n       X        n      x  yo   x      X  ho   X  ho  X       (tsuzuke)
1.2 |  0.9  |  1.0   |  1.0 |  1.1  |  0.9 |  0.9  |  0.8 |
    1       2        3      4       5      6       7      8

line 3 starting on beat 3
(te)--------------       Ko---------  no
yo---  x--------                 iya      (tsukusuma)
             n   ho  x   ho      X        (tori)
1.5    |  1.1   |  0.9  |  1.3   |
       1        2       3        4

(no)------    ya----   ma  ka  ge----   no   hi   to----   ya  do  ri  ni
-----X        n  yo--------i   x        x        iya-----  X       iya   (kashiranidanme)
     n        X        n       x   yo   x         X   ho   X   ho  X     (tsuzuke)
1.5  |  1.1   |  1.2   |  1.0  |  0.9   |  1.0    |  1.0   |  0.8 |
     1        2        3       4        5         6        7      8
```

FIGURE 8.6 Analysis of a *hira-nori* song in *Ataka*. Each frame shows the eight-beat meter unit except for the third, which consists of four beats. Each frame is composed of five tiers: (1): song text; (2): *o-tsuzumi* drumming with name of drumming pattern in parentheses; (3): *ko-tsuzumi* drumming with name of drumming pattern in parentheses (n: *komi*, x: small stroke, X: strong stroke, "yo", "ho" and "iya": *kake-goe*); (4): the time interval between beats measured by the author; (5): beat numbers from theoretical viewpoint. (Singers are ignorant of this in practice.)

produces the third beat in the meter. This stroke is usually preceded by a *kake-goe* "ho" (Figures 8.4a and 8.5c) but is omitted here, as is the practice for the first line of a song.

The first stroke falls on the fifth syllable "ra" of the first hemistich. In the recording, however, we can hear the *o-tsuzumi* player's stroke coming a little behind the syllable "ra" by about 0.1 to 0.2 seconds. Because singers give each syllable nearly equal durations, the *o-tsuzumi* player could have synchronized his stroke to the syllable. Apparently, this gap is intentional; that is, the result of a performance convention which prescribes that once one has taken *komi* or synchronized with the other parts, one should concentrate on one's own sequence without paying attention to the others. The gap between "ra" and the stroke brings about a tension among participants because the gap could be perceived as the *o-tsuzumi* player indicating that the tempo be made graver.

On the sixth syllable, "ru," the *ko-tsuzumi* player takes *komi* to start his own sequence. Because this is the first line, the first *kake-goe* is omitted. The stroke falls on the syllable "me," two syllables after the *komi* position. Here, unlike the *o-tsuzumi* player's first stroke, we cannot find any rhythmic discrepancy between the singers' attacks and strikes on the *ko-tsuzumi*. The ko-tsuzumi player takes another *komi* on the next syllable, "n." This brings forth a series of *kake-goes* and strokes toward the end of the line.

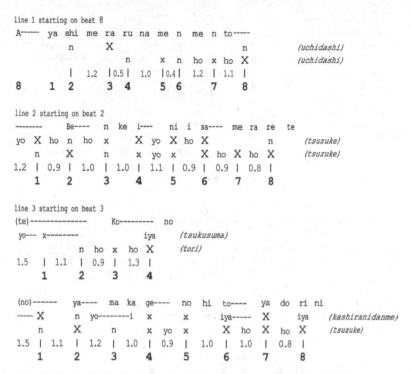

```
line 4 starting on beat 3
(ni)-----------          Sa  ra  ri----  to  ma  to----  i  shi  te---
-----X        n  yo----x---i    X                iya -------X      iya   (itsutsugashira)
     n        X        X        n   x   X        X   ho   X   ho   X     (uchihanashi)
1.0  |  1.0  |  1.0  |  0.9  |  1.0  |  0.9  |  0.9  |  1.0  |
     1        2        3        4        5        6        7        8

line 5 starting on beat 3
-----------------        To  ko  ro----   mo  ya------      ma  ji  no
----X         n  ho   x        X  yo  X   ho  X                      n   (orosu)
    n         X       n        x  yo  x       X   ho   X   ho   X        (tsuzuke)
1.1  |  0.7  |  1.0  |  0.9  |  1.0  |  0.8  |  0.9  |  1.0  |
     1        2        3        4        5        6        7        8

line 6 from 1 and half
--------  Ki  ku-----  no  sa  ke  wo----   no  mo  o  yo---------
yo  X  ho  n  ho  x        X  yo  X  ho  X                        x   (tsuzuke)
    n         X   n        x  yo  x      X   ho   X   ho   X          (tsuzuke)
0.9  |  1.0  |  0.9  |  0.9  |  0.8  |  0.9  |  0.8  |  0.9  |
     1        2        3        4        5        6        7        8

line 7 starting on beat 2
----------    O  mo  shi  ro  ya  ya  ma  mi  zu  ni----
yo----  X                                              n             (yaa)
                         n   yo   x   n   ho   x   ho   X            (kanmitsuji)
2.1        |      (3.3)       |  1.4  | 0.6 |  1.0  |  1.0  |
           1 (2)          (3) 4        5     6        7       8

line 8 starting on beat 2
----------       O----   mo  shi  ro----   ya  ya  ma  mi  zu  ni----
yo  X  ho  n  ho  x        X  yo  X  ho  X                        x   (tsuzuke)
    n         X   n        x  yo  x      X   ho   X   ho   X          (tsuzuke)
1.2  |  1.1  |  1.0  |  1.0  |  0.9  |  0.9  |  0.9  |  0.9  |
     1        2        3        4        5        6        7        8
```

FIGURE 8.6 Continued

Line 2

The last syllable "to" of the first line is prolonged until about beat one-and-a-half in the next eight-beat metrical sequence (frame/measure). This is just before the singers take a breath to start line 2. Line 2 starts from beat 2 because the number of syllables in the first hemistich is only 5 (i.e., less than the standard 7). In the same frame, singers are taught to add *mochis* on some syllables such as "be," "i," and "sa" (Figure 8.3b). Their durations become twice as long as those of the others. Since, in theory, syllables situated in certain positions in a hemistich are strictly tied to even-numbered beats, such as beats 2, 4, and 6 in Figure 8.1, it is better to say that the singing of those syllables creates those beats. In other words, the positions where those particular syllables fall become those even beats, regardless of how they might deviate from isochronous regularity. Some of those even-numbered beats are synchronized with the drummers' processes of taking *komi* (Figure 8.6). With the prolongation of syllables falling on beats 2, 4, and 6 in this example, the song unfolds in an even stream of beats that is fixed to the eight-beat meter produced by the drums.

Let us focus on the interval times between the strokes on the same eight-beat frame. The *o-tsuzumi* player's *kake-goe* and stroke stretch out the interval preceding the time point of the first beat to 1.2 seconds. Then, without performing a *kake-goe*, the *ko-tsuzumi* player strikes beat 2 after only 0.9 seconds, providing a strong durational contrast. It is plausible that the contrast is a result of the collaboration of both drummers, who together share a *yang-ying* or "wave" conception. However, we may also speculate that the *o-tsuzumi* player proposes a different tempo against the stream of even beats and that the *ko-tsuzumi* player rejects the *o-tsuzumi*'s proposal.

Importantly, here, such a contrast is permitted and does not disrupt the pattern of interlocking between the drums. The network of *komi* functions as a safety device to support this flow. The first stroke by the *o-tsuzumi* player becomes the point of *komi* for the *ko-tsuzumi* player to prepare the next beat. In turn, the second beat sounded by the *ko-tsuzumi* is taken as *komi* by the *o-tsuzumi* player to produce beat 3. The drum players usually become very conscious of taking *komi* especially when the tempo is very slow or when the tempo changes frequently. From beat 2 onward, the intervals are almost even, ranging from 0.8 to 1.1 seconds. It seems, however, that the sequence of beats is slightly accelerated toward the end of this line, possibly for the purpose of emphasizing the contrast that will ensue in the next frame, which consists of four beats.

Line 3

Moving toward the first beat of the frame containing the third line, the *o-tsuzumi* player again creates a large space of 1.5 seconds with a long *kake-goe*, "yo." Along with this *kake-goe* and a stroke marking beat 1, singers also prolong the last syllable "te" from eight-and-a-half in the second line to two-and-a-half in line 3. The third line starts on beat 3 of this four-beat frame (measure), named *tori* ("reduced"). This instance of four-beat meter was inserted by the anonymous composer. The last syllable of the second line, "te," and the first two syllables of the third line, "ko" and "no," are prolonged, providing the song "stream-and-backwater" contrast as described in Figure 8.3b. Moreover, the original durations allotted to those syllables are emphasized in actual performance when accompanied by the *o-tsuzumi* player, who provides a longer interval (1.5 seconds) on the first beats of the third and fourth frames than on those of frames 1 and 2.

I would like to make one more remark on the inserted *tori*, the four-beat metric frame: the second beat is not marked by a drum stroke. In order to provide a series of *kake-goes* and strokes, the *ko-tsuzumi* player must take *komi* on the second beat as he or she reckons it. Based on this, she or he plays the subsequent *kake-goes* and strokes. In addition, the *o-tsuzumi* player does not have any strokes or *kake-goes* until beat 4. This means that a *ko-tsuzumi* player has the right to change the tempo as they like. However, in this four-beat meter, we may say that the image of a wave is prevalent among the two players: without this image, the strong contrast in size between adjacent beats would not make sense.

From Line 4 Onward

From the fourth line (the fifth frame), each poetic line starts on a different "slot" according to the number of syllables in its first hemistich. For singers, this varied metrical placement is difficult to know theoretically because "stream and backwater" is the singers' original image of the rhythm. Additionally, the singers must prolong some syllables that fall on even beats (*mochis* in Figure 8.3b). In contrast to these complexities pertaining to the song rhythm, the drum strokes continue persistently straight until the end of line 6. The rushing stream of beats ends with the *o-tsuzumi* player's sudden stop at the beginning of line 7. The 2.1-second interval is spacious enough to set off the second portion of a song, which starts from line 7. The song rhythm in line 7 is as heavily modified as it was in line 1.

SYNCHRONIZED AND DETACHED

According to modern performance conventions, Richard Emmert notes, the various parts perform "sometimes independent of each other and sometimes not" (Emmert 1983, 5). This texture is a result of the performers taking *komi*, for after doing so, performers are required to be detached from the actual sound produced by coplayers instead of being synchronized with one other. In this regard, my teacher frequently gave the following practical instruction: "Do not listen to the song or other parts after you take *komi*. Just concentrate on your own part."[15]

Figure 8.7 shows a model that demonstrates the extemporal nature of the *hira-nori* rhythm. A drummer, in taking *komi* at definite syllables (C and F in the first hemistich and B in the second hemistich), does not have to synchronize with the following sung syllables such as D and E that are preceded by C in the first hemistich and G in the first hemistich, and A in the second hemistich that are preceded by F. Thus, the stroke on the *o-tsuzumi* does not necessarily perfectly synchronize with the text syllable E, nor does the first stroke of the *ko-tsuzumi* need to synchronize with the text syllable A in

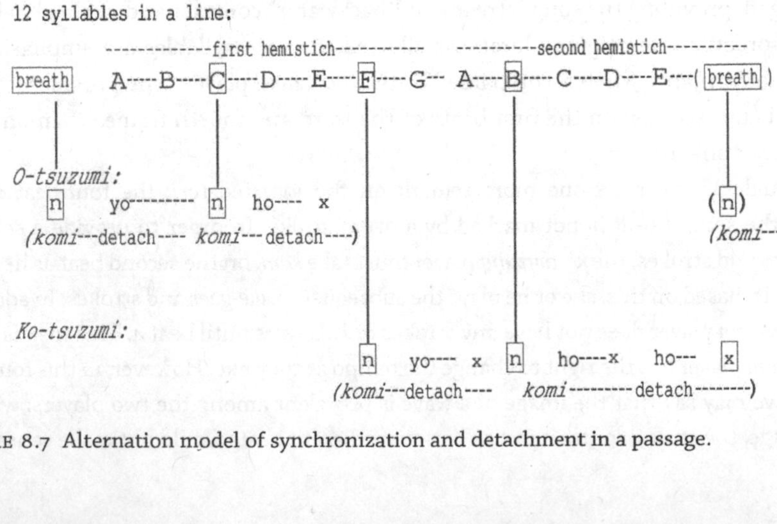

FIGURE 8.7 Alternation model of synchronization and detachment in a passage.

the second hemistich. Thus, the *hira-nori* song is realized as a layered rhythm of the singing part and the drumming part.

Detachment, in contrast to synchronization, has also brought about an elasticity of beats, which are sometimes so spacious and sometimes so contracted as to be close to breaking the continuity. The interlocking network centered on *komi* allows for this extreme spaciousness and contraction while engendering tensions among the players.

THE COMBINED FORMATION OF PATRON-AMATEUR AND PROFESSIONAL PLAYERS

What social aspects are relevant to these kinds of interaction? In order to answer the question, I will focus on the difference of social status embedded in performance, which I think would best illuminate the development of the practice centering on taking *komi*.[16] Unlike in other Japanese performance traditions, Noh is unique in that patrons participate both as amateur performers and influential transmitters of Noh dance and music.[17] In the fifteenth century, when many original works were created, Noh was only performed by a theater troupe's professional actors. However, after Noh started to gain broader patronage from political leaders in the sixteenth century, patrons became not only audience members but also performers themselves: they started to learn how to sing and dance from professional players. As mentioned earlier, *su-utai*, the unaccompanied singing of Noh drama, had become popular among aristocrats. It is likely that amateurs used to get together and sing pieces of Noh by themselves in small private circles without professional players.

At the same time, participation in full Noh plays also became popular among rulers and governors. Historical accounts of private performances at the castles of lords tell us that in the sixteenth century many aficionados among rulers/governors performed the main actor's role in full Noh plays alongside professional players.[18] Historical documents only provide the main actor's names and do not tell us about the concrete formation of amateur and professional players in performance. However, the modern conventions of amateur recitals may give us a hint of that history. Modern amateurs give recitals under the supervision of their teachers, usually once a year.[19] Interestingly, recitals featuring amateurs must have free admission. This leads me to think that amateur recitals were not open to the public in the past; maybe they were more private. In fact, even today the primary audience for amateur recitals consists of the actor's relatives, friends, and colleagues. There is seldom a public audience because the performance is not widely publicized.

An amateur must always perform with professional players in a recital. This rule holds both when the amateur acts as a protagonist, whether in a full play or simpler form such as *mai-bayashi*, and when the amateur plays musical instruments such as a drums or flute. For a full Noh drama, the amateur performs with more than fifteen professional coplayers, including supporting actors, the chorus, drummers, and a flutist.[20] Figure 8.8 shows a performance in the *mai-bayashi* format, which draws from the climactic part of a Noh play. In the picture we count three singers on the side

FIGURE 8.8 An amateur woman dancing with professional musicians at the back and choral singers at the side of the stage July 31, 2011, at the Noh theater in Otsu city (photo by the author).

and four instrumentalists in the back of the amateur dancer. Inevitably the amateur pays to hire all those professional actors and musicians, not to mention the amateur's teacher who often sits at the back of the stage as a guardian of her or his playing. Because of the great expenditure involved, we may call this person a "patron-amateur." In most cases the patron-amateur takes center stage while the professionals remain to the side or back of the stage.

The involvement of a patron-amateur along with professional players in performance seems unauthentic and exceptional from our modern aesthetic viewpoint. However, this formation is consistent with the historical documents mentioned earlier, although the strict limitation on the number of amateurs in a performance might not have been imposed before the twentieth century. We may safely say that this combination of players in performance has been common since the sixteenth century—at least in private recitals. Evidence for this can be found in a seventeenth-century treatise about Noh singing which describes the relation between singing and drumming as follows: "In most *hira-nori* songs singer[s] [are] compared to 'lord[s]' while drummers [are compared] to 'servants.' [However] in a particular type of *hira-nori* song, drummer[s] [are] compared to 'lord[s]' while singers [are compared] to 'servants.'"[21] Here, being a lord means being central and having initiative, whereas being a servant means being one who surrounds and is subordinate. That is, this representation of the relationship between Noh singers and drummers is an image of how people of different social ranks coexist in society. I suspect that the coexistence of different social ranks is not merely an image, as encapsulated by the phrase "lord and servant"; it is a social reality, internalized in the ensemble's combination of patron-amateurs and professional players.

These social relations and their articulation in Noh ensembles help us understand the layering of rhythm in Noh songs, as well as the *komi* technique by which drummers accommodate all the variants and rhythmic deviations within a frame.

CREATING A NEW RELATIONSHIP OF EQUAL STATUS

From the nineteenth to the twentieth century, a movement arose among the drummers to oppose these relationships of inequality. (Kanze 1913) Drummers began to imitate singers' practices. At this stage, taking *komi* functioned as a device for drummers to assert their rhythmic independence from the singers, as shown in Figure 8.7. Meanwhile, choral singers have had to pay increasing attention to adding *mochi* to syllables. Lately it has become common for those who wish to become professional singers to undergo drum training from a young age. This new custom, it would seem, is based on the new relationship that developed between singers and drummers over the course of the twentieth century.

ACKNOWLEDGMENTS

I am grateful to the participants of the rhythm seminar held at Harvard University on March 1–2, 2012. I must especially express my gratitude to Richard Wolf for his comments on my presentation as well as on my first draft, and for his effort in suggesting several ideas for making my chapter clearer. I am also thankful to Alison Tokita for correcting my first draft and providing some advice, to Ichiro Kichisaka, my teacher for *Kotsuzumi*, and to Yoko Takahashi, my colleague, for cooperating in producing the audio examples corresponding to figures in this chapter.

NOTES

1. Figure 8.1 is a horizontal version of the original vertical graphical notation. Showing the flow of time graphically has been popular among students of drumming since the beginning of the twentieth century, and has been used by singers to keep track of the rhythm structure. Many theoretical works and notated collections were published with the idea that singers too should know the basic eight-beat meter clearly from the beginning of their instruction. However, notations based on the format in Figure 8.1 are no longer used in singers' training.

2. *Nori*, a noun form of the verb *noru*, is used as a technical term in music and also means "to ride on" an object such as a car or horse. Tracing it back through the history of Noh performance, this word was originally found in a treatise written by Zeami (1363–1443), one of the founders of Noh. He uses this word to explain the visual illustration of a heavenly maiden's dance, saying that a dance has to "have the mood of riding on" the music (Omote and Kato 1974). It was not until about the nineteenth century that the word *nori* started to be used to classify the rhythm of Noh songs. In the early twentieth century, practitioners began commonly to use the term *nori* for rhythmic types. In addition to *hira-nori* are two other styles called *o-nori* and *chu-nori*. See Fujita (2009) for a simple illustration of the three styles. Richard

Emmert is the first scholar who focused on *hira-nori* as a "unique" rhythm (Emmert 1980); his findings are directly related to my topic.

3. In linguistic terms, they should be called *moras* rather than syllables. The length of all the Japanese phrases is easily measured by the number of *moras* they contain. Creators of Japanese traditional narrative songs and poems are always conscious of the number of moras in a phrase although there is no specific word to refer to mora in Japanese. It is simply referred to by using the word *o-n* (2 moras) that simply means "sound." We can say, for example, a basic *hira-nori* line consists of 7 + 5 *o-n*(s).

4. The audio examples for Figure 8.1 (Audio 8.1 ⊙) and Figure 8.3 (Audio 8.2 ⊙) are performed by the author, recorded on March 22, 2017. These examples were recorded for facilitating the understanding of this chapter. The audio examples for Figure 8.4 (Audio 8.3 ⊙ and Audio 8.4 ⊙) and for Figure 8.5 (Audio 8.5 ⊙, Audio 8.6 ⊙, and Audio 8.7 ⊙) were commissioned for the analysis and description conducted in this chapter, performed by Ichiro Kichisaka with substitutive beaters for *otsuzumi* and Yoko Takahashi playing *kotsuzumi*, recorded on March 24, 2017.

5. The configuration pattern of syllables shown in Figure 8.1 is not the modern one called *hira-nori*. It is the original one, which was until the nineteenth century called *hira-ji*, meaning "standard ground pattern" (Fujita 2010). It is important to know that syllables that fall on beats in even number such as beats 2, 4, and 6 never moved their positions through history. Correctly speaking, those sung syllables do not fall on those even number beats but rather create those beats through the delivery of sung syllables. Compare, for example, line 2 in Figure 8.1 and Figure 8.6. Syllables "be," "i," "sa," and "re" that come on even beats stay at the same positions in both. But other syllables that come between those even beats do not stay on the same slots.

6. In some scenes, the *taiko* stick-drum joins the ensemble to herald and accompany the appearance of supernatural characters like heavenly maidens, gods, and goddesses, and for such urgent scenes as fighting. The strokes of this drum are produced with two sticks, one in each hand of the drummer, filling all the 16 slots in 8 beats with strokes in many basic patterns. Because of this density and simplicity of strokes, the fluctuations among the 8 beats are relatively small when the *taiko* joins the ensemble.

7. Although Hare drew out "infantilization" from his observation on amateurs' training process, we may also say that there is no substantial difference in the way of training between them. Considering Johnson's observation together, infantilization is also true to the training to professional singers as long as underlying meter is concerned.

8. The most salient "iya" is the one at the end of a song or a drama. The *kake-goe* starts on the time point of beat 8 and continues to the time point of beat 1. The interval between beats 8 and 1 becomes two or three times more spacious than previous intervals. Listen for example to the final *kake-goe* and strokes on track 22 of the CD accompanying *Music in Japan* (Wade 2005).

9. The measurement of interval timings between strokes that appears in Figures 8.5 and 8.6 in this chapter were taken manually using the time-counter of a digital audio editor, audacity version 2.0.3.

10. The noun *komi* is a technical term used normally with the verb *toru*, meaning "to take, charge, or hold." In this chapter I use the English verb "take" for the Japanese verb *toru* in reference to this *komi* playing technique.

11. This modification of the same drumming pattern appears also on track 3 of the CD accompanying *Music in Japan* (Wade 2005). From 0:52 to 1:20 this drum pattern is repeated three times over the song text "bu to iedomo—, nichi gata wa imada chi ni ochitamawazu—,

Tatoi ikanaru hooben naritomo—, ma sa" (Wade 2005, 96). The starting times for each drum pattern on the track respectively are 0:52, 1:02, and 1:09.

12. Adaptations of *yin-yang* to the rhythm of Noh can be found in the treatises that were transmitted in the Iwai school of Noh singing. One original manuscript is *Royo no hyoshi* (The beat of *yang* in its climactic form), written by Iwai Naotsune, a Noh actor of the eighteenth century. The manuscript is kept in the Iwai collection at the Kyoto City University of Arts.

13. "Blur" modification of *mitsuji* also appears on track 3 of the CD accompanying *Music in Japan* (Wade 2005). Over the *sashi* section, sung without fixed meter, *mitsuji* pattern is repeated 6 times. The starting times for each drum pattern on the track respectively are 2:06, 2:21, 2:39, 2:57, 3:13, and 3:28. The transcription of the first round starting from 2:06 is appended to Figure 8.5c. The repetition is followed by a modified *tsuzuke* pattern (Figure 8.5b) in "contraction" (from 3:43 to 3:58).

14. *Ataka* has also been adapted for Kabuki performance, where it is called *Kanjincho*.

15. I am most thankful to my *ko-tsuzumi* teacher, Ichiro Kichisaka, of the Okura school. He has been giving me lessons for over twenty years. He often repeats these quoted words when his students try to synchronize their strokes to song syllables after taking *komi*.

16. Performers and scholars have so far explained the elasticity of the rhythm of Noh music exclusively from an aesthetic standpoint; the indistinctiveness of the eight-beat meter in a song performance is meant to draw more attention to the text than to the music (Emmert 1980). However, not all fluctuations are produced by an aesthetic focusing on the text nor does the prominence of eight-beat meter necessarily detract from the literary meaning.

17. The common Japanese word for amateur is *shiro-to*. This is a compound of *shiro* and *to*, Chinese characters that means "pure" and "man" respectively. The first Chinese character *shiro* is also pronounced *su*, which is often used as a prefix that means "white," "transparent," "bare," "pure," "single," "simple," and also "naïve."

18. One such historical account is *Noh no tome cho* (The records of Noh performance), written by Shimotsuma Shojin in the early seventeenth century. Shimotsuma Shojin, one of the commanders at the Hongwanji temple, was also known to be an excellent actor. He recorded the names of lords and governors who performed Noh as main actors (Nishino 1973–1976). The most famous aficionado in the sixteenth century was the ruler Toyotomi Hideyoshi (1536–1598) who started to learn and perform Noh drama as a protagonist after the age of fifty. A historical document tells us that he used a professional actor as an extra singer on stage. We may suspect it was a prompter to help with Hideyoshi's solo part. See Amano (1997) for a historical description of the rulers/governors' amateur participation in Noh performances.

19. At present there are about 1,300 professional Noh players, including actors and musicians. They derive their primary income not from public performing but from teaching amateurs and assisting in their recitals.

20. It cost more than $10,000 (US) just to play the role of a protagonist of a Noh drama at a recital held in a Noh theater. See Irmgard Johnson's preliminary report about amateur practice (Johnson 1982), which describes all aspects of amateur practice in late twentieth-century Japan.

21. See *Utai no hisho* (A secret treatise on singing), compiled in the middle of the seventeenth century. This treatise is reproduced in Takemoto (1994).

9

Rhythmic Metamorphoses

BOTANICAL PROCESS MODELS ON THE ATLAS MOUNTAINS OF MOROCCO

Miriam Rovsing Olsen

THIS CHAPTER ENDEAVORS to show how mountain farmers conceive rhythm on the central Anti-Atlas in Morocco.[1] In these regions they focus their musical life mainly on singing and dancing with drums (*aḥwaš*) and on *a cappella* songs performed during agricultural rituals (*ladkar*) or wedding rituals. For several summer months each year, villagers are collectively engaged in these festive events and rituals, devoting the rest of the year to agriculture. Each of the three repertoires unfolds in musical suites presented through large-scale performances that sometimes continue for whole nights and days. In this sense, their musical practices do not differ from others in the Maghreb, including those in cities (the *nūba*) or rural areas, though there are many variations.

Yet the rhythmic mechanisms of these dynamic forms have not always been elucidated by scientific approaches to rhythm, which has mainly been identified with drummed cycles and has been understood as a theoretical entity separate from performance, with some exceptions and regardless of the tradition from which it derives. Because these are rural musical practices of an oral tradition, in which people do not locate rhythm only in the drummed cycles and in which they endeavor to build relationships with their natural environment, examination of their local conceptualization should be the starting point for researchers seeking to understand rhythm in the musical performance of these societies.

In this chapter I explore an aspect of rhythm on the Anti-Atlas Mountains that local participants conceptualize in terms of plant growth. I approach rhythm by analyzing their repertoires and looking at how participants relate their performances to stages in the life cycle of plants. By exploring a connection with the surrounding environment, this approach might seem similar to that of Steven Feld on the Kaluli in Papua New Guinea and the concept of "lift-up-over-sounding" (1988); however, it focuses on plants rather than on the sound environment.[2]

Christopher Hasty recently stressed the need to study rhythm in performance and not "out-of-time," as a process enabling event formation[3] through repetition combined with novelty. This approach involves a concept of rhythm as temporality. Hasty sees rhythm as largely "synonymous with time, passage, becoming, change, movement, and process" (2012, 8). According to this view, in which the "unit" (also characterized as "object") has a position in time and depends on its genesis, the notions of beginning, ending, and duration naturally become particularly important. To this conception of time, compared to a "budding (creation) of events," he opposes a time in which "past, present and future are different positions on the time-line that do not affect what the unit-object is." Such units are always available; they do not change; they stay the same regardless of their positions in time; they are "independent of their genesis." Hasty characterizes this independence as "a mark of their timelessness" (14–16).

Regarding the Maghreb, Bernard Lortat-Jacob and Richard Jankowsky are unique for having also favored a dynamic approach to music. It is one of the achievements of their research to have shown that particular methods of investigation and approaches to rhythm are required for the musical forms, widespread in the Maghreb, that are performed over long periods with an accelerating tempo. Lortat-Jacob has studied the sung and danced village music (*aḥwaš*) of the central High Atlas in its dynamics (between twelve and twenty minutes) (1980, 2013). He notes the gradual acceleration led by frame drums (*tagnza* or *allun*)—about fifteen of them, two of which stand out because of their solos (*assiff* and *tḫllif*)—and by a large drum with two skins (*bengri*), giving special attention to the rhythmic change (through compression) that occurs in the cell repeated three-quarters of the way through the performance: it goes from four beats (four quarter-notes) to three and a half beats (two quarter-notes and a dotted quarter), and through the displacement of accentuation it becomes asymmetric (two / one and a half).

Jankowsky's research focuses on the *nūba* of *sṭambēlī* in Tunisia, a dance practice that may lead some participants into a trance. He considers rhythm mainly through the strokes produced by iron clappers *shqāshiq* and on the "drumhead" of the lute *gumbrī*. He shows that the temporal dynamics are structured by the "elastic rhythm" of the clappers and the "offset accentuation" of the *gumbrī* (2010, 115). The ingredients of these dynamics are transformation—through compression of the rhythmic cell, due to the gradual acceleration of the tempo (121)—and the presence of "accentual counterpoint" between the clappers and the *gumbrī*, with dancers aligning their movement with the accents of the *gumbrī* (119). In these dynamics, in which the spacing between strokes is gradually reduced during the performance (of about fifteen minutes) toward equalization (spacings measured by the author), the meter, Jankowsky states, cannot be characterized as either binary or ternary. It is "ambiguous." This dynamic is not compatible with the notion of pulsation: "the *sṭambēlī* temporal system is best understood as a succession of self-referential rhythmic cells containing short, repeated, accented patterns of articulations whose identities are based on their relative spacing from each other, rather than on an underlying series of equidistant pulses" (115).

Like Lortat-Jacob, Jankowsky focuses on percussion instruments, but he also emphasizes the interdependence of percussion with other performance parameters in mechanisms of temporal flow. However, the vocals do not seem relevant to these temporal dynamics (they are not analyzed from this point of view), even if they conform to "the same logics of rhythmic elasticity and acceleration." Still, Jankowsky emphasizes the role of melodic pitches in the most intense moments linked to the trance of the dancers, through ambiguity of tonicity or the suspension of tonal resolution (123–25).

My contribution focuses on how the protagonists connect the different components of musical practices in *aḥwaš* (melody, lyrics, dance, body movement, choreography, performance modalities, drumming) to construct a continuously evolving temporal process. But musical life on the Anti-Atlas also presents another aspect of temporality, which is developed through performances related to the two ritual *a cappella* repertoires. In that case, it is not so much the songs that convey the temporal dynamics as it is other coexisting performance dimensions. This dynamic relates to a process that is the opposite of continuous evolution; I will provisionally refer to it as a process of reduction.

This conception of time as at once a process of continual evolution and reduction on the one hand, and as a composite substance on the other hand, is rooted in the agricultural life of the people of the Anti-Atlas. For these villagers, agriculture is an activity of survival, and the flow of time is observable in plants and fruit trees. Barley and date palms are both essential for their nourishment and sacred in character, as shown by the specific religious songs *ladkar* performed *a cappella* at certain stages of the life of these plants. These provide the villagers with their main experiences of time, in repeated cycles. Renewal of growth depends on processes of expansion and contraction. "Expansion" is the plant's growth in stages from seed, pit, or transplanted shoot. "Contraction" is returning to the seed stage, extracting the seed or pit from the mature plant. The successive manifestations of growth command their attention, sometimes through color transformations, sometimes through a proliferation of components (for example leaves), sometimes through the arrangement of these components (the formation of nodes through alternating detachments from barley stalk; alternating traces of fallen leaves left on palm tree trunks) (see Rovsing Olsen 2004). In this region, observing the shoots of palm leaves is a way to measure time. Mustapha Akhmisse nicely states (2004, 96) that according to an elderly man, the palm had always been "the clock of people of Bani" (a mountain range south of the central Anti-Atlas). Although these plants are different, barley being annual and dates perennial, they provide the first source of education in concepts related to time.[4]

I identified these concepts during my various stays among the villagers, especially during performances, and by listening to my recordings after the performances, seeking to identify repertoires and sung texts.[5] Sung poetry has proven to be an important source for understanding their concepts relating to music. In the peasant world of the Moroccan Atlas Mountains—which Hassan Jouad (a specialist in Moroccan oral poetry and a native of the central High Atlas) characterized as "taciturn and rough," adding that "austerity is part of Being" (Jouad 2013)—this poetry has a special value, in contrast to reticence in everyday speech.

There is no formal instruction in these practices of singing and dancing. That kind of transmission would imply a musical specialization that would be incompatible with the social organization, in which everyone, from a young age, contributes in turn to the collective musical and agricultural practices. Even if the secrecy surrounding the practices of some ritual repertoires causes compartmentalization of the knowledge related to them, these practices involve a consensus empirically constructed in the social environment, and the way they function certainly leaves room for "individual intellectual creativity" and "intracultural variability" as suggested by Marc Perlman in his study of ethnotheories (2004, 4–5), but without giving rise to the development of expressible concepts.[6]

Before introducing the concept of temporality, I will outline the celebratory and ritual musical practices to be discussed.

A BRIEF OVERVIEW OF THE REPERTOIRES

The three repertoires presented here (*aḥwaš*, ritual agricultural songs, and wedding ritual songs) are not specific to the central Anti-Atlas. They are found all over the Moroccan Atlas Mountains. The *aḥwaš* assumes various forms depending on the tribe, and might vary in terms of choreography, elements of musical language, drumming, women's participation, and the role of women in relation to men. These local characteristics are often designated by specific names.

However, because of its musico-poetic and choreographic style, the central Anti-Atlas belongs to a region distinguished by the Tashlhiyt Berber language, which is also spoken in the western and central High Atlas and in the Sous plain. (The Berber language of the eastern High Atlas and the Middle Atlas, called Tamazight, is significantly different from Tashlhiyt.) As elsewhere in the Tashlhiyt-speaking region, in the Anti-Atlas *aḥwaš* refers to a complex collective practice of song and dance performed by men and women, usually all night long until dawn. Summer is the season for *aḥwaš*, after the harvest, and especially on the occasion of marriages. But, in fact, these practices can be occasioned by any major event assembling a large number of people from one or more villages or tribes.

In the central part of the Anti-Atlas, which is discussed here, a great deal of importance is attached to poetry contests in *aḥwaš* and among poet-singers generally as well as between male and female poet-singers. But unlike male poets who sing their own poetry, the female poets convey their poetry through female choirs to whom they whisper their verses during the performances.

Poet-singers find it easier to sing in women's *aḥwaš* than to participate in men's *aḥwaš* (*ddrst, ahnaqqar*), in which they are expected to continuously keep up the improvised poetic exchanges, on topics that concern the village, the tribe, or even the whole country. Thus these are often performed by elderly poets with some authority. As long as they have something to say, they are allowed to participate in performances. For example, in 2004 I heard the great poet-singer Lhaj Ali Bidni, who died in January 2014 at the age of ninety-nine. In women's *aḥwaš*, the poet does not keep the exchange going, but returns to the audience as soon as he has finished his contribution, receiving the female response there. Later he can participate in the *aḥwaš* again and react to the women's poetry, but usually another poet-singer will emerge from the audience, sometimes without waiting for the end of the performance.

Aḥwaš is a necessary medium of poetic creation. Villagers memorize a lot of sung words that they pick up on the spot during the *aḥwaš*, and some of the verses will later inspire conversations, especially during the long winter evenings. The sung poetry is in fact always constructed in such a way that it leads to general ideas that can later be quoted and circulated as proverbs or sayings. Although women do not travel, some poets have become very famous and travel great distances to participate in celebrations during the summer months, and this exposes them to various musical practices.

The mastering of the art of poetry is based on tacit knowledge. It has been studied in depth by Hassan Jouad, whose research reveals a common system used by the people of the Atlas Mountains and the Sous plains. The verses appear in abstract formulas that he calls *vers vides* ("empty verses") (1995, 22–38), made up of various combinations of syllables, *la, lay, lal, layl*, and variants such as *li* or *a* (at the beginning of a formula). These form series of varying length, between eight and 18 syllables, in which one always finds one of the following syllables, which Jouad calls "low": *da, day, dal, dayl*. These patterns are matrices of the verses themselves, in that they determine the number and character of their syllables (long or short) (1995, 39 on the "translexical division" of the phonemic material). Jouad has listed over one hundred and thirty patterns, but in practice, each tribal group only uses a few dozen. In the Anti-Atlas they are sung at the beginning of every poetic improvisation. However, they are not made explicit in ritual songs, which are considered to have divine origins.

The *aḥwaš* always includes a number of frame drums *tilluna* (singular *tallunt*), mostly played by men. In the central Anti-Atlas there are usually at least five or six *tilluna*, with drummers divided, according to their role, between soloists (*amnqqar*, "the one who strikes") and *lhmz* ("to spur"). Moreover, there is always a *ganga*, a large two-headed drum played with two sticks. Instruments like metal clappers *tiqrqqawin*, or more rarely the bell *naqus*, are sometimes also used.

In these *aḥwaš* performances, all villagers are present (men, women, children). They sit on the ground or on the flat roofs, in groups according to family affiliation and gender. The spectators are not passive: poets come from the audience, and the same goes for the drummers, whom the master of ceremonies asks to take turns playing the *lhmz*. Women spectators ululate when they appreciate certain words, especially those coming from male poet-singers. Finally, in the central Anti-Atlas, the emotion generated by the excitement of a successful *aḥwaš* inspires audience members to sing *tazrrart* songs (pl. *tizrrarin*) while women are singing and dancing. These *tizrrarin* belong to another repertoire. They are sung in a responsorial form (solo and choir) to specific melodies that develop over two verses. Then wherever the performers' initiatives take them, groups of spectators sing in succession until the end of the performance, their songs surrounding and overlapping those of the dancer-singers. (For research on these *tizrrarin* in other contexts, see Hoffman 2002.)

The *a cappella* repertoires discussed in this contribution are of two kinds, related to agricultural rituals and to wedding rituals. The first, called *ladkar* (sing. *ddikr*), concern the threshing and winnowing of barley and the fertilization of date palms. Unfortunately, I was unable to attend the fertilization of date palms. Barley threshing, by families working in succession, takes place in the villages shortly after the harvest. This is done early in the morning and in privacy. Over the course of several hours, a few men rotate the animals (donkeys, mules) tied in tandem to a stake planted at the center of the threshing area. The sheaves will have been piled up at the edges of this area since the harvest. The men use their forks to gradually spread them over the area, to be trampled by the animals as they rotate. A series of *ladkar* support the different phases, which are interrupted when the men turn over the sheaves. When the threshing is finished, all of the mixed straw and grain is gathered into a rectangular pile beside the threshing area, awaiting winnowing. That process requires suitable wind that is not too strong, something that might not come for several days. The winnowers (men or women of the family) then use a fork to toss the mixture into the air, so that the wind can separate the barleycorn from the straw, as they sing one *ladkar* after another. If there is not enough wind, several interruptions may occur, sometimes lasting several hours.

The ritual wedding songs are sung antiphonally by elderly women in sequences of varying length, which take place at many locations in daytime or at night over a period of several days (see Rovsing Olsen 2013). The periods that separate song suites can sometimes last hours or even several days. But the songs making up the suites can also be separated in time, especially since the songs in most suites are multilocal (a place for each song) and women change place for each new action and song. This often entails interruptions between songs. Moreover, the performers change from one suite to the next, depending on the time and place of the ceremony.

Women sing on behalf of the bride or groom's mother, or the two families, or the bride herself, who must not speak or move during the ritual. Most of the ritual songs are constructed as dialogues intended for the bride. The verses have to be sung and repeated a certain number of times (which varies depending on the song), and this is often ensured by an expert woman who whispers the beginning of a verse or the number of its repetitions. The women perform various actions while singing and handling objects, which are often linked to agriculture. In these ritual songs, the beginning and end of each song is determined by the action connected with it. The beginning of a song suite is always signaled by three ululations from one of the women, and the end simply fades out with the end of action.

CONCEPTS OF TEMPORALITY

The search for local terms and the establishment of ethnotheories has been a major ethnomusicological focus for decades. Discussions on ethnotheories and on the nature of musical vocabularies regularly make reference to ethnomusicological work (see in particular Agawu 2003; Perlman 2004; Baily 2005), but without questioning the fact that musicological theory, which favors acoustic relations between sounds, has served indiscriminately as a model for research on urban and rural areas. This has led to the search for terms equivalent to musicological concepts (Blacking 1967) or to the translation of local terms into musicological concepts of a technical nature (to enable the establishment of a *musical* theory) (Zemp 1979 and Feld 1981), especially as expressed in contexts of learning and teaching. The view, held by Agawu, that music theory in African countries is not different from what is common in the West (2003, 71–96) does not facilitate an understanding of the situation in Morocco.

As regards terms used in the Anti-Atlas that are derived from agriculture, it would be tempting to see these as agricultural metaphors and then apply them to a component of the performance stemming solely from the language of music. To proceed in this way would be to forget that the musicians are also farmers, and to ignore the implications of this usage based on dual expertise acquired through many years of experience. In the present case, it is precisely by preserving the agricultural or botanical meaning of the terms attached to musical performances that we can penetrate the conceptualization of temporality.

The use of concepts from agriculture has several implications: 1) these concepts focus on aspects of performance that are different from those of Western music theory; 2) they are situated, in the sense that they refer to key moments of temporal experience; and 3) they are subject to the fluctuations of the living. Therefore, based on these markers, villagers can infer what comes temporally before or after, by completing it mentally.

The use of a botanical field (in this case barley or date palm) is not systematic. Some of the plant stages used by villagers in their musical performance concern barley, some concern date palm, and some concern both. This is what makes it possible to view temporality (and musical performance) in reference to two plants at once, depending on whether one chooses to mentally complete the course of time based on one or the other.

I will focus on some key moments whose conceptualization is obvious: beginning, advancement, and fulfillment, which are connected with the process of continuous evolution. These concepts will be discussed based on a study of the performance of "women's *aḥwaš*" (*aḥwaš n tmġarin*); similar notions are also found in men's *aḥwaš*. The way the mountain-dwellers express the orientation of temporality will be discussed afterward, and this will include an examination of the two ritual repertoires.

Beginning

We must distinguish between two kinds of beginning: 1) The beginning of the all-night succession of *aḥwaš*; and 2) The beginning of each *aḥwaš*. The villagers see the first as equivalent to a preparation.

1) The female singer-dancers enter the place in procession, led by two or three women playing the frame drum *tallunt*. This refers to an agricultural act, *iriẓi*. According to my local contacts, this term, which could be translated as "shattering," refers to the preparation, through plowing, of a field that has not been cultivated for several years (removing stones, thorny plants, etc.). The area the women enter, *asays*, is usually located in the village and is seen as a field that will be sown. The challenge awaiting the villagers is evoked by the women of a village when, after entering *asays*, they invoke their local saint in their song, requesting that he place "forks in their hands" and that they will "winnow seeds" (see Rovsing Olsen 1997, 99). Starting with a seed, the process should lead to another seed. The area they enter is sometimes called *asarag*. This term, which refers to the place where women break fruit pits, could be the source of the term for the initiatory song performed by poet-singers called *amarg* ("the one who breaks fruit pits"). In other words, it is a term that refers to the final state of the fruit, whose nutrient heart extracted by women precedes every beginning.
2) The poet-singer's act of beginning is seen as an act of sowing. Here is an example of a poet's first verse, directed at the female choirs of an *aḥwaš*:

   a bismi llah nḫlf amud ġ lmlk(i)
   In the name of God, we renew the seed at this area

The poet-singer, whose song type is called *amarg*, is sometimes asked by an audience member to begin: "*luḥ amarg*," "throw the *amarg*." This gesture (including the object *amarg* that will be received by the female choir) is comparable to that of the sower who throws seeds on the ground, thereby triggering a growth process. Such a beginning supplies the temporal process with what Hasty terms its "potential for becoming" (1997, 74) and with a "projective potential" (84) for what follows. In front of his face, the poet holds a frame drum, which covers his *amarg* singing. At that moment the *amarg* "goes underground," as expressed by the following three verses I collected from several people. These verses suggest a strong association between *amarg* and barley:

Iġ a tiyukriznt ṭmẓin ig^{w}z amarg akal
Iġ a ttiwinġaynt ḥra d itlala igllin
Iġ a ttiwmgirnt ukan n iġli d išhr nit

When barley is plowed, the *amarg* goes underground
When it (barley) germinates it (the *amarg*) reappears
When it (barley) is harvested, it (the *amarg*) rises and becomes visible

It is not only the sowing of cereal that is evoked at the beginning. The field of the date palm is also present. The poet's melody (*rriḥ*, "air, melody") always begins on syllables belonging to the chosen formula called *talalayt*, a term built on three syllables *a*, *la*, and *lay*, the initial and final "t" simply making the word feminine or a diminutive. The variation on this word, *talayt*, refers to the spadix (inflorescence) of the male or female date palm, and the fertilization by the male pollen of the female date palm is the beginning of the fructification of dates. It therefore makes reference to two plant types, barley and date palm, from which they hope for fulfillment after sowing (barley) or fertilization (dates).

In both cases, the process should lead to fruits *aqqayn*, a term that also refers to the outcome of the lyrics. This climax common to plants and poetry is also sought through the final emotional state. The term used is *lfrḥ*, which can be translated as "ecstasy, euphoria, jubilation" or "joy, feast." "We enter *lfrḥ*" (*nkšm di s d lfrḥ*) sings a poet at the beginning of his *amarg*, a state to which all these villagers aspire, comparable to "the rain expected for the harvest in a time of drought" (*win d lġllat s unzar iġ illa fad*) (Rovsing Olsen 1997, 100). This state is also present through the term for the area where *aḥwaš* are performed, *asays*, the "boiling" area.

From the beginning, through his *amarg*, the singer sets in motion the process that will allow development to the fulfillment stage. He establishes a "shifting" process between the melody and the "empty verse" and then between the melody and the verses themselves (see Figure 9.1 and Table 9.1, where each number refers to the corresponding audio example as well as to the marker of the integral version; all figures and tables in appendix), a mechanism that the numerous participants in the *aḥwaš* alongside the poet all apply in their own way, with the same desire for collective advancement.

Advancement

The shift introduced by the poet between melody and verse is continued by the two choirs of women, who improvise their response (see Table 9.3, Figures 9.2 and 9.3). The movement toward the fulfillment of their action is seen as a path to follow (*aġaras*), a path taken by the women through "a walk" or "steps" (*bu-uḍar*, "the one of the foot," "the one of the step") in the *aḥwaš* performed by circulating in two semicircles facing the center. The alternation of the steps proceeds through an anti-clockwise movement between the ball of the left foot and the support of the body on the whole foot, and the ball of the right foot and support of the body on the whole foot (see Figure 9.4). With these movements and steps, the women make intertwining lines with the footprints left on the ground. The dancers perform their rotation while singing antiphonally: this involves outward projections of song to the opposite choir from different positions in the circle. Such an alternating movement creates intertwining song projections.

The musicians playing drums place themselves in the middle of the two choirs and alternate between two low sounding strokes of the large two-headed drum *ganga* and three strokes (high/medium/high) of the frame drums *tilluna*. Thus the 2:3 ratio is part of the mechanism set up by the unequal number of strokes distributed between the two types of drum (see Figure 9.4). So it is not so much a metrical ambiguity as in the

Tunisian *sṭambēlī* (Jankowsky 2010, 115) that fosters the advancement. It is the alternation between two sets of strokes of contrasting timbre.

To sum up, this mechanism of inequality and binary opposition is present everywhere in the organization of the whole ensemble, in ways that appear analogous (on the importance of analog processes to music theories, see Perlman 2004) between the two contributors (male soloist, women's choir); between the two types of vocal expression (melody, lyrics); between the two choirs (set out in space and in movement); between the steps of the rotating dancers; and between the two types of drum. The various constituent elements enter the performance in succession, producing a progressive density by superimposition (for the order of these contributions, see Table 9.1) in an unbroken progression of regular shifts and intersections. This is what the villagers call *amḫllf*. This term means "he or she who intersects," who "adjusts," who "replaces"; in botany it refers to "that which buds," which yields "young shoots" or "offsets." So it applies both to *aḥwaš* and to plants, but applied to plants it is the idea of growth that emerges.

These advancement dynamics based on the dual and unequal division of the various constituent parts of the ensemble will eventually adjust, at the moment of fulfillment or plenitude when the women have finished their response to the poet.

Fulfillment

To reach fulfillment, the musicians carry out the alignment of the various dual components while initiating a compression of the units of all categories and an acceleration of the tempo. The alignment takes place between the pattern of the "empty verse" and the melody; between the drums *ganga* and *tilluna*; between the two dancing choirs that now move in varying configurations (in single file, in parallel rows, two-by-two or three-by-three, one chain behind the other, or back-to-back); between the steps done to the right (right foot, left foot). By aligning their movements and expressions, the participants trigger splits: the detachment of pairs of girls from the ranks of the singer-dancers; the regular detachment of certain high strokes by the frame drum soloists; the regular detachment of the ball of the right foot in the women's dance steps; a melodic change by the women's choirs (on the initiative of one of the singer-dancers) in a higher register and with an added refrain (see Figure 9.7); these melodies with a refrain are often short phrases from popular songs of the season, but are always in the region's own style (for example, from the songs of itinerant musicians *rways*).

These mechanisms are intended to express the "trembling" manifested in the shaking movement of women's shoulders (*iġariwn*), a movement that makes their voices tremble. The pairs of girls who break rank are particularly active in effecting these shoulder movements. This trembling concept represents this stage of the temporal process.

The villagers conceptualize this stage of fulfillment as the threshing phase of the fruit harvest, *tamssust*. This term can be translated as "the one who shakes," who "trembles," who "fells," who "threshes." The same term refers to the date harvest, sometimes in variant forms (*tamnžužt, assus*). As for barley grain or dates (visible on the barley ear or on the date spadix), the lyrics have reached maturity at this stage, in the sense that the female poetic creation or response to the poet has been brought to an end. Sung poetry then passes from the status of improvised lyrics (*awal*), that is to say lyrics in development, to that of fixed words (*aqqayn*).[7]

At this stage, barley is considered "cooked" (*nwant*, "they [the barley] are cooked") with the heat of May. In the context of the *aḥwaš*, villagers speak of "boiling" (*sis* "to boil") when referring to these trembling expressions. The term *sis* is a variant of *suss* (to shake), which is the root of the term *tamssust*. This boiling point to which all participants aspire is the manifestation of the effervescence (*lfrḥ*). When it is reached, it has the effect of adding a new sound layer: produced by successive groups of spectators sitting on the ground all around the area, who sing *tazrrart* songs (these songs are also sung during the barley harvests). The conclusion of *aḥwaš* is often abrupt, and could be compared to a fall (like dates falling from the top of the palm trees[8] when shaking or cutting the date stems) or a rooting up (barley is harvested by manually rooting it up).

The Ascent

As we have seen, when a development is a continuously evolving one, as in *aḥwaš*, time is viewed as a process of ascending to get fruit (*aqqayn*), so it proceeds in a vertical direction from bottom to top. The villagers experience or observe this rise when some of them climb up (*iġli*) palm trees in bare feet to fertilize female palms with pollen from male palms, or to cut date stems.

In *aḥwaš*, the main agent of ascent is the frame drum *tallunt*. The term for the drum, *(t)allun(t)*, conveys this idea of a rise (> *all*, to "go up"). Another way of marking the rise is to warm the skins of frame-drums. Early in the *aḥwaš* or before it begins, each player ensures that the skin of his drum is heated over a fire built for the occasion near the musicians. In doing so, he "raises the drum" (*ssrġ allun*), probably referring to the sound pitch. Achieving the boiling state is in itself a representation of warming and an ascension to the heights. At this stage, the women change their melody while raising their vocal pitch (which rises continuously from the beginning of their contribution). The following phrase sung by women at the end of *aḥwaš*, presented in the appendix (Table 9.2, verse 16), illustrates the relationship between heat, rising, and pleasure:[9]

trġa tafukt yili uġaras a ššahwa šuwr

Sun is heating, the path is rising, Oh pleasure do not hurry

The conceptualization of the temporal sequence as an ascent is not specific to this region. Bernard Lortat-Jacob reports that for musicians of the central High Atlas, the *aḥwaš* "rises (*ali*)" (1980, 67 and 130–31) and that this "rise" relates to acceleration (68). He shows two distinct rhythmic parts in this upward movement: a first so-called heavy part (*ẓẓay*) and a second part, in which the rhythm changes, called the "(mountain) pass" (*tizi*). He emphasizes that the mechanics of this rhythmic shift have to proceed imperceptibly. However, in his comparison of a shift with a geographical pass, Lortat-Jacob does not specify all the implications of this transformation.

Based on what the inhabitants of the Anti-Atlas say about their *aḥwaš*, it appears that this rise is seen as vertical. The mere botanical process leading from genesis to plenitude suggests an upward direction for the temporality of *aḥwaš*. Singer-poets might also suggest this direction. In the appendix (see Table 9.2), the singer, through the idea of *mīzān* (the balance of the builder), compares this rise to the delicate construction of a wall, which threatens to fall at the slightest imbalance. The ending of *aḥwaš*, often abrupt, reinforces the idea of a vertical rising that can be stopped only by a fall.

In reference to the *aḥwaš* of the Central High Atlas, Lortat-Jacob has also pointed out the difficulty of the rise, particularly mentioning the responsibility of the "drum soloist," whose slightest deviation from the stabilization of tempo[10] can tip over the ensemble and make it "fall down"(*sḍr*). He explains that "If the soloist loses control of the *aḥwaš*, it is said to 'fall off' (*ažu*), the *ažu* verb being used to refer to an accidental fall" (1980, 68). This could speak in favor of a vertical rise.

There is also verticality in the position of the bodies. In their initial song (*iriẓi*), the singer-dancers on the Anti-Atlas move from a squatting position (on their heels) to an upright standing position, and then perform body movements that develop upward over the course of the *aḥwaš*, in what Paris (1921) and Chottin (1939, 25) have both conceived as a "verticality" in women's dance on the Central High Atlas *aḥwaš*.

Ascent and verticality are also suggested in Moroccan Arab-Andalusian music, *al-āla*. Chottin has suggested a similar idea in relation to Moroccan *nūba*. In a chapter on rhythm, meter and "general characteristics of Andalusian rhythm" (1939, 110–19), he reproduces an image of tempo development *mīzān* (also translated as "rhythmic phase," "measure") through a tambourine musician's "spontaneously drawn" sketch of a painter's ladder whose two rails become narrower from bottom to top due to acceleration and a narrowing of the time between strokes of the tambourine (*tar*). The ladder's rungs represent the succession of the songs (111–12). According to Chottin, this acceleration is imperceptible in the first half of the musical development of *nūba*. It intensifies in the second half, in which the "rhythm gets agitated." The ladder of Chottin's Moroccan informant applies to the different forms of *nūba* throughout North Africa (Saidani 2006, 267). In the Anti-Atlas, the ladder could be replaced by the palm tree trunk, which is used to produce ladders and, among mountain-dwellers, evokes the repeated experience of the ascension necessary for access to fruits. These evocations situate the urban and rural musical forms within a more general North African conception.

Through the *aḥwaš* we have seen different mechanisms of temporal process through their related concepts. Its ascent is based on the connections between the various components, and it unfolds from a beginning, rising as its density increases, and ending at its fulfillment, with a sudden fall. This fall is not without similarities to the process of reduction mentioned earlier, but it has another temporal position. It is the abrupt end of a rise or fruition, whereas the reduction process proceeds in stages. Furthermore, from an examination of the *aḥwaš* and its upward time orientation, we can infer from both ritual repertoires an opposite movement that can be viewed as a descent.

The Descent

A study of the ritual songs themselves does not suggest a downward process. These songs have the out-of-time characteristics mentioned by Hasty. There is no transformation of the poetic-melodic-rhythmic material, no changes in tempo or vocal register. The songs follow each other discontinuously and in juxtaposition, with many interruptions associated with different actions. The verses of these strophic songs, whose words are called *aqqayn*, are also juxtaposed without developing a narrative idea. They are subject to numerous repetitions, the number of which is codified. Neither is there continuity with regard to the singers, who may change from one suite to the next. However, two of the wedding songs are danced by women with one of them playing a frame drum, and the songs might therefore appear to imply ascent. But some village women spontaneously told me that the skin of this drum, called "the groom's drum," should not be heated. The conditions for rising are thus neutralized. The descent unfolds not in the songs, but rather in the other components of the performance, through a reduction process, as well as a disarticulation of the constitutive parts.[11]

We have seen that threshing and winnowing barley is a long process involving a series of operations in a reduction dynamic, ending with the isolation of the seeds (*aqqayn*). The wedding ritual is a process involving beginnings (with every song suite), hence the name *izwirrign* (from the verb *zwur*, "to begin"), which is widespread among many tribes of the Anti-Atlas. But density decreases at each stage (or suite), because of successive divisions established through the use of the performance areas (for example, developing from actions performed in the bride and groom's area simultaneously with actions performed in the groom's area, in two different rooms at the same time, and then in one room divided in two). These reductions involving various arrangements of the two choirs of women can also be conceived in terms of a decreasing dynamic (through their distance or proximity, through their separation between two rooms or their union in a circle, etc.) (Rovsing Olsen 2013).

The reduction process observed in these rituals is associated with an emotional state that also contrasts with the rise observed in the *aḥwaš*. Villagers refer to the entire process of threshing and winnowing by the term *anrar*, which designates the area specifically designated for these actions. Etymologically, this word expresses the idea of "groaning, whining, roaring," and its morphological paradigm includes *aniri*, meaning "sorrow, grief caused by the death of a loved one." Villagers see the threshing area as the place where barley is moaning (after being rooted up during the harvest). The wedding ritual is itself driven by the weeping of the bride and her relatives after her separation from her family, and this leads to a stage at the end in which she is left alone, still lamenting. Weeping and wailing are the opposite of the effervescence of *aḥwaš*. (Although joyful moments do occur during some of the long "breaks" between the performance of song suites, or in places other than those where the ritual takes place *stricto sensu*.) It is worth noting that the term for wedding ritual songs in the western High Atlas, *asallaw*, whose meaning is unclear according to my local interlocutors, conveys the ideas of "crying," "fading," and "losing color."

* * *

In conclusion, we have seen that the conceptualization of time on the Anti-Atlas Mountains requires the joint investigation of musical repertoires and references to agricultural activities. The analysis reveals temporal processes with two complementary dimensions, one ascending with a progressive density (and a sudden fall) and another descending with a decreasing density in stages. It leads to a general approach that incorporates the protagonists' structuring between the constituent parts, through either synthesis or dissociation. In the former case they develop a time in an ascendant process, using analogy to make connections between performance parts and to connect these parts with the plants; in the latter case, in a descending process, the parts are not connected in the performance, but rather juxtaposed. My research initiated in previous publications suggests an analogical way of thinking that operates at a different level in wedding rituals: at the lexical level, between the constitutive elements in the performance. But that research (still in progress) does not challenge the observations made here on time.

The study of musical practices in the Anti-Atlas helps us understand a local way of thinking about rhythmic dynamics in relation to the musicians' farming experience. The study of rhythm in such a rural area also confirms the need for great caution in making comparisons, because the approach that makes it possible to arrive at this assessment is quite different from that which applies to art music in the same region. Also different are the concepts and their development, as well as the transmission of musical practices.

ACKNOWLEDGMENTS

I wish to thank Stephen Blum, Richard Wolf, and Monique Brandily for their insightful comments on earlier drafts of this chapter, and the many Moroccan friends who contributed to this research in Morocco, especially Omar Amarir and Lahsen Hira. I am grateful to Lahsen Hira for his help with transcriptions and translations of sung poetry and to Matthew Cunningham for his help in revising my English translation of this article from the French. Finally, I would like to thank the Center for Research in Ethnomusicology at the University of Paris Nanterre for academic, logistical, and financial support; Aude Julien-Da Cruz Lima and Joséphine Simonnot were especially helpful with placing the sound excerpts on this book's website, and Giordano Marmone with the renotation of my handwritten musical transcriptions.

APPENDIX

I analyzed dozens of *aḥwaš* recorded in the central Anti-Atlas between 1977 and 2004. The various figures that follow illustrate the beginning and different phases of advancement and fulfillment of a representative "women's *aḥwaš*" recorded during a wedding in 1979. The order of the protagonists' contributions is characteristic of this type of *aḥwaš*. From the beginning of the female choirs, each contribution adds to the preceding one.

TABLE 9.1

Temporal development of a "womens' *aḥwaš*": the order of contributions to the performance.
Audio example: Ahwash n tmgharin (integral version)
Available online at:
https://archives.crem-cnrs.fr/archives/items/CNRSMH_E_2017_088_001_00/

Time Code	Audio Marker/ Item	Description
00: 00	1	Beginning of the poet-singer's sung melody (*amarg*) (see Figure 9.1)
01: 08	2	Beginning of the alternating female choirs on syllables of the "empty verse" (*talalayt*) (see Figure 9.2). The poet takes place among the spectators
02: 09	3	The women choirs replace the "empty verse" with the beginning of a verse with lexical meaning (see Figure 9.3)
02: 53	4	Beginning of the second verse by the women, and melodic extension
04: 35	5	Beginning of women's clapping, frame-drums *tilluna* and the two-headed drum *ganga*. Beginning of the rotation of the two female choirs (see Figure 9.4)
05: 28	6	Beginning of the iron clappers *tiqrqqawin*
11: 20	7	Beginning of *tamssust*, marked by a brief interruption. Rhythmic changes with the beginning of *tamssust* (see Figures 9.5 and 9.6)
12: 58	8	Beginning of the women's vocal "trembling".
14: 48	9	Melodic change (see Figure 9.7)
18: 58	10	Responsorial *tizrrarin* in the audience
22:22		End of the *aḥwaš*.

Each sequence corresponding to an audio marker in the integral audio version is also available as a separated audio item, following the time code numeration, online at: https://archives.crem-cnrs.fr/archives/collections/CNRSMH_E_2017_088_001/

TABLE 9.2

The sung poetry reconstructed in its literary form from the performance of the *aḥwaš*.

Soloist

1) *a sidi bn yaεqub ṣṣbr nbdatin*
2) *luṭrat d lmizan llan ġ ufus*
3) *nḍalb irbbi y assn timdayyin*
4) *ad ur ḫllut ur sar ak bnnaġ*

1) Oh, Son of Jacob, with patience we begin
2) Cord and weighbridge are in good hands
3) We ask God to make solid this assemblage
4) So that it doesn't get destroyed and that I shall not have to build it once again

Women's choirs

5) *nḍalb rbbi d lmusṭafa d wayyur*
6) *a yatbir ad ak iεdl ssεd nnun*
7) *issanf as ibalisn a kk ur ḍrrun*
8) *g^w ma tnġ εumar isfaw i lžamiε*
9) *lḥamdu lillahi irḍa bahra ul*
10) *ufiġ d aytma is kullu nga yan*
11) *laḥḥ lḫ^w baṛ iġab istara ignwan*
12) *llaεawn a aytma . . . ukan*
13) *ig amzwag iġab istara ignwan*
14) *iwa yatbir ad ak ndεu, ya tt hnnat*
15) *a lay la li la lay la lay da lal a ššahwa šuwr*
16) *trġa tafukt yili uġaras a ššahwa šuwr*
17) *išuwr usiyyaġ itarryalin a ššahwa šuwr*
18) *išuwr usiyyaġ i tanbalin a ššahwa šuwr*
19) *išuwr usbbab itarryalin a ššahwa šuwr*

5) We ask of God, his Prophet and the moon
6) Oh ring dove, that your fortune will augur well
7) That devils move away from you without doing any harm
8) Our brother Omar sheds light on all of us
9) Praise God! Our hearts are light!
10) We found brothers, we make up one being
11) We have no news, he disappeared while passing the sky
12) [Incomprehensible]
13) He cut himself off, he disappeared while passing the sky
14) Oh ring dove, we express wishes of peace
15) Oh pleasure, do not hurry
16) Sun is heating, the path is rising, O pleasure, do not hurry
17) The jeweler fashions the silver pieces, O pleasure, do not hurry
18) The jeweler fashions the bracelets, O pleasure, do not hurry
19) The merchant trades the silver pieces, O pleasure, do not hurry

TABLE 9.3

The sung poetry transcribed as expressed in performance.

Soloist

/ o) . . . ay la li la way lȧ l(a) ay da la l(i) 1) a sidi

/ bn yaɛqub(a) ṣṣ(u)br(a) nbdatin(i) 1) a sidi

/ bn yaɛqub(a) ṣṣ(u)br(a) nbdatin(i) 2) (a) lu

/(u)ṭrat n lmizan llan (an) ġ ufus(i) 2) (a) lu

/(u)ṭrat n lmizan llan (an) ġ ufus(i) 3) nḍalb

/ irb(i)bi y assn timdayyin(i) 4) ad ur

/(ur) ḫllut ur sar ak bnnaġ 4) ad ur

Women's choirs

I / o) . . . *la li la way la lay da la l(i) o) wa lay / la li la way la lay*

II *da la l(i) o) wa lay / la li la way la lay*

I *da la l(i) o) wa lay / la li la way la lay*

II *da la l(i) o) wa lay / la li la way la lay*

I *da la l(i) o) wa lay / la li la way la lay*

II *da la l(i) o) wa lay / la li la way la lay*

I *da la l(i) o) wa lay / 5) . . . b rbbi d lmusṭafa d wayyur(i) 5) n(a)ḍal / b rbbi d lmusṭafa*

II *d wayyur(i) 5) n(a)ḍal / b rbbi d lmusṭafa*

I *d wayyur(i) 5) n(a)ḍal / b rbbi d lmusṭafa*

II *d wayyur(i) 5) n(a)ḍal / b rbbi d lmusṭafa*

I *d wayyur(i) 6) (w)a yat / bir ad ak iɛdl ssɛd nun(i) 6) a yat / bir ad ak iɛdl ssɛd*

II *nun(i) 6)(w)a yat / bir ad ak iɛdl ssɛd*

I *nun(i) 6) (w)a yat / bir ad ak iɛdl ssɛd*

II *nun(i) 6) (w)a yat / bir ad ak iɛdl ssɛd*

I *nun(i) 6) (w)a yat / bir ad ak iɛdl ssɛd*

II *nun(i) 6) (w)a yat / bir ak iɛdl ssɛd*

I *nun(i) 6) (w)a yat / bir ad ak iɛdl ssɛd*

II *nun(i) 6) (w)a yat / bir ad ak iɛdl ssɛd*

I *nun(i) (w)a yat / 7) . . . f ibalisn a kk ur ḍ(a)rrun(i) 7)(w)issan / f ibalisn a kk ur*

II *ḍ(a)rrun(i) 7) (w)issan / f ibalisn a kk ur*

I *ḍ(a)rrun(i) 7) (w)issan / f ibalisn a kk ur*

II *ḍ(a)rrun(i) 7) (w)issan / f ibalisn a kk ur*

I *ḍ(a)rrun(i) 7) (w)issan / f ibalisn a kk ur*

II *ḍ(a)rrun(i) 7) (w)issan / f ibalisn a kk ur*

I *ḍ(a)rrun(i) 7) (w)issan / f ibalisn a kk ur*

II *ḍ(a)rrun(i) 7) (w)issan / f ibalisn a kk ur*

. . . . , etc.

The Roman numerals refer to the two choirs. The slash defines the attack of the melodic phrase. The numbers refer to lines in Table 9.2. The added vowels are in parentheses. "o" indicates the "empty verse," which includes consonant variants.

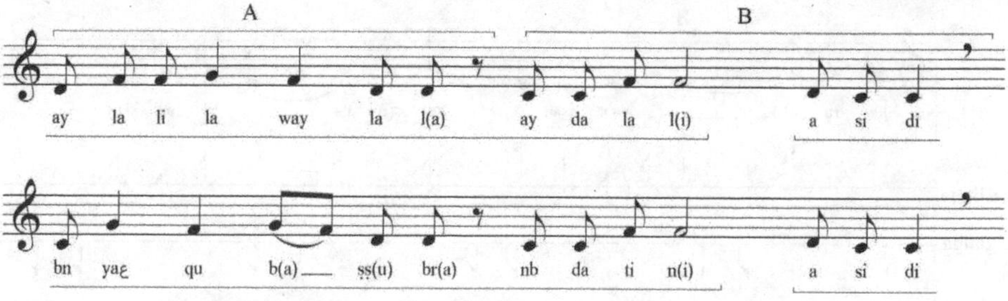
A
B
ay la li la way la l(a) ay da la l(i) a si di
bn yaɛ qu b(a) ṣṣ(u) br(a) nb da ti n(i) a si di

FIGURE 9.1 The beginning of *amarg* sung by a soloist. The soloist performs a melody consisting of two shifting fragments, the second being sung one tone below the first and the singer taking a breath (represented by a eighth-note rest) between fragment A (range D_4–G_4) and fragment B (range C_4–F_4). He begins his tune with the syllables of the "empty verse"—*a lay la li la lay la lay da lal(i)*—starting on the *second* syllable *"(l)ay."* He begins the verse itself before the end of the melodic phrase (*a sidi*) and finishes the verse before the end of the next melodic phrase, and so on (see Table 9.3).

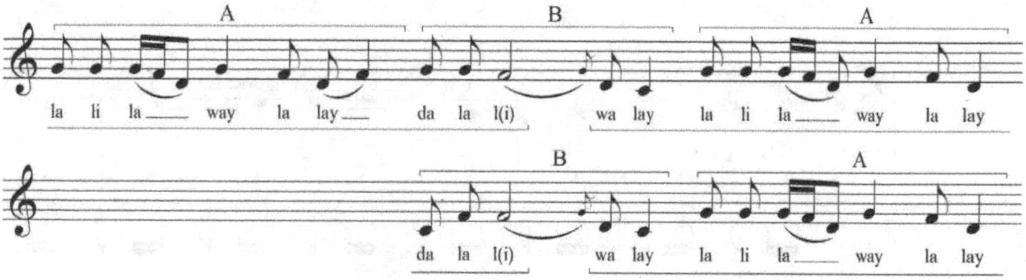
A
B
A
la li la way la lay da la l(i) wa lay la li la way la lay
B
A
da la l(i) wa lay la li la way la lay

FIGURE 9.2 *Amḫllf.* The beginning of the two female choirs. The first choir is in the upper staff, the second in the lower staff. The first choir takes up the soloist's melody (see Figure 9.1) with slight variations. Through the alternating modalities between the two groups of women, another shift is added to the one already established by the poet-singer between melody and verse (Figure 9.1). This is done from the beginning, when the women extend the melodic phrase by adding fragment A. The other female choir sings fragment B and then fragment A. In this way, both melodic fragments get inverted as soon as the second choir starts singing.

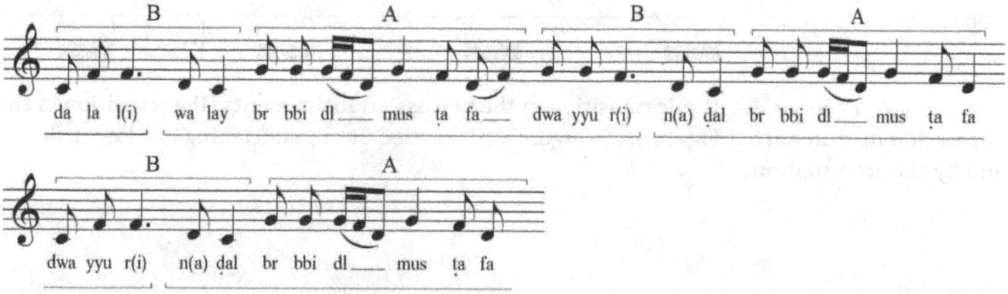
B
A
B
A
da la l(i) wa lay br bbi dl mus ṭa fa dwa yyu r(i) n(a) ḍal br bbi dl mus ṭa fa
B
A
dwa yyu r(i) n(a) ḍal br bbi dl mus ṭa fa

FIGURE 9.3 *Amḫllf.* Introduction of the first verse in the female choirs. For the introduction of the first verse with lexical meaning (see Table 9.2, line 5), the first choir starts by completing the "empty verse" (*da la li*) before taking it up again from its first two syllables (*a lay*) (see Table 9.3). It then replaces the "empty verse" with a verse with lexical meaning from its third syllable (*br*) and completes it before taking it up from its beginning (*n(a) ḍal*).

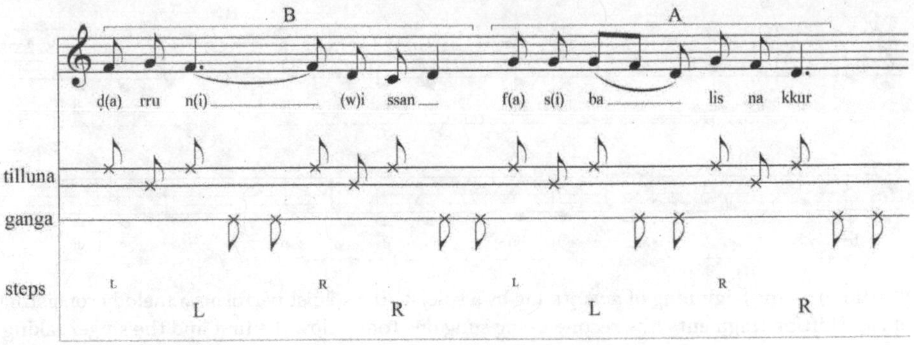

FIGURE 9.4 *Amhllf*. Beginning of the druming and the dancing. The two choirs sing the two fragments B and A antiphonally. The placing of the whole foot and the body is shown in capital letters; the ball of the foot in small letters (L = left, R = right). The two-headed drum (*ganga*) produces a low sound; the frame drums (*tilluna*) produce a high sound when played at the edge of the frame. A medium sound is produced when it is played at the center of the skin.

FIGURE 9.5 *Tamssust*. The same tune as before is sung alternately by the two choirs, but it is condensed and the drums transition from five strikes to four. The final degree is sung in a trembling voice because of the movement of the shoulders.

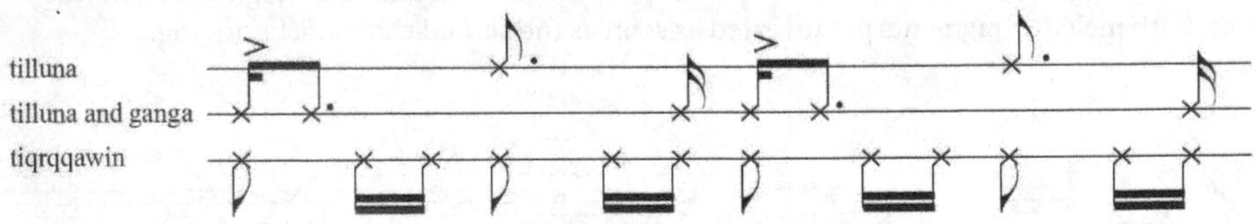

FIGURE 9.6 *Tamssust*. Rhythmic transition in the percussion instruments. The transition in the percussion instruments of Figure 9.5 to Figure 9.7 is carried out by shortening one low strike and by the accentuation.

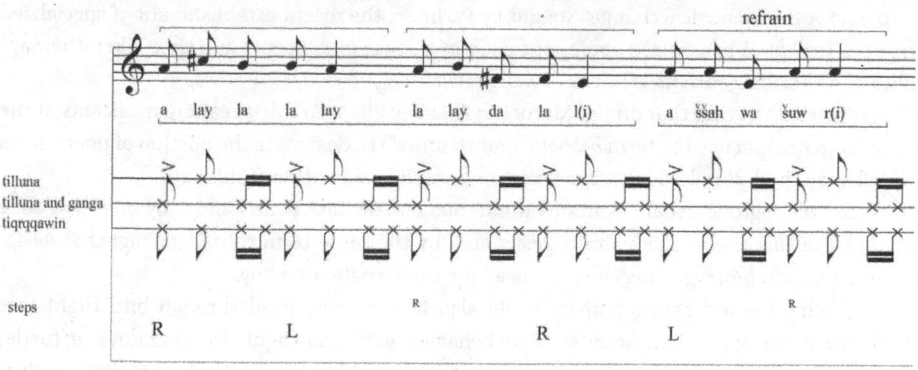

FIGURE 9.7 *Tamssust*. Introduction of a new melody. The women introduce a new melody (sung by the first choir), to which they add a refrain (sung by the second choir). The register is a semitone higher than the previous melody (taking into account the rise of a major third from the beginning of their contribution). This new melody can be divided into three segments of equal length.

NOTES

1. The Atlas is the imposing mountain chain that passes through Morocco from the northeast to the southwest. It is divided into what is called the Middle Atlas (to the north), the High Atlas and the Anti-Atlas (to the south). My research has been conducted in various mountain regions since 1975 (the western and eastern High Atlas and the central Anti-Atlas).

I focus on the music situation prior to the recent introduction of electricity into villages, and the major changes that followed (sound amplification with sound systems, night lighting, etc.), in the belief that in ethnomusicology, priority should be given to establishing the conceptual system of the music. As Bruno Nettl has pointed out (2005, 171), this system changes much faster than the music itself, yet music is given priority through the assembling of sound archives.

2. The Kaluli concept of "lift-up-over-sounding" is similar to heterophony (Feld 1988, 82), and Feld favors sound components (including timbre and texture), even if the costumes and paintings of dancers manifest themselves similarly, through multilayered materials and colors. Feld also connects this concept with Kaluli social relations and everyday verbal interactions, stating that "This patterning is also explicitly linked by Kaluli to the acoustic ecology of the rainforest environment indicating an aesthetic and ecological co-evolution" (76–77). See also Feld 1996.

3. Hasty encourages us not to view the "out-of-time abstraction of theory" as a basis of performance, because it prevents us from seeing the complexity and temporality of the concrete (2012, 6).

4. An illustration of "cross-domain mapping," a concept developed in musicology by Lawrence Zbikowski, who stresses the importance of "embodied knowledge" acquired in a culture for the selection of "mappings" (2002, 72). On the Anti-Atlas, the "source domain" is botany, which imposes certain patterns on the "target domain" of musical practice.

5. The music of the Anti-Atlas had not been studied when I started my research in this region in 1977.

6. As for the "historical change" sought by Perlman, the recent establishment of specialized troupes for *aḥwaš* has caused some confusion in the use of concepts at a time when their application to tribal contexts is not very well known.

7. It is worth noting that on the Moroccan Atlantic Plain, Arabic-speaking musicians of the popular genre *'aita* use the term *hebbat* ("grains, units") to designate the portion of poetic lines which they think should be the same from one version to another (Ciucci 2012).

8. The palm grove usually contains numerous female date palms and only one male date palm. Note that the female palm is designated by the same term *tafruḫt/tafruġt* that designates a girl, *afruḫ/afruġ* being the term used for a male palm or a boy.

9. Moving upward through space could also be conceptualized through bird flight (see Table 9.2 in the appendix). Because of its behavior, gait, and flight, the ring dove or turtledove is frequently summoned in the sung poetry of the Moroccan Atlas Mountains, and it is certainly also involved in its temporality, if only through its presence during sowing and its position high on the date palms.

10. According to Lortat-Jacob, the "rise" concept is as much based on the ability to slow down and prolong the ascent as it is to acceleration: Lortat-Jacob stresses that there is a "prevalence of form" to the point that it is not "men and women who perform the *ahwash* [*aḥwaš*], but the form itself. Furthermore, the main task of the drummers is not to accelerate the dance, but rather to slow down the metronomic speed and to control it, as if the form were provided with a natural propensity to propel in acceleration. Only powerful drummers with authority manage to contain the form within its own rules and ensure that it is not dispatched in ten minutes" (2013, 49; my translation).

11. This disarticulation can be compared to the loss of energy that Zbikowski (2002) has associated with descent. He analyzes a case of a descending scale by Palestrina, which comes in the context of his descriptive music (text painting), and suggests that "The scalar descent chosen by Palestrina . . . provides a striking analogue for the descent of our bodies through physical space . . . . Such a descent involves a lessening of potential energy and a continuous action in one direction, articulated by the regular transfer of weight from one leg to another" (73).

10

Mapping a Rhythmic Revolution Through Eighteenth- and Nineteenth-Century Sources on Rhythm and Drumming in North India

James Kippen

IN THE VERY early years of the twentieth century two outstanding works were written on North Indian rhythm (*tāl*) and drumming that in many ways represented the pinnacle of achievement in the detailed and precise notation of repertoire. One was the *Mrdaṅg aur tablā vādanpaddhati* of 1903, written in Hindi by Dattatreya Vasudev Patwardhan, alias "Gurudev," at the time vice-principal of Vishnu Digambar Paluskar's Gandharva Mahavidyalaya music school in Lahore and an active performer and teacher of both tabla and the barrel drum *pakhāvaj* (also known as *mrdaṅg*). The other was the *Risāla ṭabla nawāzī* of 1906, written in Urdu by Muhammad Ishaq of Delhi, about whom very little is known; he seems to have been an avid connoisseur with links to senior court musicians, and from the occasional insertion of his own pieces we surmise that he had some degree of practical knowledge and experience. These two works had much in common: both were pedagogical in intent, both aimed at unambiguous notational devices that promoted precision in rhythm and stroke repertoire, both presented theoretical constructs and a great many advanced pieces of music, and yet neither system was simple or practical enough to become a model for a notational consensus.

The *Mrdaṅg aur tablā vādanpaddhati* was the subject of my book *Gurudev's Drumming Legacy* (Kippen 2006). I argued that it built upon the work of late nineteenth-century educational pioneers such as Raja Sir Sourindro Mohun Tagore and Professor Maula Bakhsh (Kippen 2006, 53–69; and 2007), that analysis of its material revealed concepts about rhythm that became obsolete in the twentieth century, and yet it was forward looking in its desire to contribute to a modern, institutionalized music curriculum. The *Risāla ṭabla nawāzī* will be the subject of a future study, but what has emerged is its backward-looking perspective on the Indo-Persian scholarly tradition of which it was arguably the culmination, perhaps even its swan song. Both works have therefore raised many questions about the theory and practice of *tāl* before the twentieth century, they have led to an ever-deeper engagement with the extant Persian and Urdu works of the seventeenth to nineteenth centuries that have engaged with rhythm and drumming, and they have been useful in helping to understand and interpret past theory and practice.

In this chapter I wish to suggest that a new conception of *tāl* emerged in treatises of the eighteenth and nineteenth centuries in India. In particular, a cyclic drumming pattern called *ṭheka*, which I describe later in the chapter, comes to the fore in a new process of thinking about *tāl* as a metric framework. The rise in the prominence of *ṭheka* in discourse about the music reflects changes happening in performance practice, especially with regard to the tabla. Authors found it necessary to describe rhythm in qualitative terms, and increasingly applied Perso-Arabic terms to do so. It is through these works that we witness nothing less than a rhythmic revolution that overturned many centuries of theory and practice.

The North Indian concept of *tāl* relates to the music's rhythmic-metric system, and it consists of beats articulated by claps and waves, called *tālī* and *k̲h̲ālī* in the terminology that has dominated for most of the twentieth century onward. Claps and waves form divisions, *vibhāg*, each harboring a number of counts, *mātrā*. (*Mātrā*, etymologically linked to the term "meter," derives from Sanskrit prosody where it is a syllabic instant that equates to a short or light syllable or *laghu*; the long or heavy is two *laghus*, or one *guru*.) *Tālī*, *k̲h̲ālī*, and *mātrā* combine into patterns that recur regularly (*āvartan*, or cycle) in order to frame composition and improvisation. For example, the most common structure in contemporary music is *tīntāl*, which comprises sixteen counts divided equally into four beats: clap-2-3-4-clap-6-7-8-wave-10-11-12-clap-14-15-16. The first clap in this sequence is conceptualized as *sam*, a point of musical confluence or resolution. In performance, *tāl* as a quantitative structure is represented by *tāl* as a qualitative sequence of drum strokes of varying timbre, pitch, and often rhythm. These fixed sequences are known as *ṭheka*, a term implying support, and they are represented in oral and written notation by quasi-onomatopoeic syllables called *bols*. *Tīntāl* is:

dhā dhin dhin dhā |	dhā dhin dhin dhā |	dhā tin tin tā |	tā dhin dhin dhā ||
tālī/sam	*tālī*	*k̲h̲ālī*	*tālī*

While the abstract architecture of a *tāl* and its *ṭheka* instantiation are integrally connected, *ṭheka*s arguably assume greater importance because they define the cyclical space by imparting a recognizable musical character. For instance, there are many *tāl*s that are identical to *tīntāl* in terms of their beat-count structure but which are differentiated by their *ṭheka*s; although some of these are now rarely heard, historically they were associated with different genres, they established and maintained an appropriate pace, and they imparted a distinctive feel. Although there are infinite possibilities, in contemporary practice roughly a dozen *tāls* are in regular use in the mainstream Hindustani art tradition, and of these an even smaller handful dominates most performances (*tīntāl* 16, *ektāl* 12, *jhaptāl* 10, and *rūpak* 7).

It is important to establish these basic definitions and terminology as a point of departure because things were not always thus. Muhammad Isḥaq reminds us in a small section of his *Risāla ṭabla nawāzī* subtitled *Afsos*, or Regret (1906, 52):

> In ancient times 360 *tāls* were in general use. Afterwards in medieval times, and with a view to making it easy for people, the experts selected and put into practice 92 *tāls*. Then the contemporary masters considered the conditions of the age and, with the idea of making it easier still, selected from those 92 twelve *tāls* especially for *dhrupad* as well as a few other *tāls* and put them into common usage. However, all these *tāls* are muddled. I tried very hard to research and write down the remaining twelve of the 92 selected by the contemporary masters but I could not do so to any degree of satisfaction. Some say one thing, others another. Who can be sure what is right?

Like so many authors before him in the Indo-Persian tradition, Muhammad Isḥaq was invoking the seminal text *Tuḥfat al-hind* (1675) by Mirza Khan that was designed to introduce Mughal noblemen to the knowledge contained in Sanskrit treatises, and which was the first work to include a full chapter on *tāl*, mainly in the context of dance. In it, 92 *tāls* are named along with symbols borrowed from Sanskrit prosody that quantified their structure and duration in terms of *mātrās*, or fractions thereof: the principal durations were *pluta* (Š = 3 *mātrās*), *guru* (S = 2), *laghu* (I = 1), *druta* (O = ½), and *anudruta* (U = ¼), plus a diacritical mark for the *virām* (or *birām*), which extended a duration by half. These were *deśī tāls*, selected from many treatises ranging from the *Saṅgītaratnākara* (thirteenth century) to the *Saṅgītaśiromaṇi* (fifteenth century, see Nijenhuis 1992) to the *Saṅgītasurodaya* (sixteenth century) and many other points in between. They differed from the antiquated system of *mārga tāls* (the 360) in that they had currency in the medieval period and were relatively short (some as short as one *druta*, or in one case one *anudruta*).

The immense complexity of the rhythmic-metric system in antiquity and the medieval period is conveyed in analytical works by authors such as Narinder Mohkamsing writing on the *Nāṭyaśāstra* (Mohkamsing 2003) and Subhadra Chaudhary writing compendiously on a wide range of early treatises spanning many centuries (Chaudhary 1997). Many examples of *bol* sequences exist in these sources, and Allyn Miner (1998) detailed unique patterns called *upāśraya* in the fourteenth century *Saṃgītopaniṣat-sāroddhāraḥ* that were associated with its 73 *tāls*. Each *upāśraya* matched the length of its *tāl* but did not clearly mark out its divisions. Therefore, it remains unclear whether drummers maintained these as fixed patterns that represented *tāls* (qua *ṭheka*) or whether time was maintained externally through patterns that were clapped or marked by finger cymbals (*mañjīra*) while drummers selected freely from a series of stock patterns (the *upāśraya* being only one of these), inserted compositions, and responded in improvised rhythmic gestures to patterns created by those they accompanied. The latter strategy was, I believe, more likely: it is the one still maintained in the performance of North Indian *dhrupad*, accompanied by the *pakhāvaj*, and it predominates in South Indian performance, accompanied by *mridangam* and other drums—a possible link to a time before the two musical systems parted company. Yet it is also hard to imagine that short *tāls* were not somehow represented by relatively fixed, repetitive patterns, and one might point to a variety of folk drumming practices throughout South Asia where specific, unchanging patterns, "stroke-melodies" (see chapter 12 by Richard Wolf in this volume), are played.

The *Tuḥfat al-hind*'s chapter on *tāl* was not, however, concerned with the practices of the day. Moreover, nothing resembling a *ṭheka* is given. By contrast, the slightly earlier *Miftāḥ al-surod* (1664) by Qazi Hasan had already listed *tāls* associated with "pure" and "expressive" dance—64 and 181 respectively—and these carried quite different names from those in *Tuḥfat al-hind*: names that recur in later works, some of which even persist up to the present day (though the caveat is we cannot yet be sure that their associated structures remained unchanged). One example is *chautāla*, for which drum or dance syllables were given, though interpreting precisely what its very long sequence of syllables represents remains problematic. Later sources select and describe far fewer *tāls*, suggesting they were chosen for their practical currency: an eleven-*tāl* system is given in Ras Baras Khan Kalavant's *Shams al-aṣwāṯ* of 1698 (see also Fallahzadeh and Hassanabadi 2012, 125), and seventeen *tāls* are listed in Hakim Hasan Maududi Chishti's *Risāla-yi mūsīqī* of 1761.

THE SEARCH FOR *KHĀLĪ*

Chishti's work appears to be very important for two reasons: (1) it introduces an organizational principle wherein meters are grouped by the number of beats they contain, such as *sih-ẕarba* (three-beat) structures including *dhīma* (slow) *titāla* and *jald* (fast) *titāla*; and (2) *tāls* are clearly linked to the genres they accompany, such as those found in *dhrupad*, *qaul*, *khayāl*, *ṭappa*, and so on. Take, for instance, the description of *dhīma titāla*:

> Fourth of the *sih-ẕarba tāls* is *dhīma titāla*, which is peculiar to *dhrupad*, et cetera, but not to *khayāl* let alone *ṭappa*. Also its *burdish* is in the middle. Three *plutas* combine to form it, and in the last *kāl* the duration is one extra *pluta*. The whole of its *piṇḍ* is counted as nine *mātrās*, in this configuration: Š Š Š – .

Until and unless earlier evidence surfaces, I think that the story of *tāl* theory as it is understood today begins here in the *Risāla-yi mūsīqī*. Chishti's descriptions undeniably rationalized what had presumably been evolving in performance practice for some time, even perhaps since the seventeenth century, but they included a concept that had hitherto been absent in other treatises, a concept that is represented by the simple dash that concludes the configuration shown here. Although the word itself does not appear in Chishti's work, I believe that the dash signifies what later comes to be known as *k̲h̲ālī*.

A detailed analysis of Chishti's description of *dhīma titāla* reveals many interesting facts, but none of these helps us understand how it may have been played in the 1760s. Originally associated with *dhrupad* and presumably also the *pakhāvaj* drum chiefly connected to that genre, *dhīma titāla* became the pre-eminent *tāl* for tabla in the nineteenth century; it has long been closely associated with the *k̲h̲ayāl* vocal genre, instrumental music, and dance; and it was a direct precursor of *tīntāl*. Yet it is "almost unknown today" in *dhrupad* (Sanyal & Widdess 2004, 9) and is rarely performed on *pakhāvaj*. The structure comprises three struck beats, or *ẓarb*. Until the early twentieth century *ẓarb* was the standard term for a beat that delineated a subdivision of the *tāl* (*vibhāg* in current theory). Here, each *ẓarb* carries the duration of one *pluta* Š, or three *mātrās*, and yet there is an additional period or *kāl*, represented by the dash, that equates to one extra *pluta*. The paradox, then, is that the *piṇḍ* (now obsolete, but it meant the sum total of beats, counts and their relative proportions comprising a *tāl*) adds up to only nine and not twelve *mātrās*. This implies that only struck beats that could be represented by the traditional durational symbols of Sanskrit prosody were tangible enough to be counted, and that the additional space—real though it was as a facet of performance—was as yet unaccounted for in theory.

It is not difficult to see the links between Chishti's *dhīma titāla* and modern *tīntāl*. Nonetheless, some conceptual adjustments have to be made. First, each time unit here is a *pluta*, three *mātrās*, yet since no discrete symbol was capable of representing four *mātrās* the *pluta* was therefore the longest duration available. Second, although modern textbooks represent *tīntāl* as beginning from its *sam* (just as I represented it), traditional (i.e., non-college-educated) musicians have in my experience counted its beats differently: one, *two*, three, wave (with a heavy emphasis on two to mark the *sam*). Compare this representation:

clap | clap / *sam* | clap | wave ||

to Chishti's:

ẓarb | *ẓarb* / *burdesh* | *ẓarb* | space ||

Third, extrapolating from the examples of *dhīma titāla* found in the nineteenth century, which I will illustrate in the section on *ṭheka*, the dash or space must surely represent *k̲h̲ālī*, the "empty" or unsounded beat. This places it in diametric opposition to the *burdish*—an obscure word not so far found elsewhere but which likely derives from the Persian verb *burdan* (to carry, or to bear)—and thus aligns the *burdish* with the cycle's point of confluence or resolution, otherwise known as *sam*. Indeed, if one examines Chishti's often-indecipherable text closely, it appears that he frequently placed a small letter B beneath one of the symbols in a sequence to mark the location of the *burdish*. This letter then changes to S in certain of his examples, then again in one instance to the word *sam*. *Burdish* therefore meant *sam*.

If we accept these various interpretive transformations, then Chishti's *Risāla-yi mūsīqī* of 1761 is the earliest definitive evidence of a change in the way *tāl* was rationalized and represented. *Kh̲ālī*, the unsounded or "empty" beat, was central to that shift, notwithstanding Chishti's inability to account for it adequately.

ARABIC RHYTHMIC THEORY APPLIED TO *TĀL*

The University of Edinburgh's Oriental Manuscript 585 contains five Indo-Persian treatises on music of which the fourth is of special interest. Edin 585/4 is an anonymous, untitled, and incomplete treatise on *tāl* written in 1787–1788, and it sets out to explain rhythm with methods derived from Arabic prosody. (For an extensive discussion of Arabic rhythmic theory, see Sawa 2009; also, see chapter 3 by Stephen Blum in this volume for its application to Persian sung poetry.) *Tāl* is equated with the term *īqā'*, meaning both rhythm in general as well as a specific rhythmic mode. *Īqā'* is described as being dependent on the combination of a theoretical meter *baḥr* (pl. *buḥūr*, the system of named feet in Arabic poetry) and the practical struck beat *ẓarb*: when these combine in performance they produce a characteristic rhythmic pattern, or *wazn*. *Wazn*, meaning "weight," and implying the rhythmic feel that results from its pattern of stresses in poetry and in music, is derived from *baḥr* and is its practical instantiation (see Elwell-Sutton 1976, 42). An *īqā'* is formed with two cycles (*daur*, pl. *adwār*) of the *wazn*. Yet whether *wazn* extended from a pattern of stresses to fixed drum patterns is unclear, even though the concept is leaning in that direction. For example, *wazn* is also equated with the Indian term *lay* (rhythmic feel, or tempo; see Wolf in this volume for a discussion of many subtle differences in its usage), and as mentioned the role of *ṭheka* is to establish and maintain an appropriate pace and impart a distinctive feel. The text reads:

> And *wazn* is called *lay*. The definition of *wazn* is the arrangement of *ḥarkāt* [motions, i.e., strikes] and *sakanāt* [rests, pauses] in a certain way, so that if a change is made in a *ḥarkat* or *sukūn* [both sing.] in the arrangement, the *wazn* will move out of its proper state.

Edin 585/4 mentions many drums, and among them the finest is said to be the *pakhāvaj* (*mrdaṅg*) barrel drum. The tabla ranks next and is "extremely nice, fine and unique, and is believed to have been invented by Sultan Azam Shah [1653–1707], the son of [the Emperor] Aurangzeb Alamgir. Its treble and bass are both separate." *Tāls* are not mentioned as specific to particular drums, though they are associated with genre: the basic division being those used in *dhrupad* as practiced by the Kalāvants, a category of hereditary musicians tracing their lineage to Miyan Tansen who served at the court of the Emperor Akbar in the late sixteenth century, and those used in *qaul, k͟hayāl*, and *tirvaṭ*, the genres of the Qawwāls (although that chapter never materializes).

Edin 585/4's author's indebtedness to medieval Arabic theorists such as al-Farahidi and al-Farabi is likely reflective of a general level of interest in Arabic prosody and music theory among those who wrote, commissioned, and collected these manuscripts in the eighteenth century. Indeed, the highly influential music treatise *Kitāb al-adwār*, by Safi al-Din (d. 1294; see Wright 1995) was widely available in India in both Arabic and in Persian translation; we know that copies were in the collection of Delhi nobles in the seventeenth century (Brown 2003, 38, 210 fn42). The smallest rhythmic quantity—the indivisible *chronos protos*—is labeled interchangeably as *naqra* (Arabic) or *turit*, signifying a point of attack. *Turit* arguably derives from *truṭi* (Sanskrit), a unit of time found in the *Saṅgītapārijāta* of Ahobala (1665) measuring one quarter of a *druta*, thus a very short duration. The *naqra/turit*, when articulated as an attack or strike—*ẓarb*—is represented by the syllable *ta*; yet when denoting a space or rest (*sukūn* or *rahan*) between consecutive strikes, it is represented by *na*.

To double the durations of *ta* and *na*, either an N is added, as in *tan* and *nan* (wherein the final N is quiescent, meaning that it has practically no word-final inherent vowel) or NA, as in *tana* and *nana* (wherein the final is vocalate, i.e., the inherent vowel is articulated). The first is called a light *sabab*, the second a heavy *sabab*. A further expansion to three syllables is called *watad: tanan* and *nanan* for light, *tanana* and *nanana* for heavy. These two fundamental measures of relative duration (which may be traced to the ninth-century scholar al-Kindi; see Sawa 2009, 569) are fundamental building blocks that can be combined into longer compound strings: two *sababs* become *tananan* (i.e., heavy plus light), *sabab* plus *watad* become *tanananan*, and two *watads* become *tananananan*. These are termed short, long, and longer separators, or *fāṣila*, because they represent ever-longer durations or intervals. However, the author of Edin 585/4 invokes principles of euphony that he believes will facilitate memorizing, pronouncing, and distinguishing the patterns: he modifies the long repetitive strings of *na* by introducing the syllables *da* and *ka*, which also have the effect of emphasizing subtle rhythmic subdivisions. Thus, the seven-letter principle is notated as *tananadakadak*, eight as *tanadakananadak*, nine as *tananadakananadak*, and so on up to fourteen.

The author explains that in *dhrupad* there are four ways of dividing the *tāl: yaktāla, dotāla, titāla*, and *chautāla*. Following *Risāla-yi mūsīqī*, these are categories defined by the presence of one, two, three, and four strikes (here *ẓarb* or *tāl*) respectively. Each harbors subcategories: for example, *chautāla* has three, named *chautāla, āṛā chautāla* and *sawārī tāl* (said to have been named *chitlakan* in older treatises).

Chautāla has four *ẓarbs* that are represented in Edin 585/4 by black dots (•); the first is deliberately separated by a space (here, *kāl*) from the following three. That space is thus conceived as an event (or the conscious absence of one) and its duration is equal to a single *ẓarb*, just as it was in Chishti's *Risāla-yi mūsīqī*. The resulting sequence is notated:

•   • • •

When another cycle (*daur* or *āvart*) follows, as it must in order to form an *īqāʿ* or *tāl*, it is necessary to separate the final *zarb* in the pattern from the first in the ensuing cycle by inserting another space, *akāl* (cf. al-Farabi's *fāṣila*; see Blum in this volume). The notation is thus modified to distinguish the *ẓarbs* from the spaces (*kāl* and *akāl*) with red dots (here depicted as ○), and the result represents the framework of the *tāl* at its most basic level.

● ○ ● ● ● ○ ● ○ ● ● ● ○

Beginners are urged by Edin 585/4's author to recite the numbers one to six while clapping the pattern repeatedly: a strike on their right knee for the *ẓarbs* on counts one, three, four, and five, and a strike on their left knee for the *kāl* on two, and the *akāl* on six. Such an instruction suggests the text may possibly have had a practical, pedagogical purpose.

Hereafter, the discussion and notations serve to define more precisely three tempi that stand in fixed relation to each other: *madham lay* (i.e., *madhyam*, medium), *jald lay* (fast), and *dhīma lay* (slow). Different tempi are achieved by the insertion of red dots representing the number of *sukūn* or *rahan* between the six events: one for *jald*, two for *madhyam*, three for *dhīma*. For *madhyam lay chautāla* the *tāl*'s basic framework is therefore extended to eighteen *naqra*, meaning that a *ẓarb* will fall on 1, 7, 10, and 13, the *kāl* on 4 and the *akāl* on 16. A diagram showing one cycle is given, and the positions of *kāl* and *akāl* are marked (here notated as *k* and *a* respectively).

k (4), a (16)

● ○ ○ ○ ○ ○ ● ○ ○ ● ○ ○ ● ○ ○ ○ ○ ○

1 4 7 10 13 16

The rhythmic pattern (*wazn*) is described as containing a "longer separator" (i.e., two joined *watads*) + *watad* + *watad* + another longer separator, thus *tanadakadak tanan tanan tanadakadak*. *Madhyam lay* is conceptualized as normative, so to create *jald* and *dhīma lays* one either subtracts or adds dots. *Jald lay chautāla* is thus represented as:

k (3), a (11)

● ○ ○ ○ ● ○ ● ○ ● ○ ○ ○

1 3 5 7 9 11

The *wazn* is described as *tananan tan tan tananan*. And *dhīma lay chautāla* appears as:

k (5), a (21)

● ○ ○ ○ ○ ○ ○ ○ ● ○ ○ ○ ● ○ ○ ○ ● ○ ○ ○ ○ ○ ○ ○

1 5 9 13 17 21

Its *wazn* is *tanadakananadak tanadak tanadak tanadakananadak*. Therefore we end up with three *naqra/turit*-based ratios for these three tempi of 12:18:24 (i.e., 2:3:4).

Under the next heading of *titāla*, whose cycles comprise three strikes, are *tīvra, jald titāla, dhīma titāla, jhaptāla*, and *surfāk͟hta* (said to have been called *turaṅgalīlā* in older treatises). Unfortunately the text ends abruptly, omitting any discussion of *jhaptāla* and *surfāk͟hta. Tīvra, jald titāla*, and *dhīma titāla* have identical basic structures.

● ● ● ○

They are described respectively as the fast, medium, and slow manifestations of the *titāla* category. *Jald titāla* and *dhīma titāla* each expand and contract to different *lays* (*naqra/turit*-based ratios for *jald* are 12:16:20, while for *dhīma* they are 24:28:32). However, *tīvra* is said to have only one form (eight *naqras* in total), and it must be neither faster nor slower lest it become confused with *rūpak* or *jald titāla*. The logic of the argument for such confusion remains far from clear, but the author suggests that *rūpak* (in the *dotāla* category) may also be distinguished by the placement of its *sam* ("the third *ẓarb* would represent the *sam* of *rūpak*, not the *sam* of *tīvra*"). The reader is promised a fuller explanation of *sam* in chapter 2 of Edin 585/4, but this never materializes since the treatise is unfinished. Moreover, we never discover which other *tāls* were to be included in the *dotāla* and *yaktāla* categories.

Edin 585/4 offered a new way of conceptualizing and describing *tāl*. It likely offered particular advantages to a Mughal nobility educated in the Arabo-Persian tradition both in terms of its cultural resonance in poetic meter and its greater attention to rhythmic detail because it was capable of going beyond the quantitative confines of the *laghu-guru* system and was far more flexible in its ability to define duration, relative tempo, and rhythmic feel. Sequences such as *tananan* or *tanadakananadak* are descriptive of rhythm, duration, and flow, which are key to understanding *wazn*: the qualitative instantiation of a *tāl* that consists of a characteristic pattern of stresses distinguishing it from others. *Wazn* brings to life the *ẓarbs* of a *tāl* and the spaces between.

The concepts of *kāl* and *akāl* that mark absent events are also very important in this new conception, and unlike the dash in Chishti's *Risāla-yi mūsīqī* these could now be counted. From our current perspective it is easy to see how the *ẓarbs* equate to the claps and the *kāl/akāl* to the waves we now use to demonstrate a *tāl*'s basic structure. Although we cannot be sure where the author of Edin 585/4 would have located *sam* (as it does not seem to have been a priority), if we take the outline of *chautāla* and begin the sequence from the fifth of the six events we transform the clap-wave-clap-clap-clap-wave pattern into one we now recognize instantly as modern *chautāl* beginning from *sam*: clap-wave-clap-wave-clap-clap.

● ○ ● ● ● ○ = ● ○ ● ○ ● ●

Similarly, if we examine the *titāla* category, or at least as it applies to *dhīma* and *jald titāla* (since modern *tīvra* is quite different), we see similarities with Chishti's notation of *dhīma titāla*: S̆ S̆ S̆ – . Again, a reordering of the sequence clap-clap-clap-wave beginning this time from the second event renders the modern form clap-clap-wave-clap beginning from the *sam*:

● ● ● ○ = ● ● ○ ●

In the years following Edin 585/4, the *Uṣūl al-naghmāt-i āṣafī* of 1793 by Ghulam Raza describes eleven of the new *tāls* using a mixture of Sanskritic and Arabic methods, including the *kāl/akāl* terminology and descriptions of *wazn*. There is also the *Aṣl al-uṣūl* of Qazi Muhammad Nasir Muhammad alias "Ranj" (early nineteenth century), wherein *tāls* in common practice are listed and described using a graphical method akin to that used in Edin 585/4. Here, the lists are more complete and informative, indicating connections to genres and including differences in *tāl* terminology and practice between the Kalāvants and the Qawwāls. Notably, the *Aṣl al-uṣūl* introduces the *laghu-guru* terminology yet quickly dispenses with it before exploring *tāls* using only the new descriptive method derived from Arabic music theory.

THE RISE OF TABLA: NEW TERMINOLOGY, NEW CONCEPTS

In the early years of the nineteenth century, there appeared an anonymous, undated Indo-Persian commentary on a treatise, now lost, on the fundamentals of tabla. The *Sharḥ-i risāla-yi qawā'id-i ṭabla* is a substantial text of 156 pages, but the opacity of the language, a tendency to elliptical expression, the absence of promised examples and explanatory diagrams, references to matters having already been covered or explained in the original treatise, and incomplete or missing chapters continue to make its analysis an arduous task. What it does do is elevate the tabla, which it claims "was invented after the time of Aurang[zeb]," by not only naming and describing its various strokes (*ḥurūf* or "letters," sing. *ḥarf*) but also by personifying them using rich imagery that invokes gender (right-hand strokes are masculine, left-hand ones feminine), time of day, cardinal direction, physical beauty, height, skin color, markings on the body, attire, adornments, flowers, sound of the voice, taste and refinement, and temperament. Since its first appearance in the early eighteenth century in the northwest of India, the tabla had spread rapidly throughout the subcontinent owing to its supportive role in the popular song and dance performances (the so-called nautch) of female entertainers, as attested in myriad miniature paintings of the period. Yet it is also pictured in other contexts, suggesting that its ability to imitate and assume the musical roles of older, long-established drums such as *pakhāvaj* and *ḍholak* brought it quickly into the musical domains of the Kalāvants and Qawwāls respectively (see Kippen, forthcoming). The tabla, that "extremely nice, fine and unique" drum, as described in Edin 585/4, was clearly being taken very seriously by contemporary scholars and connoisseurs, and was competing with other instruments for drumming paramountcy: there is no similar treatise for any other drum.

In a manner consistent with Edin 585/4 and other contemporary treatises, the concept of *tāl* as musical meter is linked to *baḥr* as poetic meter whose divisions into feet (*arkān*, sing. *rukn*) parallel the occurrence of stressed beats, *ẓarb*. The resulting characteristic pattern of stresses is *wazn*, which is "fixed for every *tāl*": "each *baḥr* has a main *lay*, that is a distinct *wazn*, of its own." Yet the author goes further:

> So, in my humble opinion, *tāl* functions in the same way as *baḥr*. Just as *baḥrs* with certain *rukns* in a certain sequence are given a certain name, so is *tāl*, like *dhīma titāla* or *jald titāla* that are thus named because of the combination of *ẓarbs*. So names of *tāls* are in fact the same as *baḥr*, with *ẓarb* used instead of *rukn*; and its words [*lafẓ*] are scanned in the same way as the words of a *baḥr*. This is known as *ṭheka*, and poems like *rubā'ī*, *k̲h̲ayāl* . . . are aligned with it, in a way that one *lafẓ* corresponds to one *ḥarf* [syllable, drum stroke].

Thus, so far as we currently know, the term *ṭheka* now comes into play for the first time in Indian music history, and it signifies a pattern of words (*lafẓ*) that correspond to the individual drum strokes (*ḥarf*) described earlier in this commentary. Many *ṭheka* names are listed in the *Sharḥ-i risāla-yi qawā'id-i ṭabla*, but frustratingly there is no concrete example of one, just an unfinished chapter and many gaps where the author was to have set them out. Yet we do find statements such as "Out of the eighteen *baḥr*, *dhīma titāla* has been chosen as pre-eminent [*afẓal*] because it has an equal [*masāwī*] distribution of *lafẓ* and its *rukns* have an equal number of *lafẓ*." This implies that the *tāl* is articulated with a number of evenly spaced "words" divided into equal subdivisions, much as *tīntāl* does today.

The eighteen *tāls* to be described according to *rukn* and *lafẓ* actually number fourteen (plus some "half *tāls*" about which there is much confusion), divided into three groups: *k̲h̲afīf* (short, light) with 2 *rukn; masāwī* (equal) with 3; and *ṣaqīl* (long, heavy) with 4, as this table illustrates.

There are two types of *yaktāla* (*ektāl* in Urdu/Hindi). As a two-*rukn tāl* in the *k̲h̲afīf* category it is described thus: "*Sam* is on the first *tāl* [here, beat] and they each have two

TABLE 10.1

The three categories of *tāl* in the *Sharḥ-i risāla-yi qawā'id-i ṭabla*

***K̲h̲afīf* : 2 rukns**	***Masāwī* : 3 rukns**	***Ṣaqīl* : 4 rukns**
Yaktāla	*Yaktāla*	*Āṛā chautāla*
Qawwālī	*Dhīma titāla*	*Do-ek*
Kahna	*Jald titāla*	*Sawārī*
Kahṛa	*Holī*	*Farodast*
	Jat	
	Chat tāla	

rukns of two. . . . On its first *rukn* there are two *lafẓ* and on the adjacent second *rukn* there are three *lafẓ*." The implication is that the rhythm must comprise unequal durations (e.g., ♩♩/ ♩♫, or some other arrangement in the second *rukn*, possibly syncopated ♩♩ / ♪♩♪, or possibly even a triplet).

The second *yaktāla* is a three-*rukn tāl* in the *masāwī* category with each *rukn* comprising four *lafẓ*. It is said to give rise to all other *tāls* in this category. Subsequently, then, it is said that *dhīma titāla* "originates from this first *baḥr* and is constructed by adding one *rukn* to the existing three to create a fourth *rukn* which is omitted (*maḥẕuf-o-ẓarb*), that is *k͟hālī*."

1 2 3 4	|1 2 3 4	|1 2 3 4	|1 2 3 4 ||
ẓarb	*ẓarb*	*ẓarb*	*k͟hālī*

Compare this to Chishti's structure of Š Š Š – for *dhīma titāla* in his *Risāla-ye mūsīqī* where the final dash was left uncounted, or to the *ẓarb* structure in Edin 585/4 of • • • o. Now, in the *Sharḥ-i risāla-yi qawā'id-i ṭabla* we have finally arrived at the important term *khālī*, literally the "empty" beat.

Before moving on to other discoveries in this commentary, it is instructive to look at the description of *jald titāla*, the third *tāl* in the *masāwī* category. It is also said to be "omitted like the previous *baḥr*, except that in the first and third of its four *rukns* there are four *lafẓ* and in the second and fourth there are three *lafẓ*." As with the first of the two *yaktālas* described earlier, this configuration suggests not that *jald titāla* had 14 counts but rather that *lafẓ* here means the "words" of the *ṭheka* and that they might be expressed in irregular rhythm. There are in the later literature examples of *jald titāla ṭhekas* that incorporate syncopation (*nā dhin – nā*, or *nā - - dhin - - nā -*, viz. ♩𝅗𝅥♩ or ♩. ♩. ♩).
For example:

1 2 3 4	|1 2 – 3	|1 2 3 4	|1 2 – 3 ||
ẓarb	*ẓarb*	*ẓarb*	*k͟hālī*

Sam is a term that appears often in this text, from its metaphorical association with the compound stroke *dhā*—"masculine . . . olive-skinned . . . with eyes so beauteous and height so elegant. Except, this compound has three eyes. The third eye on his forehead makes him see the *sam* more than any other single or compound syllable"—to its location within some of the described *tāls*. However, it is mentioned inconsistently, and is absent in these *titāla* instances; therefore we can only assume that *sam* coincides with the second *ẓarb* of *dhīma* and *jald titāla*, as is the case with later nineteenth-century models.

The tabla *tāls* listed earlier in the three categories reinforce the idea that the tabla was adopting and adapting to the practices of both Kalāvants (e.g., *dhīma titāla*) and Qawwāls (e.g., *qawwālī*) and infiltrating the genres that previously were the domain of other drums. There is overlap to a small extent with named *pakhāvaj tāls*: *dhamāl, chautāla, sūrfāk͟hta, bram, lakshmī, titāla, tabūra, sūr, maha bram, maha lakshmī, maha sūr*, and *jat*. *Holī* is mentioned as a *ḍholak tāl* that crossed over to the *pakhāvaj* for use in *dhrupad* and *sawārī* (a type of suite). They also overlap in a couple of instances with *tāls* for *ḍholak: qaid, dopahr, k͟hams, kanḍah, daqaul, kul, lafs, farodast*, and *sawārī*.

Whether or not *ṭhekas* had at this point in history become the primary identifiers of *tāls*, as is the case today, is called into question by the suggestion that there were many varieties. *Dhīma titāla* is said to have eight *ṭhekas*, and no fewer than sixteen if one counted the versions from Khairabad, which was an important center of Qawwāl activity. Moreover, *jald titāla* has three *ṭhekas* but 72 *chapkās*. *Chapkā* is now obscure, but an example was described and notated by Ram Sevak Mishra in *Tāl prakāś aur tablā vijñān* (1896) as "a kind of *ṭheka*" with a simple bipartite structure that provided the basis for permutation (*bāṇṭ*) and substitution (*peṅch*) of both strokes (*bol*) and rhythmic density (*lay*). It is best understood as a *ṭheka* variant that was arguably the predecessor of the short, variable patterns now called *laggī*. It is not unreasonable to assume that there were multiple *ṭhekas* and variants in circulation in the late eighteenth and early nineteenth centuries, likely resulting from regional, stylistic, and even individual differences.

In addition to *ṭheka, sam* and *k͟hālī*, there are two other important terms that are introduced for the first time in the *Sharḥ-i risāla-yi qawā'id-i ṭabla*. Their meaning, however, is not completely clear and will require a good deal more analysis. In a long and convoluted explanation of *sawārī tāl*, the author invokes the terms *fiqra*, or phrase, and *band*, or bound. *Sawārī*, which in the nineteenth century existed in many different forms, is said to be a compound *tāl*, a contributing element of which is *dhīma titāla*.

> The first *fiqra* of *dhīma titāla* is articulated on the third *ẓarb* of *sawārī*, and the second *fiqra*, known as *band fiqra*, on the fourth *ẓarb* of *sawārī*. The beginning of the *band fiqra* in *dhīma titāla* is *k͟hālī*, and the fourth *rukn* of *sawārī* has *ẓarb*. . . . The first *fiqra* is where the *sam* is in *dhīma titāla*.

I think what this complicated description implies is that of the four *rukns* of *sawārī* the third and fourth, both marked with *ẓarbs*, house the structure of *dhīma titāla* but expressed in double tempo. We know it is double tempo because the author makes clear beforehand that "the third *rukn* is said to have seven *lafẕ* but indeed has eight *lafẕ*, the first of which is a *madd* [elongated], the repetition of which within the same time period results in eight *lafẕ*. . . . The fourth rukn has eight *lafẕ*." And so the third *rukn* contains the first *fiqra* or "phrase" of *dhīma titāla* and the fourth the second *fiqra*. In *dhīma titāla* the first of these is where the *sam* occurs, while the second is *band*, that is, where the *k͟hālī* occurs. Yet this may not imply the Persian "bound" here but rather "closed" or "damped," which is its primary meaning in Urdu and Hindi. *Band* is a term that has come to be intimately bound up with *k͟hālī* as it is articulated in tabla drumming, and it implies damping the resonance of the bass drum of the pair in a compound stroke or sequence of strokes. Typical of so much tabla repertoire are compositions bound to the *titāla* structure that comprise two phrases wherein the second mirrors the first but undergoes a partial transformation of its strokes so that the bass sonority (signified by the voiced phoneme *dh*) is damped (thus transforming it to the unvoiced *t*). This bipartite structure is apparent in *tīntāl ṭheka*,

dhā	dhin	dhin	dhā	I	dhā	dhin	dhin	dhā	I
sam					*tālī*				
- - - -	- - - -	- - - -	- - - -	- - - -	- - - -	- - - -	- - - -	- - - -	
dhā	tin	tin	tā	I	tā	dhin	dhin	dhā	II
k̲h̲ālī					*tālī*				

and may also be compared to *dhīma titāla* as notated in the next section.

Bipartite structures are found in many types of tabla composition (*qā'ida, gat, relā,* etc.). Such structures are very much the domain of *tabla*, not *pakhāvaj*, for *pakhāvaj* syllables and phrases undergo no comparable transformation.

For the first time, then, we witness in this important commentary a strong connection being made between *tabla*'s musical building blocks (*ḥarf, lafẕ*), their combination into articulations of the *wazn* by means of the *ṭheka*, and the relationship of the *ṭheka* to *tāl* structure based not only on the duration of its constituent divisions but also on the timbral qualities reflected in phrases within those divisions. *K̲h̲ālī*, linked to the notion of a *band* stroke or phrase, is now identified and named as an important structural consideration.

THE PRIMACY OF ṬHEKA

Following a gap of a few decades during which we have found no surviving sources on drumming, the Indo-Persian scholarly engagement with *tāl* continued in the 1850s and 1860s with four fascinating works. The first of these, *Ṣaut al-mubārak*, written in Persian in 1852–1853 by Wajid Ali Shah, King of Awadh, is a treatise mainly about rhythm and dance: we know the King danced, played *sitār*, was trained in tabla (Williams 2014, 100), and was also a scholar who had clearly read sources such as the *Tuḥfat al-hind* and the *Uṣūl al-nag̲h̲māt-e āṣafī*, on which he drew somewhat eclectically. Importantly, though, it is from his pen that we receive the first notated examples of *ṭheka*s for some of the *tāl*s in common usage.

As to the *tāl*s themselves, in many cases there are differences between the *ṭheka*s given and those that became standard during the twentieth century (*rūpak*, for instance) while others are recognizable. *Yaktāla* (*ektāl*) has twelve syllables (*lafẕ*). If we take Wajid Ali literally, we may represent it thus:

dhīn	dhīn	dhā	ge	I	tū	nā	kat	tīn	I	dhā	ge	tū	nā	II
sam					*ẓarb*					*k̲h̲ālī*				

Yet while the *ṭheka* is generally comparable, the beat structure differs markedly from the one widely understood now (which is clap-wave-clap-wave-clap-clap, like the structure of *chautāla*, with each gesture comprising two counts). *Yaktāla* puzzles the author because the name (lit: one beat) is incongruous with its three-beat structure. Indeed, Wajid Ali admits to a level of confusion that affects his ability to enjoy this *tāl*.

Other *tāls* of note are *chautāla* (presumably, but not explicitly here, a *pakhāvaj tāl*, though equally possible technically on tabla):

> tā dhina nak dhid | dhina nak dhina nak | dhid dhī | ghina nak |
>
> *sam*　　　　　　　　*ẓarb*　　　　　　　　　*ẓarb*　　*ẓarb*

The following is *jald titāla* (a version known as *sattārk̲h̲ānī ṭheka*, after Sattar Khan, a Qawwāl from Khairabad, featuring repetitions of the syncopated rhythm ♩. ♩. ♩ about which I speculated earlier):

> tā - - dhin - - tā - | tā - - dhin - - tā - | tā - - dhin - - tā - | tā - - tin - - tā - ||
>
> *ẓarb*　　　　　　　*sam*　　　　　　　　*ẓarb*　　　　　　　*k̲h̲ālī*

And this is *dhīma titāla*:

> dhīn kit dhīn nā | nā dhīn dhīn nā | tīn kit tīn nā | nā dhīn dhīn nā ||
>
> *sam*　　　　　　*ẓarb*　　　　　　*k̲h̲ālī*　　　　　*ẓarb*

Of special note is that *jald titāla* is notated in accordance with earlier *titāla* depictions (● ● ● ○), that is from the first *ẓarb* and not the *sam*, whereas *dhīma titāla* is notated from its *sam* and is thus a departure from earlier representations. (This may reflect a tension between the representation of a *tāl* as a series of beats and a *ṭheka* as a qualitative pattern of drum strokes that is not fully resolved until well into the twentieth century.) Although Wajid Ali says the two *titālas* are related by *piṇḍ*, the duration of the beat (i.e., *ẓarb*) in *jald titāla* is two *laghus* while in *dhīma titāla* it is doubled to two *gurus*. He thus resurrects the Sanskritic symbols for duration that were out of favor just a few decades before, arguably owing to the continued influence of the *Tuḥfat al-hind*.

The most widely known nineteenth-century work is *Ma'dan al-mūsīqī* (1869; see Qureshi 2010), an Urdu manuscript written by Muhammad Karam Imam during the 1850s and 1860s, but better known to us through its printed version (1925), and through a partial English translation by Govind Vidyarthi (1959). Although some additional *ṭhekas* are notated, including one or two of his own design, Imam relies heavily on Wajid Ali's *Ṣaut al-mubārak*, including some direct translation (for example, the puzzlement over *yaktāla*'s name and number of beats). The *G̲h̲uncha-yi rāg*, published in Urdu in 1863 by Muhammad Mardan Ali Khan, contains a chapter on rhythm that provides detailed charts for 23 *tāls*, many of which also owe a debt to *Ṣaut al-mubārak*, though it is notable that *ṭhekas* for several *tāls* are missing because they were either not known or had not been collected. A second, heavily revised, and arguably historicized edition of the *G̲h̲uncha-yi rāg* appeared in 1879, by which time Mardan Ali had clearly consulted older sources, since among other things he describes the *das prāṇ* (ten life breaths) of *tāl* whose origins lie in ancient concepts but which had cohered into a system of elemental descriptors by the sixteenth century as described in Sanskrit treatises such as the *Saṅgītasurodaya*. But Mardan Ali's interest was not original, since ten years prior the *das prāṇ* had been listed in the last work to be discussed.

The *Sarmāya-yi 'ishrat*, published in Urdu in 1869 by Sadiq Ali Khan, is an extraordinarily rich work that includes a substantial chapter on *tāl*. Yet it too historicizes the topic by beginning with a translation of sections drawn from chapter 10 of *Tuḥfat al-hind* augmented with ideas drawn from other early treatises. Moreover, one now sees where Muhammad Isḥaq drew information for his "Regret" in his *Risāla ṭabla nawāzī* of 1906: he copies from Sadiq Ali, who mentions the 360 *tāls* of antiquity and the 92 medieval *tāls* chosen by experts for their convenience. Thereafter, all of *Tuḥfat al-hind*'s 92 *tāls* are tabulated: numbered, named, spelled out for pronunciation, their *laghu-guru* structure explained in a full sentence, and finally their constituent symbols. For example, number 17, *udaichan*, has two *laghus* and one *guru*: I I S. I think this interest in archaic theory and structures represents more than pedantic erudition; it provides an important link to a deep and illustrious musical past that was considered to have echoes in contemporary theory and practice. Take, for instance, Sadiq Ali's notation of *dhīma titāla* in the section describing contemporary *tāls*:

Udaichan	I	I	S	
Dhīma titāla	1	2	3	4
	ẓarb	*ẓarb/sam*	*ẓarb*	*waqfa/k͟hālī*

he contrives to link it to *udaichan* (for despite the structural coincidence there is no evidence of one leading to the other), and *dhīma titāla*'s structure is presented as a *piṇḍ* of four *mātrās* with three beats, *sam* being on the second, followed by a pause (*waqfa*), or *khālī*.

Once again, we find that this arrangement reproduces the • • • o structure of earlier works. Yet the true focus in Sadiq Ali's *Sarmāya-yi 'ishrat* ultimately lies with the *ṭhekas*. Three versions are offered for *dhīma titāla*, and all are notated not from the first *ẓarb*, as above, but instead from *sam*, thus:

First *ṭheka*:

dhā	kiṛatak	dhin	dhin
dhā	dhā	tin	tin
tā	kiṛatak	dhin	dhin
dhā	dhā	dhin	dhin

Second *ṭheka*:

dhin	kiṭ	dhīn	nā
nā	dhin	dhīn	tā
tīn	kiṭ	tīn	nā
nā	dhīn	dhīn	tā

Third *ṭheka*:

dhā	dhīn	dhīn	dhā
dhā	dhīn	dhīn	dhā
dhā	tīn	tīn	tā
tā	dhīn	dhīn	dhā

The first of these will nowadays be recognized as *tilvāṛā ṭheka* (for which many contrasting variants existed in the nineteenth and early twentieth centuries), the second maps to *dhīma titāla ṭheka* as presented by Wajid Ali Shah in *Ṣaut al-mubārak*, and the last corresponds to the modern *ṭheka* we know as *tīntāl*.

Thirty-two *tāls* are described in *Sarmāya-yi 'ishrat*, several with more than one *ṭheka*. The reason for such abundance is that Sadiq Ali used two informants from the Ḍhāḍhī community of Delhi tabla players: Nazar Ali son of Shitab Khan, and Kala Kundu son of Ali Bakhsh. Sometimes the two supply slightly different *ṭhekas*, for example for *farodast* (whose *ṭheka* was absent in earlier treatises, and whose duration and structure here are somewhat unclear):

Kala Kundu's *ṭheka*:

dhin	kiṛatak	dhīn	kiṛatak	dhīn	kiṛatak
taghin	-ta	ghin			
dīn	kiṛatak	dīnnā	katā		

Nazar Ali's *ṭheka*:

dhīn	kiṛatak	dhīn	kiṛatak	dhīn	dhīn
taghin	-ta	ghin			
dīn	dīn	nā	kata		

At other times Nazar Ali's and Kala Kundu's *ṭhekas* are starkly different.

In addition to *ṭhekas*, Sadiq Ali also provides us with samples of repertoire such as *qā'ida* for tabla, and *paran*, *sāth*, and *ṭukṛa* for *pakhāvaj* (since both informants played both drums). Of particular interest is the ninth composition for *pakhāvaj*, where it is written, "This *sāth* is called a *ṭukṛa*":

dhā dhā dīn tā | kiṛ dhā dīn tā | kiṭ takā | gadde ghin || dhā

That pattern is now universally performed as the *ṭheka* for *chautāla*, although elsewhere in *Sarmāya-yi 'ishrat* the actual *ṭheka* is notated as almost identical to the pattern given in Wajid Ali's *Ṣaut al-mubārak*. The version from *Sarmāya-yi 'ishrat* is notated thus:

tā dhana nak dhad | dhana nak dhana nak | gi dī | kiṛa nag || tā

Ṭheka was clearly continuing to evolve, and had not yet become entirely fixed in its representations of *tāls*. Moreover, the *pakhāvaj* had not yet moved away from its use of generic "filler" sequences (e.g., *dhana nak dhad*—even today a common stock pattern used in accompaniment) to discrete compositions (*paran, sāth*) that would later come to represent the structure of its *tāls*.

THE RHYTHMIC REVOLUTION

As we ponder the trajectory of the knowledge presented in these selected works on rhythm and drumming we witness a fundamental shift from *tāl* as a quantitative structure of beats to a qualitative representation of those beats as a fixed, repeated pattern of drum strokes: *ṭheka*. I am not the first to recognize this sea change: in her highly perceptive study, Rebecca Stewart (1974) weighed up the differences between the rhythmic practices of North India's two main drums, *pakhāvaj* and tabla, noting that while tabla's *ṭheka*s bear a sonic relationship to its *tāl* structures and to the *tālī-k͟hālī* arrangement of beats, those of the *pakhāvaj* do not. Instead, they are "represented by many simple to complex patterns called parans, the primary function of which *is not* . . . to outline the internal structure of the tal" (87; emphasis in the original). Stewart felt that this difference pointed to "a type of musical revolution" and that "tabla, as a real hybrid form in itself, [was] one of the instruments of change" (78). Daniel Neuman also recognized this shift, and referred to tabla players as "autonomous timekeepers" who in the absence of an external source kept time "by playing the skeletal structure of the rhythmic cycle itself, known as the theka" (1985, 108). While I do not agree that there was no external source marking the structure of the *tāl*—since nearly all graphic depictions of musical scenes from past centuries included a *mañjīra* player marking the beats on the finger cymbals, and *mañjīra* patterns for *tāls* are explicit in *Sarmāya-yi ʿishrat*—I do agree with him when he writes, "It would appear that the entry of professional folk musicians into the classical system, beginning perhaps in the mid-eighteenth century and certainly consolidated by the end of the nineteenth, was a function of the increase in the importance of entertainment as a function of Hindustani music" (108). Setting aside Neuman's association of entertainment with Islamicization, we do know that the appearance of the tabla in the early eighteenth century coincided with the rise of the Ḍhāḍhī community's involvement in the spread of popular nautch entertainment and their gradual infiltration of the genres associated with the Kalāvant and Qawwāl communities. Muhammad Karam Imam's *Maʿdan al-mūsīqī* is full of references to Ḍhāḍhīs, who had become successful in all prestigious genres of vocal and instrumental music (as well as references to some that operated in less salubrious music-dance spheres). The mid-nineteenth century treatises on *tāl* that contain the first concrete examples of *ṭhekā* are informed by Ḍhāḍhī drummers: from Wajid Ali Shah who learned from one, to Sadiq Ali's informants for his chapter on *tāl* (and also, incidentally, the one on dance) in *Sarmāya-yi ʿishrat*.

Notwithstanding the *upāśraya* drumming patterns that appear in the fourteenth-century *saṅgītopaniṣat-sāroddhāraḥ* (Miner 1998), which I do not think qualify as *ṭhekas*, if *ṭhekas* had existed before the very late eighteenth century then I feel strongly that they would have been named and notated in some tangible form. Yet they are not. Instead, they appear as part of a new process of thinking about *tāl* that arguably responds to changes occurring in the music and consequently the need to describe rhythm in qualitative terms. I believe the rhythmic patterns used to accompany the songs and dances of the nautch contributed significantly to those changes, and specifically to the establishment of the *ṭhekas* we know today (see also Kippen 2006, 86–94). Thus, we witness a breathtaking cultural moment when the centuries-old musical order is upended in favor of an exhilarating attention to living musical practice. The tools of Arabic prosody triggered a descriptive vocabulary of *baḥr* (meter), *wazn* (rhythmic pattern), and *ẓarb* (beat), along with the precision of durational descriptors based in *sabab, watad*, and *fāṣila* units, which were powerful tools that could challenge the capacity of the old order to reflect accurately the emergent rhythmic practices. Arguably, the most important advantage of this new system was its ability to reflect the animated rhythmic flow of a metric cycle: in short, the identifiable pace, character, and cadence of a given *tāl*. I do not think it an accident that the all-important concept and practice of *ṭheka* qua fixed patterns of drum strokes evoking that very pace, character, and cadence are for the first time described in a treatise from the early nineteenth century. Moreover, it is also no accident that the term *ṭheka* first appears in a document dedicated to the *tabla*, and with it many other terms that seem quite specific to an emergent rhythmic aesthetic: *k̲h̲ālī*, the omitted beat; *band*, the strokes and sequences with damped bass sonorities associated with *k̲h̲ālī*; and *fiqra*, which indicates some kind of self-contained phrase that suggests structural repetition. At that historical moment, it appears that the tabla may well have been usurping and modifying the *tāl*s and musical roles of both Qawwāls and Kalāvants. The most important of these is *dhīma titāla*, which begins as a *pakhāvaj tāl* but which ends up as the quintessential tabla *tāl* and *ṭheka*, and the precursor of modern *tīntāl*.

Ṭhekas, however, took a long time to evolve into the uniquely representative patterns we now associate with individual *tāls* in Hindustani music; clearly, there had been many subtly and even strongly different variants of each in the past, some persisting into the early decades of the twentieth century. Indeed, I think this is what lies behind Muhammad Isḥaq's comment in his *Risāla ṭabla nawāzī* about the difficulty of establishing definitive structures and *ṭhekas* for certain *dhrupad tāls*: "all these *tāls* are muddled. . . . Some say one thing, others another." Nonetheless, *ṭhekas* were gradually consolidated and standardized, so much so that their fixity made obsolete the role of the *mañjīra* player—the external timekeeper—who quickly disappears from the graphic record in the late nineteenth century. This standardization of *ṭhekas* was, I think, due to three main interconnected factors: printing, musical notation, and the rise of the pedagogical text. The Mughal elite class that was formerly the focus of edification through written works was being replaced in the second half of the nineteenth century by a much broader readership, and thanks to the vernacular Urdu medium and lithographic printing technology the impact of works such as *G̲h̲uncha-yi rāg* and *Sarmāya-yi ʿishrat*, both published in several editions, was therefore surely much broader than that of the Persian manuscripts that had previously circulated in very few handwritten copies. Among others, Sourindro Mohun Tagore, Maula Bakhsh, Ram Sevak Mishra, Gurudev Patwardhan, and Muhammad Isḥaq all published works on *tāl* and drumming using ever more precise prescriptive methods of notation, works that were designed to be used as textbooks in instructional settings.

Standardization—in the rhythmic system as well as in other musical domains—was the result of much more than notations and books, which of course burgeoned throughout the twentieth century along with institutional music programs and their curricula. It also had to do with the interconnectedness of musical life brought about by the ease of travel, the greater exposure to a variety of performances through public concerts, and technological developments such as recordings and radio broadcasts that brought music into people's homes. But this is quite another story.

Orthography

Tabla (Urdu: *ṭabla* طبلہ, Hindi: *tabla* तबला) is not italicized and will be spelled throughout the text without diacriticals, unless part of a title. I also do not use diacriticals for proper nouns except to distinguish sh from sḥ. Macrons elongate vowels *ā* , *ī*, and *ū*. Subscript dots for *ḍ ṭ ṇ* and *ṛ* represent retroflex phonemes. Nasalization of the preceding vowel is *ṅ* or *ñ*. Final h (ہ) commutes to *a* (as in tabla طبلہ). *Ch* represents an unaspirated palatal چ while *chh* چھ is aspirated. *Sh* is the sibilant ش while Hindi श is written *ś* . *K̲h̲* is the voiceless velar fricative خ , while *g̲h̲* is the voiced velar fricative غ . Otherwise, *h* following a consonant implies aspiration. *W* and *v* (U: و , H: व) are largely interchangeable, but my practice is to differentiate Arabo-Persian-Urdu derivations as *w* and Sanskrit-Hindi as *v*. The letter ع (*'ain*) is represented by the open inverted comma ', and the *hamza* ء by the close inverted comma '. Other important diacriticals for Arabo-Persian-Urdu spellings are as follows: *ṣ* ث ; *ḥ* ح ; *ẕ* ذ ; *ṣ* ص ; *ẓ* ض ; *ṭ* ط ; *ẓ* ظ .

PRIMARY SOURCES: MANUSCRIPTS

Aṣl al-uṣūl, early nineteenth century, Qazi Muhammad Nasir Muhammadi "Ranj" [P.]
Kitāb al-adwār, c. 1260, by Safi al-Din Abd al-Mumin b. Yusuf b. Fakhir al-Urmawi [Ar.]
Kitāb al-mūsīqī al-kabīr (tenth century), Al-Farabi [Ar.]
Ma'dan al-mūsīqī, 1869, Muhammad Karam Imam [U.]
Miftāḥ al-surod, 1664, by Qazi Hasan [P.]
Risāla-yi mūsīqī, 1761, by Hakim Hasan Maududi Chishti [P.]
Saṅgītapārijāta, 1665, by Ahobala [Skt.]
Ṣaut al-mubārak, 1852–53, by Wajid Ali Shah [P.]
Shams al-aṣwāṭ, 1698, by Ras Baras Khan Kalavant [P.]
Sharḥ-i risāla-yi qawā'id-i ṭabla, early nineteenth century, anon. [P.]
Tuḥfat al-hind, 1675, by Mirza Khan [P.]
University of Edinburgh Oriental Manuscript 585/4, 1787–1788, anon. [P.]
Uṣūl al-naghmāt-i āṣafī, 1793, by Ghulam Raza [P.]

11

Time Changes

HETEROMETRIC MUSIC IN SOUTH ASIA

Richard Widdess

IN BOTH HINDUSTANI and Karnatak classical music, metrical organization is often described as "cyclic." This term refers to the fact that successive metrical units—"cycles" of the *tāla*—are identical in length and structure, and to the convention that one repeatedly comes "back to the beginning" (Powers/Widdess 2001) of the cycle, normally ending on or shortly after the first beat. The metaphor of rotation implied by "cycle" reflects indigenous terminology in both systems (*āvart*, *āvartana*, from the Sanskrit root *vṛt*, "turn, revolve"). The structure of the cycle can be articulated either by a repeated pattern of hand gestures (claps, finger-counts, and silent waves), or by a drum pattern; the former is normal in Karnatak music and in Hindustani *dhrupad*, while the latter is the case in other styles of Hindustani music, where the tabla commonly repeats or elaborates a groove-pattern (*ṭhekā*) one cycle in length. However the cycle is marked, Indian classical music appears quintessentially isometric (every cycle the same length), the metrical organization changing only if the soloist begins a new item of repertoire (*bandiś*) in a different metrical cycle (*tāla*). There may be a gradual or staged increase in tempo, but the maintenance of a cycle of consistent structure seems to be a precondition of the elaborate improvisation that is an important feature of both Hindustani and Karnatak traditions.[1]

Isometric organization is not universal in South Asian music, however. Heterometric temporal organization occurs in a variety of contexts and in a variety of different types. By heterometric, I mean a musical item in which the temporal organization, or musical "time," changes.[2] I will suggest that heterometric temporal organization features mainly in genres that fulfill different functions, and have different historical precedents, from those of concert or "classical" music as it is now commonly practiced;

in the past, such genres may have been more central to what was defined as music (*gāndharva, saṅgīta*) by South Asian music theorists.

SOME DEFINITIONS

Heterometric music could be informally described, using South Asian or Western emic terms, as music in which "the *tāla* changes," or music that "changes meter" or "changes time." To describe metrical phenomena with greater precision is a more complex matter and calls for some consideration of terminology.

I will use the term *time-unit* to denote any unit of duration. I refer to equal time-units as *isochronous* and to unequal time-units as *anisochronous*.[3] A series of time-units, normally but not invariably isochronous, constitutes a *pulse*. The existence and speed of a pulse can be cognitively inferred from the sonic events of the music, and/or from physical movements that are part of the performance, and such inference may lead to *entrainment* between performers and listeners to that pulse; that is, their external body-movements and/or their internal rhythmic expectations synchronize with the pulse.

Meter, broadly defined, denotes the grouping of smaller time-units into larger time-units. Typically, there may be several hierarchical levels of such grouping. Shorter and longer time-units may also be conceptualized or perceived as faster and slower pulses (whether isochronous or anisochronous). By *cycle* I mean the time-unit coextensive with the *time-line*—clap-pattern, cymbal-pattern or drum-pattern—and emically identified as the *tāla*; still longer time-units formed of multiple cycles will be termed *hypermetrical* units.

Table 11.1 represents the Hindustani classical *tāl*[4] Tīntāl. An isochronous time-unit of relatively short duration (its actual duration depending on the tempo (*laya*) of the music) is emically regarded as a unit of reference, called *mātrā* (see Table 11.1, pulse a): I will refer to it as the tactus or tactus beat.[5] As shown by the dots,[6] these tactus beats are grouped into larger isochronous time-units of four (*vibhāg* "segment"), eight (defined by the alternation of a clapped beat and a silent wave), and 16 (*āvart* "cycle") tactus beats (pulse-levels b–d respectively). Tīntāl can thus be conceived as a multileveled relationship between two isochronous time-units, the tactus (pulse a) and the cycle (pulse d), in the relationship 1:16. This numerical relationship is termed the *cardinality* of the cycle (London 2004, 87).

The structure of Tīntāl as represented here is explicit in pedagogy and performance. A student of this music will learn to keep time with the hands while singing or listening, by executing a standard *clap-pattern* or *time-line* corresponding in length with the cycle (Table 11.1). A firm clap on beat 1, the most emphasized tactus-beat (the *sam*, represented in writing as X), marks the beginning of each cycle (pulse d). Pulse c is denoted by a contrasting gesture (*khālī*, written 0), a silent wave of one hand, on beat 9. Pulse b is marked by subsidiary claps (*tālī*, written 2, 3) on beats 5 and 13. Thus the linear sequence of hand-gestures denotes a hierarchical metrical structure. In

TABLE 11.1

Levels of pulsation in Tīntāl (cardinality 16).

	tablā *ṭhekā*	dhā	dhin	dhin	dhā	dhā	dhin	dhin	dhā	dhā	tin	tin	tā	tā	dhin	dhin	dhā	dhā
	beat no.	1	2	3	4	5	6	7	8	9	10	11	12	13	14	15	16	1
a	pulse a (*mātrā*)	•	•	•	•	•	•	•	•	•	•	•	•	•	•	•	•	•
b	pulse b (*vibhāg*)	•				•				•				•				•
c	pulse c (*sam, khālī*)	•								•								•
d	pulse d (*āvart*)	•																•
e	clap-pattern	X				2				o				3				X

X = first clap (*sam*) 2, 3 = subsequent claps o = silent wave (*khālī*)

• = beat at corresponding level of pulsation

performance, the hand-gestures are not normally performed, because the structure is instead audibly encoded in a standard accompaniment pattern (*ṭhekā*) played on the tabla, repeated once each cycle (usually with variations, and interludes of more soloistic playing). As Kippen and others have pointed out, the *ṭhekā* does not reflect the structure of the clap-pattern in every *tāl* (Kippen 2001; Powers/Widdess 2001); but in every case it articulates the cardinality-relationship between the tactus and the cycle.

Table 11.2 represents another Hindustani classical *tāl*, Jhaptāl. This is structured similarly to Tīntāl, but comprises 10 *mātrā* to the cycle, grouped 2 + 3 + 2 + 3. Pulse b is thus, in this *tāl*, anisochronous; but the regularly alternating time-units of two and three tactus-beats group into isochronous time-units at adjacent hierarchical levels, that is, five-beat units (pulse c), and 10-beat units (pulse d). Many *tālas* in South Asia similarly feature one level of anisochronous time-units, but these are invariably grouped into longer, isochronous units including the cycle.

In the South Indian classical tradition, and in the dhrupad style of Hindustani vocal music, the time-line is executed visually as a clap-pattern by performers and members of the audience. In genres outside the concert-music tradition, especially traditions of religious music and dance, a time-line is realized audibly on cymbals; typical time-line patterns contrast a number of undamped, resonant cymbal-strokes with one or more damped, unresonant strokes. It should be stressed however that the time-line, whether performed with the hands, on tabla, or on cymbals, does not necessarily dictate the only possible grouping of tactus-beats within the cycle, nor does it determine surface-level rhythmic patterns of durations and accents in melodic or percussion music. Such surface patterns may involve subdividing the tactus into smaller units; they may vary from cycle to cycle in almost limitless variety, or articulate a groove that is not inherent in the time-line. Surface rhythmic groupings may overlap time-units at any level including the cycle itself. Especially at slow tempi, gestural or percussion time-line patterns function primarily as time-keeping devices that help performers and listeners to track the metrical cycle during complex changes of surface rhythm (Widdess 1981a, b; Powers/Widdess 2001).[7]

TABLE 11.2

Levels of pulsation in Jhaptāl (cardinality 10).

	tablā *ṭhekā*	dhī	nā	dhī	dhī	nā	tī	nā	dhī	dhī	nā	dhī
	beat no.	1	2	3	4	5	6	7	8	9	10	1
a	pulse a (*mātrā*)	•	•	•	•	•	•	•	•	•	•	•
b	pulse b (*vibhāg*)	•		•			•		•			•
c	pulse c (*sam, khālī*)	•					•					•
d	pulse d (*āvart*)	•										•
e	clap-pattern	X		2			0		3			X

Music in *tāla* is normally assumed to be *isometrical*, that is, successive cycles in a given musical item (song, instrumental composition, dance) have the same length and structure. Indeed, it is only through repetition that meter can be experienced, and can lead to entrainment to time-units longer than the pulse-beat. By *heterometrical*, I mean that change of metrical structure occurs during a single musical item: specifically, and as a minimum, change in *cardinality*—the length of the cycle in terms of the number of tactus beats. Any change in cardinality must, of course, entail change in internal groupings within the cycle, and may affect surface rhythmic patterns, but changes in internal groupings and surface rhythms without change in cardinality would be normal in any *tāla* and would not constitute heterometrical change in the sense intended here.[8] The duration of the tactus-beat may remain the same, or it may also change, leading to a double disruption of the metrical structure, but a change in speed of the tactus alone does not constitute a change in metrical structure, only a change of tempo. In other words it is that aspect of meter that is normally most resistant to change that changes in heterometric music, namely cardinality.

EVIDENCE FOR HETEROMETRIC MUSIC IN SOUTH ASIA

In this chapter I propose to focus on genres of vocal music where metrical structure is clear: music that can be emically described in terms of a *tāla* system, and in which that system is articulated by the use of percussion and gestural time-line patterns in performance. My typology does not include the quasi-heterometric organization of classical *ālāp(ana)*, because an important aspect of those forms is that isochronous units and metrical grouping, if present at all, are ambiguous or unclear.[9] *Ālāp(ana)* is never accompanied by *tāla* hand-gestures, and only exceptionally by percussion.[10]

Examples of heterometric genres in South Asia include the following.

- The Sufi Islamic song-form *qalbānā*, as still sung today by a few classical musicians of the Delhi *gharānā* (e.g., Ustad Iqbal Ahmed Khan) and some performers of *qawwālī* (Sufi devotional) music, includes heterometric songs with changing *tāls*. They form part of the repertoire attributed to the Sufi poet Amir Khusrau of Delhi (1253–1325), which is still sung at Sufi shrines in Delhi and Pakistan.
- The Sikh *gurubānī* repertoire—consisting of hymns from Sikh scripture dating from the sixteenth to the seventeenth centuries—as sung by hereditary *rāgī* or *rabābī* musicians in the Panjāb, includes a genre of heterometric songs, known as *partāl*, in which each section may be composed in a different *tāl* (Cassio 2015, 49 f.).
- Temple music (*samāj*) in Vrindaban, U.P., includes performances in which *tāl* and tempo change (Tanaka 2008).
- Some classical singers know songs in which different sections are in different *tāls*. They are sometimes called *prabandha* and may be included in the *dhrupad* repertoire. These are, however, seldom if ever performed.

Various genres of religious and ceremonial music and dance performed in the Newar cities of the Kathmandu Valley include metrical changes. This is the case, for example, in the Hindu-Buddhist *dāphā bhajan* tradition of temple singing, and in the *gūlābājā* tradition of Buddhist seasonal music, where such changes are especially conspicuous in the song genre *gvārā*.

This is certainly not a comprehensive list of South Asian heterometrical genres,[11] and it would be premature to hazard an all-encompassing characterization of the phenomenon. The diversity of examples suggests that the Indian classical music traditions, normally treated as the "classic" exemplars of South Asian musical idiom, are in fact somewhat exceptional in systematically avoiding any change of tāla during a musical item. Also notable is the fact that heterometric compositions are not the exclusive preserve of any one religious tradition, but are found in the ritual or devotional repertoires of Hinduism, Sufism, Sikhism, and Buddhism.

The variety of musical types noted here is sufficient to show that heterometric temporal organization can assume different forms. In some genres, the song comprises a number of sections in different meters; the changes of meter coincide with section boundaries, and each section is internally isometric. Such songs can be through-composed (that is, sections are not repeated between other sections but follow in linear sequence); some percussion pieces, and some maqam-related vocal suites, may be of this type. Alternatively, one section of the composition is repeated between the others as a refrain (*dhruva, ṭek, sthāyī* etc.), a pattern that is also common in isometric songs. The *partāl* of Sikh *gurubānī*, referred to earlier, exemplifies this second type. In a typical example,[12] three isometric sections are sung, in Āṛācautāl (14 beats), Ektāl (12 beats), and Rūpak *tāl* (7 beats) respectively, but the first section is repeated after the second, and again after the third, making four changes of *tāl* altogether. *Prabandhas* and *dhrupads* in changing *tāls* would also represent this type. In *gurubānī* the change of *tāla* from one section to the next can also involve a change of vocal style, so that a section in Cautāl could be sung in dhrupad style, while a section of the same song in Dīpcandī could be sung in ṭhumrī style, or if Ektāl, in khayāl style.[13]

In other cases, metrical changes occur within a single section of the song, as well as at section boundaries. This type can be observed, for example, in a *qalbānā–tarānā* of the tradition of Amir Khusrau, sung by Ustad Iqbal Ahmad Khan.[14] The *sthāyī* section begins in Āṛācautāl (14 beats), changes to Sūltāl (10 beats), and returns to Āṛācautāl; the *antarā* section starts in Ektāl (12 beats), changes to Jhaptāl (10 beats), and changes again to Tīntāl (16 beats), before returning to the first phrase of the *sthāyī*, in Āṛācautāl. In this type, *tāl* is no longer compartmentalized within isometric sections, but can seemingly change at any point.

While the heterometric organization of these different examples may reflect different motivations, functions, and constraints, they all apparently contradict a fundamental assumption, that meter is predicated on isometrical repetition. Indeed, discussions of meter in cross-cultural comparative perspective (e.g., Kolinski 1973; Clayton 2000; London 2004; Kvifte 2007; Tenzer 2011a, 2011b; Savage, Merritt,

Rzeszutek, and Brown 2012) generally make this assumption. And the assumption is surely correct: it is only through repetition that meter becomes perceptible at all. If meter were to change every cycle it would be hard to perceive cycles as such. Thus the examples considered here normally involve some repetition of each *tāla* before changing to a different one; in addition, percussion and gestural time-line patterns help to clarify the changing temporal organization.

The question then arises, therefore, *why* meter changes at all, and what are the principles of compositional construction, the cognitive experiences, or the cultural symbolisms that underlie such changes? Do changes of organization at the level of *tāla* cycles represent a surface phenomenon only, for example in order to provide a kind of playful rhythmic variety from moment to moment, or deliberately to obscure metrical structure from the less knowledgeable listener; or are they deployed in the service of some larger structural principle or regularity, for example in relation to the poetic structure of the song-text, or a hyper-metrical template, process, or symbolism of some kind; or do they generate a particular cognitive experience for the performer or listener that is typically valued in the culture concerned? As we shall see, a case could be made for any or all such possible explanations. In order to begin to investigate the question, I will analyze three examples from the Kathmandu Valley of Nepal. I will then consider evidence for possible historical antecedents, cultural/behavioral parallels, and cognitive implications of my findings, which may help us to understand heterometric music in broader South Asian contexts and cross-cultural perspectives.

HETEROMETRIC SONGS IN NEWAR MUSIC

Heterometric musical structure can be illustrated with reference to the *dāphā* and *gvārā* traditions of religious singing, practiced in the Newar[15] communities of the Kathmandu Valley, principally in the cities of Bhaktapur, Patan, and Kathmandu. Extensive economic, political, and cultural interactions between the urban centers of the Kathmandu Valley and those of India over most of the last two millennia, and the deeply embedded traces of that interaction in the culture of Nepal today, have led many scholars to regard Nepal as a living record of South Asian cultural history. Despite the formidable barriers of forest and mountain, the major traditions of Hinduism have all found homes in what was until very recently the last remaining Hindu kingdom. In addition, Buddhism, in the form in which it survived in Northern India until around the fourteenth century, coexists with Hinduism in a cultural symbiosis, having been boosted by an influx of refugee monks and scholars, often bearing precious written or oral texts, fleeing the early expansion of Muslim hegemony in the Ganges valley. Both Hinduism and Buddhism maintain Tantric elements typical of eastern India since the late first millennium A.D. Rich traditions of art, architecture, and literature show forms derived from India reinterpreted in the light of local preferences and innovations.

Similarly, in music it is not difficult to recognize elements that remind us of performing traditions current in India, or described in Indian musical *śāstras* of centuries ago. The social and religious contexts invite us to see how these elements have been selected, preserved, and transformed to serve local and changing needs. The melodic and rhythmic concepts of *rāga* and *tāla*, many of the instruments, and vocal genres of religious music can be linked to Indian antecedents, but have acquired distinctive forms. Heterometric musics appear to be a good example of this phenomenon.

Both Buddhists and Hindus in the Kathmandu Valley sing devotional songs called *dāphā* (or *dāphā bhajan* in full). These songs have texts in the local vernacular, Newari, or in Indian languages including Sanskrit and Hindi; they typically have a structure of about four verses, plus a single-line refrain that comes at the beginning and is repeated after each verse. In melodic structure they are related to *prabandha* forms (see the section entitled Prabandhas) and later classical genres such as *dhrupad*.

In Bhaktapur, the singers belong mainly to the farmer caste or other middle to low-ranking castes,[16] and they perform either daily or at important festivals; each neighborhood will have one or more such groups, which meet to sing at a local temple or wherever there is a suitable performance space. The *dāphā* group is an important focus of local culture and social identity, and represents the neighborhood at major festivals alongside music groups from other neighborhoods.

Nāndī and Cālī

Dāphā songs are normally sung as a structured sequence, with different *rāgs* and *tāls* in successive songs, and special song types for starting and finishing the sequence; a whole singing session takes between one and three hours. While the sequence varies according to different groups or individual informants, there are two main divisions of the repertoire, sometimes respectively called *nāndī* and *cālī*. The *nāndī* songs are sung in praise of the god Śiva, patron deity of music and dance, and are suitable for beginning the session as a kind of invocation. Singing therefore begins with one song from the *nāndī* section, and continues with a number of songs from the *cālī* section (this division is sometimes reflected in the organization of song books). The number of songs sung in total should be uneven, with three as the minimum; usually five or seven songs will be sung, depending on the length of time available.

The metrical organization of these repertoire divisions is very different. Songs in the *nāndī* division employ a number of otherwise rare *tāls*. It also includes heterometric songs in which two or more *tāls* are combined; very few of these songs are known today, but the songbooks contain many examples. Thus heterometric songs, of which we will examine two examples next, find a specific place at the head of the repertoire, and at the start of the sequence of *tāls* performed in the singing session. Unusual metrical structures are associated, it would appear, with the function of invocation. Indeed, the singing session begins with a solo piece on the drum *lālākhī*, called *dyaḥlhāygu* "calling the gods," which also has a heterometric structure.[17] In both vocal and instrumental pieces, the metrical structure is articulated by the singers with the help of thick-walled, high-pitched bronze cymbals (*tāḥ*). We will examine two examples from the *nāndī* division of the *dāphā* repertoire.

He Śiva Bhairava

Figure 11.1 (Audio 11.1 ⊙) is a transcription of the song *He Śiva Bhairava* (transcribed and analyzed in Widdess 2013, 269 ff.). This is a very well-known song in the *dāphā* repertoire of Bhaktapur, in praise of the god Bhairav, the fierce avatar of Śiva, and the patron deity of the city. It is often sung at the annual festival of Bhairav, Biskāḥ (Nepali: Bisket), both in regular *dāphā* singing sessions, and in special processions and gatherings of musicians to mark the festival (see Widdess 2013, 220 ff.), especially in connection with the large temple of Bhairav in the center of the city, and with the wooden chariot on which the image of Bhairav is hauled through the streets (Figure 11.2). The text, in mixed Sanskrit, Newari, and Hindi, and a provisional translation, are given in Table 11.3.[18]

As the notation in Figure 11.1 shows, this song is heterometric, and indeed it belongs in the *nāndī* section of the repertoire. There are three sections, in different *tāls*: 1) Parimān (3 quarter-note beats, as notated in Figure 11.1); 2) Cvakh (2 quarter-note beats); and 3) Partāl (7 sixteenth-note beats). If these sections were sung as a nonrepeating sequence, there would be just two metrical changes, from Parimān to Cvakh, and from Cvakh to Partāl. But the first section, in Parimān *tāl*, is repeated as a refrain (*dhuvā*) after the other sections, as shown in Figure 11.3. This repetition increases the number of metrical changes from two to four.

Figure 11.3 also shows the progressive compression of temporal space represented by the sequence Parimān > Cvakh > Partāl, which reduce in cycle–length from 3, to 2, to 1¾ quarter notes. A tendency to undergo metrical compression is common in Newar music (Widdess 2006), but in this case the repetition of Parimān after Cvakh and again after Partāl yields a more complex structure, with alternating reductions and increases in cycle length; the second reduction and the second increase are greater than the first (see the arrows in Figure 11.3). Thus not only does the meter change, the *degree and direction of metrical change* also change.

In addition, in Partāl, the tactus changes to a shorter time-unit, approximately a quarter of the previous tactus time-unit, grouped 3 + 2 + 2 (alternatively, we could say that there are three anisochronous beats, but still shorter than the previous tactus). This causes a more dramatic rupture of metrical structure than in the previous metrical changes, which only affect the grouping of a constant tactus-beat. The rupture is reversed by resuming the previous tactus in the final refrain.

The process of compression of cycle length can be seen as an example of what Henry has termed "intensification" in South Asian music (Henry 2002). This term refers to the several ways in which musical performance can become more intense as it proceeds, including acceleration of the basic pulse, high pitch, high volume, and so on. Henry shows that many genres of both classical and nonclassical music feature intensification, often

FIGURE 11.1 *Dāphā* song *He Śiva Bhairava* as sung by the Dattātreya and Bhairavnāth temple *dāphā* groups, Bhaktapur, Nepal.

very marked, which he interprets as stimulating heightened emotional engagement or response. In section C of *He Śiva Bhairava*, the intensification results from a combination of high pitch (emphasis of upper F in the melody: see Figure 11.1), high volume (resulting from the high pitch), the reduction of the tactus time-unit, and the use of an

FIGURE 11.2 Singers of the Bhairavnāth temple *dāphā* group singing *He Śiva Bhairava* at the start of the Biskāḥ festival. The chariot of Bhairav can be seen in the background. Bhaktapur, Nepal, 2003. Photo: R. Widdess.

additive meter[19] in contrast to the binary and ternary meters of the preceding sections (or alternatively an anisochronous time-unit), as well as from the reduction in metrical unit length and the increase in degree of metrical change just noted.

The composer of *He Śiva Bhairava* has maximized intensification by using the 7-beat *tāl* Partāl, the fastest *tāl* used in *dāphā*, in the last section of the song. This section corresponds to the first line of the last couplet of the poem, in which the poet, Ranjit Malla,[20] names himself. Inclusion of the poet's name in the final section of a song is widespread in South Asian devotional song poetry, including Hindustani *dhrupad* and South Indian *kriti*, and it is common in *dāphā*; it thus marks the section as in some degree final and climactic, although it is always followed by a reprise of the opening section. Many *dāphā* songs are signed by Newar kings who ruled the three cities of the Kathmandu Valley in the seventeenth and eighteenth centuries. Ranjit Malla was the last king of Bhaktapur (ruled 1722–1769), and was banished into exile by the invading king of Gorkha, Pṛthvī Nārāyaṇ Shāh, in 1769. The fall of Bhaktapur in that year set the seal on Pṛthvī Nārāyan's conquest of the Valley, which

TABLE 11.3

Text and translation of *dāphā* song *He Śiva Bhairava.*

A1	he śiva bhairava tribhuvana vande •	O Śiva Bhairava, worshipped by the three worlds!
A2	candrakalāsira bhairavi saṃge | |	[He who] has the crescent moon on his head is together with [his consort] Bhairavī.
B1	mun[ḍa]mālā hāt[h]a [kṛpāṇā] netra viśālā śobhe | |	[He has] a necklace of skulls, a knife in his hand, and large eyes, and looks graceful.
B2	tanu chavi kālā [kirīṭina] mālā sarpa vibhū[ṣi]ta aṃge | |	His body is black, his crown is garlanded, his limbs adorned with snakes.
B3	dṛmikita dṛmikita tāthaiyānā tāthaiyānā dṛgido dṛgi [do] | |	(Dance syllables)
B4	tākadhaṃtri takadhaṃtri kṛtakṛta kathaiyānā thaiyā | |	(Dance syllables)
A1	he śiva bhairava tribhuvana nande | |	O Śiva Bhairava, delight of the three worlds!
C	kahata śrī ranajita tuma [śaraṇa] | |	Śrī Ranajita who is under your shelter says
A2	jaya jaya bhairava bhayahara nande | |	"Victory to Bhairava, the one who takes away fear, [my] delight!"
A1	he śiva bhairava tribhuvana vande	O Śiva Bhairava, worshipped by the three worlds!

became the heart of his new empire; this empire later became the modern nation state of Nepal, in which Newars now constitute a minority in the Valley they used to rule. Ranjit Malla's name thus evokes powerful associations with Newar political identity and historical nostalgia. He was a prolific composer of religious songs—more *dāphā* songs bear his signature in Bhaktapur songbooks than that of any other composer by a large margin—and indeed his poetic and musical preoccupations are sometimes blamed for having contributed to his downfall. The metrical compression in section C thus contributes to a musical intensification coinciding with a verse of special significance. While there is nothing unusual about singing a *dāphā* song signed by Ranjit Malla, his authorship gains added significance in the context of Biskāḥ, because the king is symbolically present at the festival, represented by his sword carried by a royal priest (Levy 1990, 469).

In certain respects, therefore, we can understand the metrical changes in *He Śiva Bhairava* as a formal process of intensification linked to the structure, meaning and context of the song. The unusual performance challenges posed by its metrical changes

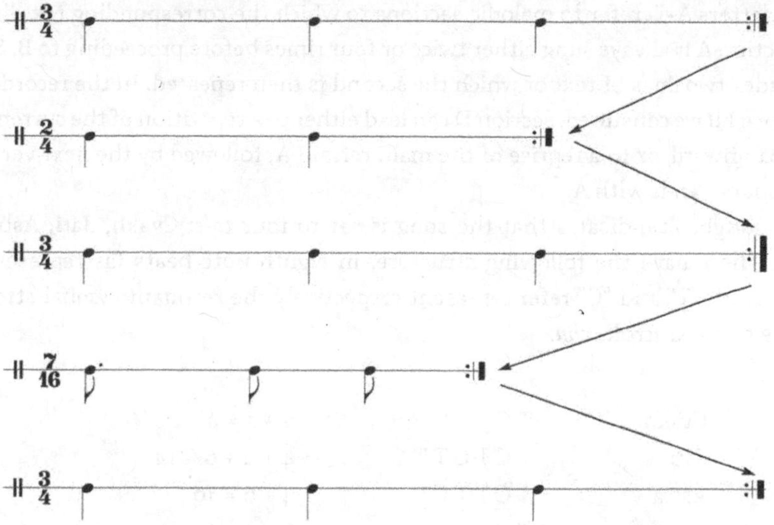

FIGURE 11.3 Changes of metrical cycle in *dāphā* song *He Śiva Bhairava.*

contribute to the exceptional exertions required by the festival, including for example the pulling of Bhairav's enormous chariot (effectively a temple on wheels) from end to end of the town. The song furthermore evokes fundamental themes concerning sacred and secular power, identity and history in Bhaktapur, which have no doubt contributed to its popularity and longevity.

Girīhe Nandinī

Girīhe nandinī is another heterometric song from the *nāndī* section of the *dāphā* repertoire that remains well-known to Bhaktapur singers. The melody is transcribed in Figure 11.4 (Audio 11.2 ▶) and the text (in Sanskrit and Newari) and translation are given in Table 11.4. Again, Ranjit Malla is named as the author/composer. As befits a song in the *nāndī* repertoire, *Girīhe nandinī* is in praise of Śiva, here addressed as Śankara. It portrays the commonly depicted scene in which Śiva and his wife Pārvatī sit together on the sacred mountain Kailāsa.

The transcription is based on my learning of the song in 2004 and a subsequent recorded performance, both reflecting the tradition of the Dattātreya Temple in Bhaktapur (Figure 11.5). The text and translation are based on three manuscript songbooks (Widdess 2013, 252 ff).[21]

This song is one of the most complex in the *dāphā* repertoire, both in poetic and in musical rhythmic structure. The primary refrain (*dhuvā̃*) is formed by the first line of the song, "Lord Śankara, [husband of] the Daughter of the Mountain!," which can be repeated after each of the three stanzas. Each stanza has three lines rather than the more usual two, and is followed in performance by a secondary refrain, "This is the salutation of 'Jitaraṇa' [= Ranjit Malla]."

The letters A–D refer to melodic sections to which the corresponding text lines are set. Section A is always sung either twice or four times before proceeding to B. Section C includes two lines of text of which the second is then repeated. In the recorded performance I have consulted, section D can lead either to a repetition of the current verse from B1 onward, or to a reprise of the main refrain A, followed by the next verse. The performance ends with A.

The songbook indicates that the song is set to four *tāls*: Cvakh, Jati, Astrā, and Ektāḥ. These have the following structure, in eighth-note beats (as represented in Figure 11.4). "T" and "C" refer represent respectively the resonant cymbal-stroke *tin*, and the damped stroke *chu*.

Cvakh	T C	2 + 2 = 4
Jati	T C T C T T C	4 + 4 + 6 = 14
Astrā	T C T T C	4 + 6 = 10
Ektāḥ	T C	3 + 3 = 6

Note that Cvakh and Ektāḥ differ in the number of tactus-beats per cymbal-stroke: the pattern of strokes is the same (T C) but the rate of striking is slower in Ektāḥ because there are three tactus-beats per stroke, the tactus remaining more or less constant in duration. Sections A–D are structured as follows:

A Cvakh: 8 cycles (repeated)

B1 Jati: 2 cycles
B2 Cvakh: 6 cycles
B3 Astrā: 2 cycles

C Ektāḥ: 6 cycles

D1 Jati: 1 cycle
D2 Cvakh: 1 cycle, plus one extra beat overlapping with the first beat of section A (Cvakh)

Here the segmentation according to text units (A, B, C, D) has been further divided to reflect metric changes: each of the segments (A, B1, B2, etc.) is isometric. Note that the boundary between B2 and B3 is marked by a dot in the manuscript song-texts, suggesting that it is perceived as an important boundary; otherwise the metrical changes are not indicated in the written text.

I suggested earlier that in *He Śiva Bhairava*, changes of meter from section to section serve to contrast different cycle lengths, and that gradual compression of the cycle length is interrupted by repetition of the refrain. In *Girī he nandinī*, metrical changes

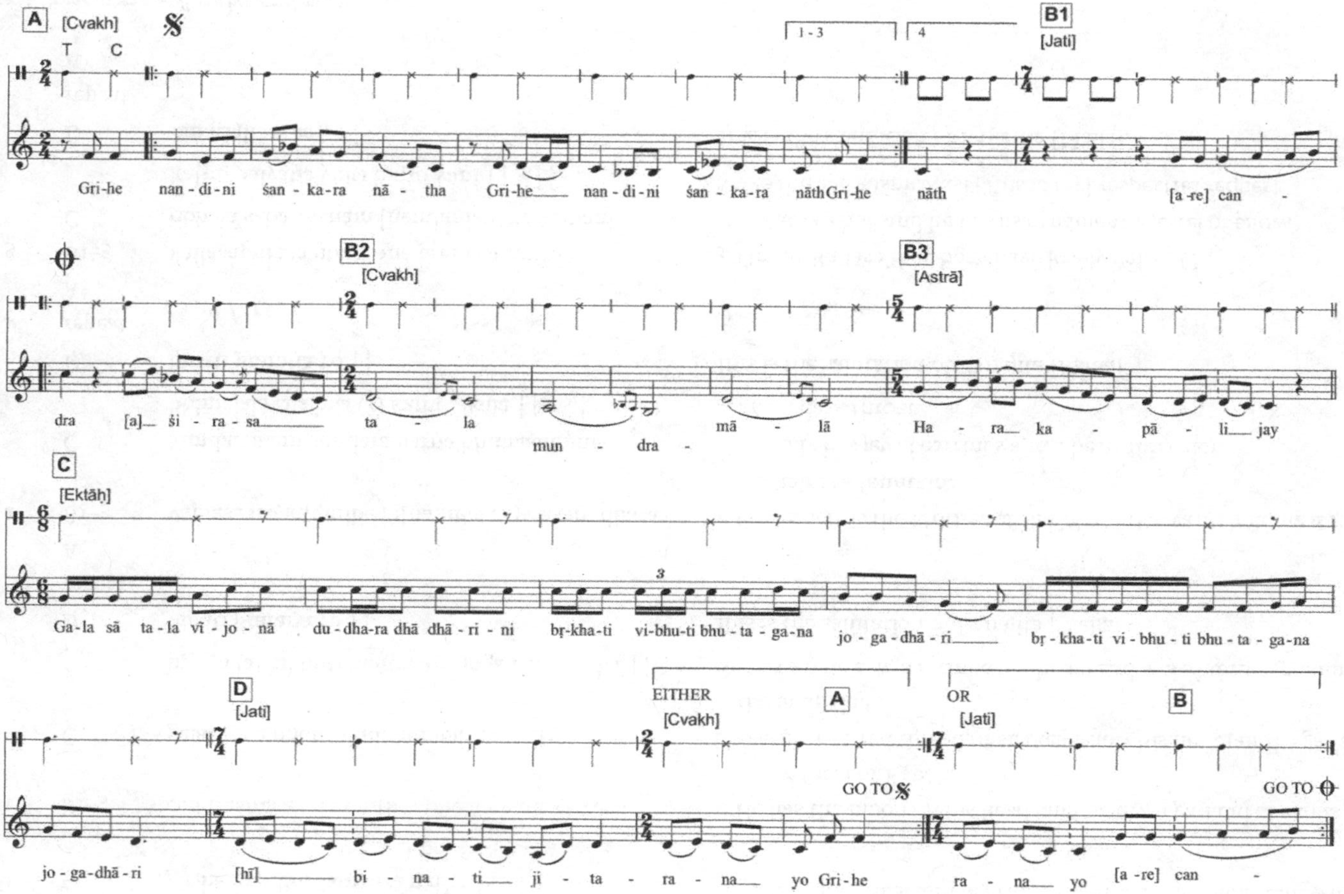

FIGURE 11.4 *Dāphā* song *Girīhe nandinī* as sung by the Dattātreya temple *dāphā* group, Bhaktapur, Nepal.

TABLE 11.4

Text and translation of *dāphā* song *Girīhe nandinī.*

<table>
<tr><td>refrain</td><td>A</td><td>girīhe nandinī śaṃkara nātha | |</td><td>Lord Śankara, [husband of] the Daughter of the Mountain (Pārvatī)!</td></tr>
<tr><td>verse 1</td><td>B1–3</td><td>candrasirasa tala mu[ṇḍa]mālā • hara kāpālī |</td><td>1. He has the moon on his head, and below, a garland of skulls. He is Śiva in the form of Kāpālī.*</td></tr>
<tr><td></td><td>C</td><td>galasatala bījonā dudharamā[lā]dhā[rī] |</td><td>He wears a sacred thread of snakes below his neck [and] a garland of thorn-apple.†</td></tr>
<tr><td></td><td></td><td>bṛṣa[bha] bibhuti bhūtagaṇa jogadhā[rī] | | 1 | |</td><td>He has a bull, ash, a retinue of ghosts and a meditative [posture].</td></tr>
<tr><td></td><td>D</td><td>binati jitaraṇa yo | |</td><td>This is the salutation of Raṇajita [Malla].</td></tr>
<tr><td></td><td>repeat
A</td><td></td><td></td></tr>
<tr><td>verse 2</td><td>B1–3</td><td>vāmasa jagad[am]be jo[ṅā] mālā • jatasaṃ dhārā |</td><td>2. On his left is the Mother of the World (Pārvatī), holding a garland. In his hair is a fountain.</td></tr>
<tr><td></td><td>C</td><td>kundalamani sundara barṇa bhimakāminī</td><td>Śiva's lady has jewel earrings and a beautiful color.</td></tr>
<tr><td></td><td></td><td>bhimajala cila bila (?) kaṃṭhakālā | | 2 | |</td><td>. . . ? . . . dark throat.‡</td></tr>
<tr><td></td><td>D</td><td>binati jitaraṇa yo | |</td><td>This is the salutation of Raṇajita [Malla].</td></tr>
<tr><td></td><td>repeat
A</td><td></td><td></td></tr>
<tr><td>verse 3</td><td>B1–3</td><td>kailāsapurasa ubhayana premasi vāni |</td><td>3. On Mt Kailāsa they both have lovely voices (?).</td></tr>
<tr><td></td><td>C</td><td>dohala saba āsanam [hem]amaṇi bhūṣaṇam</td><td>His seat is a bull and he has as ornament a jewel of snow.</td></tr>
<tr><td></td><td></td><td>ka[ra] kalyāṇa yuga biṃti vāni | | 3 | |</td><td>Make the age auspicious! [This is my] respectful request.</td></tr>
<tr><td></td><td>D</td><td>binati jitaraṇa yo | |</td><td>This is the salutation of Raṇajita [Malla].</td></tr>
<tr><td></td><td>repeat
A</td><td></td><td></td></tr>
</table>

* *An ascetic who carries a skull as a begging bowl.*

† *A fruit beloved of Śiva because of its intoxicating effect.*

‡ *Śiva's throat is dark owing to his swallowing poison. The remainder of this line is obscure.*

FIGURE 11.5 The Dattātreya temple *dāphā* group, Bhaktapur, Nepal, 2012. Photo: R. Widdess.

occur within the verse section (B), as well as between it and the refrain (A). There are more changes of cycle length than in *He Śiva Bhairava*, and these changes follow a different pattern, in which a short cycle length of 4 or 6 beats alternates with a longer cycle of 10 or 14 beats. Metrical changes thus alternate between expansion and contraction of cycle length.

Cycle length in eighth-notes:

A	Cvakh	4
B1	Jati	14
B2	Cvakh	4
B3	Astrā	10
C	Ektāḥ	6
D1	Jati	14
D2	Cvakh	4

These alternating cycle-lengths are not the only element of rhythmic design in this particular song, however. When we take into account the number of tactus-beats in each section, we find that metrical changes and matching text divisions articulate time spans of *proportionally related lengths*. This is demonstrated in Figure 11.6, where each square represents one eighth-note beat, and each *tāl* cycle is indicated by a heavy outline. Beats bearing a cymbal-stroke are marked T or C. In the upper part of Figure 11.6 we see the following structure:

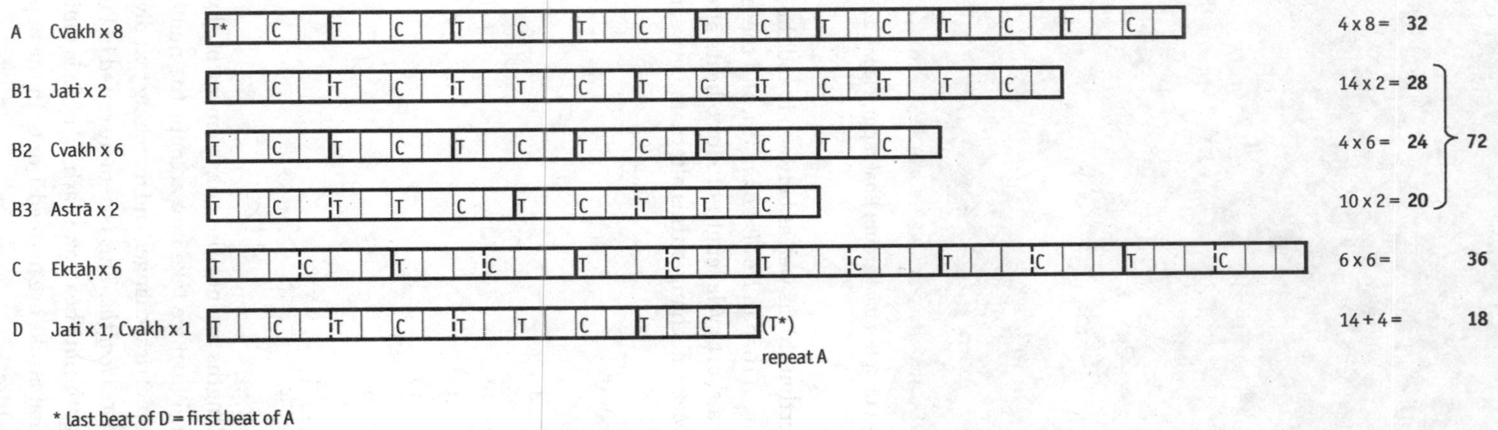

FIGURE 11.6 Proportional structure in *dāphā* song *Girīhe nandinī*.

A: 8 cycles of Cvakh occupy 4 x 8 = 32 beats.[22]

B1: 2 cycles of Jati occupy 14 x 2 = 28 beats.

B2: 6 cycles of Cvakh occupy 4 x 6 = 24 beats.

B3: 2 cycles of Astrā occupy 10 x 2 = 20 beats.

Together, sections A and B1–3 comprise four successively shorter time spans of 32, 28, 24, and 20 beats respectively, in the proportional relationship 8:7:6:5. Once again, a process of compression is revealed: not of the length of the cycle, but of the hypermetric time spans demarcated by metrical changes and corresponding to text units.

In section C, six cycles of Ektāḥ comprise the longest isometric time span in the piece, of 6 x 6 = 36 beats. At first sight, this section does not continue the progressive compression of the preceding sections; we might have expected a segment of 16 beats to continue the pattern previously established.

However, we should note that the whole of section B, corresponding to the first text line of the verse, occupies 72 beats (28+24+20). Section C, corresponding to the second line of the verse, is exactly half this length; thus B1–3 and C exhibit the relationship 2:1. This relationship is then continued in D, corresponding to the secondary refrain "This is the salutation of Ranjit Malla," which occupies one cycle each of Jati and Cvakh, totalling 14 + 4 = 18 beats. Thus B1–3, C and D comprise time spans of 72, 36 and 18 beats, in the proportion 4:2:1 (Table 11.5).

The song thus exhibits two sets of proportional relationships, 8:7:6:5 and 4:2:1, between successive hypermetric time spans that are demarcated by metrical changes and correspond to text units. In both sets of relationship, time spans undergo compression.

While we may justifiably marvel at the complexity of this heterometrical scheme, we may also wonder about the composer's intention in creating it. Do the hypermetrical proportional relationships indicate an aesthetic appreciation of certain numerical proportions, or some kind of number symbolism? Proportional formal schemes have been claimed for a number of Western composers, from Dunstable to Bartók (e.g., Trowell 1978; Howat 1983), with both aesthetic and symbolic explanations, and these

TABLE 11.5

Proportional structure in *Girīhe nandinī.*

	Tactus beats	Proportions	
A	32	8	
B1	28	7	
B2	24	6	4
B3	20	5	
C	36		2
D	18		1

are sometimes linked to heterometrical schemes. But these claims rest on notated scores; can we infer similar processes at work in an oral tradition, or should we perhaps rather infer that writing was in some way used in the process of composition? While such use of writing in the literate milieu of court and temple cannot be ruled out, we should bear in mind other means of supporting memory besides writing; these include the use of gestural and percussion patterns, and perhaps symbolic templates that are partly conceptual, partly visual in character.

In an earlier publication, I suggested that metrical compression in Newar music is the musical manifestation of a process of intensification that is also seen in the visual domain, where it appears in the ground plans and three-dimensional structures of temples and fountains, and especially in the *maṇḍala*, a map of the cosmos used in ritual and meditation (Figure 11.7; Widdess 2006). In the present example, the sequence of segments of different metrical structure and diminishing proportions suggests that the composer may have had consciously in mind the analogy of the concentric areas of a *maṇḍala*, with their differing geometry (circle, square, triangle, etc.), contracting toward the center. In the case of this musical *maṇḍala*, the smallest, "central" area, which in a visual *maṇḍala* or temple contains the image of the main deity, is the subrefrain D, in which the name of Ranjit Malla appears. As in *He Śiva Bhairava*, the name of the royal author appears at the point of maximum compression. That the human author, if he was also the composer, should put himself at the center of a musical *maṇḍala* in place of the deity is not surprising in a culture deeply permeated by the philosophy and practice of Tantra, a system of Hindu-Buddhist philosophy and practice in which the complete integration of the self with the divine and with the cosmos is sought (Gellner 1992, 190f.). Tantra has long been especially associated with kingship in South Asia (White 2000, 24 ff.), and the *maṇḍala* is a foundational metaphor in Tantra for the relationship of individual—especially the king—and cosmos.

To complete the connection with *dāphā* it is only necessary to note that this genre was originally performed in the Bhaktapur royal palace, where Ranjit Malla himself is believed to have participated in its composition and performance, and where court musicians and scholars might have had the skills and incentive to invent complex symbolic compositional schemes, and that it spread from there to the major civic temples (such as the Dattātreya and Bhairav temples in Bhaktapur) with the support of royal patronage (Widdess 2013, 47 ff.). The relationship proposed between musical and cosmic designs is therefore not merely an unmotivated resemblance or homology between otherwise unconnected cultural phenomena (as rightly called in question by Solomon [2008]), but reflects a fundamental symbolic pattern manifested in closely related cognitive domains, perhaps constituting a cultural model or "foundational schema" (Strauss and Quinn 1997; Shore 1996).

While there is more to be said in this connection in relation to the next example, what is perhaps equally important here is that the particular arrangement of *tāla* cycles is unique, at least in the current repertoire, to the present song. As far as I am

FIGURE 11.7 *Maṇḍala* of Cakrasaṃvara. Painting on cloth, Nepal, c. 1100. Metropolitan Museum of Art, New York. Public domain.

aware, no other song in the *dāphā* repertoire has exactly this structure. As my teacher put it, this song has "a special *tāl*"; as a *lālākhĩ* player, he would be particularly sensitive to this fact.[23] The same is probably true of the overall structure of *He Śiva Bhairava*. The point is that the heterometric structure of these pieces does not follow a template used in multiple items of repertoire; they are each unique. This has an important bearing on the cognitive aspects of heterometric music, to which I shall return.

Mahārudra Gvārā

The complex series of structural proportions that we have uncovered in *Girīhe nandinī* points to a connection with another repertoire of Newar religious music, called *gvārā*.[24] This is a type of composition sung and played by Buddhists in Bhaktapur and Patan, especially in connection with the festival of Gũlā, held toward the end of the rainy season in August each year. In this month-long festival, devout Buddhists of high and low caste engage in processions to worship Buddhist shrines in their locality. These processions are accompanied by groups of musicians, mostly members of the Buddhist community, playing the barrel-drum *dhã*. While walking in procession, the drummers, accompanied melodically by wind instruments,[25] play isometric pieces, each piece matched to a different section of the route (Wegner 2009). When they reach an important temple, wayside shrine, or Buddhist "monastery" (*vihāra, bahaḥ*), the group pause to play a *gvārā*.

This type of song seems to comprise a single through-composed stanza. The musical setting is quite long, however, and can include a number of metrical changes; songs are called "two-*tāl*," "three-*tāl*," "four-*tāl*," and so on (*domān, timān, caumān*), according to the number of different *tāl*s combined in the song. The whole verse is repeated six times, the drums playing different precomposed accompaniment patterns each time; indeed the drums appear to be the chief component of the music, the melody and text being of secondary importance (a feature of other South Asian musical genres: Wolf [2014, 9]). Learning to play all the variations for all the songs is a major challenge; it requires months of preparation, and is treated as a rite of passage for young members (now, both male and female) of the Buddhist community.

In addition to the *dhã*, in Patan large cymbals are clashed to mark the main *tāl* beats, and periodic blasts (coordinated rhythmically with the metrical structure) are blown on a group of *neku*—bamboo trumpets with goat-horn bells, and low-pitched trumpets made of buffalo horns (Greene 2003a; Wegner 2009). As the singers, usually seated at the center of the group, sing the song,[26] they perform large hand-gestures: claps and silent waves. These replicate the resonant and damped *tāl*-strokes (respectively) on the cymbals. The guru of the group uses these gestures to direct the whole ensemble, not unlike a Western conductor, but all the singers also perform the gestures to ensure coordination (Figure 11.8).[27] The drummers and cymbal players also follow these visual indications of the metrical structure of the piece. Thus the unfolding of the heterometric structure is a socially constructed and socially regulated process.

Figure 11.9 maps the structure of a heterometric *gvārā* performed in August 2011 in Patan, called *Mahārudra Gvārā* (Video 11. 1 ▶).[28] It comprises a sequence of *tāla*s: four cycles of 14 beats (*Dhalãjati*[29]), eight cycles of 4 beats (*Cautāl*), four cycles of 6 beats (*Palimā*), and 16 cycles of 7 beats (*Lava*). This structure features both time-span compression, in the proportions 7:4:3 and 1:1:2, and time spans of equal length but different internal articulation (Table 11.6):

FIGURE 11.8 Singers making time-keeping gestures while performing *Mahārudra Gvārā*. Ikhālakhu Nekujātrā and Matayājātrā group, Patan, Nepal, 2011. Photo: R. Widdess (still from video).

14 x 4 = 56
4 x 8 = 32
6 x 4 = 24
7 x 16 = 112

This kind of metrical architecture has also been noted in Newar Buddhist music by Ellingson, in an article titled "The Mathematics of Newar Music" (1996). Ellingson relates the proportional time spans of a *dāphā* song that he recorded in Patan to other Buddhist sonic and meditative practices based on numerical proportions, and concludes that "Buddhist music generally tends to emphasize musical structures based on organization of musical components (beats, phrases, sections, entire compositions included as parts of a larger musical suite) by multiples of prime numbers." Our earlier examples show, however, that heterometric structures are not limited to Buddhist Newar music. Indeed, as Ellingson acknowledges, it is difficult to draw a line between Hindu and Buddhist cultural forms in the Kathmandu Valley, since the two religions have coexisted and interacted there for centuries.

As we have seen, a common feature of both Buddhist and Hindu traditions in the Kathmandu Valley is the occurrence of the maṇḍala, not only as an aid to meditation (or a design to be imagined in meditation), but as a cross-domain cultural model or

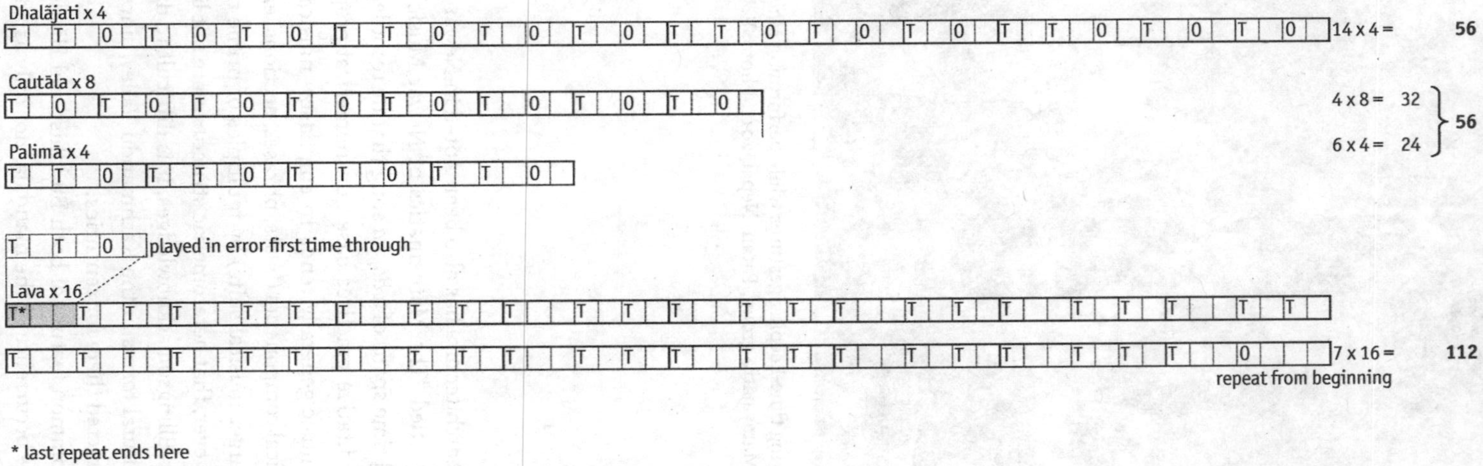

FIGURE 11.9 Proportional structure in *Mahārudra Gvārā*.

TABLE 11.6

Proportional structure in *Mahārudra Gvārā*.

Beats	Proportions		
56	7	1	
32	4		1
		1	
24	3		
112	14	2	1

foundational schema (Shore 1996, 53 f.; cf. Widdess 2006). Indeed, Wegner has described how in Bhaktapur, the processions celebrating Gūlā, in the context of which *gvārā* are performed, themselves trace conceptual maṇḍala-designs superimposed on the urban landscape (2009). Similar designs musically constructed by processional flute bands in Kathmandu, also at Gūlā, have been documented by Greene (2003b), and Ellingson has further described how a smaller-scale maṇḍala design can be constructed through dance (1990).

If metrical or time-span compression is an analog of the concentric, geometrically contrasted areas contracting toward the center of a maṇḍala, then it is no surprise to find this compositional technique in both Hindu and Buddhist contexts. What is of interest in the present inquiry is to find that heterometric temporal organization has been employed, in Newar music, to achieve metrical or time-span compression.[30] This finding helps us to understand how the pan-South Asian concept of *tāla* has been adapted to specific cultural preoccupations in a particular region.

HISTORICAL ANTECEDENTS

Given the diversity of genres in which the phenomenon of heterometric changes occurs, it is not surprising to find evidence for similar phenomena in historical literature. The sources of this evidence are music-theoretical treatises, that is, scholarly works referring to elite music of high-prestige, urban traditions. The question arises, however, in what respects these heterometric structures were analogous to those of present-day South Asian genres.

There are two principal historic genres in which heterometrical structure is described: *gītakas* and *prabandhas*.

Gītakas

The repertoire of *gītakas*, songs in praise of the gods, was performed during the preliminary ritual (*pūrvaraṅga*) before a classical Sanskrit drama.[31] They are described in the earliest surviving treatise on dramatic production, the *Nāṭyaśāstra* of Bharata, and in the earliest surviving treatise purely on music, the *Dattilam*; both texts are assumed to date from the Gupta period (second–fifth centuries A.D.), in which the Sanskrit drama reached its peak of development, but the *gītaka*s continue to be described in later music treatises up to the fifteenth century, although in practice they must have fallen out of use at the latest by the end of the first millennium A.D. They are described in the context of *tāla*-theory, because they were of exceptionally long and complex temporal structure. The temporal structure of each section was marked in performance by a clap-pattern, and the primary concern of the treatises is to codify these patterns.

The function of the *gītaka*s was to create an auspicious aura, purify the performance environment, and invite the gods to attend the drama, before the beginning of the narrative, scripted drama itself. They were performed by an ensemble comprising dancer(s), male and female singers, melodic instrumentalists (flute, harp, lute), and several percussionists (cymbals, drums of varying type). In this type of ensemble performance, which can be seen in sculptures of the Hindu-Buddhist period, any individual variation or improvisation must have been very limited in scope, as it is in *dāphā* and *gvārā*; the emphasis in the sources, and in the current genres, is on regulation and synchrony of group performance. The ensemble was coordinated by singers or other performers who marked the progress of each section by performing a set sequence of hand gestures: claps with right or left hand or both—presumably on the seated musicians' thighs—and silent gestures, with fingers closed or extended, palm up or down.[32] The audible claps could alternatively be sounded on cymbals (*kaṃsya-tāla*).

The use of sounded and silent gestures in the synchronization of a large performing group appears comparable with the Newar Buddhist *gvārā* performance practice (Figure 11.8). There are, however, important differences. Figure 11.10 represents, as an example, the structure of the *pāṇikā* genre, one of the *gītaka* forms described in early texts (Widdess 1981b). The song comprises three sections distinguished by metrical structure, composed of 32, 24, and 12 time-units respectively: the first section is composed of two identical subsections of 16 beats each, called *mukha* "face" and *pratimukha* "counterface."

The series of diminishing proportions 8:6:3 appears analogous to the proportional time-span compression we have noted in *Girīhe Nandinī* and *Mahārudra Gvārā*. It can, however, be argued that the clap-patterns prescribed for the *pāṇikā* and other *gītaka*s were not metrical but *hyper*metrical structures. The isochronous time-unit represented by squares in Figure 11.10 is not the tactus, but a measure (*kalā*) consisting of two, four, or eight tactus-beats (*mātrā*); this relationship (*mārga*) between *mātrā* and *kalā* apparently remained constant throughout a particular song. The *mātrā* was defined as a fixed time-unit of about one second in duration or slightly less (Lath 1978, 317; Clayton 2000, 77), so a *kalā*, even in its longest form, would have fallen within, or only slightly exceeded, the limits of the psychological present (2–7 seconds: London 2004, 30)[33] and short-term memory (5–9 seconds). It seems likely therefore that the *kalā* was easily perceptible as a cycle, while sections consisting of many *kalā*s would have been hypermetrical: that is, too long to be perceptible as such, but

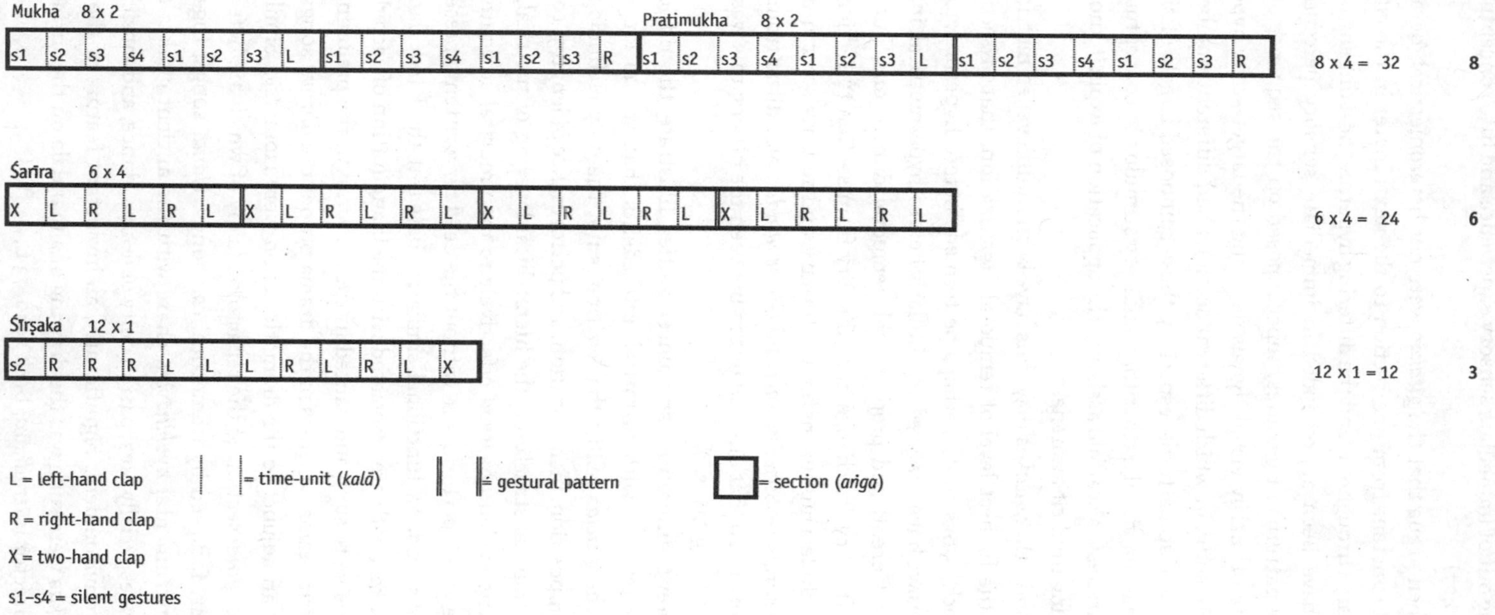

FIGURE 11.10 Structure of *pāṇikā* song.

rather "receding out of immediate sensory experience and into conceptual awareness" (Tenzer 2011b, 427).

One could then argue that the *gītaka*s were not heterometrical, because the *kalā*-cycle remained constant from one section to the next; meter in the *gītaka*s was isometric and binary throughout, and the differing hypermetrical dimensions of sections would hardly have been apprehended in immediate sensory perception. It would follow that the patterns of gestures, superimposed on the sequence of isochronous *kalā* cycles, were primarily visual signals denoting the larger-scale, hypermetrical architecture of the song, in which different sections had different numbers of isochronous *kalā*s. These clap-patterns, especially those composed largely of silent gestures, may have served as a visual, rather than auditory stimulus to conceptual, rather than perceptual awareness; a scaffold assisting the application of explicit knowledge rather than engendering implicit awareness.

The *pāṇikā* and other *gītaka*s may thus have been multilevelled metrical hierarchies in which only the highest level of temporal organization, that of sections, was heterometrical; such songs could perhaps be termed "hetero-hypermetrical." The three Newar examples we have analyzed are similarly hetero-hypermetrical, in that different sections have different, and proportional, temporal dimensions, but they are also *heterometrical*: their cycles change in cardinality from section to section, even within sections, and include a mixture of binary, ternary, and additive structures. The heterometrical *dāphā* songs *He Śiva Bhairavī* and *Girīhe nandinī* also differ from the *gītaka*s in being refrain forms, so that one *tāla* recurs between the others; this was not generally characteristic of the *gītaka*s.

These apparent differences and uncertainties illustrate the difficulty of comparing present practice with historical antecedents that are no longer performed. Nevertheless, the *gītaka*s tell us that writing is not the only technology available to support the composition, memorization, and performance of lengthy, complex hetero-hypermetrical musical structures: the hierarchical layering of metrical, melodic, and gestural patterns evidently served effectively to map musical structure conceptually and coordinate group performance without the need for written representations.[34]

We should also note a functional similarity between the *nāndī* dāphā songs and the ancient *gītaka*s: both are associated with the inauguration of sacred dance performances. *Gītaka*s were sung and danced in the *pūrvaraṅga*, the preliminary ritual preceding a Sanskrit drama, whereas in the drama proper the *dhruvā* songs sung, played, and danced as an adjunct to the dramatic action were isometric. Similarly, in *dāphā*, songs from the *nāndī* section of the repertoire, many of which are heterometrical, are performed first, followed by isometrical *cālī* songs. *Nāndī* songs, together with the preliminary instrumental *dyaḥlhāygu*, share with the ancient *gītaka*s the role of inviting the gods (especially Śiva, patron deity of drama, dance, and music) and ensuring an auspicious environment. Significantly, an important feature of the *pūrvaraṅga* in which the *gītaka*s were sung was the drawing of a maṇḍala on the surface of the stage by the stage-director (*sūtradhāra*; Beck 2012, 73 f., 81 ff.).

Although *dāphā* is not overtly a dance form today, singers believe that while the singing goes on, the gods dance invisibly in the space between the two antiphonal groups of singers. The music of *dāphā* should therefore be considered as dance music even if no dance can be seen. It is also likely that *dāphā* was closely related, in the seventeenth and early eighteenth centuries, to the Newar dance drama that was a favorite artform at court, patronized and indeed composed by many of the Newar kings themselves (Widdess 2013, 45). The term *nāndī* for the repertoire of initial songs appears in the documented dance dramas. It is a term that goes back to the *Nāṭyaśāstra*, where it denotes an introductory scene of the dance drama, following the *pūrvaraṅga* but before the start of the dramatic action proper. Songs in the current *dāphā nāndī* repertoire may have originated as *nāndī* songs performed in dance drama (see Widdess 2013, 238 ff. for an example).

We should note, furthermore, that the composers of seventeenth- to eighteenth-century dance drama, who in many cases were the same royal poet-musicians who composed the *dāphā* song repertoire, were aware of the *Nāṭyaśāstra* tradition of dance, dramatic theory, and musical theory. The earliest surviving manuscripts of the *Nāṭyaśāstra* itself, dating from the fifteenth century, are preserved in the Kathmandu National Archive. Also preserved are many later treatises in the same tradition, some imported from India, others composed locally. The local treatises are often attributed to the seventeenth-century Newar kings, and include a commentary on the *Nāṭyaśāstra* in Newari.[35] It is thus possible that some features of the ancient Indian dance drama were reconstructed in Newar dance drama on the basis of the textual tradition. This could include the creation of hetero-hypermetric compositions analogous to the *gītaka*s to serve as opening items in dance drama, spreading from there to *dāphā* and to the Buddhist *gvārā* repertoire. In the literate world of courtly culture, historical texts are not merely passive witnesses to ancient practices, but may actively support and influence the transmission or reinvention of such practices.

*Prabandha*s

Whatever connection there might be between the *gītaka*s and surviving genres, it must be an indirect one, as there is no record of the *gītaka*s themselves surviving as musical practice beyond around 1000 A.D. at the latest.[36] There may, however, have been a more direct link with the *prabandha* repertoire: a large repertoire of vocal composition-types, some associated also with dance, described in post-Bharata texts including the c. ninth-century *Bṛhaddeśī* of Matanga, the eleventh-century *Mānasollāsa*, and the thirteenth-century *Sangīta-ratnākara* (Rowell 1988, 1992b; Nijenhuis 2010). The rise of these poetic–musical types seems to reflect the decline of the Sanskrit theater with its elaborate rituals and group performance of music and dance, and the development in its place of soloistic musical performance as an artform independent of theater. Later texts, including the fifteenth-century *Saṅgīta-śiromaṇi* (Nijenhuis 1992) and the seventeenth-century *Saṅgīta-nārāyaṇa* (Katz 1987), imply the survival of some *prabandha* forms into the late medieval period, by which time the *dāphā* genre of Newar music was coming into existence.

The *Saṅgīta-ratnākara* catalogs and briefly defines 75 different *prabandha* forms, many of which have multiple varieties. The *prabandhas* are distinguished by musical and textual characteristics, but precise details of their metrical structure are not given. In some cases it is implied that a sequence of different *prabandhas* could be performed as a suite (Shringy and Sharma 1989, 221; Nijenhuis 2010), and in this case the *tālas* of successive songs might have been different. But the songs comprising such a suite are clearly considered to be separate items, complete in themselves. Still today in the dhrupad tradition, a typical performance option is to sing a sequence of compositions in the same *rāga* but in different *tāls*, and in progressively faster tempi; compositions in different *tāls* such as Cautāl, Dhamār, and Sūl or Tīvra have different musical and poetic characteristics, as the *prabandhas* of old must have done. However, these compositions are again individual items of repertoire that can be performed separately. Similarly, in *dāphā*, the daily singing session may be structured as a sequence of songs of different types and different *tāls* including *nāndi* and *cālī* songs according to a set pattern (Widdess 2013, 76 ff.). An ancient *prabandha* text that is still performed by *dāphā* groups is the *Gītagovinda* of Jayadeva (twelfth century), comprising 25 songs in different *rāgas*, *tālas*, and verse meters. The sequence of *gvārā* compositions performed at the Matyā festival in Patan where successive compositions feature different metrical, frequently heterometrical, structures, and are performed in different locations around the city, could also be regarded as a particularly elaborate and extended *prabandha*-like suite. In all these cases, again, each song is treated as a separate item that can be sung independently.

More germane to our inquiry, however, are a number of *prabandha* song-types in which two or more *tālas* were combined in a single song. In the earliest account of *prabandhas*, the *Bṛhaddeśī* of Mataṅga, which describes 48 *prabandha* types, three multi-*tāla* forms are mentioned:

śarabhalīlā has 8 lines, sung in 8 *rāgas*, and 8 *tālas* (v. 400[37])
vicitra has many regional languages, *tālas*, etc. (v. 402)
tribhaṅgī has 3 verse-meters, 3 *tālas* (v. 403)
caturaṅga has 4 *rāgas*, 4 *tālas* (v. 404)

These *prabandhas* are grouped together as song-types that exhibit multiplicity not only of *tāla* but also of other features—*rāga*, verse meter, language. We may suspect that they were intended to be particularly challenging and impressive show-pieces for their poet-composer-singers (*vāggeyakāra*).

Some centuries later, the thirteenth-century *Saṅgīta-ratnākara* lists nine *prabandhas* that have multiple *tālas* (*Saṅgīta-ratnākara* IV, vv. 145–52, 224–5, 253–86). The number of *tālas* in each song varies between two and five, with the exception of the *rāgakadambaka prabandha* (vv. 253–6), which could include four, eight, 16, or 32 *rāgas* along with the same number of *tālas*. Again, one assumes that the composition and performance of a song with so many *rāgas* and *tālas* would have been a soloistic tour de force: indeed the fifteenth-century commentator Kallinātha, commenting on these verses, cites an example of a *rāgakadambaka prabandha* with 32 *rāgas* and *tālas* composed by a famous contemporary musician, Gopāl Nāyak, implying that such an accomplishment was a rare and notable feat.

In her survey of the post-*Saṅgīta-ratnākara* history of *prabandhas*, E. te Nijenhuis (2010) shows that a number of forms with multiple *tālas*, typically also featuring the same number of *rāgas*, *rasas*, or languages, survived in practice at least into the sixteenth century and were in some cases performed at the Mughal court, presumably again as virtuoso show-pieces for their composer-singers; some of the same forms are mentioned in the seventeenth century by the Mughal writer Faqirullah (Sarmadee 1996, 93). Nijenhuis plausibly suggests that such compositions prefigure the *rāgamālā* of contemporary classical music, a composed or improvised sequence of different *rāgas* (but rarely if ever involving different *tālas*).

Considering the virtual disappearance of such multiplex forms from the classical music performance traditions today, Nijenhuis comments:

> Perhaps the musicians performing at the Mughal court preferred the less rigid [forms], such as the khayal, because song texts in strict poetical meter and songs composed in a large number of ragas and talas prevented them from showing their musical skills, their imagination, and voice culture. This may have been the reason why so many old song forms changed, disintegrated, or disappeared altogether. Sometimes, however, old musical forms are continued on various [different] cultural levels. (2010, 113)

Such cultural levels undoubtedly include Hindu devotional, Sikh, Sufi, and Newar Hindu–Buddhist religious traditions, in which we still find heterometrical compositions. Even in the classical Hindustani tradition, where skills of improvisation have become more important for professional success than knowledge of a large and varied repertoire, some musicians can still demonstrate composed songs that they call *prabandha*, some of which use different *tāls* in different sections of the song. Such songs are seldom if ever performed in public or included in notation-books, but they evidently preserve at least a distant memory of the earlier *prabandha* repertoire.

WHY DOES TIME CHANGE?

Even if we could definitively identify a channel of transmission to connect current heterometric forms in Newar music with historical traditions of South Asian music, we would still not have accounted for the existence of such forms in the first place.

What is it that commended the peculiar complexity of heterometric forms to particular communities and enabled their survival to the present? It would be premature, on the basis of an analysis of a few examples from just one local tradition, to do more than suggest possible approaches to the question, Why does time change in music? The possible answers turn out to be many and diverse, but not necessarily mutually exclusive.

In the specific examples of Newar song that we analyzed, we found that heterometrical structure is used to achieve effects of metrical compression, through contraction of the cycle or alternate contraction and expansion, which we interpreted as a process of intensification. Beyond its purely musical effect, the intensification observed highlights the composer-poet's name and the historical and political resonances evoked thereby. Heterometrical changes also articulate hypermetrical periods with proportionally related dimensions, suggesting analogies with cosmological and visual designs. But while the proportional relationships and quasi-maṇḍalic structures can hardly be fortuitous, they are likely to be a symptom of the specific historical context of Newar religious music—a literate courtly culture infused with esoteric *śāstric* and Tantric religious concepts.

Another possible answer to the question is that complex combinations of *tāla*, like multiplicity of *rāgas* or verse meters in a single song, demonstrate musical mastery of both composition and performance. The importance of tours de force can be understood in a context of competition between professional court musicians or composers, although classical musicians today prefer to demonstrate their powers of improvisation and technical virtuosity rather than of memory and structural complexity. This answer appears less immediately relevant to group performance of religious music, however, since demonstrating individual skill or knowledge is not normally the primary motivation for such performances.

For the present, and pending further research, two further answers to the question may be suggested, which certainly apply to the religious music repertoires we have been considering, and probably to others also. First, in the context of group religious ritual, the additional complexity of heterometric musical organization is of merit in itself, contributing to the overall complexity and emotional satisfaction of the ritual event. And second, periodic metric changes contribute to the attainment of a particular psychological state of collaborative engagement that is valued in the culture concerned.

Concerted Religious Effort

One might begin by observing that all of the South Asian genres I have noted in present practice that include heterometric forms are connected with religious observance. In the Newar context, they contribute to a phenomenon that I have termed elsewhere "concerted religious effort" (Widdess 2013, 218 ff.). By this expression I mean to suggest three things. First, performance of complex forms such as *dāphā* and *gvārā* requires a significant investment of time, energy, knowledge, and resources. Second, this investment is made collaboratively by members of a community, never by a single singer alone. Third, the objective of performance is not the music for its own sake, but the acquisition of religious merit and other broadly socioreligious benefits. Musical performance can be seen as analogous to, and frequently constitutive of, the many elaborate religious observances—sacrifices, vows, fasts, feasts, pilgrimages—that punctuate the Newar calendar, all demanding high levels of group exertion, expense, and social coordination—that is, concerted religious effort.

The Buddhist *gvārā* is a case in point. In Patan, the performance of heterometric *gvārā* is part of a complex religious observance, focusing on one day, Matyā, in the month of Gũlā (usually beginning in late August or early September). On this day, a group of about 40 musicians make a circuit of the town. They have been in training for several months, and they include many adolescents, both boys and girls.[38] Matyā happens every year, but each year it falls to a different neighborhood to provide the music group. As Patan is divided into 10 neighborhoods, each neighborhood is obliged to provide the music group at 10-year intervals. Consequently a new generation participates each year alongside older musicians, and the community of trained performers is renewed in each neighborhood on a regular basis—a citywide, but distributed collaborative social enterprise. In the days leading up to Matyā, rehearsals and preparatory rituals become ever more frequent, climaxing with an initiation ritual to Nāsaḥdyaḥ, the god of music and dance, at which the neophyte musicians are presented with their instruments and play together in public for the first time. The day of Matyā itself starts with a feast for all the musicians and their teachers, provided by the neighborhood. The group then makes its way from temple to temple around the city, pausing to sing a specific *gvārā* for each one. It is evening by the time they reach the former palace of the Newar kings in the center of the city, where they receive another feast. It is after midnight by the time they complete the circuit and arrive back in their own neighborhood, having sung 35 different *gvārās* in 35 different locations.

Here exceptional musical complexity seems to mirror the exceptional physical, mental, organizational, and financial effort involved in making the ritual processions and other observances undertaken at this season; the entire process is a collaborative social enterprise. The music with its complex structures is not the sole focus of activity, but neither is it dispensable. It is an integral component of the whole ritual complex that is Gũlā.[39] It could thus be argued that the performance of heterometric *gvārā* songs, requiring as it does not only collaborative performance but also extended preparation and training, is a musical expression of the ideal of concerted religious effort.

It should, however, be stressed that despite the financial and physical burdens involved in celebrating such festivals and rituals, many Newars derive palpable pleasure in such activities, and some festivals may be voluntarily extended to allow more enjoyment (especially the Gāijātrā festival: Widdess 2006). The younger musicians take obvious pride in wearing special dress and emblems declaring their membership of the music group and the neighborhood of the city that they represent (Figure 11.11). The objective of concerted religious effort may be a spiritual one, but it does not preclude enjoyment or a sense of social and individual well-being.

FIGURE 11.11 The Ikhālakhu Nekujātrā and Matayājātrā group, Patan, Nepal, 2011. Group photograph before the start of the Matyā procession around the city. The instruments used by the group are displayed on the rear wall. Photo: R. Widdess.

The Cognitive Dimension

From the point of view of cognitive processes and experience, heterometrical rhythm would seem to be an anomaly. Standard literature of musical cognition (e.g., Snyder 2000; Huron 2006; Hallam, Cross, and Thaut 2009; cf Clayton 2000) treats pulse and meter as manifestations of regularity, leading to prediction and expectation, and to bodily entrainment at the levels of tactus, cycle, and intermediate levels. Pulse and cycle are among the mechanisms by which participants and listeners make sense of music as it unfolds, and through entrainment, they become integrated into an embodied social experience. Heterometric temporal organization of the kinds we have been considering is seldom if ever considered in discussions of musical meter (a phenomenon that is itself difficult to define in a cross-culturally valid manner), and it challenges the assumption of regularity on which that concept rests.

Similarly, heterometric compositions in South Asia constitute an anomaly in the context of prevailing isometric rhythm. They tend to be less numerous, performed less frequently, and considered old, difficult, and requiring exceptional expertise or knowledge; in particular contexts they may have special significance, functions, or value. Some consideration of the cognitive psychology of music may help us to understand both the anomalous character of heterometrical music, and its significance.

Change of meter reduces the predictability of rhythmic structure. This has two consequences: first, heterometric structure constitutes explicit musical knowledge that must be learned. In Newar culture, music is traditionally a socially valued form of knowledge. For most genres, including both *dāphā* and *gvārā*, a rigorous group training process must precede licensed performance; this is a social process, conducted in secrecy, and framed by rituals (Widdess 2013, 207 ff.). Whereas in isometric music, each *tāla* (associated, in some traditions, with a drum *ṭhekā*) is a cognitive schema or template employed in many compositions, in heterometric music, the sequence of *tāla*s is probably unique to each composition (though this is hard to verify). Avoidance of standard metrical templates increases the degree to which explicit knowledge of individual compositions is required. Recall from memory is an active process of reconstruction (Bartlett 1932; Treitler 1974); heterometric compositions impose a greater burden on recall, as witness the relatively small number of them surviving in current repertoire.

The second consequence of the reduced predictability of rhythmic structure is that entrainment at the cycle level is reduced. While such entrainment may occur during isometrical sections of a song, every change of meter, at or between section boundaries, causes what London (2004, 108) calls an "indirect [metrical] dissonance": dissonant, because two metrical structures conflict; indirect, because they occur in succession rather than simultaneously. London writes that the listener's entrained expectations continue into, and therefore conflict with, the new metrical structure: the musical surface

> must contain various cues for an alternate metrical construal, such as a change in the period or phase of one or more levels of the meter. One effect of these mismatches is that listeners may become more aware of their metric sensibilities and activities; they must exert more effort to maintain an attentional framework.

In the examples we have considered, the principal cue for "alternate metrical construal" is the time-line pattern of cymbal-strokes and hand-gestures, together perhaps with drum-patterns, and in the case of the final section of *He Śiva Bhairava*, a marked change in tactus-beat. But while the listener can afford to be confused for a moment until entrainment to the new cycle sets in, performers must know in advance how and when to execute the change. This brings us back to the necessity of explicit knowledge.

It might be argued that the phenomena of cycle-length reduction and time-span compression constitute cognitive templates of a more general kind than meter, and a manifestation of the process identified by Henry (2002) as "intensification": the increase in arousal produced by increasing musical parameters such as loudness, pitch, and tempo. Reduction in cycle length no doubt produces a perceptible rhythmic intensification, although the interpolation of repetitions of a refrain in *He Śiva Bhairava* disrupts the metrical intensification produced by reduction of cycle length; in both this song and *Girīhe nandinī* the cycles alternately contract and expand again. But proportional relationships between hypermetrical time spans as in *Girīhe nandinī* and *Mahārudra Gvārā* are more difficult, if not impossible, to apprehend as such in real time. This is because the time spans concerned far exceed in length the capacity of short-term memory and the psychological sense of the present. Proportional time-span manipulation is therefore likely to be a compositional technique apparent only to experts.

It is well known that in human behavior, selected aspects of a complex cognitive task are frequently externalized, to free cognitive processing power. In vocal music the realisation of metrical or formal schemas as patterns of physical gestures or of sounds played on instruments would be a case in point. In many cultures, the use of writing, for language and music, is another. Heterometric music in South Asia is indeed associated with a cultural emphasis on writing. Repertoires like the *ravish* of Amir Khusrau, the Sikh *Ādi Granth*, and the *dāphā* and *gvārā* songbooks, are transmitted in written texts that specify the words and often convey metrical and modal information. In Patan and Bhaktapur, in what is probably a recent development, handwritten or printed notations of the *tāla* structures of *gvārā* songs are used by some music groups, in training or performance (Śākya and Śākya 1987; Śākya 1995; Śākya and Śākya 1996). In such notations, especially printed ones, changes in hypermetrical temporal organization may become visible, as geometrical shapes on the page, and hence apparent to performers in a way they may not have been before the use of such notation (Figure 11.12).[40]

Whether or not such aids are used, the additional cognitive effort required in order to recall and perform heterometric pieces may explain the physical behavior of Newar musicians, who typically make exaggerated time-keeping gestures, and watch carefully the gestures made by other members of the group, while performing such songs. Such physical behavior implies a highly alert cognitive state. Gert-Matthias Wegner, who has participated in Newar music for several decades, comments that unlike many genres of devotional and classical music in South Asia where incessant isometrical rhythm allows trance-like states of mind to occur, heterometric music such as *gvārā* "calls for an increase of presence of the performers' minds, of 'being there'" (personal email dated April 23, 2012). This perception accords with London's observation that in conditions of indirect metrical dissonance, participants "must exert more effort to maintain an attentional framework" (2004, 108).

A state of deep concentration and engagement focused on one activity to the exclusion of all others, called "flow" (Csikszentmihalyi 1990, 2002), has been associated with many participatory musical styles (Turino 2008, 4) including *dāphā* (Widdess 2013, 126ff.). We may suppose that performers in such a state would be better able to cope collaboratively with the demands of heterometric time changes than those in either a normal relaxed state, or a state of trance. Similarly, in the isometric *cālī* songs of *dāphā*, although singers do not normally have to change meter, they have to repeat each line in a complex pattern of responsorial alternation, including changes of tempo, which similarly requires considerable presence of mind to execute correctly. *Dāphā* singers value the freedom from other mental preoccupations and the social collaboration that engagement in such complex group performance confers: they are able to sustain lengthy singing sessions (two to three hours, or more for *Gītagovinda* performances) without feeling tired. These are typical manifestations of the flow state.

भगवान ग्वाराया म्येया बोल

+ १	२	० ३	४	+ १	२	० ३	४
श्री	ऽ	ऽ	ऽ	भ	ऽ	ऽ	ऽ
ग	ऽ	ऽ	ऽ	वा	ऽ	न	ऽ

+ १	२	+ १	२	० ३	४
मा	ऽ	म	ऽ	ऽ	कि
लो	ऽ	च	ऽ	ऽ	नि
प	ऽ	द्म	ऽ	ऽ	नि
ता	ऽ	रा	ऽ	हा	दे

+ १	२	० ३	४	+ १	२	+ १	२	० ३	४
च	ऽ	तु	ऽ	र्दि	ऽ	ग	ऽ	ऽ	ऽ
भ	ऽ	ग	ऽ	वा	ऽ	न	ऽ	ऽ	ऽ
मो	ऽ	क्ष	ऽ	दा	ऽ	ता	ऽ	हा	दे

+ १	२	३	+ १	२	० ३	४
त्रै	ऽ	ऽ	लो	ऽ	ऽ	क्य
इ	ऽ	ऽ	श्व	ऽ	र	ऽ
म	ऽ	ऽ	हा	ऽ	आ	ऽ
बु	ऽ	ऽ	द्ध	ऽ	हा	हादे

० १	२	३	+ १	२	+ ३	४
श्री	ऽ	ऽ	ध	ऽ	ऽ	ऽ
र्म	ऽ	ऽ	अ	ऽ	अ	ऽ
धा	ऽ	ऽ	आ	ऽ	आ	ऽ

तु

५९

FIGURE 11.12 Page from a modern notation-book showing heterometric structure of a *gvārā* song (Śākya 1995).

The involvement of young people in the performance of *gvārā* and other music for the Buddhist festival of Gūlā has a strong social element: they often wear special uniforms emblazoned with the group's name and emblems, and enjoy social interaction at rehearsals, group visits to nearby shrines, and feasts, as well as the climactic concerted religious effort of performance on festival days. As Csikszentmihalyi argues, group sports, games, and music are all *designed* to induce a shared experience of "flow" (2002, 72ff.). In combination with other musical and social factors, therefore, heterometric temporal organization may have contributed to the popularity and apparently continuous social transmission of *dāphā* and *gvārā* performance over several centuries.

But as Csikszentmihalyi also notes, achieving flow requires a balance between the competence of the participant and the technical challenge of the activity: if challenge is either too low or too high in relation to competence, flow will give way to either boredom or frustration respectively (2002, 42 ff.). In *dāphā*, the pattern of responsorial alternation and tempo changes performed in *cālī* songs is apparently neither too easy, nor too difficult for flow to occur; but heterometrical time-changes may be, for some groups at least, too challenging, with the exception of a few well-known songs. In *gvārā*, the intensive training and memorization required evidently serves to overcome the cognitive challenge of heterometrical temporal organization, at least for the duration of the festival while the repertoire is fresh in memory.

The energy and commitment shown by teachers and performers of *dāphā* and *gvārā* is remarkable, and has succeeded in maintaining complex repertoires in practice to the present day. But these repertoires did not originate in the residential neighborhoods of Bhaktapur and Patan where they are now taught and performed. Both *dāphā* and *gvārā* show unmistakable evidence of origins in the elite context of palace and royal temple, where they would have been composed and performed originally by professional musicians, scholars, and kings. These would no doubt have had the theoretical knowledge and technical skills to compose and perform songs with complex metrical structures, in the tradition of heterometrical *prabandhas* and *gītakas*. A similar historical transmission from palace musicians to the general populace, aided by the shared experience of "flow," may help explain the occurrence, albeit comparatively rarely, of heterometrical songs in other parts of South Asia.

Further investigation would undoubtedly reveal additional examples of heterometric musical forms in South Asia, and shed more light on the factors that make such forms meaningful. For the present, we can conclude that these factors include musical, historical, social, cultural, and psychological aspects, all of which need to be considered in a comparative mode embracing different religious and regional traditions in order to appreciate more fully the richness and significance of musical rhythm in South Asia.

ACKNOWLEDGMENTS

This chapter would have been impossible to write without the generous assistance of many individuals and groups in Bhaktapur and Patan. I thank them all, and especially: Shamsher Nhuchen Pradhan, Nutandhar Sharma, Buddhalal Manandhar, Panchalal Lachimasyu, Pushparatna Shakya, Mohan Shilpakar, and the following groups: Dattatreya Navadāphā and Bhairavnāth Navadāphā groups (Bhaktapur), and the Ikhālakhu Nekujātrā and Matayājātrā group of V.S. 2068 = A.D. 2011 (Patan). I thank Gert-Matthias Wegner, Simonne Bailey, the editors, and anonymous readers for their constructive comments. I am also most grateful to the Spalding Trust for financially supporting my visit to Patan in 2011.

NOTES

1. For a comprehensive account of rhythm and meter in Hindustani music see Clayton (2000). In this chapter I use "Hindustani" and "Karnatak" to denote North Indian and South Indian classical music respectively.

2. For the term *heterometric* see for example Bartók (1931, 46f.); Nettl (1964, 148); Malm (1977, 7); Savage, Merritt, Rzeszutek, and Brown (2012, 102). Some authors prefer terms such as *irregular meter* (e.g. Lomax 1968, 49), but with some risk of confusion with *additive* or *aksak* meters.

3. I use this word-form in preference to "nonisochronous" on etymological grounds (*a(n)-* being the appropriate negative prefix for words of Greek origin). No difference of meaning is implied.

4. I adopt the spelling *tāl* for specific *tāla*s of Hindustani and Newar music, following vernacular pronunciation, and *tāla* for the theoretical concept common to various regional traditions.

5. The *mātrā* can be subdivided into shorter time-units, but the *mātrā* normally remains the emic time-unit of reference, except in very slow or very fast tempo (Clayton 2000, 82 ff.).

6. For this notation of metrical hierarchy see Lerdahl and Jackendoff (1996, 19ff.) and Clayton (2000, 47ff.).

7. An analogous function is performed by the *lehrā*, a repeated melody one cycle in duration, played on sārangī or harmonium to accompany a tabla solo.

8. The existence of time-lines in *tāla*, and their role in maintaining cardinality, especially highlighted in the context of heterometric music, necessitates retaining the concept of meter as a template or schema. This, however, is not a complete representation of the cognitive experience of metrical music, for which changes of internal articulation or surface rhythm should also be taken into account (London 2004, 84 ff.).

9. See Clayton (2000, 95–106) for discussion of this issue.

10. The most familiar such exception is the style of *ālāp* practiced in Hindustānī khayāl, following the introduction of a metrical composition, during which the tablā maintains an isometric *ṭhekā* throughout. In Karnatak *periya mēḷam* music, the *tavil* drums may play a metrical cycle during *ālāpana*. In Hindustani *dhrupad*, the *pakhāvaj* drum may do likewise during the last, fast-tempo stage of *ālāp*. Such accompaniments normally seem to be isometrical.

11. One may also note various genres of percussion music, typically processional, in which metrically differing patterns or items are played in sequence (e.g., Wolf 2014, 56–8, etc.). Since this chapter was written, two further examples of vocal genres with changing tāla have come to my attention. The *Gaura-candrikā* songs of the Bengali *padāvalī-kīrtan* devotional genre feature a sequence of tālas with proportional metrical compression (see later) (Graves

2017). In songs of the *sulādi* genre of South India (fifteenth to seventeenth centuries), successive verses were in different tālas, each verse probably originating as an independent song (Rao 2015).

12. "Har jas gavho Bhagavan," recorded by Bhai Avtar Singh Ragi on CD Magnasound D6–N2701 *Gurubani kirtan* (available on iTunes).

13. Information from Baldeep Singh, whom I have heard render *partāl* compositions in this way.

14. "Qalbana—Tarana—Ustad Iqbal Ahmad Khan Sahab" (http://youtu.be/qz_hsP_hOfQ). See also "Qalbana- Ustad Bahauddin Khan Qawwal" (http://youtu.be/_9Qg8a1Itgg).

15. The Newar are an ethnic group who claim to be the original inhabitants of the Kathmandu Valley, which they ruled until 1769. Their language, Newari, belongs to the Tibeto-Burman language family, but includes many loan-words from Sanskrit, Hindi, and Nepali.

16. In the past dāphā was cultivated by high-caste participants attached to the royal court of Bhaktapur. The dāphā group of the royal Taleju Temple survived until the 1980s and was exclusively high-caste (information from G. M. Wegner, personal email dated April 23, 2012). Today the Nakhīlibi group is the only functioning high-caste dāphā group in Bhaktapur.

17. G. M. Wegner points out that there are many examples of heterometrical structure in Newar instrumental music, and also in the music of the Navadurga dancers of Bhaktapur (personal email dated April 23, 2012).

18. I am indebted to Dr Nutandhar Sharma of Patan for his expert assistance in reconstructing the song-text from manuscript songbooks and in making the provisional translation. The reconstructed text given here therefore differs from the text in Ex. 1, which is closer to that sung by the Bhairavnāth and Dattātreya groups. A definitive version of *dāphā* texts is not possible given the discrepancies between manuscripts and between singing groups.

19. That is, cycles comprising segments of unequal length, e.g., 3 + 2 + 2 beats.

20. The name, correctly Raṇajita, is usually spelled *Ranajita* in dāphā songbooks, and is commonly pronounced and spelled Ranjit.

21. I am again indebted to Nutandhar Sharma for his work on the text and translation.

22. The table does not take account of the repetitions of this section in the recorded performance; such repetition between the two groups of singers is standard practice in all dāphā songs. In the performance recorded, the last tāl cycle of A overlaps with the first cycle of its repetition, reducing the length to 7 cycles. On the last repetition, however, the full 8 cycles are performed.

23. In *dāphā*, the *lālākhī* drum does not play a repeated *ṭhekā* as does the tabla in more recent styles of classical and religious music, but a through-composed sequence of varied patterns that fit the metric dimensions of the song. My teacher was thus regarding this precomposed accompaniment as "the *tāl*" for this song.

24. In Bhaktapur, *gvarāḥ*.

25. In Patan the shawm (*mvālī*) is used to play the melody. In Bhaktapur this instrument is played for low-caste groups; for high caste groups, Western trumpet and clarinet are employed (see Wegner 2009).

26. In Patan the singing appears to be approximately on a monotone, but is hard to hear because of the loud percussion accompaniment.

27. In Bhaktapur there is no group of singers, and most of the performers are playing instruments; but the leader of the group, while playing thick-walled cymbals (*tāḥ*), and any other participants whose hands are sufficiently free, gesture in a similar way to the Patan singers.

The musicians, however, learn to sing the words, and according to Simonne Bailey the melody sung is the same as that played on trumpet and clarinet (personal email dated April 23, 2012).

28. Recorded on video by the author. Once again the assistance of Nutandhar Sharma is gratefully acknowledged. The words are again in praise of Bhairav, who is venerated by Buddhists as well as Hindus.

29. The names of *tāls* differ between Patan and Bhaktapur, and between *gvārā* and *dāphā*.

30. I cannot, however, assert that heterometric structures in dāphā and gvārā *always* display proportional time spans in quasi-*maṇḍalic* sequences. This requires further analysis.

31. See Rowell (1988; 1992a, 252 ff.); Nijenhuis (1970, 317 ff.); Lath (1978, 313); Widdess (1981b); Beck (2012, 79 ff.).

32. A number of early Buddhist reliefs showing music and dance performance include a small group of performers clapping or making silent gestures. These may also have been singers.

33. London (2004, 30) defines the psychological present as "the time interval in which sensory information and concurrent behavior are to be integrated within the same span of attention."

34. There is no evidence that melodic musical notation was used to represent the *gītaka*s at the time of the *Nāṭyaśāstra*. Notated songs in the *Sarasvatīhṛdayālaṃkāra* of Nānyadeva (c. 1100) may well be late reconstructions or recompositions, and those in the fifteenth-century *Saṅgīta-rāja* of Kumbhakarṇa manifestly are.

35. An early seventeenth-century rāgamālā set painted in Bhaktapur includes a named figure of Bharata holding the text (Wegner and Widdess 2004).

36. Abhinavagupta, author of a commentary on the *Nāṭyaśāstra* around 1000 A.D., is alleged to have based his interpretation of that text on direct experience of the music described, in his native Kashmir (Lath 1978, 76 ff.). This claim appears rather tenuous.

37. I follow the numbering of verses in the edition and translation by Sharma and Beohar (1994).

38. The involvement of women in Newar musical performance has been an ongoing development during the last two decades.

39. See Wegner (2009) for parallel rituals in Bhaktapur.

40. The figure shows part of a representation of a *gvārā* (*Bhagavān Gvārā*) with five sections in different *tāls*, as performed in Bhaktapur, from Śākya (1995). Each small rectangle corresponds to one tactus beat; each row represents one or two cycles of the *tāl*. o and + denote damped (*chu*) and undamped (*tin*) cymbal-strokes respectively; beats are numbered beginning from each +. Syllables of the song-text are arranged in the grid for each *tāl*; S = continuation of the preceding syllable.

12

"Rhythm," "Beat," and "Freedom" in South Asian Musical Traditions

Richard K. Wolf

IN THIS CHAPTER I argue that a family of common rhythmic conceptions underlies many of the musical traditions of South Asia despite sometimes dramatic regional differences in language, culture, and religion. I'll focus on two contrasting kinds of rhythmic representation: one that objectifies through names and numbers, and one that points toward freedom and resists numeration. As representations, both of these lie in the realm of what Christopher Hasty calls R2 in this volume. Yet an emphasis on freedom and unboundedness points toward subjective experience, the realm of Hasty's R1.

Philosophical traditions in many parts of the world touch on some aspect of the divide between theorizing music through the act of labeling and understanding music through unmediated experience. This divide is manifested in South Asian musical worlds through the ways in which reflective individuals of diverse background think about music in relation to prevailing spiritual commonplaces. Various forms of emphasis on "the word" in Islam and Hinduism, for instance, inform the tendency of some musicians to map instrumental patterns onto the structure of verbal phrases. Quasi-spiritual ideas about improvisation, by contrast, may undergird the resistance some Karnatak musicians express toward the idea that *rāga ālāpana* flows in accordance with definable rhythmic principles.

A tiny window into the range of sentiments associated with improvisation is provided by the way Karnatak music theorists classify their music into *manodharma* (improvisational) or *kalpita* (composed). The term *dharma* means "duty," "practice," or "law," and carries a heavy moral burden in Hindu discourse in association with religious merit. As part of a compound with the Indic term for the heart-mind (*manas*) as a bodily locus of thought, creativity, and emotion, *manodharma* means something like "dharma of the heart/mind" or "guided by imagination." In contrast, the adjective for the realm of composed music is *kalpita*, meaning "fabricated" or "well arranged." Anxieties about the realm of the imagination inform the ways theorists in South Asia have treated both tone and time. As Lewis Rowell put it, the emphasis of early theorists on rhythmic control seemed to respond to a worry that "time's power must be continually held in check lest it run away with us" (1992b, 181). A concern for the converse is common among musicians who treat the *ālāpana* as a protected domain, seemingly impervious to the strictures of composition or *tāla*: any attempt to keep time in check would be tantamount to treading on *ālāpana*'s dharmic status.

To understand the tension between constraint and freedom in South Asian music, we need to consider what are, for musicians, the fundamental units of rhythmic thought: pulses, beats, phrases, goal tones or anchor points, phrases, syllables and other linguistic utterances, or something different still.[1] We must also consider how these are interrelated and/or set against a background or reference system. This background might be manifested through repeating instrumental patterns or hand gestures; it might exist solely in a musician's conscious awareness; or we might infer it from practice, hypothesizing that a tacit system is maintained through what psychologists call implicit learning.

Before turning to specifics it will be helpful to note that the dominant reference system for rhythm in South Asia concerns *tāla*. A *tāla*, in South Indian classical (Karnatak) music, is a metrical structure articulated with a series of claps and finger counts. In Hindustani (North Indian and Pakistani classical) music, the *tāla* can be also be shown through hand gestures, but unlike in the South it can be directly embodied in drum patterns (*ṭhekas*), and melodies (*lehra*). *Tāla* theories currently in use and some of the rhythmic theory available to scholars via historical treatises (e.g., the thirteenth-century *Sangītaratnākara* and the eleventh-century *Abhinavabhāratī*) shed comparative light on contemporary practices outside the classical mainstream. However, new models are needed to understand the relationships among a variety of other genres, both within the classical repertoires and throughout the wider world of functional performance: in Sufi shrines, at temples, in religious processions, and a variety of other contexts outside the cloisters of art-music exposition and pedagogy. Scholars have not often considered possibilities for understanding rhythmic coherence across diverse genres in South Asia in terms that extend beyond the canonical *tāla*-related principles. A growing body of scholarship does, however, identify rhythmic properties that are idiosyncratic to *ālāp* (Widdess 1994; 1995; Clayton 1996; 2000), folk drumming (Manuel 2015; Sykes 2011; Schreffler 2002) and even tanbura playing (Clayton 2007); and in this volume Richard Widdess describes what he calls "heterometric temporal organization"—successive pulse groupings of different lengths organized into a larger structure—which, he suggests, can be found in a number of South Asian functional musics.

My attempt to offer frameworks for such a comparative discussion draws from fieldwork spanning the years 1982–2019 in India (about seven years), Pakistan (a year),

Tajikistan (two years), Northern Afghanistan (short visits once or twice a year, 2015–2019) as well as 37 years' experience as a South Indian classical *vīṇā* player. In the present context I'll be making brief reference to musical examples that are discussed more fully in chapters 3 and 4 of my book *The Voice in the Drum: Music, Language and Emotion in Islamicate South Asia* (Wolf 2014). In that book and in this chapter I understand "rhythm" as *the organization of events in time*. In accepting this widespread general understanding of rhythm, I make no assumptions concerning the isochrony of constituent units at any level of rhythmic activity. This inclusive definition of rhythm differs from others that, explicitly or implicitly, rely on the idea of regularly recurring units. Regularity is but one possible aspect of rhythmic organization. Every action has rhythm because it unfolds over time; thus events might exhibit different degrees of rhythmic regularity or dynamic emphasis, but not, in my usage, "more" or "less" rhythm per se. The point is to describe the specific qualities of a given rhythmic texture.

My use of the term melody takes into account a number of related ethnomusicological concepts, including A. M. Jones's notion of African drumming "tunes" (1959, I:61ff.), José Maceda's idea of melodies as arrangements of articulations "with or without pitch" (Maceda 1974, 247), and Meki Nzewi's neologism *melo-rhythm*, "a rhythmic organization that is melodically conceived and melodically born. This kind of organization should be recognized as having a different orientation than the kind in which the rhythm of a music has a more independent derivation and function" (Nzewi 1974, 24). Nzewi was arguing for the distinctiveness of "West African folk music" in comparison with "Western percussive style," but I believe the problem is not one of cultural difference but one that arises from the imprecision of the term melody, especially when it is explicitly or implicitly contrasted with "rhythm."[2]

"Melody," as commonly understood, depends on horizontal sequences of tones. "Rhythm" is already built into melody: without time, melody would collapse into a set of pitches (even if, in the case of South-Indian-classical and other melodies involving portamento, an infinitesimal set of pitch gradations would be needed to capture a contour—analogous to derivatives in differential calculus). An unfortunate slippage in the English language equates "a rhythm" with a particular pattern articulated on the drums. However, a percussion pattern is no more rhythmic than is a melody. The pattern has a rhythm but the drummed articulation should not be confused with "a rhythm." A drum pattern is rather a kind of melody that is (usually) dominated by timbral rather than tonal distinctions. With this in mind, I find it useful to think of melodies as patterns of tones and timbres and to distinguish between tone-melodies and stroke-melodies rather than between melodies and rhythms. Stroke melodies are patterns differentiated by aspects of timbre and articulation more than by discrete tones. As we shall see, strumming patterns on a stringed instrument and drum patterns are, each in their own ways, stroke-melodies.

My discussion of *rāga ālāpana* branches out from my 2010 article on the rhythmic properties of this genre. *Ālāpana* is often characterized in terms of its lack of meter, pulse, and, according to some usages, rhythm. However, based on the idea that all melodies have rhythm it is necessary to investigate what characterizes the rhythm(s) of *rāga ālāpana*. Percussion-dominated ritual genres may seem oddly matched with *rāga ālāpana* for a discussion of rhythm. However, comparing phenomenally disparate material can, through the "very disparateness" of the subject matter lead to "deeper understanding" (Blum 1975, 226; Geertz 1968, 55; see also Wolf 2009). Already it should be apparent that drum patterns can be viewed as kinds of melodies and that *rāga ālāpana*, as a melodic form, ought to receive rhythmic attention. Moreover, the genres to be examined here, each in their own ways, call into question concepts of "rhythm," "beat," and "freedom," used to varying degrees in both vernacular and scholarly discourses (in and beyond South Asia).

The concern here is not merely with the ways in which English terms such as beat or rhythm are used, for these terms are readily borrowed (with varying degrees of precision) by speakers of Tamil, Hindi/Urdu, and other South Asian languages. More important are uses of analogous terms in several languages of South Asia, which include or contain derivations from Tamil, Sanskrit, Persian, and Arabic. These may point toward cognitive processes that are nevertheless culturally and socially shaped (cf. Blacking 1971, 95 and passim).

RHYTHM IN SOUTH ASIA

In India and Pakistan as in America, the English term rhythm is used with considerable flexibility. Rhythm may refer to temporal phenomena including tempo and meter; it may refer to the instrumental accompaniment for a song, embracing but not limited to the percussion part (much in the way some use the English word music for instrumental music and not for singing); and it may refer to the presence of a discernible beat. There is little point in attempting to enumerate all the possible uses of the term in scholarship and everyday speech.

The Sanskrit term *laya*, with its variety of local derivatives including *lay* in Hindi-Urdu and *layam* in Tamil, holds a similar range of meanings, both broad and narrow (see, e.g., Powers 1980, 118 and Kippen in this volume). The musical definitions for *laya* in the authoritative Monier-Williams Sanskrit dictionary include "(in music) time (regarded as of three kinds, viz. *druta*, 'quick,' *madhya*, 'mean or moderate,' *and vilambita*, 'slow,')" and "a kind of measure, *Saṃgīt*; the union of song, dance and instrumental music." Tempo is the most common narrow definition of *laya* in modern Indian languages.

A key meaning of the term *laya* is "the act of sticking or clinging to," with additional usages including "lying down, repose," and "melting . . . absorption in." What are the connections between the obviously musical and nonmusical meanings of this term? Many words are polythetic, possessing meanings that are not reducible to a singular idea. We might imagine how "tempo" and "the act of sticking to" would be related, but no link between these ideas is self-evident. For the purpose of understanding historical conceptions of a term, an etymology resulting in lists of definitions into which we can only imagine interrelations is insufficient. We need to know if and how users of such a term have drawn connections among its possible meanings. The *Abhinavabhāratī* (c. 1000 C.E.), theorist Abhinavagupta's commentary on Bharata's *Nāṭyaśāstra*, provides a helpful clue in this regard by describing a divinely embodied equilibrium of worldly activities composed of *kalā, kāla*, and *laya*. Abhinavagupta likens the relations of these three to the oft-mentioned cycle of creation (differentiation—*kalā*), maintenance (time flow—*kāla*), and destruction (dissolution, entropy, rest—*laya*) of the universe in Hindu cosmology. The relation between the musical divisions of time (*kalā*) and the periods of quiescence or rest that separate the articulations of those divisions is what, for Abhinavagupta and others, composes *laya*.[3] *Laya*, then, is the metaphorical glue holding together musical articulations, whether these be struck, plucked, blown, sung, or merely felt.[4] The tension between action and repose inherent in the performance of much *tāla*-based South Asian music is well modeled by this idea of stickiness—with all the possibilities of elasticity it might imply. *Laya* as "rest" is also compatible with the idea of a musical rest in European notation: if one increases the distances between articulations, the tempo slows; if one reduces them, the tempo increases.[5]

The use of the term *laya* by performers in the drumming tradition associated with the shrine of Nizamuddin Auliya in New Delhi is consistent with broader North Indian and Pakistani usages and illustrates further the idea that *laya* is not merely a measurement or a tempo but is also akin to a substance. Exponents of the Nizamuddin drumming tradition include a professional Hindu troupe of professional musicians in India led by a master named Mamraj and a group of laborers in Karachi, Pakistan, who are otherwise unskilled in music. The ancestors of the drummers in Karachi once lived near the Nizamuddin shrine and migrated to Pakistan at the time of the partition of India and Pakistan in 1947. In Jacob Lines, Karachi they established a parallel set of religious and musical practices for their own transplanted Nizamuddin shrine.

In Delhi, Mamraj, band-leader and master of the shallow, bowl-shaped drum called the *tāsha*, described the role of his drum in as "building the *lay*" (*lay bāndhnā*; Wolf 2014, 103) in the ensemble. The *ḍhol* (a cylindrical drum providing the bass) provides the sparse cycle of articulations that defines the repertoire item; the accompaniment *tāsha*s fill in the bass strokes with continuous subdivision patterns; and then individual *tāsha* players, one by one, "build the *lay*" by performing improvisational solos against this background.

Moving to the Pakistani counterpart of this group, the *ḍhol*-playing floor-maker Hashim referred to *lay* analogously as getting "built" by the *tāsha* inside a piece of *marsiyah* lament poetry whose words are outlined on the *ḍhol* (Wolf 2014, 304n2). In both the Delhi and Karachi branches of the Nizamuddin tradition, the drummers are talking about the ways in which the improvisational part, which can vary dense and sparse strings of articulations, creates interest *in relation* to a fixed frame articulated by the *ḍhol*s. It doesn't merely fill in the intervals between *ḍhol* strokes, but "builds" something called *lay*. *Lay* entails a process of pushing and pulling, or relating to temporal anchor points (Wolf 2005). *Lay* is substantial and deeply implicated in the musicality of this tradition.

Laya in South India can mean tempo, but it can also refer to one's sense of musical time. It is related to *kālapramāṇam* ("time-measure" or "time-rule"), the pace of a performance. In Karnatak music today, *kaḷā* refers to the first level of possible subdivisions of a *tāla* count: for example, an 8 count *tāla* such as *ādi* can be reckoned in terms of one, two, or four subcounts depending on the overall tempo of the composition; and those subcounts may be filled with varying numbers of pulses depending on details of the musical surface, whether that surface is composed or improvised.[6] *Kālam* (in Tamil) refers to time-period in general and to fixed speeds of rendition in music: the same musical material can be played in different *kālams*, speeds that are integer or simple-fraction multiples of the base speed. Modern uses of the terms *laya, kalā/kaḷā*, and *kāla* in South India, then, are strikingly consistent with those of Abinavagupta more than a millennium ago.

Experiencing *laya*, like rhythm more generally, entails awareness of multiple hierarchical levels: in this case, an outer layer that is sparse and (relatively) fixed, an inner layer of denser, variable texture, and the possibility of an intervening stratum. Rhythmic processes in South Asia may involve elements that are audible in the music as well as those conceptually abstracted from it. The following case studies will investigate relations among various levels of articulation and how these configurations are named or otherwise theorized.

First, it will be helpful to describe the basic principle for generating *tāla* structures in South India and to specify how various levels in a *tāla* hierarchy are marked. We will then be equipped to discuss metric and rhythmic thinking as resembling or differing from classical formulations to various degrees. In Karnatak music, *tāla* is a metric structure (distinct from the surface structure of the music) against which singing or playing makes rhythmic sense. In our *ādi tāla* example as shown in Figure 12.1, three basic levels of reckoning are relevant: *akṣarakālas* (syllable-time units), the 8 counts marked out by the primary hand gestures (*kriya*)—claps, finger counts, and waves; *kaḷā*, two or four subcounts to help keep track of the counts if they are very slow in tempo; and *naṭai*, pulses within the counts or subcounts that can vary in number according to the song or according to the imagination of the performer during periods of accompaniment or improvisation.

The three kinds of hand gestures, clap, finger-count, and wave, are qualitatively distinct and provide means of time-reckoning and orientation. The time points made most prominent either visually or sonically are the claps. The presence of claps,

Akṣarakāla: (♩)	1	2	3	4	5	6	7	8
Kriya (hand gestures): (♩)	clap	pinky	ring	mid	clap	wave	clap	wave
(kaḷā) (♩)	/ /	/ /	/ /	/ /	/ /	/ /	/ /	/ /
naṭai (♪)	....	....	....	....	....	....	....	....

FIGURE 12.1 *Ādi tāla* with 2 *kaḷā*.

however, does not mean that the *tāla* has "accents" in the way that $\frac{3}{4}$ time or $\frac{4}{4}$ time has metric accents in European classical music. Rather, the clapped moments in the cycle serve as reference and sometimes goal points for musicians as they perform a segment of a composition or an improvisation. The hand gestures help musicians distinguish between analogous parts of the time cycle—for example, between the metrically similar beats on counts 1 and 5 in *ādi tāla*. The beginning of a composition is a significant point of rhythmic reference in South Indian music that does not rely on direct marking in the *tāla*: it occurs before, after, or on count 1 of the *tāla*.

The South Indian *tāla* system comprises formulas into which one of five sets of clap-plus-finger counts (3, 4, 5, 7, 9) can be inserted to create *tālas* of different lengths.[7] So for instance, *ādi tāla* can be transformed into the 7-count *tripuṭa tāla* by substituting the first 4-count "limb" of the *tāla* (consisting of one clap and 3 finger counts) for one of 3 counts (a clap and 2 finger counts). The sequence of claps alone is a reduction that retains the essential elements of the *tāla* structure. Instrumentalists, whose hands are occupied playing their instruments, cannot articulate the whole *tāla* but may articulate the claps using other parts of their bodies (otherwise they need to keep the whole *tāla* in their heads): violinists, for instance, often use their knees or feet and *vīṇā* players use their right pinky fingers to stroke side strings.

In North Indian terminology a clap is called a *tālī*, a beat, from the Sanskrit *tāḍa* ("beating," also related to the term *tāla*). With this notion in mind, I will reserve the term "beat" for elements of a cycle marked out by a clap or other form of emphasis and not for the constituent homogeneous units (counts) that separate beats.[8] In this view, *ādi tāla* has 3 beats and 8 counts. While Hindustani *tāla* differs from Karnatak *tāla* in that an instrument (usually the tabla) carries the *tāla* explicitly and usually makes it unnecessary to show the *tāla* with the hand, in the South, the mridangist does not play a version of the *tāla*. All the performers in a South Indian ensemble are playing in relation to the *tāla*, and often in counterpoint to it. The idea of *tāla* as extensible formula based on an arrangement of beats with variable counts extends beyond the Karnatak musical world; however, the idea of *tāla* as an abstract structure separable from the music is apparently limited to the classical world. As one examines the variety of drumming traditions in South Asia, one finds forms of rhythmic organization that are largely distinct from the classical *tāla* systems as described, some relate to the classical systems through common terms (which may vary in their meaning), and some have been made classical by the efforts of individual drummers who have been trained in more than one tradition.

In most of the drumming traditions outside the purview of art music *tāla* refers not to an abstract metrical pattern held fixed outside of the musical surface structure, as is found in Karnatak music, but to a fixed pattern—a stroke-melody akin to a Hindustani *ṭheka*—that is audibly prominent in the music. The pattern may rely on multiple instruments including percussion and tone-melody instruments such as double-reed aerophones and bagpipes. The pattern may be called *tāl* or by other generic names such as *cāl* (Hindi: gait) and *aṭi* (Tamil: beat). It may function as a gridlike substratum for other musical activity, or it may constitute its own center of attention, possibly swelling and contracting, living and breathing, with dynamic changes of tempo instigated by a leader and tempered by the rate of group responses. The naming of patterns in many traditions refers to the number or arrangements of *beats* according to the usage I've outlined, and not necessarily according to the number of constituent counts—that is, the durations between the beats may vary. The conceptual basis for such naming, then, has parallels with ideas underlying the South Indian *tāla* system today and suggests others found in ancient Indian writings on musical time, which describe musical forms that can be temporally "inflated" in nonuniform ways (when we substituted 3 counts for the 4 counts in the *ādi tāla* example, we created a 7-count *tāla* out of an 8-count one. Because only the clap-and-finger-count section was inflated, the *tāla* increased its number of beats in what I am calling a nonuniform way). According to James Kippen (this volume), the first Indo-Persian source which groups "meters" by their number of "beats" (not counts) is Maudūdī Chishtī's *Risāla-ye mūsīqī* (1763). However, the concept is so widespread across language families, regions and genres today, and the implications for such an idea is so strong in ancient discussions of inflatable *tāla* structures, that it is hard to assess how new M. Chishti's work was seen at the time and how much it may have contributed to what might have been a firmly established habit of thinking about meter and rhythm in many parts of South and Central Asia already.

In the following case studies I will present a variety of examples in which stroke-melodies are labeled by numbers of beats. Comparing these examples helps us grasp the *different* ways in which rhythmic flexibility fits within the various beat structures. Retaining the metaphor of *lay* as a substance, to put this another way, I would like to explore how this substance inhabits the spaces between the beats.

COUNTING BEATS IN INDIA AND PAKISTAN

We begin in South India where musical terminology draws from the Dravidian family of languages in the region as well as from words in these languages with Sanskrit etymologies. A key term in this regard is *aṭi* in Tamil (the letter /ṭ/ in Tamil is pronounced /ḍ/ between two vowels), meaning "beat" or "strike."

Among the Kotas, a South Indian hill tribe (Wolf 2005), drumming serves as accompaniment for melodies played on the double-reed *koḷ*. Drum patterns consist of three parts: a frame drum (*tabaṭk*) which leads and the cylinder drums *dobar* and *kiṇvar* whose bass and treble sounds interlock. Kotas recognize three "types" (*dāk*) of drum pattern: "plain" (*cādā*), "turning-dance" (*tiruganāṭ*), and one using the Kota name for a Telugu-speaking drummer caste on the plains (*kolāḷ*). The term for generic drum pattern, *dāk*, is in all likelihood cognate with the Tamil term *tākku-* (to beat), although Kotas with whom I discussed the term said it means "type" and is related to the Kota term *dākl*, meaning "like" or "similar to."

Three different drum patterns, with 6, 7, and 10 pulses respectively, are encompassed within the term *cādā dāk* ("plain type") (Audio 12.1, 12.2, 12.3 ▶). The three share the relative proportions long-short-long-long after structural drum strokes (Kota, *aṛy*, beat—cf. Tamil, *aṭi*) and some Kota musicians have described them as versions of the same idea played at different tempos. However, the pulse counts of the three versions actually vary because the internal durational ratios of each pattern do not remain constant (see Wolf 2000–2001, 23). The structure of this Kota drumming practice is consistent with the idea of nonuniform inflation, as expressed in both the modern Karnatak *tāla* system and the *mārga tāla*s of ancient India (Rowell 1992b, 201 and passim). In the Kota case, the concept of *cādā dāk* relies on an implicit acceptance of rhythmic elasticity that takes place at the microlevel in between the "anchoring" (Wolf 2005) strokes of the frame drum.

Within each of the particularizations of the *dāk*s, it is possible to play a set of variations whose density is labeled according to the number of "beats" (*aṛy* or *dāk*)—the word beat referring, as it usually does in South Asia, to stressed strokes (here on the frame drum). In the case of the simple duple pattern for *tiruganāṭ*, three of the possible variations are shown in Figure 12.2. Vertical arrows show the beats that are counted for the purpose of naming the variations "one-beat" (Video 12.1), "two-beat" (Video 12.2), and "three-beat" (Video 12.3), respectively (from Wolf 2014, 93–95).

Unlike the three versions of the *cādā dāk* pattern, these variations are not generated by inflation or deflation, but rather of nonuniform densification; they can be mixed and matched at will by the lead frame drummer (Audio 12.4) without suggesting any significant changes for the other drummers or dancers (not so for the three varieties of *cādā dāk*, which are associated with different melodies and dances or rituals). The naming practice has nothing to do with counts, only with "beats." On three levels then, the level of the generic pattern/type/beat (*dāk*), and the level of the specific subvariety (e.g., one of the three versions of *cādā dāk*), and the level of elaborating a subvariety through varying the density of "beats" (*aṛy* or *dāk*), Kota musical thinking involves a focus on stressed strokes and not on counting subdivisions. Indeed, in the case of *cādā*

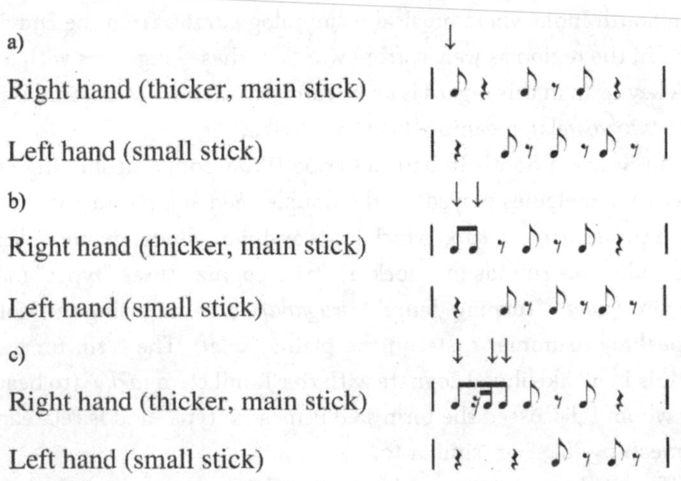

FIGURE 12.2 (a) *Tiruganāṭ* basic version on *tabaṭk*, "one-beat" (*or aṛy*). (b) *Tiruganāṭ* variation on *tabaṭk*, "two-beat" (*eyṛ aṛy*). (c) *Tiruganāṭ* variation on *tabaṭk*, "three-beat" (*mūṇḍ aṛy*).

dāk, counting subdivisions would lead Kotas to challenge their own understanding of the relation among *cādā dāk* varieties as merely ones of tempo: they are deformations of one another.

In the Tamil countryside, the Dalit community after which the Kota *kolāḷ dāk* is named is a Telugu-speaking caste known in Tamil as Cakkiliyār. Members of this caste and (in their own separate tradition) the Paṟaiyār caste perform on cognate sets of frame drums, cylinder, kettle, and clay spherical drums for festivals and funerals. They also perform compound drum patterns in which the lead instrument is a frame drum (*tappaṭṭai*) referred to, appropriately, as the King (*rājā*). Naming practices for patterns vary (Wolf 2014, 63–64, 69). The vast majority of specific patterns bear the name of the contexts for which they are played. The generic term for pattern means beat or strike (as in the Kota *dāk* or Tamil *aṭi*) or is the name of an instrument or an ensemble on which the pattern is played (e.g., Tamil *mēḷam*). The patterns themselves are small motives that the frame drummer iterates and the other instruments elaborate with filler patterns that sometimes interlock. Although the specifics vary, the patterns do not generally resemble Hindustani *ṭheka*s: no overarching metric frameworks persist continuously. Rather, successive iterations of short phrases consist of highly contrasting forms of stress, timbre, and pitch. In some cases, musicians refer to a sequence of patterns in terms of numbers of "beats" (*aṭi*), such that each successive pattern in a suite has a larger number of stressed strokes.

In the website accompanying this book is an example of a sequence of such *aṭi*s played at a festival in Dharmapuri district of Tamil Nadu in April of 1991 (Video 12.4 ▶). Prominent is the responsorial relationship of the "king" frame drum (*tappaṭṭai*) to the spherical clay drum with two heads (*maṉmattāḷam*). The frame drummer leads with a mid-range timbral articulation while the *maṉmattāḷam* players provide bass and treble strokes that timbrally surround that of the frame drum. Heard filling in the sound in the background are *tāshā* drums (locally pronounced *tājā*). The tempo and texture of the patterns change in relation to the cues from the frame drum player.

As we think about "rhythm" in this context, one option is to analyze the texture at any given stable segment in this flow—much in the way I have given a snapshot of rhythmic process in some of the other examples considered in this chapter. But it is also worth considering rhythm in a less countable manner, taking into consideration the ebb and flow of group reactivity. It is as if the frame drummer performs the musical equivalent of what Mikhail Bakhtin called an "utterance" in speech (Bakhtin 1986, 71, 94–95, and passim). A speech utterance differs from a word, sentence, or paragraph (outside of an actual speech context) in that it has an addressee, broadly defined, and it is bounded by a change in speaker. When we listen to a story being told, or the flow of a conversation, it is often possible to sense a rhythm of exchange, each utterance of which is shaped and finalized by the many expressive features available in spoken language. Sensitive participants in a conversation know when it is appropriate to respond, and sensitive speakers know when they should leave room for a response. Some kinds of rhythmic interactivity in which such regulating frameworks as *tāla*, song structure, or chord sequence do not serve to dictate changes in musical speaker, might well be considered in terms analogous to the exchange of utterances.[9]

COUNTING STRESSED STROKES IN OTHER TRADITIONS OF SOUTH AND CENTRAL ASIA

The phenomenon of using numbers of stressed strokes to represent rhythmic configurations is widespread in South Asia, even though the specific ways in which the stresses relate to the configurations are diverse. Those familiar with Hindustani music will recognize the phenomenon in the common 16-count *tīntāl*. Meaning "three beats," it refers to a structure marked by *tālīs*, or beats/claps, on counts 1, 5, and 13. However, neither this method of naming *tāls* nor the method of indicating *tāl* structure in terms of "beats" is uniform within the Hindustani *tāla* system.[10] The numbering phenomenon is similarly episodic outside of the classical music world.

When the crisp, trebly *tāshā* is paired with a bassier drum, usually the *ḍhol*, the main strokes of the latter drum lend primary definition to the resulting compound pattern—whether or not this involves counting. So central is this bass pattern that some musicians call it the *naġmah*, meaning "tune" (Arabic: "to read or sing in a low voice"). The term *naġmah* normally applies to tone-melodies in North India and Pakistan, especially ones that are instrumental iterations of verbal formulas (Wolf 2000, 103; Qureshi 2006, 45). We must look to the bass pattern, then, to find the significant numbers of "beats" as well as outlines of verbal phrases and other characteristic phrases.

In Hyderabad, Andhra Pradesh, the *tāshā* drum may be paired with one of several other bassier drums that produce a contrasting, sparse texture. In ensembles of *tāshā* and *dugga* (a narrow cylindrical drum), some Dalit drummers perform stroke-melodies called *do mār* (Urdu/Hindi: "two strike") and *tīn mār* ("three strike"), so named for the number of strokes on the bass head of the *dugga* in each cycle (Video 12.5 ▶), as in Figure 12.3.[11]

This kind of naming, often limited to one or two patterns in a repertoire, is common in drum ensembles associated with public rituals, both Hindu and Muslim, throughout India and Pakistan. It's important to stress that the repertoires of folk and ritual drumming ensembles of South Asia can vary tremendously in their variety and range, from

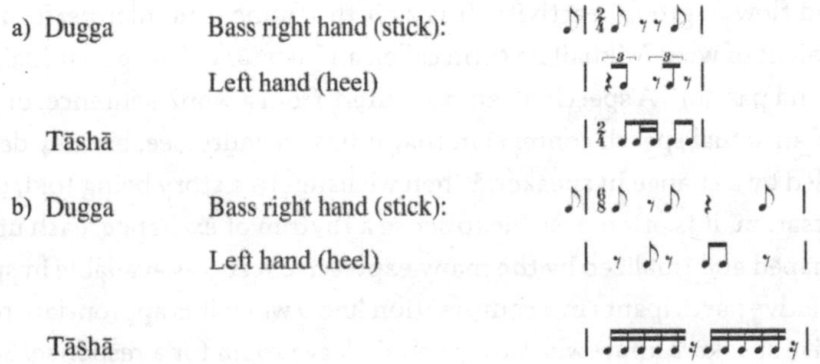

FIGURE 12.3 (a) *Do mār*. (b) *Tīn mār*.

as few as one or two items to several dozen. Usually, only a small subset of patterns is named according to beat numbers.

In rare instances, beat-focused pattern naming maintains formulaic consistency across a repertoire. Such is the case in Hyderabad, Sindh, where a group of male *ḍhol* drummers performs the patterns in Table 12.1 exclusively for the first ten days of Muharram (Wolf 2014, 98–102). The eldest member and leader of the group migrated from Agra in India at the time of Partition, so this represents one of many transported Indian drumming traditions and not one native to Sindh. The individual pattern-names correspond with prominent strokes in the bass. During Muharram, the only context for performance the performers consider legitimate, the leader cues the rest of the group to switch among these patterns (according to his preference) without inserting breaks in between (Video 12.6 ▶).[12]

The practice of naming these stroke-melodies according to stressed strokes rather than isochronous counts links this tradition to those already discussed. This Hyderabad-Agra tradition differs from the others by virtue of its unison texture and its relative lack of rhythmic elasticity, partly owing to the absence of interaction with other instrumentalists who improvise or otherwise fill out the texture. Creating sequences of *cāl*s does, however, involve the leader's moment-to-moment decision-making and an interval of adjustment as the rest of the group catches on to the new pattern (they play only once a year over 10 days, so the group's technique remains perpetually rusty). By contrast, in the Dharmapuri example discussed earlier, the lead

TABLE 12.1

Beat structure of *cāl*s performed by *ḍhol* group in Hyderabad, Sindh, Pakistan.

<table>
<tr><th>Tempo</th><th>Pattern</th></tr>
<tr><td>Ek kī cāl ("cāl of 1") ♪. ♪♪ = 93</td><td>>
|♪. ♪♪ | ♪. ♪♪ |</td></tr>
<tr><td>Do kī cāl ("cāl of 2") ♪. ♪♪ = 84</td><td>> >
|♪. ♪♪ |♪. ♪♪| ♪. ♪♪ |</td></tr>
<tr><td>Cār kī cāl ("cāl of 4") ♪. ♪♪ = 91</td><td>> > > >
|♪. ♪♪ |♪. ♪♪ |♪. ♪♪ |♪. ♪♪ | ♪. ♪♪|</td></tr>
<tr><td>Tīn kī cāl ("cāl of 3" ♩ = 50</td><td>> > >
|♩ ♪♩ ♩ |♪♩ ♩ ♩ ♪|</td></tr>
<tr><td>Pānc kī cāl ("cāl of 5") ♩ = 66</td><td>> > > > >
|♩ ♪♩ ♩ |♩ ♪♩ ♩ |♪♩ ♩ ♩ ♪|</td></tr>
<tr><td>Cheh kī cāl ("cāl of 6") ♩ = 66</td><td>> > > > > >
|♩ ♪♩ ♩ |♩ ♪♩ ♩ |♩ ♪♩ ♩ | ♩ ♩ (♪)|</td></tr>
<tr><td>Sāt kī cāl ("cāl of 7") ♩ = 66</td><td>> > > > > > >
|♩ ♪♩ ♩ |♩ ♪♩ ♩ |♩ ♪♩ ♩ |♪♩ ♩ ♩ ♪|</td></tr>
</table>

frame drummer proceeds from repetitions of one stressed stroke, to two, to three, and so on in order, increasing the number and density of strokes with each subsequent pattern. The Tamil ensemble's responses to these changes involve controlled temporal ebb and flow. In the Kota case of *cādā dāk*, different still, some rhythmic elasticity prevails *in between* the structural strokes on the frame drum; the frame drummer, meanwhile, will be making slight adjustments in interaction with the double-reed players and dancers. In each of these cases, much as in Bakhtin's idea of speech genres, the musical genre is defined in part by what constitutes an utterance and who or what constitutes the "addressee." Inasmuch as these interactions result in changes in pulse groupings, they are examples of what Richard Widdess terms heterometric rhythmic structure; one of the genre-defining characteristics is the degree to which the heterometric structure depends on predetermined sequences, and shared understandings of how many times one structure should recur before it is appropriate to change to another.

The generic term for the stroke-melodies played by the Hyderabad-Agra group is *cāl*, meaning "gait." One way in which *tāl*, be it an abstract metrical frame or a specific stroke-melody (like a *ṭheka*), can be distinguished from *cāl* is through so-called empty (*k̲h̲ālī*) units—a feature of the Hindustani tradition that emerged relatively late, but at least by the early nineteenth century.[13] In the Hindustani *tāl* gesture system, the period of such a unit corresponds to a wave of the hand rather than to a clap and is marked with special drumming techniques—usually one or more damped strokes on or near the time point indicated by the wave. *Cāls* are usually seen as less complex entities than *tāls*—they are grooves rather than metric structures. The repertoires of many percussion-dominated ensembles in South Asia include items called both *cāl* and *tāl*, in which case the structural difference between the two might be significant. In this Hyderabad-Agra *ḍhol* repertoire the term *tāl* does not appear, but the use of *cāl* as a pattern that is less internally differentiated than a *tāl* (or *ṭheka*) is consistent with wider labeling practices.

The repertoire of Mamraj's band, mentioned earlier in connection with the term *lay*, is especially broad and hybrid with regard to naming practices. The term for "beat" found prominently in this repertoire is *jarba*, a Hindi pronunciation of the Urdu word *zarbah* (from Arabic via Persian) meaning strike, beat, or a kind of drum. In this case, the *jarbas* are long, through-composed stroke melodies that may be played only once. They maintain a two- or three-part textures; *ḍhols* define the pattern with their number of stressed strokes, and *tāshās* play filler patterns of varying density (it is not clear whether the *tāshās* improvise as they do for some of the simpler patterns). The precise number of counts that separate the "beats" of the *ḍhol* appears flexible, but the arrangement of beats remains constant in terms of relative density—which I represent in simplified form as beat clusters separated by filler patterns. The stroke-melody is named for the sum of all the beats, regardless of the patterning. For example, "32 beats" (*batīs jarbe̲n̲*) is clustered 1-9-5-3-2-9-1-1-1, where each of the numbers in between the hyphens represents a cluster (or a single stroke). The cluster pattern for the stroke-melody called "62 beats" (*bāsaṭh jarbe̲n̲*), 8-8-8, 6-6, 3-3-3, 2-2-2, 11, follows a logic of diminution (which is then disrupted with the cluster of 11) that Mamraj described explicitly to me during my first interview with him in 1998 (Audio 12.5 ▶). This adds another dimension to Widdess's notion of heterometric rhythm: here it is not a sequence of pulse groupings but a sequence of "beat" groupings in which pulse is not the relevant unit of reckoning.

As the examples suggest, the habit of naming drumming patterns and metric structures according to nonisochronous units that are usually conceptualized as "beats" covers a diverse array of actual drumming practices and appears in a diversity of South Asian languages (notably here in both Indo-Aryan and Dravidian language families). Sometimes the beats refer to cycles, sometimes they do not; sometimes they refer to punctuations in gridlike structures, sometimes to frameworks within which elastic rhythmic activity is possible, and sometimes to frameworks that are themselves elastic. Examples in which *ṭheka*s from Hindustani music have been transferred directly onto the *ḍhol* or ensembles of *ḍhol* and *tāshā* have not been discussed, but many examples of this phenomenon exist as well. Classical *tāl*s exist side by side along with folk repertoire in many ensembles, whether or not all the practitioners themselves are aware of the common distinctions South Asians typically draw between folk and classical musical practices.

In some instances of number-naming, I have not yet been able to determine what is being counted. I suspect that in most such cases, either "beats" or "counts" (homogeneous units often called *mātras*) were originally the objects of counting, but that, in time, successive generations of practitioners have altered the patterns in ways that hide the original logic. This may have been the result of creative manipulation or imperfect reproduction of materials inherited from the past. Two instances of puzzling numbering can be found in the stroke melodies called *das kī gintī* (Video 12.7 ▶) and *bīs kī gintī*, meaning "ten count" and "twenty count" respectively. A *ḍhol-tāshā* ensemble with ancestrals roots in Bharatpur, India, perform these as part of a repertoire of about a dozen stroke melodies in Hyderabad, Sindh in connection with Muharram. "*Gintī*" means "count," but neither *mātra*s nor stressed strokes in these patterns as they are currently played add up to 10 or 20 respectively.

STRUMMING IN CENTRAL ASIA

Many of the percussion-dominated ensembles of South Asia perform their repertoires in set suites or in sequences that involve choices among alternatives. Part of the musical interest in these drumming traditions lies in elaborations on and improvisations around a particular groove. As drummers transition from one pattern to another, they also try to maintain the listener's interest by balancing elements of continuity and surprise. The choice for such transitions may also depend on what other instrumentalists, singers, breast beaters (in rituals of mourning during Muharram), and/or dancers are doing or wish to do.

Moving from Pakistan, with its drum-based suites, into Northern Afghanistan, Tajikistan, Uzbekistan, and Xinjiang, China, one encounters suites in which each successive item may retain common tonal materials and vary such aspects of rhythm as poetic meter, rhythmic mode (*usul*) performed on a drum, and strumming pattern. Suites and other sequences based on rhythmic contrast in Central and West Asia are found in folk (*xalkī*) and classical (*klasikī*) music as well as in Muslim religious practices. In *sineh zani* (breast beating) as part of Muharram observances in Iran (and its counterpart of *mātam* in South Asia) for instance, participants chant couplets in the *nauheh* genre while striking their chests in choreographed beat patterns. These may fall in set sequences and involve antiphonal structures between two or more groups of chanters.

Sufi chanting of *zikr*s involves a similar production of beats. A *zikr*, literally "remembrance," is a repetitive verbal formula meant to focus the chanter's mind on God. The performance of *zikr*s often involves creating accents with the breath; cycles of breath accents are arranged in ascending sequences of beats (Mijit 2016, 404; see also Djumaev 2002, 943–44).

The term *zarba* or *zarb* in items of Central Asian (mainly Persianate) repertoire may refer to several possible elements: downward strokes or stressed beats in a strumming pattern; different patterns in a suite; or units of text. For example, Wakhi poet and singer Qurbonsho follows a local practice of referring to strumming patterns on the Pamiri rabāb with such names as *du zarba* ("2 beats") and *se zarba* ("3 beats"; Video 12.8), indicating that the numbers refer to the strokes. Yet I have also observed him note, when asked to show clearly how the strokes were counted, that the number in certain pattern names failed to correspond to the number of strokes. Instead of revising his playing or questioning the system, he would revise the name of the pattern, saying something like, "actually, the name of this is 5-beat not 2-beat."

Ismoil Nazriev, doyen of the so-called Darvoz style in Tajikistan, taught me a "*se zarb*" ("three *zarb*") in which "three" referred to the number of pieces in the suite, each with a contrasting strumming pattern. *Zarb* in this instance refers to rhythmic organization at a generic level—similar to a usage of the word beat in English to refer to a kind of pattern rather than a pulse or a strike. Instead of 3 strikes, then, 3 *zarb* in this case refers to three different kinds of rhythmic groove. (This is a common usage of the term *zarb* in Tajik, not one idiosyncratic to Nazriev or the Darvoz style.)

Ikromuddinov Abdulloxon, a Wakhi singer of the Ismaili religious genre known as Qasoid or Maddoh, came up with what seemed to be ad-hoc explanations for *zarb* numbers, claiming that a *du zarb* (2 beat) was so named because of the two hemistiches covered in one cycle of the strumming pattern, while other numbers for *zarb*s referred to strums. I have also found other Maddoh singers who linked *zarb* numbers to lines of text, but in each instance it was an attempt to account for a numbering system they had trouble defining in words.

Although the musics of India and Pakistan are different from those in Tajikistan in many respects, the episodic occurrence of naming stroke-melodies by numbers of nonisochronous "beats" joins them in surprising ways.

TEXT AS THE ORGANIZING PRINCIPLE FOR DRUMMING PATTERNS

Another way in which musicians have drawn upon the prominence of "beats" in naming and organizing drum patterns is by conceptualizing their internal durations in relation to verbal phrases. The most common instance of this corresponds with the Sufi *zikr* and Muslim statement of faith in one god, **lā** il-**lā**ha **illa**l-**lāh** muḥ**amm**a**dur** ras**ūl allāh**. Taking into account durations of long and short syllables in this phrase and the dynamic emphasis given to the syllables in bold (when chanted), several *ḍhol-tāshā* groups use the riff in Figure 12.4 as the framework around which *tāshā* soloists take turns improvising.

Of particular interest is the riff's irregular recurrence; the riff returns not after a fixed number of counts (the accompaniment *tāshās* play a filler pattern throughout), but rather after the soloist finishes and plays a cue for the group's return—that is, after his "utterance." I term this a "riff-based pattern" to distinguish it from "*mātra*-based patterns," which rely on the recurrence of a fixed number of counts in a cycle (Wolf 2014, 105). It would not be fruitful to analyze this as a form of heterometer in Widdess's sense because the pulse groupings in between the iterations of the "riff" are not conventionally fixed; nor, however, is the drumming "isometric," unless meter and tactus are collapsed (Video 12.9).

The ways in which texts correspond with durational relationships among "beats" varies. Some are fairly straightforward iterations of poetic meter. Others are impressionistic replications of speech rhythms. In one case a line of *marsiyah* poetry in the Nizamuddin tradition was represented by only 3 strokes on the *ḍhol*. Based on abstractions of the poetic meter in combination with stresses in a sung version of the *marsiyah*, I suggested that listeners who claimed to recall the text through the sound of the drums did so through their impressions of three internally flexible durations that remained in the relative proportions of short, long, and prolonged (Wolf 2014, 259–60). In performance, the number of counts separating the three strokes varied, but the general proportions were retained.

DISCUSSION

In seeking broader possibilities for describing rhythmic patterning in music cross-culturally, it may be useful to consider approaches to rhythm in speech and poetry. The forms of such rhythm also involve hierarchies of "beats" (through various forms of accent and stress) and lower level articulations (e.g., syllables), and have been the object

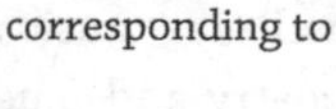

FIGURE 12.4 The *kalmah*, a beat pattern corresponding to the Muslim statement of faith in one god.

of discussions concerning linguistic isochrony. Although speech and poetic recitation are forms of sound distinct from music according to convention in some cultures, they cannot be inherently different because no culturally neutral definition of music exists that can categorically distinguish musical and nonmusical uses of language. Meter in language may involve regulating proportions or relative weights of syllables, numbers of syllables, numbers of virtual minimal time units, positions of syllables with particular qualities (e.g., long/short; heavy/light; hard-medium-soft), and fixed numbers or kinds of elements in each position of a colonic structure. What does not get regulated strictly is the set of durations within a poem as it is actually recited. Even if a language features phonemic vowel length, for instance, other factors may prevail in regulating speech and poetic recitation.

Derek Attridge, specialist on rhythm and meter in English, defined meter as "an organizing principle which turns the general tendency toward regularity in rhythm into a strictly-patterned regularity, that can be counted and named" (Attridge 1995, 7). "Count[ing]" and "nam[ing]" in meter may be more important than some aspects of "regularity." Evidence suggests, for instance, that ideas of "syllable-timing" and "stress-timing" in languages are based more on perceptions of regularity at the syllable or stress level than on the measurable presence of isochronous durations. Readers perhaps emphasize perceived regularities at the syllable or stress levels when providing a metrical reading of poetry, just as musicians may or may not emphasize the equality of eighth notes or other units of musical time-reckoning when they perform.

Since meter involves not only the organizations of syllables and stresses but also the meanings of words, metrical analysis in language needs to take semantic and grammatical matters into account as well (Attridge 1995, 56). Syntactic functions of other kinds are also critical in understanding the multiple levels in which rhythm and meter operate in musical works (whether or not text is involved). In our examples, the return of the "riff" in response to a cue is more important to the musical structure than the "regularity" of isochronous counts separating iterations of the riff. Only a rather limited view of rhythm and meter would present theoretical difficulties in accounting for this kind of musical process, but the very surprise I experienced in discovering this form of musical organization shows just how much certain principles of musical meter may be taken for granted in both Western theoretical traditions and those of South Asia, where *tāla* reigns supreme. The idea of rhythm as a trade in utterances may be intuitively more useful in some instances than in terms of counted pulses.

John Lotz, a linguist who defined poetic meter as "the numerical regulation of certain properties of the linguistic form alone" (Lotz 1972, 2), emphasized that music cannot be the basis for metric analysis [of language] because "both temporal and dynamic relations in music are much stricter and organized in a different way from those in poetry" (1972, 3). Distinctions between music and poetry need to be recognized in a culturally sensitive manner. Nevertheless, assumptions about "regularity" in rhythm built into the notion of what constitutes music are likely to hide deeper similarities between metrical properties of poetry and musics such as those presented in this chapter.[14] If we allow for the difference between what Lotz calls "metric performance" (the actual recitation of poetry) and "metric score" (nonmeasurable relations based on linguistic function) in language, we should be able to recognize similar distinctions in music. I'm arguing for more than the obvious fact that performances of a melody scored in one meter might suggest (or be made to suggest) other metric possibilities. Rather, I would like to begin from a "metric score" that is more flexible than one implied by Western staff notation. Does musical meter need to rely on isochronous units at all? Might we expand our notions of musical meter to include the kinds of pattern definitions discussed here, defined by "beats"—regulated by number and or verbal phrase—and the relative proportions that separate them?

ISOCHRONY, RHYTHM, AND *RĀGA ĀLĀPANA*

In a groundbreaking article, Geniche Tsuge attempted to account for some of the durational configurations in the Persian *āvāz* through reference to Perso-Arabic poetic meter, *'arūz* (Tsuge 1970). *Āvāz* is a rhythmically elastic form of vocal improvisation in Persian classical music. Tsuge found that singers deform the poetic meters in somewhat predictable ways when they perform *āvāz*. They begin their singing with a dense burst of syllables and then spread out the syllables, embellishing them with melismas and a technique of glottal ornamentation called *taḥrīr*. Tsuge's model has been challenged (e.g., Wright 2009) and tested for other languages using the *'arūz* metrical system (for Urdu, see Qureshi 1981; 2006), but no alternative model has yet been proposed.

Attention to differences in vowel quantity also proved useful for my analyses of (sometimes elastic) stroke-melodies that were said to articulate *zikrs*, chants, and lines of poetry. However, poetic meter is only one of many resources performers draw upon in creating rhythmic sense. Like *āvāz* in Persian music, *rāga ālāpana* is an example of a widespread kind of musical opening section in which performers explore typical melodic features of a mode or tune-type and gradually move into sections that are more rhythmically regular or metrically marked. In North India, the *ālāp* section is the center of attention and often takes up the bulk of a performance. In South India, the *ālāpana* is only mandatory in certain sections of the concert sequence and usually leads into the performance of a composition (in North India the composed part of a performance is comparatively brief). Richard Widdess, Ritwik Sanyal, and Martin Clayton have investigated the question of whether *ālāp* in selected North Indian genres has a pulse and if so, how one might measure or perceive it. Ritwik Sanyal, who is a *dhrupad* singer as well as musicologist, reports feeling a pulse when he sings. Richard Widdess was able to measure that pulse as precisely 1.6 seconds in length (Widdess 2005).[15] By contrast, Martin Clayton argued that sarod-player Amjad Ali Khan separates his iterations of the tonic after a period of rapid melodic activity in such a way as to destroy a listener's sense of periodicity (Clayton 2000, 102).

In listening to North Indian *ālāp*, with its long durations between tones, the suggestion that performers might be keeping track with a mental time grid, whether consciouslless or unconsciously, is quite surprising. On the surface, the rhythmically more active *ālāpana* of South India might seem a more plausible candidate for analysis in terms of pulse. However, as we have seen, performers take it as a kind of credo that *ālāpana* is rhythmically free, and perhaps that is one of the reasons musicological discussions of rhythm among scholars in South India have focused on the parts of the performance that are governed by *tāla*.

The equation of *tāla* with "rhythm" and organization of time more generally is deeply rooted in Indian musicological discourse. Arun Kumar Sen, former director of the Bhatkande Institute of Music and Musicology, presented the extreme view in his book *Indian Concept of Rhythm* that "Just as lack of definite time sequence in life leads to lack of happiness and prosperity, so too music without tāla makes it meaningless and ineffective" (Sen 1994, 13). Whereas a more common belief holds that *ālāp* and *ālāpana* are genres in which performers tap into a sense of unbounded spiritual flow, Sen criticizes *ālāp* in Hindustani music for failing to live up to the standard of great art as that "which unites with the Supreme Bliss like the soul (Ātman). . . ." because of its failure to be "rhythmic" (Sen 1994, 13). Although these South Asian views of rhythmic elasticity provide cultural information on time and perception in music, they do not help us understand what is actually happening in musical performance. My intention here is merely to summarize a small portion of what I've observed and report a few instances in which South Indian performers have themselves acknowledged the rhythmic qualities of *ālāpana* in spite of the contrary ideology among their peers.

Although I argued earlier that conceptions of rhythm in South Asian drumming do not necessarily depend on the existence, recognition, or counting of isochronous units, I do not believe this is entirely the case for rhythm in *rāga ālāpana*. I believe that a musically acceptable performance of *rāga ālāpana* does presuppose maintenance of a quite precise pulse—even though the performers themselves are not, to my knowledge, aware of it while they are performing and almost always deny pulse is present if asked.[16] However, performers will generally acknowledge that *rāga ālāpana* has *kālapramāṇam*—pace. In my view, pace presupposes pulse without specifying where that pulse resides.

One of the leading Karnatak vocalists today, Sanjay Subramanyan, relayed to me a critical moment in his development as an artist. He had just returned from performing a concert and received a phone call from his *guru*. His *guru* said, "Sanjay, you have finally mastered the *kālapramāṇam* of *ālāpana*." Now, when Subramanyan teaches children of Indian heritage during concentrated visits to America, he tries to teach them how *ālāpana* is paced. He is one of the few artists who had himself thought about what I had newly discovered—that one can not only find a pulse in *ālāpana*, but also snap or tap to it consistently, right through sections of long, held tones.

The importance of maintaining pace in *ālāpana* is illustrated further in a commonly encountered form of musical incompetence. The majority of Karnatak music concerts consist of a vocalist accompanied by a violinist and mridangist. The violinist's role is to play along with the vocalist during compositions, shadow her or him during *ālāpana*, and respond with his or her own improvisations during that and other improvisational interludes. If the violinist fails to maintain the same pace as the lead singer when taking turns in the *ālāpana*, it can be jarring and annoying for the singer, who is forced either to take up the changed pace in the *ālāpana*, or create another discontinuity by returning to her/his own pace.

The one situation in which a drummer accompanies *rāga ālāpana* as a matter of course is that of double-reed *nāgasvaram* performance, normally found in South Indian Hindu temples and weddings but also on the classical concert stage. The accompanists, who play a type of barrel drum called *tavil*, will intersperse drum cadences and occasional strokes in between sections of *ālāpana*. *Ālāpana* performed on *nāgasvaram* is no more obviously pulsed than any other type of *ālāpana*. Yet it provides a special listening opportunity: if one projects forth the pace set on the drums, one can usually hear the *nāgasvaram* player maintain (or fail to maintain) the same pulse rate until the drum again returns, seamlessly driving the music forward at the same rate.

When I discussed this phenomenon with the *nāgasvaram*-playing Chennai musician Murugavel, he attributed the maintenance of *kālapramāṇam* to the method of training in Karnatak music. One learns to perform *rāgas* first by performing exercises in multiple speeds (*kālams*), the slowest speed with, say, four oscillations, and faster speeds with proportional reductions in these oscillations—2 or 1. This way, from the very beginning, the performer's body is entrained to maintain a steady pace at all levels of detail—no speeding up or slowing down, only increasing or decreasing the density. That is, even when a performer intersperses a rapid passage into an *ālāpana*, the base rate remains unchanged because the density will merely double or quadruple. I spoke with another vocalist on this topic and he added that some of today's musicians never properly mastered the proportional reduction of oscillations in moving from one speed to another, and this has resulted in their inability to move from one speed (*kālam*) to another in the correct proportions even in the sections governed by *tāla*. It affects their ability to accurately return to the first *kālam* as well.

It is not merely on the basis of the existence of a pulse in *rāga ālāpana* that I argue for its status as "rhythmically organized," but rather on the basis of what the listener can become aware of through hearing such a pulse (there is more than one way to hear pulse). For instance, it helps one realize how like melodic gestures recur in different rhythmic contexts. Melodic kernels are not just presented floating in space, and they are not presented in simple periodic sequences lined up with a pulse. They cross-cut the pulse (however you hear it) in different ways while remaining bound, ideally, to a commonly held *kālapramāṇam*;[17] this renders each rhythmic gesture on the micro-level comparable with every other one. When these internal melodic kernels are not rhythmically comparable—when they do not share the same pace—the performance sounds unmusical.

There are other, more specific analytical benefits of exploring the rhythmic aspects of *rāga ālāpana*. In some cases, ways of handling the rhythm of particular *gamakas* distinguishes *rāgas* or as well as schools/styles of playing (*bāṇi*; see Wolf 1991). In the Karaikudi style of *vīṇā* playing (and seemingly in general), for example, the way of handling the fourth scale degree in the *rāga nīlāmbari* is rhythmically different from

FIGURE 12.5 Approximate oscillation rhythm on *svara ma* in *nīlāmbari*.

FIGURE 12.6 Approximate oscillation rhythm on *svara ma* in *śankarābharaṇam*.

that in *śankarābharaṇam*: both involve an oscillation between E and F (taking C as tonic), but in Nīlāmbari the oscillation involves remaining on the lower tone (E) longer and then only briefly touching the upper tone (F), four oscillations of which might be represented as in Figure 12.5.

As these oscillations decay in amplitude, the tones often dissolve into more equidistant alternations (Audio 12.6 ▶). This profile contrasts with the energetic and more even alternation of tones approximated by Figure 12.6 for the *rāga śankarābharaṇam* (Audio 12.7 ▶).[18]

Audio 12.8 ▶ presents a *rāga ālāpana* in *śankarābharaṇam* sung by Voleti Venkateswarlu accompanied by my finger snaps to show one possible reckoning of the pulse.

This observation about the difference between *śankarābharaṇam* and *nīlāmbari* is nothing special for most Karnatak musicians. Any trained musician can talk about how one *rāga* can be distinguished from another by something subtle, often involving timing. What has not happened, however, is for the ideas of temporal regulation that musicians know through their bodies and in piecemeal fashion to be incorporated into the larger narrative on how classical music works.

The point of this chapter, then, has been to turn many of the common conceptions rhythm, beat, and freedom in South Asian music on their heads. Drum music, taken for granted as the most "rhythmic" and most temporally regulated kind of music in the subcontinent, may be organized according to rhythmic signposts or "anchor points" (Wolf 2005) that are often called "beats" in South Asian languages. The rhythmic space in between these beats may be variable, sometimes involving counting isochronous units and sometimes not. *Rāga ālāpana*, taken to be the most rhythmically "free" (termed elastic in this chapter), is most musical when it is most regulated at the level of the pulse, but this level of rhythmic organization is not acknowledged by most musicians and the perceived absence of temporal regulation has led to strong moral opinions regarding music and spiritual attainment.

NOTES

1. Because some of the contexts under discussion involve Islam, the status of particular repertoires as "music" is controversial. "Music" or not, performers and listeners recognize "rhythm" in these performances and I will use the terms "music" and "musician" liberally in the limited context of this chapter.

2. See also Hornbostel, who writes, "the variety of colours (timbre) brought about by beating the drum-head at different places, e.g., in the middle or on the rim, may be of some help in distinguishing the individual 'voices' of a polyrhythmic structure, at least for native hearers" (1928, 55), as well as distinctions of rhythm in terms of pattern in Knight (1974) and Kauffman (1980).

3. My understanding of Abhinavagupta's writings is based on the writings of Lewis Rowell (1992b, 189, 191, 202).

4. See also Kippen's discussion of Edinburgh Oriental Manuscript 585/4, which discusses *lay* in relation to *wazn*—here, meaning rhythmic pattern consisting of strikes and spaces.

5. In the case of South Indian music, the tempo of the *tāla* is not supposed to change, so it would be more accurate to refer to changes in density, and not tempo, within a particular performance. In Hindustani music, the pace of the *tāla* itself changes—speeding up over the course of a long *rāg* rendition.

6. *Kalā* and *kaḷā* (or *kaḷai* in Tamil) are cognates. It is common to find retroflex consonants in Dravidian language terms where their counterparts in Indo-Aryan languages are not. This is especially true for /l/. The widespread word *tāl* or *tāla*, for example, is pronounced *tāḷam* in Tamil.

7. This refers to the *sulādi tāla*s, which consists of many more *tāla*s than are commonly in use, and excludes some very common *tāla*s.

8. This use of the term "beat" for discussing Indian music was suggested to me by the late Harold Powers.

9. See also Chernoff, who discusses "hearing" in West Africa as entangled with the relationships of multiple parts (1997, 24 and passim).

10. James Kippen has explored some of the puzzles and anomalies of this system with reference to the tabla and *pakhāvaj* drums (Kippen 2001, 2006; and this volume).

11. Transcriptions based on my field recordings of two ensembles in Secunderabad, Andhra Pradesh, November 1998.

12. For further discussion of this example, see Wolf (2014, 98–102). The patterns follow two basic formulas and bear a surprising resemblance to the structure of some *deśi tāla*s.

13. Kippen (this volume) identifies the *Sharḥ-e risāla-ye qavāid-e ṭabla*, or commentary on the *Risāla-ye qavāid-e ṭabla*, an as yet undiscovered treatise on the fundamentals of tabla, as the earliest known source discussing the *k̲h̲ālī* function in *tāla*s. It is presumed to date from the first decade of the nineteenth century.

14. See also Mathiesen (1985) for discussion of the highly complex relations between poetic meter and music in the earliest extant examples of Greek music.

15. Widdess also obtained similar results by analyzing an *ālāp* sung on a recording by Aminuddin and Moinuddin Dagar, although we do not know whether these musicians actually experienced a sense of pulse while singing it (Widdess 1995).

16. In 2019, as an update to my original investigation in the mid-2000s, I would now qualify this statement. After I interacted with a number of musicians and musicologists in Chennai and discussed with them the issue of rhythm in *ālāpana*, the idea that *ālāpana* is pulsed may no longer seem to them so novel. The vocalist T. M. Krishna indicated that he'd enlisted a group of students to investigate the matter further, though I have not seen the results of their investigation.

17. This would be comparable, on a small scale, to what Mieczyslaw Kolinski (1973) identifies as contrametric patterning—the analogue of meter, here, being pulse. Listeners to Karnatak music are accustomed to musicals accents after (*atīta*) and before (*anāgata*) key positions in

the *tāla*, which, though offset, act to mark those points in the *tāla*. When listening to *ālāpana* while snapping our fingers, my consultants applied the same principles to their understanding of the pulse: "offbeat" articulations did not disturb the feeling of common pace/pulse.

18. In the comparative study of Karnatak and Hindustani *rāgas*, *Rāganidhi*, B. Subba Rao simply notes, "In this raga andolan [type of gamaka] on Ma with Ga as grace note as [ga ma ga ma ma . . .] is beautiful and characteristic of this raga" (Subba Rao 1984 (K-P), 201), whereas nothing is mentioned about the *ma* of *śankarābharaṇam* other than its pitch position.

13

New Music—New Rhythm

Christopher Hasty

NOTE ON TERMINOLOGY: IN this chapter I would like to explore metrical experiments/innovations in several pieces of late twentieth-century music that come out of European classical tradition. A customary label for an enduring trend that began early in the twentieth century is "New Music," or sometimes "the New Music" (in a more openly hegemonic gesture).[1] The other customary choice at this level of generality would have been "Contemporary Music," in which the new gets stretched out into a century in a kind of utopian stasis. Compared to the claim of being "new," the political stakes for being "contemporary" might seem small until one thinks how much of the actually contemporary world is excluded from this "contemporary music." I opt for "New Music" because it claims a sort of adventure or risk and because the word "new" is so interesting.[2] For New Music, "newness" itself would become focal, or perhaps bifocal: as a resistance to or rejection of the old or as a utopian movement where now is conjoined to a bright future of novelty as freedom (with or without nostalgia for the past). In the first case, there need be no end of resistance. For as long as there is resistance there is the self-consciously New, and since there seems no dearth of what is old to resist, this sort of New can last indefinitely as ongoing and ever-New resistance. "Resistance" and "rejection" thematize the opposition of new and old. If, on the other hand, the New is a utopian movement into new and *higher* spiritual realms in which the old is absorbed as decorative or is forgotten, the New can be (like resistance to the old) indefinitely sustainable; but only if progress is guaranteed. In this nisus toward perfection, there can be imagined an entry into a New Age (Schoenberg once imagined a hundred-year age of German dominance), a place that is no place.[3]

Below the generic level of "New" and "Contemporary" come the labels "modern," "avant-garde," and "experimental" ("modern" recently cut off from "postmodern," and so a label for old music). From here labeling proliferates quickly and with increasing clarity as we focus on smaller bodies of work (e.g., early Cage).

* * *

If musical rhythm can be understood as an eventfulness that involves all the innumerable dimensions that can come into play in music-making, then an inquiry into the rhythmic innovations of European-grounded (deeply-notational) modernist or avant-garde music ought to involve much more than "meter" as the central or sole dimension—especially if meter be reduced, via a technologically useful but ultimately misleading abstraction, to an autonomous arrangement of "time-units." I will, nonetheless, focus here on meter as a namable dimension in the measuring of duration, but I will try to allow for both the actual complicity of such specialized measuring in the measuring of other specialized dimensions, and a complexity of measuring durational "quantity" itself that might exceed the pedagogical simplifications of counting. The few excerpts of pieces I will consider in detail—Toru Takemitsu's *Rain Tree* for percussion (1981), Salvatore Sciarrino's *Muro d'Orrinzonte* (1997), and Morton Feldman's *De Kooning* (1963)—in one way or another both resist and play with "equal" measure or isochrony characteristic of the old music. I take resistance as a characteristic or generic marking of New Music that in its many and various exemplars may, or may not, engage a dialectical spirit of play with the very reproduction it resists. I have chosen as focal examples excerpts from pieces that offer to keep such play in rhythmic motion. These few examples may serve to open questions that might be carried farther in other pieces and other "genres," more narrowly defined.

Among the topics I will address, a focal one will be the role of new and challenging notation as an invitation to performers to make new sorts of sense of music. Measure will also be a focal topic. But against the grain of received theory, I would ask that "meter" or measure be understood here as a measuring, a creative activity performed by players and their audiences. New forms of notating and measuring can be a challenge to all parties (audience, performer, composer, and theorist) to explore hearing, feeling, and thinking in new ways. To talk about ways (new or old) of hearing, feeling, and thinking is to talk about process. To speak of process it will be useful to shift from a nominal (noun-like, substantive) "meter" to a verbal action of "measuring." I would therefore ask that meter as measuring be understood actively as a dynamic category and therefore as something not separate from rhythm understood as the ongoing and continuous process of event formation. I will begin with a brief account of meter from a processive or temporal perspective in which meter is understood as durational-quantitative measuring or what I have elsewhere called "durational projection."[4]

From the perspective of process, a new or present event is becoming and is not fully determined so long as it is going on. Once it is no longer becoming but become, the event is determined and past, no longer going on. But the past is not without issue. The new, present event doesn't come out of nowhere; it comes out into (*evenire*) a world it must deal with. This is a world inhabited (in part) by the determinacies of past events that will help to shape the new event's becoming—this sound is, for example, longer or shorter, higher or lower, louder or softer than its predecessor. We might be tempted to say that the past determines what the present is to become, or that the present event is measured *by* its predecessor (say, meted out by the predecessor as efficient cause). These ways of putting it seem to make the past an active agent ("it determines"). But, so put, this seems to have everything backward—the present is active or becoming; the past in itself is not active—it is determined, ended, already become, dead. If it can be admitted that the present is active, it would be better to say that the present measur*es* (present tense) itself against the past, and that the present event tak*es* (active, agent) *its own* measure from the past. If, however, we wish to eliminate such temporal complications (and, indeed, the temporal is not simple), we could say that the new or present "metered" duration is determined by an a priori set of counts set up in the meter signature, or set out in an endless stream of isochronous pulses. To say this would be to deny process by substituting for a temporal development (which involves both determinacy and indeterminacy) the determinism of an abstract, out-of-time schema or imaginary mechanism. The power of this abstraction (i.e., reduction or elimination of complexity) is in its intense focus on one or another category and the ways it can lead to a multitude of categories that can themselves create a complex play, or a play of complexities—rather like an artwork, but working with abstract concepts rather than sensible concepts.

Although I will trade freely in abstraction, I shall attempt to circumvent time-excluding abstractions and their necessary reduction from complexity. The following exposition will be an excursus into the world of the speculative-theoretical in order to find a contemplative foothold in the world of the temporal, where things happen. This is in preparation for a second section composed of several excursions (or incursions) into music, drawing on whatever domain of sensing (kinesthetic/aural/visual) and whatever intensity or valuing the reader can bring.

* * *

In an attempt that I hope might allow for the complexities of time and tense, I would suggest thinking of rhythm (and meter) in terms of events, beginning with immediately successive events of the very simplest sort: one followed by another. This is, of course a severe abstraction. Rhythm (and indeed, event) is always more than just two—so very many things are happening, have happened, and might happen, indeed more than can be counted. To take a processive-temporal perspective is to be open, in principle, to a complexity that goes beyond counting. But I believe this minimal, two-beat (one-another, *primus-secundus*) approach might be a useful place to start thinking about complexity—provided that complexity is built into succession.

To illustrate one approach to the problem of internal or felt measure in the creation of the rhythmic event I offer the diagrammatic representation shown in Figure 13.1. The vertical symbol | marks the emergence of an event; in a sense it *stands* for the whole event. Here two sonic events are represented (*A* and *B*, initiated with asterisks).[5]

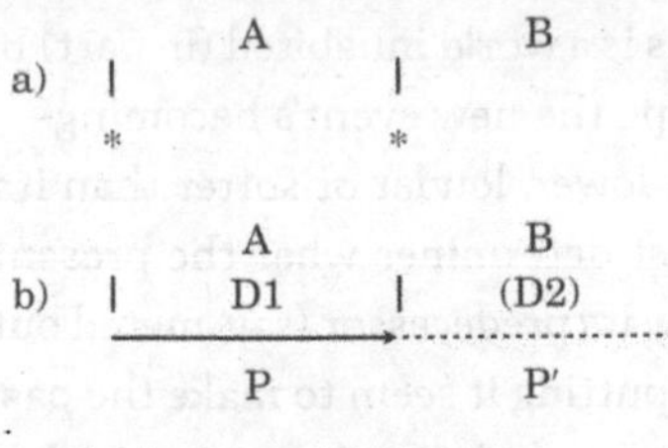

FIGURE 13.1a-b Scheme for simple durational projection.

To imagine temporal passage, Figure 13.1a) might be read by covering the figure with your hand and sliding your hand across the page, left to right to uncover a gradually expanding "space of time" represented by a "time-line." The first mark of emergence will not end in a determinate duration until the second has appeared. With the appearance of a second mark there will now, for the first time, *be* a first event *A* with just this length or duration. From the beginning of the emergence of what will become *A* there is (by our definition of the "mark") a present event be-coming, or coming into being. With the second mark the first event is now a being *in itself*—determined and past, finally come to be. Now, there is no going back to change what has now become. Think of playing. Once you have played this note or figure or phrase, there's no going back. If it was unsatisfactory—too short, out of tune—you'll have to live with it. Perhaps you can make something out of this mistake and discover in your continued playing something useful to work with, something you wouldn't have been given to work with otherwise; or if not so useful, you might just try to regain your balance and try to forget about it. In any case, what's done is done—but not necessarily done with.

The second mark labels a new becoming, "new" in being now. I wish to grant this "new/now" an ultimate freedom or creativity to construct itself out of its parental heritage, out of a settled past but with a view to its own life and destiny in what future it might aspire to or, willy-nilly, become party to. Such freedom is not unlimited or unconditioned. (As we shall see, "free" rhythm can be especially, precisely sensitive to the complex conditions of its environment.) In the case of Figure 13.1a, imagine hearing two sounds (symbolized by asterisks). With the second sound we will hear something not heard in the first—the promise of a more or less definite duration, a duration more or less equal to the first event *A*. With this (provisional) determinacy we can feel about how long the second event might go on, or when we might expect a third event, and if there does come a third event, we might feel if it is early or late.

In Figure 13.1b I have added symbols intended to point to this opportunity for determinacy the second event takes from the first. In this diagram we take a synoptic view of the whole sequence in which the first event is past and the second event is present. D1 is the now past and fully determined (terminated, no longer going on) duration of *A*; D2 is the present and as yet undetermined duration of the ongoing event *B*. (I've placed D2 in parentheses to indicate its indeterminacy and its gradually emerging determination—on its way to determinacy.)[6] The solid line with arrowhead labeled P is not D1—D1 is event *A*'s alone. Rather, P represents the potential of D1 to be taken by event *B* as a factor in its process of self-determination. The arrowhead signifies that it is not for itself but for another. P might be regarded as a potential model or pattern (which, as potential, may or may not be actualized). P' represents the relevance of P for event *B* as a potential that can inform *B*'s becoming in one way or another. The dotted line indicates the openness of this potential for actualization.[7]

The entire process schematized in Figure 13.1b) I call "projection" as a throwing forth (hence the arrow) of the old *into* the new. In this scheme *B* takes *its* measure from *A*, and (at least in the domain of durational quantity) such process is what I will mean by "meter." It should be pointed out right away that projection/meter can never be so simple as the situation represented in this diagram. Since the notion of projection is all about potentiality, it implies nothing fixed or determined in the processes of measuring or taking into account. Potentiality (or virtuality) is precisely indeterminate and endlessly complex in the interweaving of all that can in any actual situation be taken into account: this person, these people, their histories (culturally, bodily), the environment into which this present moment occurs—the countless "set" of circumstances into which the new event occurs and which involve needs and goals that exceed (but still involve) the present moment.

In spite of its extreme simplification, Figure 13.1b) can offer a way of understanding meter as something essentially free and creative. It can also offer a way of seeing in the innovations of modernist music a novel playing with meter, even with the goal of ultimately destroying its virtual (and, as some modernists might argue, not so virtuous) powers. To pursue this line of inquiry I shall have to introduce a few more distinctions and symbols that would engage the issue of "metrical hierarchy," a sort of process that modernists have characteristically sought to limit or to avoid altogether. In Figure 13.2a a third event *C* takes its measure from its predecessor *B* in the projection Q-Q'. But as Figure 13.2b illustrates, with a third event the possibility is opened for the emergence of a new level or scale of measuring. Here the new event *Beta* is given a mark of emergence (|) that makes it a second event in the context of *Alpha*.[8] In this case, a potential R will not be relevant for the beginning of *Beta* (as in Figure 13.2a, a potential Q was relevant for the beginning of event *C*). And yet potential R can be relevant for a later phase or continuation of *Beta*, precisely as it is a later phase or continuation of *Alpha*. In Figure 13.2b) event *B* continues a larger event *Alpha*. The backward-slanting line \ is a mark of (articulated) continuation.[9] The initiation of *B* still ends event *A*, but it does not end *Alpha*.

For an understanding of this diagram two important points must be made. First and foremost, there is continuation during the entire becoming of *Alpha*, even from its very beginning—with and from the mark of emergence | which, though a mark of articulation, is not durationless; indeed, it is the mark of the entire duration, whatever that may become. Emergence and continuation are coextensive. For this reason the two marks, | and \ do *not* label two beats or two parts of the duration. We might say that | extends over \. It is important to note in this connection that the | of *Alpha* is not the | of *A*. (Since the mark of continuation in the figure does happen to correspond to a second "beat" *B* equal to a first beat *A*, I should point out again that

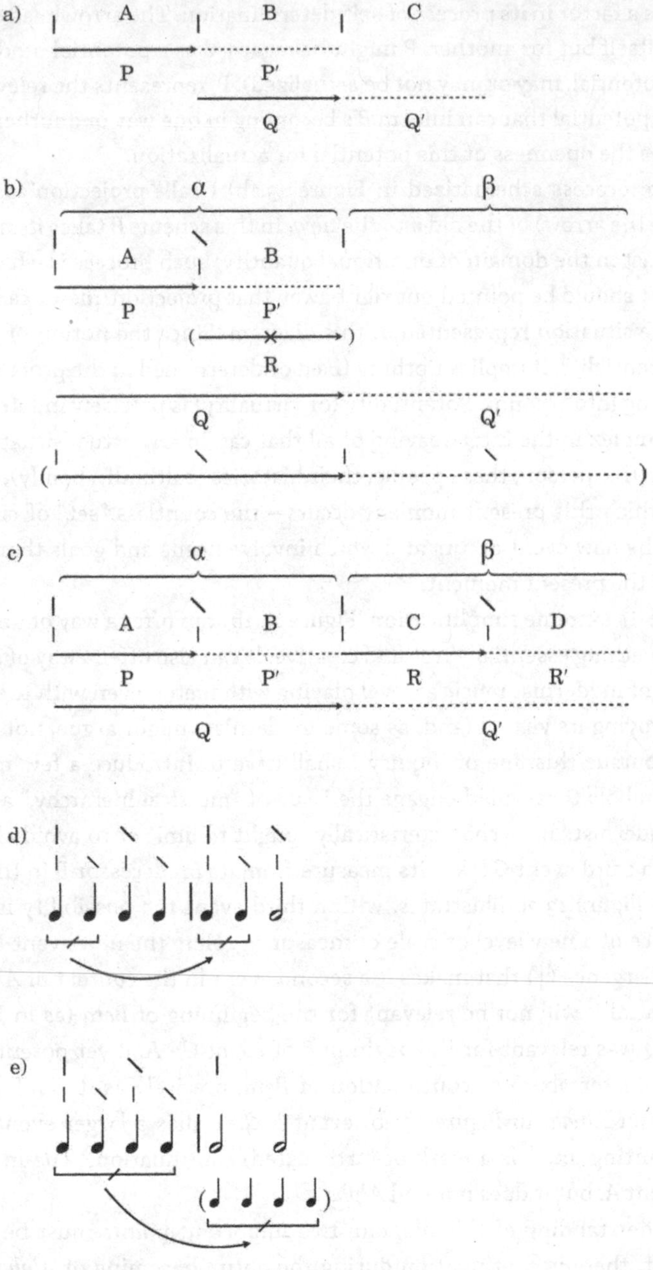

FIGURE 13.2a-e Schemes for compound projections.

any articulation within the event can bear a mark of continuation; that is to say, the symbol \ is not reserved for and does not imply "equal division.") This perspective argues against the opposition of "strong" and "weak" beats as *separate entities* and can also eliminate the need for making a distinction simply on the basis of acoustic stress (however calibrated).[10]

My second point concerns the potential Q in Figure 13.2a, seen in 13.2b as a potential R denied and thus crossed out. Continuation is not projective for a new emergence. One outcome of this observation is the denial of autonomous pulse or beat levels. The lower level is not untouched by or ignorant of the higher. All levels are interaffecting. Although there appears no reason in Figure 13.2b to mark the beginning of *Beta* with a | at the lower level, in Figure 13.2c there is; here an event *C* does form to offer its successor a measure of duration.[11] And yet, in Figure 13.2b if there can emerge a feeling, however faint, of a silent continuation or "offbeat" in *Beta* (D in Figure 13.2c) a potential for the situation shown in Figure 13.2c must have been engendered by the specific form of the *Alphas* of both Figure 13.2b and Figure 13.2c. In this regard it is crucial to note that event *A* of *Alpha* is relevant for event *C* of *Beta*, as *B* of *Alpha* is relevant for *D* of *Beta*. The hierarchic shift to *Alpha-Beta* withdraws the possible projective relevance of *B* for *C* (or *A* for *D*).

Figures 13.2d) and 13.2e) introduce note values (arbitrarily, quarter- and half-notes) and barlines to make the same point and to argue against the notion of autonomous pulse streams going on at the same time. Event *Beta* is a complex duration, not an abstract "*length* of time." It "remembers" something of what *Alpha* became (and something quite special as the one-and-only immediate successor to *Alpha*). In Figure 13.2d I have shown a congruence of the early phases of *Alpha* and *Beta* in which the first and second quarters of *Beta* are inherited from the first and second quarter of *Alpha*. As shown in Figure 13.2e, *Beta* has the potential (given from *Alpha* and shown here in parentheses as realized) of repeating or continuing quarter-note pulses. In this sense, whole precedes part. Such a process is not entrainment as an automatic (infinite) pulse stream that once set up continues of its own accord (though the notion of "entrainment" might be adjusted to allow for ongoing, evolving complexities so barely sketched in Figure 13.2). There may be situations in which we can more or less vividly sense a continuation of pulses that are not sounded. Thus, in Figure 13.2e *Beta* might inherit something of the succession of quarter note events explicit in *Alpha* if we should for any reason need to feel "subdivisions" here, but whether and how vividly a continuation of quarters might be felt is fully, openly, "subjectively" contextual/situational. The becoming of an event *Beta* is free to deny or adjust potentials from *Alpha* in light of other more relevant and possibly conflicting potentials. In a processive theory the emergence of events is highly context-dependent and always adjusting to new situations. Rather than positing a metrical hierarchy, we might as well speak of heterarchy.

Before turning to some of the ways composers (or, we might say, "notaters," puters-together of symbols for performance) have sought to limit or break the inherent "doubling" of durational measure (within and without the bounds of traditional metric notation) I must give a brief processive or "projective" account of triple or unequal measure.[12] In Figure 13.3 I outline a process of mediation or "deferral" as a complication of the immediate succession of equal measure (notice that the sign = is a division in two). In this figure the possibility of a projection Q-Q' is denied or abrogated when a new, second event (*Beta*) emerges with a greater potential S'. To indicate deferral, the two consecutive and equal marks of continuation will be shown connected with a

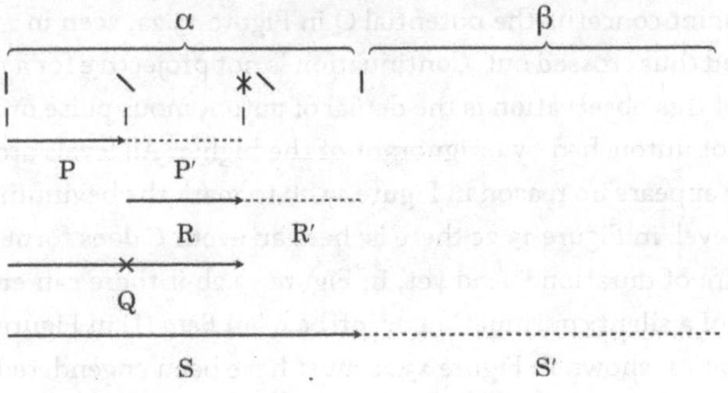

FIGURE 13.3 Scheme for triple unequal projection (deferral).

horizontal line to symbolize the possibility of feeling a suspension or lengthening of continuation, thus: | \—\. There are countless feelings that can arise from deferral—from suspended or held up, or limping, or off-kilter, or galloping, or the heart's "lub, dub" (or any of the other countless characters that can be imagined) to smooth with little if any sense of "unevenness." In the latter case, a clear sense of *pattern* or character in deferral will have disappeared, and in such cases we may have to count to identify "triple meter."[13] Where qualitative pattern has quite disappeared we may, nonetheless, feel the projective consequences of deferral at what might be called a "deeper," perhaps more primitive, quantitative level. But whether deeper or higher, more primitive or more superficial, there is a difference of kind, however we chose to name it.

***

Although modernist music is most often characterized by experiment in pitch or tonal domains, experiment with new rhythmic-metric procedures is no less characteristic. Indeed, the two factors are intricately entwined. Thus, in the case of the atonal ("*frei-tonale*" free-tonal) music of the Second Viennese School (Schoenberg, Webern, Berg, et al.) metrical innovation was prominent from the start. Schoenberg's "emancipation of dissonance" annulled the traditional distinction of consonance and dissonance, or rather treated traditional dissonances as consonant—thus any tone or combination of tones could, in principle, sound together with any other in harmony. This homogenization removes conventional harmony as a clear means of articulation (and thus the difficulties of segmentation in set-class analysis—what notes to circle?).[14] Emancipation of dissonance is thus also a rhythmic-metric emancipation. Without the distinction of consonance (sounding together) and dissonance (sounding apart) "harmonies" (*harmonia*, joining or fitting together) need not arise as sharply defined units that succeed one another. Thus, no clear opportunity for "cutting at the joint"—no "natural" (or rather, conventional) joints. Without clearly felt chord change and harmonic cadence new rhythm will be quite unlike that of the older music that depended on and fostered such tonal heterogeneity. New means would have to be found to create articulations and difference. Were the new means of articulation invented to differentiate new tonal vocabularies, or were these vocabularies created to serve the interests of experiments with a new rhythm? Although this question may be seen as a chicken-and-egg problem,

I am inclined to favor the latter alternative in view of the greater scope I would accord "rhythm."[15]

In his late essay "Brahms the Progressive" (1975/1947), Schoenberg praises the virtues of a "musical prose"—"prose" as unbound ("free") speech in distinction from the bound (strict) speech of verse.[16] Musical prose involves "asymmetry and imparity of structural elements" (429). Although he censures the literal or simply ornamented repetition of melody, Schoenberg gives more attention to the similarly anesthetizing effects of the four-bar phrase and eight-bar period. His examples from the music of Mozart and Brahms (among others) all show departures from the "squareness" of quadratic meter or the progressive doubling of measure (2, 4, 8, 16, 32) in larger durations. I do not take Schoenberg as an authority on the history and fortunes of New Music (or even as a reliable witness to his own practice), but I do think that an intense aversion to the consolations of extended durational doubling has characterized New Music from its emergence in the early twentieth century as a radical alternative to nineteenth-century norms through to the present day.[17]

Why would the "doubling" of thematic repetition and large-scale projection on the order of phrase have seemed undesirable? I imagine that the reason lies in an aversion to a *telos* that in its extent and relative determinacy could permit a relaxation of attention, an "easy listening" enabled by tonal-rhythmic conventions.[18] If the new event promises a repeated melody or a second "equal" phrase length (measured by a tonal/harmonic progression that forecasts cadence) it could be argued that we may not be challenged to attend to the novelty the new event might offer. Such repetition creates a sort of convention of its own, "apart" from, or rather alongside, other stylistic conventions. Resistance to convention as passive habit (let's say with the Modernists) is resistance to a numbing or anesthetizing repetition in which significant difference is attenuated. Of course, we need not use such repetition as an opportunity to relax our attention and forfeit intensity of feeling. Schoenberg does not (nor do other composers, Feldman for example) criticize Mozart for his repetitions and parallel periods. Indeed, he praises such techniques for their contribution to music's "comprehensibility," a supreme value for Schoenberg. But times change and so do audiences. Schoenberg's cultivated and culturally savvy Viennese milieu was enchanted with songs of the post-Hegelian *Geist* of progress mixed with many other voices of spiritual progress such as those of Swedenborg and Rudolf Steiner. The call for spiritual advancement was for many a call for a development or expansion of human reason; moreover, a reason not divorced from sense. As William Blake (2008), an important forerunner of modernist aesthetic spirituality wrote, "Reason, or the ratio of all we have already known, is not the same as it shall be when we know more." For Schoenberg, the need for comprehensibility (as a sort of *ratio*) is a constant in music, but comprehensibility can be accomplished in many ways that vary in their demands and rewards. Schoenberg believed, as did many others, that his time was ripe for heightened complexity as a challenge to comprehensibility and thus a road to spiritual advancement.[19]

* * *

In the early twentieth century the new avant-garde aesthetic asked for a change in the scale and character of repetition, and especially for speed, for a rapid and demanding flux in presentation (Marinetti's Futurism, for example, explicitly exalted speed). Concentrating here on the new use of the "materials" or dimensions of timing and meter, I would like to set the stage by imagining a scale from largest measures or durational projections to the smallest which approach the suppression of projective activity altogether. The largest might be examples of 4-, 8-, 12-, 16-, or 32-bar measures. The limits are imposed by the limits of memory. Durational quantity can be felt most vividly in the range of what is called "the conscious present"—an identifiable span of attention, identified in experimental psychology as a span of time. Estimates are quite various, ranging from 2 to 12 seconds.[20] Hierarchical organization promotes larger durations that can be more or less accurately estimated or reproduced (and that in music might exceed psychologists' measures of much less complex durations/situations). Smaller projections, on the order of 1–2 seconds, are more vividly and differently felt and require less contextual complexity. There is difference of feeling among various hierarchical levels. Indeed, without significant differences of feeling there could be no levels. In classical music, large projections (the glory of nineteenth-century music) drew crucially on melodic and harmonic support to create hierarchic order and to provide a sort of arc or telos that can hold together constituent events. The New Music was happy to give up the old support system to find its new rhythmic complexities.

These new complexities would involve weakening or eliminating projection and in this way challenging or defeating memory. Reducing projective potential might begin with a departure from the repetition of equal 4-bar phrase measures, and then lead to a departure from repetition on the order of bar measures, and so on to the absence of durational projection altogether. But suppressing projection altogether will require various innovative compositional/notational techniques (some of which we will consider shortly). Indeed, it requires special effort to produce "arrhythmic" or ametrical sequences. Paul Fraisse (1982, 165) writes, "If rhythm is order, arrhythmia is disorder . . . A computer can produce this type of sequence. Can Man?" His answer is, only barely and with great difficulty.[21] Projection is an automatic or spontaneous feature of human memory (think the tic-toc of a clock) that requires special measures to defeat—ways of denying or at least minimizing the quantitative durational relevance of an event for a successor.

At the other end of our scale then are situations in which projection is severely limited or eliminated. I suggest two general means for achieving this reduction or elimination: 1) through brief, conflicting durations that do not support one another and thus fail to form even a flexible isochrony; or 2) through protracted lack of significant difference that exceeds the bounds of some form of memory (say, "present memory" into "working memory"). These two categories bear some resemblance to Whitehead's (1985) notions of "triviality" and "vagueness" which together with "narrowness" and "width" constitute "depth" of relevance in experience and the promote "intensity" of feeling (thus the negative connotations of "triviality" and "vagueness" should not be taken to deny their value for rhythm).

> Triviality arises from lack of coordination in the factors of the datum, so that no feeling arising from one factor is reinforced by any feeling arising from any other factor. . . . Thus "triviality" arises from excess of incompatible differentiation. On the other hand, "vagueness" is due to excess of identification. . . . By reason of vagueness, many count as one, and are subject to indefinite possibilities of division (Whitehead 1978, 111–12).

Think, for example, of the dense complexities of articulation in Ferneyhough that can (through their particular "triviality") obscure virtually any feeling of beat, and of Ligeti's *Atmospheres* that begins (in an eloquent tribute to "vagueness") with almost a minute of relatively unarticulated sound and only fleeting, vague feelings of meter. Of course, in music, metrical order is just one dimension of event formation and when suppressed can have the positive result of allowing attention to be drawn to other dimensions, such as timbre and texture. Both "triviality" and "vagueness" can lead to the emergence of large-scale events unbroken by projective articulation, a sort of continuity where possibilities of focusing and holding on to a comfortable conscious present are withdrawn. Such events may at the same time offer opportunities for focusing on fine detail, though this make take some effort or practice. Indeed, for some listeners encounters with "difficult" New Music can seem to offer nothing to focus on if triviality and vagueness are merely destructive (chaos or bland stasis). Focus is a sort of "narrowness" that for the production of high intensity requires a massive "width" of subsidiary sensation as a sort of background in which focusing can take place. In terms of intensity as "speed," think of the focal narrowness as the restriction of a pipe and the width of the subsidiary as the force of the water moving through that pipe. As Whitehead writes, "Intensity is the reward of narrowness" (1978, 112). How novel intensities can be created is the question of how new rhythms can be made.[22]

Although our interest will be focused on intensities of new rhythm, it may be useful to catalog some of the ways in which meter can be reduced or eliminated through an abundance of "incompatible differentiation." In his essay "Musical Technique," Boulez (1971/1963) writes of the need for a "smooth time" (or "amorphous time") as opposed to the "striated time" of "static distribution."[23]

> Western music has ingeniously developed recognized "markers" within recognized forms, so that it is possible to speak of an "angle of hearing" as we speak of an angle of vision [i.e., field of view—the extent of what can be seen at any instant], thanks to a more or less conscious and immediate "memorizing" of what has gone before. But with the object of keeping the listener's attention alerted, these "markers" have become increasingly asymmetrical, and indeed increasingly "unremarkable" . . . Listening is tending to become increasingly instantaneous, so that points of reference are losing their usefulness . . . Frontiers have been deliberately "anesthetized" . . . (Boulez 1971, 178)

Due to our proclivity for hearing projection most vividly in the succession of events on the order of, say, .5–2 seconds it will take special measures to create a "smooth time" in musical textures that involve the articulation of events in this range of duration. Boulez remarks on the difficulty of producing the effect of smooth time from "chronometric" or conventional notation that, for Boulez, ultimately takes its measure from the clock in terms of seconds where a second is translated "M.M.=60":

> The performer, instead of producing smooth time, will *automatically* return to striated time, where the unit of reference is the second—he will fall back on the metronomical unit equal to 60; this confirms how false and illusory directly chronometric notation is in most cases, since the result will directly contradict the [composer's/notater's] intention [the elimination of projection]. True smooth time is that over which the performer has no control (Boulez 1971, 94; emphasis added).

Boulez the notater does have the control to bypass the performer's uncontrollable and "automatic" feeling for beat and projection. Boulez writes that the performer will "return to," "fall back on" striation (measuring) in a gesture of regression. The implication is that ahead lies Boulez's new sort of freedom (perhaps an absolute freedom) born of smooth time. But again, this plastic freedom of the "arrhythmic" is for human beings very difficult to achieve. Acquiring such smooth control or mastery over the performer's natural inclinations requires a careful, sophisticated compositional/notational technique. Indeed, such control could not be exercised without the apparently autonomous, and masterful hammer of a notation.

From a look at the opening of Boulez's "bel edifice et les pressentiments" (double) from *Le Marteau sans maître* (1954) we can identify several devises for the attenuation or elimination of projective potential that operate within the environment of conventional notation. In connection with Figure 13.4, I would list six ways (at least) in which durational projection can be resisted:

1. The timbral diversity of Boulez's vocal-instrumental ensemble can reduce the connection of consecutive sounds. For example, in the first bar (not measure) maraca does not interact with viola to form a triple measure (deferral); similarly, voice and xylorimba in bar 1 are metrically uncoordinated.
2. Fermati can create hiatus or the dissolution of measure. And yet, it should be noted that such negative, "durationless" spaces can be opportunities for subsequent reclamation as positive spaces. Notice, for example, that the hiatus or unmeasured gap created by the longer fermata at bar 3 can (in favorable circumstances) be energized and thus bridged by feeling the stepwise connection of xylorimba and vibraphone (G♯-B♭), similar in timbre (xylorimba sounds an octave higher than written).
3. Meter signatures change sporadically, and change in their denominations ($\frac{2}{4}$, $\frac{7}{16}$, and, continuing: $\frac{5}{8}$, $\frac{3}{8}$, $\frac{3}{4}$, $\frac{3}{8}$, etc.).

4. Ties are used across notated beats, which are thereby suppressed without giving rise to syncopation (see especially the voice part). Since events are rarely ended with silence, silence following sound can have the same effect as a tie—thus the second event in xylorimba bar 1, D♭, is (indefinitely) longer than the first which can thereby become anacrusis.
5. Here grace notes function as anacrusis, but they can in other contexts, especially when appearing in groups of two or more, be used to displace notated beats (see Takemitsu Figure 13.10).
6. In other movements, and later in this movement, frequent changes of tempo, ritardandi, and accelerandi function to weaken a sense of pulse.[24]

It should be noted that these devises are not new. The last of Webern's *Six Bagatelles for String Quartet*, Op. 9 (Figure 13.5) composed in 1913 turns the normally and quintessentially homogeneous ensemble of the string quartet into a vehicle for metrical heterogeneity, segregating sound streams by means timbral, registral, harmonic/intervallic difference and otherwise subverting a sense of pulse, except for a brief hint of triple meter in the opening that soon vanishes.[25] The score is notated in $\frac{3}{4}$ time throughout. But none of these 9 bars is a measure—what would it take, for example, to hear bar 6 as the beginning of a measure of a sonic event? For the player the barline could be a signal to keep the energy of the beginning going rather than planting the C at the end of b.5 as an arrival, as it is otherwise likely to sound (hearing aścending and anacrusitc B and E ending in C). The violinist has freedom and responsibility in making some sort of decision along these lines or, responding to some other sort of

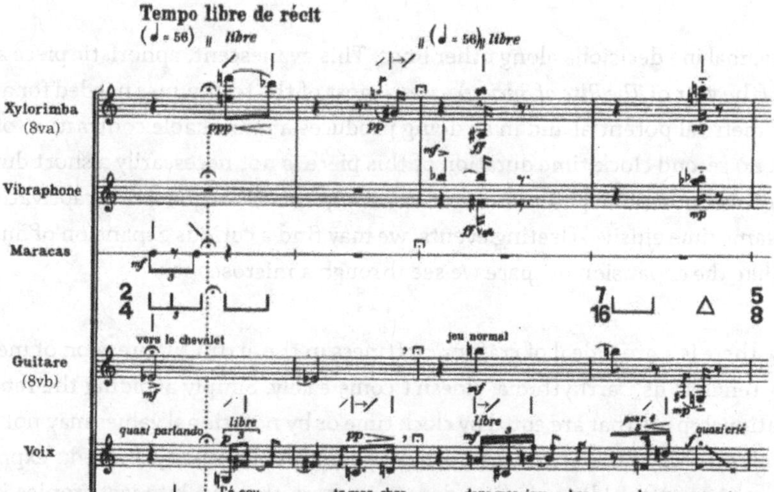

FIGURE 13.4 Pierre Boulez, *Le Marteau sans maître*, no. 9, "bel edifice et les pressentiments" double bs. 1–4.

FIGURE 13.5 Anton von Webern, *Six Bagatelles for String Quartet*, Op. 9 no. 6, bars 1–6.

impulse, making decisions along other lines. This evanescent, aphoristic piece already in 1913 (the year of *The Rite of Spring*) essays most of the techniques needed for a reduction of metrical potential and in so doing produces a remarkable contraction of scale. The ca. 40 second clock-time duration of this piece is not necessarily a short duration. Lost in this "far from equilibrium" and relatively chaotic sequence of captivating and at the same time elusive, fleeting events, we may find a curious expansion of duration, rather like the expansion of space we see through a microscope.

***

Clearly, there is a great deal of craft or craftiness in the artful suppression of meter. As Fraisse reminds us, "arrhythmia" doesn't come easily. Simply avoiding the repetition of durational spans that are equal by clock time or by notational values may not suffice to dissolve meter or the actual measuring of durational quantity. Indeed, "expressive" performance of the old music (i.e., departure from the absolute isochronies implied by the notation) can involve durations far from isochrony—and indeed, far beyond notation.[26] Such performance, though requiring high craft from the performer, does not result in a "difficult" experience for a cultured/acculturated listener, but rather serves as a vehicle to lead to heightened attentiveness. The robustness of projective imagination thus not only survives difference/variation—it seems to be intensified by certain creative forms and degrees of difference. Jeanne Bamberger has provided an instructive example of notational difference. David Lewin (1981, 101–2) relates an experiment Bamberger undertook presenting subjects with a series of five brief synthesized pulses "separated by successive durations of 2, 3, 4, and 5 time units, at a brisk tempo," as illustrated in Figure 13.6a where Lewin has represented the time unit as an eighth note. Subjects were told they would be hearing an ametrical sequence. To their surprise, what they heard was something resembling Figure 13.6b (Lewin's notation, modified). In Figure 13.6b I have added metric-functional symbols and have given a whole note duration to the 5th sound event (a dot in Lewin's example) suggesting that its duration will continue through silence, as indeed is implied by the notated $\frac{4}{4}$ meter signature.

In New Music there are many cases in which a rhythmic figure that looks ametrical sounds fully metrical but with a sort of nuance that resembles a more spontaneous "expressive" (or, if edgier, "expressionistic") timing. Perhaps the motivation for composing such figures is to insert such nuance in a "style" that does not offer performers reason to provide it on their own. I say "resembles" because, for the player, counting may (at least, initially) replace feeling and because very precise notation can ask for exact replication in every performance and thus allow little freedom for the player. As an example, consider the figure shown in Figure 13.7a from Toru Takemitsu's *Rain Tree* (1981) for three percussionists and a silent fourth—the "light player," who I imagine might also be a percussionist skilled in "counting." For purposes of reference I have numbered bars (both dotted and solid). Figure 13.7a is from page 6 of the score (approximately 1.7 minutes into the piece). Since this new and second section is preceded by a double bar, I will for convenience label these bars 1–8.

On a darkened stage spotlights illuminate, in turn, two of the three percussionists: on the far left, performer *A* and on the far right, performer *B*.[27] Each plays marimba and also 3 crotales (differently pitched for *A* than for *B*). The middle position occupied by the third performer *C* playing vibraphone and 11 crotales is dark for now. Both *A* and *B* have cues for one another in their respective notated parts, but only for the first 11 or 12 bars (with bar 13 lights go on and stay on for the two players). The

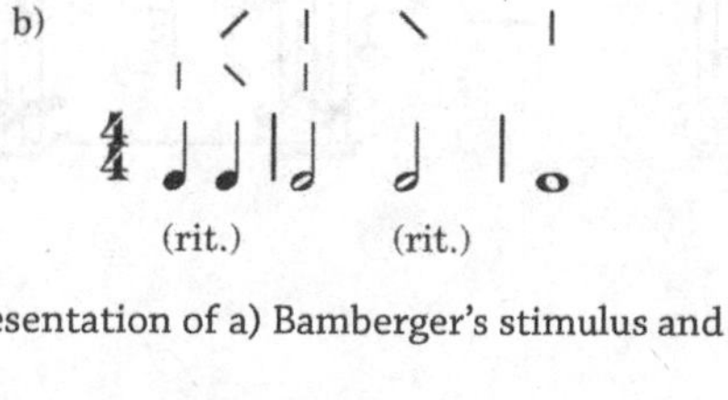

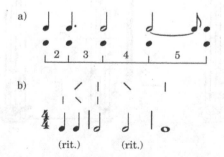

FIGURE 13.6 Lewin's representation of a) Bamberger's stimulus and b) her subjects' interpretation (modified).

(a)

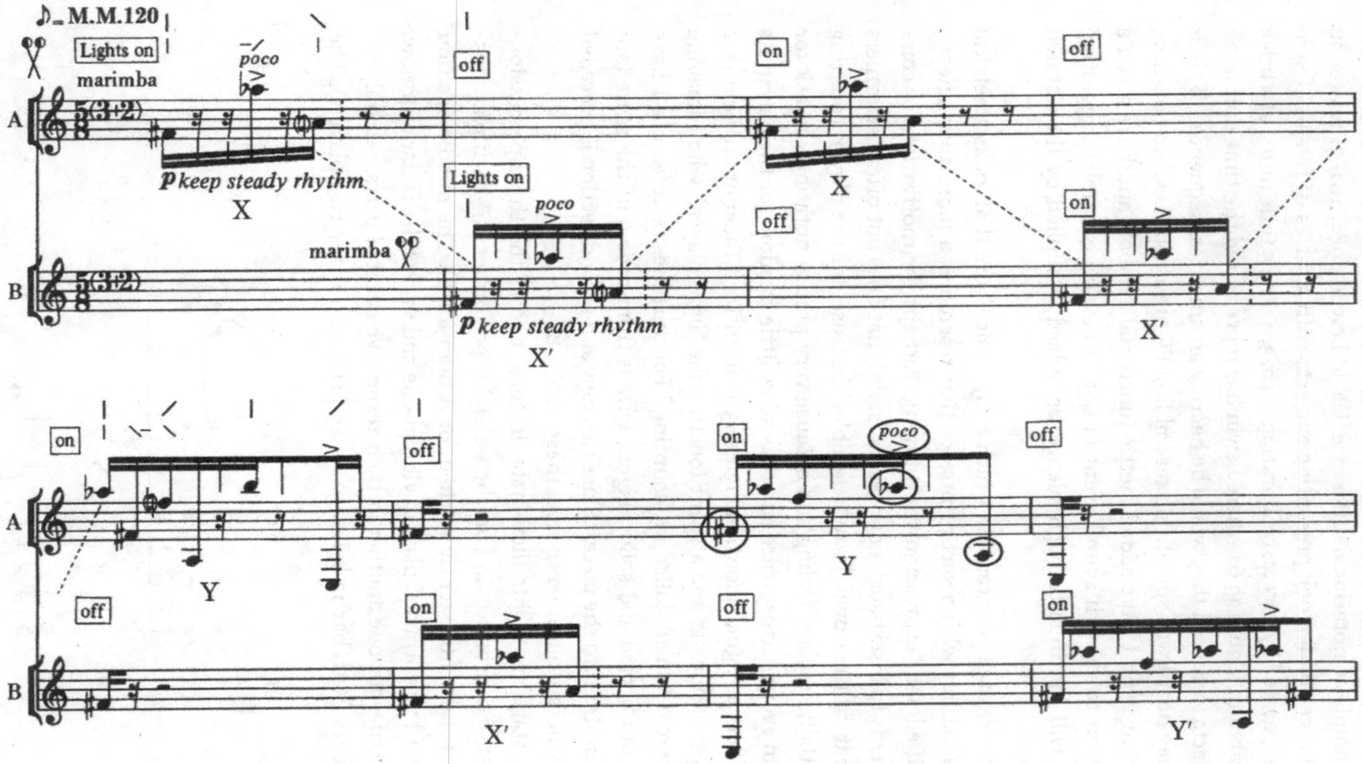

(b)

FIGURE 13.7 Toru Takemitsu, *Rain Tree*, a) second section bs. 1–8 (bottom of page 6); b) interpretation of figure X.

pattern the two marimba players exchange is notated to be counted in 3+2 eighths, the second and third sounds (A♭ and A) falling on off-beats, perhaps to give the players a feeling of syncopation as anacruses suspended over a silenced beginning. But for the listener not counting, the effect is more complicated, as I indicate in Figure 7b. In two graduate seminars I taught, all but two of the approximately 16 students vividly felt, from the first hearing, triple or unequal measure in which the second beat, A♭ (deferred continuation) seemed a bit too long, a slowed beat momentarily suspended, hesitating before moving to a second measure (beginning with A-natural), itself continuing a larger measure. Some found the following entrance of Marimba *B* unpredictable. The two students who initially resisted this interpretation were able to identify a 3+2 pattern by counting sixteenths. Eventually everyone could hear it both ways and also hear it strangely between the two.[28]

The two students who searched for and found the 3+2 pattern were percussionists at heart. Because the performers (light player included) are to be precisely coordinated, they will have to count. And yet how the three players count need not be fully determined by the notation—the only requirement is to make their timings accurate. Subdividing, counting (10) sixteenths, rather than eighths, could give more security—thus, 3+3+4 (playing A♭ on the beat) or 5 (3+2) + 5 (two equal measures). Or, in the course of practicing, players (individually) might experiment with a variety of solutions. Could the players with practice come also to hear something of Figure 13.7b, or must they remain deaf to a rhythm they produce for some of their audience? It is difficult to say, but I believe that hearing/feeling might accommodate such complexity. (Notice that only in bars 1–4 and bar 6 are there dotted lines explicitly indicating $\frac{3}{8}+\frac{2}{8}$.)

As this (third) section continues, the initial figure becomes submerged in an increasingly complex texture (later vibraphone and crotales join, and the stage becomes fully lighted). In a second "phrase" event new figures—bars 5, 7, and 8 in Figure 7a—give rise to new rhythmic sensations sharpened by pitch repetitions that are enhanced by the limited pitch material (in order of presentation: F♯, A♭, A, F, B, and E) and fixed register (with the exception of A which appears in two registers). In Figure 7a I have labeled the initial "fixed" figure, X (X' in marimba *B*) and the sharply contrasting "variable" figure, Y (Y' in marimba *B*). Notice that after the two-bar repetitions in bars 1–4 (marimba *A*–marimba *B*, repeated) a potential for a new two-bar (or four-bar) measure is systematically withdrawn: bar 5 promises a new, second event, but then X' returns—a beginning-again? But then with bar 7, could there be a new pairing—bars 4–5 (X'-Y) and bars 6–7 (X'-Y)? And yet with bar 8, a new pairing emerges—here Y' closely reenacts Y (bar 7) through pitch repetition—the first 5 pitches of Y' repeat the pitches of Y (notice too the low Cs)—and both these events depart from Y in bar 5; in their new sort of repetition they can forget the first Y and the larger event Y-X' (not to mention the larger event, bars 1–4). A lot is going on here. But I would mention one detail in light of Takemitsu's choice to (re)write *poco* above the accented A♭ in bar 7—this *is* the suspended A♭ of X, but now farther held up and isolated. There is so much going on to be heard/felt/thought.

Salvatore Sciarrino's *Muro d'orizzonte* (1997) provides a comparable example of precisely notated flexible rhythm/meter in the alto flute figure shown in Figure 13.8, bar 14.[29] Here precision of notation and the precision of perception cannot be so easily sorted out. For one thing, we now have a conductor and a player (the flutist) who does not have to coordinate with another player. Certainly, the player is asked to respond conscientiously to the notated instruction and to achieve a consistency in the three varied repetitions of this initial figure in the following bars (14–19). But this will be a different sort of counting than we observed in Figure 13.7 and involve a creative working/playing with a different sort of repetition. Notice that in the course of bars 14–19 the figure changes as the notated B♭ (sounding F, a fourth below) becomes increasingly detached metrically and with bar 16 changes timbrally, forfeiting some of its pitchness in a half-step fall (here the pitch is produced by blowing air through the flute without producing a full sound). Thus far in the piece B♭ has been the only note played *ordinario* with distinct pitch. Thus the emergence here of a line, B♭-A-A-G, is new and can ask for special attention. The pitches notated this line are fingered, resulting in timbral and pitch modification of the four sounds (notice the acceleration across the four).

Above bar 14 in the example I have indicated a likely perception from the position of an "outsider," that is, a hearer not privy to the notation and not responsible for the production of its effects. I suggest a perception of something like a "$\frac{3}{8}$ meter" where the second sound is continuative for the first and the third is continuative for the second. (The only other possibility is a perception of | \ | \ where the repeated the pitch A initiates a new event; but this possibility is withdrawn in succeeding iterations of the figure.) In this case the second sound is slightly too long, and the third is slightly too short. So there is no process of getting longer or getting shorter (no ritardando or accelerando). Rather there is a slight instability (perhaps the short third sound can give a bit of energy to the fourth as the flutist negotiates the 32nd-note offbeat) contributing to uncertainty and fragility of the sounds. In its succeeding iterations the figure becomes gradually broken. The distance from B♭ to the first A is progressively lengthened (from 1 to 3 to 5 to 7 eighths) as the distance from G to the new downbeat (B♭ in bars 16–19) is shortened. With bar 19 the process is suddenly and shockingly accelerated or truncated. Here the bass clarinet's E tongue slap interrupts the figure—no G and a sudden starting over with the delayed B♭ (now mezzo forte).

Notice that this process doesn't get underway until bar 16. In bar 15 there is a rather surprising return to the pervasive fortissimo overblown flute (see Figure 13.9), which will reassert itself again in bars 20–24 ($\frac{3}{8}$ is one of only two departures from $\frac{4}{4}$ in the first 37 bars). In bar 14 the bass clarinet's repeated 16th-note figure is taken up again from bar 11 (Figure 13.9) where it entered as something new and, till now (without issue) seemed forgotten. (Incidentally, without watching the conductor, how would you know in bars 11 and 14 that the clarinet begins with an "offbeat"?) Now in bar 15 it is continued, higher and louder, in English horn under which the clarinet introduces a new sound, a multiphonic. These promising developments are abandoned as the focus turns to our initial 4-note figure, but with bar 20 overblown flute and the

FIGURE 13.8 Salvatore Sciarrino, *Muro d'orizzonte* bs. 13–22.

new bass clarinet sound return and take over for five bars taking with them the liberated B♭ glide. A new and second section of the piece (not shown here) then slides into becoming—the new section is clearly underway in bar 28 when it emerges that it had already begun with bar 25 and that the fifth flute blast in bar 24 was indeed an ending of sorts (it "ends" again in bar 28, but in bar 29 it has no effect against the new tongue-trilled sounds, and in bar 31 is transformed into a new composite figure with bass clarinet).

I mention these details to give a general idea of this music's rhythmic behavior, how it moves. This is a behavior that is constantly changing in unpredictable ways making up new "rules" as it goes. There are always many processes going on simultaneously—aligning, parting, forgotten, remembered, transforming one another in interaction and thus transforming into new processes. In some ways this procedure is reminiscent of "process" or "phase" music, but with far less rigidity. It is not so unlike any musics that in their complexity reward close attention, but the speed of change is remarkable. To follow this course of events will require extraordinary attention to detail or nuance in sound and timing of sound. (In live performance, it will also require stillness on the part of the audience—many of the sounds are barely audible, and extraneous sounds can easily be assimilated into "the music" where they can have significant sonic and rhythmic/metric consequences). Exploring the behavior of the music that precedes bar 14 (Figure 13.9) will give us an opportunity to see something more of Sciarrino's rhythmic invention and help to give a fuller picture of Sciarrino's multidimensional, heterarchic technique, and to place Figure 13.8 in its proper context.

The piece opens with four violent blasts from the alto flute, an overblown fingered C (the flute's lowest note) producing the overtones notated C, D, and E. The low, soft bass clarinet tongue slaps, changing in (fairly indeterminate) pitch, can be heard with close attention. In the middle, the even softer English horn key clicks are largely masked but can gradually become perceptible in their delays. At eighth note = 60 each bar lasts 8 sec. The conductor does not beat but does provide a quick upbeat preparation for the beginning of the four events. Of course, neither the players nor the audience are counting. Eight seconds would seem to far exceed the bounds of projective potential for this single isolated sound soon lost in echoic rehearsal.[30] The blasts, which can be painful, like an electric shock, are unpredictable except for the conductor's quick upbeats that suddenly call them forth. This loud, piercing sound (*furiosa, crudele*) is going to happen again, but when? Not watching the conductor or hearing a recording can intensify the anxiety this opening provokes (I have seen students flinch at each of these sounds, as I have myself). Even if fully, quantitatively unmeasured, these four events may, nonetheless, give rise to a sort of doubling if there is an inclination toward pairing, that is, coming to feel not just a third event but a second 2-bar event. In any case, the fourth (or perhaps second) event is cut short with the entrance "too soon" of a new phrase, a beginning-again and the beginning of something new. The sudden, novel profusion of key clicks in bar 4 has no issue, goes nowhere (this sort of figure won't be encountered again for another 29 bars). A new behavior forms with new sounds. The

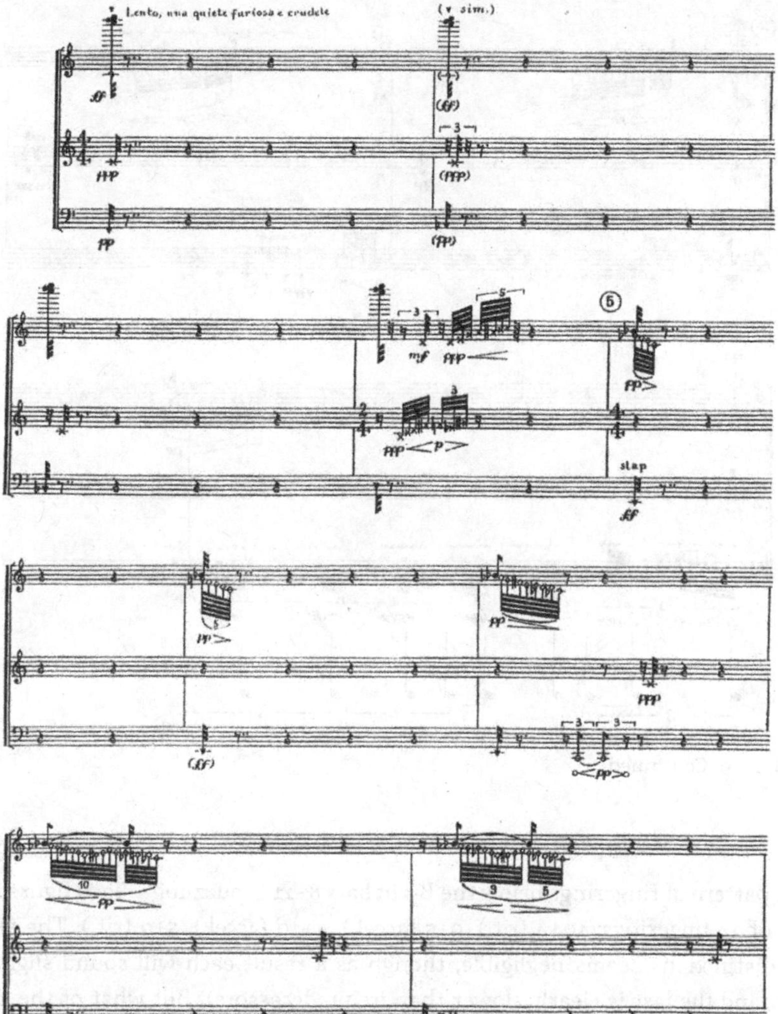

FIGURE 13.9 Salvatore Sciarrino, *Muro d'orizzonte* bs. 1–12.

pitched B♭ and low fortissimo tongue slap (bar 5) will survive for another 15 bars. This second phrase develops a process (much clearer than the first) of lengthening and complicating. After the first 2 bars (again paired?) a new sound appears in clarinet coupled with a return of English horn key click. In bar 8 the lengthening of flute continues, but no bass clarinet. Let's say we're waiting for the clarinet—waiting, but now the key click, late. Thus, I suggest that the absence can draw attention to the click and give it fresh meaning. From here the flute gets progressively later and so does the English horn, becoming an ever sooner anacrusis to the returned flute blast. Then flute late (bar 9); and click even later, which makes the return to the opening blast early (as we have seen, a similar sort of "phasing" occurs in bars 14–19.)

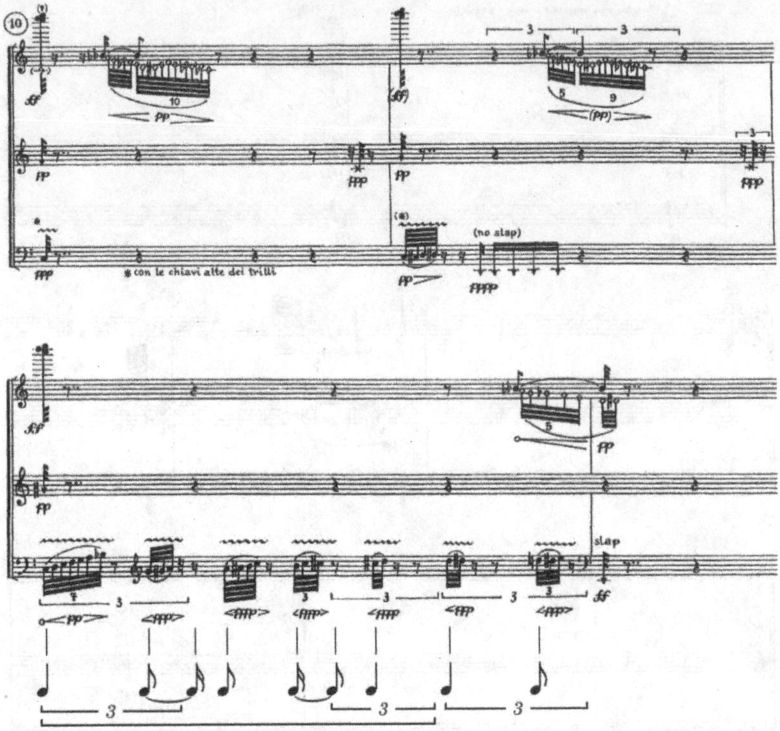

FIGURE 13.9 Continued

The pattern of fingerings below the B♭s in bars 8–11 is puzzling—each figure is composed of 14 fingerings: 10+4 (rit.), 9+5 (accel.), 4+10 (accel.), 5+9 (rit.). The effect of these distinctions seems negligible, though as a result each will sound slightly different (and the last is clearly slower than its predecessors). But what of the notated pattern: 10+4, 9+5 | 4+10, 5+9? What does this notated pattern mean? Consider another curiosity: the notation of the new (bar 11) sonic strand in bass clarinet (trilled from above) in bar 12 is also rather esoterically patterned but has a clear effect. The clarinet line here is precisely notated in order to avoid any trace of meter. Below bar 12 I have notated the durations of these seven events from their onsets. In the absence of pulse, the acceleration-retard-acceleration I have shown has no musical (i.e., sensible) reality. Possibilities for durational projection cancel one another out in an excess of uncoordinated detail ("triviality"). The reduction to two trills toward the end has an effect as does the compression into three covering the flute (*da niente*, from nothing) and then suddenly slapping us back into an earlier behavior (bars 5–11) but now (bar 13) out of order, with the flute Bb preceding the clarinet fortissimo tongue-slap. And now a long, 8-second "rest." (Things are changing.)

But the question remains: if the point of bar 12 is to block a metrical/projective feel, then why the notated measuring? My renotation in Figure 13.9 sharpens visual measuring and reveals a chiasmus that is certainly visible, if not audible. As is shown, the first five events display the same pattern read right-to-left and left-to-right. This would be an example of Messiaen's "non-retrogradable rhythm," that is, "a rhythm" (really, an abstract pattern) that if played "backward" can't be distinguished from its purported "forward" version.[31] Such symmetrical or palindromic patterns, which do not as such block projection, are produced by a simple rule—"*write* the same pattern backward." That such a pattern occurs here could well be pure coincidence, but imagining that Sciarrino did use this procedure in notating, what might be the rationale? If the primary object is to block projective potentials, and there are very many ways to do this, and you don't want to choose, then why not simply invoke a rule. Similarly, if the "moaning" figures in bars 8–11 are to be repeated with slight difference, and the specific differences are inconsequential ("vagueness"), why choose them individually rather than by (global) rule? (How exact do the 10's, 9's, 5's, and 4's have to be?) Here two ways of dividing 14 are chosen (10+4 and 9+5), each with its two possible orderings. Although these examples are inconclusive, they do point to the value of algorithmic procedures in general. When particular details don't much matter—where a variety of different details would produce essentially the same global effect—the choices are arbitrary, and the services of an "outside" arbitrator can be called for, an arbitrator (algorithm) that makes its own binding ruling. Serialized musical dimensions can be organized by rule when particularity of decisions does not matter (where "narrowness" is not asked to contribute to "depth," or rather a certain kind of "depth"). Boulez's serialism, Ligeti's microcanons, Xenakis's stochasticism, and Cage's yarrow sticks work along similar lines. But of a different generation, Sciarrino is not much interested in the charms of rule, and, in any case, with the following phrase, beginning bar 14, the emergence of significant/meaningful contrast promotes a new "depth," taking everything together.

* * *

Returning to *Rain Tree*, the second section shows another solution to the problem of dissolving projective potentials (Figure 10). Here the two players of crotales (antique cymbals, written two octaves below sounding) are asked, in darkness, to improvise "softly and irregularly like raindrops falling from the leaves."[32] The crotales provide a nonfocal background, which could be compromised by any emergence of pattern. But no pattern is at all likely to emerge; even if individually an inclination to repeat were to surface (as Boulez fears it must), the interference from the other player will cancel out any patterning available to the audience. Darkness insulates the players from one another (moreover, the two are placed on either side of the central vibraphone) and hides them from the spectator; and, of course, in a recording all is darkness. This "background" is not intended to interact with the focal and spotlighted vibraphone, which offers a precise and elusive measuring of durational quantity.

Vibraphone is asked to play "soloistic, freely" (in contrast to Figure 13.7a, "keep steady rhythm")—freely because solo, no need to coordinate with another player.

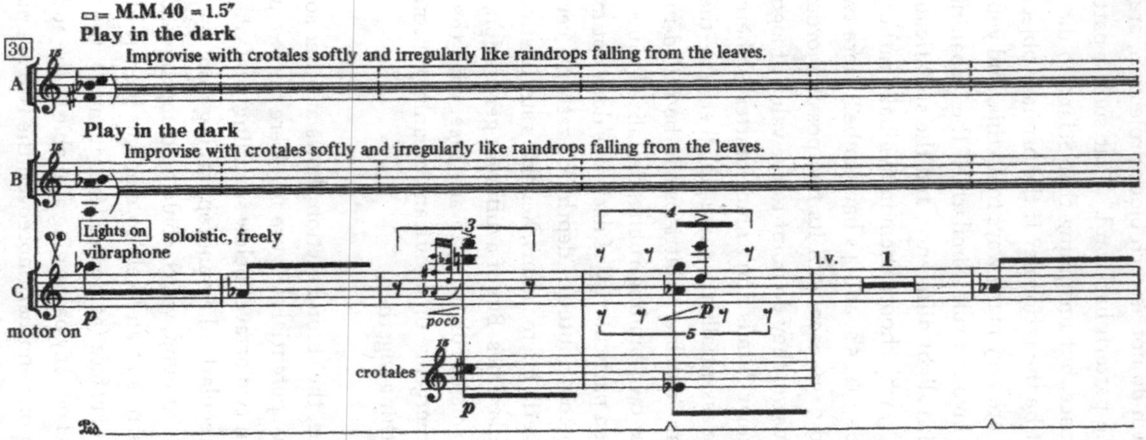

FIGURE 13.10 Toru Takemitsu, *Rain Tree*, first section bs. 30–45 (page 5 of score).

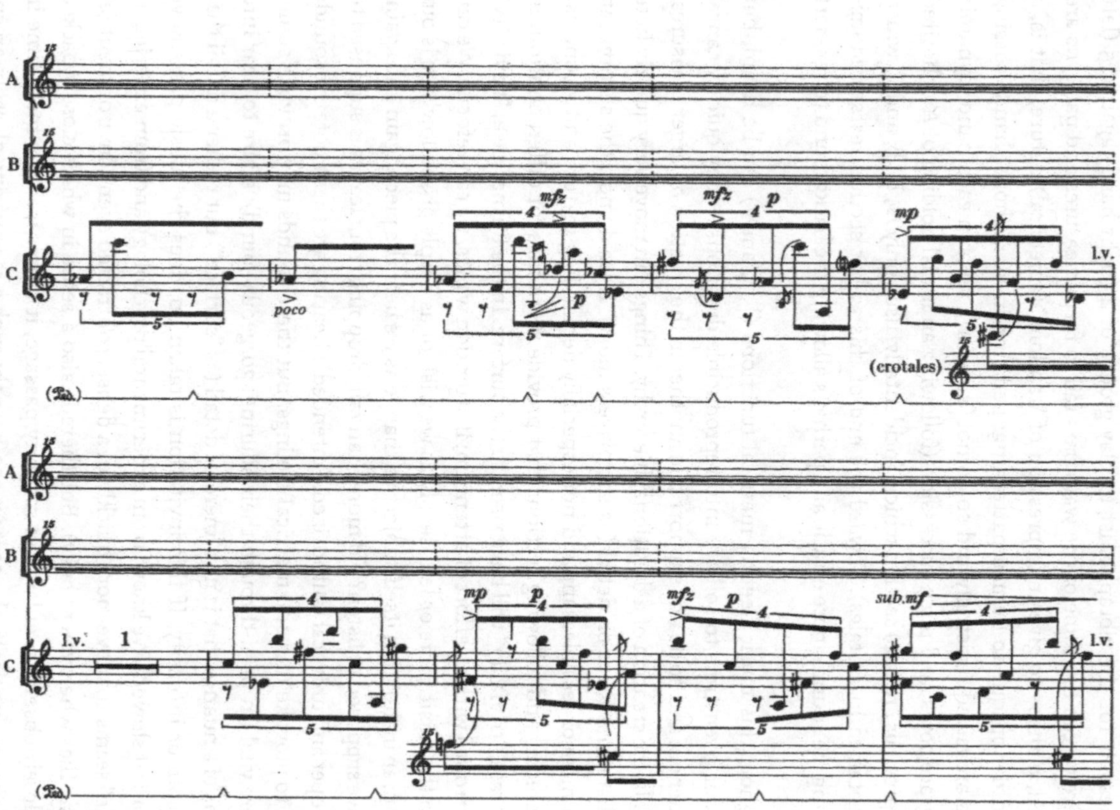

FIGURE 13.10 Continued

The vibraphonist also plays crotales, which do not duplicate pitches of the other two players. Takemitsu's notation is metrically less conventional than Sciarrino's—no meter signatures, just bars (dotted for crotales) of 1.5 seconds duration divided into 3s, 4s, and 5s as needed. 1.5 seconds is well within the projective potential for single sounds (that is, clapping at this "interval" can be quite precise and confident) and provides a measure for the vibraphonist to play groups of 4 (right hand) against 5 (left hand). Here we can list some of the ways bars fail to form measures and patterns are suppressed, perhaps to give an impression of "random" (ametrical) nature, that is, a complex order opaque to human patterning: pedaling in vibraphone, hand crossing (4s and 5s are mixed registrally and so do not "stream"), rests in each hand, dynamic accents, grace notes, and pitch succession (following an initial holding of A♭ inherited from the previous crotales section which, incidentally, used only A♭, B♭, B, and C, which are here retained in crotales). Toward the end of this 32-bar section rests predominate making the sounds more erratic and perhaps allowing the background to reassert itself.

Throughout this music fleeting metrical functions (|, \, and /) can be heard, but they are not given time to solidify into reproducible durations—they quickly cancel one another out and so do not support one another in the creation of larger measures, much less in the creation of a durational hierarchy. Things can move very quickly here if we (as listeners) focus on detail (as the players must). If we do not, the section can become a more or less pleasant and not especially demanding texture and a contrast to the preceding and following sections that provide more cues for differentiation. In the latter case, "triviality" will have risen to the surface. In the former case, "triviality" will be narrowed with an effort of attention; if attention wanes, we can refocus. We can enter into the music more or less deeply as we wish or as deeply or shallowly as is our inclination, an inclination itself subject to change as we hear the piece again and again. How are we supposed to listen? No more than rain dropping from leaves is supposed to elicit a proper and univocal (authorized, "intended") hearing are these notated sounds intended to provoke univocal metrical feelings. But these sounds may provoke something more vital (in part, through their alluring, gorgeous sound): a lure to hear into the depths of a nuance that is not "merely" detail (as "surface") but rather a detail that invites depth or intensity. If this invitation is taken up, does the music pass/move quickly, or is it slowed? We know, from experimental psychology and from experience, that "time" seems to move more quickly in a dense, contracted event environment (at work, time flies when you're busy). But there is also a sense in which closely packed events, closely observed, enlarge or magnify passage; it seems we have more time in which to observe/notice/feel—as if we see/hear through a magnifying glass. In an environment such as Takemitsu has assembled here, a listener is free to focus in a deepened awareness, a paradoxically smaller and larger scale of "presence"—or not.

***

Coincidentally, *Rain Tree*, like *Muro*, begins with a sort of regularity, an engagement (at arm's length) with the old doubling. In the first section of *Rain Tree* (Figure 13.11) such

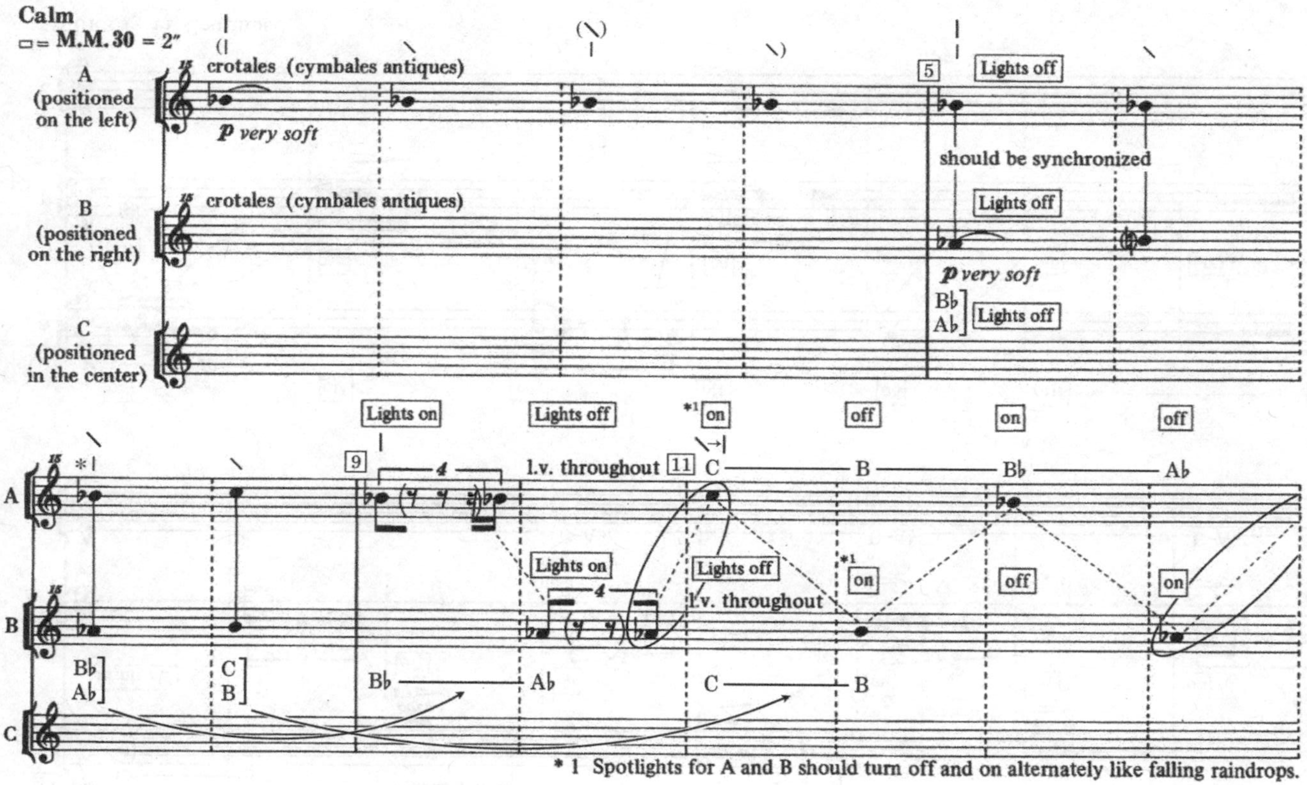

FIGURE 13.11 Toru Takemitsu, *Rain Tree*, opening bs. 1–29.

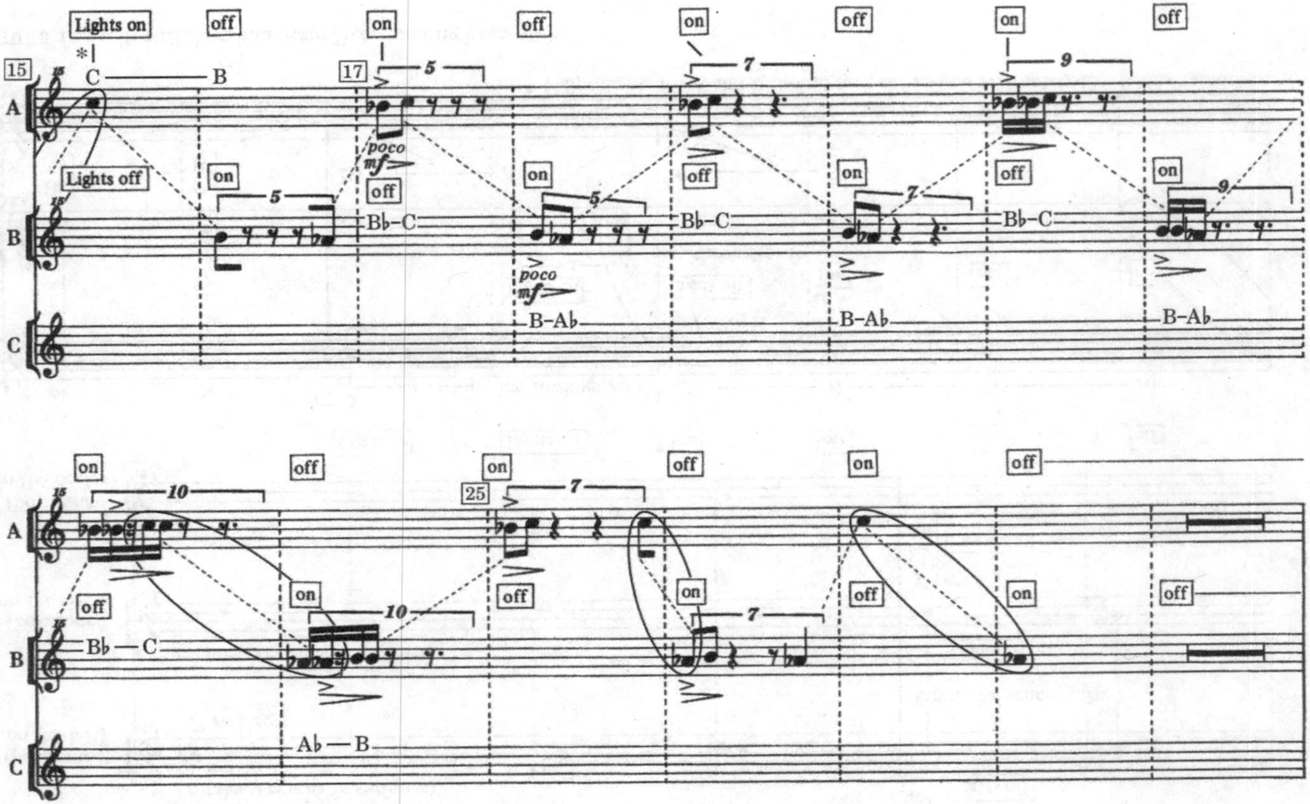

FIGURE 13.11 Continued

doubling is far more explicit, which is to say, more palpable. Two-second durations are well within the sort of conscious present that for single impulses can (with attention) give rise to fairly vivid projective potentials. Here they must be vividly felt for the three players to coordinate their timings. The larger potentials I will propose are not so vivid, but they can, nonetheless, serve in various ways to place us in larger phrase or phase events. Notice that Takemitsu has designated three sections/events with solid bar lines: the first with lights on, the second with lights off, and the third with alternating spotlights ending in darkness. For the lights-off section the players must rely on an internalization of the preceding 2-second durations set up by crotales *A*.

The piece opens with a homogeneous succession of single sounds. The second sound is a continuation of some sort, if only of the piece that has begun. The third might be just that, another continuation on the same level—merely a "third" sound. But there is the possibility that it could become the initiation of a second event if a spontaneous and barely audible "subjective grouping" takes hold. With bar 5 that possibility, if felt, will have in a sense prepared the new event. Here the projective functions I have marked are certain—the beginning-again (*) with bar 7 (B♭ -A♭) articulates two events, as does pitch contour (up-up). I have also indicated the possibility of a larger 4-bar measure ended with the new and third event beginning in bar 9. The second (4-bar) event (bars 5–8) does not need the first to be heard with these projective functions, but the first is projective for the contrast that we hear in the second—a contrast that might involve a more or less implicit metrical order ("2+2") becoming explicit. If this connection of the two 4-bar events is a form of doubling it is quite different from the old doubling.

Now with the more robust potential of the second 4-bar event in play, a third event beginning with bar 9 can begin more or less straight away as a projected potential and one that, for some time, seems to be working—notice the inverted repetition of pitch contour that preserves a 2+2 grouping (now down-down) and the repetition of the pitch dyads B♭-A♭ followed by C-B. But somewhere in bars 11–14 things change. The stopped sounds (indicated by rests) and the anacruses in bars 9–10 disappear, and a descending line through the four pitches (C-B-B♭ -A♭) emerges. What might have been, and perhaps initially was a continuation with bar 11 has now become the beginning of a 4-bar (8 sec.) measure. The beginning again with bar 15 (C–B) and change of contour signal a new measure with a relatively robust potential inherited from bars 11–14 (relative to this relatively large scale of duration); but again anacrusis (now a cue?) leads into a reinterpretation. The new patterning, mezzo forte, in 17–20 (now clearly "2+2") can form a 4-bar measure followed by another that continues the process of accelerating and multiplying strokes. Such a process, however, is ended or reversed with bars 25–29. The slowing, perhaps coupled with a dissolution of larger measure leads to cadence. Notice the new complication here: bar 24 breaks the pattern by ascending in pitch (A♭-B). The pitch succession in bars 23–24 is now B♭-C-A♭-B, the same as bars 25–26 which dissolves the rhythmic pattern in preparation for the cadential descent C-A♭, from top to bottom of the pitch set: C,B,B♭,A♭ (up until bar 24, C was never directly followed by A♭).

All these tenuous and carefully balanced complexities prevent the music from foregrounding a regular periodicity and thus do not (or need not, even in theory) index the old world of doubling. The tenuousness of 8-second projective potentials, the delayed functional reinterpretations or overlappings, and the focus on constantly paired bars enhanced by lighting allow the larger measures to do their articulative work subcutaneously. These articulations are necessarily marked by sonic details as lures for attention; thus, such "markers" become more remarkable as they come to function in the creation of larger becomings.[33]

* * *

Both *Rain Tree* and *Muro* display a great variety of rhythmic behaviors different from those few we have explored so far in this chapter. Such variety and novelty, which involves changes of density, speed, scale, character, and intensity, is itself rhythmic in the very broad sense of the characterful shaping and play of events. In contrast to this marked heterogeneity, many pieces by Morton Feldman offer behaviors that are less obvious in their difference but no less inventive and no more or less hetero-hierarchical. I have chosen music composed by Feldman to conclude this essentially (fundamentally) open-ended survey of techniques and notations in view of its rhythmic invention and in view of its focus on notation as intrinsic to composition rather than simply an instrumental means for recording visibly what has been and is to be heard.[34] Indeed, much of my commentary has been focused on notation in these various attempts to create a new music that might use the old notational conventions for new ends. But these ends can involve explicitly problematizing the symbolic-diagrammatic medium of the score. This is not to say that the notations of older musics aren't problematical even in the performance of the standard eighteenth- and nineteenth-century repertory ("don't just play the notes").[35] But New Music has pointedly questioned the apparent transparency of notation as a neutral, objective, and ultimately invisible medium for magically reproducing the same properly musical effects/affects. Moreover, New Music on the avant-garde side has worked or played with the power of notation, even as a political power that might interestingly be explored and tested in music. If music can connect the symbolic-graphic and the symbolic-aural/kinetic, then music is a complex multimedia—and if symbolic-graphic, why not move all the way to symbolic-verbal (conceptual), and thus allow music a critical voice.

Throughout his career Feldman used symbolic-graphic notations in puzzling or problematic ways to point beyond the page to what is not and cannot itself be represented—in a word, *rhythm*, which is nothing if not presented and *per*formed (i.e., *actually* formed/shaped/made to appear). In Feldman's always-experimental notation the bar or (more generally) "the grid" can serve as sources of irony or paradox that are not separate from "the music." Irony and paradox are vehicles and perhaps themselves notations (*notatio*, explanation or observation) for thinking/feeling farther, farther than the apparently "given." Toward the paradoxical I would cite two of many examples. On the first page *Spring of Chosroes* for violin and piano (1977) shown as Figure 13.12, a note (**) appears to assure the reader that the anomaly of bar 5 is not a printer's error: "This bar is slightly longer than the $\frac{5}{8}$ but stands as the composer intended." The

** violin part bar 5: this bar is slightly longer than 5/8 but stands as the composer intended

FIGURE 13.12 Morton Feldman, *Spring of Chosroes* bs. 1–7.

preceding and following bars are peculiar in their own way with their "delayed triplets." Are the delayed triplets (differently delayed in bars 5–6) meant to resist or break the bar/grid (how rigid)?

In the 1983 composition *Crippled Symmetry* (not just *asymmetry*) for flute/bass flute, vibraphone/glockenspiel, and piano/celeste (Figure 13.13), a lack of notated coordination among the three players is coupled with a great "rhythmic" specificity within each part. This peculiar and paradoxical coupling may, nonetheless, present opportunities for other sorts of coordination or interaction not exactly "controlled" by the notation but nonetheless fostered by it.[36] Each part presents a sequence of distinctive or characteristic patterns or patterned behaviors defined by similarity/difference in various dimensions. The patterns are short (often four notes) and vary constantly in various dimensions without losing their "identity" as pattern. The patterns/behaviors/sounds of the three parts often have potentials for closely interacting in pitch and contour. And, more than simply interacting, the two "percussion" parts (especially glockenspiel and celeste) can sometimes become confused. Again, and most remarkably, the players are notationally uncoordinated—each reads from their part and is not asked to synchronize with the others. The score is barred, but each bar contains wildly incommensurate durations/measures (signatures from $\frac{7}{2}$ to $\frac{3}{32}$). But need sounding duration and graphic length be the same? Unlike the sounding durations, the bar lengths here are not graphically incommensurate—in Feldman's hand-written score they are all of precisely the same width. Consequently, every system contains the same number of bars—nine bars per system (though three to eight systems per page). Figure 13.13 shows the first system (note the repeats in piano).

How are the players to play together/listen/interact while attending to their own intricately changing and "metrically" demanding patterns? Players read from score (obviously, no conductor); and although the three players can sometimes catch a glimpse of another part, they can at times be more than two pages apart (think of how exciting this could be for the players). Metaphorically, we might say that Feldman's figures form a "surface" working in the "depth" of their changing interactions (rather different from Takemitsu's "figure-ground" setup in Figure 13.10). For the player and listener the (notated) variation within figures is not separable from the (unnotated) variation brought about by interaction with other figures (again, glockenspiel and celeste, vibraphone and piano can sometimes become quite confused). How seriously to take this notation/music, or how to take this seriously? Might not this notation present opportunities to take music/rhythm seriously, in new ways?

* * *

The piece I would like to consider in a bit more detail, *De Kooning* (1963), is not quite so overt in its challenges. The opening is shown as Figure 13.14. There are no bars (until later in the piece). Dotted lines connect successive sound, and solid vertical lines indicate simultaneity. The vertical lines are numbered and so can perhaps function as rehearsal numbers (do some of these mark "phrase" events?). Durations of events are left up to the performers. The question here is when to play, how long to hold?

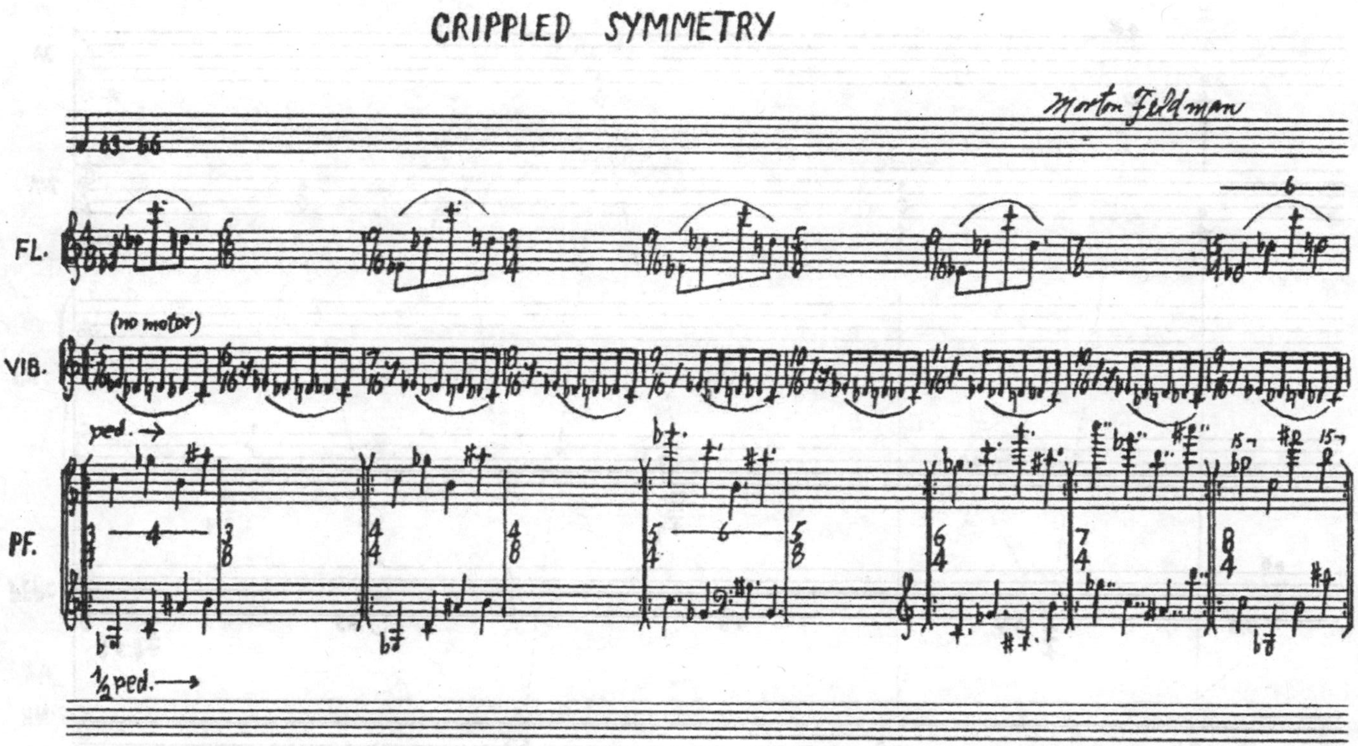

FIGURE 13.13 Morton Feldman, *Crippled Symmetry* first system (bs. 1–9).

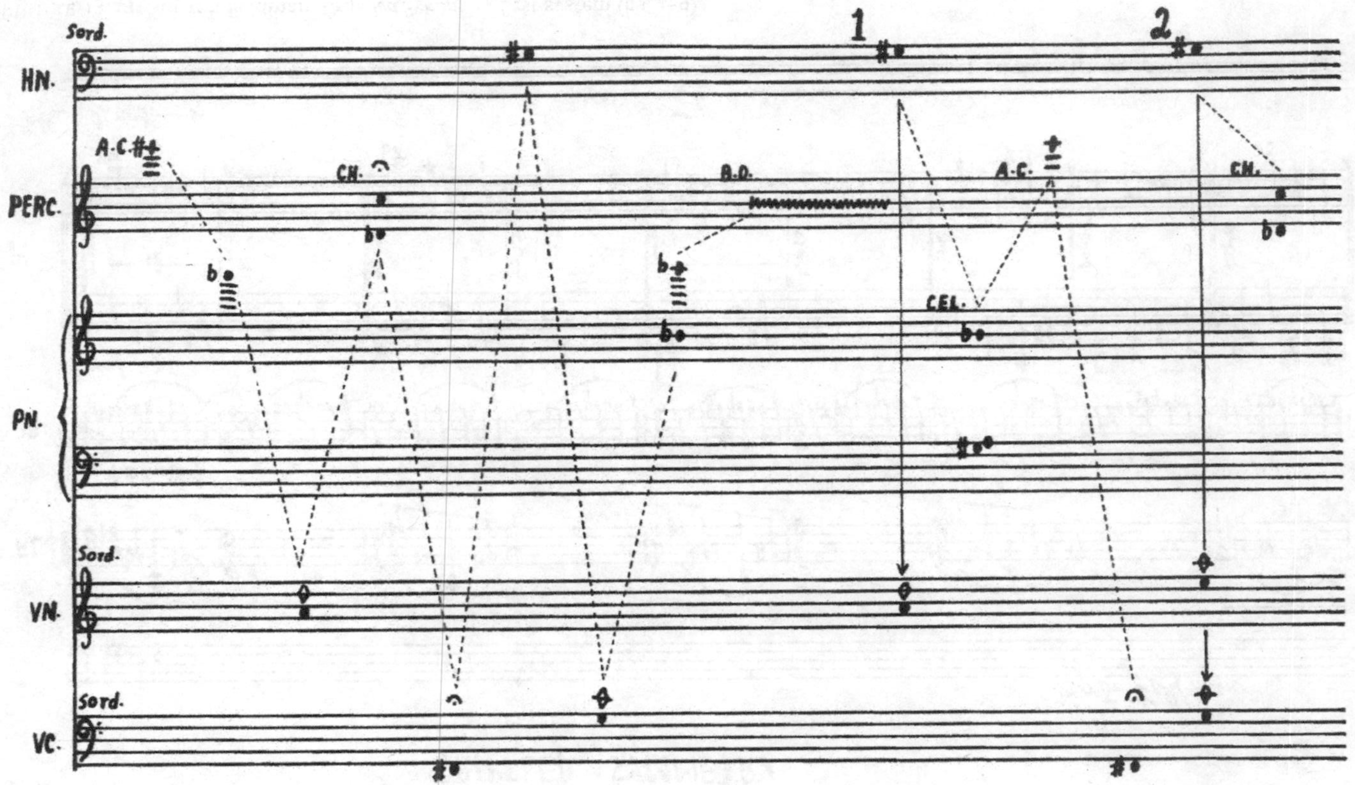

FIGURE 13.14 Morton Feldman, *De Kooning* first system.

Some notes appear under fermati, and sometimes fermati appear with no note; but the spacing of notes on the page is homogeneous, even for the fermati. The conductor is required to coordinate the simultaneities but need not conduct successive entries since the players play from score. (Even if the conductor cues successive sounds, how precisely need the players follow?) The performance instructions ask for the sounds to be played softly with a minimum of attack and that each instrument enter "when the preceding sound begins to fade." But this last instruction is problematic, for "fading" is highly variable. Percussed and plucked sounds fade differently depending on material, register, and force of attack (e.g., chimes versus cello pizzicato). By comparison, sustained sounds (e.g., horn) are already played very softly and don't so easily fade away. More problematically, is "fading" only a matter of acoustic audibility or also "echoic" memory? If the latter, then silences can be admitted. (Need we separate sound from memory?) In all the recordings I've heard, silences (sometimes quite long) do appear along with varying degrees of overlapping. Most remarkably, long (7–8 second) and very precisely notated silences do appear around the middle of the piece. They are notated with a puzzling precision—rests are notated with changing time signatures ($\frac{6}{8}$, $\frac{5}{4}$, $\frac{3}{2}$) and changing metronome markings. These silent "sections" are marked internally with barlines and externally (marked off from preceding and following sound) by double bars. Is the conductor to beat time through these silences? If not, why the notational instructions? How precisely would the conductor beat time? Is this just a paradox for the score reader or a visual-aural demonstration of a "musical" paradox? Finally, there is a question of silence at the end of the piece, the departure of both sound and sound's trailing silence as moments that might, but will not, continue *this* event. At the very end of the piece (Figure 13.15) horn, chimes, violin, and cello start at the same time to initiate the last sound. This moment is specially marked in notation—the last sound is written (for the first time) in whole notes, and there is no vertical line. It is preceded and followed by a double bar, exactly like the earlier bars of silence, but now with neither time signature nor tempo marking, and without fermata. Above and below the final double bar are two fermati, and so the symbol marking end itself comes to bear the symbol of holding on. How are the players to take this? Is it their first, and perhaps specially challenging request to "fade" or depart together, perhaps taking the lead of the chime to fade imperceptibly into silence (where does sound end)? Is the final double bar with fermati a signal to prolong silence as the music "still" going on, sound-into-silence?

Why all these notational decisions and, indeed, countless other decisions regarding other dimensions (pitch, contour, timbre, etc.)? Might this problematic question lead beyond particular answers to more general questions of what musical/rhythmic dimensions are or might be? For example, at the very beginning of the piece antique cymbal and piano are written as enharmonic versions of the "same" pitch (G♯/A♭). Untunable antique cymbals and an already tuned piano are unlikely to be perfectly in tune with one another (but they might be). Does the enharmonic spelling signal a microtonal change in pitch abandoned with the following violin A? Or does this signal an opportunity for violin, cello, and horn players to adjust pitches in sensitive, creative ways?

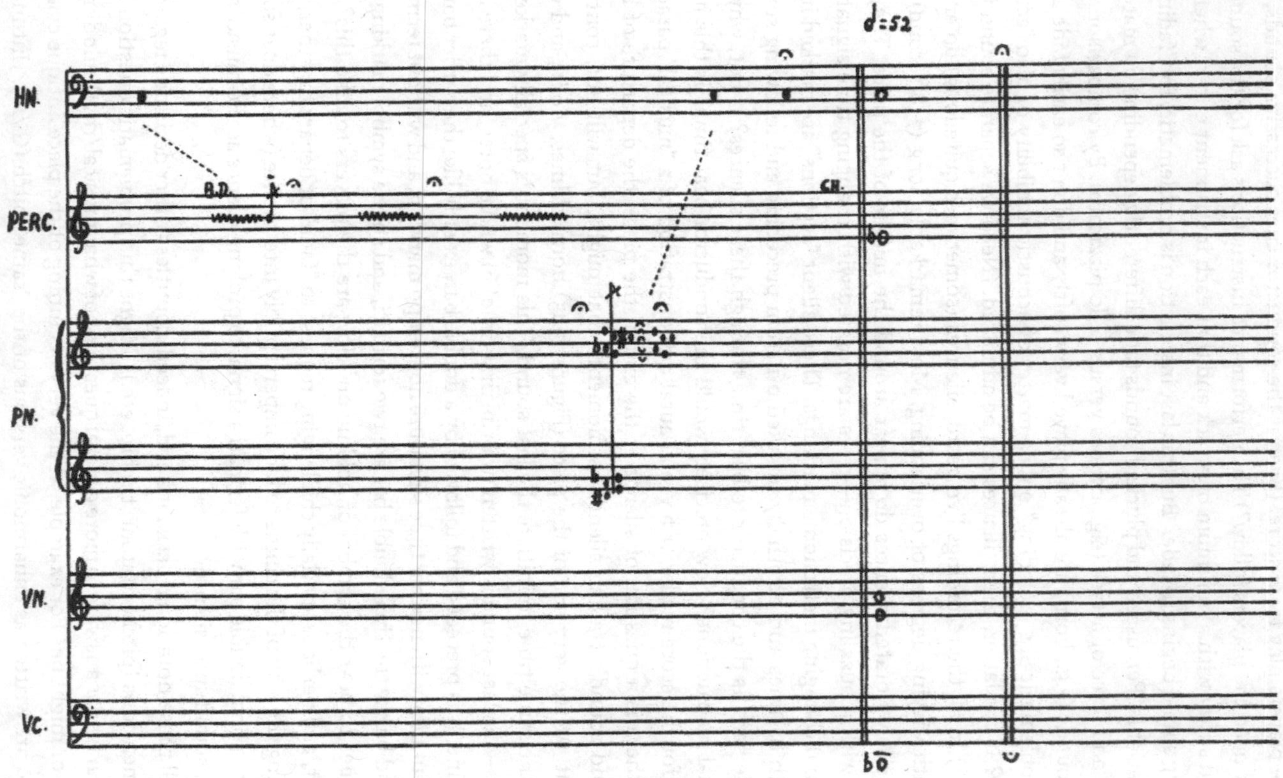

FIGURE 13.15 Morton Feldman, *De Kooning* final system.

(How is the violinist to tune her A; how to tune in simultaneities that involve the harmonic instabilities of many of the percussion instruments; how do clearly focused pitches change the perceptions of the not so clearly focused, and vice-versa?) What is the dimension of pitch? Are there many dimensions—how many? Such questions need not be merely speculative; they can have practical ramifications for performance. Notation need not be seen simply as a set of instructions for what to do again and again, but complexly as an invitation for creative experimentation that would make things new.

Indeed, it will be by experimentation that players (with or without conducting) will answer questions of when and how long to play: when the time is/feels right, where "rightness" is determined in evolving and changing situations in which little is taken for granted and all musical dimensions can come into play. ("Rhythm" might be a word for "evolving situations.") Sound-to-sound measuring is most palpable—this sound is longer-shorter, higher-lower, more or less "resonant," "brighter-darker" than the other (how many dimensions could we name?). These successive sounds, intriguing and "beautiful" as they might be, are not "the sounds themselves," that is to say, identities. They are *for* one another; they *are* what they give to and take from one another (how could successive sounds be for themselves, autonomous, identities?). Beauty, like rhythm is nothing if not contextual or "situational."

But larger measurings are also available. Let's say, speculatively, that the simultaneity labeled #1 emerges as the beginning of a new, second event (perhaps a third even shorter event could emerge in #2–#3). There are many factors that might present such an opportunity: 1) the possibly "articulative" sound of the bass drum, following the rather surprising double octave in piano (has Feldman given a clue in the relatively long and separated notational image of the drum roll?); 2) the contour of the first 8 sounds (down-up) returning to the high register of the opening (piano B♭ is a half step above violin A); or 3) the repetition of pitches in the putative second event—G♯, A, B♭, and F♯ (might we hear a "closing" retrograde in the horn G♯ falling to the cello F♯?). There are also opportunities for smaller events—the first 3 sounds, for example, with chimes perhaps promising a second, commensurate event, but not delivering if cello and horn fail to cohere with chimes (contour changes with cello and horn). On a smaller scale, might successive sounds pair as a second becomes continuation for a first? I believe traces of this sort of projective behavior can emerge with attentiveness, but only fleetingly and unstably—thus the piano might be heard as continuative for the beginning with antique cymbal, but if so, be denied as a larger beginning if chimes are not felt as continuative from violin. All these analytic speculations separate out a few factors. And yet in performance, everything works together, spontaneously. Individual sounds determine and are determined by the larger events that take shape. Further analysis of this piece would reveal a variety of rhythmic behaviors and far-ranging resonances of characteristic sounds (for example, the piano double octave, the drum roll).[37] This piece is not nearly as homogeneous as it might look at first glance. Indeed, participating in this piece will involve many encounters involving ear and eye in which new sensations and questions emerge. Again, as a well-crafted artifact, this piece is meant to be repeated. How we repeat it is an open and challenging question.

***

In closing I would like to suggest that although the rhythms of New Music may be challenging and require close attention, they need not be thought especially esoteric or resistant to the "natural" deliverances of the ear. We can hear in them the failure of measure as well as a variety of successes and partial successes/failures. There may be, as Schoenberg and Webern insist, very general laws of comprehensibility (and incomprehensibility). But rather than think of rigid and timeless laws, think instead of flexible and mobile rules, rules of thumb, rules that are asked to work in the exigencies of (present) practice, and that actually *practiced* can change, develop, be refined, or lose their efficacy and leave us perplexed. Such rules are not and cannot in principle be fixed; neither can they be precisely stated. They are always new and changeable in their always new and changeable operation in situations that cannot, in principle, be the same. There may be degrees of novelty—say from a staleness of habit where intensity of attending wanes in a kind of anesthesia, to an overload of nonhabit (nonrepetition/nondifference) that leads to an anesthesia of a different sort, an active withdrawal of attending and thus a forfeit of opportunities for intense feeling. Both these possibilities can present their own challenges and so need not be despised—each might lead to new/other intensities born of boredom and frustration.

A problem with (the) New Music is an often implicit (sometimes explicit) definite article and the exclusionary claim of novelty for a sort of music that would *in itself* be new. In a world where "Music" meant European "concert/art" music, the construction of the old and new was narrowly imagined. We might now see things differently. But in generosity it could be granted that the problematic novelty of musical experiment in this modernist tradition has opened and continues to open new possibilities for the laws of comprehensibility, possibilities that if felt can change our feeling and understanding of other musics—old and new.

Indeed, in its opposition to European tradition New Music's experimentation with alternatives has opened possibilities—especially notational possibilities—that can invite the participation of traditions outside the (proper) European classical cultural sphere. With current technologies of notation involving, for example, tablatures that can direct players of any instrument precisely how to move, virtually any possible sound on any instrument can be produced and produced in excruciating temporal-notational (if not necessarily *rhythmic*) detail. With the new notation any musical culture can be represented. Is this an opportunity for non-European composers to participate in a global musical culture in which non-European cultures might contribute something of their own traditions and, indeed, in a quite "non-Modernist" frame of mind, seek to honor their traditions? Or is this inclusion an opportunity for a sort of colonization, the fulfillment of a modern (sixteenth- and seventeenth-century) European dream of universality (a *mathesis universalis*, a universal language)? Clearly, such questions lie beyond the scope of this chapter, but I would hope that this chapter might make some room for them.

NOTES

1. "New Music" refers broadly to modernist, avant-garde, and experimental musics dating from the first decade of the twentieth century to the present. These practices emerged as paradoxical continuations and rejections of classical European music traditions and show resistance especially to nineteenth-century Romantic practice (which itself began as explicitly revolutionary). In a real sense, all music is new—it is now, or it never is. Born into a contemporary world, the actually new cannot be divorced from the formative powers of the past, even (or perhaps especially) where the new would be deliberately destructive of the old (and thus possibly obsessed with the old). For Europeans, the so-called New Music came to be a complex, active, revolutionary (and extraordinarily well-theorized) denial of tradition in the wake of the terrible destruction of the Second World War in the aftermath of a physically and spiritually devastating First World War (especially in view of the utopian optimism that preceded the First World War)—or at least, that's one story. *Ars nova*, *"Le nuove musiche," Zukunftsmusik, die neue Musik* (Futurism, Acmeism) are a few names for the incessant churning of the new in countless traditions, churnings that move at different rates and with different intensities. Such change might also be called rhythmic, a rhythm of cultural change, of large movements that are far from regular or homogeneous; they are perhaps closer to the chaotic but, let's say, still rhythmic, coherent, and meaningful in their succession. Indeed, they might be understood as deeply rhythmic precisely because of their complexity. If history is rhythmic is it free (never the same) or strict? In this volume Kippens' rhythmic revolution presents us with a large vista for the play of cultural change and one open to great complexity of perspectives. Sumarsam's historical purview is narrower and more or less matches mine. The coincidences (and entanglements) of our histories are remarkable, and I think the pairing of our two topics can be rewarding.

2. An early and influential use of the term "die neue Musik" is found in Paul Bekker's 1919 essay of the same name (Bekker 1923). See also Christoph von Blumroeder *Der Begriff "Neue Musik" im 20. Jahrhundert* (1981) and Heile *The Modernist Legacy: Essays on New Music* (2009).

3. The utopian New can take many forms, from mild hubris to a declaration of war against others who are contemporaries and yet are Past, that is, all who do not pledge to this New—this can lead to the most incredible violence (as in Russia and Germany).

4. For fuller account of the notion of durational-quantitative projection see Hasty (1997). Calling such projection quantitative is an abbreviation and simplification. The sort of measuring I have in mind mixes quantity and quality. Here durational quantity as how much or how long is not detached from the particularities of qualitative difference that are also in a sense "measured" in their difference. Meter or measuring here is meant to take into account anything that can make a difference. In analyzing and describing music we must isolate various factors, but rhythm and the measuring of "meter" knows of no such separations.

5. The sign * symbolizes any sound or sound complex that comes to be taken as the initiation of an event. Although I will not use asterisks in the following figures, I include these symbols here as a reminder that this series of diagrams aims to represent a dimension of (real-time) sensible/aural experience.

6. Here the terms "determined" or "determinacy" will mean ended (*de-terminare*), no longer present or going on. "Indeterminate" will mean present, still going on, not ended. In this sense "indeterminate" will not mean vague or deficient in detail or particularity.

7. Compare Fujita's "*haku* or *hyoshi*. . . . the temporal interval from the end of the previous beat to the point of articulation of the beat in question. For clarity, I will distinguish beat as 'time point' from beat as a temporal interval between time points. However, the native conception—which obscures this distinction—is important to grasp: Japanese Noh musicians refer to beat 1 as the space or time interval separating beat 8 from beat 1" (this volume, chapter 8).

8. "Second" here should be understood not as an ordinal number but rather as the immediate follower (*sequi*). Akin perhaps to Pierce's category of "secondness," the second ends or determines its erstwhile present predecessor. Second might mean always more than one, where one is never truly without another (taken as number "one" means, unit, self-same, identity—all concepts foreign to process). Such a notion of "secondness" can be part of a strategy for dealing with succession and continuity together—the paradox of continuous succession. The Latin *secundus* meant following and also favorable, prosperous (we can still hear this latter meaning in the verb "to second"—to support or carry farther, as in the seconding or assisting in a duel, or in the supporting and carrying forth of a recommendation). Things follow *from* one another. Incidentally, "time points" (durationless) can't follow—how can we get from one durationless instant to another? Indeed, time-points have been used precisely to model continuity; but, paradoxically, this is a continuity in which nothing can happen—no duration for things to happen "in."

9. The symbol / that will appear in some of the following examples indicates anacrusis as a variety of continuation, a continuation that "points forward" to a new event/emergence. The distinction of "thetic" (\) and "anacrusic" (/) continuation is the distinction between "how long will *this* event last" and "how long till the *next*." Both are event-durational ("how long do I now have"), but one points to a present-to-become-past and the other to a present-to-become-future. This sort of distinction is as complex, subtle, and variable as any present must be; and so these two marks are very crude indicators of an "orientation" that depends on the particular situation, never quite the same.

10. In the Western classical tradition it is well understood, at least by performers, that the consistent dynamic stressing of "downbeats" (at any level) can have a deadening effect on rhythm (and, I would suggest, "meter" as the rhythmic measuring of duration). Theorists of the eighteenth century were especially wary of associating meter and dynamic or stress accent. The later was deemed external or extrinsic, opposed to "intrinsic temporal quantity" (*quantitas temporalis intrinsica*) in which the downbeat is intrinsically longer than the upbeat though the two be equal in duration. It was intrinsic quantity that constituted the measure which itself could involve a great variety of extrinsic accentuations. See George Houle (1987, chapter 4).

11. To avoid confusion I should point out that projective/projected labels beginning with *P* (i.e., *P*, *P'*, *Q*, *Q'*, *R*, *R'*, etc.) are applied uniquely in each example more or less in order of emergence. Thus, the projective function by, say, *Q* or *R* in one example has no necessary connection or correspondence to *Q* or *R* in another example.

12. From an eighteenth-century perspective triple meter was called "*un*equal time" (*temps inegal, ungleich*). The term "triple" was also used but not to the exclusion of a feeling that could not be exhausted in the idea of number. In the present chapter the feeling triple or unequal is understood as a process of "deferral" in the projection of durational quantity.

13. On this view, measures of 5, 7, 10 pulses (i.e., measures that are not multiples, times 2 or 3, of 2 or 3) to be confidently replicated (projected) require a serviceable reproduction of pattern (e.g., 3+2, 2+2+3, 4+4+2).

14. The solution in most cases has been to circle tones, i.e., identify pitch-class sets that form set *classes* or *types* that can be found *repeated* (that is, to identify sets of pitch classes that are transformationally related in one-to-one mappings under the operations of transposition and inversion). This analytic project is, in large measure, a search for a surrogate for (consonant) harmonies or chords where replication or identity/same is the primary criteria for identification. The practice frequently results in selecting entities composed of nonsimultaneous and nonadjacent pitches without, however, satisfactorily accounting for the excluded, nonparticipating pitches as "dissonances." If inclusion/exclusion is based on repetition of set-class then we have a tautology: the inclusion ("consonance") of pitches is based on their involvement in repetitions of the set class, which to be a class must (to be "extensional") involve repetition, the repetition of the more than one thing that *makes of them that kind of thing* (class, category, concept). For a construction of set class that takes a different view of repetition see Hasty (1987).

15. See Alban Berg's (1974 [1924]) essay "Why is Schoenberg's Music so Difficult to Understand?" In this thoughtful and admiring essay, written for the occasion of Schoenberg's fiftieth birthday, Berg attributes the difficulty of hearing Schoenberg's music primarily to its rhythm rather than to its melody or harmony. The challenges that Berg explicitly and convincingly points to are irregularity and speed.

16. "Brahms the Progressive" in *Style and Idea* (1947). Although Schoenberg may have intended in part to legitimize his music by an appeal to continuity with the old masters (and to claim equal status), I hear a tone of sincerity in his claims to carry the old music forward and *farther* into a new cultural/historical climate (and thereby renewing and saving German music).

17. There are, of course, many other texts that could testify to a resistance to what has been seen as the pathological boundedness of meter, or rather meter conceived as an inherently abstract and coercive constraint on rhythm (a conception I am at pains to refute). Here I would mention a couple of instances from the many: The "tyranny of the bar" is now a cliché. The formula was introduced in by Daniel Gregory Mason (1919), for whom "meter is a dangerous enemy of rhythm" (31). Mason's critique is aimed at performances in which "metrical" stress accents are mechanically applied destructive of an organic ("improvised") wholeness that is necessarily complex and highly nuanced. Although his complaint is leveled at performers actions rather than at meter as such, he is stuck with a traditional definition of meter based on regularity of stress. Edward T. Cone (1968), while he does not disparage meter in the small (in its proper measuring of bars), does see meter as a threat if it attempts to exceed its bounds. Cone criticizes the "hypermeasures" ("hyper-" means *too* much) of some nineteenth-century music as an incursion of the "regularity" of meter into the phrase: "In the Classical period . . . when measures combined to form phrases, they did so not in any regular metrical way but as components of freely articulated rhythmic groups whose structure depended on their specific content. In Romantic music, on the other hand, one can find long stretches in which the measures combine into phrases that are themselves metrically conceived—into what I call hypermeasures . . . It is here, and not in the preceding style, that we can justly speak of the tyranny of the four-bar phrase!" (79). The notion of such a tyranny has, unfortunately, infected attitudes toward both Western and non-Western musics that trade in something like "bound" rhythm and that seem to offer only a simple, i.e., primitive repetition of fixed pattern. I suggest that such judgments arise from an inadequate conceptualization of measure that can

lead to unproductive oppositions of strict and free, simple and complex. To what extent the post-World War II and present aversion turns on a resistance to popular music in which largish beats are not despised is a question worth pursuing.

18. And yet it could be argued to the contrary that in classical music the use of large and vividly felt measures enhances attentiveness and both asks for and rewards a demanding cocreative work from the hearer. The gift to the hearer is the opportunity to form some aural image of the new phrase to come. Having sufficient time to do this is strongly fostered by feeling doubling as continuation, that is to say, a feeling of the space you're now in and how much time you have before coming into the next event. This opening for imagination is an ancient practice shared by language in which endings are formalized as falling (*cadere*) or dropping, not necessarily or only in pitch but, more generally, falling or dropping in interest (the thought is done, let it go). Europe experienced a remarkably long-lived cadence tradition and one that led to very large closings such as closing *sections* or codas. In the process of cadence the end is announced in advance; and since the cadence material is the most conventional and unremarkable ("uninteresting"), we may, given some time, be encouraged to think ahead, to imagine what might come (or in the case of codas, perhaps to reflect on what has been done and focus on a moment of ending). In 1854 Eduard Hanslick, champion of the German classical tradition Haydn to Brahms (and not including Wagner's "Music of the Future"), writes: "The most important factor in the mental process which accompanies the act of listening to music, and which converts it into a source of pleasure, is frequently overlooked. We here refer to the intellectual satisfaction which the listener derives from continually following and anticipating the composer's intentions—now, to see his expectations fulfilled, and now, to find himself agreeably mistaken. It is a matter of course that this intellectual flux and reflux, this perpetual giving and receiving takes place unconsciously, and with the rapidity of lightning flashes. Only that music can yield truly aesthetic enjoyment which prompts and rewards the act of thus closely following the composer's thoughts, and which with perfect justice may be called a pondering of the imagination."

19. And yet I imagine that mixed with feelings of utopian optimism were anxieties arising from an impending loss of tradition. Some ardent supporters of the classical tradition (Mason and Schenker, for example) felt it slipping away in contemporary performances that lacked rhythmic vitality. This crisis of performance was attributed to the insensitivity and inattention of performers and conveniently symbolized by the relaxed regularity of repeating large measures, what William Rothstein (1989, 184), echoing Cone's "tyranny of the four-measure phrase," has called the "Great Nineteenth-Century Rhythm Problem." This crisis of rhythmic performance at the end of the nineteenth century was the well-motivated fear that the spirit of the old music was in danger of being lost, and that its loss would mean the passing of an era. For Schoenberg and for many other modernists the passing was bittersweet—a great loss but also, at the same time, a great opportunity for something new.

20. See Edwin Boring (1942) on the findings of Dietze et al. In view of the complexity of duration hierarchies, it is not surprising that estimations of the length of a held or "remembered" present would be quite various. Moreover, different modes of memory can generate a variety of categories, such as echoic memory (5–20 seconds), iconic memory (.5-1 seconds), and working memory (20–30 seconds).

21. The reader can test this difficulty by trying to produce a series of claps that seem fully disordered or nonmetrical. See also Martin Clayton's (2000, 97–103 and 203–206) discussion of the difficulties of avoiding a clear sense of "periodicity" in connection with *ālāpana* movements of Hindustani music.

22. Thinking about music (Ferneyhough and Ligeti), the difference of triviality and vagueness is crucially a difference of timespan. Whitehead, theorizing event in general, does not give much attention to temporal scale apart from the broad distinction of "actual occasion" (for human beings on the order of one-tenth of a second) and "societies" of occasions that hold larger durations in emergent/habitual patterns or behaviors. Perhaps, because of its intense connection to the feeling of duration, music could offer clues for human-specific potentials for event formation that involve critical differences of scale and, more generally, make "scaling" a central concern.

23. Deleuze/Guattari (2003) took up Boulez's terms "striated" and "smooth" without, I think, appreciating the music theoretical ramifications and ideological commitments involved. See Martin Scherzinger (2010). I imagine that Deleuze might have found a more sympathetic guide in the thought and writings of Stefan Wolpe.

24. For a more detailed analysis of this and other excerpts from *Le Marteau* see Hasty (1997, 284–93).

25. See the six long essays on this piece in Obert (2012).

26. For a demonstration of such variation in timing see Olivier Senn, Kilchenmann, and Camp (2009) analysis of a recording of a 1975 performance by Martha Argerich of Chopin's E minor Prelude, Op. 28 no. 4. Notice also the frequent lack of coordination of the two hands. These discrepancies might be seen as a more intricate sort of coordination, or "participatory discrepancy" of two hands.

27. In his instructions for performance in the score Takemitsu writes, "It is preferable for the piece to be performed with the lighting effects indicated on the music. However, it is also possible to perform it without lighting effects." And he writes, "This piece can also be played using any combination of keyboard instruments."

28. In the end, everyone wanted to keep a feeling of deferral and enjoyed playing with its weaving into and out of sixteenth note patterns. As the section develops there is a great wealth of opportunities for such play—more than can quite be taken in.

29. The tempo is very slow, "Lento, una quiete furiosa e crudele." In performances I have heard, the eighth note is around M.M. 60 or 1 sec. The conductor beats a subdivided pattern, i.e., 8 beats per bar. I have relied primarily on the recording by Ensemble Recherche (Kairos 0012132KAI). *Muro d'orizzonte* was written for and dedicated to the Ensemble Recherche.

30. I was therefore surprised to find that after listening many times to the Ensemble Recherche recording I could very accurately coordinate a clap with the third and fourth sounds without counting or beating. The accuracy always surprised me—I was never confident that I would clap with the next sound. Musical practice seems to foster abilities that experimental psychology might find surprising.

31. For Messiaen non-retrogradable rhythm was symbolic—a cycle that symbolized a sort of moving image of eternity. "A final symbol—that moment which I live, this thought which crosses my mind, this movement which I accomplish, this time which I beat, before it and after it lies eternity: it is a non-retrogradable rhythm" (Messiaen 1995, 77).

32. The title "Rain Tree" is taken from Kenzaburo Oe's novel *Atama no ii, Ame no Ki* (*The Ingenious Rain Tree*) 1980. In the front matter to the score Takemitsu quotes from Oe, "It has been named the 'rain tree,' for its abundant foliage continues to let fall rain drops collected from last night's shower until well after the following midday. Its hundreds of thousands of tiny leaves—finger-like—store up moisture while other trees dry up at once. What an ingenious tree, isn't it?"

33. In contrast to Takemitsu's experiment, Helmut Lachenmann's "Schattentanz" from *Ein Kinderspiel* offers a very explicit and witty play with periodicity (dance) and its periodic (shadowy, ghostly) undoing.

34. Feldman often writes about notation, for instance in his essay "Crippled Symmetry" (1981): "The degree to which a music's notation is responsible for much of the composition itself is one of history's best kept secrets. . . . Many composers and theorists will disagree with the almost hierarchical prominence I attribute to the notation's effect on composition. They would argue that the new musical concepts, resulting in innovative systems, necessitated changes in notation. . . . This interpretation cannot be refuted, but some room should be left open to question it. My speculation over how a notational look may have contributed to the music of Webern, or for that matter Boulez (who, incidentally, has composed a work called *Notations*), might appear dubious. But *notation can have an aspect of 'role playing,' and I feel it as a very strong voice, if not onstage, then off*" (144–45, emphasis added). Commenting more specifically on his own notational/rhythmic practice Feldman writes, "the patterns that interest me are both concrete and ephemeral, making notation difficult. If notated exactly, they are too stiff; if given the slightest notational leeway, they are too loose. Though these patterns exist in rhythmic shapes articulated by instrumental sounds, they are also in part notational images that do not make a direct impact on the ear as we listen. A tumbling of sorts happens in midair between their translation from the page and their execution. To a great degree, this tumbling occurs in all music—but becomes more compounded in mine, since there is no rhythmic 'style,' a quality often crucial to the performer's understanding of how and what to do" (143).

35. See David Hyun-Su Kim (2009) on the nineteenth-century European innovation of "hairpin" notations as guides for making sense of then New Musics that could not be read with the old feelings of rhythm and that thus called for a notational supplement that might educate performers into new ways of hearing-feeling. Kim understands these symbols broadly and intensively to mean, "becoming more/less" (rather than specifically, becoming louder/softer). In a provisional taxonomy, Kim identifies a variety of functions such as "closing," "accelerating," "lingering."

36. See Feldman's *Why Patterns?* for flute percussion and piano (1978) for a different approach to the decoupling of metrical notation from the coordination of parts.

37. For a more detailed analysis see Hasty (2014).

GLOSSARY

This glossary covers many of the foreign-language terms and specialized usages in this volume. In the parenthetical abbreviations following each entry, the most pertinent or immediate language of origin generally appears first. These indications are simplified and are not intended to be comprehensive etymologies. In the case of widespread Indic terms, the abbreviation "Ind." is used in addition to a source language. Hindi and Urdu are essentially the same language, with different emphases in vocabulary and written in different scripts; for this reason identical terms may be spelled differently according to the orthography (the determination of a word as belonging primarily to one versus the other language is a problem not entirely resolved here). In general, Urdu draws more heavily from Persian and Arabic. Some but not all variant spellings of terms are listed, but readers can easily access all usages through the page-number references. Authors are listed in cases of multiple or special usages of terms.

MASTER GLOSSARY: LANGUAGES AND ABBREVIATIONS

Ar. Arabic
B.I. Bahasa Indonesia
Ewe
H. Hindi
Ind. Indic, which appears in several South Asian languages. Usually the musical term will be of Sanskrit or Persian origin and used in a specific technical sense in a spoken Indic language.

J. Japanese
Jv. Javanese
Khorasani Turkish
Nw. Newari
P. Persian
Panjabi
Skt. Sanskrit. See "Ind."
T. Tamil
T.B. Tashlhiyt Berber
Tj. Tajik
U. Urdu

accent A moment toward which a listener's attention is drawn by some feature in the music, such as duration or loudness (agogic accent, dynamic accent) (Locke).
additive meter Metrical structure comprising unequal groupings of pulse-beats, e.g., 3 +2 + 2.
afterbeat Time-point coming after an onbeat moment (Locke).
Agbadza (Ewe) A type of performance art of the Ewe-speaking people of West Africa (Ghana/Togo) whose expressive means are dance, vocal music, and drum-ensemble music.
āhang (P.) Persian for tune, melody type, equivalent to some senses of Arabic *laḥn* (Blum).
aḥwaš (T.B.) A complex collective practice of song and dance performed with drums by men and women in Tashlhiyt-speaking regions of Morocco.
aḥwaš n tmġarin (T.B.) Women's *aḥwaš* of the Anti-Atlas in Morocco.
akāl (H.) Lit., "out of time." An unsounded beat in Hindustani rhythmic theory; an interval (*fāṣila*) in a *tāl* (Kippen).
ālāp(ana) (Skt., Ind.) In Indian classical music, an unmeasured, improvised exposition of a *rāga*, usually introducing a measured composition in the same *rāga*. (Called *ālāp* in Hindustani, *ālāpana* in Karnatak music; see also "rāga ālāpana.")
amarg (T.B.) Sung poetry in Tashlhiyt-speaking regions of Morocco.
amḫllf (T.B.) Stage of advancement in the *aḥwaš* of the Anti-Atlas in Morocco.
anchor point A reference point in (space) time with a subjective quality of gravity that has the effect of altering human experiences of temporality immediately preceding and following it. Originally coined by Richard Wolf as a way to describe rhythmic planning in Kota instrumental music.
andhegan (Jv.) A stop in the middle of the piece, which resumes again after a *pesindhèn* singer sings an interlude.
anisochronous Of unequal duration (see also "nonisochronous").
antarā (Skt.) The second section of a composition in Hindustani vocal music, followed by a return to the first section (*sthāyī*).
anudruta (Skt./Ind.) A duration equal to one quarter of a *mātrā* in South Asian classical rhythmic theory, symbolized as U (Kippen).
aqqayn (T.B.) Fixed sung words in Tashlhiyt-speaking regions of Morocco.
āṛā chautāla (H./U.) Originally a *pakhāvaj tāl*, now played on tabla (Kippen).
'arūḍ (Ar., *'aruz* in P.) System of Arabic prosody, first codified in the eighth century C.E.
asallaw (T.B.) Ritual wedding songs in parts of the Western High Atlas of Morocco.

atānin (Ar., P.) Systems of syllables used in Arabic and Persian treatises and pedagogies to represent rhythmic cycles, poetic meters, and rhythmic patterns (for examples, see *naqra*, *sabab*, and *watad*).

aṭi (T.) "Beat." Both a strike and a generic term for rhythmic patterns in folk drumming.

āvart (H., Ind.) A cycle or *āvartan* (equivalent to *daur*) in Hindustani rhythmic theory.

āvāz (P.) A rhythmically elastic vocal style of Iran.

awal (T.B.) Improvised sung lyrics in Tashlhiyt-speaking regions of Morocco.

backbeat Colloquial term for onbeats two and four within a measure of four onbeats (Locke).

baḥr (Ar., pl. *buḥūr*, P., spelled *bəhr* in Azerbaijani) (1) Arabic term for a quantitative poetic meter, composed of named feet; (2) a musical meter that can be represented by a time signature using the conventions of Western notation (Blum, Kippen).

balungan (Jv.) Melodic skeleton of *gendhing*.

band (H./U.) Persian for "bound, closed, stopped": a sequence of tabla strokes where the bass sonority is stopped.

baxši (Khorasani Turkish, P.) A bard in Iranian Khorasan who performs sung poetry in Persian, Khorasani Turkish, and Kurmanji Kurdish to his own *dotār* accompaniment.

bayt (Ar., P.) Arabic term for one line of verse composed of two hemistiches.

beat zone Time span of one beat or count including the pickup (Locke).

bedhug (Jv.) A large hanging drum.

bell (Ewe) Iron instrument struck by wooden stick to sound a recurrent temporal pattern that shapes and structures musical rhythm.

Bhairav (Skt.) The fierce, terrifying form of the Hindu god Śiva; the patron deity of Bhaktapur.

bhajan (Skt., Ind.) A devotional song.

Bhaktapur A town in the Kathmandu Valley; formerly the capital of a Newar kingdom (until 1769).

bol (H./U.) A drum syllable or stroke in Hindustani rhythmic theory.

bonang (Jv.) An instrument consisting of a set of ten to fourteen horizontal kettle gongs arranged in two rows, placed on cords strung through a wooden frame.

bonang barung (Jv.) Medium size, middle-to-high-octave *bonang*.

bonang panerus (Jv.) Small size, highest-octave *bonang*.

buka (Jv.) Introductory melodic phrase of a gendhing, usually played by *rebab* or *bonang*.

burdish (P.) Obsolete Indo-Persian term equivalent to *sam* in Hindustani rhythmic theory.

cāl (H./U.) "Gait." Generic term for a kind of rhythmic pattern that in some folk traditions is designated by a number indicating stressed strokes.

cāli (Nw.) A type of song in the *dāphā* repertoire, sung to one *tāl* throughout.

call-and-response What "comes before" is followed by what "comes after," thus making a musical relationship (Locke).

cardinality The number of pulse-beats in a metrical cycle.

čarx (P.) Persian for circular motion, cycle.

chapkā (H.) In Hindustani rhythmic theory, a variant of the *ṭheka*, or a short, variable pattern substituting for it. Perhaps equivalent to *laggī*. Obsolete.

chautāla (H.) "Four-beat"; a category of *tāls* comprising four beats; a *tāl* structure primarily associated with *dhrupad* and *pakhāvaj*.

clap-pattern A pattern of claps and silent waves lasting one cycle of a *tāla*, performed to aid in counting and coordinating performance.

clempung (Jv.) A plucked zither set on four legs.

dā'ira (Ar., pl. *dawā'ir*, P.) Arabic for "circle," used in the theory of prosody for diagrams displaying rotations of quantitative poetic meters.

dāphā (Nw.) A type of group devotional singing performed by farmers in the Kathmandu Valley, believed to have originated in the seventeenth century in the palaces of Bhaktapur and other towns.

darāmad (P.) The section of Persian classical song that introduces the musical materials.

das prāṇ (H.) The "ten life breaths" of *tāl*, a medieval system of elemental descriptors for rhythm that was resurrected in Hindustani rhythmic theory in the late nineteenth century.

dastgāh (P.) A modal system of Persian classical music.

daur (Ar., pl. *adwār*, P.) Arabic for "cycle," "rhythmic cycle."

demung (Jv.) Large-size, middle-octave range of *saron*.

deśī-tāla (Skt.) "Provincial-*tāla*." A system of *tāls* described in medieval treatises which replaced *mārga tāls*.

dhā A horizontal barrel-drum, played with a stick on the lower-pitched head and the hand on the higher-pitched head.

dhīma (H./U.) "Slow" in Hindustani rhythmic theory.

ḍhol (H., Ind.) Barrel or cylindrical drum used in South Asia.

ḍholak (H./Ind.) (diminutive of *ḍhol*). South Asian barrel drum used extensively in folk music and in the genres of the Qawwāls.

dhrupad (H.) The oldest genre of Hindustani classical vocal music, accompanied by the drum pakhāvaj. Vocal genre of the *Kalāvants*.

dotāla (H.) "Two-beat." In Hindustani rhythmic theory, a category of *tāls* comprising two beats.

downbeat First onbeat in a measure (Locke).

drum language Words in language played on a drum or other sonorous object.

druta (Skt., Ind.) In South Asian classical rhythmic theory, a duration equal to one half of a *mātrā*, symbolized by o.

dyaḥlhāygu (Nw.) An instrumental piece played at the start of a performance of Newar music to invoke the blessings and presence of the gods.

dzimeɣe (Ewe) The basic Agbadza dance (lit. "dance of the middle-of-the-back").

ektāl See *yaktāla*.

fāṣila (Ar., P) In Arabic rhythmic theory, an interval whose duration comprises a combination of *sabab* and *watad*, or an interval separating two rhythmic cycles (Blum, Kippen).

fiqra (U.) Arabic term used in Hindustani rhythmic theory for a phrase, possibly one of the two halves of a tabla *tāl*.

gambang (Jv.) A wooden xylophone with seventeen to twenty-one keys.

ganga (T.B.) A large two-headed drum played with two sticks (Morocco).

garap (Jv.) Melodic interpretation or treatment.

gatra (Jv.) A unit of four notes of the melodic skeleton (*balungan*) of *gendhing*.

gendèr (Jv.) A metallophone with ten to fourteen keys.

gendhing (Jv.) (1) A generic term for any gamelan composition; (2) a generic term for a gamelan composition with a long structure (*gongan*), consisting of two major parts, *mérong* and *inggah*.

Gītagovinda A sequence of 25 songs in Sanskrit, composed by the twelfth-century Indian poet Jayadeva, on the theme of the love-play of Krishna and Radha.

gītaka (Skt.) A repertoire of sacred songs in Sanskrit performed in the pūrvaraṅga of an ancient Sanskrit drama.

gongan (Jv.) The basic structural unit of gendhing between two strokes of large gong.

groove Propulsive reiteration of successive marked moments in time, that is, beats (Locke); regularly repeating accentual patterns sometimes rooted in bodily movement (Wolf and passim).

gropak (Jv.) Ending the piece in a fast tempo.

Gūlā (Nw.) A month of the Newar calendar in which Buddhists perform religious observances for the acquisition of merit.

guru (Skt.) In South Asian classical rhythmic theory, a duration equal to two *mātrās*, symbolized by S.

gurubānī (Panjabi) A repertoire of sacred songs in the Sikh tradition.

guše (P.) "Corner." Persian for one unit in the *radif* of *musiqi-ye sonnati*.

gvārā (Nw.) A repertoire of sacred songs in the Newar Buddhist tradition, typically sung in the Gūlā season.

ḥaraka (Ar., P.) Arabic for a motion, action, or strike.

ḥarf (Ar., pl. *hurūf*, P.) Arabic term for a consonant, qualified in prosody as either "movent" (*mutaḥarrik*), i.e., vowelled, or "motionless" (*sākin*) (Blum); a drum stroke in Hindustani rhythmic theory (Kippen).

heterometric music Music in which the meter changes in cardinality.

hidda (Ar., P.) Arabic for acuity of a musical tone, equivalent to Greek *oksytēs*.

Hindustani music The classical, concert music of North India and adjacent regions (Bangladesh, Pakistan, Nepal).

hypermetrical A pattern or structure longer in duration than the cycle, i.e., comprising two or more cycles.

imbal (Jv.) An interlocking playing technique.

in-one Metric pace by downbeats (Locke).

inggah (Jv.) See "gendhing."

intensification Increase in the arousal experienced by performers and listeners, generated by increasing musical parameters such as loudness, pitch, tempo, etc.

interonset interval A duration defined by the onsets of two attacks.

intiqāl (Ar., P.) Arabic term for passage or modulation.

iqā‘ (Ar., pl. *īqā‘āt*, P.) Arabic for rhythmic cycle or rhythmic mode, and rhythm in general.

irama (Jv.) (1) Tempo; (2) a musical concept defined by the expanding and contracting of structural units of gendhing, accompanied by changes of density level of instruments. There are four levels of *irama: tanggung, dadi, wilet*, and *rangkep*.

iriẓi (T.B.) Sung and drummed entrance into procession by performers of *aḥwaš* (Anti-Atlas in Morocco).

isochronous Of equal duration.

isometric Having metrical cycles of equal duration.

izwirrign (T.B.) Ritual wedding songs in parts of the Anti-Atlas of Morocco.

jald (H.) "Fast," in Hindustani rhythmic theory.

javāb-e āvāz (P.) Response to vocalizing in performances of *musiqi-ye sonnati*.

jhaptāl (H.) A *tāl* of 4 beats, 10 counts (2+3+2+3).

kake-goe (J.) Lit. "vocal emissions." As a technical term in music, *kake-goe* are the vocal calls "iya," "ha," and "ei" that precede drum strokes. The Noh drummer produces *kake-goe* to inform coplayers where the drum stroke will fall in an 8-beat cycle and what tempo change may follow in order to create dramatic effects.

kāl (Skt., Ind.) In Hindustani rhythmic theory, a unit of time, or period; an unsounded beat; an interval (*fāṣila*) in a *tāl* (see also *kālam*) (Kippen).

kālam (T.) Speeds of rendition in Karnāṭak music. In exercises and in particular musical genres, a particular passage may be performed in multiple *kālams*, integer or simple-fraction multiples of the base speed (see also *kāl*) (Wolf).

kālapramāṇam (T.) Lit. "time-measure" or "time-rule," the pace at which a performance of Karnatak music proceeds, which should remain steady.

Kalāvant South Asian community of musicians historically specializing in *dhrupad*.

karawitan (Jv.) The art of Javanese gamelan and vocal music.

Karnāṭak music The classical, concert music of South India.

kawya (Jv.) A form of Indian poetry.

kekawin (Jv.) A form of Indian-derived Javanese poetry.

kendhang (Jv.) A two-headed asymmetrical drum with heads attached to leather loops interlaced in a Y pattern. There are a number of *kendhang*, depending on the size and its technique/usage in the ensemble: *kendhang satunggal* and *kalih* (technique); *kendhang ageng* and *ketipung* (names according to size); *kendhang ciblon* and *wayangan* (names, technique, and usage).

kenongan (Jv.) A musical phrase delineated by the stroke of kenong, a set of large horizontal gong kettles placed on a wooden rack.

keplok (Jv.) Hand-clapping, enhancing the lively mood of the music.

k͟hafif (U.) Arabic for "light, short": a category of *tāls* with two beats.

khālī/k͟hālī (H./U.) A silent gesture in the clap-pattern of a Hindustani tāla; a beat or segment of the cycle marked by this gesture.

khayāl/k͟hayāl (H./U.) The predominant style of Hindustani vocal music, accompanied by the tabla drum. Formerly associated with Qawwāls.

kidi (Ewe) Response drum in Agbadza.

klenèngan (Jv.) A gamelan performance held just for the sake of listening.

komi (J.) Noun form of verb *komu*, "to take, hold, concentrate." In Noh drumming, *komi* refers to the silent beginning point of a drumming pattern. This is followed by series of vocal calls, *kake-goe* and strokes. Drummers say "m," "n," or "tsu" in their minds to realize and sense that silent point properly.

kriti (Skt., Ind.) The predominant composition form in Karnatak vocal music.

ladkar (s. ddikr) (T.B.) Songs with religious words performed in rituals in Morocco.

ladrang (Jv.) One of the formal structures of *gendhing*, 32 pulses per *gongan* unit.

lafẓ (Ar. pl. *alfāẓ*, U.) "Word." In Hindustani rhythmic theory, equivalent to *bol*, a constituent word or stroke in a *ṭheka*.

laghu (Skt.) In South Asian classical rhythmic theory, a duration equal to one *mātrā*, symbolized by I.

laḥn (Ar., pl. *alḥān)* Arabic for melody, melody type, tune and verse as an integral whole.

lālākhĩ (Nw.) A horizontal barrel-drum played with the hands, used to accompany *dāphā* singing and some dance genres in Newar music.

lancar (Jv.) One of the *irama*, performed during transitions.

lancaran (Jv.) One of the *irama*, eight pulses per *gongan* unit.

laya (Jv.) A Javanese musical term for tempo deriving from Sanskrit *laya*.

laya/lay (Skt., Ind.) In South Asian rhythmic theory, tempo or rhythmic feel (Kippen, Wolf).

lomba (Jv.) A playing style of *gendèr*.

madhyam "Medium" tempo in Hindustani rhythmic theory.

maḥẕuf-o-ẓarb (U.) An "omitted" beat in Hindustani music.

maṇḍala (Skt., Ind.) A symmetrical design representing the cosmos in the form of concentric geometrical regions, used in Hindu and Buddhist religious practice and architectural forms.

mañjīra (H.) South Asian finger cymbals used widely up to the twentieth century to maintain the beat structure of a performance (Kippen).

maqṭaʿ (Ar.) Arabic for syllable, classified by prosodists as "short" (*kasīr*) or "long" (*tawīl*).

mār (H./U.) "Beat." used as a generic term for rhythmic patterns in folk drumming.

mārga-tāla (Skt.) "Way, path"-*tāl*. System of *tāl* described in ancient treatises.

masâwī (Ar.) Arabic for "even, equal": a category of *tāls* with three beats.

matra (B.I.) The main smallest unit of gamelan and poetry.

mātrā (Skt., Ind.) In Hindustani rhythmic theory, a count equal to one *laghu*; frequently said to be the duration of a healthy person's pulse; tactus referred to in counting beats.

mbanyu mili (Jv.) Aesthetic and treatment of melody, like "the flow of water."

mérong (Jv.) See "gendhing."

miṣrāʿ (Ar., P.) Arabic for one of the two hemistiches in a line (*bayt*) of poetry.

mora A minimal unit of duration in verse, often equivalent to a short syllable or an unvowelled consonant (see *ḥarf*) (Blum, Fujita).

mrdaṅg (Skt., Ind.) Another name for the South Asian *pakhāvaj* (Kippen).

musiqi-ye navāhi (P.) Any of the recognized "regional musics" of Iran.

musiqi-ye sonnati (P.) "Traditional music" of Iran, also called *musiqi-ye dastgâhi* and *musiqi-ye klassik*.

nağam (Ar., P.) Arabic for a musical tone, equivalent to *Greek phthongos*.

nāndī (Nw.) A type of *dāphā* song performed at the beginning of a singing session, in praise of Śiva or a related deity, using one or more special *tāls*.

naqqāl (Ar., literally "transmitter," P.) In Iran, a vocalist who recites and/or sings verses from Ferdowsi's *Shāh-nāma*, the national epic of Iran, often with prose summaries of the stories.

naqra (Ar., P.) "Strike." In Hindustani rhythmic theory, a short syllable, ta; a very short duration (equivalent to *turit*).

Nāṭyaśāstra (Skt.) The oldest surviving Indian treatise on dramaturgy, music, and dance, probably written in the Gupta period (c. second–fifth centuries C.E.). Attributed to the sage Bharata.

Newar An ethnic group, formerly the main inhabitants of the Kathmandu Valley, who created an elaborate urban civilization there based on the Hindu and Buddhist religions.

nonisochronous (beat) A series of felt impulses that have some qualities of a regular beat, but are not regular (see also "anisochronous") (Roeder).

nori (J.) Noun form of verb *noru*, "to ride on." As a technical term in traditional Japanese music, *nori* refers to the delivery of beats or to rhythm more generally. It is also a suffix for names of different rhythmic patterns in traditional genres. In Noh music the three types of song rhythm are named *hira-nori, o-nori*, and *chu-nori*.

nūba (Ar.) Suite form of classical urban music in the Maghreb.

nuqla (Ar.) In Arabic rhythmic theory, a progression or movement from one attack to the next.

offbeat A contra-metric moment that is not in unison with the first time-point within a metric beat, i.e., onbeat (Locke).

ompak (Jv.) Transitional phrase.

onbeat A commetric moment on the first time-point within a metric beat (Locke).

pakhāvaj (H.) Barrel drum of northern India, used mainly in *dhrupad*.

pamurba irama (Jv.) Those who have the authority to regulate the tempo and *irama* of *gendhing*, the *kendhang* player.

pāṇikā (Skt.) A type of sacred song (*gītaka*) performed during the *pūrvaraṅga* of an ancient Sanskrit drama.

paran (H.) A composition for the Indian barrel drum *pakhāvaj*.

partāl (1) (Panjabi) A type of Sikh devotional song in the *gurubānī* repertoire, characterized by the use of multiple *tāls*.

partāl (2) (Nw.) A particular tāl of Newar music, having seven beats (3 + 2 + 2), sung in fast tempo.

pathetan (Jv.) Preludes or postludes to *gendhing* performed by a few elaborating instruments (*rebab, gendèr, gambang*, and *suling*).

pélog (Jv.) One of the gamelan tuning systems, seven notes per octave.

pesindhèn (Jv.) Female solo singer in the gamelan.

piṇḍ (H.) In Hindustani rhythmic theory, quantity, or collection; the sum total of the beats, counts, and their relative proportions comprising a *tāl*. Obsolete.

pipilan (Jv.) Style of *bonang* or *gendèr* performance in which the player strikes notes one at a time.

pluta (Skt.) In South Asian rhythmic theory, a duration equal to three *mātrās*, symbolized by Š.

polyrhythm Simultaneous presence of more than one rhythmic figure (Locke).

prabandha (Skt., Ind.) General term for forms of vocal composition in India, classified in theoretical treatises from around the ninth century onward.

process thought Characterized by concern with change and movement and so with temporality; sometimes contrasted with "substance thought," whose concerns rest with permanences.

projection A hypothetical process of event formation in which the present event comes into being by taking into account the past, especially the immediately or fresh past. One aspect of projection especially prominent in music, poetry, and dance is that of durational quantity (Hasty).

pūrvaraṅga (Skt.) The preliminary ritual, including musical and dance pieces, performed on stage before an ancient Sanskrit drama, invoking the gods and ensuring the success of the performance.

qā'ida (U.) A composition for tabla.

qār' (Ar.) Arabic for "strike" or "stroke."

qaul (Ar., U.) Vocal genre of the Qawwāls.

Qawwāl Member of a South Asian community of musicians historically specializing in genres such as *qaul* and *k͟hayāl*.

radif (P.) The repertory of melodic and rhythmic units (*gušes*) taught to performers of Persian *musiqi-ye sonnati*, parts of which are selected and interpreted by musicians to serve as bases for composition and for improvised performance.

rāga/rāgam (Skt., Ind) A melodic mode of Indian classical music, also occurring in some religious music traditions such as *dāphā* (Widdess). More loosely, may refer to melody in nonclassical repertoires.

rāga ālāpana (Skt., Ind.) Elaboration of a *rāga*, usually without accompaniment, in a rhythmically elastic manner. The large-scale form of a *rāga ālapana* is an arc, beginning in a relatively low range and ascending to a peak, followed by a descent. (See also "ālāp[ana].")

rāh (P.) Persian for "road, way," equivalent to Arabic *ṭarīqa* as a musical term.

rahan (H.) In Hindustani rhythmic theory, rest (equivalent to Arabic *sukūn*).

rangkep (Jv.) (1) An irama; (2) a playing technique of a certain instruments by doubling the density level of the existing melodic patterns by repeating sections of a pattern and adding more whimsical melodic ornamentation.

rebab (Jv.) A two-stringed bowed lute with a heart-shaped body of wood covered with a membrane made of parchment.

rhythm The organization of events in time (Wolf).

rriḥ (T.B.) Air, melody (Morocco).

rukn (Ar. pl. *arkān)* A metric foot in Arabic poetry; equivalent in Hindustani rhythmic theory to a *ẓarb* that delineates a subdivision of the *tāl* (*vibhāg* in modern usage).

rūpak (H.) In Hindustani music, a *tāl* of seven counts whose form has changed greatly over time.

sabab (Ar.) A duration in Arabic theory equal to two syllables, *tan* (light) or *tana* (heavy).

sam (H., Ind.) In Hindustani rhythmic theory, a beat in a *tāl* considered to be a point of confluence or resolution.

sam/samam (Skt., Ind.) The first beat of a metrical cycle in Indian classical music.

Sanskrit The classical and sacred language of India.

ṣaqīl (P., Ar. *thaqīl*) "Heavy, long." In Hindustani rhythmic theory, a category of *tāls* with four beats.

saron (Jv.) A generic name for a metallophone with six or seven keys (one octave of one octave and one tone) placed on a wooden frame.

śāstra (Skt.) A text in Sanskrit expounding the theory of a particular branch of knowledge; theory in general, as opposed to practice (*prayoga*).

sāth (H.) A type of *paran* for pakhāvaj.

sawāri (P., Ind.) A compound tāl said to originate with Amir Khusrau (thirteenth–fourteenth century).

sekatèn (Jv.) An honorable gamelan, larger in size, performed each year to commemorate the birth of Prophet Muhammad.

sèlèh (Jv.) Resolving or ending, the end of a musical phrase.

senggakan (Jv.) Syllables or brief melodic passages performed by male singer, to enhance a lively mood of the piece.

senggrèngan (Jv.) A brief melodic cue of rebab, signaling that a gendhing is about to be performed.

sesegan (Jv.) Fast and loud style of playing a section of a piece.

se-zarba *See sih ẓarba* (P., Tj.).

sih-ẓarba/se zarba "Three-beat." A category of *tāls* comprising three beats (Kippen); classification of strumming patterns in Tajikistan with three emphasized strokes (Wolf).

sléndro (Jv.) One of the gamelan tuning systems, five notes per octave.

slenthem (Jv.) A metallophone with six or seven keys.

sogo (Ewe) Lead drum in Agbadza.

sthāyī (H.) The first section of a composition in Hindustani vocal music.

stroke melody A pattern of strokes on a drum or stringed instrument differentiated primarily by timbre (Wolf).

su-utai (J.) One of the performance formats of Noh drama performance: the singing of dramatic texts without accompaniment of drums and flute and without dance.

sukūn (Ar. pl. *sakanāt*) Arabic for pause, rest, or silence.

suling (Jv.) An end-blown flute made of bamboo.

sūrfāk͟h͟ta (U.) A tāl in Hindustani music, now uncommon.

suwuk (Jv.) End or ending.

tabla A pair of small hand-beaten kettledrums used to accompany most genres of Hindustani music.

tactus (1) in fifteenth- and sixteenth-century European polyphony, a beat marked by two hand motions (*arsis*, upward and *thesis*, downward) which regulated the treatment of dissonance and cadences (Hasty, ch. 1); (2) in current academic theory, a regular and continuous beat, generally maintained at a moderate rate to orient musicians and listeners to subdivisions and larger groupings; (3) by extension, "an isochronous time-unit of relatively short duration" that is treated as a unit of reference (e.g., the *mātrā* in North Indian classical music; Widdess).

taḥrir (P.) A yodel-like melismatic manner of singing that is featured in the *āvāz* style of Iran.

tāl/tāla/tāḷam (Skt., Ind.) In South Asian classical music, a metrical framework kept in a musician's mind, displayed with hand gestures, or articulated on an instrument (as with a fixed configuration of drum strokes known as *ṭheka*). In folk treatments, *tāla/tāl* may refer to a specific drum pattern and not a metric abstraction.

tālī (Skt., Ind.) A sounded clap in the clap-pattern of a Hindustani tāla; a beat or segment of the cycle marked by this gesture (equivalent to *ẓarb*).

tamssust (T.B.) Stage of fulfilment in the *aḥwaš* of the Anti-Atlas in Morocco.

tantra/tantric A set of philosophical concepts and religious practices common to Hinduism and Buddhism, emphasizing the esoteric identification of the individual with the cosmos.

ṭappa (H.) A vocal genre often associated with Qawwāls.

ṭarīqa (Ar., P.) Arabic for "way": as a musical term has often referred to a rhythmic cycle that supports one or more tunes.

tāshā (H./U.) Shallow, bowl-shaped drum, made of clay or metal, used in South Asia.

tazrrart (pl. tizrrarin) (T.B.) Anti-Atlas in Morocco, song performed in a responsorial form (solo and choir).

tempus (tempora, pl.) A global level of duration in the European mensural system (c. 1400–1600) designating by mensural sign the breve as primary unit, worth either 2 (if imperfect) or 3 (if perfect) semibreves.

ṭhekā (H.) In Hindustani music, an instrumental time-line in the form of a repeated pattern of sonorities played on the accompanying *tablā* or *pakhāvaj*, marking the metrical cycle of a particular *tāl*.

thiql (Ar.) Arabic for gravity of a musical tone, equivalent to Greek *barytēs*.

tilluna (s. tallunt) (T.B.) Frame drums (Moroccan Atlas mountains).

tilvāṛā (H.) A 16-count *tāl* that existed in many versions in the nineteenth century.

time feel Metric framework that organizes perception of rhythm (Locke).

time-line A pattern of gestures or instrumental sounds defining the length of a particular metrical cycle, repeated once each cycle (Widdess).

time-point Precise moment within the time span of the measure on which the onset of a fast pulse occurs (Locke). Point of time in an abstract metric frame that may or may not be marked by a sound (Fujita).

tīntāl (H.) The most common tāl in Hindustani music today.

tiqrqqawin (T.B.) Metal clappers (Anti-Atlas in Morocco).

tirvaṭ (H.) Vocal genre often associated with Qawwāls.

titāla (H.) "Three-beat," a category of *tāls* comprising three beats; a *tāl* structure that preceded *tīntāl* in slow (*dhīma*) and fast (*jald*) forms with three sounded beats and one unsounded.

tīvra (H.) A *tāl* now of seven counts but formerly perhaps of eight.

tone melody A melody articulated primarily by distinctions in tone (see "stroke melody") (Wolf).

ṭukṛā (H.) A composition for *pakhāvaj*.

turit (H.) A very short duration (equivalent to *naqra*), likely derived from *truṭi*, one eighth of a *mātrā*.

udaichan (H.) A tāl structure listed in the *Tuḥfat al-hind*, comprising two *laghus* and one *guru*.

upāśraya (H.) A pattern of drum strokes associated with *tāls* mentioned in the fourteenth-century Saṇgītopaniṣat-sāroddhāraḥ.

upbeat Midpoint between two onbeat moments (Locke).

vibhāg (H.) A subdivision of a *tāl* (equivalent to *rukn* in Arabic).

vīṇā (Skt./Ind.) South Indian lute with 7 strings and frets set into wax.

virām (H.) A diacritical symbol extending the duration of a laghu, druta, etc. by half its value (also *birām*).

waqfa (Ar.) Arabic term for a pause.

watad (Ar.) A duration in Arabic theory equal to three syllables, *tanan* (light) or *tanana* (heavy).

wazn (Ar., pl. *awzān*;) Arabic for "meter, weight"; in Hindustani rhythmic theory, the characteristic rhythm produced by the arrangement of beats.

wirama (Jv.) An older term for irama.

yaktāla (U.) "One-beat;" a category of *tāls* comprising one beat; the name of at least two different *tāl* structures, one of which preceded modern-day *ektāl*.

zamān (Ar., P.) Arabic for "duration."

ẓarb (Ar. pl. *ẓurūb*, U.) Arabic for "beat": in Hindustani rhythmic theory, marks a subdivison of a *tāl* or indicates the number of beats in a *tāl* (see *seh-zarba*) (Kippen); in Central Asia, indicates the number of stressed articulations, instrumental or vocal, in an item of repertoire; or a suite consisting of poetry set to contrasting rhythmic patterns (Wolf).

zarb/zarba (Tj.) In Central Asia, a term indicating the number of stressed articulations, instrumental or vocal, in an item of repertoire; or indicating a suite consisting of poetry set to contrasting rhythmic patterns.

zarbah/jarba (U./H.) "beat." Stressed stroke in a drum pattern. Through-composed stroke melody (Wolf).

zikr (U.) verbal formula often uttered with rhythmic regularity and sometimes articulated on instruments.

BIBLIOGRAPHY

Abdurashidov, Abduvali. 2002. *Omūziši avzoni še'r va musiqī (arūz va musiqī)* [Instruction in Prosody and Music (Aruz and Music)]. Dushanbe: Izdatel'stvo "Qonuniyat."

Abdurashidov, Abduvali. 2009. "Tašakkuli avzoni ruboi dar matni advori zarbii muziki [The Formation of Ruboi Meters in Terms of Musical Rhythmic Rotations]." In *Falak va mas'alahoi ta'rikī-nazariyavii musiqii tojik*. The 3rd international symposium on Falak organized by Faroghat Azizi. Ministry of Culture, Republic of Tajikistan. Dushanbe: Adib. English ed., Society for Ethnomusicology Online Translation Series, trans. Evan Rapport, ed. Richard Wolf. https://scholarworks.iu.edu/journals/index.php/emt/article/view/23933.

Agawu, Kofi. 2003. *Representing African Music. Postcolonial Notes, Queries, Positions*. New York: Routledge.

Agawu, Kofi. 2006. "Structural Analysis or Cultural Analysis? Competing Perspectives on the 'Standard Pattern' of West African Rhythm." *Journal of the American Musicological Society* 59 (1): 1–46.

Akhmisse, Mustapha Docteur. 2004. *Le journal d'un médecin chez les Berbères du Bani*. Casablanca: Editions Kortoba.

Alorwoyie, G. Foli, with David Locke. 2013. *Agbadza: Songs, Drum Language of the Ewes*. St. Louis, MO: African Music Publishers.

Amano, Fumio. 1997. *No ni tsukareta kenryokusha* [A Ruler Intoxicated with Acting Noh]. Tokyo: Kodan-sha.

Amoozegar-Fassaie, Farzad. 2009. "Ritme dar musiqi-ye irāni." *Ketāb-e Sāl-e Shaydā* 10/11: 152–73.

Amoozegar-Fassaie, Farzad. 2010. "The Poetics of Persian Music: The Intimate Correlation Between Prosody and Persian Classical Music." MA thesis, University of British Columbia.

Andersen, Mark, and Mark Jenkins. 2003. *Dance of Days: Two Decades of Punk in the Nation's Capital*. New York: Akashic Books.

Anku, Willi. 2000. "Circles and Time: A Theory of Structural Organization of Rhythm in African Music." *Music Theory Online* 6 (1). http://www.mtosmt.org/issues/mto.00.6.1/mto.00.6.1.anku.html.

Anyidoho, Kofi. 1983. "Oral Poetics and Traditions of Verbal Art in Africa." PhD diss., University of Texas at Austin.

Aristides Quintilianus. 1963. *De musica libri tres*. Ed. R. P. Winnington-Ingram. Leipzig: Teubner.

Aristotle. 1963 [1929]. *The Physics*. Ed. and trans. Philip H. Wicksteed and Francis M. Cornford. 2 vols. Loeb Classical Library. London: Heinemann and Cambridge, MA: Harvard University Press.

Aristoxenus. 1990. *Elementa Rhythmica: The Fragment of Book II and the Additional Evidence for Aristoxenean Rhythmic Theory*. Ed. and trans. Lionel Pearson. Oxford: Clarendon Press.

Arom, Simha. 1991. *African Polyphony and Polyrhythm: Musical Structure and Methodology*. Trans. Martin Thom, Barbara Tuckett, and Raymond Boyd. Cambridge: Cambridge University Press.

Asafiev, B. V. 1947. *Muzykal'naia forma kak protsess, kn. 2-aia: Intonatsiia* [Musical Form as Process, Book 2: Intonation]. Moscow and Leningrad: Muzgig.

Attridge, Derek. 1995. *Poetic Rhythm: An Introduction*. Cambridge: Cambridge University Press.

Avicenna. 1966. *Kitāb al-Šifā', I, al-Mantiq* [Logic], 9, *al- Ši'r* [Poetics], ed. A. Badawī. Cairo: al-Dār al-Miṣriyyah li al-Ta'līf wa 't-Tarjamah. English translation in Dahiyat 1974.

Azadehfar, Mohammad Reza. 2004. "Rhythmic Structure in Iranian Music." PhD diss., University of Sheffield.

Azadehfar, Mohammad Reza. 2006. *Rhythmic Structure in Iranian Music*. Tehran: Tehran Arts University Press.

Baily, John. 2005. "La théorie de la musique dans les cultures de tradition orale." In *Musiques: Une encyclopédie pour le XXIe siècle, vol. 3: Musiques et cultures*, ed. Jean-Jacques Nattiez, 911–29. Paris: Actes Sud/Cité de la musique.

Bakhtin, Mikhail. 1986. "The Problem of Speech Genres." In *Speech Genres and Other Late Essays*, trans. Vern W. McGee, ed. C. Emerson and M. Holquist, 60–102. Austin: University of Texas Press.

Barker, Andrew, ed. 1989. *Greek Musical Writings: Volume 2, Harmonic and Acoustic Theory*. Cambridge Readings in the Literature of Music. Cambridge: Cambridge University Press.

Bartlett, Frederic C. 1932. *Remembering: A Study in Experimental and Social Psychology*. Cambridge: Cambridge University Press.

Bartók, Bela. 1931. *Hungarian Folk Music*. London: Oxford University Press.

Beauvillain, C., and Paul Fraisse. 1984. "On the Temporal Control of Polyrhythmic Performance." *Music Perception* 1 (4): 485–99.

Beck, Guy. 2012. *Sonic Liturgy: Ritual and Music in Hindu Tradition*. Columbia: University of South Carolina Press.

Becker, Alton, and Judith Becker. 1979. "A Grammar of the Musical Genre Srepegan." *Journal of Music Theory* 23 (1): 1–43.

Becker, Judith. 1979. "Time and Tune in Java." In *The Imagination of Reality: Essays in Southeast Asian Coherence Systems*, ed. A. L. Becker and Aram A. Yengoyan, 197–210. Norwood, NJ: Ablex.

Becker, Judith. 1981. "A Southeast Asian Musical Process: Thai Thaw and Javanese Irama." *Ethnomusicology* 24 (3): 453–64.

Bekker, Paul. 1923. "Neue Musik." In *Gesammelte Schriften* 3: 100–1. Berlin: Deutsche Verlaganstalt.

Benadon, F. 2009. "Time Warps in Early Jazz." *Music Theory Spectrum* 31 (1): 1–25.

Benamou, Marc. 2010. *Rasa: Affect and Intuition in Javanese Musical Aesthetics*. Oxford: Oxford University Press.

Bendix, Regina. 2000. "The Pleasures of the Ear: Toward an Ethnography of Listening." *Cultural Analysis* 1: 33–50.

Benveniste, Emile. 1971. "The Notion of 'Rhythm' in Its Linguistic Expression." In *Problems in General Linguistics*, trans. Mary Elizabeth Meek, 281–88. Coral Gables, FL: University of Miami Press.

Berg, Alban. 1974 [1924]. "Why Is Schoenberg's Music So Difficult to Understand?" In *Alban Berg*, ed. Willi Reich, 189–204. London: Thames and Hudson.

Bergson, Henri. 1965 [1922]. *Duration and Simultaneity: With Reference to Einstein's Theory*, trans. Leon Jacobson. Indianapolis: Bobbs-Merrill.

Berliner, Paul. 1994. *Thinking in Jazz: The Infinite Art of Improvisation*. Chicago: University of Chicago Press.

Binesh, Taqi, and Jean During. 1989. "Boḥur al-alḥān." In *Encyclopaedia Iranica: iranicaonline.org* (last updated December 15, 1989).

Blacking, John. 1967. *Venda Children's Songs: A Study in Ethnomusicological Analysis*. Johannesburg: Witwatersrand University Press.

Blacking, John. 1971. "Deep and Surface Structures in Venda Music." *Yearbook of the International Folk Music Council* 3: 91–108.

Blake, William. 2008. "There Is No Natural Religion." In *The Complete Poetry and Prose of William Blake*, ed. David V. Erdman, 2. Berkeley: University of California Press.

Blum, Stephen. 1975. "Towards a Social History of Musicological Technique." *Ethnomusicology* 19 (2): 207–31.

Blum, Stephen. 1991. "European Musical Terminology and the Music of Africa." *Comparative Musicology and Anthropology of Music: Essays in the History of Ethnomusicology*, ed. Bruno Nettl and Philip V. Bohlman, 3–36. Chicago Studies in Ethnomusicology. Chicago: University of Chicago Press.

Blum, Stephen. 2003. "Analyzing the Rhythms of Musical Responses." In *Third International Symposium, "Music in Society," Sarajevo, October 24–26, 2002: Collection of Papers*, 178–85. Sarajevo: Muzikološko Društvo F BiH.

Blum, Stephen. 2006. "Navā'i, a Musical Genre of Northeastern Iran." In *Analytical Studies in World Music*, ed. Michael Tenzer, 41–57. Oxford: Oxford University Press.

Blum, Stephen. 2009a. "Modes of Theorizing in Iranian Khorasan." In *Theorizing the Local: Music, Practice, and Experience in South Asia and Beyond*, ed. Richard K. Wolf, 207–24. New York: Oxford University Press.

Blum, Stephen. 2009b. "Şah Xətā'i as Name and Genre." In *Proceedings of International Musicological Symposium "Space of mugham,"* March 18–20, 2009, 92–97. Baku: Şərq-Qərb.

Blum, Stephen. 2013. "Foundations of Musical Knowledge in the Muslim World." In *The Cambridge History of World Music*, ed. Philip V. Bohlman, 103–24. Cambridge: Cambridge University Press.

Blush, Steven. 2001. *American Hardcore: A Tribal History*. New York: Feral House.

Boring, Edwin. 1942. *Sensation and Perception in the History of Experimental Psychology*. New York: Appleton-Century Crofts.

Boulez, Pierre. 1971. *Boulez on Music Today*. Trans. Susan Brown and Richard Bennett. Cambridge, MA: Harvard University Press.

Bregman, Albert S. 1990. *Auditory Scene Analysis: The Perceptual Organization of Sound*. Cambridge, MA: The MIT Press.

Brinner, Benjamin. 1995. *Knowing Music, Making Music: Javanese Gamelan and the Theory of Musical Competence and Interaction*. Chicago: University of Chicago Press.

Brown, Katherine Butler [Schofield]. 2003. "Hindustani Music in the Time of Aurangzeb." PhD diss., School of Oriental and African Studies, University of London.

Burns, James. 2010. "Rhythmic Archetypes in Instrumental Music from Africa and the Diaspora." *Music Theory Online* 16 (4). http://www.mtosmt.org/issues/mto.10.16.4/mto.10.16.4.burns.html.

Burns, James. 2012. "'Doing It With Style': An Ethnopoetic Study of Improvisation and Variation in Southern Ewe Drum Language Conversations." *African Music Journal* 9 (1): 154–205.

Burrows, David. 2007. *Time and the Warm Body: A Musical Perspective on the Construction of Time*. Vol. 2: Supplements to the Study of Time. Boston: Brill.

Busoni, Ferruccio. 1974 [1916]. *Entwurf einer neuen Ästhetik der Tonkunst, mit Anmerkungen von Arnold Schönberg und einem Nachwort von H.H Stuckenschmidt*. Frankfurt am Main: Suhrkamp. Text of the 2nd ed. first published Leipzig, 1916.

Butler, Mark. 2006. *Unlocking the Groove: Rhythm, Meter, and Musical Design in Electronic Dance Music*. Bloomington: Indiana University Press.

Čapek, Milič. 1961. *The Philosophical Impact of Contemporary Physics*. New York: Van Nostrand.

Caron, Nelly, and Dariouche Safvate. 1966. *Iran*. Les traditions musicales. Paris: Buchet/Chastel.

Cassio, Francesca. 2015. "Gurbānī Sangīt: Authenticity and Influences." *Sikh Formations: Religion, Culture, Theory* 11: 1–2, 23–60. http://dx.doi.org/10.1080/17448727.2015.1023105.

Charry, Eric. 2000. *Mande Music: Traditional and Modern Music of the Maninka and Mandinka of Western Africa*. Chicago Studies in Ethnomusicology. Chicago: University of Chicago Press.

Chashchina, Svetlana. 2013. "Theory of Intonation Rhythm: The Ways of Development." In *Principles of Music Composing: The Phenomenon of Rhythm*, translated and edited by Zuzana Šiušaitė, 28–33. Vilnius: Lithuanian Academy of Music and Theatre.

Chaudhary, Subhadra. 1997. *Time Measure and Compositional Types in Indian Music: A Historical and Analytical Study of Tāla, Chanda, and Nibaddha Musical Forms*. New Delhi: Aditya Prakashan.

Chernoff, John Miller. 1979. *African Rhythm and African Sensibility*. Chicago: University of Chicago Press.

Chernoff, John. 1991. "The Rhythmic Medium in African Music." *New Literary History* 22 (4): 1093–102.

Chernoff, John. 1997. "'Hearing' in West African Idioms." *The World of Music* 39 (2): 19–25.

Chopin, Frédéric, Etude Op.10 No.1, Advanced Tutorial, Paul Barton, piano. YouTube video, 45:24. February 15, 2013. https://www.youtube.com/watch?v=S6vp8QIfcIg&t=1s.

Chottin, Alexis. 1939. *Tableau de la musique marocaine*. Paris: Paul Geuthner.

Ciucci, Alessandra. 2012. "'The Text Must Remain the Same': History, Collective Memory, and Sung Poetry in Morocco." *Ethnomusicology* 56 (3): 476–504.

Clayton, Martin. 1996. "Free Rhythm: Ethnomusicology and the Study of Music Without Metre." *Bulletin of the School of Oriental and African Studies, University of London* 59 (2): 323–32.

Clayton, Martin. 2000. *Time in Indian Music: Rhythm, Metre, and Form in North Indian Rāg Performance with Audio CD*. Oxford: Oxford University Press.

Clayton, Martin. 2007. "Observing Entrainment in Music Performance: Video-Based Observational Analysis of Indian Musicians' Tanpura Playing and Beat Marking." *Musicae scientiae* 11 (1): 27–59.

Clinton, Jerome W. 1987. *The Tragedy of Rostam and Sohrab*. Seattle: University of Washington Press.

Cohn, Richard. 1992. "Metric and Hypermetric Dissonance in the Menuetto of Mozart's Symphony in G Minor, K.550." *Intégral* 6: 1–33.

Cohn, Richard. 2001. "Complex Hemiolas, Ski-Hill Graphs and Metric Spaces." *Music Analysis* 20 (3): 295–326.

Colaiuta, Vinnie. 1987. "Superimposed Metric Modulation." *Percussioner International* 1 (4). http://www.vinniecolaiuta.com/Interviews/Superimposed_Metric_Modulation.

Colannino, Justin, Francisco Gómez, and Godfried Toussaint. 2009. "Analysis of Emergent Beat-Class Sets in Steve Reich's Clapping Music and the Yoruba Bell Timeline." *Perspectives of New Music* 47 (1): 111–34.

Conant, Faith. 1988. "Adjogbo in Lome: Music and Musical Terminology of the Ge." MA thesis, Tufts University.

Cone, Edward T. 1968. *Musical Form and Musical Performance*. New York: Norton.

Cooper, Grosvenor, and Leonard Meyer. 1960. *The Rhythmic Structure of Music*. Chicago: University of Chicago Press.

Cooper, Grosvenor. 1969. "Rhythm." In *Harvard Dictionary of Music*, ed. Willi Apel. 2nd ed. Cambridge, MA: Harvard University Press.

Cotgrave, Randle. 1611. *Dictionary of the French and English Tongues*. London: Adam Aslip, printer. http://www.pbm.com/~lindahl/cotgrave/.

Csikszentmihalyi, Mihaly. 1990. *Flow: The Psychology of Optimal Experience*. New York: Harper and Row.

Csikszentmihalyi, Mihaly. 2002. *Flow: The Classic Work on How to Achieve Happiness*. London: Rider.

Dahiyat, I. M. 1974. *Avicenna's Commentary on the Poetics of Aristotle*. Leiden: Brill.

Darvishi, Mohammad Rezā. 1995 [1373]. *Negāh be ğarb: Baḥsi dar ta'sir-e musiqi-ye ğarb bar musiqi-ye Irān* [Westward Look: A Discussion on the Impact of Western Music on the Iranian Music]. Tehran: Māhur.

David, Dick, trans. 2006. *Shahnameh, the Persian Book of Kings: A New Translation*. New York: Viking/Penguin.

DeFord, Ruth. 2015. *Tactus, Mensuration, and Rhythm in Renaissance Music*. Cambridge: Cambridge University Press.

Dehlavi, Hoseyn. 2000 [1379]. *Peyvand-e še'r va musiqi-ye āvāzi* [The Relationship of Poetry and Vocal Music]. Tehran: Māhur.

Deleuze, Gilles, and Félix Guattari. 2003. *A Thousand Plateaus: Capitalism and Schizophrenia*. Trans. Brian Massumi. London: Continuum.

Demaine, Erik, Francisco Gomez-Martin, Henk Meijer, David Rappaport, Perouz Taslakian, Godfried Toussaint, Terry Winograd, and David Wood. 2009. "The Distance Geometry of Music." *Computational Geometry* 42(5): 429–54.

Dewantara, Ki Hadjar. 1930. *Sari Swara*. Groningen-Den Haag-Weltevreden: J. B. Wolter.

Dewey, John. 1887. *Psychology*. New York: Harper and Brothers.

Dihlavi, Muhammad Isḥaq. 1906. *Risāla ṭabla nawāzī*. Delhi: Qasimi Press. [U.].

Djakoeb and Wignyaroemeksa. 1913. *Layang Anyumurupake Pratikele Bab Sinau Nabuh Sarta Panggawene Gamelan*. Batavia: Drukkerij Eertijd H. M. van Dorp.

Djumaev, Alexander. 2002. "Sacred Music and Chant in Islamic Central Asia." In *The Garland Encyclopedia of World Music*, vol. 6: The Middle East, ed. Virginia Danielson, Scott Marcus, and Dwight Reynolds, 276–329. New York: Routledge.

Dor, George. 2000. "Tonal Resources and Compositional Processes of Ewe Traditional Vocal Music." PhD diss., University of Pittsburgh.

Dournon, Geneviève. 1980. *Comp. Inde: Musique tribal du Bastar*. Paris: Collection C.N.R.S.-Musée de l'Homme. LP with notes.

During, Jean. 1996a. 18. Iran. *Liner notes to Les voix du monde: Une anthologie des expressions vocales*, 149. Le Chant du Monde CMX 3741010.12 Compact Disc.

During, Jean. 1996b. "La voix des esprits et la face cachée de la musique: Le parcours du maître Ḥātam 'Asgari." *Le voyage initiatique en terre d'Islam. Ascensions célestes et itinéraires spirituels*, ed. M. A. Amir-Moezzi, 335–73. Louvain: Peeters.

Easthope, Antony. 1983. *Poetry as Discourse*. London: Routledge.

Elders, Willem. 2000. *New Josquin Edition*, vol. 4. Koninklijke Vereniging Nederlandse Muziekgeschiedenis: Utrecht.

El Hefny, Mahmoud. 1931. *Ibn Sina's Musiklehre hauptsächlih an seinem "Nağat" erläutert: Nebst Übersetzung und Herausgabe des Musikabschnittes des "Nağat."* Berlin: Otto Hellwig.

Eliade, Mircea. 2000. *The Myth of the Eternal Return: Cosmos and History*. Princeton, NJ: Princeton University Press.

Ellingson, Ter. 1990. "Nāsa:dya:: Newar God of Music." *Selected Reports in Ethnomusicology* 8: 221–72.

Ellingson, Ter. 1996. "The Mathematics of Newar Buddhist Music." In *Change and Continuity: Studies in the Nepalese Culture of the Kathmandu Valley*, ed. S. Lienhard, 447–81. Alessandria: Edizioni dell'Orso.

Ellis, Catherine. 1985. *Aboriginal Music, Education For Living, Cross-Cultural Experiences from South Australia*. St. Lucia: University of Queensland Press.

Elwell-Sutton, Lawrence P. 1976. *The Persian Metres*. Cambridge: Cambridge University Press.

Emmert, Richard. 1980. "Hiranori: A Unique Rhythm Form in Japanese No Music." In *Musical Voices of Asia*, ed. Richard Emmert and Minegishi Yuki, 100–7. Tokyo: Japan Foundation.

Emmert, Richard. 1983. "The Maigoto of No: A Musical Analysis of the Chu-no-mai." *Yearbook for Traditional Music* 15: 5–13.

Erlanger, Rodolphe d'. 1930. *La musique arabe*, I. Paris: Paul Geuthner.

Erlanger, Rodolphe d'. 1935. *La musique arabe* II. Paris: Paul Geuthner.

Fallahzadeh, Mehrdad, and Mahmoud Hassanabadi. 2012. Shams al-aṣvāt: *The Sun of Songs by Ras Baras (an Indo-Persian Music Theoretical Treatise from the Late 17th Century)*. Acta Universitatis Upsaliensis. Studia Iranica Upsaliensia and South Asian Studies. Uppsala: Uppsala Universitet.

Fallon, Daniel M., and James Harding. 2001. "Saint- Saëns, (Charles) Camille." *Grove Music Online*. March 11, 2019. http://www.oxfordmusiconline.com/grovemusic/view/10.1093/gmo/9781561592630.001.0001/omo-9781561592630-e-0000024335.

Fārābī, Abū Naṣr al-. 1959. *Kitāb al-shi'r* [Book on Poetry]. Ed. Muḥsin Mahdi. *Shi'r* 3: 90–95.

Fārābī, Abū Naṣr al-. 1961. *Fusul al-madani: Aphorisms of the Statesman*, ed. with an English trans., introduction, and notes by D. M. Dunlop. Cambridge: Cambridge University Press.

Fārābī, Abū Naṣr al-. 1967. *Kitāb al-mūsīqā al-kabīr* [*Great Book on Music*]. Ed. Ghaṭṭās 'Abd al-Malik Khashaba and Muḥammad Aḥmed al-Ḥifnī. Cairo: Dār al-Kātib al-'Arabī. First chapter on rhythm, 435–81; second chapter on rhythm, 983–1055; second section on melodic composition, 1063–188. French translation of entire work in d'Erlanger 1930 and 1935. For English translations of the three sections named see Sawa 2009 (rhythm) and Madian 1992 (melodic composition).

Fārābī, Abū Naṣr al-. 1971. *Al-Fārābī's* Fuṣūl muntaza'ah *(Selected Aphorisms): Arabic Text*, ed. Fawzī Mitrī Najjār. Beirut: Dār al-Mashriq.

Fārābī, Abū Naṣr al-. 1981. *Al-Farabi's Commentary and Short Treatise on Aristotle's De Interpretatione*. Ed. F. W. Zimmermann. Oxford: Oxford University Press for the British Academy.

Fārābī, Abū Naṣr al-. 2001. *Alfarabi's Political Writings: "Selected Aphorisms" and Other Texts*. Trans. C. E. Butterworth. Ithaca, NY: Cornell University Press.

Farhat, Hormoz. 1989. "Bīdād." In *Encyclopedia Iranica* IV (3): 240. http://www.iranicaonline.org/articles/bidad-dastgah.

Farhat, Hormoz. 1990. *The Dastgāh Concept in Persian Music*. Cambridge Studies in Ethnomusicology. Cambridge: Cambridge University Press.

Feld, Steven. 1981. "'Flow like a Waterfall': The Metaphors of Kaluli Musical Theory." *Yearbook for Traditional Music* 13: 22–47.

Feld, Steven. 1982. *Sound and Sentiment: Birds, Weeping, Poetics, and Song in Kaluli Expression*. Philadelphia: University of Pennsylvania Press.

Feld, Steven. 1988. "Aesthetics as Iconicity of Style, or 'Lift-Up-Over-Sounding': Getting Into the Kaluli Groove." *Yearbook for Traditional Music* 20: 74–113.

Feld, Steven. 1996. "Waterfalls of Song: An Acoustemology of Place Resounding in Bosavi, Papua New Guinea." In *Senses of Place*, ed. Steven Feld and Keith H. Basso, 91–135. Santa Fe, NM: School of American Research Press.

Feldman, Morton. 2000. *Give My Regards to Eighth Street*. Cambridge, MA: Exact Change.

Ferdowsi, Abolqasem. 2006. *Shahnameh, the Persian Book of Kings*, trans. Dick Davis. New York: Viking.

Folio, Cynthia. 1995. "An Analysis of Polyrhythm in Selected Improvised Jazz Solos." In *Concert Music, Rock, and Jazz Since 1945: Essays and Analytical Studies*, ed. E. W. Marvin and R. Hermann, 103–34. Rochester, NY: University of Rochester Press.

Fraisse, Paul. 1952. "La perception de la durée comme organisation du successif. Mise en évidence expérimentale." *L'année psychologique* 52 (1): 39–46.

Fraisse, Paul. 1982. "Rhythm and Tempo." In *The Psychology of Music*, ed. Diana Deutsch, 149–81. Orlando, FL: Academic Press.

Fraisse, Paul. 1987. "A Historical Approach to Rhythm as Perception." In *Action and Perception in Rhythm and Music*, ed. Alf Gabrielsson, 7–18. Stockholm: Royal Swedish Academy of Music.

Friedson, Steven. 2009. *Remains of Ritual: Northern Gods in a Southern Land*. Chicago: Chicago University Press.

Frigyesi, Judit. 1993. "Preliminary Thoughts Toward the Study of Music Without Clear Beat: The Example of 'Flowing Rhythm' in Jewish 'Nusah.'" *Asian Music* 24 (2): 59–88.

Frigyesi, Judit. 1999. "Transcription de la pulsation, de la métrique et du 'rythme libre.'" *Cahiers d'ethnomusicologie* 12: 55–73.

Frishkopf, Michael. 2007. *Kinka, Traditional Songs from Avenorpedo*. Self-published CD.

Frolov, Dmitry. 2000. *Classical Arabic Verse: History and Theory of 'Arūḍ*. Studies in Arabic Literature 21. Leiden: Brill.

Fujita, Takanori. 1986. "Structure and Rhythm in Nô: An Introduction." *The Oral and the Literate in Music*, ed. Tokumaru Yosihiko and Yamaguti Osamu, 88–95. Tokyo: Academia.

Fujita, Takanori. 2009. "No and Kyogen: Music from the Medieval theater. Trans. Alison McQueen Tokita." In *The Ashgate Research Companion to Japanese Music*, ed. Alison McQueen Tokita and David W. Hughes, 127–44. Aldershot: Ashgate Publishing Ltd.

Fujita, Takanori. 2010. *No no Nori to Jibyoshi* [Nori and Basic Rhythm in Noh: Ethnomusicology of Rhythm]. Tokyo: Hinoki-Shoten.

Geertz, Clifford. 1968. *Islam Observed: Religious Development in Morocco and Indonesia*. New Haven, CT: Yale University Press.

Geertz, Clifford. 1973. "Person, Time and Conduct in Bali." In *The Interpretation of Cultures: Selected Essays*, 360–411. New York: Basic Books.

Gell, Alfred. 1992. *The Anthropology of Time: Cultural Constructions of Temporal Maps and Images*. Oxford: Berg.

Gellner, David. 1992. *Monk, Householder, and Tantric Priest*. Cambridge Studies in Social and Cultural Anthropology. Cambridge: Cambridge University Press.

Gendlin, Eugene. 1962. *Experiencing and the Creation of Meaning*. Evanston, IL: Northwestern University Press.

Graves, Eben. 2017. "The Marketplace of Devotional Song: Cultural Economies of Exchange in Bengali Padāvalī-Kīrtan." *Ethnomusicology* 61(1): 52–86.

Greene, Paul. 2003a. "Sounding the Body in Buddhist Nepal." *World of Music* 44 (2): 93–114.

Greene, Paul. 2003b. "Ordering a Sacred Terrain: Melodic Pathways of Himalayan Flute Pilgrimage." *Ethnomusicology* 47 (2): 205–27.

Groneman, J. 1890. *De Gamelan te Jogjakarta*, with a foreword "Over Onze Kennis der Javaansche Muziek" by J. P. N. Land. Amsterdam: Johannes Muller.

Haas, Max. 2006. "Griechische Musiktheorie in arabischen, hebräischen und syrischen Zeugnissen." In *Geschichte der Musiktheorie, II, Vom Mythos zur Fachdisziplin: Antike und Byzanz*, ed. T. Ertelt, H. von Loesch, and F. Zaminer, 635–716. Darmstadt: Wissenschaftliche Buchgesellschaft.

Hajibeyov, Uzeyir. 1988 [1945]. *Azərbaycan xalq musiqisinin əsasları*. Tehran: Entešārāt-e Donyā. Azerbaijani text in Arabic script. First published in Russian as *Osnovy azerbaïdzhanskoï narodnoï muzyki*, Baku, 1945. English translation from the Russian ed., *Principles of Azerbaijan Folk Music*, Baku: Yazichi, 1985.

Hallam, Susan, Ian Cross, and Michael Thaut, eds. 2009. *The Oxford Handbook to Music Psychology*. Oxford: Oxford University Press.

Hanon, Charles-Louis. 1986 [1928]. *The Virtuoso Pianist in Sixty Exercises for the Piano*. New York: G. Schirmer, Inc.

Hanslick, Eduard. 1885. *The Beautiful in Music: A Contribution to the Revisal of Musical Aesthetics*. Trans. Gustav Cohen. Leipzig: Novello.

Hare, Thomas B. 1996. "Try, Try Again: Training in Noh Drama." In *Teaching and Learning in Japan*, ed. Thomas P. Rohlen and Gerald K. LeTendre, 323–44. Cambridge: Cambridge University Press.

Ḥasan al-Kātib al-. 1975. *Kitāb kamāl adab al-ghinā'*. Ed. Muḥammad Aḥmad al-Ḥifnī and Ghaṭṭās 'Abd al-Malik Khašaba. Cairo: al-Hayat al-Miṣriyat al-Ammah lil-Kitāb. French translation by Amnon Shiloah. 1972. *La perfection des connaissances musicales*. Gueutner: Paris.

Hasty, Christopher. 1987. "An Intervallic Definition of Set Class." *Journal of Music Theory* 31 (2): 183–204.

Hasty, Christopher. 1997. *Meter as Rhythm*. New York: Oxford University Press.

Hasty, Christopher. 2012. "What Is Rhythm?" Paper presented at the Conference on Rhythm, Harvard University, March 3–4.

Hasty, Christopher. 2013. "Rhythmicizing the Subject." In *Musical Implications: Studies in Honor of Eugene Narmour*, ed. Lawrence Bernstein and Lex Rozin, 169–90. Hilsdale, NY: Pendragon Press.

Hasty, Christopher. 2014. "Rhythmusexperimente-Halt und Bewegung." In *Rhythmus—Balance—Metrum*, ed. Christian Gruny and Matteo Nanni, 155–207. Bielefeld: Transcript Verlag.

Heile, Bjorn, ed. 2009. *The Modernist Legacy: Essays on New Music*. Surrey: Ashgate.

Heinrichs, Wolfhart. 1969. *Arabische Dichtung und griechische Poetik: Hâzim al-Qartăğannīs Grundlegung der poetik mit Hilfe aristotelischer Begriffe*. Beiruter Texte und Studien, 8. Beirut: Orient-Institut der Deutschen Morgenlaendischen Gesellschaft.

Heller-Roazen, Daniel. 2007. *The Inner Touch: Archaeology of a Sensation*. New York: Zone Books.

Henry, Edward O. 2002. "The Rationalization of Intensity in Indian Music." *Ethnomusicology* 46 (1): 33–55.

Heylin, Clinton. 1993. *From the Velvets to the Voidoids: A Pre-Punk History for a Post-Punk World*. London: Penguin.

Heylin, Clinton. 1998. *Never Mind the Bollocks, Here's the Sex Pistols*. New York: Schirmer Books.

Hikosaka, Okihide, Kae Nakamura, Katsuyuki Sakai, and Hiroyuki Nakahara. 2002. "Central Mechanisms of Motor Skill Learning." *Current Opinion in Neurobiology* 12 (2): 217–22.

Hoffman, Katherine. 2002. "Generational Change in Berber Women's Song of the Anti-Atlas Mountains, Morocco." *Ethnomusicology* 46 (3): 510–40.

Hopkins, Gerard Manley. 1967 [1918]. "Author's Preface." In *The Poems of Gerard Manley Hopkins*, 4th ed., ed. W. H. Gardiner and N. H. Mackenzie, 45–49. London: Oxford University Press.

Hornbostel, Erich M. von. 1928. "African Negro Music." *Journal of the International African Institute* 1 (1): 30–62.

Hoshino, Shizuko. 1978. *Utai no Naraikata* [How to Learn Singing in Noh]. Tokyo: Hinoki-Shoten.

Houle, George. 1987. *Meter in Music, 1600–1800: Performance, Perception and Notation*. Bloomington: Indiana University Press.

How to Play Son Clave—for Beginners. 2010. YouTube video, posted by Rqshquesada. http://www.youtube.com/watch?v=eel1mqQrJIQ.

Howat, Roy. 1983. "Bartók, Lendvai and the Principles of Proportional Analysis." *Music Analysis* 2 (1): 69–95.

Huron, David, and Ann Ommen. 2006. "An Empirical Study of Syncopation in American Popular Music, 1890–1939." *Music Theory Spectrum* 28 (2): 211–31.

Huron, David. 2006. *Sweet Anticipation: Music and the Psychology of Expectation*. Cambridge, MA: The MIT Press.

Imam, Muhammad Karam. 1925. *Ma'dan al-mūsīqī*. Lucknow: Hindustani Press. [U.].

Ingold, Tim. 2011. *Being Alive: Essays on Movement, Knowledge and Description*. Hoboken, NJ: Taylor and Francis.

Jankowsky, Richard. C. 2010. *Stambeli: Music, Trance, and Alterity in Tunisia*. Chicago: University of Chicago Press. Accompanying CD.

Jazayeri, Mehrdad, and Michael N. Shadlen. 2010. "Temporal Context Calibrates Interval Timing." *Nature Neuroscience* 13 (8): 1020–26.

Jeppesen, Knud. 1946. *The Style of Palestrina and the Dissonance*. Oxford: Oxford University Press.

Johnson, Hafiz Shabazz Farel, and John Chernoff. 1991. "Basic Conga Drum Rhythms in African-American Musical Styles." *Black Music Research Journal* 11 (1): 55–73.

Johnson, Irmgard. 1977. "The Child Player and His Training for the Noh Profession." *Denver Quarterly* 12 (2): 190–95.

Johnson, Irmgard. 1982. "The Role of Amateur Participants in the Arts of No in Contemporary Japan." *Asian Music* 13 (2): 115–33.

Jones, A.M. 1954. "African Rhythm." *Africa* 24(1): 26–47.

Jones, A. M. 1959. *Studies in African Music*. 2 vols. Oxford: Oxford University Press.

Jones, Mari Reiss. 2016. "Musical Time." In *The Oxford Handbook of Music Psychology*, 2nd ed., ed. Susan Hallam, Ian Cross, and Michael Thaut, 124–41. Oxford: Oxford University Press.

Jouad, Hassan. 1995. *Le calcul inconscient de l'improvisation: Poésie berbère—Rythme, nombre, sens*. Paris-Louvain: Peeters.

Jouad, Hassan. 2013. Lecture at the International Conference "Anthropology of Morocco and the Maghreb," Essaouira, Morocco, September 8–10, 2013.

Kanze, Motonori. 1913. "Hayashi-kata reizoku-shi [History of Noh Musicians' Subservience to Noh actors]." *Nohgaku* 15 (5): 34–38.

Kartomi, Margaret. 1990. *On Concepts and Classifications of Musical Instruments*. Chicago: University of Chicago Press.

Katz, J. B. 1987. "The Musicological Portions of the *Saṅgītanārāyaṇa*: A Critical Edition and Commentary." PhD diss., University of Oxford.

Kauffman, Robert. 1980. "African Rhythm: A Reassessment." *Ethnomusicology* 24 (3): 393–415.

Keeler, Ward. 1987. *Javanese Shadow Plays, Javanese Selves*. Princeton, NJ: Princeton University Press.

Khan, Muhammad Mardan Ali. 1862–1863. *G͟huncha-yi rāg*. Lucknow: Munshi Naval Kishore. (Second edition, 1879.) [U.].

Khan, Sadiq Ali. 1869. *Sarmāya- yi 'ishrat*. Delhi: Faiz-i am. [U.].

Khānlari, Parviz Nātel. 1994 [1958]. *Vazn-e še'r-e fārsi* [Meter in Persian Poetry]. Sixth printing. Tehran: Entešārāt Tus.

Khazrāi, Bābak. 2012. "Āyā Forṣat Širāzi nevisande-ye ketāb Boḥur al-alḥān ast? [Was Forsat Shirazi the Author of the Book Boḥur al-alḥān?]." *Faṣl-nāme-he Māhur* 14 (56): 125–29.

Kim, David Hyun-Su. 2009. "Hairpins and Notation as Metaphor." MA thesis, Harvard University.

Kippen, James. 1988. *The Tabla of Lucknow: A Cultural Analysis of a Musical Tradition*. New York: Cambridge University Press.

Kippen, James. 2001. "Folk Grooves and Tabla Tāls." *ECHO: A Music-Centered Journal* 3 (1). http://www.echo.ucla.edu/Volume3-Issue1/kippen/.

Kippen, James. 2006. *Gurudev's Drumming Legacy: Music, Theory and Nationalism in the* Mrdaṅg aur Tablā Vādanpaddhati *of Gurudev Patwardhan*. SOAS Musicology Series. Aldershot: Ashgate.

Kippen, James. 2007. "The *Tāl Paddhati* of 1888: An Early Source for Tabla." *Journal of the Indian Musicological Society* 38: 151–239.

Kippen, James. Forthcoming. "An Extremely Nice, Fine and Unique Drum: A Reading of Late Mughal and Early Colonial Texts and Images on Hindustani Rhythm and Drumming." In *Paracolonial Soundworlds: Music and Colonial Transitions in the Eastern Indian Ocean*, ed. Katherine Butler Schofield, Julia Byl, and David Lunn.

Knight, Roderic. 1974. "Mandinka Drumming." *African Arts* 7 (4): 24–35.

Kolinski, Mieczyslaw. 1973. "A Cross-Cultural Approach to Metro-Rhythmic Patterns." *Ethnomusicology* 17 (3): 494–506.

Kramer, Jonathan D. 1988. *The Time of Music: New Meanings, New Temporalities, New Listening Strategies*. New York: Schirmer Books.

Krebs, Harald. 1999. *Fantasy Pieces: Metrical Dissonance in the Music of Robert Schumann*. New York: Oxford University Press.

Kubik, Gerhard. 2010. *Theory of African music*, vol. 2. Chicago: University of Chicago Press.

Kunst, Jaap. 1973 [1949]. *Music in Java*. 2 volumes. The Hague: Martinus Nijhoff.

Kvifte, Tellef. 2007. "Categories and Timing: On the Perception of Meter." *Ethnomusicology* 51 (1): 64–84.

Laade, Wolfgang. 1979. *Australia: Songs of the Aborigines and Music of Papua, New Guinea*. Liner notes. Lyrichord LYRCD 7331 compact disc.

Ladzekpo, S. Kobla, and Hewitt Pantaleoni. 1970. "Takada Drumming." *African Music* 4 (4): 6–31.

Lath, Mukund. 1978. *A Study of* Dattilam: *A Treatise on the Sacred Music of Ancient India*. New Delhi: Impex India.

Lehmann, Bertram. 2002. "Syntax of 'Clave': Perception and Analysis of Meter in Cuban and African Music." MA thesis, Tufts University.

Lerdahl, Fred, and Ray Jackendoff. 1983. *A Generative Theory of Tonal Music*. Cambridge: The MIT Press.

Lerdahl, Fred, and Ray Jackendoff. 1996. *A Generative Theory of Tonal Music*. 2nd ed. Cambridge: The MIT Press.

Lester, Joel. 1986. *The Rhythms of Tonal Music*. Carbondale: Southern Illinois University Press.

Levin, Flora. 1972. "*Synesis* in Aristoxenian Theory." *American Philological Society Transactions* 103: 211–34.

Levy, Robert I. 1990. *Mesocosm: Hinduism and the Organization of a Traditional Newar City in Nepal*. Berkeley: University of California Press.

Lewin, David. 1981. "Some Investigations into Foreground Rhythmic and Metric Patterning." In *Music Theory: Special Topics*, ed. Richmond Brown, 101–37. San Diego, CA: Academic Press.

Locke, David. 1978. "The Music of Atsiagbekor." PhD diss., Wesleyan University.

Locke, David. 1982. "Principles of Offbeat Timing and Cross-Rhythm in Southern Ewe Drumming." *Ethnomusicology* 26 (2): 217–46.

Locke, David. 1992. *A Performance of Kpegisu by the Wodome-Akatsi Kpegisu Habobo*. Tempe, AZ: White Cliffs Media.

Locke, David. 2009. "Simultaneous Multidimensionality in African Music: Musical Cubism." *African Music* 8 (3): 8–37.

Locke, David. 2010. "Yewevu in the Metric Matrix." *Music Theory Online* 16 (4). http://www.mtosmt.org/issues/mto.10.16.4/mto.10.16.4.locke.html

Locke, David. 2011. "The Metric Matrix: Simultaneous Multidimensionality in African Music." *Analytical Approaches to World Music* 1 (1). http://www.aawmjournal.com/articles/2011a/Locke_AAWM_Vol_1_1.htm.

Locke, David. 2012. *Agbadza: The Critical Edition*. http://sites.tufts.edu/davidlocke/files/2012/01/Agbadza-Critical-Edition-final-DL1.pdf.

Locke, David. 2013. "Call and Response in Ewe Agbadza Songs." *Analytic Approaches to World Music Journal* 3 (1). http://aawmjournal.com/articles/2014a/Locke AAWM Vol.3.1.html.

Lomax, Alan. 1968. *Folk Song Style and Culture*. New Brunswick, NJ: Transaction Books.

Lomax, Alan. 1976. *Cantometrics: An Approach to the Anthropology of Music*. Berkeley: University of California Extension Media Center.

London, Justin. 2001. "Rhythm." *Grove Music Online*. March 11, 2019. http://www.oxfordmusiconline.com/grovemusic/view/10.1093/gmo/9781561592630.001.0001/omo-9781561592630-e-0000045963.

London, Justin. 2004. *Hearing in Time: Psychological Aspects of Musical Meter*. Oxford: Oxford University Press.

London, Justin. 2012. *Hearing in Time: Psychological Aspects of Musical Meter*. 2nd ed. Oxford: Oxford University Press.

Lord, Albert. 1960. *The Singer of Tales*. Cambridge, MA: Harvard University Press.

Lortat-Jacob, Bernard. 1980. *Musique et fêtes au Haut Atlas*. Paris: Mouton-EHESS.

Lortat-Jacob, Bernard. 2013. "L'ahwash berbère du Maroc: Le passage difficile d'un 'col musical.'" *Cahiers de Littérature Orale 73–74 (D'un rythme à l'autre)*: 41–70.

Lotz, John. 1972. "Elements of Versification." In *Versification: Major Language Types*, ed. William K. Wimsatt, 1–21. New York: New York University Press.

Maceda, José.1974. "Drone and Melody in Philippine Musical Instruments." In *Traditional Drama and Music of Southeast Asia*, ed. Mohd Taib Osman, 246–73. Kuala Lumpur: Dewan Bahasa dan Pustaka.

Madian, Azza Abd al-Hamid.1992. "Language-Music Relationships in Al-Farabi's 'Grand Book of Music.'" PhD diss., Cornell University. Eng. trans. of Fārābi's second section on melodic composition, 261–364.

Madison, Guy, and Björn Merker. 2002. "On the Limits of Anisochrony in Pulse Attribution." *Psychological Research* 66(3): 201–7.

Magill, Jonathan, and Jeffrey Pressing. 1997. "Asymmetric Cognitive Clock Structures in West African Rhythms." *Music Perception* 15 (2): 189–221.

Malm, William P. 1977. *Music Cultures of the Pacific, the Near East, and Asia*. Englewood Cliffs, NJ: Prentice-Hall.

Manuel, Peter. 2015. *Tales, Tunes and Tassa Drums: Retention and Invention in Indo-Caribbean Music*. Urbana: University of Illinois Press.

Mason, Daniel Gregory. 1919. "The Tyranny of the Bar-Line." *New Music Review* 9 (December): 31.

Massoudieh, Mohammad Taqi. 1978. *Radīf vocal de la musique traditionnelle de l'Iran par Maḥmūd-e-Karīmī: Transcription et analyse*. Tehran: Ministère de la Culture et des Arts.

Massoudieh, Mohammad Taghi. 1992. "Der Begriff des Maqām in der persischen Volksmusik." In *Von der Vielfalt musikalischer Kultur. Festschrift für Josef Kuckertz*. ed. Rüdiger Schumacher, 311–34. Anif/Salzburg: Ursula Müller-Speiser.

Massoudieh, Mohammad Taghi, ed. 1997 [1376]. *Radif-e āvāzi-e musiqi-e sonnati-e Irān be revāyat-e Maḥmud Karimi*. 2nd ed. Tehran: Māhur.

Mathiesen, Thomas J. 1985. "Rhythm and Meter in Ancient Greek Music." *Music Theory Spectrum* 7(1): 159–80.

Matsuno, Kiochiro. 1989. *Protobiology*. Boca Raton, FL: CRC Press.

Matsuno, Kiochiro. 2000. "The Internalist Stance: A Linguistic Practice Enclosing Dynamics." *Annals of the New York Academy of Sciences* 901: 332–49.

Mazo, Margarita. 1990. "Stravinsky's *Les Noces* and Russian Folk Wedding Ritual." *Journal of the American Musicological Society* 43 (1): 99–142.

Meade, Fionn, and Joan Rothfuss, eds. 2017. *Merce Cunningham: Co:mm:on Ti:me*. Minneapolis: Walker Art Center.

Messiaen, Olivier. 1995. *Music and Color: Conversations with Claude Samuel*. Milwaukee, WI: Amadeus.

Mijit, Mukaddas. 2016. "Sufism and the Ceremony of Zikr in Ghulja." In *The Music of Central Asia*, ed. T. Levin, S. Daukeyeva, and E. Köchümkulova, 388–405. Bloomington: Indiana University Press and Aga Khan Trust for Culture, Music Initiative.

Miller, Lloyd Clifton. 1999. *Music and Song in Persia: The Art of Āvāz*. Richmond, UK: Curzon.

Miner, Allyn. 1998. *The* Saṅgītopaniṣat-Sāroddhāraḥ: *A Fourteenth-Century Text on Music from Western India, Composed by Vācanācārya-Śrī Sudhākalaśa*. New Delhi: Indira Gandhi National Centre for the Arts and Motilal Banarsidass Publishers.

Mirka, Danuta. 2009. *Metric Manipulations in Haydn and Mozart: Chamber Music for Strings, 1787–1791*. New York: Oxford University Press.

Mishra, Ram Sevak. 1986. *Tāl prakāś aur tablā vijñān*. Benares: Bharatjivan Press. [H.]

Mohkamsing, Narinder. 2003. "A Study of Rhythmic Organisation in Ancient Indian Music: The Tāla System as Described in Bharata's *Nāṭyaśāstra*." PhD diss., University of Leiden.

Montague, Eugene. 2012. "Instrumental Gesture in Chopin's Étude in A-Flat Major, Op. 25, No. 1." *Music Theory Online* 18 (4). http://mtosmt.org/issues/mto.12.18.4/mto.12.18.4.montague.html.

Munn, Nancy. 1986. *The Fame of Gawa: A Symbolic Study of Value Transformation in a Massim (Papua New Guinea) Society*. Durham, NC: Duke University Press.

Nakajima, Y., E. Hasuo, M. Yamashita, and Y. Haraguchi. 2014. "Overestimation of the Second Time Interval Replaces Time-Shrinking When the Difference Between Two Adjacent Time Intervals Increases." *Frontiers in Human Neuroscience* 8. https://doi.org/10.3389/fnhum.2014.00281.

Neisser, Ulrich. 1967. *Cognitive Psychology*. Engelwood Cliffs, NJ: Prentice Hall.

Ness, Sally Ann. 2008. "The Inscription of Gesture: Inward Migrations in Dance." In *Migrations of Gesture*, ed. Carrie Noland and Sally Ann Ness, 1–30. Minneapolis: University of Minnesota Press.

Nettl, Bruno. 1964. *Theory and Method in Ethnomusicology*. New York: Schirmer.

Nettl, Bruno. 1987. *The Radif of Persian Music*. Champaign, IL: Elephant and Cat.

Nettl, Bruno. 2005. *The Study of Ethnomusicology: Thirty-One Issues and Concepts*. 2nd ed. Urbana: University of Illinois Press.

Neubauer, Eckhard. 1968–1969. "Die Theorie vom Īqā'. I. Übersetzung des *Kitāb al-īqā'āt* von Abū Naṣr al-Fārābī." *Oriens* 21–22: 196–232. Reprinted in Neubauer 1998a with facsimile of the Arabic text.

Neubauer, Eckhard. 1994. "Die Theorie vom Īqā'. II. Übersetzung des *Kitāb iḥṣā'al-īqā'āt* von Abū Naṣr al-Fārābī." *Oriens* 34: 103–73. Reprinted in Neubauer 1998a with facsimile of the Arabic text.

Neubauer, Eckhard. 1995–96. "Al-Halīl ibn Ahmad und die Frühgeschichte der arabischen Lehre von den 'Tönen' und den musikalischen Metren." In *Zeitschrift für Geschichte der arabisch-islamischen Wissenschaften* 10: 255–323.

Neubauer, Eckhard. 1998a. *Arabische Musiktheorie von den Anfängen bis zum 6./12. Jahrhundert. Studien, Übersetzungen und Texte in Faksimile*. Publications of the Institute for the History of Arabic-Islamic Science: The Science of Music in Islam, 3. Frankfurt: Institute for the History of Arabic-Islamic Science, 1998. Invaluable "Register von Fachwörtern aus der Musik und verwandten Gebieten," 349–425. Reprints of Neubauer 1968–1969 and 1994 with facsimiles of the Arabic texts.

Neubauer, Eckhard. 1998b. "Al-Khalīl Ibn Aḥmad and Music." In *Early Medieval Arabic: Studies on al-Khalīl ibn Aḥmad*, ed. Karin C. Ryding, 63–91. Washington, DC: Georgetown University Press.

Neuman, Daniel. 1985. "Indian Music as a Cultural System." *Asian Music* 17 (1): 98–113.

Nijenhuis, Emmie te. 1970. Dattilam: *A Compendium of Indian Music*. Leiden: Brill.

Nijenhuis, Emmie te. 1992. Saṅgītaśiromaṇi: *A Medieval Handbook of Indian Music*. Leiden: Brill.

Nijenhuis, Emmie te. 2010. "Musical Forms in Medieval India." In *Hindustani Music: Thirteenth To Twentieth Centuries*, ed. Joep Bor, Françoise 'Nalini' Delvoye, Jane Harvey and Emmie te Nijenhuis, 95–115. New Delhi: Manohar.

Nishino, Haruo, trans. 1973–1976. *Shimotsuma Shojin-shu* [Anthology of Works, 3 vols.] Tokyo: Wanwa-Shoten, Showa.

Nketia, J. H. Kwabena. 1963. *African Music in Ghana*. Evanston, IL: Northwestern University Press.

Noë, Alva. 2009. *Out of Our Heads: Why You Are Not Your Brain, and Other Lessons from the Biology of Consciousness*. New York: Hill and Wang.

Noland, Carrie. 2009. *Agency and Embodiment: Performing Gestures/Producing Culture*. Cambridge, MA: Harvard University Press.

Nooshin, Laudan. 2015. *Iranian Classical Music: The Discourses and Practice of Creativity*. SOAS Musicology Series. Farnham, UK: Ashgate.

Nzewi, Meki. 1974. "Melo-Rhythmic Essence and Hot Rhythm in Nigerian Folk Music." *The Black Perspective in Music* 2 (1): 23–28.

Nzewi, Meki. 1997. *African Music: Theoretical Content and Creative Continuum; The Culture-Exponent's Definitions*. Olderhausen: Institut fur Diaktik Popularer Music.

O'Hara, Craig. 1993. *The Philosophy of Punk: More Than Noise*. Oakland, CA: AK Press.

Obert, Simon, ed. 2012. *Wechselnde Erscheinung: Sechs Perspectiven auf Anton Weberns sechste Begatelle* (Webern Studien, *Beihefte der Anton Webern Gesamtausgabe*, Band I). Vienna: Lafite.

Omote, Akira, and Shuichi Kato. 1974. *Zeami Zenchiku*. Tokyo: Iwanami-Shoten.

Paris, André. 1921. "Haouach à Telouet." *Hespéris* 1 (January 1): 209–16.

Patwardhan, Dattatreya Vasudev (*alias* Gurudev). 1903. *Mrdaṅg aur tablā vādanpaddhati*. Lahore: Mufid-i am. [H.]

Perlman, Marc. 2004. *Unplayed Melodies: Javanese Gamelan and the Genesis of Music Theory*. Berkeley: University of California Press.

Phillips-Silver, Jessica, Petri Toiviainen, Nathalie Gosselin, Olivier Piché, Sylvie Nozaradan, Caroline Palmer, and Isabelle Peretz. 2011. "Born to Dance But Beat Deaf: A New Form of Congenital Amusia." *Neuropsychologia* 49 (5): 961–69.

Polak, Rainer. 2010. "Rhythmic Feel as Meter: Non-isochronous Beat Subdivision in Jembe Music from Mali." *Music Theory Online* 16(4). (mtosmt.org)

Polak, Rainer, and Justin London. 2014. "Timing and Meter in Mande Drumming from Mali." *Music Theory Online* 20 (1). http://mtosmt.org/issues/mto.14.20.1/mto.14.20.1.polak-london.html.

Polanyi, Michael. 1969. "Knowing and Being." In *Knowing and Being*, ed. Marjorie Grene, 123–37. Chicago: University of Chicago Press.

Poudrier, Ève, and Bruno Repp. 2013. "Rate Limits of On-Beat and Off-Beat Tapping with Simple Auditory Rhythms." *Music Perception* 23 (2): 165–88.

Powers, Harold S. 1980. "India, Subcontinent of, I: The Region, Its Music and Music History; II: Theory and Practice of Classical Music." In *The New Grove Dictionary of Music and Musicians*, ed. Stanley Sadie, 69–141. London: Macmillan.

Powers, Harold S./Richard Widdess. 2001. "India, Subcontinent of, III.1–5, Theory and practice of classical music." In *The New Grove Dictionary of Music and Musicians*, ed. Stanley Sadie, 9: 178–88. 2nd ed. London: Macmillan.

Powers, Harold S. 1986. "Rhythm." In *The New Harvard Dictionary of Music*, ed. Don M. Randel, 700–5. Cambridge, MA: Harvard University Press.

Pressing, Jeffrey. 2002. "Black Atlantic Rhythm: Its Computational and Transcultural Foundations." *Music Perception* 19 (3): 285–310.

Qureshi, Regula. 1969. "Tarannum: The Chanting of Urdu Poetry." *Ethnomusicology* 13 (3): 425–68.

Qureshi, Regula. 1981. "Islamic Music in an Indian Environment: The Shi'a Majlis." *Ethnomusicology* 25 (1): 41–71.

Qureshi, Regula. 2006. *Sufi Music of India and Pakistan: Sound, Context and Meaning in Qawwali*. Oxford: Oxford University Press.

Qureshi, Regula Burckhardt. 2010. "A Mine of Music History from Nineteenth-Century Lucknow." In *Hindustani Music: Thirteenth to Twentieth Centuries*, ed. Joep Bor, Françoise 'Nalini' Delvoye, Jane Harvey, and Emmie te Nijenhuis, 221–37. New Delhi: Manohar.

Rahâti, Bābak. 2012a. "Mafhum-e maqām dar musiqi-ye baxši-hā-ye šomāl-e Xorāsān [The Concept of *maqām* in the Music of the Baxšis of Northern Khorasan]." *Fasl-nāme-he Māhur* 14 (56): 43–59.

Rāhati, Bābak. 2012b. "Tajzie va taḥlil modāl maqām-hā-ye haftgāne-ye musiqi-ye baxši-hā-ye šomāl-e Xorāsān [Description and Modal Analysis of the Seven Maqams of the Baxšis of Northern Khorasan]." *Faṣl-nāme-he Māhur* 14 (57): 35–64.

Randel, Don M. 1976. "Al-Farabi and the Role of Arabic Music Theory in the Latin Middle Ages." *Journal of the American Musicological Society* 29(2): 173–88. Includes the Arabic text of the music section of Fārābi's *Ihsā' al-'ulūm* with Randel's translation.

Rao, Arati. 2015. "Discovery of Suḷādi notations with 'Raṅganāyaka' mudra in Thanjavur manuscripts." *Journal of the Music Academy of Madras* 86 (December): 74–93.

Rapport, Evan. 2016. "Prosodic Rhythm in Jewish Sacred Music: Examples from the Persian-Speaking World." *Asian Music* 47 (1): 64–102.

Rios, Rosetta de, ed. 1954. *Aristoxeni Elementa harmonica*. Rome: Typis Publicae Officinae Polygraphicae.

Rosch, Eleanor. 1973. "Natural Categories." *Cognitive Psychology* 4(3): 328–50.

Rothstein, William. 1989. *Phrase Rhythm in Tonal Music*. New York: Schirmer Books.

Rovsing Olsen, Miriam. 1997. *Chants et danses de l'Atlas (Maroc)*. Paris-Arles: Cité de la musique/Actes Sud. Accompanying CD.

Rovsing Olsen, Miriam. 2004. "Le musical et le végétal: essai de décryptage: Exemple berbère de l'Anti-Atlas." *l'Homme ('Musique et Anthropologie')* 171–72: 103–24. Accompanying CD.

Rovsing Olsen, Miriam. 2013. "A Common Motivation—A Specific Style for Each Culture: Towards a Comparison of Wedding Rituals in Morocco." *Yearbook for Traditional Music* 45: 164–86.

Rowell, Lewis. 1988. "Form in the Ritual Theatre Music of Ancient India." *Musica Asiatica* 5: 140–90.

Rowell, Lewis. 1992a. "The Prabandhas in Mataṅga's Bṛhaddeśī." In *The Traditional Indian Theory and Practice of Music and Dance*, ed. J. Katz, 107–41. Leiden: Brill.

Rowell, Lewis. 1992b. *Music and Musical Thought in Early India*. Chicago: University of Chicago Press.

Rqshquesada, 2010. "How to Play Son Clave—for Beginners." YouTube video, 5:13. http://www.youtube.com/watch?v=eel1mqQrJIQ.

Rumi, Jalāl al-Din Mohammad Balkhi. 1990. *Masnavi*. Ed. Mohammad Este'lāmi. 2nd ed. 7 vols. Tehran: Zavvār.

Rumi, Jalāl al-Din Mohammad Balkhi. 1992. *Masnavi-ye ma'navi*. Tehran: Iran University Press. Facsimile of Konya manuscript redacted in 677 AH.

Rumi, Jalāl al-Din Mohammad Balkhi. 2004. *The Masnavi, Book One*. Trans. Javad Mojadeddi. Oxford World's Classics. Oxford: Oxford University Press.

Sachs, Curt. 1953. *Rhythm and Tempo: A Study in Music History*. New York: Norton.

Saidani, Maya. 2006. *La musique du constantinois: contexte, nature, transmission et définition*. Alger: Casbah Éditions.

Sakai, Katsuyuki, Okihide Hikosaka, and Kae Nakamura. 2004. "Emergence of Rhythm During Motor Learning." *Trends in Cognitive Sciences* 8 (12): 547–53.

Śākya, Jogamān, and Śākya, Dharmaratna 1996 [V.S. 2053]. *Dāphā bhajanayā rāg tathā gvārā myẽ va cālī myẽyā rūparekhā*. Yale (Lalitpur): Hiraṇya Varṇa Mahāvihāra, Tāremām Saṅgha.

Śākya, Kīrtimān, and Śākya, Jogamān. 1987 [V.S. 2044]. *Jhīgu bājā jhīgu saṃskriti (dāphā bhajanayā gvāra saṃgraha)*. Yale (Lalitpur): Hiraṇya Varṇa Mahāvihāra, Tāremām Saṅgha.

Śākya, Puṣparatna 1995 [V.S. 2052]. *Khvapayā gūlā bājā*. Bhaktapur: Bhaktapur Buddhist Heritage Society.

Sambamoorthy, Pichu. 1958. *South Indian Music: Book 3*. 5th ed. Madras: Indian Music Publishing House.

Sanyal, Ritwik, and Richard Widdess. 2004. *Dhrupad: Tradition and Performance in Indian Music*. SOAS Musicology Series. Aldershot: Ashgate.

Sarmadee, Shahab. 1996. *Tarjuma-i-Mānakutūhala & Risāla-i-Rāgadarpaṇa by Faqīrullāh (Nawab Saif Khan)*. Kalāmūlaśāstra Series. New Delhi: Indira Gandhi National Centre for the Arts.

Savage, Jon. 1992. *England's Dreaming: Anarchy, Sex Pistols, Punk Rock and Beyond*. New York: St. Martin's.

Savage, P. E., E. Merritt, T. Rzeszutek, and S. Brown. 2012. "CantoCore: A New Cross-Cultural Song Classification Scheme." *Analytical Approaches to World Music* 2 (1): 87–137. http://aawmjournal.com/articles/2012a/Savage_Merritt_Rzeszutek_Brown_AAWM_Vol_2_1.htm.

Sawa, George. 1989. *Music Performance Practice in the Early 'Abbāsid Era, 132–320 AH/750–932 AD*. Toronto: Pontifical Institute of Mediaeval Studies.

Sawa, George. 2004. *Music Performance Practice in the Early Abbasid Era, 132–320 AH/750–932 AD*. 2nd ed. Toronto: Institute of Mediaeval Music.

Sawa, George. 2009. *Rhythmic Theories and Practices in Arabic Writings to 339 AH/ 950 CE*. Annotated translations and commentaries. Ottawa: The Institute of Mediaeval Music. English translation of all Fārābi's writings on rhythm, including the two chapters in the *Kitāb al-mūsīqā al-kabīr*, 128–57 and 164–235. Arabic–English glossary, 512–29; English–Arabic glossary, 530–80.

Sawa, George. 2015. "Al-Fārābī on Music." In *Encyclopaedia of Islam Three*, fascicle 4, ed. Kate Fleet, Gudrun Krämer, Denis Matringe, John Nawas, and Everett Rowson, 129–32. Leiden: Brill.

Schachter, Carl. 1976. "Rhythm and Linear Analysis: A Preliminary Study." *The Music Forum* 4: 281–334.

Scherzinger, Martin. 2010. "Enforced Deterritorialization, or the Trouble with Musical Politics." In *Sounding the Virtual: Gilles Deleuze and the Theory and Philosophy of Music*, ed. Brian Hulse and Nick Nesbitt, 103–28. Farnham: Ashgate.

Schoenberg, Arnold. 1975. "Brahms the Progressive." In *Style and Idea*, ed. Leonard Stein, trans. Dika Newlin, 398–441. New York: St. Martin's.

Schreffler, Gibb. 2002. "Out of the Ḍhol Drums: The Rhythmic 'System' of Punjabi Bhangṛā." MA thesis, University of California, Santa Barbara.

Schütz, Alfred. 1951. "Making Music Together: A Study in Social Relationship." *Social Research* 18 (1): 76–97.

Seidel, Wilhelm. 1980. "Rhythmus/numerus." In *Handwörterbuch der musikalischen Terminologie*. Wiesbaden: Steiner.

Sen, Arun Kumar. 1994. *Indian Concept of Rhythm*. Delhi: Kanishka.

Senn, Olivier, Lorenz Kilchenmann, and Marc-Antoine Camp. 2009. "Expressive Timing: Martha Argerich Plays Chopin's Prelude op. 28/4 in E Minor." In *Proceedings of the International Symposium on Performance Science*, ed. Aaron Williamon, Sharman Pretty, and Ralph Buck, 107–12. Utrecht: Association européenne des conservatoires, académies de musique et Musikhochschulen (AEC).

Setāyeshgar, Mehdi. 1374–1375 [1995–1996]. *Vāženāme-he musiqi-ye Irānzamin [Dictionary of music in Iranian lands]*. 2 vols. Tehran: Entešārāt-e 'Eṭṭelā'āt.

Sharma, Premlata, and Anil Bihari Beohar. 1994. *Bṛhaddeśī of Śrī Mataṅga Muni II*. New Delhi: Indira Gandhi National Centre for the Arts.

Shiloah, Amnon, trans. 1972. *La perfection des connaissances musicales*/Kitāb kamāl adab al-ğinā'. *Traduction et commentaire d'un traité de musique arabe du XIe siècle*. Paris: Paul Geuthner.

Shirāzi, Nasir Forsat al-Dawla. 1966 [1914]. *Bohur al-alhān dar 'elm-e musiqi va nesbat-e ān bā 'aruz [Meters of melodies in the science of music and their relation to the system of poetic meter]*. Tehran: Forughi. Facsimile of book published in Bombay, 1914.

Shore, Bradd. 1996. *Culture in Mind*. Oxford: Oxford University Press.

Shringy, R. K., and P. L. Sharma. 1989. *Saṅgītaratnākara of Śārṅgadeva*, 2. Delhi: Munshiram Manoharlal.

Simms, Rob, and Amir Koushkani. 2012. *The Art of Avaz and Mohammad Reza Shajarian: Foundations and Contexts*. Lanham, MD: Lexington Books.

Sindusawarno, Ki. 1955. *Ilmu Karawitan* [The Knowledge about Gamelan Music], 1. Surakarta: Konservatori Karawitan Indonesia. English translation by Martin Hatch in *Karawitan: Source Readings in Javanese Gamelan and Vocal Music*, ed. Judith Becker, 2: 311–38. Ann Arbor: Center for South and Southeast Asian Studies, The University of Michigan, 1987.

Snyder, Bob. 2000. *Music and Memory*. Cambridge, MA: The MIT Press.

Soderland, Gustave. 1947. *Direct Approach to Counterpoint in Sixteenth Century Style*. New York: Appleton-Century Crofts.

Soelardi, Raden Bagus. 1918. *Serat Pradongga*. Weltevreden: Widya-Poestaka nr. 2.

Solomon, Thomas. 2008. "Music as Culture? Reflections on an Ethnomusicological Moment." *Studia Musicologica Norvegica* 34 (1): 68–90.

Spiro, Michael. Congamasterclass, Son Clavé. 2008. YouTube video, 6:55. http://www.youtube.com/watch?v=oDPRzoJ45gc.

Stewart, Rebecca. 1974. "The Tabla in Perspective." PhD diss., University of California at Los Angeles.

Stockhausen, Karlheinz. 1963 [1955]. "Struktur und Erlebniszeit." Reprinted in Stockhausen, *Texte zur elektronischen und instrumentalen Musik, I, Aufsätze 1952–1962 zur Theorie des Komponierens*, 86–98. Cologne: DuMont. First publ. in *die Reihe* 2: Anton Webern. Vienna: Universal Edition, 1955.

Strauss, C., and N. Quinn. 1997. *A Cognitive Theory of Cultural Meaning*. Cambridge: Cambridge University Press.

Subba Rao, B. 1984 [1966]. *Raganidhi: A Comparative Study of Hindustani and Karnatak Ragas*. 4 vols. Madras: The Music Academy.

Sudnow, David. 2001. *Ways of the Hand: A Rewritten Account*. Cambridge, MA: The MIT Press.

Sumarsam. 1995. *Gamelan: Cultural Interaction and Musical Development in Central Java*. Chicago: University of Chicago Press.

Supanggah, Rahayu. 2011. *Bothèkan—Garap karawitan: The Rich Styles of Interpretation in Javanese Gamelan Music*. Surakarta: ISI Press Surakarta in collaboration with Garasi Seni Banawa Surakarta.

Sutton, Anderson. 1993. *Variation in Javanese Gamelan Music: Dynamics of a Steady State*. Monograph series on Southeast Asia, Special Report No. 28. DeKalb: Center for Southeast Asian Studies, Northern Illinois University.

Sutton, Anderson, and Roger Vetter. 2006. "Flexing the Frame in Javanese Gamelan Music: Playfulness in a Performance of Ladrang Pangkur." In *Analytical Studies in World Music*, ed. Michael Tenzer, 237–72. Oxford: Oxford University Press.

Sykes, James. 2011. "The Musical Gift: Sound, Sovereignty and Multicultural History in Sri Lanka." PhD diss., University of Chicago.

Tahmāsebi, Aršad. 1995 [1374]. *Javāb-e āvāz bar asās-e radif-e āvāzi be ravāyat-e Ostād Mahmud Karimi barā-ye tār va setār* [Instrumental Response to Avaz, Based on Master Mahmud Karimi's Version of the Vocal Radif, for Tar and Setar]. Tehran: Māhur.

Tahmāsebi, Aršad. 2001 [1380]. *Vazn-xāni važegāni(raveši ebdā'i)* [Reading Meters Lexically (An Innovative Method)]. Tehran: Māhur.

Takemoto, Mikio.1994. *Nogaku Shiryo-shu (Anthology of Treatises of Noh)*, 2. Tokyo: Waseda University Press.

Talā'i, Dariush. 1983. "Musique et poésie persanes: Analyse du rythme de la musique traditionnelle à travers la prosodie." Master's thesis, Université de Paris VIII.

Talā'i, Dariush. 1993. *Negāreši now be te'uri-ye musiqi-ye irāni* [A New Approach to the Theory of Persian Art Music]. Tehran: Māhur. Full text in both Persian and English. English text repr. in Talā'i 2000, 4–33 and Talā'i 2002.

Talā'i, Dariush. 2000. *Traditional Persian Art Music: The Radif of Mirza 'Abdollah*. Musical notation, commentary and performance by Dariush Talā'i [5 CDs]. Costa Mesa, CA: Mazda Publications.

Talā'i, Dariush. 2002. "A New Approach to the Theory of Persian Art Music: The Radif and the Modal System." In *The Garland Encyclopedia of World Music Vol. 6: The Middle East*, ed. Virginia Danielson, Scott Marcus, and Dwight Reynolds, 865–74. New York: Routledge.

Talā'i, Dariush. 2016. *Tahlil-e radif bar asās-e not-nevisi-ye radif-e Mirzā 'Abdollāh bā namudār-hā-ye tašrihi* [Radif Analysis Based on the Notation of Mirza Abdollah's Radif with Annotated Visual Description]. Tehran: Našr-e Ney.

Talero, Maria. 2006. "Merleau-Ponty and the Bodily Subject of Learning." *International Philosophical Quarterly* 46 (2): 191–203.

Tanaka, Takako. 2008. "The Samāj-Gāyan Tradition: Transmitting a Musico-Religious System in North India." In *Music and Society in South Asia: Perspectives from Japan*, ed. Yoshitaka Terada, 87–101. Senri Ethnological Studies. Osaka: National Museum of Ethnology.

Tehrāni, Farāmarz Najafi, and Asdollāh Hejāzi. 1991. *Ritm-hā-ye varzeši (ritm-ha-ye zarb-e zurxān'i)* [Rhythms of Athletics (Rhythms of the Zurxane Drum)]. Tehran: Entešārāt-e Pārt.

Tenzer, Michael. 2011a. "Generalized Representations of Musical Time and Periodic Structures." *Ethnomusicology* 55 (3): 369–86.

Tenzer, Michael. 2011b. "A Cross-Cultural Typology of Musical Time." In *Analytical and Cross-Cultural Studies in World Music*, ed. Michael Tenzer and John Roeder, 415–40. Oxford: Oxford University Press.

Tenzer, Michael. 2011c. "Temporal Transformations in Cross-Cultural Perspective: Augmentation in Baroque, Carnatic and Balinese Music." *Analytical Approaches to World Music Journal* 1 (1): 152–75.

Thackston, Wheeler M. 1994. *A Millennium of Classical Persian Poetry*. Bethesda, MD: Ibex.

Toussaint, Godfried T. 2005. "The Geometry of Musical Rhythm." In *Proceedings of the Japan Conference on Discrete and Computational Geometry*, ed. J. Akiyama, J. Kano, and X. Tan. Lecture Notes in Computer Science, vol. 3742: 198–212. Berlin: Springer.

Toussaint, Godfried T. 2013. *The Geometry of Musical Rhythm: What Makes a "Good" Rhythm Good?* Boca Raton, FL: CRC Press, Taylor & Francis Group.

Treitler, Leo. 1974. "Homer and Gregory: The Transmission of Epic Poetry and Plainchant." *Musical Quarterly* 60 (3): 333–72.

Trowell, Brian. 1978. "Proportion in the Music of Dunstable." *Proceedings of the Royal Musical Association* 105 (1): 100–41.

Trubetzkoy, N. S. 1969 [1939]. *Principles of Phonology*, trans. Christiane A.M. Baltaxe. Berkeley: University of California Press. First published as *Grundzüge der Phonologie (Travaux du Cercle linguistique de Prague*, no. 7).

True, Everett. 2002. *Hey Ho Let's Go: The Story of the Ramones*. London: Omnibus Press.

Tsuge, Gen'ichi. 1970. "Rhythmic Aspects of the Āvāz in Persian Music." *Ethnomusicology* 14 (2): 205–27.

Tsuge, Gen'ichi. 1974. "Āvāz: A Study of the Rhythmic Aspects in Classical Iranian Music." PhD diss., Wesleyan University.

Turino, Thomas. 2008. *Music as Social Life: The Politics of Participation*. Chicago: University of Chicago Press.

Urmawī, Safī al-Dīn al-. 2001. *Ketāb al-adwār fi al-musiqā (Persian Translation and Arabic Text)*, ed. Āryu Rostami. Tehran: Mirās-e Maktub.

Vidyarthi, Govind. 1959. "Melody Through the Centuries." *Sangeet Natak Akademi Bulletin* 11–12: 13–26, 33.

von Blumroeder, Christoph. 1981. *Der Begriff "Neue Musik" in 20. Jahrhundert. Freiburger Schriften zur Musikwissenschaft 12*. Munich/Salzburg: Katzbichler.

Wade, Bonnie C. 2005. *Music in Japan*. New York: Oxford University Press.

Wason, Robert W. 2002. "Two Bach Preludes/Two Chopin Etudes, or Toujours Travailler Bach-ce sera votre meilleur moyen de progresser." *Music Theory Spectrum* 24 (1): 103–20.

Wegner, Gert-Matthias. 1986. *The Dhimaybājā of Bhaktapur*. Wiesbaden: Franz Steiner.

Wegner, Gert-Matthias. 2009. "Music in Urban Space: Newar Buddhist Processional Music in the Kathmandu Valley." In *Theorizing the Local: Music, Practice, and Experience in South Asia and Beyond*, ed. Richard Wolf, 113–40. Oxford: Oxford University Press.

Wegner, Gert-Matthias, and Richard Widdess. 2004. "Musical Miniatures from Nepal: Two Newar Ragamalas." In *Nepal: Old Images, New Insights*, ed. Pratapaditya Pal, 81–91. Mumbai: Marg Publications.

Wegner, Ulrich. 1993. "Cognitive Aspects of Amadinda Xylophone Music from Buganda: Inherent Patterns Reconsidered." *Ethnomusicology* 37 (2): 201–41.

Weil, Gotthold. 1960. *'Arūḍ. Encyclopaedia of Islam*, 2nd ed. 1: 667–77, eds. H. A. R. Gibb and P. J. Bearman. Leiden: Brill.

White, David G., ed. 2000. *Tantra in Practice*. Princeton, NJ: Princeton University Press.

Whitehead, Alfred North. 1967. *Science and the Modern World*. New York: The Free Press.

Whitehead, Alfred North. 1978. *Process and Reality*. New York: The Free Press.

Widdess, Richard. 1981a. "Rhythm and Time-Measurement in South Asian Art-Music: Some Observations on Tāla." *Proceedings of the Royal Musical Association* 107: 132–38.

Widdess, Richard. 1981b. "Tāla and Melody in Early Indian Music: A Study of Nānyadeva's Pāṇikā Songs with Musical Notation." *Bulletin of the School of Oriental and African Studies*, University of London XLIV (3): 481–508.

Widdess, Richard. 1993. "Sléndro and Pélog in India." In *Performance in Java and Bali: Studies of Narrative, Theatre, Music, and Dance*, ed. Ben Arps, 186–96. London: University of London, School of African and Oriental Studies.

Widdess, Richard. 1994. "Involving the Performer in Transcription and Analysis: A Collaborative Approach to Dhrupad." *Ethnomusicology* 38 (1): 59–80.

Widdess, Richard. 1995. "'Free Rhythm' in Indian Music." *EM. Annuario degli Archivi di Etnomusicologia dell'Accademia Nazionale di Santa Cecilia* 3: 77–95.

Widdess, Richard. 2005. "'Free Rhythm' in Alap: Performers' Perspective." Paper delivered at the National Conference of the Society for Ethnomusicology, Atlanta, Georgia, November 19, 2005.

Widdess, Richard. 2006. "Musical Structure, Performance and Meaning: The Case of a Stick-Dance from Nepal." *Ethnomusicology Forum* 15 (2): 179–213.

Widdess, Richard. 2009. "Dāphā: Dancing Gods, Virtual Pilgrimage and Sacred Singing in Bhaktapur, Nepal." *Musiké* 5 (6): 55–79.

Widdess, Richard. 2011. "Dynamics of Melodic Discourse in Indian Music: Budhaditya Mukherjee's Ālāp in Rāg Pūriyā-Kalyān." In *Analytical and Cross-Cultural Studies in World Music*, ed. Michael Tenzer and John Roeder, 187–224. New York: Oxford.

Widdess, Richard. 2013. *Dāphā: Sacred Singing in a South Asian City: Music, Performance and Meaning in Bhaktapur, Nepal*. London: Ashgate.

Williams, Richard David. 2014. "Hindustani Music Between Awadh and Bengal, c. 1758–1905." PhD diss., King's College London.

Wolf, Richard K. 1991. "Style and Tradition in Karaikkudi *Vīṇā* Playing." *Asian Theatre Journal* 8 (2): 118–41.

Wolf, Richard K. 2000–2001. "Three Perspectives on Music and the Idea of Tribe in India." *Asian Music* 32 (1): 5–34.

Wolf, Richard K. 2000. "Embodiment and Ambivalence: Emotion in South Asian Muharram Drumming." *Yearbook for Traditional Music* 32: 81–116.

Wolf, Richard K. 2005. *The Black Cow's Footprint: Time, Space and Music in the Lives of the Kotas of South India*. Delhi: Permanent Black. (Also Urbana: University of Illinois Press, 2006.)

Wolf, Richard K., ed. 2009. *Theorizing the Local: Music, Practice and Experience in South Asia and Beyond*. New York: Oxford University Press.

Wolf, Richard K. 2010. "The Rhythms of *Rāga Ālāpana* in South Indian Music: A Preliminary Introduction." *Perspectives on Korean Music: Sanjo and Issues of Improvisation in Musical Traditions of Asia* 1: 121–41.

Wolf, Richard K. 2014. *The Voice in the Drum: Music, Language and Emotion in Islamicate South Asia*. Urbana: University of Illinois Press.

Wolpe, Stefan. 1967. "Thinking Twice." In *Contemporary Composers on Contemporary Music*, ed. Barney Childs and Elliot Schwartz, 274–307. New York: Holt Rinehart Winston.

Wright, Owen. 1978. *The Modal System of Arab and Persian Music, A.D. 1250–1300*. London Oriental Series 28. Oxford: Oxford University Press.

Wright, Owen. 1983. "Music and Verse." In *Arabic Literature to the End of the Umayyad Period*, ed. A. F. L. Beeston, T. M. Johnstone, R. B. Serjeant, and G. R. Smith, 433–59. Cambridge: Cambridge University Press.

Wright, Owen. 1995. "A Preliminary Version of the *Kitāb al-Adwār*." *Bulletin of the School of Oriental and African Studies* 58 (3): 455–47.

Wright, Owen. 2009. *Touraj Kiaras and Persian Classical Music: An Analytical Perspective*. SOAS Musicology Series. Farnham: Ashgate. Accompanying CD.

Yeston, Maury. 1976. *The Stratification of Musical Rhythm*. New Haven, CT: Yale University Press.

Youssefzadeh, Ameneh. 2002. *Les bardes du Khorassan iranien: Le* bakhshi *et son répertoire*. Travaux et mémoires de l'Institute d' études iraniennes, 6. Leuven and Paris: Peeters. Accompanying CD.

Youssefzadeh, Ameneh. 2010. *Rāmešgarān-e šomāl-e Xorāsān: Baxši va repertwār-e u*. Tehran: Māhur. Accompanying CD.

Youssefzadeh, Ameneh, and Stephen Blum. 2016. "Kontrol-e ritm dar do ejrā'i-ye dāstān-e Šāh Esmā'il dar Xorāsān [Control of Rhythm in Two Performances of the Story of Šāh Esmā'il in Khorasan]." *Faṣl-nāme-he Māhur* 18 (71): 41–57.

Zarlino, Gioseffo. 1573 [1558]. *Istitutioni harmoniche*. 2nd ed. Venice: Francesco de i Franceschi Senese.

Zbikowski, Lawrence M. 2002. *Conceptualizing Music: Cognitive Structure, Theory, and Analysis*. Oxford: Oxford University Press.

Zemp, Hugo. 1979. "Aspects of 'Are'are Musical Theory." *Ethnomusicology* 23 (1): 5–48.

Zonis, Ella. 1973. *Classical Persian Music, an Introduction*. Cambridge, MA: Harvard University Press.

INDEX

Abhinavagupta, 313n36, 318. See also *Abhinavabhāratī*
Abhinavabhāratī, 315, 318
abstraction, 23–24, 147, 339, 341
accent/accentuation, 5, 9
  agogic, 102
  accomplished by particular instruments, 101
  commetric, 102
  as "feeling tone," 10, 102
  variety of options for, 118, 129
actual, the, 21, 23, 32, 49n4
addressee, 323, 326
affect
  analysis in relation to, 142n10
  anchor points and, 13
  changes of *irama* and, 211
  climatic, common to plants and poetry, 240
  of drumming and related performance elements, 201
  metric fields and, 106, 143n19
  of pleasure, associated with "rising," 242
  sorrowful, 244
  technics for generating lively, 203, 206
African music
  in Anti-Atlas Mountains, Morocco, 232–52
  of Ewe in Ghana and Togo, 100–45
  oral notation of, 6, 120
  rhythm in, 3, 4
Afrikania Cultural Troupe, 100
Agawu, Kofi, 142n5, 238
Agbadza, 8, 9, 10, 100–145
  form in, 132–34
Agra, India, 325, 326
aḥwaš, 15, 232–52 passim
  defined, 235
akāl, 260, 261, 262, 382
akṣara, 19n1
ālāp/ālāpana, 6, 18, 277, 382, 389
  accompanied by drums, 311n10, 333
  analysis of, 335n15
  in Hindustani and Karnatak music, 311n10, 331
  incompetent performances of, 332–33
  "offbeat" articulations of, 73n6, 336
  performers' perspectives on, 332, 333, 335n16
  pulse in, 6–7, 66, 73n6, 332–34, 335n15, 335n16, 336n17

ālāp/ālāpana (*cont.*)
in Pūriyā-Kalyān *rāga*, 66–70
rhythmic properties of, 73n6, 73n10, 314–17, 331–34
spiritual associations, 332, 334
Alorwoyie, Gideon Foli, 100–1, 105, 107, 110, 113, 120, 127, 129, 130, 136, 141, 145
amateur musicians
in Noh, 226–28
(singers) in Iran, 87
amḫllf, 241, 248, 249, 250, 382
Amoozegar-Fassaie, Farzad, 91–93
anacrusis, 56–57, 64–65, 52n29, 376n9
anchor point, 13, 17, 315, 322, 318, 334, 382. *See also* synchronization
anisochrony (unequal time units), 5, 55, 62, 274, 276, 281, 283, 311n3, 327, 328. *See also* isochrony
at one level grouped into isochronous units at another, 276
Anti-Atlas Mountains, music and dance of, 5, 13, 15, 232–52
anudruta, 255, 382
aqqayn, 240, 242, 244
āṛā chautāla, 259, 263, 278, 382
Argerich, Martha, 379n23
Aristides Quintilianus, 94n3, 94n4
Aristotle, 75–77, 86, 94n3, 95n7, 95n10, 95n17
Aristoxenus, 77, 94n4, 95n7, 95n12
Arom, Simha, 144n32
articulations, *see* attacks
'arūz/ 'arūḍ, 78, 86, 91, 331, 382
aṛy (beat), 322
Astrā (*tāl*), 286, 289, 291
Ataka, 213, 214, 216, 217, 222–226, 231n14
aṭi (beat), 9, 320, 321, 322, 323, 383
atonality, 344–345
attack(s), 76–78, 95n8, 95n10. *See also* event(s)
as constituents in rhythmic thinking, 5, 19n1
strong, moderate, or soft, 78
synchronization of, 37
Attridge, Derek, 33, 330
Australian Aboriginal performance, 17
āvart/āvartan, 9, 254, 260, 273–276 passim, 383
āvāz, 57–62, 73n4, 73n10, 86, 92, 96n26, 97n31, 331, 383
Avicenna, 75, 86, 95n8
Azadehfar, Moḥammad Rezā, 91, 98n43
axatsɛ (rattle), 107, 109
background, musical, 315, 329
multiple conceptions of, 15–16
baḥr, 92, 258, 263, 264, 271, 383
Bakhtin, Mikhail, 323, 326
balungan, 200, 201, 203, 209, 211n4, 383
Bamberger, Jeanne, 351
band, 265, 266, 271, 383
Barton, Paul, 172n14
baxši, 80–85, 96n25, 97n29. *See also* Yegāneh, Zambilbāf
beat(s), 4, 317. *See also* count
beat zone, 102, 113, 144n26, 383
clarity of, variable, 201
clusters, organization in terms of, 326–27
contraction of (*see* contraction)
elasticity of, 84, 227
empty, 6, 10
in Hindustani *tāls*, 254
isochronous, 5, 8, 214
Japanese concepts of, 213–14, 217, 218 (see also *haku* or *hyoshi*)
light versus heavy (*see* light and heavy as characteristics of beat, rhythm and meter)
naming items according to number of, 256–272 passim, 321–29 passim
nonisochronous, 5, 8, 11, 12, 55
offbeat versus onbeat, depending on phrasal context, 118
predictable, 82
qualities of, 9, 11, 13, 218, 221
strong and weak, 342
terms related to, 9, 218, 320
tones before and after, 199
zarb (see *zarb*)
beginnings of cycles, 9, 10, 11, 105, 109–10, 214, 217, 236, 238, 244
South Asian, 254, 274 (see also *sam*)
Bekker, Paul, 375n2
bell phrase/pattern, 108, 195n9
as defining West African music, 100, 144n24
division of, 102
as source for ideas in songs, 136
Benveniste, Émile, 2
Berg, Alban, 377n15

Bergson, Henri, 2, 24
Bhaktapur, Nepal, 279–294, 297, 305–311 passim, 383
Bharatpur, India, 327
Black Cow's Footprint: Time, Space and Music in the Lives of the Kotas of South India, The, 17
Blake, William, 345
Blum, Stephen, 26, 33, 49n8
body, the
  breath accents of, 328
  coordinating movements in part of, 14
  "handedness" in, musical implications of, 110, 120, 144n27, 154, 262
  heartbeat compared to musical beat, 207
  restricted movement of, 214, 223
  rhythm and, 5
  rhythmic grouping based on bilateral symmetry of, 102
  trembling of, resulting in vocal trembling, 241
bols, 10, 254, 255, 265, 383. *See also* vocables
bonang, 201–205, 211n2, 383
Boring, Edwin, 378n20
Borumand, Nur 'Ali, 92, 98n39
Boulez, Pierre, 347–349, 359, 379n23
  Le Marteau sans maître, 348–349
Brenneis, Don, 94n3
Bṛhaddeśī, 301
Buddhism, 279
  genres and practices in, 278 (see also *dāphā; gvārā*)
buka, 202, 208, 211, 383
burdish, 256–258, 383
Burrows, David, 146

Cage, John, 17
cāl, 320, 326, 383
  as less complex than *tāl*, 326
cālī songs, see *dāphā*
Čapek, Milič, 49n6
cardinality, 274–277, 383
  changing of, at different levels of piece, 300
  in *jhaptāl*, 276
  ṭhekā as representing, 276
  time-line in relation to, 311n8
  in *tīntāl*, 275
Caron, Nelly, 90–91
Central Asia, music of, 327–28
chapkā, 265, 383
chautāla, 256, 259, 260, 261, 264, 266, 267, 269, 383
Chernoff, John Miller, 19n4, 144n30, 171n5, 335n9
Chishti, Hakim Hasan Maududi, see *Risāla-yi mūsīqī*
Chopin, Frédéric, Étude in C major, Op. 10 no. 1, 157–163
Chottin, Alexis, 243
chronos protos, see *protos chronos*
cikārī, 6, 67–70
Clayton, Martin, 55–56, 59, 70–71, 76, 94n6, 198, 210, 311n1, 331, 378n21
clempung, 201, 384
cognition, 18, 306–311
  shared, culturally shaped, 317
  temporal, 56
coincidence, musical, 16–17, 209. *See also* synchronization
  compared to calendrical systems, 211n5
  overlapping, 127, 138
  periodic, 87 (*see also* periodicity)
  as *sam* in Hindustani music, 254
Colaiuta, Vinnie, 194n2
  "Live at Catalina's," 182–186
colotomic structure, 13, 203, 209. *See also* gongan
comparison, 141, 245
  approaches to, 14, 15, 317, 321
  as taking measure, 27
  of terminologies
  temporality of, 51n24, 66
comprehension, *see* synesis
compression, rhythmic and metric, 47, 233, 241, 311n11, 358
  in Newar music, 281, 284, 289–98 passim, 303, 307
Cone, Edward T., 377n17, 378n19
consonant(s), vowelled or motionless, 78
continuation (projective), 37, 51n23, 56–57, 64–65, 341–44, 376n9
contraction, 67, 38
  of beats, 219–221, 227, 231n13
  and expansion of metric cycles, 289, 303
  and expansion in torso movements of dancers, 10, 101, 102
  geometric, 292, 297
  of scale, 350

Cooper, Grosvenor, 22, 23, 24
coordination in performance, 15, 200
of syllables and beats, 84–87
Cortázar, Julio, 195n12
counterpoint, rhythmic, 84
count(s), 320. *See also* beat(s)
as beat zone, 102
differentiation of, 102
as division of beats in Hindustani music, 254
cross-domain cognitive phenomena, 234, 251n4, 295. *See also* cognition; schema, foundational
Csikszentmihalyi, Mihalyi, 308
cues, musical, 94n4, 202, 208. *See also* drumming
Cunningham, Merce, 17
Cvakh, 281, 286, 289, 291
cycles, 4–6, 10–11. See also *āvart/ āvartan*; *daur*
as background, 210
beginnings of (*see* beginnings of cycles)
circular versus linear, 108, 210
compound (see *īqā'*)
constituent parts of a cycle, 9
countability of, 11
defined, 8, 274
differentiation within, 12, 219
melodic and rhythmic, 80–81
metric, 94n6, 273
multiplicity of in a perfomance, 17–18
of pitches, 62–66, 73n8
positions within, 11, 128, 135, 137–138, 214, 219
rhythmic, 8, 76–88. 95n14, 96n21
dadi, 200, 202, 203, 205, 283
literal meaning of, 209
dāk, 9, 321–23, 326
cādā, 321–23, 326
tiruganāṭ, 321, 322
Dalit, 323, 324
dance, 8, 10, 101
accents created by, 10
cadence in, 104
choreography of aḥwaš, 240, 241
conceptualized in terms of plant growth, 15
creativity of dancers with respect to temporal structures, 101
dzimeɣe, 101–105
of gods, 301
importance for analysis of rhythm, 101
as indicator of beat, 5, 142n5
interdependence with music, 17, 326
kakeri, 219
mazurka, rhythm of, 8
rhythm different from accompanying music, 220
tāl discussed in context of, 255, 256
dāphā, 278–311 passim, 384
nāndī and *cālī* songs of, 280, 300
darāmad, 58–62, 64–65
Darvoz, Tajikistan, 328
das prāṇ, 267, 268
dastgāh, 58, 82–83, 86, 96n26
daur, 76, 80, 258, 260
deferral (projective), 53n33, 343–344, 376n12
DeFord, Ruth, 53n33
Deleuze, Gilles, 24, 379n23
density of articulation, 4, 6, 366. *See also* *irama*; *laya*; tempo
Anti-Atlas music, 241, 243, 244, 245
in Javanese gamelan music, 198, 200, 201, 204, 207, 210
in Japanese music, 230n6
nonuniform change in, 322
South Asian music, 265, 322, 318, 326, 333, 335n5
Des Prez, Josquin, *Pange lingua* Mass, *Sanctus*, 41–47
determinacy and indeterminacy, 340–341, 376n6
Dewey, John, 49n7
dhā (barrel drum), 294, 384
Ḍhāḍhī (drumming community), 269, 270
dharma, 314, 315
Dharmapuri, Tamil Nadu, India, 323, 325
dhīma titāla, 256, 257, 261, 263–269, 271, 391
ḍhol (drum), 318, 324–327, 329, 384
as defining item of repertoire, 318, 326
ḍholak, 262, 264, 265, 384
dhrupad, 255–259 passim, 265, 384
ālāp accompanied by drum in, 311n10
clap pattern produced for, 273, 276
melodic structure related to *dāphā*, 280
poet's name in final section of, 283
pulse in *ālāp* of, 331

singing songs with contrasting *tāls* in, 277, 278, 302
ṭhekās for *tāls* in, 271
dhruva, 278, 300
dialogue(s)
in musical process of gamelan, 15
ritual songs as, with the bride, 237
Dihlavi, Muhammad Isḥaq, *see* Isḥaq, Muhammad
dimensions (musical), 31–32, 34, 347, 359
diminution, 326–27
dobar, 321
do mār, 324
dotāla, 259, 261, 384
dotār, 80–85
doubling (isochrony), 345, 362, 365–366
Dournon, Geneviève, 17
downbeat (various senses of), 10, 219, 376n10
drum call, 214, 218–226, 230n8, 386
as signaling position within meter, 219
drumming
contrasting timbres in, 14, 113, 120, 240
cueing in, 9, 15, 120, 201, 202, 203, 208, 209, 307, 323, 325, 329, 330
decision-making in, 325
folk, in South Asia, rhythmic properties of, 315, 327
formulaic consistency in a repertoire of, 325
leading transition of *irama*, 200
interlocking, 127, 128, 220, 225, 227, 321, 323
mood in relation to other parts of performance, 201
out of sync with syllable, 224
patterns, modification of in Noh, 219–221
precedence over (tone) melody, 294
in relation to rhythm, 2, 215, 232
"riff based" patterns of, 323, 329, 330
tunes, 316 (*see also* stroke melody)
as utterances, 323, 329
druta, 255, 259, 317, 384
du zarba, 328
dugga (drum), 324
duration, 7
determination of, 75–79
durational projection (*see* projection)
as process, 34–37
dyaḥlhāygu, 280, 300, 384
dynamics
change in, as generative of rhythmic process, 208
Easthope, Anthony, 50n20
Ektāḥ (*tāl*), 286, 289, 291
ektāl, 256, 263, 266, 278, 384
Ellingson, Ter, 295–96, 297
emergence, 27–28, 36, 38, 339–343, 353
Emmert, Richard, 226, 229n2
emotion, *see* affect
"empty verses"
as generative of poetic structure, 236
entrainment, 55–56, 64, 343
challenges for the listener, 16
defined, 274
flexibility allowed by, 17
to unwavering pulse, 333
entry, interval of, 96n19
eternal return, 11
etymologies, limits of, 317–18
event(s), 25–29, 338–339
complexity of, 28, 29, 30–31, 37, 45, 48–49n1, 339
onset of, 56, 59, 64–66
succession of, 56–57, 77
expansion, *see* contraction
experience, 18. *See also* R1
performer's, of rhythm, 7, 14, 142n12
qualitative aspects of rhythm, 13–14, 261
rhythmic, 20–21
subjective musical, 6, 314
total musical, 2–3
Fallon, Daniel, 152
Fārābī, Abū Naṣr al-, 5, 75–80, 86, 259
attributes of tones by, extended in work of al-Kātib, 96n18
emphasis on attacks, 95n10
fāṣila as defined by, 87, 260
nuqla defined by, 95n7
point metaphor in rhythmic theory of, 95n17
syllable as defined by, 95n16, 96n21
translated works of, 94n1
zamān as defined by, 96n19
farodast, 263, 265, 269
Feld, Steven, 143n20, 207, 233, 251n2

Feldman, Morton, 380n34
Crippled Symmetry, 368–369
De Kooning, 368–373
Spring of Chosroes, 366–368
Why Patterns? 380n36
Ferdowsi, Abolqāsem, 86–90
figure-ground relations, 69, 108, 186, 368. *See also* perception
fiqra, 265, 271, 384
flow, 2, 15, 16, 22, 23, 50n18, 57, 234, 308
in the Anti-Atlas, 234
grid versus, 13
in Indonesian music, 198–200, 206–208, 210
"inflow," 37
in Japanese Noh, 219, 220, 225, 229n1
in Jewish *nusach*, 59
in South Asian music, 16, 261, 271, 308, 311, 314, 318, 323, 326
in West African music, 100–145 passim
form, musical, 33–4, 71
in Agbadza, 132–34
as agentive, 252n10
heterometric, 273–313 passim
irama as, 207–9
irregular, in drumming, 320
Noh drama, reduced and full, 228
perception of, 57
projections of, 65
questioning the powers of, 21
responsorial, 236
rhythmic, of melodiy, 2
tīntāl, development of modern, 261–62
of *tīvra*, 261
formulas, melodic, 81
Fraisse, Paul, 20, 48n1, 146, 346
"freedom", 13, 314, 317. *see also under* rhythm
in connection with flow state, 308
versus constraint, 315, 360
of drummer to adjust position of motive, 180
novelty as, 357
questioning, 317, 354
types of, in rhythm, 61
Frigyesi, Judith, 59–60, 73n10
Frolov, Dmitry, 95n13
Gadd, Steve, 194n2
"Clave Solo," 188–193
"Three Quartets," 176–179
gamaka, 333–34, 336n18
gambang, 201, 206, 209, 384
gamelan, 196–211
distinctive rhythm of, 204
Indian music in relation to theory of, 197, 211n1
theory, 196
ganga (drum), 236, 240, 241, 246, 250
gaŋkogui (bell), 107. *See also* bell pattern
gatra, 4, 8, 198, 203, 209, 384
gaura-candrikā songs, 311n11
gender, 236, 262
of date palms, 240
differentiation in musical roles, 15, 235
grouping by, in *aḥwaš* performance, 236
instruments associated with, 222
oppositions in parallel domains, 241
of right- versus left-hand strokes, 262
gendèr, 201–209 passim, 384
Gendlin, Eugene, 24, 50n17
genres, "strong" and "soft," 97n33
gesture, 5, 6
functions of, 320
in Javanese dance, 197
pattern of, 7
in South Asian music, 9, 254, 260, 261, 273, 298, 319–20
G̱huncha-yi rāg, 267, 271
Gibson, J. J., 24
gintī, 327
Girīhe Nandinī, 285–91, 298, 300, 307
Gītagovinda, 302, 308, 385
gītaka, 297–300, 301, 310, 313n34, 385
function of, 298
Gizra people, Papua New Guinea, 62–66
gongan, 8, 200, 203, 208, 210, 211, 385
grid, musical time envisioned as a, 320, 327, 331–32. *See also* flow
groove, 7, 16, 164, 167, 176, 328, 385
in Agabadza, 50n18, 105, 111, 140, 142n12, 142n13, 143n14
in South Asian music, 4, 273, 276, 327
grouping, 101
Gūlā, 294, 297, 305, 310, 385
gūlābājā, 278

Gurtu, Trilok, 194n2
"Belo Horizonte," 179–180
guru (long syllable), 254, 255, 261, 262, 267, 268, 385
gurubānī,, *see* Sikh forms and practices
"Gurudev", *see* Patwardhan, Dattatreya Vasudev
gvārā, 278, 274, 294, 295–313 passim, 385
gvarāḥ, 312n24

haku (beat), 11, 218, 376n7
handclapping, 105
Hanon, Charles-Louis, 172n11
Hanslick, Eduard, 378n18
ḥarf, 77, 95n13, 262, 263, 266, 385
Ḥasan al-Khatib, al-, 83–84
Hasty, Christopher, 56, 66–71, 75, 77, 93, 172n8, 195n11, 208, 233, 239, 251n3
Haydn, Franz Joseph, String Quartet Op. 76 no. 4 ("Sunrise"), 38–40
heavy, *see* light and heavy as characteristics of beat, rhythm and meter
He Śiva Bhairava, 281–85, 289, 292, 300, 307
Heile, Bjorn, 375n2
Henry, Edward O., 281, 307
hetero-hypermetric composition, 301
heterometrical organization, 9, 13, 273–313 passim, 315, 326, 327
as requiring concentration, 307, 309
significance of, 291–92, 303–305
special functions of, 273, 279, 280
use of term in other literature, 311n2
hierarchies, 7
metric, 12, 105, 300
multiplicity of levels, 16, 300, 319
of pulse, 55
rhythmic and metrical differences within musical, 8
Hinduism, 197, 278, 279, 314
cosmology in, 318
Hindustani music, 6, 9, 10, 15, 16, 18, 66–70, 76, 204, 273, 274, 276, 283, 302, 311n1, 311n4, 311n10, 315, 320, 323, 324, 326, 327, 332, 336, 378n21, 385
changing *tāla* conceptions in, 253–272
differences from Karnatak music, 315, 335n5
hira-ji, 230n5
hira-nori (Noh song-rhythm type), 212, 217–219, 223, 226, 227, 229, 398
etymology of, 229n2, 387
theory of, 213–14
Hopkins, Gerard Manley, 84
Hornbostel, Erich M. von, 5, 10, 335n2
Hyderabad, Andhra Pradesh (now Telangana), 324
Hyderabad, Sindh, 325, 327
hyoshi (beat), 11, 218, 376n7

iambic pentameter, 33
Ilxāniān, Moḥammad, 86
imagination, 319, 378n18
anxieties regarding, 315
factors that restrict, 302
projective, 40, 351
Imam, Muhammad Karam, see *Ma'dan al-mūsīqī*
imbal, 202, 203, 205, 385
improvisation, 15, 17, 92, 147
in Agbadza, 118, 126, 127, 129, 140
of drum solos, 12, 147–195
function of prosody in, 92
in Iranian music, 91, 92
in New Music, 359, 377
poetic, 235, 236, 240, 242
process of moving from, to fixed composition, 242
quasi-spiritual ideas about, 314, 332
in South Asian music, 70–71, 254, 256, 273, 298, 302, 303, 314–336 passim (see also *manodharma*)
Indonesia, 5, 196–211
Inggah, 203, 209, 384
Ingold, Tim, 155
inherent rhythmic structures, 19n3, 165, 167. *See also* meter
"intensification," 281–284, 292, 304, 307, 385
intensity, 29, 47, 346–347, 374
interaction, 14–17, 29, 100–45 passim
as critical in gamelan music, 201, 208
measurement with regard to, 49n10
between singers and drummers in Noh, 222–227
interonset interval, 96n19
īqā', 4, 76, 78, 79, 83–84, 96n20, 258, 260, 385
etymology, 94n5

irama, 4, 8, 13, 197–210
Iranian music, 75–99 passim
  Persian classical, 57–62, 80, 82, 91
  "regional" and "traditional," 80, 84, 86
Isḥaq, Muhammad, 253, 255, 268, 271, 272
Islam, genres associated with, 87, 277, 314, 328, 334n1
isochrony, 8, 12, 13, 33, 37, 79, 276, 277, 298, 299, 316, 325, 330, 331, 332, 334, 338, 339, 346, 350–351, 385. *See also* anisochrony
  defined (isochronous as equal time units), 274
  implied in some understandings of rhythm, 316
  meter and, 331
  near, 184
isometric organization, 273, 277, 278, 289, 291, 294, 300, 306, 307, 309, 311n10, 329, 385

Jaladara, 208, 210
jald titāla, 256, 261, 263–265, 267, 391
James, William, 24
Jankowsky, Richard, 233, 234
jarba, 326, 391. See also *ẓarb*
Jati (*tāl*), 286, 289, 291
Java, *see* Indonesia; Gamelan
Jeppesen, Knud, 53n33
jhaptāl(a), 255, 261, 276, 278, 385
Johnson, Irmgard, 231n20
Jones, A. M., 316
Jouad, Hassan, 235, 236

Kabuki, 230n14
kagaŋu (support drum), 107, 109–110
kake-goe, *see* drum call
kāl, 256–262
kāla, 318, 319
kalā, 298, 299, 318, 319, 335n6
kālapramāṇam, 319, 332, 333, 386
  internalized in performer of *ālāpana* through training method, 333
Kalāvant, 258, 262, 264, 270, 271, 386
kalmah, 329
kalpita (composed) , 314, 315. See also *manodharma*
Karimi, Maḥmud, 82, 97n37
Karnatak music, 15, 19n2, 73n6, 93n6, 273, 311n1, 311n10, 314, 315, 319, 320, 322, 332, 333, 334, 335n17, 336n18, 386
  timeline visually executed as clap pattern, 276
Kathmandu valley, Nepal, 278–280, 283, 295, 297, 301, 312n15. *See also* Bhaktapur; Patan
Kauffman, Robert, 335n2
kendhang ciblon, 201, 202, 205, 284
kendhang kalih, 201, 202, 386
kenong, 202, 203, 206, 209, 386
k͟hafīf, 263, 386
k͟hālī ("empty beat"), 254, 256–258, 264–271 passim, 274–276 passim, 326, 335n13, 386. *See also* beat
  appearance of term in *Sharḥ-i risāla-yi qawāʾid-i ṭabla*, 264
Khalīl ibn Aḥmad, al-, 77–79
Khan, Muhammad Mardan Ali, 268. See also *G͟huncha-yi rāg*
Khan, Sadiq Ali, see *Sarmāya-yi ʿishrat*
k͟hayāl, 256, 257, 259, 263, 278, 303, 311n10, 386
Khorasan, 80–90
Kichisaka, Ichiro, 231n15
kidi (drum), 14, 100, 111–18
Kim, David Hyun-Su, 380n35
kingship, 284, 292
kiṇvar, 321
Kippen, James, 4, 9, 16, 18, 95n14, 276, 321, 335n4, 335n10, 375n1
Kitāb al-adwār, *see* Urmawī, Ṣafī al-Dīn al-
Knight, Roderic, 335n2
koḷ, 321
komi, 6, 15, 212–31 passim
  sequence of taking, with two performers, 225
  "to take" (*toru*), 232n10
Kota (tribal people), 9, 13, 17, 321–23, 326
ko-tsuzumi, 212, 214, 218, 220–227, 230n4, 230n15
Kramer, Jonathan, 195n11
Kubik, Gerhard, 8, 51n23

Lachenmann, Helmut, 380n33
ladkar, 232, 234, 237, 386
ladrang Pangkur, 201, 202, 410

lafẓ, 263, 264, 265, 266, 386
laggī, 265
laghu, 19n2, 254, 255, 261, 262, 267, 268
laḥn (pl., *alḥān*), 77, 80
lālākhī (drum), 280, 293, 312n23, 386
lamentation, 244–45
language, 10, 330–31
drum, 110–11
mapping instrumental patterns onto verbal phrases (*see* verbal phrases)
mixed language songs, 281
music and, analogies, 15
music shaped by, 107
shared features of music and, 378n18
laya/lay, 4, 5, 260, 387
as "act of sticking of clinging to," 317
"building the," (*lay bāndhnā*), 318
concept of in South Asian music, 8, 258, 274, 317–319, 321, 326
in Javanese, 8, 197, 198
related concepts compared, 204, 258, 263, 265, 335n4
learning, implicit, 315
Lerdahl and Jackendoff, 311n6
Lewin, David, 351
light and heavy as characteristics of beat, rhythm and meter, 9, 13, 95n14, 102, 132, 198, 208, 254, 259, 263, 330, 342
line or linearity
as model of progress, 11
of musical motion, 108, 132, 210, 278
musical time-, 4, 5, 11, 108
time-, 24
local
approaches, 1, 3
representations of rhythm, 5
Locke, David, 33, 50n18, 145n36
lomba technique, 201, 202, 203, 387
London, Justin, 4, 141n1, 146, 307, 308, 312n33
Lortat-Jacob, Bernard, 233, 242, 243, 252n10
Loṭfi, Moḥammad Rezā, 91
Lotz, John, 330
metric performance versus metric score, 330–331

Maceda, José, 23, 316
MacKaye, Ian, 164–165, 170, 173n22
Ma'dan al- mūsīqī, 267, 270
Maddoh, 328
Mahārudra Gvārā, 294–97, 298, 307
Malla, Ranjita (Newari poet), 283, 284, 285, 312n20
manas, 315
maṇḍala, 293, 294, 296, 297, 300, 387
as quasi-maṇḍalic structure, 303, 313n30
mañjīra, 256, 270, 271, 287, 291, 292, 387
maṉmattāḷam, 323
manodharma (composed), 314–315. See also *kalpita*
maqām, 96n23
vocal suites, 278
Mardan Ali, *see* Khan, Muhammad Mardan Ali; *G͟huncha-yi rāg*
marsiyah (lament poetry), articulated on drums, 318, 329
masāwī, 263, 264, 387
Mason, Daniel Gregory, 377n17
Massoudieh, Moḥammad Taqi, 83, 97–98n37
Mathiesen, Thomas, 94n4
mātrā/matra, 4, 8, 9, 298
based pattern, 329
defined, 274
as emic time-unit of reference, 311n5
etymology, 254
hierachical position of, 19n1
in Indonesian, 198
matrix, musical, 7, 9, 16, 32–33, 50n18, 79, 105, 106, 107, 135
Matsuno, Koichiro, 49–50n10
Mayer, Jojo, 194n2
"Jabon," 186–188
Mazo, Margarita, 17
measure. *See also* measurement
laya as, 317
mīzān, 243
proportional durations of drum parts in a cycle, 128
measurement, 2. *See also* time intervals
counting, 6, 9, 10, 220
internal, 27–29, 35, 37, 47, 49–50n10, 339
mechanical, 6–7, 230n9
of pulse, 331
of time by observing palm leaf shoots, 234
mēḷam, 311n10, 323

melody
  composition of, 76–78
  dependence on rhythm, 199, 316
  identity of, in gamelan music, 200, 203
  modal shift as contributing to rhythm, 131
  movement toward tonal goal, 136
  phrases of, in difference rhythmic contexts, 333
  "stroke" (*see* stroke-melody; tone melody)
memory, 35
  echoic, 35
  immediate, 94n6, 95n11
  span for duration, 298, 307, 346–348, 378n20
Mensurstriche, 41, 52n31
Mérong, 203, 209, 387
Messiaen, Olivier, 359, 379n31
metaphoric projections of rhythm, 5, 135, 145n39, 207–208, 219–22
  in cooking, 242
  in plants' growth, 232–252
  yin-yang, 13, 221, 222, 225, 230n12
meter, 4, 11–13. *See also* beat; *baḥr; wazn* and *tāla/tāl*
  additive (*see* rhythm: additive)
  ambiguous, 233
  defined, 274, 330
  hetero (*see* heterometrical organization)
  hypermeter, 298, 329, 377
  implicitness of, 12
    in Ewe music, 101, 106, 108, 110, 129, 136
  iso (*see* isometric organization)
  "many meters hypothesis," 4
  multiplicity of, 135
  musical in relation to poetic, 330
  numeric representation of, 5, 9
  obscured by context-driven modifications of drum pattern, 219
  "performance" versus "score," 330–31
  in phase, out of phase, 12, 128, 207
  poetic, 78, 79, 81, 82, 84, 86, 90, 91, 92, 94, 96n21, 96n42, 261, 263, 328, 329, 330, 331, 335n14
  as a referent within multiple hierarchical levels, 16
  semantic and grammatical factors involving poetic, 330
  surface rhythm as integral to, 311n8
  as a universal, 105
microtiming, 4
Miller, Lloyd, 97n37
Miner, Allyn, 255, 270
Minor Threat, "Straight Edge," 163–170
mitsuji (drum pattern), 218, 221, 222, 230n13
mode, rhythmic, 76
Moḥammad Ḥasan Naqqāl, 87–89
mora, 7, 79, 95n13, 95n14, 229n3, 387
moral character, melodious intonation as imitation of, 86
morshed, 88–90, 97n35
movement
  bodily, 2–3, 5, 7, 77 (see also *dance*)
  forward, feeling of, 91, 118, 128, 138, 144n28, 144n31, 188, 333
  restrictions on bodily, 214
mrdaṅg, see *pakhāvaj*
mridangam, 256, 320, 332
  player of, does not play *tāla* explicitly, 320
Muharram, 325, 327, 328
Mukherjee, Budhaditya, 66–70
naḍai, 19n2
naġmah, 324
naming of rhythmic units, 9. *See also* beat(s)
  obscure, 327
nāndī songs, see *dāphā*
naqqāl, 86–90, 97n32. *See also* Ilxāniān, Moḥammad; Moḥammad Ḥasan Naqqāl; Ṣādeq ʿAli Shāh; Ṣalaḥshur, Ḥasan
naqra, 259, 260, 261, 387
Nāṭyaśāstra, 210n1, 255, 297, 301, 313n34, 313n36, 318, 387
nauheh, 328
Neisser, Ulrich, 35
neku (bamboo trumpet), 294
Nelson, Jeff, 164–165
Nepal, 18. *See also* Newar
Ness, Sally Ann, 155
Nettl, Bruno, 73n5
Neubauer, Eckhard, 94n1, 95n7, 96n24
Neuman, Daniel, 270
New Music, 12, 337, 374, 375n1, 375n2
  rhythmic challenges face by composers of, 16
Newar (ethnic group), 312n15, 387
  music of, 279–297, 298–307 passim, 311n4, 312n17
  Newari (language) of, 280, 281, 285, 301, 312n15
  women in musical performance, 313n38
Nijenhuis, Emmie te, 303

nīlāmbari rāga, 333–34
Nizamuddin Auliya shrine in Delhi
drumming tradition of, 318, 329
post-Partition practices of, in Karachi, 318
Nketia, J. H. Kwabena, 144n24
Noë, Alva, 155
Noh, 7, 8, 9, 11, 13, 212–31 passim
changing hierarchies in, 15
Noland, Carrie, 155
nonisochronous, *see* anisochrony
Nooshin, Laudan, 98n38
norazu (blurring of meter), 219, 221
notation. *See also* transcription
beat placement in, 4–5, 6, 105
excluding meter from, 214–15
gestural patterns rendering, unnecessary, 300
graphic, changing usage of, 213, 229n1
heterometric music associated with, 307
intentional differences from, in performance, 214–227
oral, 6, 7
proportional form schemes associated with, 291
responding to, 14–15, 17
rhythmic, 41–43, 52–53, 147, 338, 351, 366–373, 380n34
rhythmic, for South Asian music, 253–72 passim
score reading, 13, 14
staff, for African music, 107, 142n6
syllable, 216
now, the, 76–77, 95–96n17. *See also* actual, the
as new, 340, 345
nūba, 232, 233, 243, 387
number(s). *See also* measurement
as defining rhythm in terms of attacks, 19n1
in history of representing rhythm, 9
order, 84
prominence in naming South Asian metric patterns, 314–36 passim
rational, 79
Nusah, *see* flow, in Jewish *nusach*
Nzewi, Meki, 23, 135, 144n23, 145n37, 316
objects and objectification. *See also* R2
through names and numbers, 314, 315–36 passim
of performance, 1
rhythm as embodied in things, 6
Omumi, Ḥoseyn, 58
ostinato, 6, 8, 12, 14
drummed, as background for improvisation, 174–175 (see also *ṭhekā*)
drum themes in relation to bell, 128
o-tsuzumi, 212, 214, 218, 220–227, 230n4
pace, 208, 255, 258, 271, 319, 332, 333, 336n17
Hindustani versus Karnatak music in terms of, 335n5
pakhāvaj, 253–272 passim, 311n10, 335n10
pāṇikā genre, 298, 299, 388
parallelism, 64, 69, 82
paran, 269, 270, 388
Partāl (Newar *tāl*), 281, 283, 388
participation in performance, 304–305
appropriateness of, 16
learning through, 217
motivations for, 16
Patan, Nepal, 279, 294–295, 302, 304–312 passim
passage, 14, 21–23, 48–49n1, 76, 78, 97n32, 340
pathet, 208, 210
path, 7, 240. See also *ṭarīqa*
patronage, 227–237, 292
Patwardhan, Dattatreya Vasudev, 253, 272
pedagogy, 9, 92, 170, 274
African approaches to, 5, 142–43n14
avoidance of representing meter in, 215
changes in, 15
counting, role of, 9
modern institutionalized, 254
musical, in Western institutions, 1
patrons involved in, 227
Peirce, Charles Sanders, 376n8
perception, 4. *See also* figure-ground relations
ambiguity of, 14, 111
changing objects of focus, 9, 19n3, 128–129
of meter in light of variable syllables counts, 214
of meter through repetition, 279
orientation, 9, 105
potentials for, 106, 113, 144n25
problems of insider, 62, 106, 140, 143–44n22, 197
of regularity in syllable-timing of languages, 330
in relation to background, 16, 315
temporal, 56–57, 61, 78–79
performance vs. (abstract) form, 21–25

periodicity, 10–11, 76, 208, 331, 366, 378n21, 380n33
of conjunctions, 87
measurements of, 62, 72
in polymetric context, 192
preconceptions concerning, 59, 60
pulse level, 55
syllable sequences creating, 84
pesindhèn, 201–204, 388
Philebus, 2
piano, technique as productive of rhythmic complexity, 15
piṇḍ, 256, 257, 267, 268, 388
pipilan, 201, 202, 388
Plato, 2, 94n3
pluta, 256, 256, 257, 388
poetry. *See also* text
Agbadza songs as, 129–30
contests, 237
fitting to musical meter, 212–31 passim
improvising of, 235, 242
length of poems contributing to rhythm, 132
marsiyah (*see marsiyah* (lament poetry), articulated on drums)
meter of, as basis for drum patterns, 329
musical setting affective semantics of, 130
periodic complexity of performed, 10, 12, 33–34
recitation of, not strictly regulated, 330
significance of, compared to speech, 235
variable syllable counts in Japanese, 214
used in and inspired by conversation, 236
whispering versus singing, 15, 235, 237
Polanyi, Michael, 45–46, 50
polymeter and polyrhythm, 105, 113, 144n23, 175, 174–195
potential (or virtual), 16, 29, 32, 33, 48, 341–344, 365–366
Powers, Harold, 19n1, 199–200, 204, 335n8
prabandhas, 277, 278, 280, 297, 301–303, 310, 388
present tense, 22, 338–339
Pressing, Jeff, 142n13
printing technology, lithographic, 271
process, temporal, 11, 13, 22, 338–344
process philosophy, 58
processions, music associated with, 239, 281, 294, 297, 304, 305, 311n11, 315
professional performers, changing roles of, in Noh, 227–29, 231n19
progression, 76–77
projection, 5, 6, 56–74, 77, 89, 142n9
of drum pace in between periods of *ālāpana*, 333
durational, 338, 339–344, 375n4
projective potential, 79, 82–83, 89, 239
proportionality, 9
prosody, Arabic, 78–79
prosody, Persian, 55–56, 79–81, 91–93
protos chronos, 8, 259
psychological present, *see* memory: span for duration
pulse, 4, 6
in cycles, 8, 106
defined, 274
in gamelan music, 198
internal, 62, 73n6
isochronous, 79, 84
maintenance of, 73n6
problems of analysis in terms of, 234
stream of, 56, 63–64
unit of reckoning other than, 327
pūrvaraṅga, 297, 300

qā'ida, 266, 269, 388
qalbānā, 277, 278, 312n14
qaul, 256, 259, 388
qawwālī, 263, 264, 277

R1 (realtime experience of rhythmic processes), 7, 13, 26, 31, 38, 43–44, 47–48, 51n24, 52n27, 75, 314
R2 (objectifications of rhythm), 7, 13, 26, 31, 38, 43–44, 47–48, 51n24, 52n27, 75, 314
rāga, rhythmic characteristics of, 333–34
rāga ālāpana, see *ālāp/ālāpana*
rahan, see *sukūn*
rangkep, 200–204, 206, 385, 389
Rapport, Evan, 93
Raza, Ghulam, see *Uṣul al-naghmāt-i āṣafī*
rebab, 201–210 passim, 389
reference system, 15
referent, instrumental, 82
religion and spirituality
"concerted religious effort" in producing heterometric music, 16, 285, 304–305
merit (religious), 304, 314

rhythm associated with, 332
spiritual commonplaces, 314
temporal transformation in relation to enhanced, 201
repetition, 11, 26–27
choices regarding, 133
response to vocalizing, 86, 97n31
rests and pauses, 5, 6, 7, 198
resultant rhythm/pattern, 108, 109
rhythm, 1–3, 199, 317. *See also* rhythm as subentry under region names
additive, 108, 129, 283, 300, 311n2, 312n19
Arabic terms for (*see īqā'*)
avoidance of teaching, directly, 215
compression of (*see* compression, rhythmic and metric)
concepts of, historical changes in, 253–272
concepts of, related to environment, 233–252
defined, 316
drumming as only partial to understanding, 232, 316
elasticity of, 2, 6, 12, 13, 17, 18, 212–31 passim, 322, 326, 327, 331–36 passim
etymologies for, 2
"free", 1, 26, 53n33, 55–56, 59–60, 314, 340, 345 (*see also* rhythm: elasticity of)
gestural, 154
Greek (see *rhythmos*)
Indonesian term for (see *ritme*)
inherent, 19n3
melody in relation to, 2, 13, 131, 316
multidimensionality of, 3, 18, 100, 140
nonisochronous, 62
as an object, 1
prosodic, 93
qualitatively described, 254, 258, 261, 316
regularity of, 2, 5, 332
representations of, 3–7, 332
South Asian terms for, 317–321
units pertaining to, 7–10
rhythmos, 9, 16, 76
Risāla-yi mūsīqī, 256, 257, 258, 259, 261, 264, 321
ritme, 197
rituals, music associated with
agriculture, 232, 237, 238–45
death, 100, 214, 323
wedding, 232, 237, 244–45
robā'I, see *rubā'ī*
Roeder, Geoffrey, 73n11
roles, musical, 235, 70, 88, 118
compared to "lord" and "servant," 229
improvisational, 318
maintaining or varying texture, 8
of notation as "role playing," 380n34
performers' rhythmic responsibilities in New Music, 17
preparing for, 9
in terms of gender, 237 (*see also* gender)
timekeeping, 4, 258, 262, 271, 311n8
of violin in Karnatak music, 332
Rothstein, William, 378n19
Rowell, Lewis, 315, 322
Rqshquesada, 150–151
rubā'ī, 79, 263
rukn, 263, 264, 265, 389
Rumi, Jalāl al-Din, 82–83, 97n27
rūpak tāl, 255, 261, 266, 278, 389

sabab, 78, 95n14, 259, 271, 389
Sachs, Curt, 2, 52–53n33
Ṣādeq 'Ali Shāh, 88–89
Sa'di, 88–89
Sadiq Ali Khan, see *Sarmāya-yi 'ishrat*
Safi al-Din, *see* Urmawī, Ṣafī al-Dīn al-
Safvat, Dariush, 90–91
Saint-Saëns, Camille, *Le Carnaval des Animaux* ("Pianistes"), 152–157
Ṣalaḥshur, Ḥasan, 89–91
sam/samam, 9, 10, 254, 274–76 passim, 389
changing conceptualizations of, 257–258, 261–265, 267, 268
samāj, 277
Sambamoorthy, P., 19n2
saṅgīta, 274
Saṅgītaratnākara, 255, 301, 315
Saṅgītaśiromaṇi, 255, 301
Saṅgītasurodaya, 255, 268
śankarābharaṇam rāga, 334
Sanyal, Ritwik, 7, 257, 331
ṣaqīl, 263, 389
Sarmāya-yi 'ishrat, 268, 269, 270, 271
saron, 201, 389
sāth, 269, 270, 389
Ṣaut al-mubārak, 266, 267, 269
Sawa, George, 75–76
sawārī, 259, 263, 265, 389

scheme, 87, 97n34
schema, foundational, 16, 292, 296–97, 307. *See also* cognition
Scherzinger, Martin, 379n23
Schoenberg, Arnold, 345, 377n15, 377n16
Schütz, Alfred, 2
Sciarrino, Salvatore, *Muro d'orizzonte,* 354–359, 379n29
se zarba/se zarb, 328. See also *sih-ẓarba*
Sen, Arun Kumar, 352
senggrèngan, 202, 208, 389
Senn, Olivier, 379n26
sesegan, 203, 209, 287
set class, 344, 377n14
Shah, Wajid Ali, 270. See also *Ṣaut al-mubārak*
Shajariān, Moḥammad Rezā, 86
Shapiro-Wilks test, 71–72, 73n11
Sharḥ-i risāla-yi qawā'id-i ṭabla, 262–265
shidai (entrance music), 220, 221
Shirāzi, Naṣir Forṣat al-Dowle, 86
Sikh forms and practices, 278, 303, 308
  gurubānī, 277, 278, 385
  partāl, 277, 278, 312n13, 388
sih-ẓarba, 256. See also *se zarba/se zarb*
Sindusawarno, Ki, 2, 9, 196–199, 207, 211n3, 211n4
Singing, as act of sowing, 239
situation-environment, 21, 28–29, 50
slenthem, 201, 209, 390
social relations
  creating consensus in musical and agricultural practices, 235
  in distribution of melodic phrases, 134
  as factor in rhythmic process, 15, 131–32
  and social status as contributing to musical interaction, 227–29
Soderlund, Gustav, 53n33
sogo (lead drum), 100, 104, 118–29
son clavé, 148–152, 171n5, 172n7
South Asia. *See also* entries for individual musical terms and countries
  Hindustani music (*see* Hindustani music)
  Hindustani versus Karnatak metric notions, 4
  Karnatak music (*see* Karnatak music)
  rhythm in, 4, 10, 15, 18 (see also *tāla*)
  Muria Gond music in, metrical complexity of, 17
  underlying common conceptions of rhythm in, 314– 36 passim
South Indian classical, see *Karnatak*
space, 2, 5
  bell phrase in musica, 108
  descending in, 244– 45, 252n11
  irama and, 197
  rising in, 242– 44, 252n9
  spatializing time, 5
speech, rhythm of, 19n1
spirituality, *see* religion and spirituality
Spiro, Michael, 150– 151
sṭambēlī, 233, 234, 241
Stewart, Rebecca, 270
sthāyī, 278, 390
Stockhausen, Karlheinz, 96n19
Stravinsky, multiple time streams in music of, 17
strokes, 8, 263. *See also ḥarf*
  metaphorical associations of drum, 262, 264
  stressed, as basis for conceptualization, 322– 27
stroke melody, 17, 256, 316, 320– 328, 331, 390
  strumming pattern as, 316
succession as secondness, 26, 29, 35– 36, 40, 376
Sudnow, David, 172n10
Sufi-related forms, 277, 278, 302, 315
  zikr, 328, 329, 331, 391
suites, musical. See also *maqām*; *nūba*
  in Atlas mountains, 232, 237, 244
  Buddhist, 295
  Central Asian, 328
  named for number of metric changes, 295
  South Asian, 265, 301, 323
sukūn, 77, 258, 259, 260, 390
sulādi genre, 311n11
sulādi tālas, 320, 335n7
suling, 209, 388, 390
su-utai (singing without instruments), 214, 215, 217, 227, 390
surfākhta, 261, 264, 390
suwuk, 206, 209, 211n4, 390
syllables, 7, 78– 79
  as attacks in musical rhythm, 8, 259
  coordinated with dance steps, 15
  creating beats, 225, 230n5
  definition of, 78
  formula of, used at beginning of song, 240

"holding on" (*mochi*) to, 217, 225, 226, 229
length of, 213, 217 (*see also* mora)
mental synchronization with, 223
rhythmic notation using, 259
sequences of, used as rhythmic models (*see also* "empty verses")
syllabic meter in Japanese poems, 213
synchronization, 57. *See also* coincidence
absence of, in "taking komi," 222, 226
alignment with bell cycle (Agbadza), 113
avoidance of, 17, 224
mental, in "taking komi," 223
rampak-rempeg (unity and synchrony), 206
synchronization space, 14, 17, 18, 174–175
syncopation, 16, 100–145 passim, 174–195 passim
dependence on regular accents, 52n33
quantification of, 194n3
sense of depending on listener's attention, 353
in South Asian music, 264
synesis, 77, 95n12

tabaṭk, 321, 322
tabla, 4, 275, 276, 311n7, 313n23
accompanying *ālāp*, 311n10
bipartite structure of compositions for, 266
as carrying *tāla* explicitly, 320, 253–72 passim
historical development of rhythmic thought in relation to, 253–72 passim, 335n10, 335n13
as part of Trilok Gurtu's training, 194n2
tactus, 43, 45, 53n33, 274, 329, 390
change in, 307
comparison of *tāl*s and sections in terms of, 286, 289, 290
entrainment to, 306, 333
markers for, 53
in Partāl, 281
reduction of, 304
relation of, to cycle, 274, 276
as represented in figure, 313n40
Ruth DeFord's three measurings in terms of, 53n33
subjective, 6
tactus beat, 47, 274, 276, 277, 298
"theoretical," 48, 53n33
Tagore, Sourindro Mohun, 253, 272
tāḥ, 281, 312n27
taḥrīr, 60, 61, 73n4, 331, 390
taiko (drum), 215, 230n6
Takemitsu, Toru, *Rain Tree*, 351–353, 359–366, 379n27, 379n32
tāla/tāl, 4, 13, 76, 94n4, 253–272 passim, 273–313 passim. *See also* under individual *tāl* names
as abstract, 320
changing of, 274, 278
counting, aloud, 260
deśī, 255, 335n12, 384
equation with "rhythm," 332
as fixed pattern, 320
instrumentalists marking out, 320
in Karnatak music, 319
Karnatak and Hindustani compared, 315, 320
mārga, 255, 322, 387
spelling of, 311n4
as reference system, 15, 315
as series of beats versus qualitative pattern of strokes, 267, 270, 271
through-composed sequence as, 278, 294, 312n23, 326
Ṭalā'i, Dariush, 91–93, 97n42–43
talalayt, 240, 246
Talero, Maria, 155
tālī, 254, 270, 274, 320, 324, 390
tallunt, see *tilluna*
tamssust, 241, 242, 246
tanbura playing, rhythmic properties of, 315
tanggung, 200, 202, 203, 208, 209, 385
Tantra, 279, 292, 304, 390
tappaṭṭai, 323
ṭarīqa, 80–81, 96n24
tāsha/tāshā/tājā, 318, 323, 324, 326, 327, 329, 390
as "building the *lay*" by improvising solos, 318
tavil (drum), 333, 311n10
tazrrart songs, 236, 242, 250, 251, 390
ṭek, 278
template for composing and singing verse, 84, 87, 97n34

tempo, 4
acceleration of, in central High Atlas, 233, 242, 252n10
categories of, 198
dhīma, madh(y)am and *jald* (slow, medium, fast), 260
negotiation of, between performers, 225, 226
relation to changes in *gongan* structure, 200
in relation to other meanings of *laya*, 317–18
temporality, 10–11, 237–38. *See also* time
process of reduction, 234, 244
in terms of "mental completion," 238
rhythm as, 233
tempus, 41, 52, 53n33
Tenzer, Michael, 3, 201, 300
text. *See also* poetry
as factor in elasticity of Noh rhythm disputed, 230n16
drums highlighting verbal messages and phrases, 139, 324
emphasis on textual lines as units, 215
implicit, 107, 110
texture, rhythmic, 8
call and response, 100, 131–32, 321, 326
timing of alternation between light and heavy, 132
Thackston, Wheeler, 97n28
ṭhekā, 4, 6, 273, 315
bipartite structure of, on basis of damping, 266
emerging in eighteenth- and nineteenth-century treatises, 254–272
as endowing cyclical space with specific character, 16
first notations of, 266
first usage of term, 263
as qualitatively differentiated cycle of counts, 10, 254
theorizing
agricultural process as grounding for, 13, 18, 238
of Iranian performers, 80
implicit, 1
tension between, and experiencing music without mediation, 314
theory, music
accounting for only struck beats, 257–258
as generated through interactions, 14
insider versus outsider, 62, 60, 196–197, 274
limits of existing, for vernacular music, 315
Noh, and variance with practice, 212–31 passim
tilluna (frame drums, s. *tallunt*), 236, 239, 240, 241, 242, 246, 250
tilvāṛā, 269, 390
timbre, 14
changes in, as generative of rhythmic process, 208
stroke melodies as patterns differentiated by, 316
tonal palette, 120
vocal, 76–79
time, 2. *See also* temporality
deflation of, 322
experience of, provided by life cycle of plants, 234, 242–45
inflation of, 321, 322
irama and, 197
as "rising," 242–45
"tension in time," 138
time intervals, 2, 5, 7
drum improvisation "builds" *lay* within, 318
flexibility of, in Noh, 212, 220–23, 225, 226, 230n7, 230n9
qualities associated with, 218
time points, 5
critiqued, 376n8
in definitions, 382, 388, 391
marked by gesture in South Asian music, 261, 294, 319, 326
as pulse in David Locke's notational system, 102
in reference to Japanese concept of beat, 213–14, 218, 220, 221, 376n7
timekeeping, 6, 176, 270, 271, 276, 295, 308
time-line, 4, 5, 11, 55, 144n24, 233, 340, 391. *See also* bell phrase/pattern
on cymbals, 276
gestural, 276, 277, 279, 307
lehrā articulating, 311n7, 315
in reference to South Asian music, 274, 276, 277, 279, 306, 311n8

time-unit, 274
timing, 7
tīn mār, 324
tīntāl, 9, 10, 254, 255, 263, 266, 269, 271, 274, 275, 276, 278, 324, 391
  relation with *titāl*, 257
tīvra, 261, 301, 391
tone melody, 77, 316, 391
tori (reduced measure), 225, 226
Toussaint, Godfried, 148– 151, 171n6
trance, 309
  related to musical ambiguity, 233, 234
  related to "incessant isometrical rhythm," 308
transcription. *See also* notation
  time-proportional, 62, 67
translation, of musical terms and experiences, 3– 8
triviality, 346– 347, 358, 362, 379
Tsuge, Geniche, 56, 58, 73n4, 91, 331
tsuzuke (drum pattern), 218, 219, 221, 230n13
Tuḥfat al-hind, 255, 256, 266, 267, 268
ṭukṛā, 269, 391
turit, see *naqra*

udaichan, 268, 391
ululation, 236, 237
universalism
  local terminologies with degrees of, 5, 8
  of meter as a category, 12, 105
  universalist approaches, 1, 3
Upaniṣad, 2
upāśraya, 255, 256, 270, 391
Urmawī, Ṣafī al-Dīn al-, 95n14, 96n24, 259, 272
usul, 6, 328
Uṣul al-naghmāt-i āṣafī, 262, 266

vagueness, 346– 347, 359, 379
vazn, see *wazn*
verbal phrases, rhythm of drum patterns organized according to, 314, 329– 31
vibhāg, 9, 254, 257, 274– 276 passim, 391
vīṇā, South Indian classical, 316, 320, 333, 391
virām (or *bīram*), 255, 391
vocables, 84, 120. See also *bols*
voice, 163– 169
  ideology of, 4
  and instrumental music, fusion of in Agbaza, 100
  moral evaluations of, 86
  trembling of, 241
Voice in the Drum, the, 316
von Blumroeder, Christoph, 375n2

waqfa, 77, 268, 391
watad, 78, 95n14, 259, 260, 271, 391
wazn, 76, 92, 94, 2658– 66 passim, 271, 335n4, 391
Webern, Anton, Six Bagatelles for String Quartet, Op. 9 no. 6, 349– 350
Weckl, Dave, 194n2
  "Master Plan," 180– 182
Wegner, Gert-Matthias, 19n3, 308, 312n17
Whitehead, Alfred North, 346– 347, 379n22
  fallacy of misplaced concreteness, 22, 24, 49n3
Widdess, Richard, 4, 5, 6, 7, 9, 16, 18, 66, 68, 70, 73n6, 77, 97n34, 210n1, 315, 326, 327, 329, 331, 335n15
wilet, 200– 203, 205, 385
wirama, 197, 198, 201, 391
Wolf, Richard, 52n27, 73n6, 93
Wolpe, Stefan, 50n13
Wright, Owen, 58, 98n41

yaktāla, 259, 261, 263, 264, 391. See also *ektāl*
Yāvari, Hāj Ḥoseyn Xān, 87– 88
Yegâneh, Moḥammad Ḥoseyn, 81– 82
Youssefzadeh, Ameneh, 82, 93, 96n23

Zambilbāf, Moxtār, 80– 81, 84– 85
ẓarb, 9, 261. See also *jarba*
  beat as delineation of *tāl*, 257
  in Central Asia, 328
  conflicting accounts in explaining, 328
  enumerating hemistiches, 328
  in relation to *sam*, 267, 268
  struck beat, 258, 259, 260, 261, 263, 264, 265
Zarlino, Gioseffo, 94n3
Zbikowski, Lawrence, 251n4, 252n11
Ziā'i, Afsāne, 57– 62
Zinzir, 62– 66